NEW TESTAMENT

Contemporary English Version

Commerative Edition

**GRACE & GLORY
LUTHERAN CHURCH**

PROMISE KEEPERS®
MEN OF INTEGRITY

Dear Men,

This special commemorative Bible is a gift to you from Promise Keepers and the American Bible Society. We trust it will serve as a tangible reminder of your participation in *Stand In The Gap: A Sacred Assembly Of Men* and of the solemn commitment you will make today to live a life wholly set apart for Almighty God.

Yours is one of one million New Testaments that the American Bible Society has provided for this occasion. Written in contemporary English, it is easy to read and also contains a daily devotional section that will add to your understanding and help you become more like Jesus. As part of your dedication to live a life pleasing to the Lord, I encourage you to get in the habit of reading the Bible every day! Revival and spiritual awakening are at the heart of God's desire for our country, and it begins with you and me consistently spending time in his Word, getting to know him and developing a passion for him and for the things of his kingdom. As Jesus said in John 17.3, *"Eternal life is to know you, the only true God, and to know Jesus Christ, the one you sent."* Our prayer is that the Lord will use this New Testament to help you get to know him intimately.

We thank the American Bible Society for their generosity to Promise Keepers and for their partnership with us in "uniting men through vital relationships to become godly influences in their world." However, most of all, we want to thank you for being here today and for being part of this historic *Sacred Assembly*. May Almighty God hear our cries, see the sincerity of our hearts and bring revival to his Church and spiritual awakening to our land!

Your servant,

Bill

Bill McCartney
Founder & CEO

Dear Friends:

Sharing God's Word is the core mission of the American Bible Society and it is especially gratifying to provide these New Testaments in the *Contemporary English Version* (CEV) for distribution at the *Stand In The Gap: A Sacred Assembly Of Men* Gathering in Washington, DC on October 4, 1997.

Through partnership with organizations like Promise Keepers, we help make all the difference in the world for millions of people whose lives are touched by the hope-filled message of God's Word. It's compelling work... challenging work... rewarding work. Knowing that someone else has been given the opportunity to understand what eternal life through Jesus Christ really means is the greatest benefit anyone involved with the American Bible Society can ever receive. You are our indispensable co-workers in the Bible cause helping to make a greater witness for Jesus Christ in the world today.

As you read your CEV New Testament — in your home, your place of business, or wherever you choose — our prayer is that you will be encouraged by it, and that it will remind you of the joy that God's Word brings to your own life.

Please remember to pray for the American Bible Society as we pray for you, and that many would come to know Christ as a result of his Word.

Sincerely,

Eugene B. Habecker

Eugene B. Habecker
President

INTRODUCTION

An Introduction to Your Daily Devotional Readings

These devotionals are designed to lead you on a path to a deeper relationship with Christ. This will involve an openness and vulnerability with God, repentance as a lifestyle (not a single event), and consistency in the process of your spiritual walk. They include practical, daily demonstrations of a revived life.

The devotionals were written by different authors with varying backgrounds and cultures. Thus, while you will follow a similar format, you will find various styles exhibited. As you work through these devotionals, it is imperative that you read each daily Scripture passage first.

This devotional is focused toward men; the issues are not only true of men but are illustrated in the lives of men. Each devotional deals with issues with which men struggle and which often cause stumbling blocks in their pursuit of God. They are also presented in a linear style, which men often find easier to grasp. This linear style establishes a process and leads to a point of action.

The devotionals are written to be used either personally or included in a weekly meeting with others. We encourage you to choose a pattern that will fit you. Interaction with another person will help you face issues in your life. Consider a small group of men, couples in your church, an adult class, a father and teenage son, or a married couple.

The time-line can begin immediately following *Stand in the Gap* until the end of the year. Any time, however, is equally good to read, reflect, interact, pray and grow.

Isaiah chapter 6 gives one of the clearest models for us to follow if we are to move into practical applications in the area of a repentant lifestyle. The first six weeks of this devotional follow the processes modeled in Isaiah 6.

The devotional readings are in sections:
First: the process of repentance.
Second: personal issue.
Third: the pursuit of the heart of God.

WEEK 1—The Attributes of Jesus

A God Worthy of the Name
John 1.14 *(NT p. 102);* 2 Corinthians 3.17,18 *(NT p. 190)*

"A picture of God"

GROUP DAY
DAY 1

When you think of God, what comes to mind? Do you see him as all-knowing and all-powerful, the creator and sustainer of life? Do you think of his holiness? God embodies all these qualities and more. As mortals, we can never be like him in those ways.

But God demands that we become holy. What can he mean? Logic indicates that such a challenge is impossible. Since, as sinners, we're already destined to fail, why try? We have enough failure in our lives, just trying to live up to the standards of our bosses, families, and friends. We find ourselves falling short all of the time. It would be impossible if God was "out there" somewhere and we were forever left "down here" to ourselves. But that's not the case.

Reflection

God became a man in Jesus so that we could "see" how to become like him and identify with his humanness, as he lived to please God. Everything Jesus said and did was to model the love God intended for us. The key is to remember that Jesus' mission was two-fold. He was sent to be both a tender-hearted shepherd and a tough-minded Savior. As the shepherd, he showed compassion to those who were broken and in need. But, as our Savior, Jesus also took a stand for the truth. His love was based on kingdom values which implied standards of behavior and judgment.

Accountability and Application

Some men are strongly oriented toward truth: principles and projects. Others are drawn primarily to kindness: the needs of people. Both are "right" if they are willing to learn from each other.

Why do we need to keep both attributes in "creative tension"?

What must I do now to be more like Jesus? Who will hold me accountable?

Your temptation will be to quit when the true you surfaces. But, don't! That tension you feel is the beginning of understanding yourself and where you need to grow to be more like Christ.

Prayer

Lord, make me more like Jesus. I want to be filled with your kindness for those in need. And, I want to be willing to take a stand for the truth even when that is tough to do. So, make my heart tender, and toughen my mind to respond rightly to the challenges of a fallen world. May your Spirit live out Christ's life through me!

WEEK 1—The Attributes of Jesus

Righteousness
Matthew 4.1-11 *(NT p. 7, 8)*; 22.34-40 *(NT p. 30)*

"What's the bottom line?"

DAY 2

Bill, the president of a chain of convenience stores, received a letter from a group of parents who were concerned about minors having easy access to "soft-core" pornographic magazines. As a Christian and a parent, Bill understood. But, he had been hired to turn the stores around, since they had been losing money for years.

In examining the figures, Bill found that the magazines in question represented a significant yearly profit. Knowing that the "bottom line" would rule finances, he wrestled with the issue in prayer. And God answered.

By telling the board it was necessary to give the chain a "new look," he predicted that profits would rise if the stores were perceived to be more "family friendly." And they did!

Reflection

Righteousness is just plain rightness. We make it too theological because it's a biblical word. Rightness is not easily defined, but we all know it when we see it. Our conscience affirms it.—Harry Lathrop Reed

Testing and tempting are two sides of the same coin. Satan tempts us in the tough times by asking, "Would a loving God let a man struggle in the wilderness?" He argues that God does not care and that we are free to satisfy our appetites and ambitions any way we wish.

Jesus fought Satan's lies by quoting the Word. By knowing God's Word, he thwarted Satan's attack and gained victory. And so can we!

Accountability and Application

Expect the wilderness. Though there are times when we all feel alone, the truth is that men need "brothers" who can help when they're wrestling with the truth and with issues of standing for righteousness. If you don't have any "brothers," pray for and actively seek out such a fellowship of committed men.

Are you currently in a situation where righteousness is at stake?
What can you personally do to "make a difference"?
How could our ambitions be twisted if we are not careful?
Do you have a "bottom line" when it comes to righteousness? Does it show?

Prayer

Father, I realize that there will be times when you put me to the test. I know that as I cling to your Word, I will emerge as a man who is more like Jesus. But, I need the help of other committed men. Lead me to "brothers" who will faithfully help me through the wildernesses of life.

WEEK 1—The Attributes of Jesus

Forgiveness
Matthew 18.21, 22 *(NT p. 25)*

"A hard one to forget"

DAY 3

During the Nazi occupation of France, a young novitiate was returning to the convent from the village market. A soldier on his motorcycle saw her and pulled over. Although she initially thought it was to help her with the heavy basket of food, she quickly learned of the conqueror's real motives. As he forced her into the woods, she screamed, but no one heard her.

The trauma that occurred that night haunted her with nightmares for years. But, gradually, with the help of friends, she forgave and was able to forget. Years later, she was chosen to host a meeting of German teachers as a gesture of post-war reconciliation. Among them was her aggressor.

It all came back! The bitterness and the thoughts of revenge were unbearable until she spent the night in prayer. Crying out to God, she eventually found the grace to serve them—all of them. She was finally free!

Reflection

God's forgiveness is free, but it's not cheap. We cannot meditate on the cross without being shocked by the price Jesus paid for our redemption. There was not only the physical pain, there was also the pain of rejection and abandonment. Add to that a crowd of spectators who couldn't have cared less that he was dying for them, and we finally begin to understand how deep his love is. He forgave all of that, and he forgives us of our sin! And because he does, so should we.

That means we must pardon and cease blaming and resenting one another.

Accountability and Application

Until we forgive, we are the prisoner of the person who has offended us. We are caught in an emotional and psychological trap. Whether we want to or not, we meditate on the offender and the offense until our mind is obsessed. And though we might not be aware of it, others may be.

Are you a prisoner of unforgiveness? Do you meditate on an offense over and over?

Can you find it within yourself to let go of past offenses, even though you "deserve" to hang on to them? Jesus did—on the cross!

Prayer

Almighty God, please forgive my lack of forgiveness, and guide me through the minefield of my feelings. I want to forgive and forget, but I just can't seem to do it. So, whatever is hindering that process, I ask you to remove it by the power of Christ's blood...and for his glory.

WEEK 1—The Attributes of Jesus

Judgment
Mark 7.6-9 *(NT p. 49)*; Matthew 20.20-28 *(NT p. 27)*

"Status or service?"

DAY 4

They were successful. In every sense of the word, they had established themselves as one of the premier players in the industry. But, David, an executive who had been invited for a job interview, was not satisfied with some of the answers he was getting. It appeared that customer service had been lost in corporate politics and the scramble for status within the organization.

As an experienced corporate executive, David knew when the rules of success were being violated. When he refused to accept their very lucrative job offer, he told them why. "There's too much politics. The resultant handling of the money is fast and loose and there is visceral resistance to the idea of accountability. It's all gonna' come down." A year later, it did!

Reflection

God judges a man not by the distance he has covered, but by the direction he has taken.—James S. Stewart

Here, Jesus is calling men to sound judgment by openly challenging hypocrisy. He calls the hypocrites "show-offs," whose hearts are far from God. Why would Jesus be filled with so much anger at hypocrisy? It is because it's a lie; it says one thing and does another. Hypocrisy creates rites and rituals, a show of respectability that must be served. But, true religion creates relationships based on trust and follow-through.

Accountability and Application

Do you serve? Or, do you think that because of your level of experience, you should be in charge? If you are thinking that you are now "above" serving others, then you need to assess your own heart and your work environment. Ask yourself honestly:

Why do you think Jesus was so hard on hypocrisy?
Must you have it your way?
Do you find it difficult to admit to mistakes?
Do you have to prove that you are right?
Are there any practices in your life that you need to re-evaluate?
On what basis do you have the right to judge?

Whether in business or in volunteer work of any kind, when we become more concerned with our status than our service, we are no longer available to others...and to God.

Prayer

Lord, you made me to serve you and others. Take away the pride in my heart that keeps me from serving. Remind me that I'm not in charge, and that everything doesn't have to be my way. Live through me to once again reach out to others...in service.

WEEK 1—The Attributes of Jesus

Grace
John 8.3-11

"In spite of it all!"

DAY 5

George's wife, Sue, ran off with her old college boyfriend shortly after their class reunion. Convincing herself that she would be happier with him, she married him right after the divorce was final. It took George over a year to recover but, through much prayer and long hours at work, he avoided bitterness and got on with his life.

Eventually, George got word that Sue and her new husband had had a child and had moved overseas to pursue his career. Then, Sue wrote him an unexpected letter to announce that she had terminal cancer. Not only that, her husband, unable to face it, had abandoned her and the child. She was destitute!

George sent her some money. Then, he took an unpaid leave of absence to go see them. He stayed there for several months and was at her side when she died. Then, he adopted her son and raised him as his own.

Reflection

Jesus had nothing against the law. In fact, he stated that he had come to fulfill it. The problem here was with the experts in the law. And the issue was not their interpretation of the law, but their hearts.

Law without grace becomes cruel—even torturous. Because the hearts of the legalists were so far from God, Jesus felt compelled to remind all men everywhere that if only law reigned, who could stand? Jesus gently reminded the woman who was caught in adultery of the law when he said, "Go now, but don't sin any more"; replacing deserved punishment with grace.

Accountability and Application

It's a "guy thing" to focus in on the rules. We often judge ourselves and others too harshly. The way that Jesus led and corrected, through parables and reminders of laws that were given by a loving God, produced far more good.

How does what George did challenge you?

What does this incident say to you about the law?

Are there areas in which you are too "rule" driven, and you could show grace?

Prayer

Lord, please help me to be merciful when it's required—to look beyond the rules and penalties to the importance of the relationships involved. Help me to be a balance to the law when I need to be so that lives will be positively re-oriented because of your grace.

WEEK 1—The Attributes of Jesus

Truthfulness
Matthew 16.21-28 *(NT p. 23, 24)*

"Saying what needs to be said"

DAY 6

"Who do you think you are...talking to me that way?"
But, it needed to be said, and Harry wasn't about to back down. Jim was going to leave his wife for his secretary and he was looking for some "biblical" justification for it. He said that he was not obligated to see it through because they never really "became one" in God's sight, in spite of two kids.

Harry went right to the heart of the matter. "Whether you can admit it or not, Jim, you are living in sin...cheating on your wife and your children. Because of some bad choices, you are now caught in some very wrong thinking. You will live to greatly regret any decisions that you make in this current state of mind, and I care enough to tell you that. Change your mind. Repent. There is still time. I will help you put it all back together. But, you have to repent."

Reflection

Everyone wishes to have truth on his side, but few wish to be on the side of truth.
—Richard Whateley

Jesus zeroes in on Peter's real motives and painfully exposes them before his peers. Peter's motives were very worldly. He had left his small business expecting to be rewarded by a Savior-King who was going to be placed on the throne of a greater Israel. Jesus was making it very plain that he came to establish another kingdom with different values. And the relationship he had with Peter, plus the hopes that he had for Peter, permitted him to be truthful, even painfully so.

Accountability and Application

Do you find Harry's "in your face" style appropriate?
 Why did Harry have the right to talk that way?
 Would you be able to stand for truth and speak that way to a friend?
 Would you be able to receive this from a friend?
 Truthfulness is making our words conform to fact, reality and standard. There is a stigma attached to direct, truthful communication in the church today. It implies that there is a lack of spirituality if anger is ever expressed. This could not be further from the model of Jesus. When he needed to be, he could be confrontational, direct, and brutally honest. We've been called to be like him—not a watered down, culturally acceptable, polite substitute.

Prayer

Lord, if I am afraid to speak up for the truth, help me. Prepare my heart and give me the words to say. Don't let me be ashamed of you or your standards. Don't let me hide in the culturally acceptable. I want to be all that you'd have me be. And if I need this kind of talk, let me be able to receive it with an open heart.

WEEK 1—The Attributes of Jesus

Faithfulness
John 21.15-19 *(NT p. 126)*

"It's falling apart!"

DAY 7

"I feel like you're putting the nails in my coffin!" Tom stormed out of the house, leaving his friends speechless. He had been depressed for months. A recent job change, created by downsizing the company, had left him off balance. He was earning less and had to move into a smaller place. So, to cheer him up, his friends came over to help paint the house. But, he felt such a failure that his friends' efforts appeared to be saying with pity, "Boy, do you need us!"

John went after him. "We're just trying to help. We know you're struggling, but God still loves you and so do we, brother. It's not over; it'll get better."

But it didn't. Tom needed to hear of God's love again and again, and John made sure that he did. In time, Tom was back on his feet, positive and better placed for promotion than he had been before. And to this day, he remembers the fact that John was "there for him," a faithful friend who wouldn't give up on him...even though he gave up on himself!

Reflection

Peter spoke up, "Even if all the others reject you, I never will!" (Matthew 26. 33). Peter was sure that he was better than all the rest, that he would finish well, even if it cost him his life! But, Jesus knew that Peter was self-deceived and he calmly said, "before the rooster crows tonight, you will deny me three times."

And he did! At the cross, Peter lost his self-respect. He now knew that he, too, was a moral coward. So, Jesus went looking for him, knowing that Peter still had a place in the kingdom and a major role to play. As a faithful friend, he still believed in Peter even though Peter no longer believed in himself. So, three times Jesus commissioned him to "feed my sheep" and in doing so, he erased three denials and restored a man to heroic service to his God.

Accountability and Application

What does Christ's faithfulness to Peter say to you?
How do you feel when a friend proves himself faithful to you?
How are you at being a faithful friend?
Men like to solve problems. But "being there" for someone doesn't mean having all the answers—just a listening ear. You don't give advice, you listen. It takes energy and emotion. Most of all, it takes availability, and communicating that you care.

Prayer

God, please open my eyes to those around me who are struggling. Help me to "be there" for them, to communicate availability and care. Make me your instrument of faithfulness in their lives.

WEEK 2 — My Condition in God's Reflection

God's Standard

Philippians 2.1-11 *(NT p. 208)*; 1 John 3 *(NT p. 259)*

LAST WEEK IN REVIEW: *God sent Jesus as a living model of his attributes and characteristics. Though we can never attain them on our own, we are motivated to live by godly standards. In what ways were you challenged last week to change any of your actions or attitudes?*

"Under Dad's shadow"

As Jon walks through the park, he is oblivious to the beautiful setting. He is preoccupied with this haunting question: Would he ever be able to fill his father's shoes? Would he ever measure up? When he is with his contemporaries he feels adequate and fulfilled. But when he imagines his father's standards, inadequacy sets in. This standard seemingly leaves him "less" no matter what he does or how hard he tries. Can this nagging measurement determine his self-concept? His self worth?

It was about two years ago that Jon teamed up with his buddies and drove to a Promise Keepers conference. When the invitation was given to go forward, Jon responded. For the first time in his life he really felt that he measured up, not because of his goodness but because of what Christ had done for him. He didn't feel sub-standard.

Reflection

What is God's standard? The answer comes by seeking God, realizing our sinfulness before a holy God, and embracing by faith the salvation Christ provided for us on the cross. In Philippians 2, we are told to have Christ's attitude and thoughts. Even though we are sinful, we have been justified by the blood of Jesus and are "children of God." All other standards of comparison seem insignificant.

Accountability and Application

Have you felt the tension that Jon feels? How have you responded?
  What's wrong with measuring yourself against the standards of man?
  Who or what is your standard?

Prayer

Lord, help me to see you as you are, and to see myself by your standards, not man's. I cannot change myself, so transform me by your power. As I look at your attributes, begin making me like you.

WEEK 2 — My Condition in God's Reflection

Christ's Attitude
Philippians 2.1-4 *(NT p. 208)*

"Feeling overlooked"

DAY 2

Joe moved through the dining room and took his seat at one of the tables. The program started, and young Christians began sharing their ministry experiences. One after another they were honored by the group. Joe began to feel uneasy, even anxious. He was a successful Christian businessman, well-known in the Christian community. Why were they honoring these young people and not him? Didn't they know who he was and what he had done for the community?

As the evening drew to a close, the coveted "Philanthropist of the Year" award was about to be announced. Joe sat up, believing himself to be a likely candidate. When the recipient was announced, the audience cheered as Joe declined the award, naming a more deserving winner.

Have you ever had feelings similar to Joe's? Have you wanted to be recognized for your accomplishments?

Reflection
Philippians 2 shows us the proper attitude, the one Christ had. He willingly gave up his ruling position with God to live as a servant on earth. "Don't be jealous or proud, but be humble and consider others more important than yourselves." (v.3) This is convicting. God doesn't care nearly as much about what Joe had done, as he cares about what Joe was becoming.

Accountability and Application
How does your mindset compare to Christ's?
   Are you focused on who you are in Christ, or what you do?
   What can you do to change your attitude and to exhibit Christ's attitude?
   Think like Christ thought. He readily gave up a position that was duly his.

Prayer
Father, help me to lay down my positions in life.

WEEK 2 — My Condition in God's Reflection

My Rights
Luke 23.32-43 *(NT p. 98)*

"Taken for a ride"

"They can't do that! I know my rights," Harvey yelled. They just couldn't treat him that way. A wild group of troublemakers had slid their car into his fence with no intention of paying for the damage. His mind raced in anger. He would get even. He determined that he would take them to small claims court and get every last penny. And, he would make a point to tell everyone in town how irresponsible they were and what an injustice he had experienced.

Have you ever thought these kind of thoughts?

Have you ever acted on these thoughts and feelings?

As Harvey drove his car down the road, he started to cool down. He parked the car and entered the church, and the music started. Harvey felt his spirit begin to soften as he entered into worship. The pastor read from the 23rd chapter of Luke. When he got to the 34th verse, Harvey began to feel uncomfortable. The words of Jesus cut deep: "Father forgive these people! They don't know what they're doing." Harvey hadn't been thinking the way Jesus thought. He'd not forgiven this group. He didn't even take time to find out who they were. He'd hung onto his right to have his fence free from invasion.

Reflection

Jesus willingly gave up his right to be in position with his Father when he came to earth as a servant. And he willingly gave up his right to life on earth when he sacrificed himself on the cross, fully capable of calling for help and freeing himself from the trauma and death. Yet, when our possessions are tampered with, we hold on to our rights. When our positions at work or in the community are threatened by unfair intrusions, we protest emphatically. What are our rights, really?

Accountability and Application

At what times do you demand your rights?

In what area of your life is God calling you to give up your rights?

Pay attention to the way you tend to hold on to your perceived rights the next time you feel them threatened. Find a way to release what really isn't yours anyway. See if it makes a difference in the way you view situations and in the way you deal with them.

Prayer

Lord, show me where I am demanding my rights and keeping you from being able to use me fully. Help me trust you enough to release my rights and trust in your mercy.

WEEK 2 — My Condition in God's Reflection

Enslaving Habits
Romans 6.15-18 *(NT p. 166)*

"No one is looking"

DAY 4

Jon checked into the hotel, picked up his room key and headed for the elevator. The door opened at the third floor, and he walked down the hall to his room. The room was pleasant enough. He unpacked his clothes, put them on hangers and sat down on the bed. He looked to the nightstand, picked up the remote control for the TV and turned it on. That old familiar gnawing started to twist his insides. Was he going to be drawn into a night of the sensual programming that was available to him? Was he going to be a slave to it again?

What are you a slave to? Work? Lust? Hobbies? Accomplishments? Money? The thrill of risk? Or are you a slave to righteousness, purity, love and other godly things?

Jon looked around the room trying to free his mind of these thoughts. His eyes fell on the Gideon Bible on the nightstand. He picked it up, opened it, and began to read.

Reflection

Romans 6.15-18 teaches that we can either be a slave to sin, which leads to death, or obedience, which leads to righteousness. The very God of the universe had voluntarily become a slave so that you could live free. Our response is obvious. We can only be a slave to one master, the Lord Jesus.

Accountability and Application

Have you found yourself in a similar dilemma?

What did you do?

Think of all of your habits, desires, and attitudes. Are you a slave to any of them? Do any of them have you in bondage?

What do you need to do to be able to respond to these struggles with the mind of Christ?

Prayer

Lord, so many times I am a slave to my wants and desires. Fill me with your power to overcome these struggles and cause me to pursue righteousness in all I do.

WEEK 2 — My Condition in God's Reflection

True Humility
1 Peter 5.5-11 *(NT p. 253)*

"Follow the leader"

DAY 5

Five men were trekking for days across a wide plateau in western Colorado. One man declared himself the leader and attempted to control and direct the others' every move. He was abusive and demanding. Three of the others complained, resisted and demanded their rights. The fifth did not resist or complain. Instead, he pitched their camp, cooked their food, and attended to their blisters. He offered suggestions to their route but did not insist on his own way. The others continued to gripe and complain. Finally, the fifth man had it, and he left the group. The reality of their situation began to dawn on them. They were lost, and they could not get back to where they started. They didn't possess the skills to find food or shelter, and their relationships were so fractured that they were not even speaking to one another.

Have you experienced or observed a similar situation?
Was a legitimate leader in the group? Who was that?

The sixth and seventh days brought snow with below-freezing temperatures. The four men were growing desperate. They could die, and no one would even know where they were. One of them looked to the west and saw a thin wisp of smoke. Moving toward the smoke, they found the man they had driven away. He gave them food and shelter, and he led them out. It was his humility and desire to serve that saved their lives.

Reflection

Arrogance, pride, and demand for leadership disqualifies one to lead. Yet humility and service establishes leadership. Christ did not demand leadership. Yet throngs of people followed him, as he spent his earthly life serving. He chose to lower himself to our level to save us.

Accountability and Application

Is it natural for us to exhibit humility?
What does 1 Peter 5.5 tell us will happen if we refuse to humble ourselves?
Do you ever demand leadership or resist the established leader?

Prayer

Lord, as my view of you becomes clearer, I see that there is little about me that I can be proud of. Help me to walk in your humility so that you can use me.

WEEK 2 — My Condition in God's Reflection

Obedience
Matthew 26.36-45 *(NT p. 36)*

"Running from the Master"

DAY 6

Winston was a cute year-old Springer Spaniel puppy. His cuddly appearance masked his rebellion. It was his first trip into the mountains and I took him for a hike. As we hiked, he picked up an elk dropping in his mouth. Telling him to drop it, I could see by his response and reaction that he understood what I wanted him to do, but he was unwilling to do it. Rather than obeying me, he started to run away. He ran all the way back to camp. Further situations with him proved to be the same. I thought that I was never going to be able to trust him as a hunting dog, for he refused to "soft-hold" in retrieving game, and he displayed numerous uncooperative tendencies. Future actions verified that he would not be obedient, even when he was forced to. Discipline had to be so severe that he would growl before it would have any effect. Necessarily, we had to remove him from the household five years later when a new baby came into the home and he could not be trusted with that child.

Do you ever find yourself resisting what you know God wants you to do?
Can you be trusted with what God treasures?
Is there something that God has forbidden that you are holding on to?

Reflection

Isaiah 53.4, 5 tells us how brutal the assignment was that Christ accepted and fulfilled. "He suffered and endured/great pain for us,/but we thought his suffering/was punishment from God./He was wounded and crushed/because of our sins;/by taking our punishment,/he made us completely well."

The prophet goes on to say, in the 10th verse, "The LORD decided his servant/would suffer as a sacrifice/to take away the sin/and guilt of others./Now the servant will live/to see his own descendants./He did everything/the LORD had planned."

Accountability and Application

Are you being obedient to all the Lord is asking you to do today?

It is easy to respond in obedience to pleasant, simple or enjoyable tasks. How are you at responding in obedience to difficult directives? Commit this area to the Lord.

Can you be obedient in your own strength? Remember to ask the Lord for strength in obedience.

Prayer

Lord, continue to transform me into your image. I desire to be that living sacrifice that you have called me to be. I need your power to become obedient.

WEEK 2 — My Condition in God's Reflection

Dying to Self

2 Timothy 2.11-13 *(NT p. 226)*; 4.6-8 *(NT p. 227)*

"A clearer look"

DAY 7

Pete had had it. Life was just too difficult. Maybe he would just check out. Things were difficult at home, his job was falling apart, and the church was not appreciating all of his extra work. Pete's friend, Jim, saw his condition and knew that Pete needed perspective. The two of them met at a trail-head for a hike up the mountain. Eventually, Pete began to view his situation more clearly. He had been competing with others to have his needs met. His wife and children were guarded around him. His coworkers were pulling back from him. The people at church were sensing that they didn't meet his needs adequately, but they didn't know what to do. Jim helped Pete see that he was becoming self-focused, that he had viewed others as a means for encouraging himself. He needed to die to his own needs and begin to focus on others.

Reflection

We often lose the will to live when we live only for ourselves. While it would seem logical as needy human beings to seek to have physical and emotional needs met, if we become consumed with only our own needs, we begin to have tunnel vision. We miss the big picture around us. We miss the needs of others, and life becomes self-serving. The result is a sad, lonely person. The reality is that if, like Christ, we can die to our own needs and wants, and focus on others' needs, we will find purpose in life.

Accountability and Application

Do you usually seek to have primarily your own needs met?
 When you meet someone else's needs, do you feel angry later?
 Do you equally value your needs and the needs of others?
 Ask a friend to confront you when you begin to focus only on yourself. It may be hard to hear, but it will be the best thing they could do for you.
 Ask God to help you become more focused on others.

Prayer

Many times I think it would be easier to die physically than to be a living sacrifice. Lord, help me to trust you enough that I will enter into the process of being formed in your image. Thank you for the fact that I don't have to do it in my own strength. I only need to desire that you transform me, and to begin to participate with you in this process.

WEEK 3—Humility

Learning Humility from Christ
Philippians 2.1, 2 *(NT p. 208)*

GROUP DAY
DAY 1

LAST WEEK IN REVIEW: *What one or two issues surfaced in last week's study that you need to change? Did you find it difficult to be compared with Christ's standard? Did you feel defeated? Don't give up! The rest of the process will help you to begin to see the mind of Christ increasingly exhibited in your life. Will you trust God with those areas and begin to allow yourself to be held accountable?*

"Jack the 'go-getter'"

"Keep your eye on the ball, Danny," urged Jack to his son. Jack is a hard worker, good husband and father, and a faithful church member. At work, he's known as a "go-getter"—driven. The words "strive to be the best" have driven him his entire life. From his first baseball practice at age 7 until now, he has struggled with the demands of the competitive computer industry. Now, it's Jack's turn to teach his son the lessons he learned from his dad. But sitting there in the bleachers, there was that nagging, restless feeling again, deep down on the inside. Sure, Jack's a Christian; he accepted the Lord into his heart years ago. But that peace that the pastor keeps preaching about continues to elude him. How can Jack have this peace?

Reflection

Jesus tells us in Matthew 11.29, "Take the yoke I give you. Put it on your shoulders and learn from me. I am gentle and humble, and you will find rest." Many times that restlessness is a result of a lack of humility. That constant, inward striving could be because we have never learned true humility from the Master himself.

Accountability and Application

Do I have to give up wanting to be the best if I am to be humble?
  Describe the character of someone you know who is humble.
  How do people who are driven help each other practice humility?
  Plan to read Philippians 2.1-11 every day this week during your quiet time.

Prayer

Lord, help me to commit to reading the Philippians passage daily and to seek your face. Help me to learn what it's like to have Christ-like humility. Lord, work true humility in me.

WEEK 3—Humility

Consider Others
Philippians 2.3 *(NT p. 208)*

"I'll take it!"

DAY 2

Jack paused from his work to think about the new job coming up. "Even though it's not my strong area, it'll look good on my resumé." Jack knew that the best person for this job was Margaret, and he probably should have put in a good word for her, but he resisted.

Later that morning, Mr. Watkins came by Jack's office. "Jack, as you know, we've got to fill this new position. Since you have seniority, you have first crack at it."

"I'll take it," replied Jack without hesitation.

"Are you sure, Jack?" asked Mr. Watkins, a little surprised. "Okay, Jack, if you're sure, you've got the job. It's yours."

"Oh, by the way, Jack," he added as he was leaving, "our president will be looking for some sharp analysts to manage a special, high-profile project that would have been right up your alley. Since you're now tied up, do you think Margaret can handle it?"

Jack was speechless.

Reflection

This is a tough spot for Jack. Would you have taken the job? He didn't know a better job would be coming his way so soon. The problem is that Jack was thinking more about his selfish desire to move up the corporate ladder than who was the best fit for the job, or what was best for the company. Jesus Christ wants to impart to us the "I will trust the Lord; therefore I will wait on him" aspect of humility. Jack missed an opportunity to employ the "consider others more important than yourselves" concept. He knew that Margaret was better suited for this new position, yet he convinced himself that he was more deserving.

Accountability and Application

Confess to the Lord where you have been guilty of selfish ambition. Then be alert for the Lord to provide opportunities to consider others above yourself.

Have you ever found yourself in a situation like this?
Is it selfish to want to move up the ladder?
Is there any way to move up the ladder and still exhibit humility?

Prayer

Lord, forgive me where I've let my ambition get in the way of your perfect will for my life. May your Holy Spirit prompt me when I yield to the temptation of selfish ambition, and may I heed the Spirit's voice.

WEEK 3— Humility

Setting Aside Our Own Agendas
Philippians 2.4 *(NT p. 208)*

"Date night"

Heading home on a Friday evening, Jack looks forward to his date with his wife. As he turns into the driveway, he catches the eye of a new neighbor moving in. He grabs his briefcase and dashes into the house to change. He only has an hour before they leave for the evening, and he wants to get a good workout in at the gym. So, to avoid having to meet the new neighbor, he slips out the side door.

As Jack and his wife leave for their date, she notices the neighbor and suggests a quick meeting. But Jack is anxious to go out with his wife, so he promises they'll meet them another time.

At church on Sunday, it is Jack's turn to serve as greeter. Sam, one of the deacons, finds Jack. "Hey, Jack, I want you to meet someone who just moved into your neighborhood," says Sam. They approach, but the visitor does so hesitantly, tentative about meeting Jack.

Jack extends his hand to the new visitor, the one whom he avoided in order to get to his workout a few days earlier.

Reflection

Is your time so precious that you have no room to think of spending time reaching out to someone else? One very important aspect of humility is thinking beyond your own needs and caring about your neighbor's. Jack was so concerned with his own agenda that selfishness caused him to miss an opportunity to reach out to someone in need.

Accountability and Application

Allow time for unexpected chances to reach out to others. Don't be so driven by your own schedule that you miss an opportunity for ministry. Remember, your time is not your own; it is given to you by God. You should always be available to be used of the Lord. It may not always be convenient, but it's a matter of an attitude that says that your brother's interests are more important than yours.

Have you ever done something like Jack did?
How can you change to make yourself more available to God?

Prayer

Lord, help me to be less selfish about the time that you've entrusted to me. Help me to humbly submit each day to you.

WEEK 3—Humility

The Nature of a Servant
Philippians 2.5-7 *(NT p. 208)*

"All dressed up"

DAY 4

"Honey, I'm gone!" says Jack as he rushes out the door. There's no way he's going to be late. He's the emcee for this year's fund-raiser. The mayor and other VIPs will all be there, and so will Jack, decked out in his tux. As Jack makes his way down the freeway, he notices a young woman waving frantically. "Not now," thinks Jack. But, he pulls to a stop, jumps out of his car, rolls up his sleeves, and heads for her wheel well. He changes the tire in record time noticing the grease spots on his knees, lapel and collar. "Well, can't do anything about it now," sighs Jack, and hurries to the dinner. As Jack takes the podium, he resists the temptation to relate his heroics in explanation of his appearance. Rather, he diffuses the embarrassing situation by pointing out his inability to dress himself.

Reflection

If Jesus Christ, who is God incarnate, can lay aside the glory that was his with the Father, then surely we can lay aside our titles, positions, and tuxes, that we wrap around ourselves, to reach out to a need. Have a servant's heart. Paul admonishes us in Romans 12.3, "I tell each of you not to think you are better than you really are. Use good sense and measure yourself by the amount of faith that God has given you."

Accountability and Application

What "suit" in your life are you willing to lay down?

Describe a situation in your life where you had to choose between title/position and serving.

Have you ever been tempted to say, "Do you know who I am?"

Avoid telling someone what you do before you tell them who you belong to.

Prayer

Thank you, Father, for laying down your glory, that you might become one of us. Help me today, Lord, to have the mind and heart of a servant.

WEEK 3 — Humility

Humble Yourself
Philippians 2.8 *(NT p. 208)*

"30 bucks!"

It's vacation time for Jack's family. In order to get the family minivan ready for the road trip, they have to rent a car while the minivan is being repaired. It's close-of-business Wednesday, and Jack and Susan are on their way home from the repair shop. "Well, that's 30 more bucks we'll have to put out," grumbles Jack.

"What do you mean by that?" asks Susan.

"You told me the service guy told you that Thursday is the best day to bring it in," explains Jack. "So I went on what you told me, and rented this car today. Well, guess what? I just found out they're all booked up Thursday and can't get it in until Friday. Now we have to pay for another day of rental!"

"So, Jack, why did you leave the car there? We could have gone to another shop!"

Jack knows that she is right, but he's too proud to go back and get the car to take it to another shop.

Reflection

Daily, especially if we live with a spouse and/or children, we are constantly given a number of occasions in which we have a split-second opportunity to either demonstrate true humility or "fire one back." God has granted us the ability to discern our motives in the many conversations we have. The issue is making the decision to humble ourselves rather than insisting on our own way. We must simply humble ourselves.

Accountability and Application

What could he have said to avoid this argument?

Would members of your family say that you sometimes demonstrate Jack's attitude?

Which arguments in your home could be avoided if your responses weren't motivated by an "I'm right, and you're wrong" attitude?

For the next 24 hours, try to keep count of the number of times you have the opportunity to start an argument. Take note of your response options.

Prayer

Lord, thank you that we have the example of Christ who humbled himself. Even when opponents beat him and spit on him, he didn't strike back. Lord, teach me how to humble myself like that. I need your Holy Spirit to empower me to humble myself.

WEEK 3—Humility

Humble Obedience
Philippians 2.8 *(NT p. 208)*

"One special evening"

DAY 6

"This has been a long day!" Jack grabs his briefcase, then decides to go through the park on the way to Leroy's. It's fight night with the guys. He always enjoys a night of sandwiches and pay-per-view fights at Leroy's.

But as he approaches an elderly gentleman sitting on a bench, he feels extraordinarily prompted to sit and talk with him. Thinking it odd, he hesitates, and moves on past him. But wrestling with that nagging feeling, he obediently returns to the bench. Soon Jack is sharing his Christian testimony, and explaining how the elderly man, too, can find peace for his life. Just when the old man starts to show interest, he grabs his chest and starts gasping for air. Jack rushes him to the hospital, hands him over to the hospital staff, and goes to phone the guys at Leroy's.

As fight night continues without him, Jack is led into the old man's room, where Jack leads the man to salvation in Christ.

Jack missed fight night, but his obedience resulted in a soul saved to Christ for eternity.

Reflection

Jack's obedience resulted in an exciting, unexpected evening, but his obedience cost him something. Jesus Christ also paid a price at the cross. Love took him there—an unbelievable love for humanity. But he was also motivated by obedience to his Father's will. In our "I'll do it my way" society, it takes courage to overcome the tendency to think your way is best. Let it be said of you that, in your life, you chose to do it not your way, but God's way, and that you were obedient. Humility creates the environment for obedience.

Accountability and Application

Are you obedient in these types of situations?
  What might have happened if Jack ignored God's prompting?
  How often do you share your faith? What stops you?
  Be particularly attentive to opportunities God may grant you. Be bold and share your faith, or just obey whatever God has you to do.

Prayer

Lord, if there is one area in my life that needs work, it's this area of obedience. Take me to the cross again and again so that my will matches yours. Help me to choose your way, not my own. Give me boldness to be obedient in sharing my Christian testimony with others.

WEEK 3 — Humility

God Will Exalt
Philippians 2.9 *(NT p. 208)*

"Leave the driving to us"

DAY 7

Jack had just finished teaching the junior high Sunday school class, when one of his students, Mike, questioned him. "You coming tonight? I know my mom's receiving that service award. She really does a lot."

"I wouldn't miss it," replied Jack to his student. Jack works hard to go to events that are important to his students. Many times he's gone to their basketball or soccer games, piano recitals and plays, or to their award night. They call him at home too. Jack really goes the extra mile for these kids, and it doesn't bother him that his pastor doesn't know all he does. Really, Jack doesn't expect anything. He just likes getting involved in the kids' lives.

Mike's mom is Liz McCormick. She's on the pastor's Aide Board, the Missions Committee—you name it. She really gives of herself. At the banquet, to no one's surprise, she won the service award. Although this is usually the last presentation, the pastor did something a little different this year. "I have been inspired by the servant's heart that many of you exemplify. But there's one individual who is willing to spend countless hours in ministry without taking any credit or needing to be seen. Jack, would you come up here please?"

The longstanding ovation floored Jack.

Reflection

The Greyhound bus commercial has the catchy slogan, "Leave the driving to us." God wants us to leave the rewarding to him. Many times we do things that exalt ourselves: accept high-profile tasks, talk about our spirituality or remind our associates of what we deserve. Let us humbly serve God because we love him, and let him decide just when and how he wants to honor us. When you think that he's forgotten you, just rest in him. Don't try to push your way to the front to be seen by others. Don't be a spiritual backseat driver. Leave the exalting to God.

Accountability and Application

Are your good works behind the scene, or are they always up front and visible?

Do you have a Jack in your church? Describe him.

Can you pinpoint an area in your life regarding your desire for exaltation that you need to work on?

Take a moment to take inventory of your recent conversations, thought patterns, etc., and look for self-exaltation tendencies.

Prayer

Lord, forgive me for those times when I have sought to exalt myself. Take away my desire to be noticed, honored, rewarded and promoted. Make my motives to serve pure.

21

WEEK 4—Confession

Turning Toward God
Mark 1.4 *(NT p. 42)*

LAST WEEK IN REVIEW: Asking yourself if you are willing to be nothing, so that God may be something in you is hard. It is difficult to practice humility, because you're fighting your flesh and desires all of the time. How did you do last week in the area of humility? Did anything significant take place that provided either victory or defeat for you?

"What will it take to come clean?"

It had seemed like a great idea at the time—pieces of gray duct tape layered on the cat, like overlapping armor plates. In the eye of any imaginative five-year-old, this was both genius and art. With his sister holding Puff's legs, he pressed strips of tape on the cat's sides. But when Mom saw the cat and wanted to know whose idea this was, he wanted to hide. Somehow, saying the words, "I did it," was the furthest thing from his mind, as he raced to find a scapegoat.

King David knew that feeling. He had a guilty conscience, and it haunted him relentlessly. He had abused his power as king and loitered too long looking at Bathsheba bathing next door. As David's gaze turned to lust, he snared and bedded Bathsheba while her husband Uriah was away fighting David's wars. Deceit led to treachery, as David tried to cover up his adultery. David thought he had hidden it from everyone—but God knew.

David could not escape the hand of God on his spirit. "When I kept silent, my bones wasted away..."(Ps 32.2) (NIV) Because David knew God, continuing to hide from him was not an option. "So I confessed my sins and told them all to you." (vs. 5) (CEV)

Confession is God's remedy for a fractured relationship with him. It's the key to the door that locks shut between God and us when we sin. It's the way out from under the hand of God pressing our conscience about our "hidden" sins.

Reflection

If confession is good for the soul, why do I wait so long to confess? Surely it is the temptation of the enemy whispering lies in my ear about my loving God. For God loves me, he calls me his own, and will forgive my sins, if I will only turn to him.

Accountability and Application

Are you a blessed man "in whose spirit there is no deceit?"

Is God nudging you about a past act, a present disobedience or a pattern of hidden sin?

Act on it. The hour of confession is now.

Prayer

Lord, let nothing in my life separate me from fellowship with you. Give me the willingness to acknowledge my sin and turn from my wicked ways.

WEEK 4—Confession

Confessing and Cleansing
1 John 1.9 *(NT p. 257)*

"Scrubbed up"

DAY 2

As he looked up from the dentist's chair, that old clammy feeling spread from his knotted stomach to his tense shoulders and over his furrowed brow. Today, Dr. Ferguson was not going to drill, cut, pull, or even clean Dave's teeth. Today was for x-rays that indicated how much pain was ahead. Dave had ignored his teeth for twelve years, and his failure to have regular cleanings had led to serious decay. Destructive bacteria had lived for years under his gums, beyond the reach of the toothbrush or floss. Though serious infection had even taken some bone mass, Dave had felt nothing. Now he would need deep cleaning, surgery and good insurance.

Sin, like any biological infection, can be ignored. Yet the effects of neglect are undeniable and damaging. Sin can corrode the soul and without cleansing, can deal a deadly blow.

Confession is God's deep cleaning for sin. In his epistle, John writes, "If we confess our sins to God, he can always be trusted to forgive us and take our sins away."

How does he clean us up? By the washing of the Word of God. God's Word runs deep into the very fiber of our being and cleanses us at the unconscious level of all unrighteousness. As with a serious infection whose effects cannot be readily seen, so it is with sin whose effects may go unnoticed. It is God's desire to free us from sins.

Reflection

Sin is not just an action; it is also a condition. And the "self-performed" spiritual deep cleaning is as futile a task as self-performed oral surgery. I need God to search me, to know my heart, to try me and know my thoughts, keeping in mind that he is faithful to cleanse and forgive me.

Accountability and Application

Pause and ask God to sort though your life. If he convicts you of a sin, ask him to cleanse you.

Prayer

Lord, I've neglected to confess many of my sins. And because I've not been keeping clean with you, sin has taken root. I'd like to deal with these sins. Please wash me clean. Dig up the roots and reveal the unseen areas. Help me to stay clean in you.

23

WEEK 4—Confession

Confessing and Healing
James 5.13-19 *(NT p. 248)*

"Can we talk?"

DAY 3

In the late1980's, comedienne Joan Rivers popularized a phrase and set off a trend for TV candor that has gone from bad to worse in the succeeding decade. Set in the casual style of her talk show, Rivers moved beyond her guest's remark to a pointed, stinging truth: "Can we talk?" Americans spread this catchy phrase, reading it as code for cutting facts.

Challenging a friend to speak plainly, without mincing words, dodging the truth or glossing over the facts, is a mark of integrity and an earnest desire for relationship. To say to someone, "Can we talk?" should say something deep, without superficiality or false sincerity.

In the Epistle from James, we get such a challenge. He says to "tell each other what you have done...you can pray for one another and be healed." Just short of prayer, personal confession may be the most candid talk we can have with another person. James is telling us to talk plainly about what grieves God's heart, verbally with another believer. Unlike the staged "tell all" tabloid confessions of our day, James calls the Christian to something deeper, more intimate and healing.

It is only God who forgives our sins. But the act of going to another believer in confession exposes to the light that which was hidden in darkness, and through this confession of sin, we can disarms sin's power. Can we talk? Yes, to God. And can we talk to a brother in Christ? Yes, for accountability is part of what Christ's body, the church provides.

Reflection

I fear sharing my struggles with someone else. I fear more the sharing of my sins. It seems that I prefer the darkness of my guilt to the clean light of a clear conscience. I find the thought of telling my sins to another an impossibility. God's prompting to confession to another believer is for my good; his call to me to confess my sins is for my wholeness.

Accountability and Application

Is God nudging you about confessing a sin? Has he drawn to your mind a mature believer who will hear you and, in Jesus name, receive your heart's confession with gentleness and discretion?

Prayer

Lord, I have not practiced confession of my sins to others. It's difficult enough for me to deal with them with you. Please give me the opportunity and the openness to expose the dark areas of my soul to another in Christ.

WEEK 4—Confession

Owning My Sin
John 9.35-41 *(NT p. 113)*

"Who am I fooling?"

The prison ministry leader was speaking to a group of trainees who would help men coming out of prison make the transition to the outside world. He addressed the problem of the alarming rate of repeat offenders to emphasize the importance of the role the trainees were about to have. Then he explained a chronic problem with recovering inmates. In order to get past their personal history, it is important that the men first own, or take responsibility for, their crime. As long as the inmate denied the harm he had caused, he would continue to view himself as a victim—a victim of his environment, his home or the system that had apprehended and imprisoned him.

Reflection

The story of the blind man who had been healed by Jesus is about a wonderful miracle of restoration, but it also is about the sin of the Pharisees. They were angry and jealous that Jesus had healed a man, and they were powerless. The blind man was thrilled to observe the leaders. They were upset that Jesus did this work on the Sabbath when he should not be working. The Pharisees didn't want to accept the positive testimony of the healed man so they started to assassinate his character. Jesus interrupted the conversation by saying he had come to give sight to the blind and to affirm both the healed man and the healing act.

The Pharisees asked, "Are we blind?" Jesus said, "If you were blind, you would not be guilty. But now that you claim to see, you will keep on being guilty." (v. 41)

Accountability and Application

Although we are not guilty of crimes punishable by prison, we each have our own sins. What sin or sins have you not yet admitted? Do you believe that you are less guilty of offending God because you haven't come clean? Or do you see that you're the only one who is fooled?

Prayer

Right now, Lord, I will stop pretending that I'm clean before you. I admit that I need a house cleaning. You run a spiritual janitorial service. Please accept my prayer as an invitation to start the clean up!

WEEK 4—Confession

Agreeing with God
Romans 10.8-11 *(NT p. 169)*

"This is serious!"

DAY 5

This crime has been described as the most reprehensible ever committed on American soil—an act of terrorism targeted at a sight including a child care facility in the Federal Building. The nation followed the trial day by day. The prosecution built a factual case detailing people, locations, phone calls and conversations. Some of the evidence was circumstantial, but the facts regarding who, what, where and when became clear. The verdict was decisive.

Reflection

The facts build the case! In Romans 10, Paul is not talking about confession in the negative sense, but in the positive sense. To believe and tell—these are the two aspects of saving faith in this text. However, what the believer tells is linked to the facts! To make a true confession is to agree with God about Jesus Christ, to agree with God about the resurrection and to agree about my need for salvation.

Confession of sin has the same element of agreement. What I confess is not my excuse, nor is it my complaint for getting caught. I don't deny it, I don't excuse it and I don't trivialize it. True confession is agreeing with God that sin is serious. It is so serious that Jesus Christ, God's Son, died to free me of the consequences of my sin.

Accountability and Application

Do I identify issues in my life that I have come to tolerate that God condemns?

Is my casual attitude about the seriousness of sin one of ignorance, or "in-your-face" arrogance before a holy God?

Identify one person that you will share your thoughts with on confession.

Prayer

Lord, I know the feeling of not being taken seriously. Please forgive me for taking lightly the sacrifice you made for me. I see more clearly that without your intervention I would have no hope.

WEEK 4—Confession

Taking Responsibility for My Sin
1 John 1.6-10 *(NT p. 257)*

"I'm on the hook"

DAY 6

Frank, a father of three, had experienced a rocky marital relationship. His inconsistencies and especially his lack of integrity in being faithful to his wife, on at least four known occasions, had caused lack of trust and intimacy in their marriage. They had turned to a marriage counselor for help. Frank's wife, while still hopeful, expressed caution, even though the words of commitment seemed genuine to get back on the path of rebuilding. Only accidentally did the counselor happen to overhear a conversation in a restaurant when Frank was sharing with a friend about his troubled marriage. "I need to play along for at least six months," he said. "My wife will inherit about ten thousand dollars from her dad, and I'd like to get a piece of that before I hang it up."

Reflection

Thoughts or motivations are sometimes hard to know. People can be fooled by the right words, then be disappointed by inconsistent behavior which shows the true motive of the heart. God knows our thoughts and the intent of our heart. In fact, sometimes we have even fooled ourselves as to our motive, and only the conviction of the Holy Spirit helps bring to light how phony we are. God does not listen to false motives. He is not taken in by our games or deception. When we come clean in prayer, asking with a right heart, God will hear and respond.

Accountability and Application

If there were a TV screen above us as we talked, which would print out our motives or second agendas, would our intentions and promises be more truthful? Realizing that God already knows even the hidden thoughts, what do I need to confess to God, and what forgiveness do I need to seek from my wife, family or others whom I may have "conned"?

Prayer

Thank you, Lord, for making me come clean. I want to ask that the Holy Spirit will convict me each time I start to deceive someone or myself with a false motive in my heart and mind. Don't let me be the victim of my own deception. Without your truth I could easily self-destruct.

WEEK 4—Confession

Confession Is More Than Words

Romans 8.13, 14 *(NT p. 167)*

"I quit"

DAY 7

"Racing is in your blood," Jim's brother noted. "Dad was hooked on it too, but you are pulled to racecars like a magnet pulls steel." It was true. Jim had been sucked into various racecars and races and was making a mess of his life. Lately, he was spending more and more money just to get to the races.

And, he put a down payment on his own racecar, which he could not afford. Now, he was making deals to get into the business. There seemed to be no end to it. The more he became involved, the more he wanted. And, his wife had no idea just how deep into it he really was.

At first he rationalized it as entertainment. Now, separated from his wife, and about $80,000 in debt, he had to face that his addiction had caused this mess. The problem was clear. The missing piece was, however, that "Jim didn't want to change!"

Reflection

Confession in words only is insincere and even deceptive. Change is the proof that makes confession genuine. From a statement of intention, to a specific and a consistent pattern of avoiding the behavior and practicing the new right way, is proof positive that a change has taken place. Here are four steps to lead you from mere words to change:

1. State your sin and the need for a change.
2. Describe what you will do and what you will no longer do.
3. Understand the principles from the Bible that form the basis of your choice.
4. Establish an accountability plan.

Accountability and Application

Do I have a trusted friend to whom I will give permission to hold me accountable? Have I specifically shared the area of struggle with this person and asked for a regular checkup on how I'm doing? Am I willing to give that person permission to probe beyond what I say, to talk with my wife and others to see how I'm doing in my change?

Prayer

Habits die hard, Lord. I need your help, first with courage to do what I need to do, and then with openness to an accountability partner, to keep me on track. When I fail, give me the grace to admit it quickly and turn around to get back on the path of following you, Lord.

WEEK 5— Brokenness

A Place of Beginning
John 1.14 *(NT p. 102)*

LAST WEEK IN REVIEW: *When you are at the end of yourself and you allow yourself to be broken before God, there is no more of your "self" to hold on to. It is then that God has an open field in which to work. What area of last week's study particularly challenged you? Were you able to experience brokenness in any way? How?*

"Exposed"

Former presidential aide, Chuck Colsen, writes about the moments just prior to his salvation. The words of C. S. Lewis penetrated his heart: "For pride is a spiritual cancer: it eats up the very possibility of love, contentment or even common sense." It was at that precise moment that Colsen surrendered everything. "I was exposed," he later wrote, "unprotected, for Lewis' words were describing me."

Says Colsen, "As I drove out of the driveway, the tears were flowing uncontrollably. I pulled to the side of the road not more than a hundred yards from the entrance of my friend's driveway...I remember hoping that my friend wouldn't hear my sobbing.... With my face cupped in my hands, head leaning forward against the wheel, I forgot about machismo, about pretenses, about fears of being weak. And as I did, I began to experience a wonderful feeling of being released."

Reflection

Most believers go through a period of breaking as they truly come to know and understand God's grace. Brokenness is when you are stripped before the Lord. There's no rock to hide behind. And although you fool others, the Lord knows who you are. So, in brokenness, you crumble under your own strength and cry out to him.

This occurs when a man is at the end of himself. And it is usually when this occurs, when he is totally broken, that God can finally work in his life. But, it is not a one-time event. Brokenness is an on-going process, a way of thinking.

Accountability and Application

Have you ever been broken?

Has God revealed himself to you deeply, where you saw him more clearly than you ever could have without having been broken?

How has he stripped you of the "props" that you generally lean on (things, positions and pretenses), and forced you to depend completely on him?

Would you be willing to be broken by him, and to surrender those props?

Prayer

Lord, I am not asking for things this time. I'm asking you to break me in such a way that I can no longer see me, only you, and in such a way that I know you more deeply than ever before. Take me to the next level with you. Remove my dependency on earthly things, positions and pretenses. Make me want nothing but you.

WEEK 5—Brokenness

A Pathway to Intimacy
John 1.14 *(NT p. 102)*

"No excuses"

DAY 2

One hot evening, a man stepped out onto the balcony of his home. Perhaps he had walked outside to gaze at the sunset, or to watch busy people return to their homes after a day at work. Certainly, he was not prepared for what he saw.

He likely did a "double-take" when he looked next door. Out on her balcony was his neighbor, bathing at dusk. It was her moment to relax at the end of the day, but her choice of a bathing spot was questionable. This man, known as King David, became preoccupied with this woman and with his own lust. His struggle may have been compounded by the fact that he wasn't doing what he should have been doing. It was the time for kings, like him, to be out fighting battles against his nation's enemies. Because he was not participating this time, he began to fight his own inward battle. When the whole episode was over, this man had committed adultery with the woman, concealed the matter from his staff and deceived her husband. Ultimately, he was party to the husband's murder.

Soon this information became public through his friend Nathan. David was crushed. He had no defense. He gave no excuses for his behavior. Instead, he allowed God to break him, and he became exposed to God. In the process, David wrote a song of brokenness—Psalm 51. In it, he reveals the path he took from brokenness to intimacy with God.

Reflection

Much of the time when spiritual leaders fail morally, they only repent when someone else has brought their sin to public attention. David could not have experienced intimacy with God in his state of denial and deception. Unfortunately, it took someone else to bring his denial to his attention.

Accountability and Application

Are you hiding any secret sins right now? Are you pretending that all is well, when really you need a Nathan to give you some straight-talk?

Are you willing to be honest about yourself?

Can you find someone with whom you can be brutally honest? Will you share these secret sins before they ask, or will it take their confrontation to bring them to the surface?

Prayer

Lord, search my heart. Show me if there are any dark places inside. Enable me to take initiative and confess whatever you show me. Bring me to the place where I desire intimacy with you more than I desire to protect my reputation.

WEEK 5—Brokenness

A Recognition of Weakness
Romans 7.15-25 *(NT p. 166)*

"More than I married"

DAY 3

Pastor John confided his weakness to his close friend. "I'm totally committed to my wife. We've been married for years, and I really love her. But, I'm just not attracted to her any more."

His friend Pete began to set him straight. "But you don't understand," John objected. "There's forty more pounds of her than what I married. It's really a struggle. And then there's... Cynthia, my church secretary. She's so sweet."

The time came for clear thinking. "Pastor, you're not playing on an even field. When you see your wife in the morning, she's not yet brushed her hair or teeth; she has no make-up on. But when you see Cynthia, she's all done up. You see her with no 'flaws' sticking out. Now this is what you need to do. First, realize, that you are at the end of your rope, you're broken, and you can't solve this on your own. Confess to God your weakness. Ask him for help in seeing the beautiful wife he gave you. Concentrate on her good points. And as far as Cynthia...get yourself another secretary. Don't even put that stumbling block in front of you."

Reflection

One vital aspect of brokenness is realizing your weakness, admitting it, confronting it, and taking any steps necessary to deal with it. Know that you are a weak human vessel, and that in your own strength you are not capable of living morally. Then ask God to give you the strength you lack. When you develop an "I am undone" attitude, God can work well with you, because you are constantly aware of your need for him."

The Apostle Paul knew this well. He said that the good that he wanted to do, he never seemed to be able to do. And that which was wrong which he didn't want to do, he kept doing. He too, fought his flesh, and found himself broken before the Lord.

Accountability and Application

Have you ever struggled with feelings and/or thoughts that are contrary to your good intentions?

Do you attempt to solve them on your own, hiding them from all so that you will still appear "together" before a watching world?

Prayer

Lord, I am undone. Immorality plagues me. Help me with the struggles which I alone cannot face.

WEEK 5—Brokenness

A Cry for Help
Romans 12.1, 2 *(NT p. 170)*

"At the end of my rope"

DAY 4

Paul Cedar, director of Mission America in the AD2000 and Beyond movement, once shared about his early ministry, when God called him to minister to pastors. The cash flow was miserable, and he didn't feel he could ask for compensation from those he was serving. His financial state grew worse. Ultimately, things reached a climax.

"In addition, I felt attacks of discouragement and disillusionment—even humiliation. One final straw was when an area hospital named us as one of the neediest families in the community and presented us with a food basket for Thanksgiving. The Lord brought us to a point of total brokenness before him. We were completely dependent on him.

"On a given evening, while I was driving alone in my car, I cried out to God in pain and frustration. It was the only time that I remember being angry with God. I rehearsed for him all of the sacrifices that we had made for him, and reminded him of the embarrassment and humiliation we had suffered. I said in desperation, 'Why don't you just take my life?' I felt his answer, 'Son, I already have taken your life.' Immediately, I was broken before him. I pulled over and sobbed."

Reflection

If you examine servants of Christ Jesus who are powerfully and effectively used by God, you will almost always find that they have experienced a desert and/or time of complete brokenness in their lives. It is this brokenness which enables them to be vessels used for God.

Joseph is a perfect example of this. His brokenness came during his exile in Egypt. Realizing that his life was no longer his own to control, he became completely surrendered to God. And, he was used by God in a mighty way.

Accountability and Application

How have you expressed surrender in your life? Have you turned over absolutely every part of your life to God? Are there any areas which you still control? Why is that area difficult to relinquish? It will help you to identify the reason and deal with it.

Prayer

Lord, I have not surrendered my entire life to you. I feel remorse for failing to follow you completely surrendered. Today I'm offering my life to you without reservation, without taking back control.

WEEK 5—Brokenness

A View of Yourself
John 15.5, 6 *(NT p. 120)*

"Nobody special"

DAY 5

With his retirement approaching, Joe became pensive. He had worked 30 years now for this supermarket chain. Many times he had wanted to quit, but he had stuck with it, knowing that his grit would pay in the end. He waited with anticipation for the dinner where he would be honored. Finally he would make them proud. But, make who proud?

His wife Mary would be there for his great moment. The bitterness of that tightened his jaw, though, as Joe was keenly aware that Mary never liked his job. Even though he'd been a store manager for the last 16 years, she always thought he could do better. And although his father was now long in the grave, he would finally make his name mean something. It frustrated him that his father was not here to see it. And, it angered him that his own grown children didn't care enough to attend his big night.

As Joe straightened his tie, the gnawing thought plagued him that really, of the things that counted most in life, he had nothing to show for it, nothing to be proud of. He was really getting a reward for endurance. He didn't have a marriage that was exemplary—not at all. He'd wanted to work on it, but kept putting it off, settling for "keeping the peace." He had almost no relationship with his kids. He didn't really like his job, and his job didn't give him any self-worth. Worst of all, he'd never really done anything to help anyone or serve anyone but himself. Who was Joe, anyway? He was a nobody.

Reflection

When you stand back to look at who you really are, your true colors will show when you recognize your true spiritual state apart from God. Have you ever really looked first-hand at your own "spiritual bankruptcy," or do you continue to project an image of being completely together? You see, Joe is normal—completely normal. It is only when we stand broken before a holy God, that we rise above "normalcy." For it is only then that others see Christ in us, and not the "nobody special" that we are.

The Apostle Paul was nobody special, yet he did amazing things for Christ's kingdom. In fact, he called himself the "least important of all the apostles," and said he didn't "deserve to be called an apostle." (1 Corinthians 15.9) Paul was broken, standing as nobody special, doing great things for God.

Accountability and Application:

Look at who you really are. Then get with a friend and discuss your discovery. Are you standing on your own merits? Or are you nobody special, letting Christ be great in you? Ask him to increase in you, so that you might decrease.

Prayer

Lord, I've been standing on my own merits; but they are nothing. I'm broken. Please break me further, and allow me to see myself as worthy only in you. Let me see myself as nobody without you, and my life as nothing without you.

WEEK 5—Brokenness

A Lost Hope
1 Peter 4.12-14 *(NT p. 252)*

"Losing the race"

DAY 6

Heading for home in his pick-up, Paul Broken Arrow hoped for the best. Tomorrow was the state championships for the 10K. It was a once-in-a-lifetime opportunity, and there were no second chances.

Paul was probably the fastest runner in the state. He'd already won state once, and he'd beaten runners at several regional levels. But this time, he was competing for a place on the Olympic ticket. He wasn't doing this to provide a way out. No, Paul liked living in this little town with his family. This was Paul's chance to make a name for his family and people—that was why he was preparing.

Paul had been training for this race for a year now. Sacrificing lots of free time, he'd committed to an austere diet and weight training program. Most of his friends and family knew of his commitment, and they were all behind him. But not one of them knew of his 4 a.m. exercise sessions. Not one of them knew of the extent of his sacrifice.

He planned to get a good night's sleep before the Olympic preliminaries. He ate well, exercised, and headed for bed. At three in the morning, he woke in a cold sweat. It wasn't nerves. Paul's appendix was inflamed. As he rode to the hospital in despair, he held the pain in his side, but felt it in his heart. A broken man with a broken heart—he'd been banking his all on this one day.

Reflection

There are two kinds of brokenness—voluntary and involuntary. Most of the time, people experience involuntary brokenness. We don't willingly ask for it or welcome it, but it breaks us just the same. It comes when we have tried everything else to make life work. Hopefully, when life bottoms out, we turn to the Lord in our despair.

Voluntary brokenness involves viewing yourself undone in God's sight—in desperate need of him.

Accountability and Application

My challenge to you is to choose brokenness, today, voluntarily.

If it comes to you involuntarily, without your invitation, accept it—even embrace it. For in brokenness you will find your wholeness in Christ.

Have you found insurmountable problems that bring brokenness your way? How do you respond?

Do you submit to brokenness voluntarily, allowing your "self" to be lost in Christ? In what way?

Prayer

Lord, I fight it when bad things come my way. Instead of responding rightly, I become angry. Help me to allow myself to be broken, leaning on you. Let me respond with a broken and contrite heart.

WEEK 5—Brokenness

A New Perspective

Philippians 1.20b-23 *(NT p. 208)*

"Legless"

DAY 7

Years ago, the Veterans of Foreign Wars sponsored a dinner to honor the war veterans in that area. At the dinner, a veteran soldier was introduced as one of the speakers. In making the introduction, the presiding officer referred to the fact that the man who was about to speak had lost a leg in World War II; the veteran was greeted with loud cheering as he arose to make the address. He began disavowing the introduction.

"No," he said, "that was a mistake. I lost nothing in the war, you see, for when we went to the war we resolved to give our country our all—even if it meant our lives. We reckoned that we would not even be coming back. So you see, in returning at all, everything that we brought back was clear gain."

Reflection

This is how we must view our spiritual journey with God. When we offered Christ lordship of our lives, we gave him everything we had, including our very lives. We died, in effect. Therefore, all that he allows us to keep is clear gain. We don't own anything in our own right, nor do we deserve any blessing. It is all grace.

Accountability and Application

How far short do you fall from this perspective?

Do you hold a "life owes this to me" attitude, or can you see it all as clear gain?

Would you be willing to adopt this mindset, as the veteran had?

How would it change any of your situations?

Prayer

Lord, when I give something up, I'm either bitter or self-righteous. I confess my own possessiveness and control of my life. I often demand my "rights." Help me to release them to you. Give me a proper perspective.

WEEK 6—Cleansing and Forgiveness

God's Call for Personal Holiness
1 Peter 1.15, 16 *(NT p. 250)*

GROUP DAY — DAY 1

LAST WEEK IN REVIEW: When you are at the end of yourself and you allow yourself to be broken, there is no more "self" to hold on to. It is then that God has an open field in which to work. Were you challenged and able to experience brokenness in any way last week? How?

"What will they say?"

Your interview seems to be going well until the vice president asks you an unexpected question—to list three words that best describe who you are as a person outside of work. Then he shows you a couple of hand-written pages and smiles, saying he just finished calling a number of your family members and close friends and asked them the same question. You begin to ponder what impression you have left with family and friends. Sure, they like you—even support you. But boil it down to three words? You begin to reflect on all of the situations that you've had with these people. You wonder exactly what they do think of you. Is the "you" that you are portraying the "you" that you really want them to see?

What would be the three words you would select about yourself? What words would you want selected about you? What picture of you would surface? Now here's a startling question: Would anyone even consider the word "holy" as a possible choice for you?

Reflection

Consider for a moment how God would describe you at this precise moment. What would be the Lord's three words describing you? God is holy and he says that you and I must be holy too—not just holy at church, but at home and in the marketplace; not just Sunday morning holiness, but Friday night holiness; holy when you're with other Christians, and holy when no one can see you.

Accountability and Application

The person you really are is the person you are when nobody else is around. Make a decision that who you really are is one who reflects the good and holy attributes of God.

Are you a person of holiness? Or do you think holiness is only for clergy?

How can you make holiness a lifestyle, and not just a one-time event at church?

What would you have to change to become a person of holiness?

Prayer

Lord, I'm a long way from being holy. I've never turned my heart, and my habits, toward holiness. Forgive me. Transform me. Incline my heart to holiness.

WEEK 6—Cleansing and Forgiveness

The Hidden Areas of the Heart
Romans 12.1 *(NT p. 170)*

"I do!"

DAY 2

Go back in your memory to your wedding—or the wedding of a close friend. Remember how sincerely those sacred vows were spoken: "in sickness or health, for richer or poorer, until death do us part." Those words mark one of the defining moments in life. Never again would life be the same. From that moment on, all your time, energy, plans, emotions, dreams and money are to be shared with another because you have promised to give yourself wholly to another person. From that moment on, all secrets, wrong thoughts, and selfish motives become painfully visible to another person.

Not only can a person commit himself to another person, he can also commit himself to the Lord God with the same level of intensity, devotion, transparency and significance.

The Apostle Paul begs these believers to give themselves over to the Lord. It is only because God is so incredibly faithful, merciful and committed to you that you would find yourself willing to give him your life. Like your spouse, he knows you and your innermost being, and what you're really like—but even more.

Reflection

Why does a man give his heart to a woman and commit himself to her for life? It is only because of his deep love for her that has developed through time and meaningful experiences. When others might have given up on him because of his failures, she stood by him determinedly. The Bible calls all men to experience the reality of a meaningful relationship with the Lord and to commit themselves to him for life. Similar to marriage, that specific act of dedication to Jesus Christ is one of the most significant decisions that a true believer will ever make.

Accountability and Application

Amazingly, God has already made that "heart commitment" toward you and proved his loyal love to you by sending his Son to die for you.

Have you responded to him in like commitment? Have you once and for all given him your whole self?

Have you stood before him transparent, willing to let him see what you are really like?

Are you hesitant to let the Lord see the real you?

Prayer

Lord, I bow my knee and hold my heart up to you. I do not hold back anything anymore from you. I present myself to you as a living sacrifice. I want to be holy. Do what it takes to make me holy, Lord.

WEEK 6—Cleansing and Forgiveness

A Holiness Check
2 Timothy 2.19b, 21b *(NT p. 226)*

"Marking the mileposts"

DAY 3

You spent some time at the hospital this morning with your father-in-law who is close to death. As you drive home with your wife, you listen as she tearfully reminisces and marks his mileposts. This "looking back" leads you to a little introspection yourself.

You remember the time that you walked the city streets at night with your son, looking at the barely discernable figures of homeless folks under the street lights. You had explained to him the need to make a difference in this world. When his friends from school got caught popping tires one night, you had a long talk with him about choosing not to follow the wrong crowd. When he hung out with a group—a gang—that restricted kids from other races, you explained to him for hours that he was no better than they.

But was it all talk? Did you do anything, or model in any way, a man who changed the world? Did you actually reach out across racial boundaries to understand what others feel? Have you added anything of significance to this world, or to anyone else's life? If someone were marking *your* mileposts, what would stand out? Would there be one significant time when you determined to turn from sin and wrongdoing? Is your "lifeline" filled with lots of highs, lows, bouts with sin, or decisions against sin? These defining moments determine our entire lives.

Reflection

You confess to others that you are a Christian, but you still tolerate acts of unholiness and selfishness, and find yourself making wrong decisions. Somewhere in the lifeline of the growing Christian is a defining decision toward holiness. Habits of unholiness that have been tolerated for years finally become intolerable, and you finally take responsibility to allow God to cleanse you.

A godly man makes a decision to turn away from evil and to seek cleansing and purity. First, he turns from evil; second, he stops doing evil by putting a final end to habits of unholiness; and third, he pursues righteousness in his heart and habits.

Accountability and Application

We tend to think holiness is just a matter of the heart. It isn't. It starts in the heart, but it must transform the habits.

How about a holiness check on yourself? In the past three years, what sinful areas in your life have you turned from? What areas in your life provide proof that you are indeed pursuing righteousness?

Prayer

Lord, forgive my sinful habits. Cleanse me as I open myself to the work of your Spirit. Help me to turn from evil. Empower me by your Spirit to stop specific sinful habits. Strengthen me in my pursuit of holiness.

WEEK 6—Cleansing and Forgiveness

A Clean Conscience
1 Timothy 1.5-7 *(NT p. 220)*

"You owe me!"

DAY 4

Standing with your two kids at an amusement park, you make the next turn in a snake-like line and find yourself face-to-face with your past—a neighbor from whom you once borrowed $200 when the transmission on your car gave out. When you were 19 and were ready to take on the world with no money or job, he had helped you. Shoveling his snow and hauling his trash were your exchanges for jumpstarts and fixed tires. Kind enough to make a loan, he understood your hard times, and you made a vow to repay.

Normally your folks would have supervised your follow-through on that commitment, but they weren't even together anymore, and this was the last thing on their mind. And so, eventually you forgot about that debt. The thought of it had surfaced a few times, but you had always pushed it back with the rationalization that you didn't even know this man's phone number.

You avoid the neighbor's glance and look down, but you are sure that his eyes are fixed on you, and you really don't know what to do or say.

Reflection

No matter how much we may try to keep the past buried, the Lord inevitably brings to light the issues in our lives that we haven't been willing to face. Unresolved sin is a huge weight on our lives. Although we confess our sins to God, if we've offended someone, we must make restitution in order to experience a true clear conscience and to enjoy God's fullest blessing. Although God's forgiveness awaits us if we ask, we must not assume people we've wronged have forgiven us. We must ask!

Accountability and Application

Having a clean conscience before God and man is an absolute requirement for personal holiness. Here's what you can do:
1. Slip away for some uninterrupted time.
2. Ask the Lord to reveal specific sins or problems that are still unresolved.
3. Write down every person and situation that comes to mind.
4. Put a #1 next to the most difficult to handle, then a #2, and so on.
5. Commit to the Lord that you will work at resolving these, starting with #1.
6. Call a close friend and tell him what you've decided.

Prayer

Lord, I realize that even though you have forgiven me, there are issues and offenses that I have against other men and women that I am responsible to bring to resolution. I don't have the strength to do this on my own. I need your help.

WEEK 6—Cleansing and Forgiveness

Reconciliation with God
Luke 15.11-32 *(NT p. 87)*

"Going back"

DAY 5

Have you ever gone back to your parents, as an adult yourself, to ask forgiveness for the sins of your youth? If you're like most, you probably weren't the easiest person to raise. You might have ripped your parents' hearts either with rebellion against them and their standards, or with your ungodly lifestyle choices of immorality or wild living. It may be 20 years later when you finally "see the light" and express your most humble apology. If you do, that moment will surely be one of the priceless treasures in your parents' lives.

Your heavenly Father has also loved you with parental love that is unconditional. When you were rebellious and/or ungodly in your behaviors and decisions, his love for you was just as strong as it is today. If you want to pursue holiness, there must come a time when you return to the Lord with apologies. It's time to come clean.

Reflection

The first time this hits you, you'll never be the same. It's a profound thought that the Lord takes every one of your sins personally. He views your sin as directly against him! King David said, "You are really the one I have sinned against; I have disobeyed you and have done wrong." (Psalm 51.4) The Apostle John knew this principle very well. He understood that if your walk with the Lord is going to be real and personal, there must not be anything between you and God. John instructs us, "But if we confess our sins to God, he can always be trusted to forgive us and take our sins away." (1 John 1.9)

Accountability and Application

One of the keys to walking with the Lord closely and personally is to confess and apologize to the Lord for the ways you have disobeyed and grieved him.

Are there sins and wrong attitudes in your life, past and present, which need to be reconciled with the Father? Are there unconfessed areas that you are hiding?

How would your walk with the Lord change if you were willing to set these areas straight?

Prayer

Lord, I apologize for taking so long in getting to this point, but I want to ask your personal forgiveness for _____.

WEEK 6—Cleansing and Forgiveness

The Foundation for Forgiveness
Luke 15.11-32 *(NT p. 87)*

"You're outta here!"

DAY 6

My teenager Juan is no different than most teens. Seeing only his own wants, he seems to miss the big picture. He'll argue with us because he thinks he knows it all. Sometimes he acts rebellious. And when he will have the best of intentions and motives, he will still blow it—again and again. When I have dared to expect something from him, he lets me down. So, he resolves to change his ways, only to return to the same behavior.

There usually comes a time that you tell a teen, "If you want to live in this house, and in harmony with this family, you'll follow the standards of the house. If not, you're outta here!" This demonstrates that your standards will reign over their desire to rebel. But when your teen asks forgiveness for walking in disobedience and unholiness, are you able to open your arms to him again?

Reflection

Once you have enjoyed the depth of relationship with the heavenly Father, you want more and more. You may turn back for a short time, thinking that life is easier to live on your own. Soon, though, you will run back to the Father who has known you, forgiven you, understood you, and made a place for you.

From the beginning, when Adam and Eve sinned in the garden, they were ashamed and could no longer walk in the coolness of the day with God. Again and again the Bible records that the Lord will not walk with those who continue to live in disobedience and unholiness.

Accountability and Application

The closer you walk with the Lord, the more sinful you will appear to yourself. There will always be times when you feel that walking with him is just too difficult, and certainly life on your own terms must be easier. These brief times soon bring a short period of repentance.

Do you honestly believe that the Lord welcomes you back when you ask forgiveness after you stray?

When you have been rebellious, what pierces your heart to return to him?
What can you do to keep yourself living his will and not your own will?

Prayer

Lord, I have come to you many times when I've blown it, seeking your forgiveness. Still, I stray, living with my own agenda, and ignoring you. I've messed up so many times that it's embarrassing coming again. I trust that you will once again extend your mercy. Help me to find the strength to keep pursuing your holiness.

WEEK 6—Cleansing and Forgiveness

The Incredible Reward of Holiness
1 Peter 1.6 *(NT p. 250)*

"Providing a lap"

DAY 7

Walking to the park with your daughter, you listen as she confidently relates what she wants to be when she grows up. Her speech reveals a child who has great security in her dad. The security she knows did not come overnight. Every day that you made your way from providing a living, to providing a lap for her in the easy chair, you added a block to the foundation for this relationship. Her entire trust is in your strong arms, listening ear, and warm heart. She trusts you completely, and, she is not daunted that you know her inside and out. In fact, your acute understanding of her zealous and impulsive nature draws her to you even more. You've forgiven her mistakes and selfishness again and again. And, to the extent that your forgiveness has been extended, and your patience tried, your love for each other has cemented.

Reflection

When a man who knows Christ begins the pilgrimage of holiness, the Lord reveals himself at deeper and deeper levels. Time spent with the Lord, restoration in times of failure, and promises to remain faithful, all serve to cement the relationship. Peter drew closer and more determined as a follower when he had failed the Lord and had to face the Lord with his failure. He then looked to the future with new resolve to remain close at the Lord's side.

Accountability and Application

Determine that in order for you to be solid in relationship with the Lord, you must be totally transparent with him.

Are there areas of your life which you are holding on to, resisting to show the "real you" to the Lord?

Would you like to have a deep relationship with him that results from that kind of dependency and transparency?

Do you want to be dependent on the Lord? What will it cost you?

Prayer

> Lord, I'm not sure about this deep relationship bit. I know I'm not as close as I can be. I hold back a lot. Help me to give it up to you. Cement us, Lord.

WEEK 7 — Pursuing God with a Whole Heart

Communicating with God

Romans 8.12-17 *(NT p. 167)*

GROUP DAY
DAY 1

LAST WEEK IN REVIEW: *When we ask for forgiveness and come clean before God, we provide a platform for a strong and ongoing relationship with God. What specific areas last week challenged you?*

"Full steam ahead"

Remember how it felt to fall in love? Feelings ran high. You always wanted to be with her. And you didn't seem to mind that she had caused some changes in your life.

You cleaned up your talk. You shaved a little closer. You opened car doors. Your dreams seemed to revolve around her and what might become of your life together. For the first time, your focus was on something more than a goal. It was on a relationship! And though you weren't good at it, you sure were eager to learn. You were willing to give it a try. That's the way it should be with God.

Reflection

Because of the cross, we can move beyond religious rituals to a relationship with God. We now have the right to call Almighty God "Abba." That's the word Jesus used in his more intimate moments with the Father (Mark 14.36).

We must examine worship, prayer and his Word, in light of the promised relationship—not a ritual. Jesus said that the Holy Spirit would come to help us and to teach us as a friend (John 14.26).

Will we let him?

What is the key to relationship with God?

Accountability and Application

The key to any healthy relationship is mutually honest and respectful communication. And, the command to be filled with the Holy Spirit means that we are not passive. We are always actively seeking relationship. We do this through worship, as we talk to him in prayer, and as he talks to us through his Word. Isn't that the way it is with any relationship? As we work together in honest dialogue, the relationship grows.

Prayer

Lord, thank you for "sonship" and for the privilege to move beyond rituals into a meaningful relationship with you. Forgive me for not relating to you in the past and help me to do so.

WEEK 7—Pursuing God with a Whole Heart

Worship As an Activity
Acts 2.43-47 *(NT p. 131)*

"Style or substance"

DAY 2

"Wow!" said Bob, "I could hardly believe it. Thousands of guys singing and praising God. The teaching was great. So was the prayer. And the thousands that were saved! I wouldn't have missed it for the world."

"I would," replied Ron flatly. "I just don't get into all of that showy stuff. I'd rather worship more quietly, more intimately. I want a teacher who is going to go through the Bible verse-by-verse, so I can learn. As for the singing, give me those old hymns that we sang in church when I was a kid. These tunes make me nervous. They're just too much."

Reflection

When you think of worship, what comes to mind? Songs? Prayer? If you have a religious tradition, you may think of the style you grew up with. As long as the traditions continue to point us toward an intimate relationship with God, they are good. But that is not always the case. Sometimes, instead of merely providing a framework for a relationship with God, traditions have a tendency to replace it.

This is not the fault of the clergy. It's just human nature. Routines often replace relationships. As the focus gradually shifts from what is loving to what is "right," worship can create an exclusive atmosphere rather than one that includes everyone. To put worship and relationship in perspective, let's take a look at the early church described in today's Scripture passage.

What did they spend time doing?
What was the ultimate outcome of their worship?
What does it say about your personal devotional life?

Accountability and Application

Worship in the early church was the result of a relationship with God experienced with others. Rituals and routines were far off. The bottom line was that they wanted reality with God in their everyday lives.

Think of worship not as an event, but as a process—an ongoing expression of our relationship with Christ.

Write about your perception of worship. How is it narrow? Now write a commitment to worship the Lord in a larger context, as an ongoing process of everyday life.

Prayer

Lord, forgive me where I've been narrow or hypocritical. Lead me to be more genuine in my worship of you. Lead me to be more open with you. Help me to take risks where necessary, and to expand my concept and practice of worship.

WEEK 7—Pursuing God with a Whole Heart

Worship As a Lifestyle
1 Corinthians 12.12-18 *(NT p. 183)*

"Moving beyond the pew"

DAY 3

Jim was content with his Anglo church in the deep South. He was involved in the church life there. He worked hard, gave to the church and was involved in the youth programs. One thing about this church—it was very white.

Jim had everything going for him. God had obviously "blessed" his efforts and Jim was comfortable with his religious identity. Many thought of Jim as a "godly man."

Then it happened. A black family, moving to town to join ministry efforts with their friends, showed up at church one Sunday. The congregation didn't know how to react. Neither did Jim. In fact, because he didn't know what to say, he avoided them. Sadly, the pastor did too. So, they visited but were ignored. But they weren't daunted.

This family walked right up to the pastor and asked him about the church's programs and offerings. It was obvious they were there to stay.

Reflection

Today's passage teaches that all parts of a body are important. If you have allowed a lifestyle or mindset which excludes certain groups of people or "parts of the body," you are wrong! God wants us to view each and every person as a member of his body.

What do you think of Jim's reaction in the story?

What type of reaction do you think God would desire? How would you react?

What does the Scripture passage teach you personally?

Accountability and Application

God is way ahead of us. His Spirit is preparing the hearts of those he will bring into our lives to respond to the message of his love. However, our hearts must be prepared not only to teach that love, but also to live it out. Jesus stepped out of the cultural and religious norms of his day in order to respond to the call of God's love. So did Peter. So should we!

Write an incident in which you are, or were, stretched to step out of the cultural norms. Why was it difficult? Write a commitment to God to be open to move "religion" out of the pew and into real life.

Prayer

Lord, I have locked myself in rituals that guarantee my spiritual comfort. I need and want a deepening relationship with you. I now see that if I am to have it, I must step out in faith into areas that stretch me beyond comfort. Help me to do so.

WEEK 7—Pursuing God with a Whole Heart

Prayer: Confession, Repentance and Forgiveness
1 John 1.7-10 *(NT p. 257)*

"Too big to forgive"

DAY 4

Dave was in turmoil. It had all happened so fast. All he was going to do was a few drug deals. Everybody else does, right? In his neighborhood, it was only the next logical step in the struggle for survival. He's already had run-ins with the law, so drugs wouldn't matter that much.

Now, he'd been caught in the act. The "buy" was part of a large sting operation. After reading him his rights, the police threw him in a holding cell and the legal process was set in motion. He was sentenced to five years. During that time he began to read his Gideon New Testament. Little by little, light invaded his dark world. He began to see where he'd gone wrong and why.

But, the message was too good to be true. Total forgiveness? No way—not after what he'd done. Not after all the other things the cops didn't even know about. The fact is, though, that God did.

Reflection

Many of the heresies of our time deny that immorality disrupts our communion with God. In short, many deny the concept of sin.

Have you ever felt the way Dave feels? Can you trust your emotions in these matters?

What is true confession? What will God do if we confess? Why?

Accountability and Application

The blood of Christ was shed for all people. The acceptance of this blood is three-fold: 1) Confession begins by stepping out of denial to acknowledge our sin. 2) Repentance continues the process by turning from the sin, to be cleansed and purified. 3) Forgiveness is God's personal assurance of his love for us in Christ, in spite of our sin.

Christians need the Gospel, too! We may not be able to identify with Dave, but there is surely something that is hindering our walk with God. To experience forgiveness, we must walk through the process and return to our loving Father. He's the God of second chances.

Prayer

Father, it's against you that I have sinned. Worse yet, I've rationalized it away. I've tried to ignore it. I repent of this sin. I want you to take it away. Wash me in the blood of your Son that I may once again be the son you'd have me to be. Lead me in the path of righteousness.

WEEK 7— Pursuing God with a Whole Heart

Prayer: Thanksgiving and Supplication
Ephesians 3.14-21 *(NT p. 204)*

"How do I pray now?"

DAY 5

John had tried to be a good dad...so what happened? His teenage son was clearly hanging around with the wrong crowd. It was worse than language, cigarettes and beer. John feared for his son's life.

It's not that John Jr. hadn't seen a clear alternative. John and his wife had been missionaries. Since returning from the field, they'd led exemplary lives in the community, and all their friends were positive role models. So, it was surprising that John Jr. would stray so far from the mark. No one seemed to know why—least of all, John!

Finally, it all came to a head. While John was gone on a business trip, his son came home "stoned" and threatened his mother with a knife. The police came, disarmed the boy and took him away. Not knowing what to do, John left his son in the county jail for a few days to "cool off and think about it." And then he tried to pray....

Reflection

In Philippians 4.6,7, Paul exhorts us not to worry about anything, but to pray about everything. Anxiety is self-centered, counter-productive worry. As legitimate as it seems, however, it is unbelief.

Have you ever experienced anything like John did in the story? How did you feel?

Did it change your impression of God? Should it? What is still true of God's character?

What should John pray for?

Accountability and Application

You're praying "Santa Claus" prayers! You think anything you ask for will be delivered. Why? You've lived as you should. Why should you struggle?

Isn't that the way we treat God? We spend very little time with him, just praising him for who he is and thanking him for what he has done for us.

Paul didn't pray that way, and neither should we. Adoration, confession and thanksgiving are as much a part of prayer as supplication. In fact, they are the best preparation for our petitions, because they prepare our hearts.

Prayer

Oh Lord God! Thank you for who you are. Thank you for your love that you so lavishly shed upon all of us at the cross. Help me to be a channel of that love to others.

WEEK 7—Pursuing God with a Whole Heart

Prayer: The Importance of His Word
2 Timothy 3.16, 17 *(NT p. 227)*

"What's the answer?"

DAY 6

Bill was a busy man! And he made sure that everyone knew it. He was a husband, a father, a deacon of the church, a board member of several non-profit organizations and a member of various clubs in town. And if that weren't enough, Bill was also part of the executive team of a large publicly-owned company.

Like everyone, he was a man with bills to pay, schedules to keep, people to see and places to go. He would say that he was trying to make his faith relevant to the marketplace. But, he had the sneaking suspicion that he was missing something. He didn't seem to know what it was. Bill was restlessly looking for something more than the routine things of life.

Lately he was in conflict with his family, and even his relatives. So, he tried to solve problems with logical solutions—his way. It never occurred to him that he had a resource to draw from which would help him find solutions to the everyday problems which plagued him. But then, as involved as Bill was in activities of the church, he never spent any time reading the Bible.

Reflection

When we spend time reading the Word of God, we find out who we really are in light of who God is. We discover how Jesus responded to human situations, and we are exhorted to make godly choices.

Do you "make time" for the Word?

What can you gain from the Holy Spirit's interpretation of the Word?

Have you neglected to turn to the Bible as a resource for everyday life problems?

Accountability and Application

The Bible is the perfect Book! It was written over a period of 1500 years by many different authors, in three different languages. Starting with Moses, a former Egyptian prince, we see that the inspiration of God touched a wide variety of authors. Not only were there prophets, priests and kings, but there were many common men like Peter, a fisherman and follower of Christ. The story starts in the Middle East and progresses throughout North Africa and Europe as disciples, soldiers, slaves and traders spread the news of Christ to any and all who would listen.

Among the major themes of the Bible is included who God is, what he expects of his creation, and how he, himself, is willing to help us attain it. It is too marvelous a Book to be ignored. And yet, we're just too busy.

Prayer

Lord, please forgive me for ignoring your Word. Give me a desire to learn from it and to turn to it constantly as a resource for life. Help me to listen to your Holy Spirit as I struggle to apply what you say to me about my daily life.

WEEK 7— Pursuing God with a Whole Heart

Prayer: His Word and Victory
John 14.21-24 *(NT p. 119)*

"Because you say so, Lord"

DAY 7

She was beautiful! There she was, about 10 years younger than Sam and applying for the job of his administrative assistant. During the interview, everything seemed to go well and she appeared to be quite business-like. But as the months passed and they were continually working together, his respect for her gradually changed into something more intimate. Though he hadn't yet pursued her, he was sensing a gentle nudge from her. His fantasies soared.

As a married Christian man, his conscience was tormented. How could he have let this happen? He was completely under her spell. So much so that, while his wife and children were preparing dinner, he was in the bedroom contemplating the divorce.

Then God spoke. It wasn't audible; rather, it was that small voice that comes within our hearts. He fell to his knees. Then he lay prostrate before God and pleaded with him to set him free of this lust that would destroy everything. He laid there for a long time, and God's Word kept breaking through the storm of his emotions sternly warning him to let it go and become a man of God. The struggle continued. But, when he heard his wife's voice calling him to dinner, the siege was lifted. He knew he'd won—because of God's Word.

Reflection

The Word of God comes to the fore when it has been hidden in your heart, when you have spent enough time with God to know what his Word is about, what he judges, accepts, condones, and celebrates. When you are faced with a huge trial, will the Word of God set your course?

What does this story tell you about the Word of God?

How does this victory encourage you in your present circumstances?

Accountability and Application

Bible scholarship, is not the sole key to greater revelation of God. It is the combination of the Word and a heart prepared by prayer. When the Word falls on a heart that has been in prayerful humility, it brings about obedience. Therefore, anyone, big or small, rich or poor, whose heart is in the right place can obey God.

Prayer

Lord, thank you for the victory we have over sin because of Christ Jesus. Thank you for your Word that we can rely on to bring us into closer relationship with you as we seek to obey. Thank you for your willingness to reveal yourself to those whose hearts belong to you.

WEEK 8—My Relational Response to God and Others

The Object of Your Worship
Matthew 4.7-11 *(NT p. 8)*

GROUP DAY / DAY 1

LAST WEEK IN REVIEW: *As we've studied the Word, prayer and worship, it is evident that they are vehicles of communication with God. How have you reached God through these? Has there been a change?*

"Worshiping work"

When writing of many American Christians, Gordon Dahl said that they:

> "...tend to worship their work,
> to work at their play, and to play at their worship.
> As a result...their lifestyles resemble
> a cast of characters in search of a plot."

Gordon Dahl's quote suggests a picture of worship. God is an audience of One! We, the worshipers, are the cast. Worship leaders, musicians and ministers are the coaches. The plot is the glory of God and his triumph and victory. The story line is human history.

The true worship of God is the highest goal of the Church. From it flow the other aspects of the Christian life. In worship we adore God and ascribe worth and value to him.

Scripture is central in preparing us to worship, teaching us the acts and character of God. Then, what we experience in worship is its complement. Our experience makes God's truth personal to us.

Reflection

In our worship, as in drama, symbols are frequently used. Stylistic elements in form and music, both old and new, give the security of tradition or the freshness of new expression. Each unique Christian brings his or her own needs, joys and aspirations to worship. True worship is giving up to the Lord all that we are, all that we have, and all that demands our highest loyalty. If you're not sure what demands your loyalty, ask yourself what it is that draws most of your time, resources, and attention.

In false worship, the object of worship is not worthy of our loyalty. Men find it easy to affix loyalty to possessions and accomplishments. It has been said, "The guy who dies with the most toys wins." Accumulation, loyalty, and attention all speak of worship.

Accountabilty and Application

If you were standing before God, what would you say in honor or thanksgiving to him? Take time now to say it out loud in your group or write it down. What idols do you need to confront in your life? Ask God to make you willing to let go.

Prayer

God, you are worthy. Jesus Christ, I honor you. Holy Spirit, thank you for indwelling me. Let all my deepest loyalty be to you. Pull me away from any distractions that prohibit me from worshiping.

WEEK 8—My Relational Response to God and Others

Clarifying Your Priorities
Matthew 6.19-21 *(NT p. 11)*

"Where's your treasure?"

DAY 2

A missionary was speaking at a church service. He challenged his congregation abruptly: "I want your money, I want your children and I want your prayers, and I want them in that order!" He clearly understood the thrust of Matthew 6.21.

It is our treasure that leads our loyalty. If our wealth is committed, we become involved. We often see churches sending out youth on short-term mission trips. Parents who have committed to "spend" tend to "send" their young people. When you have your money committed and your children involved, you'll keep them on the top of the prayer list, and you'll spend more time, effort and attention in helping them.

Reflection

The most sensitive nerve in a man's body is the one connected to his wallet! Money is very important in a man's life. He spends his entire life in work. And aside from the experience gained, and hopefully some pride of accomplishment, its chief benefit is a paycheck.

Because resources are so tied to our identity, as well as to our sense of well being, we can often fool ourselves. If I had unlimited funds, what would I like to do? If I had $5,000 and only one week to live, what would I do with it?

Accountability and Application

Have you ever discussed with your wife the subject of your giving to the Lord's work? If not, you should do it soon. Try involving your family in a special project for the Lord which would demand your resources and time. Design it so that it involves not only giving, but praying and some "hands-on" action too.

Prayer

Lord, I admit that money can grab me in a way that is hard to break. I believe that all that I have is truly yours, but sometimes I act as though I am the owner and not the steward. Please forgive my tight-fistedness. Free me to become a vessel of your blessing to others.

WEEK 8—My Relational Response to God and Others

Giving to God
2 Corinthians 8.1-5 *(NT p. 192)*

"Worshiping with my wallet"

DAY 3

Roger had a good job in construction. He and his wife both had good incomes. They had a comfortable home, adequate cars and all of their needs met. They were talking with their pastor about the blessing of their current financial situation.

"We've been feeling a special calling to give above our regular tithe. We want to ask you about personal needs that you may know about in the lives of others in the congregation or among our missionaries." The pastor was able to direct them to church members in need. On three other occasions, Roger and his wife had already given special, "over-and-beyond" gifts. Each time they had experienced the Lord's blessing and a deep feeling of purpose.

Reflection

Roger and his wife have experienced a part of worship that many Christians have not yet tapped in to. These experiences of worship could be more frequent if we understood the principle of the church meeting needs. Those with the ability to share wealth should give to those in need. Giving is only one of several areas of worship in which Christians should increase their experience. It has been said that you can tell a person's heart and loyalties by observing where they spend their money. If your checkbook register were exposed, what would it show?

Accountability and Application

If you are currently not giving to God according to the biblical standard, what plan could you make to correct the pattern?

If a man in an accountability group asked to see your checkbook, would you be ashamed or proud of how it reflects your integrity in giving to God?

Prayer

Lord, I acknowledge that all I have belongs to you. Help me to manage your resources in a way that honors you and meets the needs of my family.

WEEK 8— My Relational Response to God and Others

My Circle of Influence
Matthew 6.31-33 *(NT p. 11)*

"Making a difference"

DAY 4

George, a committed Christian, was growing in his awareness of God's expectations for his life and influences. He was owner of a mid-size metal business in an industrial state. In response to a challenge at a Promise Keepers meeting he determined to change the hiring practices of his plant. Instead of only looking for experienced men, he chose to seek men of ethnic diversity where possible. If the prospective employee was lacking in a certain skill or machine operation, he determined that if possible, he would provide training. Over a period of two years he has now given employment to five new men. Four of the five were productive. The fifth was re-directed to another line of work where he could excel. One of the new men became a believer through the witness of a fellow employee. He confided to George that his increased income had not only benefited his family, but it had also allowed that family to increase support to their church.

Reflection

In this story you see a progression of the use of influence and power to show intention as a Christian and toward the fulfillment of reconciliation. All of the areas of our lives tend to spread out like rings on a pool of water: our marriage, our children, our friends, our church, our work, and even the scope of our work in some cases. Would someone say of you that your life is ultimately influencing someone else?

This is the point. We need to build solid foundations in each area of our lives. God wants us to serve him by serving our spouse, by loving our children, etc. Each area is an area of obedience to Christ.

Accountability and Application

If the loyalty that I demonstrate to the body of Christ, the Church, were measured by God's loyalty to me, how would I be doing?

Prayer

Lord, you have given me many areas of influence. Help me to show my devotion to you by those that I serve.

WEEK 8—My Relational Response to God and Others

Caring for Kids
Ephesians 6.1-4 *(NT p. 206)*

"Caring for kids"

DAY 5

A 50-plus-year-old man spoke of his late father and had this to say, "He was a wonderful dad, not perfect, but outstanding. The thing I remember best is how my dad would answer my questions." He went on to say, "He never was harsh, never out of control. His whole life was one of teaching me. There never was a question off limits. When I think back on the fifteen years I had with him before he died, I think of the saying, 'A wise teacher makes learning a joy.'"

Reflection

The text in Ephesians tells us, as parents, not to be hard. Another translation uses the word "exasperate" or "frustrate." In our desire to be correct and play by the rules, we often find it difficult to make a transition year-by-year with our children as they develop. The relationship of a man to his sons and daughters is critical. A man teaches his son how to treat a lady by the way he treats his wife, how he speaks of her to others and how he allows others to speak to her. From her father, a girl learns much of what to expect from a man and what to look for in a future husband.

Men, you are God's personal tutor placed in the lives of your children.

Accountability and Application

Am I allowing my preoccupation with my work, my hobbies or my toys to make me miss the blessing of being the dad that God has designed me to be? What specific issues have caused me to be too severe in training my kids?

Prayer

Lord, let me be strong, honest and loving in my relationship with my kids. When I mess up, give me humility to apologize. When I do it well, allow me to glance over my shoulder and see your smile. I'll smile with you because they are also your children.

WEEK 8—My Relational Response to God and Others

Faith or Idols
Luke 12.13-21 *(NT p. 83)*

"More than a statue"

DAY 6

One day when the Sunday school teacher had given a lesson on idols, the eight-year-old Trent asked his father on the drive home, "Dad, do you know what an idol is?" His thoughts were interrupted by the question, and Dad replied without giving it much thought. He hadn't planned on exploring the subject to any extent.

"Well, it is something that people worship or bow down in front of, like a carving, or a statue," Dad answered. As with any child-like discourse, the next question followed logically, then what is worship?

"When you worship something, you care about it so much that you give it attention, honor, and respect. You think very much of it," the father attempted to explain. This was a tough one. "An idol can be anything or anybody that takes the place of God, or of our highest loyalty. So when we worship it, we give all of our attention and honor to something that takes our loyalty, or the place of God."

Trent thought for a moment. "Dad, Grandpa has an idol, doesn't he? That old car that he keeps so perfect and won't let us touch—that's his idol."

Reflection

In the Scripture passage today we see a father and a boy. The father is scratching for all the faith he can pull together, and then he asks for more. There are two great issues we all face about our belief—intensity and object. Many of us are very intense in our commitment to a pet idol. We invest time, money, attention, practice and thought into the object of our loyalty. If our obsession with anything takes away from the intensity of our loyalty to God, we are practicing idolatry. God must be our focus. When God is number One in our loyalty and attention, then we have freedom to enjoy the things he gives us.

It doesn't need to be a carved image; it might even have four sport wheels.

Accountability and Application

A clarifying question is: Do I own it, or does it own me? Think about that. Think about the things in your life that may be idols to you. Do they own you? Could you easily rid yourself of them? Make a note of those things, and describe the idolatry. Describe their control over you. Purpose to make a change.

Prayer

God, I confess that I get ensnared by things. Sometimes I get so lured into my job and success that I begin to think I'm the center of it all. Let me see you as the center around which I order my life. Forgive my selfish preoccupation.

WEEK 8—My Relational Response to God and Others

Doubting the Truth

John 20.19-29 *(NT p. 125, 126)*

"I'll believe it when I see it"

DAY 7

The middle-aged computer engineer sat across the table as he expressed his struggle. "I was raised as a Christian, attended church and I personally made a commitment to God years ago, at 20. Even today, sometimes I doubt. It's like all of my time and energy in work are related to hard science. Demonstration of results and cause-and-effect—this is how I think. So sometimes I wonder, "Is he really there? Does he really want to be involved in my personal life? Even though it is hard for a fact-driven person like me to accept things like Christ's resurrection and ascension into heaven, or the fact that he's the Son of God, somehow I manage to accept these by faith. But the fact that he wants to be personally involved in my life! That's a hard one to believe with no evidence."

I responded with the story of today's Scripture passage: Even Thomas, a disciple of Christ, struggled with doubt. You are not alone!

Reflection

When we are consumed with a certain perspective, we try to put all of life into the same box. If all of life were based on proven facts, how would you answer some of the big questions: Where did I come from? Where am I going? If we find our thinking concentrated on only the physical realities of life, then the spiritual, non-tangible will not fit into this paradigm. As we grasp to keep balance, let's remember that Jesus didn't rebuke, but offered his hand of confirmation.

Accountability and Application

What areas of life cause you to question? Have you shared your struggles with another believer?

What good can come out of doubting and questioning your faith? Write down your thoughts on this.

If you were the parent of a teenager, how might you help him or her to strengthen his/her belief in a skeptical world?

Prayer

Even the things I can see make me stretch, not to mention those I can't. Lord, let me not be like Thomas—see and believe. The next time I wonder and question, help me to remember the last time you proved your presence and power. Let my questioning lead to a firmly planted faith in you.

WEEK 9— Personal Issues

Making Your Anger Work for You
Ephesians 4.25-28 *(NT p. 205)*

GROUP DAY — DAY 1

LAST WEEK IN REVIEW: *Learning to relate to God in prayer and in his Word has been crucial for your growth. What specific areas from last week challenged you?*

"Watch out!"

For many years Tom had struggled with his anger. "It seems like I can go along for a while and it doesn't bother me, and then all of a sudden, I lose my temper and say things that I'm usually sorry for later. I'm not the only one in my family with an anger problem. My father, who is a wonderful Christian man, has for many years had a reputation for being 'hotheaded.' He doesn't get angry very often, but when he does, watch out!"

Although Tom is embarrassed and thinks himself "atypical," many men are like him. They tend to view anger as a problem, something that must be avoided, and something negative that they must conceal. In reality, research tells us that most people experience this emotion 8-10 times a day. When we begrudge, or are annoyed, irritated, frustrated, offended or cross, we're experiencing anger in some form.

Reflection

Anger is energy. While we may have minimal control over when and how we become angry, we do have control over how we choose to express it. We can either spend it or invest it. Because it involves physical and emotional energy, it is up to us whether to use that energy in constructive ways or to abuse ourselves and others. We could utilize it as an opportunity to channel energy into positive change in our lives.

Part of what it means to be made in God's image is that we, like God, have a variety of emotions. The Lord Jesus, a human reflection of God, experienced anger as well as joy, sorrow as well as peace. And, he directed his anger to be used for a purpose.

Accountability and Application

Write about a situation that consistently makes you angry. Although you feel the anger in this situation, are you able to see that your response to it is your choice? Commit in writing your choice to deal with your anger constructively.

Do you "stuff" your emotions and then boil over?

Who can you discuss your anger with?

Prayer

Lord, please help me to get honest with you, myself and others. Help me seek the help I need to deal with my anger in more constructive ways.

WEEK 9—Personal Issues

Making Your Anger Work for You
Ephesians 4.31 *(NT p. 205)*

"What's on the inside?"

DAY 2

Carl would not be considered an angry person. He rarely appears to be angry. One of the many myths regarding anger is that if a person doesn't look or appear angry on the outside, then they don't have a problem with anger, and they are clearly not an angry person. While he doesn't appear angry on the outside, his insides are a battlefield. He's been taking medication for ulcers for several years, and he frequently experiences migraine headaches.

Reflection

First of all, accept responsibility for your anger. Don't say, "he made me angry." It's yours. You own it. Even though the feeling may have come without your beckon, you chose to react in anger. Second, don't allow it to control and dominate you. Rely on the help of the Holy Spirit to make a choice about how you will express it. Third, look at the facts. Identify the source and cause of it. Fourth, choose your response. When you are angry, ask yourself: Is it really that important? How can I express my anger in a way that is biblical and that will bring resolution and reconciliation?

We must make a choice. In the same way that Joshua said, "choose this day whom you will serve," (NRSV). God asks us to choose, we can serve our anger or control and invest it.

Accountability and Application

Think for a moment about the things that easily ignite you. Do you observe a root to those things? For some, it may be when their material possessions, titles or positions are threatened. For others, it may be when they are mistreated or misrepresented, or when their expectations are not met. Any number of things can trigger anger. Write about normal situations that make you angry. What is your response?

What have I learned about myself and how I handle anger?

Prayer

Lord, I see in the life of Christ how he was able to channel his anger and frustration, caused by a sinful world, into positive, redemptive action. Make me more like Jesus in this area.

WEEK 9—Personal Issues

Fear

Ephesians 4.31 *(NT p. 205)*

"Are you running?"

DAY 3

David experienced fear as he hid from the rage of Saul. After seeing that God caused fire to rain from heaven and destroy the false prophets of Baal, Elijah's fear of Jezebel caused him to run and hide. His unhealthy response to fear led to his severe depression and his desire to die. Peter's fear caused him to deny three times the Christ he had defended in the garden. The disciples' fear caused them to run and hide after the crucifixion of their Lord.

You may be thinking, "Well, if I have fear, I should confront it like a man and beat it." But remember, the fear isn't the problem. Fear is a God-given emotion. It drives you to flee danger or rappel down the side of a cliff to safety. By pretending that we don't fear, we fail to grow. Identify your fears, and learn to understand their source. Then you can begin to discriminate between legitimate and irrational fears.

Reflection

Normal or rational fear is healthy and valuable. It serves as an invaluable protective function, especially in times of crisis. Irrational fear involves an exaggeration and overreaction to normal fear. When we don't learn how to identify normal fear, when we ignore its signs or repress, deny, or ignore its alarm, we become more vulnerable to irrational fear.

Many of us react normally to fear. For some, the flight response causes us to run. At times, we run to something that will either numb, or take our mind off the fear. Alcohol, drugs, work, television—these become destructive refuges. For some, the fight response causes us to attack in times of fear. And for others, the response is to freeze, making us unable to take positive action.

Accountability and Application

Which of these responses is most characteristic of you? What do you think you can do about it? Write about normal fears for you, and your normal responses. Are they healthy?

Prayer

Lord, help me to respond more constructively to my fear. Please help me to deal with the things that bring me fear, and to work through those fears in a way that is acceptable to you.

WEEK 9—Personal Issues

Fear
2 Timothy 1.7 *(NT p. 225)*

"No fear"

DAY 4

Exodus 3—6 tells the story of God's call to Moses to lead the children of Israel out of Egypt and into the promised land.

When God first approached Moses with this idea, he panicked. On five different occasions he gave God five different reasons why he couldn't do it, why he was the wrong man, why God needed to find someone else. Finally Moses agreed to do it and the first thing that happened was that the people turned against him. Pharaoh not only commanded the people to make more bricks, but he also said that they had to go out and gather their own straw.

Moses said to the Lord, "O Lord, why hast Thou brought harm to this people? Why didst Thou ever send me? Ever since I came to Pharaoh to speak in Thy name, he has done harm to this people; and Thou hast not delivered Thy people at all." (NASB) That's his way of saying, "Lord, I've had it, this is the last straw!"

Reflection

What can I do to eliminate or decrease my fear? Usually the solution will involve facing the fear in some way. Face it, but face it gradually. Don't rush into it. Go slowly. Let your confidence build. Reach out for support and encouragement.

Gaining the victory over fear can take time. Remember what God says in Psalm 27.14, "Trust the LORD! Be brave and strong and trust the LORD."

There is no such thing as fearlessness. But, that fear which exists can be faced with the courage that comes from God. Most of the time you will discover that the reality of the situation is not nearly as bad as you thought it would be.

Paul had left Timothy in Ephesus as the leader of the church. He was a young man, and had been given a huge responsibility and authority. He was timid in nature. Timothy was a bit overwhelmed by it all and had some fears and apprehensions. Paul reminded Timothy of his call and said, "God's Spirit doesn't make cowards out of us. The Spirit gives us power, love, and self-control."

Accountability and Application

Have you ever felt like Moses? Like Timothy? What does Paul's encouragement to Timothy say to you? Write about experiences from your heritage that could be of encouragement as you face your fears.

Prayer

Lord, forgive my fear. I know I need to learn from you and to walk in faith. Help me to learn what I am really capable of doing through you as I choose to believe in you.

WEEK 9— Personal Issues

Lust
1 Peter 2.11 *(NT p. 251)*

"A tragic downfall"

DAY 5

Samson grew up with it all—looks, body, respect, power, authority and influence. When we first meet him, we find a somewhat immature, impulsive and selfish young man. When you hear the name of Samson, what comes to your mind is his unbelievably stupid mistake of trusting Delilah. But his foolish downfall didn't happen overnight. It was what Samson did (and didn't do) that set him up for a catastrophic failure. Samson was lured by Delilah, and experienced defeat due to his lust for her. Yet God was with him and blessed him.

Much of Samson's life was characterized by stability and success. Yet Samson was a man who hadn't completely dealt with his "stuff." He was a walking time-bomb waiting to explode. Over time the hidden weakness and covert compromises exploded, and the walls came tumbling down. Before our very eyes, we see the unnecessary and tragic fall of one of the strongest men who had ever lived. We see the vulnerablility of a man who had the strength to control others but who never learned how to control himself.

Reflection

"Losing self-control leaves you as helpless as a city without a wall." (Proverbs 25.28)

When it comes to dealing with temptation, the best defense is a good offense. Determine when and where you are the weakest, and develop a plan to deal with it. For example, if you are weakest when you see immoral magazine covers, stay away from the stands. If you weaken at the sight of a woman in a bikini, propose that you won't go to the beach without your wife. When you first hear the seductive voice of temptation, fight it. Don't analyze it. Run from it! The battle is won or lost in the first 60 seconds.

Many men have allowed themselves to move from lust to blatant immorality. An often shared remorse is, "If I had only known what this relationship would cost me, I never would have gotten involved."

Accountability and Application

A fresh start begins with a fresh end. Is there something you need to let go of? Is there a habit you are tempted to rationalize away? Is there an activity that, while it is not sin, is clearly leading you "away from," rather than "closer to," your Lord Jesus?

Have you determined where the "line" is for you? Do you usually walk as closely to the line as possible?

Write where your "line" is and write a plan which will keep you from crossing it.

Prayer

Lord, when I step over the line into lust, I take what is beautiful and destroy it. I'm ashamed. Please forgive me, and strengthen me to stand firm.

WEEK 9—Personal Issues

Lust

*The words of an immoral woman
may be as sweet as honey
and as smooth as olive oil.
But all that you really get from being with her
is bitter poison and pain.*
                                   Proverbs 5.3, 4

"Dealing with a temptress"

DAY 6

You find that the new office that you've been transferred to has a secretary that is a total come-on. This isn't really a problem, because you're committed entirely to your wife. But it sure would be easier if she'd dress differently, and contain herself a little. Knowing the right thing to do seems easy enough. But every time you have determined to look the other way, there she is, right in your face. It seems to you like she knows, like she does it purposely. In all honesty, it's difficult not to lust after her every time you see her. You determine that you will not let this get to you.

Now would be a good time to ask yourself: To whom can I go for help?

Reflection

Do I have any relationships with other Christian guys or a small group of men with whom I can be transparent? Who is committed to me, who will give me an accountability check, asking tough questions, to keep me on track? Or, have I simply chosen to be isolated and alone?

If you isolate yourself from others, it is highly probable that you will not become the "sharpened" individual that God so wonderfully created you to be.

Accountability and Application

One way to keep yourself accountable is to develop a plan. For example, when traveling and alone in a hotel room, if you are tempted by destructive television programming, take a picture of your family and put in on top of the television, phone the front desk and ask them to shut off the adult channels, and call home each night.

Would you be willing to share these times of struggling with lust with a person of accountability?

How do you sharpen each other?

Prayer

Lord, I have a lot of trouble in this area of lust. Actually, I deal with it more than most know. I do want to handle it in a godly manner. Give me the strength that only comes from you to war against my lustful thoughts and habits. Keep me clean, God.

WEEK 9—Personal Issues

Temptation That Is Hot!

*Losing self-control leaves you as helpless
as a city without a wall.*
Proverbs 25.28

"Doing it right"

DAY 7

The most classic story of a man who demonstrated self-control comes from the Bible. Joseph is the man. Sold into slavery, living as a manager in Potiphar's household, he eventually became a leader in Egypt. The story is in Genesis 39; you may want to read it for details.

Potiphar's wife asked Joseph to make love to her. Again and again she tried to seduce him, but he declined. He had strong character and convictions. The climax of the story comes when she grabbed his cloak, wanting to seduce him. He did what any man of integrity would do—he ran! She lied. He was framed. He landed in jail. Story over!

Reflection

Wait! The story was not quite over. God needed Joseph in jail to interpret dreams for the Pharoah. This way, by interpreting the dream of the famine which was to come, he was used by God to save God's people from starvation.

Does this sound complicated? Almost unbelievable? It's not. When we respond to God's way, he can use us, to complete his plan and bless his people. When we mess up and yield to temptation, many people are hurt. In this case, perhaps a whole nation would have been damaged.

Accountability and Application

Have I ever been that close to giving in, but I held back through the strength of the Holy Spirit? Stop right now and thank him again!

If you were asked by a friend what to do in the face of temptation, what would you say? Try running!

Prayer

Lord, let me see lust as the door to failure—for me, for my testimony of you, for my marriage, for my future. Help me to have the foresight to read temptation for what it is—Satan's attack at my weak point. Help me to run from it every time.

WEEK 10—God's Heart...Biblical Unity

An Issue of the Head
John 17.20-23 *(NT p. 122)*

GROUP DAY
DAY 1

LAST WEEK IN REVIEW: *First, we studied the basis for a revived life. Then the section on personal issues addressed how we may be impacted. The concluding weeks will focus on our pursuit of God. As human beings, our own sin nature conquers, and we fall short of his nature in our anger, lust and pride. God desires that we confess our weakness and sin to him, ask for forgiveness, repent, and purpose to allow him to impact our flesh and decisions. How were you impacted last week? What areas of challenges did you face?*

"Whose idea was it anyway?"

The high school chemistry teacher bellowed out, partly in surprise but more in panic, "Whose idea was this experiment?" All the boys just looked at each other and shifted their eyes as if to pass the blame. The unauthorized little experiment had erupted from the lab sink, sending kids scurrying away, and foul smelling foam into the air and onto the desks. The culprit's experiment misfired. However, the teacher blamed a junior standing in the aisle. He didn't have a clue, but he got a bad grade and a reprimand.

Reflection

The idea for biblical unity was not created by one "culprit" or by a group of theologians attempting to solve biblical problems. We can't claim it, nor shift credit to some earthly figure. No, the idea was God's.

When we pursue biblical unity, our goal is to be Christians who accept each others' differences, but join in truth. Jesus said, "I want all of them to be one with each other, just as I am one with you, *Father*, and you are one with me." (John 17.21) Along with the idea, we are equipped with the power and plan. The power is the Holy Spirit, enabling us to live obediently. The plan comes with directions in a "how-to" manual. Paul exhorts us to affirm each other as better than ourselves, accepting one another, playing as a unified team. If we use our heads, we'll listen to our coach. He wrote the playbook, he gifted the players, and he will have the victory.

At Promise Keepers we are not preoccupied with a man's denominational label, nor do we wish to see all church distinctives disappear. We are committed to reach beyond labels and enter relationships with each other based on our common faith in Christ.

Accountability and Application

What position do you see yourself playing on the Lord's team?

In what specific ways will you head toward biblical unity? What changes will you have to make in your thoughts and actions?

Prayer

Lord, let me improve my serve and begin to view those with different opinions as important players on the same team. Show me where I've been self-righteous and judgmental, and help me to pursue unity.

WEEK 10—God's Heart...Biblical Unity

A Matter of the Heart
1 Peter 1.22-25 *(NT p. 250)*

"A warm port in the storm"

DAY 2

Red stood in shock as he watched the ambulance pull away. He had been driving his welding truck when he saw his brother-in-law going the other way on the highway. His brother-in-law had made a U-turn and had not seen an eighteen-wheeler. The truck hit at full speed. His brother-in-law—his best friend—was gone. Red, the big Irishman, stood there weeping. He knew he must call his priest, and take close friends to be with his wife when she would hear that her only brother had been killed. Then he had to drive to the small Colorado mountain town where he must tell his relatives, awaiting the return of their husband and father, that his brother-in-law had been killed. How could he break the news?

His head was still spinning as he pulled into the driveway of a little house several miles down the road. Still dazed, he knocked on the door. A burley man with jet-dark hair and a warm smile opened the door. He spoke Spanish, and only a limited amount of English.

The Irishman began, "I was told that you folks attend that church across the road," he stammered, holding back the emotion. "I need to use your phone." The owner of the home didn't hesitate, but welcomed him in to make his call. As the family overheard his tragedy, they gathered in the next room. Only as he finished the phone call did the Irishman realize that the homeowner, his mother and another person in the house were in the next room praying for him. Not knowing the situation or even his name, these people had taken his grief to the Lord in prayer. Red was in need. They sensed his pain and did the most compassionate and helpful thing a believer could do.

Reflection
Love may be something we *do* for another person or on behalf of another. In any case, it is our love in *action*, which unite us in Christ, not only our words. Words can be hollow when not supported by action. But actions demonstrate a unifying love which breaks all sorts of barriers.

Accountability and Application
Would it surprise you to know that the family who welcomed Red into their home and prayed so earnestly for him were Hispanic? If you were hurting and in need of help, would you find just as much comfort from the prayers and support of someone from a denomination or culture different from your own?

Will you purpose to seek biblical unity and love in your *actions*?

Prayer

Forgive me, Lord, when I've been harsh, uncaring and not willing to open my heart or my door. May I demonstrate active love to others to your glory.

WEEK 10—God's Heart...Biblical Unity

A Lend of the Hand
1 Corinthians 10.31; 11.1 *(NT p. 182)*

"Old hands"

DAY 3

An inner-city ministry had developed an effective mentoring program for elementary and middle school youth. One would never expect that Bill, a 74-year-old retired postal worker would find a niche there. The guys who went on a monthly basis into the inner-city for fellowship told him of the need. He asked if he could help, wondering if he was too old.

He began working with 10- to 12-year-old boys. Bill was perfect as the grandfather that many of them had never had. A couple of boys in particular, John and Carlos, found him to be a great friend. They looked forward to his visits, as he would listen to their dreams, plans and stories. Then he would share with them his own experiences at that age. Bill never laughed at them. In fact, he made them feel quite important, and understood all of their dreams.

It wasn't that he was brilliant; he didn't need to be. He was just wise from experience, mellow with age, and loving with the love of Christ.

Reflection

Men are especially good at "doing." Given a defined task they can "do it." In fact, sometimes the task itself becomes the goal. The compulsion to conquer takes over, and they may find themselves caught between the extremes of doing nothing, so as to not overstep their bounds, or doing it all, and running right over other people in the process. In any case, a demonstration of commitment in the body of Christ, often presents a "doing" opportunity. Sometimes a man who is short on words can demonstrate a heartfelt commitment by putting his hand to the task.

Have you noticed that the contrast in today's Bible is cultural? It's easy to bump into one another when our history and perspectives vary. It is your choice, but when you serve, do it to demonstrate reconciliation and unity in the body of Christ. Do it as a testimony and witness for Christ. Mostly, do it to honor God.

Accountability and Application

What are my opportunities to do physical acts of service for someone for Jesus' sake?

Would I need public acclaim to be motivated to participate, or would it be thanks enough to receive a "well done" from the Lord?

What skills do I most enjoy using to serve others? Could I stretch to serve a person of a different denomination, race, age or socio-economic group?

Prayer

Jesus Christ, you came from heaven to serve me! You didn't make me learn your language, wear your style of clothes or look like you. Motivate me to reach out like you did, rather than retreat inward to my "safe space."

WEEK 10— God's Heart...Biblical Unity

The Use of Your Feet
Romans 10.14-17 *(NT p. 169)*

"Running the race"

DAY 4

In between speaking at Wake-Up Calls in Kona, Hawaii, Dave Wardell, co-founder of Promise Keepers, was challenged by witnessing the Iron Man Triathlon. Early one Saturday morning he observed a participant eating breakfast. The athlete was in his sixties, and although already bald and wrinkled by years in the sun, his body had the muscle tone of a 19-year-old. Dave, motivated by this man's conditioning, wondered how well he would do swimming two and a half miles, riding a bicycle 112 miles and immediately running a 26.2-mile marathon?

The verse I Timothy 4.8 came to mind, "Exercise is good for your body, but religion helps you in every way. It promises life now and forever." "God wants me to go deeper," Dave determined, "both physically and spiritually." What challenges you? What keeps you going? Runners follow this rule: Pick up your foot and put it in front of the other!

Reflection

AT&T encourages us to "Reach out and touch someone." At the core is a message carried by a messenger. This is also true of a reconciler. God sent Christ to bring us into a relationship of peace—reconciled to God. Now we are commanded to carry the same message. And biblical unity is the result: a relationship, an end to hostility, full participant in the family of God. It all began when Christ was sent. Our part begins when we follow instructions and step out.

Accountability and Application

Who do I desire to see reconciled to God through Jesus Christ?

Who is my brother in Christ that I have not yet engaged as even a friend?

Would I be willing to exert myself in the effort to be a reconciler, to bring about biblical unity?

Prayer

"I'll go where you want me to go, dear Lord...I'll say what you want me to say, and I'll be what you want me to be." (Mary Brown) Help me to make these words true, Lord.

WEEK 10—God's Heart...Biblical Unity

A Matter of the Eyes
1 Corinthians 3.1-9 *(NT p. 177)*

"See it in my eyes"

DAY 5

The 1994 Promise Keepers conference in Indianapolis, Indiana, was packed as men heard one speaker after another. Perhaps though, the most quoted phrase of the event came from the lips of Pastor Jeffery Johnson who said, "If God's your Father, then I'm your brother."

Leaving the stadium, the stands were united with the sounds of men challenged by the words they had heard. Johnson's words hung in the air. New commitments of brotherhood abounded. And for many, there was a resolution to look into another's eyes and try to feel their pain and assume their brotherhood.

Johnson is an African-American. To hear his words carried only half the message. His face carried the passion of this call for inclusion and full partnership in the family of believers—this was not a message to be heard only. You had to see it in his eyes.

Reflection

Eyes are said to be the windows of the soul. Our physical eyes pick up messages of people, places and things. Eyes also carry the message of our understanding. They enable us to understand our brother's situation, feeling his grief or his joy. When we assume the place of brotherhood in Christ, when we understand that we can be united in the truth of Scripture, accepting our differences, we have achieved biblical unity.

Accountability and Application

Do you think that praying over the hurts of others will give you understanding of them?

What further step could you take to understand another's hurts?

Are you willing to commit to this?

Use your eyes to "see" the message you hear, when someone shares his grief. See it on his face. Understand what he is really saying.

Prayer

Lord, your eyes view the whole world. They look deep into my heart and understand what's there. I ask that you'll find my heart wanting to see everything as you see it.

WEEK 10— God's Heart...Biblical Unity

Involving Our Ears
Matthew 11.15-19 *(NT p. 16)*

"Pay attention"

DAY 6

Listening is sometimes the hardest thing we can do. Sometimes we are distracted, like the husband who said to his wife, "Talk fast, honey, the Bulls' game starts in three minutes. You know I can't pay attention to two things at once."

Sometimes we don't listen because the words are not comfortable. A woman told a pastor that she likes the church her children attend through bus ministry. She even tried it herself. The people were friendly, and her grandson loved his class. "But," she told him, "the songs are different, and they don't use *my* Bible translation. It feels foreign."

John the Baptist and Jesus were very different in style. John was intense. Jesus, although intense and often referred to as the great teacher, was also social and fun. He marched to his own drummer. He offended the religious and pious by accepting the outcast underclass. He said things to people that were uncomfortable to hear. So some didn't listen.

Would you listen to Jesus, or would you tune him out, because his style didn't fit your own? If you would listen to him, would you be willing to listen to the people he loves?

Reflection

Sometimes what is being said stops some of us from listening. Other times the message taps into unresolved pain that we're still carrying.

We need to park our preoccupation at the curb of attentiveness. This means a concerted effort to listen to those who may have ideas different than our own. We must stretch our comfort zone to accommodate the expressions of others. Tune-out can result not only from disagreeing with the message but also from prejudice, racism, or a belief of superiority of worship style, church, or denomination. Although God loved us enough to accept us as we were, he continues to love us too much to leave us this way. "Speak, Lord, in the stillness while I wait on Thee; hushed my heart to listen in expectancy." (E.M. Grimes) Listening to God is always important.

Accountability and Application

What experiences or practices from another group's worship help me to open the door to closeness to God?

Where could I visit for worship that might stretch my experience?

If any of your friends have cultural or worship practices that are different from yours, purpose to find out about them, even try them out.

Prayer

Lord, help me to realize that your family is going to be of every race, tribe and worship style. As one of your sons, help me to grow in accepting my brothers and sisters in faith.

WEEK 10—God's Heart...Biblical Unity

Using Your Nose
1 Corinthians 9.24-27 *(NT p. 181)*

"Keep at it"

DAY 7

The case of a missing little girl caught the attention of the metro area. Her grandfather made public appeals, police went from door-to-door searching for clues, but nothing surfaced. No clues, no girl, no body. But then they brought in an old bloodhound. That dog followed his nose, sniffing, retracing his steps, seemingly losing the scent, then picking it up again. That bloodhound just wouldn't give up. Eventually, the search came to a close. The sad conclusion was that the little girl had been murdered. The dog, however, was a total success. The child's body was found more than twenty miles away!

Reflection

When listening and looking are not enough, sometimes to get to the bottom of an issue you'll just have to "sniff it out." This may take patience and persistence, maybe more than you now have, so you'll have to stretch. You'll have to keep at it again and again.

An African-American pastor says of his early relationship with a white pastor, now a close friend, "He just wouldn't quit! He'd leave an encouraging message. He'd show up at my church, he'd include me in invitations to events. Soon I had to say 'This guy's for real...he's committed to me.'"

Accountability and Application

What relationships have I just looked at but not yet "sniffed out"?

Am I serious about winning the prize?

How could I demonstrate commitment to a person with whom I want to be reconciled?

How could I demonstrate persistence with someone with whom I have differences?

Prayer

Lord, let me never give up the trail of a brother or sister in need of my caring pursuit. When I want to say "why bother," let me remember that you went all the way to the cross for me.

WEEK 11—God's Heart...Promise Keeping

A Man of His Word
James 5.12 *(NT p. 248)*

GROUP DAY / DAY 1

<u>LAST WEEK IN REVIEW</u>: *Pursuing Christ in your life involves accepting all members of his body, even when they are different. What conscious choices did you make in this area last week?*

"Maybe next time"

"I'm sorry son, another job just came in. I promise I will come next time."

This was the third time in a month Joe had backed out of watching his son's baseball game so that he could stay late at the repair shop. He was finishing up a job that would bring in bigger bucks than usual. Joe was torn between the opportunity to make a little extra—or to be there for his son. He had made the wrong choices too many times before. In his son's eyes, Joe's words were meaningless.

Three years earlier Joe had broken a big promise—his wedding vows. Growing tired of "hanging out" with the family, he was always gone. One day, it became too much for his wife. The fatigue of a neglected marriage had now left Joe alone.

Confusion, deep disappointment, sometimes a loss of hope—we have all felt it. We've all been on the receiving end of a broken promise. There is an old saying regarding a man's character: "A man is only as good as his word." Actually, it might be stated, "A man is only as good as he *keeps* his word!"

Reflection

Keeping the promises you make to others speaks volumes about your character. Have you ever considered why God keeps his promises in spite of our failures? Is it duty—or devotion? Consider the value you place on God making and keeping his promises.

Accountability and Application

Are you characterized as a "promise keeper" out of your devotion to another? Or, are you a "promise breaker," selfishly pursuing something you prefer?

Prayer

Father, I bow before you incapable of keeping promises. Search my heart, and reveal to me my weaknesses, for it is in you alone that I seek the enabling strength to fulfill my word. Teach me to be a man of promise keeping and of integrity.

WEEK 11—God's Heart...Promise Keeping

Preparation

1 Timothy 4.6-10 *(NT p. 222)*

"Are you ready?"

DAY 2

Scotty hung his head as he lumbered out of the locker room and headed dejectedly to his car. He had just been cut from Tennessee's national championship football team. "I can't believe it. I've been cut! How could I get cut?" Scotty thought to himself.

Scotty Gramere had easily been the most talented quarterback to transfer from Tennessee State Junior College. He was regarded as a remarkable player and became one of the most dazzling athletes to come along in decades.

But, Scotty's summer practice sessions were miserable. He had been forced to miss several practice sessions due to poor conditioning. At a time when Scotty needed to be prepared, he was not. Unfortunately, he had gotten caught up in the "star status" of his budding football career and had failed to work out and stay in shape. After all, he never practiced very hard in high school or junior college—it just came "naturally."

Reflection

In nearly every facet of life, preparation is needed in order to carry out our mission. Professional athletes will tell you that their success followed disciplined training. In the same manner, preparing your heart is a process that will help enable you to keep promises. This is not a quick, easy formula, but a discipline that requires commitment. It requires your prayers, worship and devotion.

A pure, prepared heart before the Lord will set the course for keeping promises.

Accountability and Application

Begin your heart preparation by doing daily devotions. This discipline will begin your day thinking correctly—starting with the Lord.

Also, begin heart-preparation through your prayer life. The Nike slogan gives us the best advice when it comes to prayer—"Just do it!" It's that simple. Your comfort with prayer will grow with practice.

These simple approaches will prove to be powerful preparation to being a man of integrity. The next time you are faced with an integrity slip, check your heart. Is it prepared?

Prayer

Lord, I know that I've broken promises, even to my family. I commit to following you, but I keep slipping on my promises for one reason or another. Allow me to be a person who keeps promises. Help me to prepare my heart to be a person of integrity.

WEEK 11 — God's Heart...Promise Keeping

Isolation

Galatians 6.7-10 *(NT p. 201)*

"I'm doing this for you"

DAY 3

Leo looked up from his pile of reports just to check the time. It was already 10 p.m. and he was still at the office! Leo had been working 14-hour days for years! By 5 a.m. he was sending or checking his e-mail; and every night he would come home exhausted long after dinner had been served. Besides, his kids were usually gone, and his wife had other things to do. He could work a little bit longer and "get ahead." And it was paying off. His family was able to move to a nicer home, pay off the mortgage, and get a nice new family car. On weekends, Leo would sleep late or go to the office. Rarely did he take his family anywhere. After all, he was a busy man. In reality, Leo was a workaholic.

Hiding behind long hours and "mounting" paperwork has created a place of safety for Leo. He has very few friends, and he likes his "space."

Recently, though, he's been feeling like a failure. His teen-age children have become rebellious. His wife seems to be in her own little world. Frustrated, he ponders the source of the problem. After all, he has worked hard to give them everything they want.

Reflection

God tells us in Genesis 2.18 that it was not good for Adam to be alone, so he created Eve. This Scripture gives us an important principle inherent to humanity. Relationships are important!

Because relationships take time and effort, men often avoid them. It's easier to bury yourself in your own private world than to make the effort to get to know and trust someone. The reality is the richness that you can have in the Lord when you have an accountability partner is very much worth the time and effort. It provides a sounding board for you and an anchor to rely on.

Accountability and Application

Pray for a few committed relationships that will encourage you to grow in the Lord. Ask the Lord to help you to become transparent and encourage you to keep your promises to God and others.

Is there anyone who you can trust with whom you can share your victories and defeats, and who will keep you on a straight path? Will you be able to accept their advice and counsel?

Prayer

Lord, enable me to pursue the relationships with friends who will help me pursue godliness. I know that it is not your desire that I remain in isolation.

WEEK 11—God's Heart...Promise Keeping

Honesty
Ephesians 5.8-13 *(NT p. 205)*

"Did you think you could hide?"

DAY 4

At 35, Patrick already had everything going for him in the banking industry. As First Trust Bank's youngest vice president, Patrick had no experience that qualified him, but demonstrated ability and an eagerness to learn.

People knew Patrick as personable, and he had earned a reputation of honesty; in fact, he'd been invited by U.S. Banking Services to speak on "honesty in banking." What others didn't know was that Patrick was leading two lives—a public and a private life. Patrick's wife and children didn't even know of his secret sin. And it hadn't just occurred overnight. It had been progressive over time. On the outside, he was "squeaky-clean." On the inside, he was hiding from his own dishonesty and spiraling toward certain ruin.

At first, Patrick felt a little guilty "fudging" on his expense reports, but this practice soon became a habit. He avoided searching his heart, and this secret sin had taken a firm hold on him. In public, Patrick had plenty of accountability; in his private world, he had none. What appeared to be a man of integrity was, in fact, not.

Reflection

"If you don't do what you know is right, you have sinned." What conviction this quote brings to the heart when we have been dishonest. There should be two things that follow when we have sinned. Confess it to God. Say your sin aloud, and allow your ears to hear what you did wrong. Then obey Jesus' command to repent and turn away from the sin.

Accountability and Application

Has your thought life been less than godly? Are you struggling to keep it focused on godly things?

When you give your word, do you have a pure motive? When you struggle with integrity and keeping your promises, do you share that with a friend? If not, plan to.

Prayer

Pray this powerful Psalm back to God:
Psalm 86.11: *"Teach me to follow you, and I will obey your truth. Always keep me faithful."*

WEEK 11—*God's Heart...Promise Keeping*

Protection

Romans 7.15 *(NT p. 166)*

"Avoiding traps"

DAY 5

Fury raged in Jerry's heart as he left the angry face of his wife, Beth. Another road trip, another fight with her. Why couldn't he just leave on good terms? It seemed as if every time he was called out, an argument would send him on his way for another week. Didn't Beth realize how hard it was for him to drive all week for the van lines, unload someone's belongings, and then return home totally beat?

They continually struggled to make ends meet and frequently argued about money. For the last six months, Jerry had given Beth his credit cards to prove he had his spending habits under control. But here was the real test: Jerry struggled with gambling—the lottery, poker, slots—any kind of quick, easy money.

Jerry was on his way to Sacramento traveling through Nevada. He had received a big bonus check from his home office, and Beth did not know about it. Twenty-four hours later, the flashing lights of Las Vegas were drawing him right in. Ready for a good meal, Jerry pulled into the parking lot of a popular casino that was advertising free prime rib while you "play the tables."

Reflection

Self-control comes from the Word of God being written on our hearts. This happens when we spend time with him and with the Word. It will require your determination and commitment.

Additionally, you can guard your heart and keep your promises by avoiding tempting situations. Much like a recovering alcoholic knows to flee the bar scene, you should identify weak areas and prepare yourself for battle. Avoid those situations whenever possible, and ask a friend to help you out of them.

Accountability and Application

Are you spending adequate time in the Word? Committing to this will help you to keep your promises in tempting situations.

Do you put yourself in situations that cause you to stumble? What specific situations could you change which would help you to avoid falling into defeat?

Prayer

Lord, I keep falling in those very areas that I commit to you. Help me to avoid those situations. Help me to pick myself back up when I blow it. Help me to walk in your strength, and not my own.

WEEK 11—God's Heart...Promise Keeping

Submission
John 6.38 *(NT p. 109)*; Luke 22.42 *(NT p. 96)*

"Are you protected?"

DAY 6

Having worked for your boss for two years, you are now witnessing his "true colors." The charming $100 words and surface pats-on-the-back no longer work to motivate you. You've given your word that you'll deliver this project flawlessly, with his name attached. Your stomach tightens as you imagine his puffed-up response to the accolades he'll receive. And if that were not enough, the next project that he's assigned you to is definitely beneath you. It is long, mindless, lacks creativity, and probably could be handled by someone else. Nevertheless, it has to be done, and he chose you.

There are some things you could do to change this situation. But, none of them hold the integrity that you've committed to. Gritting your teeth, you're reminded that submission means surrendering even under difficult circumstances—even when you're "in the right."

You've most likely discovered that keeping our promises takes place when we submit our will to God. Knowing that God's will is best for us encourages us to submit to him, through understanding who he is and who we aren't.

Reflection

Consider Jesus' prayer in the Garden of Gethsemene before his crucifixion. Knowing that he was "in the right"—not guilty of anything—made it perhaps even more difficult. He tells us that his purpose for coming to earth was not to do his will but to do the will of his Father.

In each case, Jesus, in his deity, was fully capable of doing what he wanted to do, but he chose to submit to his Father. We too, must submit to him.

Accountability and Application

Give the men in your small group permission to check whether you are surrendering all that you are to God.

Are you keeping your word, even in the worst of situations when you have no control?

Do you find yourself trying to change a situation rather than surrendering the circumstances to God?

Submit to God's will. He will make your paths straight and enable you to act accordingly.

Prayer

Lord, I am strong-willed and selfish. I confess my weakness to you. Please enable me to submit to you fully. I am desperate to please only you.

WEEK 11 — God's Heart...Promise Keeping

Endurance
Romans 5.1-5 *(NT p. 165)*

"I want to quit!"

DAY 7

After a week, Kevin didn't know if he was going to make it. With a couple more weeks to go, he was already tired of throwing papers for his friend, Ty. When Ty had asked him to fill in so that he could drive his wife to be with her sick mother, Kevin said that he'd be happy to help. Ordinarily Ty wouldn't ask someone to do his work for him. But, Kevin had been looking for work for some time now, and when this opportunity came along to bring in some steady cash, he didn't want to lose it. So, Kevin was filling in for 3 weeks.

Actually, it was harder than Kevin would have guessed. For one thing, he wasn't used to walking the streets in that area of town. But it was the hours that really made it tough. He had to collect the papers at 2:30 a.m., fold them, deliver them, and he usually made it home about 6:30 a.m., only to shower and head for his regular job. He wondered how Ty did it.

Kevin pondered quitting. His feet were tired, and he was exhausted. In fact, the last few days he fought sleeping on the job in the afternoon. But Kevin also thought about the promise he'd made. And that meant his word; it meant his integrity. So, he re-committed himself to a few more sleepless weeks.

Reflection

When you give your word on something, it is expected that you will follow through. Good intentions are not enough. One cannot take good intentions to the bank. When you break your word, you reduce your character, because you have demonstrated yourself as a person who cannot be trusted. When the situation is difficult, and it takes great endurance to follow through with promises, it is your character and your dependence on God that will see you to the finish line.

The apostle Paul wanted to quit his missionary work on a number of occasions. At times it was so tough that he didn't feel like it was worth it. But he knew and was convinced of the kingdom of God, and of his promises to the people and churches which he had touched. So, he endured.

Accountability and Application

Think of a time, past or present, when you have promised, or committed to something, and it was difficult to keep that promise. Did you feel like quitting? This is normal. The question is, what kept you going at the times when you wanted to throw in the towel? How can you become a person who endures to the end and keeps his promises?

Prayer

Lord, I admit it. I am weak. It's easy for me to give my word to something. When I feel like quitting, help me find the endurance through you to keep my word.

WEEK 12—Reaching the World

Multiplying Your Witness
Matthew 28.16-20 *(NT p. 40)*

GROUP DAY
DAY 1

LAST WEEK IN REVIEW: *The measure of active pursuit of God is in keeping promises—to family, to others, and to God. When you took the time to examine your heart, and then bolstered yourself to prepare and commit your heart to your promises, your relationship with God was strengthened. Which of these areas were particularly challenging this last week?*

"Too big a task?"

Near the beginning of the 20th century, a long drought plagued southern China. A hard-working man saw no way to provide for his family, so he risked all and moved to America. Now a Christian, his hard work, frugal spirit, and devoted family found a place to flourish. Eventually, a promising young Chinese-American engineer graduated from the University of California, Berkley. But, he forfeited a lucrative career to preach the Gospel. He started a mission church in Sacramento, California. One of his early converts to Christ became involved in bringing students to a seminary. The seminary, in turn, now sends them to all the world with the Gospel.

Often we view the world as too big of a place to achieve anything of significance or to make a difference. But, as Jesus told his disciples, "Those are some things that people cannot do, but God can do anything." (Mark 10.27). Remember, your work will multiply. Those whom you lead to Christ can, in turn, each lead several more to Christ, and so on. The world is not nearly as big as the power of the Gospel—the Gospel is far reaching!

Reflection

Is the world too big for any one man to have an impact? Jesus said, "Go to the people of all nations and make them my disciples." (Matthew 28.18). His command includes every human being. He is not asking us to be selective with people—just the opposite. God commands us to take the Gospel to all peoples. If each of us would significantly influence those who enter the circumference of our lives, then the sum of those who hear about Jesus would be staggering. We cannot do it alone. We can do it as we find strength in him. If each of us were to be obedient in this way, the world could be reached for Jesus Christ.

Accountability and Application

If I thought that any of my co-workers had the potential to be an international evangelist, sharing the Gospel with other nations, would I be quicker to be a witness for Christ?

What is it that keeps me from sharing the Gospel? Is it fear? Apathy? What would it take to overcome any of these barriers?

Prayer

Father, thank you for the faithful lives of those who influenced my life spiritually. Help me to do the same for others, telling those around me about Jesus. Help me start in my workplace and in my community. I desire to be part of reaching this world for your sake.

WEEK 12—Reaching the World

People Who Are Different
Ephesians 2.14-18 *(NT p. 203, 204)*

"Not help from him—no thanks!"

DAY 2

In the movie "The Tuskegee Flyers" two Anglo B-17 bomber pilots were relieved and grateful when unassigned P-51 Mustang fighters shot down enemy fighters who were after their bomber. Once on the ground, they went in search for those pilots who had saved their lives. The bomber pilots found their rescuers, but also discovered that they were black pilots. The highest ranking officer, too steeped in his own racial prejudice, turned and left without delivering his thanks. The rescued pilot never denied being rescued, but because the rescuers were black, he refused to thank them.

To this pilot's credit, he later learned that the all-black pilot squadron never lost a bomber that they were assigned to escort. Then, he requested them as he flew a bombing mission into Berlin.

Reflection

Similarly, every Christian has been rescued by Jesus Christ's grace. And this wonderful work of Christ has rescued people of all ethnic backgrounds. If he has accepted all, rescued all, and loves all, then all of us who have been similarly rescued should be enjoying our affinity with each other. We should be joined by our rescue, not separated by our biases.

This world consists of all kinds of people. To be a man of God, we must love the people of the world as Christ does. That is without preference or prejudice. The more one becomes like Jesus Christ, the more he will accept others, even those who are different from himself.

Accountability and Application

Have you ever felt acceptance from those who were once prejudiced against you?

Who in the sphere of your influence is of a different ethnic backgound than yourself that you could begin a friendship with for God's sake?

Would you be willing to "rescue" anyone, or are there some you would keep at arm's length?

Would you be willing to accept help or "rescue" from the same?

Prayer

Lord, thank you for saving me even though I once acted like your enemy. You have been very gracious to me when I did not deserve it. Please help me be just as gracious to others. Give me the love to reach out to someone of a different ethnic background than I am.

WEEK 12—Reaching the World

No Lost Causes
Mark 1.40-42 *(NT p. 43)*

"Impossible!"

DAY 3

Watching a death-row inmate plead another appeal, we shook our heads in disgust. Here was a mass-murderer and a rapist who had left a trail of death, destruction and pain. For this person, there was no hope—he was a miserable human being.

Mass murderers are often viewed as lost causes—no hope for them. In a similar way, we think that there are some people who can never come to faith in Christ—it's simply impossible. They are so evil and wicked that there is no hope for them. Yet, God does the impossible.

Reflection

When Jesus walked on this earth, a man with the incurable disease of leprosy begged for healing. He was a desperate man. If he married and had a family, he would have been forbidden to touch his wife or hug his children. What a lonely existence! He no doubt felt the pain of rejection and despise of the crowds. Jesus, sensed the man's needs and touched him—Jesus accepted the leper as he was. It was the first touch that the man had felt since he was branded an outcast. Then Jesus cleansed him of his incurable disease. God does the impossible. There is no one who is so lost, so evil, so low that God cannot do a miraculous work in his life.

Accountability and Application

Think about someone at work, in your family, in your neighborhood, or even people in the world whom you think are so awful that they can't ever be in relationship with God. Determine that there is hope for their salvation and relationship with God.

Pray for God to work in that person's life.

Develop a plan to look beyond their presumptuous behavior.

Make yourself available and purpose to cross any barriers to extend yourself for them.

Prayer

God, remind me of your great power to change the seemingly impossible people of this world. When I read about a people gripped by evil or torn by strife, move me to pray for their salvation and stop my feelings of judgment or condemnation.

WEEK 12— Reaching the World

Busyness
Mark 4.35-41 *(NT p. 46)*

"Take off!"

DAY 4

Inching his way in bumper-to-bumper traffic, Ben was anxious. His thoughts jumped from the meeting he would have tonight to the meeting he just came from. He looked at his watch, aware that it was getting late. He saw the coloring books on the seat next to him and smiled, thinking of his 3-year-old, Paul. Suddenly Ben was paralyzed. Today was the day his wife wasn't able to pick up Paul from his mother's house. He had committed to picking up Paul on his way home. He was almost home now, with no Paul. What a dilemma!

In our busyness we often put our work on "auto-pilot" and simply go through the motions. When this happens, we may miss a huge need, or work, that needs to be accomplished.

Reflection

Jesus commanded his disciples to go to the other side of the lake. Once out on the lake a massive storm swept across the waters and threatened the boat and all of its passengers. But, several of the disciples were valiantly fighting the storm. After all, sailing on the Sea of Galilee was how they made their living. Jesus slept. He did not wake until his disciples roused him. These were men pushed to the limit in the one area in which they had the most confidence—the area of their expertise.

It's good to be busy at our area of expertise. But our dependence should never be apart from a clear focus on Christ. If we are depending our own abilities, we may miss what he can do through us.

Accountability and Application

Watch how often you use the excuse "I'm too busy" to avoid an opportunity to serve or to be a witness for Christ.

If someone were to compare your ability and effort in your profession with your ability and effort in serving others or witnessing for Christ, would there be a big gap?

Prayer

Lord, I am pursuing so many things that keep me too busy. I have failed to make the effort to be a witness and testimony for you and to use my abilities for you. And I have tried to operate in my own expertise. Help me to be busy about you, Lord.

WEEK 12—Reaching the World

Cost of Evangelism
Luke 9.57-62 *(NT p. 79)*

"A risky meeting"

DAY 5

"You ready, Tony?" asked John, sticking his head around the corner of the garage. Tony nodded hesitantly, hoping no one in the back had seen John. He turned the power saw off, punched his timecard, grabbed his jacket, and headed for the door. John was waiting outside.

They'd been planning for some time to get away for lunch and talk, and now that John was having problems in his marriage, Tony thought the time had come. Tony had been looking for an opportunity to share the Gospel with him, but there never seemed to be an opportunity to bring up the subject. So, building a bridge of friendship seemed like the best idea. And he liked John. John was fair, and never put himself above others. There was a problem, though.

Tony's friends in the shop were really prejudiced. When they were working they'd crack jokes about blacks. Not only was John black, but he wore a suit and pushed papers for a living—something that these guys just couldn't relate to. They'd really give it to Tony when they found out about lunch. Their jokes made Tony's stomach tighten. He knew it wasn't right, but he was more ashamed of himself for not setting them straight. Tony never could understand how they thought they were better than everyone else. He knew this much—they needed Christ in their lives.

Reflection

Here's an example of facing repercussions from mocking peers. There was a great price to pay in the eyes of people, but what was gained was of far greater value. Being a witness for Jesus sometimes comes with a price. Reaching the world with the Gospel is threatening. But those who risk it discover that they gain much more than they ever lose.

This is the core of Jesus' admonition in Luke 9 when he asks us to follow him. But those who pay the price discover that they gain far more than they could ever lose.

Accountability and Application

What would you fear or risk losing which might keep you from being a witness for Christ?

Do the things that you fear losing really matter on an eternal scale?

Prayer

Lord, sometimes witnessing for you can cost a lot; there can be great risk. I need from you the courage to respond in obedience. Please give me the strength to step out in faith for your sake.

WEEK 12— Reaching the World

Accepting Differences
Matthew 9.9-13 *(NT p. 14)*

"Don't put 'em in a box"

DAY 6

On his way into a coffee shop for a Saturday-morning doughnut, Dan ran into a man that he had led to Christ a year ago. Dan had been reading the Bible over an early morning coffee and doughnut, when he'd gotten into a discussion with Jesse about "truth."

Jesse, a 25-year-old student at UCLA, loved to read, study and ride his Harley. He drove with a "chain and leather" gang, most of whom were students too. Intrigued by Dan's tenacity to study, Jesse entered a "debate" which resulted in his salvation.

Sharing about his latest Bible studies, Dan now told Jesse all about his rich involvement with his own church. Jesse, too, was now involved in a fellowship, and had himself led several to Christ. But his fellowship didn't look like Dan's. They didn't put on a suit and tie and sit on pews Sunday morning. Instead, their group, of about 40, met every Sunday night at a coffee house. A local pastor was bringing them a lesson every week and helping them establish worship and prayer for their culture.

Driving home, Dan was frustrated. He'd done everything right when he'd witnessed to Jesse. But Jesse was still riding his motorcycle, still wearing chains and a beard, and still hanging with the same crowd. He hadn't "cleaned up" his act. His group didn't even really go to church. Dan wondered if he'd been a failure in this situation.

Reflection

When Christ came to Peter, he found him at the shore about his business. He didn't take the fisherman out of Peter. Rather, Christ allowed Peter to use his abilities for his Kingdom.

Sometimes we Christians have an expectation of what we think a "saved" person should be. While sins must be abandoned, lifestyles are an expression of ourselves. Maintaining them can actually be a tool for leading others to Christ.

Accountability and Application

Do you think of others as "less spiritual" if their Christian lifestyle does not fit your mold?

Would you be willing to allow for cultural differences when you share the Gospel? Determine that your brand of evangelism does not presume a particular lifestyle of Christianity.

Prayer

Lord, I know that you made many types of people. Help me to understand that Christianity can have many different faces and contexts. Use me as a tool in any context.

WEEK 12—Reaching the World

A Look Around You
James 4.11, 12 *(NT p. 247)*

"Who's under that hood?"

DAY 7

Looking out the window, Lee noticed his neighbor Glen working on his car again. Glen was always doing something to it. "He ought to spend as much time with his wife," thought Lee. He had noticed that Glen and his wife never did anything together, never went anywhere together. You never even saw them leave together in the car. Of course, Lee never went out of his way to go over and talk to Glen either. No, you never saw Lee showing interest in what Glen was doing under that hood. All he ever did was watch from the window and judge Glen's family life.

Lee was very involved in his community and church life. He spent one Saturday a month with a boy's group picking up aluminum cans around the neighborhood. And he was on two different church communities—one which organized a food closet for needy people, and one which organized small Bible studies with church families around the city. He also met with other men two times a week early for prayer. The rest of his time he devoted to his family. Lee set aside a night a week to go on a date with his wife, and another for game night with the kids. He loved his family, and just couldn't understand why his neighbor didn't act the same way.

Reflection

Too often we Christians spend all of our time with other Christians and forget that to be a witness we need to be building relationships with those who do not yet know Christ. Like a doctor needs to spend time with the sick, we who are witnesses for Christ must be a light to those who are living in darkness.

Accountability and Application

When I examine how I spend my hours, are any of them spent with those who need to hear the Gospel? Or are any of the people with whom I interface lost?

Who has God already brought into my life that I could build a relationship with that may lead into an opportunity to witness to him?

Prayer

Lord, thank you for all of my Christian friends. They are a real encouragement to me. Now let me be open to recognize others that you have already placed around me who are in need of salvation. Prompt me to build those relationships where I may be a witness for you.

WEEK 13—Following Through

Where Do We Go From Here?

Just as iron sharpens iron,
friends sharpen the minds of each other.
Proverbs 27.17

GROUP DAY
DAY 1

LAST WEEK IN REVIEW: *The past three weeks have focused on God's heart. When we think his thoughts, hold his priorities and display his passion for those both inside the family of faith and those outside, our lives are different. As we close the final days of the devotional, we choose to address specific high points that keep us in tune and keep us together in our task.*

"Don't be alone"

Fred, a dock worker in an air freight company, had experienced a "so-so" type of Christian walk. Encouragement came from Allen, an African-American pastor. "Bi-vocational" was how he described his dual role of working a secular job along with pastoring a small congregation in the evenings and on Sundays. The two men decided that they would take Wednesday lunchtime together. Instead of eating a meal together, they'd talk, pray for each other and for each other's families, and support one another during times of challenge. Over the period of two years, two more men also became part of their small group.

Reflection

The impact of one man on another is powerful. The sharpening occurs because there is a balance of truth, love and accountability. This may happen, as with Fred and Allen, in a setting outside a single local church. Most often it will be among a few men within a local church. These groupings need to be simple, clear in purpose and honest.

Accountability and Application

Men can only hold one another accountable if they have given each other permission to do so. There are many questions which guys agree to be free at any time to ask and even probe. You'll need to work on your own set of questions. The following may help get you started.
1. What has God shown me from the Word this week?
2. What challenges am I facing that I need you to pray for for me?
3. What temptations are facing me for which you should hold me accountable for my response?
4. Am I honoring my wife and children?
5. Have you told me the truth without guarding yourself?

Prayer

Lord, thank you for brothers who will help hold me accountable. I know you always see me. It's also helpful to feel the support of another Christian.

WEEK 13—Following Through

Intentional Reconciliation
2 Corinthians 5.17-21 *(NT p. 191)*

"We are commissioned"

DAY 2

It was a remarkable request, "Can we help?" It came from a group of young men who were part of an Asian church. Being on the receiving end of service was a new mindset for them, and was a little difficult for them to embrace at first. A "Serve the City" project had included their church as one of twenty churches in the metro area. At the end of an exhausting but very productive day, the men were asking if they could be the ones serving next. "When you're working in a black or Hispanic church, can we go with you? We don't know anybody there, but we care and want to show it." Because men of various denominations and cultures had come to serve this church, it opened the door to partnership. They realized that it was not a matter of being a charity case. Rather, they were part of a project of reconciliation, of breaking down barriers. These men committed to no longer keep Christianity at arm's length from one another. "We're not alone, even if our worship is non-English. We still feel a new sense of being one with Christ."

Reflection

God has passed along the ministry of reconciliation to us. Reconciliation begins with the Gospel—"make peace with God" (v. 20). Ephesians 2.14 speaks of bringing together ethnic division, illustrated by the wall separating Jews and Gentiles. "On the cross Christ did away with our hatred for each other" (v. 16). Natural man is given to hate. It is only when we're born anew that loving our brother becomes a priority. If you have lingering questions about the relationship between loving God and loving your brother, read 1 John 4.7-21. "But if we say we love God and don't love each other, we are liars." (v. 20).

Accountability and Application

Do you personally have a plan to expand your path of love to others who are different from you?

Are you becoming more aware of others and their needs by reading, talking and ministering?

Prayer

Lord, I was a long way from you—sinful, and not easy to love. Now that I think of it, I can't understand why you wanted to love me, but you did! Lord, let me love my brothers with that same intensity.

WEEK 13 — Following Through

A Vital Prayer Network
Matthew 18.18-20 *(NT p. 25)*

"Prayer that changes things"

DAY 3

Kim said of her husband, "He never used to pray out loud, or with me or with the family. Even our table blessing was left up to me or, as they got older, to the kids. Then it all changed. When Bill started praying with a group of men, it was like he was free to pray simply and honestly. Now he prays with me daily and has confidence to lead out in family gatherings or in church. I'm so happy for his new leadership."

When Kim told Bill how she had been feeling for years about the lack of their prayer life together, he was surprised. He hadn't known of her desire. She told him that she had desperately wanted him to take spiritual leadership in that area, but she hadn't wanted to nag him. So, she kept this desire to herself, and prayed about it. Bill agreed that nagging wouldn't have helped, but admitted that praying with his small group really had opened the door.

Reflection

Prayer is powerful and dynamic. Many have only experienced personal prayer. Surveys tell us that more than 80% of Americans say they pray. The most basic form of prayer, in a word, is "help." We all have asked God for his help in our lives. Prayer is much more than a listing of our needs. It is praise, adoration and worship of God. It can be our confession and repentance of sin. Prayer can take its focus to the needs of others; this is called intercession. Our text today would suggest that whatever the focus or subject of our prayer, the effect of it is increased by doing it in agreement with others. We are calling on men in every church to form prayer networks to pray for God's work among men and also to pray for their local church, their pastor, priest or leader, and for the expansion of the cause of Christ everywhere. Here are a couple of suggestions to help you:
1. Simple, honest and direct is best.
2. "Just do it." The details will follow.

Accountability and Application

If you're uncomfortable praying out loud with someone else, continue to pray silently, but start jotting down the things you're requesting or saying to God. Try reading your request out loud as you pray again.

Have you selected anyone to share your praying with? If not, start this week.

Do you have a way in your church to share information about the needs of members, missionaries and your staff so that you can support them in prayer?

Prayer

Lord, your disciples said to you, "teach us to pray." I need that help also. Thanks for the millions of other believers who will agree with me in my prayer. Thank you that you always hear and that I'm not alone.

WEEK 13—Following Through

Unity in the Word
2 Timothy 3.14-17 *(NT p. 227)*

"I can do that"

DAY 4

Richard, a leader in men's ministry in his local church, reported a practice that has developed among his men. They are all reading through the New Testament. And Mike, though hearing impaired, is joining them. For a long time, Mike has wanted to be a part of the group, reading through the Bible with them. When he approached Richard with this, Richard was doubtful that the group could accommodate him.

Unaware of his insensitivity, Richard was confronted by the pastor. It was part of the church's ministry, and Mike had a special need and deserved ministry the same as any other man. Faced with his oversight, Richard began to make plans to accommodate Mike. Mike now joins them with an interpreter for group sessions. They find it easy to talk about sections they've just read, and find that the expectations of each other give a gentle nudge of accountability. As they work through their issues and struggles together, they find the Word uplifting. Richard is pleased that the group has been able to "gel" and hopes to bring in even more guys. He really has a desire to include everyone and bring unity to the men's group.

Reflection

The reading plan that Richard's group is using follows on the next four pages. Here are some facts about it. The plan separates the Gospels there by revisiting a Gospel account of the life of Jesus four times during the year. The basic outline starts with Matthew followed by Acts. The second cycle takes Mark followed by the Letters of Peter, James and Jude. Luke, the third Gospel, was written by the companion in ministry of Paul. It is followed by the Letters to the churches ascribed to Paul. Lastly, the Gospel of John is followed by the Letters of John and the Revelation.

These daily readings are simple to do. Young people can handle the checklist and they find it easy to follow. This plan can be started at any point. Check off the days as you read. If you want to go faster, do it. If you're doing it as a family, or in your men's group, be sure to talk about insights the Lord is showing you.

Accountability and Application

Have you made a commitment to read the Word of God each day?

Do you want companionship as you learn about Jesus and the early church?

Are you willing to include everyone, even if they have personal struggles or impairments which may make it a little more difficult to communicate?

Prayer

Lord, thank you for your Word that lets us know you. Thanks for preserving the Bible through history and for translations in our language that allow us to understand.

A NEW TESTAMENT READING PLAN

The following plan will lead you through the entire New Testament in one year. To keep track of your progress, just check off each passage as you read it. Consistency is the key to success!

Date   Passage   Page #

January

1	☐ Matthew 1	1
2	☐ Matthew 2	6
3	☐ Matthew 3	7
4	☐ Matthew 4	7
5	☐ Matthew 5.1-20	8
6	☐ Matthew 5.21-48	9
7	☐ Matthew 6.1-18	10
8	☐ Matthew 6.19-7.6	11
9	☐ Matthew 7.7-29	11
10	☐ Matthew 8.1-27	12
11	☐ Matthew 8.28-9.17	13
12	☐ Matthew 9.18-38	14
13	☐ Matthew 10.1-25	15
14	☐ Matthew 10.26-11.1	15
15	☐ Matthew 11.2-30	16
16	☐ Matthew 12.1-21	17
17	☐ Matthew 12.22-50	18
18	☐ Matthew 13.1-23	19
19	☐ Matthew 13.24-43	19
20	☐ Matthew 13.44-14.13	20
21	☐ Matthew 14.14-36	21
22	☐ Matthew 15.1-28	21
23	☐ Matthew 15.29-16.12	22
24	☐ Matthew 16.13-17.13	23
25	☐ Matthew 17.14-18.14	24
26	☐ Matthew 18.15-35	25
27	☐ Matthew 19.1-15	26
28	☐ Matthew 19.16-20.16	26
29	☐ Matthew 20.17-34	27
30	☐ Matthew 21.1-32	28
31	☐ Matthew 21.33-22.14	29

February

1	☐ Matthew 22.15-46	30
2	☐ Matthew 23	31
3	☐ Matthew 24.1-28	32
4	☐ Matthew 24.29-51	33
5	☐ Matthew 25.1-30	34
6	☐ Matthew 25.31-26.2	35
7	☐ Matthew 26.3-30	35
8	☐ Matthew 26.31-57	36
9	☐ Matthew 26.58-75	37
10	☐ Matthew 27.1-26	37
11	☐ Matthew 27.27-44	38
12	☐ Matthew 27.45-66	39
13	☐ Matthew 28	39
14	☐ Acts 1	129
15	☐ Acts 2.1-21	129
16	☐ Acts 2.22-47	130
17	☐ Acts 3	131
18	☐ Acts 4.1-31	132
19	☐ Acts 4.32-5.11	133
20	☐ Acts 5.12-42	133
21	☐ Acts 6	134
22	☐ Acts 7.1-29	135
23	☐ Acts 7.30-8.4	135
24	☐ Acts 8.5-40	137
25	☐ Acts 9.1-31	138
26	☐ Acts 9.32-43	138
27	☐ Acts 10.1-23	139
28	☐ Acts 10.24-48	139

March

1	☐ Acts 11.1-18	140
2	☐ Acts 11.19-30	141
3	☐ Acts 12	141
4	☐ Acts 13.1-25	142
5	☐ Acts 13.26-52	143
6	☐ Acts 14	144
7	☐ Acts 15.1-21	144
8	☐ Acts 15.22-35	145
9	☐ Acts 15.36-16.15	146
10	☐ Acts 16.16-40	146
11	☐ Acts 17.1-15	147
12	☐ Acts 17.16-34	147
13	☐ Acts 18.1-22	148
14	☐ Acts 18.23-19.20	149
15	☐ Acts 19.21-41	150
16	☐ Acts 20.1-16	150
17	☐ Acts 20.17-38	151
18	☐ Acts 21.1-16	151
19	☐ Acts 21.17-40	152
20	☐ Acts 22.1-21	153
21	☐ Acts 22.22-23.11	153
22	☐ Acts 23.12-35	154
23	☐ Acts 24	155
24	☐ Acts 25.1-22	156

25	☐ Acts 25.23-26.11	156
26	☐ Acts 26.12-32	157
27	☐ Acts 27.1-26	157
28	☐ Acts 27.27-28.10	158
29	☐ Acts 28. 11-31	159
30	☐ Mark 1.1-20	41
31	☐ Mark 1.21-45	41

APRIL

1	☐ Mark 2.1-22	43
2	☐ Mark 2.23-3.12	44
3	☐ Mark 3.13-35	44
4	☐ Mark 4.1-20	45
5	☐ Mark 4.21-41	46
6	☐ Mark 5.1-20	46
7	☐ Mark 5.21-43	47
8	☐ Mark 6.1-29	47
9	☐ Mark 6.30-56	48
10	☐ Mark 7.1-23	49
11	☐ Mark 7.24-8.10	50
12	☐ Mark 8.11-26	50
13	☐ Mark 8.27-9.13	51
14	☐ Mark 9.14-32	52
15	☐ Mark 9.33-50	52
16	☐ Mark 10.1-31	53
17	☐ Mark 10.32-52	54
18	☐ Mark 11.1-26	55
19	☐ Mark 11.27-12.17	55
20	☐ Mark 12.18-44	56
21	☐ Mark 13	57
22	☐ Mark 14.1-26	58
23	☐ Mark 14.27-52	59
24	☐ Mark 14.53-72	60
25	☐ Mark 15.1-23	61
26	☐ Mark 15.24-47	61
27	☐ Mark 16	62
28	☐ 1 Peter 1.1-12	249
29	☐ 1 Peter 1.13-2.10	250
30	☐ 1 Peter 2.11-3.7	251

MAY

1	☐ 1 Peter 3.8-22	251
2	☐ 1 Peter 4	252
3	☐ 1 Peter 5	252
4	☐ 2 Peter 1	254
5	☐ 2 Peter 2	255
6	☐ 2 Peter 3	256
7	☐ James 1	245
8	☐ James 2	246
9	☐ James 3	247
10	☐ James 4	247
11	☐ James 5	248
12	☐ Jude 1	264
13	☐ Luke 1.1-25	65
14	☐ Luke 1.26-56	65
15	☐ Luke 1.57-80	66
16	☐ Luke 2.1-21	67
17	☐ Luke 2.22-52	67
18	☐ Luke 3	68
19	☐ Luke 4.1-15	69
20	☐ Luke 4.16-44	70
21	☐ Luke 5.1-16	70
22	☐ Luke 5.17-39	71
23	☐ Luke 6.1-19	72
24	☐ Luke 6.20-49	72
25	☐ Luke 7.1-29	74
26	☐ Luke 7.30-50	74
27	☐ Luke 8.1-21	75
28	☐ Luke 8.22-39	76
29	☐ Luke 8.40-56	77
30	☐ Luke 9.1-17	77
31	☐ Luke 9.18-36	78

JUNE

1	☐ Luke 9.37-62	78
2	☐ Luke 10.1-24	79
3	☐ Luke 10.25-42	80
4	☐ Luke 11.1-13	81
5	☐ Luke 11.14-36	81
6	☐ Luke 11.37-54	82
7	☐ Luke 12.1-21	83
8	☐ Luke 12.22-40	83
9	☐ Luke 12.41-59	84
10	☐ Luke 13.1-21	84
11	☐ Luke 13.22-35	85
12	☐ Luke 14.1-24	86
13	☐ Luke 14.25-15.10	86
14	☐ Luke 15.11-32	87
15	☐ Luke 16	88
16	☐ Luke 17.1-19	89
17	☐ Luke 17.20-18.14	89
18	☐ Luke 18.15-43	90
19	☐ Luke 19.1-28	91
20	☐ Luke 19.29-48	92
21	☐ Luke 20.1-19	93
22	☐ Luke 20.20-21.4	93
23	☐ Luke 21.5-38	94
24	☐ Luke 22.1-30	95
25	☐ Luke 22.31-53	96
26	☐ Luke 22.54-23.12	97
27	☐ Luke 23.13-46	97
28	☐ Luke 23.47-24.12	98
29	☐ Luke 24.13-53	99
30	☐ 1 Thessalonians 1	215

July

1	☐	1 Thessalonians 2.1-16	216
2	☐	1 Thessalonians 2.17-3.13	216
3	☐	1 Thessalonians 4	216
4	☐	1 Thessalonians 5	217
5	☐	2 Thessalonians 1	218
6	☐	2 Thessalonians 2	219
7	☐	2 Thessalonians 3	219
8	☐	1 Corinthians 1	176
9	☐	1 Corinthians 2	176
10	☐	1 Corinthians 3	177
11	☐	1 Corinthians 4	177
12	☐	1 Corinthians 5	178
13	☐	1 Corinthians 6	178
14	☐	1 Corinthians 7	179
15	☐	1 Corinthians 8	180
16	☐	1 Corinthians 9.1-23	180
17	☐	1 Corinthians 9.24-10.14	181
18	☐	1 Corinthians 10.15-11.1	181
19	☐	1 Corinthians 11.2-34	182
20	☐	1 Corinthians 12	183
21	☐	1 Corinthians 13	183
22	☐	1 Corinthians 14	184
23	☐	1 Corinthians 15.1-34	185
24	☐	1 Corinthians 15.35-58	186
25	☐	1 Corinthians 16	187
26	☐	2 Corinthians 1	188
27	☐	2 Corinthians 2	189
28	☐	2 Corinthians 3.1-4.6	189
29	☐	2 Corinthians 4.7-5.10	190
30	☐	2 Corinthians 5.11-6.10	190
31	☐	2 Corinthians 6.11-7.16	191

August

1	☐	2 Corinthians 8	192
2	☐	2 Corinthians 9	193
3	☐	2 Corinthians 10	193
4	☐	2 Corinthians 11	194
5	☐	2 Corinthians 12.1-13	195
6	☐	2 Corinthians 12.14-13.14	195
7	☐	Romans 1.1-16	161
8	☐	Romans 1.17-32	162
9	☐	Romans 2	162
10	☐	Romans 3	163
11	☐	Romans 4.1-22	164
12	☐	Romans 4.23-5.11	165
13	☐	Romans 5.12-21	165
14	☐	Romans 6.1-14	165
15	☐	Romans 6.15-7.6	166
16	☐	Romans 7.7-25	166
17	☐	Romans 8.1-17	166
18	☐	Romans 8.18-39	167
19	☐	Romans 9.1-29	168
20	☐	Romans 9.30-10.21	168
21	☐	Romans 11.1-15	169
22	☐	Romans 11.16-36	170
23	☐	Romans 12	170
24	☐	Romans 13	171
25	☐	Romans 14.1-18	171
26	☐	Romans 14.19-15.13	172
27	☐	Romans 15.14-33	173
28	☐	Romans 16	173
29	☐	Galatians 1	197
30	☐	Galatians 2	198
31	☐	Galatians 3.1-14	198

September

1	☐	Galatians 3.15-29	199
2	☐	Galatians 4.1-20	199
3	☐	Galatians 4.21-5.9	200
4	☐	Galatians 5.10-26	200
5	☐	Galatians 6	201
6	☐	Ephesians 1.1-14	202
7	☐	Ephesians 1.15-2.10	203
8	☐	Ephesians 2.11-22	203
9	☐	Ephesians 3	204
10	☐	Ephesians 4.1-16	204
11	☐	Ephesians 4.17-32	205
12	☐	Ephesians 5.1-21	205
13	☐	Ephesians 5.22-6.9	205
14	☐	Ephesians 6.10-24	206
15	☐	Philippians 1.1-20	207
16	☐	Philippians 1.21-2.11	208
17	☐	Philippians 2.12-30	208
18	☐	Philippians 3.1-4.1	209
19	☐	Philippians 4.2-23	210
20	☐	Colossians 1.1-20	211
21	☐	Colossians 1.21-2.7	212
22	☐	Colossians 2.8-3.4	212
23	☐	Colossians 3.5-4.1	213
24	☐	Colossians 4.2-18	214
25	☐	Philemon	232
26	☐	Hebrews 1	234
27	☐	Hebrews 2	235
28	☐	Hebrews 3	236
29	☐	Hebrews 4.1-13	236
30	☐	Hebrews 4.14-5.10	237

October

1	☐	Hebrews 5.11-6.20	237
2	☐	Hebrews 7	238
3	☐	Hebrews 8	238
4	☐	Hebrews 9.1-14	239

5	☐ Hebrews 9.15-28	240
6	☐ Hebrews 10.1-18	240
7	☐ Hebrews 10.19-39	241
8	☐ Hebrews 11.1-16	241
9	☐ Hebrews 11.17-40	242
10	☐ Hebrews 12.1-17	242
11	☐ Hebrews 12.18-13.6	243
12	☐ Hebrews 13.7-25	243
13	☐ Titus 1.1-2.8	229
14	☐ Titus 2.9-3.15	230
15	☐ 1 Timothy 1	220
16	☐ 1 Timothy 2	221
17	☐ 1 Timothy 3	221
18	☐ 1 Timothy 4	222
19	☐ 1 Timothy 5	222
20	☐ 1 Timothy 6	223
21	☐ 2 Timothy 1	225
22	☐ 2 Timothy 2	226
23	☐ 2 Timothy 3	227
24	☐ 2 Timothy 4	227
25	☐ John 1.1-18	102
26	☐ John 1.19-51	102
27	☐ John 2.1-22	103
28	☐ John 2.23-3.21	104
29	☐ John 3.22-36	104
30	☐ John 4.1-30	105
31	☐ John 4.31-54	106

NOVEMBER

1	☐ John 5.1-23	106
2	☐ John 5.24-47	107
3	☐ John 6.1-21	108
4	☐ John 6.22-40	108
5	☐ John 6.41-7.1	109
6	☐ John 7.2-30	109
7	☐ John 7.31-8.11	110
8	☐ John 8.12-30	111
9	☐ John 8.31-59	112
10	☐ John 9.1-17	112
11	☐ John 9.18-38	113
12	☐ John 9.39-10.18	114
13	☐ John 10.19-42	114
14	☐ John 11.1-27	114
15	☐ John 11.28-54	115
16	☐ John 11.55-12.19	116
17	☐ John 12.20-50	116
18	☐ John 13.1-30	117
19	☐ John 13.31-14.14	118
20	☐ John 14.15-31	119
21	☐ John 15.1-16	119
22	☐ John 15.17-16.15	120
23	☐ John 16.16-33	121
24	☐ John 17	121
25	☐ John 18.1-27	122
26	☐ John 18.28-19.16	123
27	☐ John 19.17-42	124
28	☐ John 20	125
29	☐ John 21	126
30	☐ 1 John 1	257

DECEMBER

1	☐ 1 John 2.1-17	258
2	☐ 1 John 2.18-29	258
3	☐ 1 John 3	259
4	☐ 1 John 4	259
5	☐ 1 John 5	260
6	☐ 2 John	261
7	☐ 3 John	262
8	☐ Revelation 1	266
9	☐ Revelation 2.1-17	266
10	☐ Revelation 2.18-3.6	267
11	☐ Revelation 3.7-22	268
12	☐ Revelation 4	269
13	☐ Revelation 5	269
14	☐ Revelation 6	270
15	☐ Revelation 7	270
16	☐ Revelation 8	271
17	☐ Revelation 9	271
18	☐ Revelation 10	272
19	☐ Revelation 11	272
20	☐ Revelation 12	273
21	☐ Revelation 13	274
22	☐ Revelation 14	275
23	☐ Revelation 15	275
24	☐ Revelation 16	276
25	☐ Revelation 17	276
26	☐ Revelation 18	277
27	☐ Revelation 19.1-10	278
28	☐ Revelation 19.11-20.6	279
29	☐ Revelation 20.7-21.8	279
30	☐ Revelation 21.9-22.5	280
31	☐ Revelation 22.6-21	281

STAND IN THE GAP

NEW TESTAMENT

Contemporary English Version

Commerative Edition

Published for

PROMISE KEEPERS
MEN OF INTEGRITY

by

ABS

American Bible Society
New York

The New Testament
Contemporary English Version

Quotation Rights For The Contemporary English Version

The American Bible Society is glad to grant authors and publishers the right to use up to one thousand (1,000) verses from the *Contemporary English Version* text in church, religious and other publications without the need to seek and receive written permission. However, the extent of quotation must not comprise a complete book nor should it amount to more than 50% of the work. The proper copyright notice must appear on the title or copyright page.

When quotations from *CEV* are used in a non-saleable media, such as church bulletins, orders of service, posters, transparencies or similar media, a complete copyright notice is not required, but the initials *(CEV)* must appear at the end of each quotation.

Requests for quotations in excess of one thousand (1,000) verses in any publication must be directed to, and written approval received from, the American Bible Society, 1865 Broadway, New York, NY 10023.

Cover, daily devotionals and syllabus material provided by Promise Keepers.
Cover and syllabus color design created by Kirk DouPonce/International Bible Society

Promise Keepers Project Director: Gordon England

Promise Keepers Contributing Authors: Paul Edwards, Tim Elmore, Gordon England, Bruce Fong, Jim Gordon, Geoff Gorsuch, John Maxwell, Gary Oliver, Ken Moldenhauer, Lawrence Reed, Dan Schaffer, Bruce Wilkinson

Promise Keepers Editors: Linda Dunlap, Ashley Nearn

Printed in the United States of America
Eng. N.T. CEV250-106271
ABS-10/97-1,025,000-W1

Promise Keepers Evangelism Plan © 1996, Promise Keepers
Promise Keepers Daily Devotionals © 1997, Promise Keepers
New Testament Text: © 1995, American Bible Society
Maps: © 1976, 1978, 1979, United Bible Societies

THE CONTEMPORARY ENGLISH VERSION

Translation it is that opens the window, to let in the light; that breaks the shell, that we may eat the kernel; that puts aside the curtain, that we may look into the most holy place; that removes the cover of the well, that we may come by the water ("The Translators to the Reader," King James Version, 1611).

The most important document in the history of the English language is the King James Version of the Bible. To measure its spiritual impact on the English speaking world would be more impossible than counting the grains of sand along the ocean shores. Historically, many Bible translators have attempted in some measure to *retain the form* of the King James Version. But the translators of the Contemporary English Version of the Bible have diligently sought to *capture the spirit* of the King James Version by following certain principles set forth by its translators in the document "The Translators to the Reader," which was printed in the earliest editions.

This is the Word of God, which we translate

Accuracy, beauty, clarity, and dignity—all of these can and must be achieved in the translation of the Bible. After all, as the translators of the King James Version stated, "This is the Word of God, which we translate."

Every attempt has been made to produce a text that is faithful to the *meaning* of the original. In order to assure the *accuracy* of the Contemporary English Version, the Old Testament was translated directly from the Hebrew and Aramaic texts published by the United Bible Societies (*Biblia Hebraica Stuttgartensia*, fourth edition corrected). And the New Testament was translated directly from the Greek text published by the United Bible Societies (third edition corrected and compared with the fourth revised edition).

The drafts in their earliest stages were sent for review and comment to a number of biblical scholars, theologians, and educators representing a wide variety of church traditions. In addition, drafts were sent for review and comment to all English-speaking Bible Societies and to more than forty United Bible Societies translation consultants around the world. Final approval of the text was given by the American Bible Society Board of Trustees on the recommendation of its Translations Subcommittee.

We desire that the Scripture . . . may be understood

That the Scripture may be understood even by ordinary people was a primary goal of the translators of the King James Version. And they raised the question, "What can be more available thereto than to deliver God's book unto God's people in a tongue which they understand?" Martin Luther also did his translation for the common people, and he established the following guidelines:

the CEV   IV

> We do not have to inquire of the literal Latin, how we are to speak German . . . Rather we must inquire about this of the mother in the home, the children on the street, the common man in the marketplace. *We must be guided by their language, the way they speak, and do our translating accordingly.*

Today more people *hear* the Bible read aloud than read it for themselves! And statistics released by the National Center for Education indicate that "almost half of U.S. adults have very limited reading and writing skills." If this is the case, a contemporary translation must be a text that an inexperienced reader can *read aloud* without stumbling, that someone unfamiliar with traditional biblical terminology can *hear without misunderstanding*, and that everyone can *listen to with enjoyment* because the style is lucid and lyrical.

In order to attain these goals of clarity, beauty, and dignity, the translators of the Contemporary English Version carefully studied every word, phrase, clause, and paragraph of the original. Then, with equal care, they struggled to discover the best way to translate the text, so that it would be suitable both for *private* and *public* reading, and for *memorizing*. The result is an English text that is enjoyable and easily understood by the vast majority of English speakers, regardless of their religious or educational background.

In the *hearing* of a translation, even the inclusion of a simple word like "and" can make a significant difference. Matthew 2.9 of the Contemporary English Version reads as follows: "The wise men listened to what the king said, and then left. *And* the star they had seen in the east went on ahead of them until it stopped over the place where the child was."

"And" at the beginning of the second sentence assists both the person who reads the text aloud and those who must depend upon hearing it read. Like all other punctuation marks, the period after "left" is silent, and so the text without "And" could possibly be *heard* as, "The wise men listened to what the king said and then left the star they had seen in the east." However, as the text now stands, the oral reader must pause briefly for a breath before "And," which will signal the hearer that a new sentence has begun.

As another example, try reading the following two sentences aloud: "You yourselves admit, then, that you agree with what your ancestors did" and "for it was better with me then than now." Both suffer from potential tongue twisters ("admit, then, that" and "then than"). But the first is doubly difficult because it consists of a lengthy series of unaccented syllables that do not allow the reader to take a breath. In the Contemporary English Version every attempt has been made to avoid these and other kinds of constructions that could possibly prove problematic for oral reading.

According to the rules of English grammar, the pronoun *he* must refer back to God in the following sentence: "The other, however, rebuked him saying, 'Don't you fear God? You received the same sentence *he* did.'" But the reference is actually to Jesus, who is mentioned earlier in the passage. Traditional translations assume that the reader can study the printed text and finally figure out the meaning, but the Contemporary English Version is concerned equally with the reader and the *hearer*. And in many situations, the hearer may have only *one* chance to understand what is read aloud.

In poetry, the *appearance of the text on the page* is important, since in oral reading there is a tendency to stress the last word on a line and to pause momentarily before going to the next line, especially if the second line is indented. Compare the three following examples, where the lines of the same text have been broken improperly (left column) and properly (right column):

He brought me out into a broad place.	He brought me out into a broad place.
With the loyal you show yourself loyal.	With the loyal you show yourself loyal.
The Lord my God lights up my darkness.	The Lord my God lights up my darkness.

No fault is to be found with the translation itself. Yet there is a significant difference in the *appearance* of the text on the page, because the lines on the right have been *measured*, in order to prevent unfortunate runovers. In this form, the text not only looks better on the page, but it is easier to read and memorize, and it avoids such disastrous combinations as "He brought me out into a broad" or "With the loyal you show yourself" or "The Lord my God lights up." Moreover, both formats require exactly the same amount of lines.

The first translation in the history of the English Bible to develop a text with measured poetry lines is the Contemporary English Version, in which the translators have consciously created a text that will not suffer from unfortunate line breaks when published in double columns. *Accuracy* is the main concern of translators, but it must be realized that in the translation of biblical poetry, what the reader *sees* is what will be *said*, and what others will *hear*. This means that lines improperly broken can easily lead to a misunderstanding of the text, especially for those who must depend upon *hearing* the Scriptures read.

Hebrew poetry has its own systems of sound, rhyme, and rhythm, as well as a *form* that involves much repetition. It is impossible in English to retain the sounds, rhymes, and rhythms of the Hebrew text, but traditional translations have attempted to reproduce the frequent repetition, in which a second line will repeat or expand, either negatively or positively, the thoughts of the previous line. However, this repetition is often ineffective for those English speakers, who are unaccustomed to the poetic style of the biblical authors. And so, the translators of the Contemporary English Version have followed the example of Martin Luther in the translation of poetry:

> Whoever would speak German *must not use Hebrew style*. Rather he must see to it—once he understands the Hebrew author—that he concentrates on the *sense* of the text, asking himself, "Pray tell, what do the Germans say in such a situation?" Once he has the German words to serve his purpose, let him drop the Hebrew words and *express the meaning freely* in the best German he knows.

The qualities that many critics value most in modern poetry are effortless *economy* and *exactness* of language. It is hoped that readers will discover similar features in the poetry of the Contemporary English Version, which strives for beauty and dignity, as much as for accuracy and clarity. In this translation, the poetry often requires fewer lines than do traditional translations, but the *integrity*, *intent,* and *impact* of the original are consistently maintained. Note, for example, the rendering of Job 38.14,15:

> Early dawn outlines the hills   But its light is too much
> like stitches on clothing   for those who are evil,
>   or sketches on clay.   and their power is broken.

Whenever the contents of two or more verses have been joined together and rearranged in the poetic sections of the *CEV,* this is signaled by an asterisk (*) before the first verse number in the series.

In everyday speech, "gender generic" or "inclusive" language is used, because it sounds most natural to people today. This means that where the biblical languages require masculine nouns or pronouns when both men and women are intended, this intention must be reflected in translation, though the English *form* may be very different from that of the original. The Greek text of Matthew 16.24 is literally, "If anyone wants to follow me, *he* must deny *himself* and take up *his* cross and follow me." The Contemporary English Version shifts to a form which is still accurate, and at the same time more effective in English: "If any of *you* want to be my followers, *you* must forget about *yourself. You* must take up *your* cross and follow me."

Variety of translations is profitable

The translators of the King James Version said, "... variety of translations is profitable for the finding out of the sense of the Scriptures" and "We affirm and avow that the very meanest translation of the Bible in English, set forth by men of our profession ... contains the Word of God, nay is the Word of God." They even stated, "No cause therefore why the Word translated should be denied to be the Word, or forbidden to be current, notwithstanding that some imperfections and blemishes may be noted in the setting forth of it."

Each English translation is, in its own right, the Word of God, yet each translation serves to meet the needs of a different audience. In this regard, the Contemporary English Version should be considered a *companion*—the *mission* arm—of traditional translations, because it takes seriously the words of the apostle Paul that "faith comes by *hearing."*

It has pleased God in his divine providence

Translating the Bible may be compared to living the life of faith. God has not given us all the answers for our pilgrim journey, but we have been provided with all that we need to know in order to be saved. As the translators of the King James Version observed:

> ... it has pleased God in His divine providence here and there to scatter those words and sentences of that difficulty and doubtfulness, not in doctrinal points that concern salvation (for in such it has been vouched that the Scriptures are plain), but in matters of less moment, that fearfulness would better beseem us than confidence ...
>
> For as it is a fault of incredulity, to doubt of those things that are evident; so to determine of such things that the Spirit of God

has left (even in the mind of the judicious) questionable, can be no less than presumption.

Bible translators do not have the privilege and luxury of working from the original manuscripts of either the Old or New Testament. Indeed, there are numerous difficult passages where decisions must be made concerning what word or words actually belong in the text, and what these words may, in fact, mean. At such places, the best a translator can do is to give what seems to be one possible meaning for the difficult text and to indicate this by a note, which was also what the King James translators did: "... so diversity of signification and sense in the margin, where the text is not clear, must needs be good; yea, is necessary, as we are persuaded." Fortunately, these "words and sentences of that difficulty and doubtfulness" do not in any way leave unclear the central message of the Bible or any of its major doctrines.

Having and using as great helps as were needful

The translators of the Contemporary English Version have not created new or novel interpretations of the text. Rather, it was their goal to express mainstream interpretations of the text in current, everyday English. To do so required *listening* carefully to each word of the biblical text, to the way in which English is spoken today, to the remarks of their reviewers, and especially to the Spirit of God. Once again the comments of the translators of the King James Version are appropriate:

Neither did we think much to consult the translators or commentators ... but neither did we disdain to revise that which we had done, and to bring to the anvil that which we had hammered; but having and using as great helps as were needful, and fearing no reproach for slowness, nor coveting praise for expedition, we have at the length, through the good hand of the Lord upon us, brought forth the work to that pass that you see.

Accordingly, the translators of the Contemporary English Version are indebted to all translators and biblical scholars who have gone before them and have made it possible to understand something of the languages, cultures, and history of biblical times. And, together with the apostle Paul, they confess: *We don't have the right to claim that we have done anything on our own. God gives us what it takes to do all that we do.* (2 Corinthians 3.5)

Offer praise to God our Savior because of our Lord Jesus Christ! (Jude 24,25)

CONTENTS
(with book abbreviations)

THE GOSPELS
- Matthew .... Mt 5
- Mark .... Mk 41
- Luke .... Lk 64
- John .... Jn 101

HISTORY
- Acts .... Ac 128

PAUL'S LETTERS
- Romans .... Ro 161
- 1 Corinthians .... 1 Co 175
- 2 Corinthians .... 2 Co 188
- Galatians .... Ga 197
- Ephesians .... Eph 202
- Philippians .... Phil 207
- Colossians .... Col 211
- 1 Thessalonians ...... 1 Th 215
- 2 Thessalonians ...... 2 Th 218
- 1 Timothy .... 1 Ti 220
- 2 Timothy .... 2 Ti 225
- Titus .... Titus 229
- Philemon .... Phm 232

GENERAL LETTERS
- Hebrews .... He 234
- James .... Jas 245
- 1 Peter .... 1 P 249
- 2 Peter .... 2 P 254
- 1 John .... 1 Jn 257
- 2 John .... 2 Jn 261
- 3 John .... 3 Jn 262
- Jude .... Jd 263

PROPHECY
- Revelation .... Rev 265

WORD LIST 283
SPECIAL READER'S HELPS 289
MAPS 305

MATTHEW

ABOUT THIS BOOK

The Sermon on the Mount (5.1—7.28), the Lord's Prayer (6.9-13), and the Golden Rule (7.12: "Treat others as you want them to treat you") are all in this book. It is perhaps the best known and the most quoted of all the books that have ever been written about Jesus. That is one reason why Matthew was placed first among the four books about Jesus called Gospels.

One of the most important ideas found here is that God expects his people to obey him, and this is what is meant by the Greek word that appears in many translations as *righteousness*. It is used seven times by Matthew, but only once by Luke, and not at all by Mark. So it is an important clue to much of what Matthew wants his readers to understand about the teaching of Jesus.

Jesus first uses this word at his own baptism, when he tells John the Baptist, "We must do all that God wants us to do" (3.15). Then, during his Sermon on the Mount, he speaks five more times of what God's people must do to obey him (5.6, 10, 20; 6.1, 33). And finally, he reminds the chief priests and leaders of the people, "John the Baptist showed you how to do right" (21.32).

Matthew wanted to provide for the people of his time a record of Jesus' message and ministry. It is clear that the Old Testament Scriptures were very important to these people. And Matthew never fails to show when these texts point to the coming of Jesus as the Messiah sent from God. Matthew wrote this book to make sure Christians knew that their faith in Jesus as the Messiah was well anchored in the Old Testament Scriptures, and to help them grow in faith.

Matthew ends his story with the words of Jesus to his followers, which tell what they are to do after he leaves them:

I have been given all authority in heaven and on earth! Go to the people of all nations and make them my disciples. Baptize them in the name of the Father, the Son, and the Holy Spirit, and teach them to do everything I have told you. I will be with you always, even until the end of the world. (28.18b-20)

A QUICK LOOK AT THIS BOOK

The Ancestors and Birth of Jesus (1.1—2.23)
The Message of John the Baptist (3.1-12)
The Baptism and Temptation of Jesus (3.13—4.11)
Jesus in Galilee (4.12—18.35)
Jesus Goes from Galilee to Jerusalem (19.1—20.34)
Jesus' Last Week: His Trial and Death (21.1—27.66)
Jesus Is Alive (28.1-20)

The Ancestors of Jesus
(Luke 3.23-38)

1 Jesus Christ came from the family of King David and also from the family of Abraham. And this is a list of his ancestors. ²⁻⁶ᵃFrom Abraham to King David, his ancestors were:

Abraham, Isaac, Jacob, Judah and his brothers (Judah's sons were Perez and Zerah, and their mother was Tamar), Hezron;

Ram, Amminadab, Nahshon, Salmon, Boaz (his mother was Rahab), Obed (his mother was Ruth), Jesse, and King David.

Matthew 1.6b-11

6b-11 From David to the time of the exile in Babylonia, the ancestors of Jesus were:

David, Solomon (his mother had been Uriah's wife), Rehoboam, Abijah, Asa, Jehoshaphat, Jehoram;

Uzziah, Jotham, Ahaz, Hezekiah, Manasseh, Amon, Josiah, and Jehoiachin and his brothers.

12-16 From the exile to the birth of Jesus, his ancestors were:

Jehoiachin, Shealtiel, Zerubbabel, Abiud, Eliakim, Azor, Zadok, Achim;

Eliud, Eleazar, Matthan, Jacob, and Joseph, the husband of Mary, the mother of Jesus, who is called the Messiah.

17There were fourteen generations from Abraham to David. There were also fourteen from David to the exile in Babylonia and fourteen more to the birth of the Messiah.

The Birth of Jesus
(Luke 2.1-7)

18This is how Jesus Christ was born. A young woman named Mary was engaged to Joseph from King David's family. But before they were married, she learned that she was going to have a baby by God's Holy Spirit. **19**Joseph was a good man[a] and did not want to embarrass Mary in front of everyone. So he decided to quietly call off the wedding. **20**While Joseph was thinking about this, an angel from the Lord came to him in a dream. The angel said, "Joseph, the baby that Mary will have is from the Holy Spirit. Go ahead and marry her. **21**Then after her baby is born, name him Jesus,[b] because he will save his people from their sins."

22So the Lord's promise came true, just as the prophet had said, **23**"A virgin will have a baby boy, and he will be called Immanuel," which means "God is with us."

24After Joseph woke up, he and Mary were soon married, just as the Lord's angel had told him to do. **25**But they did not sleep together before her baby was born. Then Joseph named him Jesus.

The Wise Men

2 When Jesus was born in the village of Bethlehem in Judea, Herod was king. During this time some wise men[c] from the east came to Jerusalem **2**and said, "Where is the child born to be king of the Jews? We saw his star in the east[d] and have come to worship him."

3When King Herod heard about this, he was worried, and so was everyone else in Jerusalem. **4**Herod brought together the chief priests and the teachers of the Law of Moses and asked them, "Where will the Messiah be born?"

5They told him, "He will be born in Bethlehem, just as the prophet wrote,

6 'Bethlehem in the land
of Judea,
you are very important
among the towns of Judea.
From your town
will come a leader,
who will be like a shepherd
for my people Israel.' "

7Herod secretly called in the wise men and asked them when they had first seen the star. **8**He told them, "Go to Bethlehem and search carefully for the child. As soon as you find him, let me know. I want to go and worship him too."

9The wise men listened to what the king said and then left. And the star they had seen in the east went on ahead of them until it stopped over the place where the child was. **10**They were thrilled and excited to see the star. **11**When the men went into the house and saw the child with Mary, his mother, they knelt down and worshiped him. They took out their gifts of gold, frankincense, and myrrh[e] and gave them to him. **12**Later they were warned in a dream not to return to Herod, and they went back home by another road.

The Escape to Egypt

13After the wise men had gone, an angel from the Lord appeared to Joseph in a dream and said, "Get up! Hurry and take the child and his mother to Egypt! Stay there until I tell you to return, because Herod is looking for the child and wants to kill him."

14That night, Joseph got up and took his wife and the child to Egypt, **15**where they stayed until Herod died. So the Lord's promise came true, just as the prophet had said, "I called my son out of Egypt."

The Killing of the Children

16When Herod found out that the wise men from the east had tricked him, he was very angry. He gave orders for his men to kill all the boys who lived in or near Bethlehem and were two years old

---

[a]**1.19** *good man*: Or "kind man," or "man who always did the right thing." [b]**1.21** *name him Jesus*: In Hebrew the name "Jesus" means "the Lord saves." [c]**2.1** *wise men*: People famous for studying the stars. [d]**2.2** *his star in the east*: Or "his star rise." [e]**2.11** *frankincense, and myrrh*: Frankincense was a valuable powder that was burned to make a sweet smell. Myrrh was a valuable sweet-smelling powder often used in perfume.

and younger. This was based on what he had learned from the wise men.

17So the Lord's promise came true, just as the prophet Jeremiah had said,

18 "In Ramah a voice was heard
   crying and weeping loudly.
Rachel was mourning
   for her children,
and she refused
   to be comforted,
because they were dead."

The Return from Egypt

19After King Herod died, an angel from the Lord appeared in a dream to Joseph while he was still in Egypt. 20The angel said, "Get up and take the child and his mother back to Israel. The people who wanted to kill him are now dead."

21Joseph got up and left with them for Israel. 22But when he heard that Herod's son Archelaus was now ruler of Judea, he was afraid to go there. Then in a dream he was told to go to Galilee, 23and they went to live there in the town of Nazareth. So the Lord's promise came true, just as the prophet had said, "He will be called a Nazarene."[f]

The Preaching of John the Baptist
(Mark 1.1-8; Luke 3.1-18; John 1.19-28)

3 Years later, John the Baptist started preaching in the desert of Judea. 2He said, "Turn back to God! The kingdom of heaven[g] will soon be here."[h]

3John was the one the prophet Isaiah was talking about, when he said,

"In the desert someone
   is shouting,
'Get the road ready
   for the Lord!
Make a straight path
   for him.' "

4John wore clothes made of camel's hair. He had a leather strap around his waist and ate grasshoppers and wild honey.

5From Jerusalem and all Judea and from the Jordan River Valley crowds of people went to John. 6They told how sorry they were for their sins, and he baptized them in the river.

7Many Pharisees and Sadducees also came to be baptized. But John said to them:

You bunch of snakes! Who warned you to run from the coming judgment? 8Do something to show that you have really given up your sins. 9And don't start telling yourselves that you belong to Abraham's family. I tell you that God can turn these stones into children for Abraham. 10An ax is ready to cut the trees down at their roots. Any tree that doesn't produce good fruit will be chopped down and thrown into a fire.

11I baptize you with water so that you will give up your sins.[i] But someone more powerful is going to come, and I am not good enough even to carry his sandals.[j] He will baptize you with the Holy Spirit and with fire. 12His threshing fork is in his hand, and he is ready to separate the wheat from the husks.[k] He will store the wheat in a barn and burn the husks in a fire that never goes out.

The Baptism of Jesus
(Mark 1.9-11; Luke 3.21, 22)

13Jesus left Galilee and went to the Jordan River to be baptized by John. 14But John kept objecting and said, "I ought to be baptized by you. Why have you come to me?"

15Jesus answered, "For now this is how it should be, because we must do all that God wants us to do." Then John agreed.

16So Jesus was baptized. And as soon as he came out of the water, the sky opened, and he saw the Spirit of God coming down on him like a dove. 17Then a voice from heaven said, "This is my own dear Son, and I am pleased with him."

Jesus and the Devil
(Mark 1.12, 13; Luke 4.1-13)

4 The Holy Spirit led Jesus into the desert, so that the devil could test him. 2After Jesus had gone without eating[l] for forty days and nights, he was very hungry. 3Then the devil came to him and said, "If you are God's Son, tell these stones to turn into bread."

---

[f]2.23 *He will be called a Nazarene*: The prophet who said this is not known.   [g]3.2 *kingdom of heaven*: In the Gospel of Matthew "kingdom of heaven" is used with the same meaning as "God's kingdom" in Mark and Luke.   [h]3.2 *will soon be here*: Or "is already here."
[i]3.11 *so that you will give up your sins*: Or "because you have given up your sins."
[j]3.11 *carry his sandals*: This was one of the duties of a slave.   [k]3.12 *His threshing fork is in his hand, and he is ready to separate the wheat from the husks*: After Jewish farmers had trampled out the grain, they used a large fork to pitch the grain and the husks into the air. Wind would blow away the light husks, and the grain would fall back to the ground, where it could be gathered up.   [l]4.2 *without eating*: The Jewish people sometimes went without eating (also called "fasting") to show their love for God or to show sorrow for their sins.

Matthew 4.4

⁴Jesus answered, "The Scriptures say:

'No one can live only on food.
People need every word
  that God has spoken.' "

⁵Next, the devil took Jesus to the holy city and had him stand on the highest part of the temple. ⁶The devil said, "If you are God's Son, jump off. The Scriptures say:

'God will give his angels
  orders about you.
They will catch you
  in their arms,
and you won't hurt
  your feet on the stones.' "

⁷Jesus answered, "The Scriptures also say, 'Don't try to test the Lord your God!' "

⁸Finally, the devil took Jesus up on a very high mountain and showed him all the kingdoms on earth and their power. ⁹The devil said to him, "I will give all this to you, if you will bow down and worship me."

¹⁰Jesus answered, "Go away Satan! The Scriptures say:

'Worship the Lord your God
  and serve only him.' "

¹¹Then the devil left Jesus, and angels came to help him.

Jesus Begins His Work
(Mark 1.14, 15; Luke 4.14, 15)

¹²When Jesus heard that John had been put in prison, he went to Galilee. ¹³But instead of staying in Nazareth, Jesus moved to Capernaum. This town was beside Lake Galilee in the territory of Zebulun and Naphtali.ᵐ ¹⁴So God's promise came true, just as the prophet Isaiah had said,

¹⁵ "Listen, lands of Zebulun
    and Naphtali,
  lands along the road
  to the sea and east
    of the Jordan!
  Listen Galilee,
    land of the Gentiles!
¹⁶ Although your people
    live in darkness,
  they will see
    a bright light.
  Although they live
    in the shadow of death,
  a light will shine
    on them."

¹⁷Then Jesus started preaching, "Turn back to God! The kingdom of heaven will soon be here."ⁿ

Jesus Chooses Four Fishermen
(Mark 1.16-20; Luke 5.1-11)

¹⁸While Jesus was walking along the shore of Lake Galilee, he saw two brothers. One was Simon, also known as Peter, and the other was Andrew. They were fishermen, and they were casting their net into the lake. ¹⁹Jesus said to them, "Come with me! I will teach you how to bring in people instead of fish." ²⁰Right then the two brothers dropped their nets and went with him.

²¹Jesus walked on until he saw James and John, the sons of Zebedee. They were in a boat with their father, mending their nets. Jesus asked them to come with him too. ²²Right away they left the boat and their father and went with Jesus.

Jesus Teaches, Preaches, and Heals
(Luke 6.17-19)

²³Jesus went all over Galilee, teaching in the Jewish meeting places and preaching the good news about God's kingdom. He also healed every kind of disease and sickness. ²⁴News about him spread all over Syria, and people with every kind of sickness or disease were brought to him. Some of them had a lot of demons in them, others were thought to be crazy,ᵒ and still others could not walk. But Jesus healed them all.

²⁵Large crowds followed Jesus from Galilee and the region around the ten cities known as Decapolis.ᵖ They also came from Jerusalem, Judea, and from across the Jordan River.

The Sermon on the Mount

5 When Jesus saw the crowds, he went up on the side of a mountain and sat down.ᑫ

Blessings
(Luke 6.20-23)

Jesus' disciples gathered around him, ²and he taught them:

³ God blesses those people
  who depend only on him.
  They belong to the kingdom
    of heaven!ʳ

ᵐ**4.13** *Zebulun and Naphtali*: In Old Testament times these tribes were in northern Palestine, and in New Testament times many Gentiles lived where these tribes had once been.
ⁿ**4.17** *The kingdom of heaven will soon be here*: See the two notes at 3.2.   ᵒ**4.24** *thought to be crazy*: In ancient times people with epilepsy were thought to be crazy.   ᵖ**4.25** *the ten cities known as Decapolis*: A group of ten cities east of Samaria and Galilee, where the people followed the Greek way of life.   ᑫ**5.1** *sat down*: Teachers in the ancient world, including Jewish teachers, usually sat down when they taught.   ʳ**5.3** *They belong to the kingdom of heaven*: Or "The kingdom of heaven belongs to them."

⁴ God blesses those people
   who grieve.
      They will find comfort!
⁵ God blesses those people
   who are humble.
   The earth will belong
      to them!
⁶ God blesses those people
   who want to obey him^s
      more than to eat or drink.
   They will be given
      what they want!
⁷ God blesses those people
   who are merciful.
   They will be treated
      with mercy!
⁸ God blesses those people
   whose hearts are pure.
      They will see him!
⁹ God blesses those people
   who make peace.
   They will be called
      his children!
¹⁰ God blesses those people
   who are treated badly
      for doing right.
   They belong to the kingdom
      of heaven.^{t}

¹¹God will bless you when people insult you, mistreat you, and tell all kinds of evil lies about you because of me. ¹²Be happy and excited! You will have a great reward in heaven. People did these same things to the prophets who lived long ago.

Salt and Light
(Mark 9.50; Luke 14.34, 35)

¹³You are like salt for everyone on earth. But if salt no longer tastes like salt, how can it make food salty? All it is good for is to be thrown out and walked on.

¹⁴You are like light for the whole world. A city built on top of a hill cannot be hidden, ¹⁵and no one would light a lamp and put it under a clay pot. A lamp is placed on a lampstand, where it can give light to everyone in the house. ¹⁶Make your light shine, so that others will see the good that you do and will praise your Father in heaven.

The Law of Moses

¹⁷Don't suppose that I came to do away with the Law and the Prophets.^{u} I did not come to do away with them, but to give them their full meaning. ¹⁸Heaven and earth may disappear. But I promise you that not even a period or comma will ever disappear from the Law. Everything written in it must happen.

¹⁹If you reject even the least important command in the Law and teach others to do the same, you will be the least important person in the kingdom of heaven. But if you obey and teach others its commands, you will have an important place in the kingdom. ²⁰You must obey God's commands better than the Pharisees and the teachers of the Law obey them. If you don't, I promise you that you will never get into the kingdom of heaven.

Anger

²¹You know that our ancestors were told, "Do not murder" and "A murderer must be brought to trial." ²²But I promise you that if you are angry with someone,^{v} you will have to stand trial. If you call someone a fool, you will be taken to court. And if you say that someone is worthless, you will be in danger of the fires of hell.

²³So if you are about to place your gift on the altar and remember that someone is angry with you, ²⁴leave your gift there in front of the altar. Make peace with that person, then come back and offer your gift to God.

²⁵Before you are dragged into court, make friends with the person who has accused you of doing wrong. If you don't, you will be handed over to the judge and then to the officer who will put you in jail. ²⁶I promise you that you will not get out until you have paid the last cent you owe.

Marriage

²⁷You know the commandment which says, "Be faithful in marriage." ²⁸But I tell you that if you look at another woman and want her, you are already unfaithful in your thoughts. ²⁹If your right eye causes you to sin, poke it out and throw it away. It is better to lose one part of your body, than for your whole body to end up in hell. ³⁰If your right hand causes you to sin, chop it off and throw it away! It is better to lose one part of your body, than for your whole body to be thrown into hell.

---

^{s}**5.6** *who want to obey him*: Or "who want to do right" or "who want everyone to be treated right." ^{t}**5.10** *They belong to the kingdom of heaven*: See the note at 5.3. ^{u}**5.17** *the Law and the Prophets*: The Jewish Scriptures, that is, the Old Testament. ^{v}**5.22** *someone*: In verses 22-24 the Greek text has "brother," which may refer to people in general or to other followers.

Divorce
(Matthew 19.9; Mark 10.11, 12; Luke 16.18)

³¹You have been taught that a man who divorces his wife must write out divorce papers for her.^w ³²But I tell you not to divorce your wife unless she has committed some terrible sexual sin.^x If you divorce her, you will cause her to be unfaithful, just as any man who marries her is guilty of taking another man's wife.

Promises

³³You know that our ancestors were told, "Don't use the Lord's name to make a promise unless you are going to keep it." ³⁴But I tell you not to swear by anything when you make a promise! Heaven is God's throne, so don't swear by heaven. ³⁵The earth is God's footstool, so don't swear by the earth. Jerusalem is the city of the great king, so don't swear by it. ³⁶Don't swear by your own head. You cannot make one hair white or black. ³⁷When you make a promise, say only "Yes" or "No." Anything else comes from the devil.

Revenge
(Luke 6.29, 30)

³⁸You know that you have been taught, "An eye for an eye and a tooth for a tooth." ³⁹But I tell you not to try to get even with a person who has done something to you. When someone slaps your right cheek,^y turn and let that person slap your other cheek. ⁴⁰If someone sues you for your shirt, give up your coat as well. ⁴¹If a soldier forces you to carry his pack one mile, carry it two miles.^z ⁴²When people ask you for something, give it to them. When they want to borrow money, lend it to them.

Love
(Luke 6.27, 28, 32-36)

⁴³You have heard people say, "Love your neighbors and hate your enemies." ⁴⁴But I tell you to love your enemies and pray for anyone who mistreats you. ⁴⁵Then you will be acting like your Father in heaven. He makes the sun rise on both good and bad people. And he sends rain for the ones who do right and for the ones who do wrong. ⁴⁶If you love only those people who love you, will God reward you for that? Even tax collectors^a love their friends. ⁴⁷If you greet only your friends, what's so great about that? Don't even unbelievers do that? ⁴⁸But you must always act like your Father in heaven.

Giving

6 When you do good deeds, don't try to show off. If you do, you won't get a reward from your Father in heaven.

²When you give to the poor, don't blow a loud horn. That's what show-offs do in the meeting places and on the street corners, because they are always looking for praise. I can assure you that they already have their reward.

³When you give to the poor, don't let anyone know about it.^b ⁴Then your gift will be given in secret. Your Father knows what is done in secret, and he will reward you.

Prayer
(Luke 11.2-4)

⁵When you pray, don't be like those show-offs who love to stand up and pray in the meeting places and on the street corners. They do this just to look good. I can assure you that they already have their reward.

⁶When you pray, go into a room alone and close the door. Pray to your Father in private. He knows what is done in private, and he will reward you.

⁷When you pray, don't talk on and on as people do who don't know God. They think God likes to hear long prayers. ⁸Don't be like them. Your Father knows what you need before you ask.

⁹You should pray like this:

Our Father in heaven,
help us to honor
   your name.
¹⁰ Come and set up
   your kingdom,
so that everyone on earth
   will obey you,

---

^w*5.31 write out divorce papers for her*: Jewish men could divorce their wives, but the women could not divorce their husbands. The purpose of writing these papers was to make it harder for a man to divorce his wife. Before this law was made, all a man had to do was to send his wife away and say that she was no longer his wife. ^x*5.32 some terrible sexual sin*: This probably refers to the laws about the wrong kinds of marriages that are forbidden in Leviticus 18.6-18 or to some serious sexual sin. ^y*5.39 right cheek*: A slap on the right cheek was a bad insult. ^z*5.41 two miles*: A Roman soldier had the right to force a person to carry his pack as far as one mile. ^a*5.46 tax collectors*: These were usually Jewish people who paid the Romans for the right to collect taxes. They were hated by other Jews who thought of them as traitors to their country and to their religion. ^b*6.3 don't let anyone know about it*: The Greek text has, "Don't let your left hand know what your right hand is doing."

as you are obeyed
in heaven.
11 Give us our food for today.^c
12 Forgive us for doing wrong,
as we forgive others.
13 Keep us from being tempted
and protect us from evil.^d

¹⁴If you forgive others for the wrongs they do to you, your Father in heaven will forgive you. ¹⁵But if you don't forgive others, your Father will not forgive your sins.

Worshiping God by Going without Eating

¹⁶When you go without eating,^e don't try to look gloomy as those show-offs do when they go without eating. I can assure you that they already have their reward. ¹⁷Instead, comb your hair and wash your face. ¹⁸Then others won't know that you are going without eating. But your Father sees what is done in private, and he will reward you.

Treasures in Heaven
(Luke 12.33, 34)

¹⁹Don't store up treasures on earth! Moths and rust can destroy them, and thieves can break in and steal them. ²⁰Instead, store up your treasures in heaven, where moths and rust cannot destroy them, and thieves cannot break in and steal them. ²¹Your heart will always be where your treasure is.

Light
(Luke 11.34-36)

²²Your eyes are like a window for your body. When they are good, you have all the light you need. ²³But when your eyes are bad, everything is dark. If the light inside you is dark, you surely are in the dark.

Money
(Luke 16.13)

²⁴You cannot be the slave of two masters! You will like one more than the other or be more loyal to one than the other. You cannot serve both God and money.

Worry
(Luke 12.22-31)

²⁵I tell you not to worry about your life. Don't worry about having something to eat, drink, or wear. Isn't life more than food or clothing? ²⁶Look at the birds in the sky! They don't plant or harvest. They don't even store grain in barns. Yet your Father in heaven takes care of them. Aren't you worth more than birds?

²⁷Can worry make you live longer?^f ²⁸Why worry about clothes? Look how the wild flowers grow. They don't work hard to make their clothes. ²⁹But I tell you that Solomon with all his wealth^g wasn't as well clothed as one of them. ³⁰God gives such beauty to everything that grows in the fields, even though it is here today and thrown into a fire tomorrow. He will surely do even more for you! Why do you have such little faith?

³¹Don't worry and ask yourselves, "Will we have anything to eat? Will we have anything to drink? Will we have any clothes to wear?" ³²Only people who don't know God are always worrying about such things. Your Father in heaven knows that you need all of these. ³³But more than anything else, put God's work first and do what he wants. Then the other things will be yours as well.

³⁴Don't worry about tomorrow. It will take care of itself. You have enough to worry about today.

Judging Others
(Luke 6.37, 38, 41, 42)

7 Don't condemn others, and God won't condemn you. ²God will be as hard on you as you are on others! He will treat you exactly as you treat them.

³You can see the speck in your friend's eye, but you don't notice the log in your own eye. ⁴How can you say, "My friend, let me take the speck out of your eye," when you don't see the log in your own eye? ⁵You're nothing but show-offs! First, take the log out of your own eye. Then you can see how to take the speck out of your friend's eye.

⁶Don't give to dogs what belongs to God. They will only turn and attack you. Don't throw pearls down in front of pigs. They will trample all over them.

Ask, Search, Knock
(Luke 11.9-13)

⁷Ask, and you will receive. Search, and you will find. Knock, and the door will be opened for you. ⁸Everyone who asks will receive. Everyone who searches will find. And the door

---

^c**6.11** *our food for today*: Or "the food that we need" or "our food for the coming day."
^d**6.13** *evil*: Or "the evil one," that is, the devil. Some manuscripts add, "The kingdom, the power, and the glory are yours forever. Amen." ^e**6.16** *without eating*: See the note at 4.2.
^f**6.27** *live longer*: Or "grow taller." ^g**6.29** *Solomon with all his wealth*: The Jewish people thought that Solomon was the richest person who had ever lived.

will be opened for everyone who knocks. ⁹Would any of you give your hungry child a stone, if the child asked for some bread? ¹⁰Would you give your child a snake if the child asked for a fish? ¹¹As bad as you are, you still know how to give good gifts to your children. But your heavenly Father is even more ready to give good things to people who ask.

¹²Treat others as you want them to treat you. This is what the Law and the Prophets*ʰ* are all about.

The Narrow Gate
(Luke 13.24)

¹³Go in through the narrow gate. The gate to destruction is wide, and the road that leads there is easy to follow. A lot of people go through that gate. ¹⁴But the gate to life is very narrow. The road that leads there is so hard to follow that only a few people find it.

A Tree and Its Fruit
(Luke 6.43-45)

¹⁵Watch out for false prophets! They dress up like sheep, but inside they are wolves who have come to attack you. ¹⁶You can tell what they are by what they do. No one picks grapes or figs from thornbushes. ¹⁷A good tree produces good fruit, and a bad tree produces bad fruit. ¹⁸A good tree cannot produce bad fruit, and a bad tree cannot produce good fruit. ¹⁹Every tree that produces bad fruit will be chopped down and burned. ²⁰You can tell who the false prophets are by their deeds.

A Warning
(Luke 13.26, 27)

²¹Not everyone who calls me their Lord will get into the kingdom of heaven. Only the ones who obey my Father in heaven will get in. ²²On the day of judgment many will call me their Lord. They will say, "We preached in your name, and in your name we forced out demons and worked many miracles." ²³But I will tell them, "I will have nothing to do with you! Get out of my sight, you evil people!"

Two Builders
(Luke 6.47-49)

²⁴Anyone who hears and obeys these teachings of mine is like a wise person who built a house on solid rock. ²⁵Rain poured down, rivers flooded, and winds beat against that house. But it did not fall, because it was built on solid rock.

²⁶Anyone who hears my teachings and doesn't obey them is like a foolish person who built a house on sand. ²⁷The rain poured down, the rivers flooded, and the winds blew and beat against that house. Finally, it fell with a crash.

²⁸When Jesus finished speaking, the crowds were surprised at his teaching. ²⁹He taught them like someone with authority, and not like their teachers of the Law of Moses.

Jesus Heals a Man
(Mark 1.40-45; Luke 5.12-16)

8 As Jesus came down the mountain, he was followed by large crowds. ²Suddenly a man with leprosy*ⁱ* came and knelt in front of Jesus. He said, "Lord, you have the power to make me well, if only you wanted to."

³Jesus put his hand on the man and said, "I want to! Now you are well." At once the man's leprosy disappeared. ⁴Jesus told him, "Don't tell anyone about this, but go and show the priest that you are well. Then take a gift to the temple just as Moses commanded, and everyone will know that you have been healed."*ʲ*

Jesus Heals an Army Officer's Servant
(Luke 7.1-10; John 4.43-54)

⁵When Jesus was going into the town of Capernaum, an army officer came up to him and said, ⁶"Lord, my servant is at home in such terrible pain that he can't even move."

⁷"I will go and heal him," Jesus replied.

⁸But the officer said, "Lord, I'm not good enough for you to come into my house. Just give the order, and my servant will get well. ⁹I have officers who give orders to me, and I have soldiers who take orders from me. I can say to one of them, 'Go!' and he goes. I can say to another, 'Come!' and he comes. I can say to my servant, 'Do this!' and he will do it."

¹⁰When Jesus heard this, he was so surprised that he turned and said to the crowd following him, "I tell you that in all of Israel I've never found anyone

---

*ʰ***7.12** *the Law and the Prophets*: See the note at 5.17. *ⁱ***8.2** *leprosy*: In biblical times the word "leprosy" was used for many different kinds of skin diseases. *ʲ***8.4** *everyone will know that you have been healed*: People with leprosy had to be examined by a priest and told that they were well (that is "clean") before they could once again live a normal life in the Jewish community. The gift that Moses commanded was the sacrifice of some lambs together with flour mixed with olive oil.

with this much faith! [11]Many people will come from everywhere to enjoy the feast in the kingdom of heaven with Abraham, Isaac, and Jacob. [12]But the ones who should have been in the kingdom will be thrown out into the dark. They will cry and grit their teeth in pain."

[13]Then Jesus said to the officer, "You may go home now. Your faith has made it happen."

Right then his servant was healed.

Jesus Heals Many People
(Mark 1.29-34; Luke 4.38-41)

[14]Jesus went to the home of Peter, where he found that Peter's mother-in-law was sick in bed with fever. [15]He took her by the hand, and the fever left her. Then she got up and served Jesus a meal.

[16]That evening many people with demons in them were brought to Jesus. And with only a word he forced out the evil spirits and healed everyone who was sick. [17]So God's promise came true, just as the prophet Isaiah had said,

"He healed our diseases
  and made us well."

Some Who Wanted To Go with Jesus
(Luke 9.57-62)

[18]When Jesus saw the crowd,[k] he went across Lake Galilee. [19]A teacher of the Law of Moses came up to him and said, "Teacher, I'll go anywhere with you!"

[20]Jesus replied, "Foxes have dens, and birds have nests. But the Son of Man doesn't have a place to call his own."

[21]Another disciple said to Jesus, "Lord, let me wait till I bury my father."

[22]Jesus answered, "Come with me, and let the dead bury their dead." [l]

A Storm
(Mark 4.35-41; Luke 8.22-25)

[23]After Jesus left in a boat with his disciples, [24]a terrible storm suddenly struck the lake, and waves started splashing into their boat.

Jesus was sound asleep, [25]so the disciples went over to him and woke him up. They said, "Lord, save us! We're going to drown!"

[26]But Jesus replied, "Why are you so afraid? You surely don't have much faith." Then he got up and ordered the wind and the waves to calm down. And everything was calm.

[27]The men in the boat were amazed and said, "Who is this? Even the wind and the waves obey him."

Two Men with Demons in Them
(Mark 5.1-20; Luke 8.26-39)

[28]After Jesus had crossed the lake, he came to shore near the town of Gadara[m] and started down the road. Two men with demons in them came to him from the tombs.[n] They were so fierce that no one could travel that way. [29]Suddenly they shouted, "Jesus, Son of God, what do you want with us? Have you come to punish us before our time?"

[30]Not far from there a large herd of pigs was feeding. [31]So the demons begged Jesus, "If you force us out, please send us into those pigs!" [32]Jesus told them to go, and they went out of the men and into the pigs. All at once the pigs rushed down the steep bank into the lake and drowned.

[33]The people taking care of the pigs ran to the town and told everything, especially what had happened to the two men. [34]Everyone in town came out to meet Jesus. When they saw him, they begged him to leave their part of the country.

Jesus Heals a Crippled Man
(Mark 2.1-12; Luke 5.17-26)

9 Jesus got into a boat and crossed back over to the town where he lived.[o] [2]Some people soon brought to him a crippled man lying on a mat. When Jesus saw how much faith they had, he said to the crippled man, "My friend, don't worry! Your sins are forgiven."

[3]Some teachers of the Law of Moses said to themselves, "Jesus must think he is God!"

[4]But Jesus knew what was in their minds, and he said, "Why are you thinking such evil things? [5]Is it easier for me to tell this crippled man that his sins are forgiven or to tell him to get up and walk? [6]But I will show you that the Son of Man has the right to forgive sins here on earth." So Jesus said to the man, "Get up! Pick up your mat and go on home." [7]The man got up and went home. [8]When the crowds saw this, they were afraid[p] and praised God for giving such authority to people.

---

[k]8.18 *saw the crowd*: Some manuscripts have "large crowd." Others have "large crowds."
[l]8.22 *let the dead bury their dead*: For the Jewish people a proper burial of their dead was a very important duty. But Jesus teaches that following him is even more important.
[m]8.28 *Gadara*: Some manuscripts have "Gergesa." Others have "Gerasa." [n]8.28 *tombs*: It was thought that demons and evil spirits lived in tombs and in caves that were used for burying the dead. [o]9.1 *where he lived*: Capernaum (see 4.13). [p]9.8 *afraid*: Some manuscripts have "amazed."

Jesus Chooses Matthew
(Mark 2.13-17; Luke 5.27-32)

9 As Jesus was leaving, he saw a tax collector[q] named Matthew sitting at the place for paying taxes. Jesus said to him, "Come with me." Matthew got up and went with him.

10 Later, Jesus and his disciples were having dinner at Matthew's house.[r] Many tax collectors and other sinners were also there. 11 Some Pharisees asked Jesus' disciples, "Why does your teacher eat with tax collectors and other sinners?"

12 Jesus heard them and answered, "Healthy people don't need a doctor, but sick people do. 13 Go and learn what the Scriptures mean when they say, 'Instead of offering sacrifices to me, I want you to be merciful to others.' I didn't come to invite good people to be my followers. I came to invite sinners."

People Ask about Going without Eating
(Mark 2.18-22; Luke 5.33-39)

14 One day some followers of John the Baptist came and asked Jesus, "Why do we and the Pharisees often go without eating,[s] while your disciples never do?"

15 Jesus answered:

The friends of a bridegroom don't go without eating while he is still with them. But the time will come when he will be taken from them. Then they will go without eating.

16 No one uses a new piece of cloth to patch old clothes. The patch would shrink and tear a bigger hole.

17 No one pours new wine into old wineskins. The wine would swell and burst the old skins.[t] Then the wine would be lost, and the skins would be ruined. New wine must be put into new wineskins. Both the skins and the wine will then be safe.

A Dying Girl and a Sick Woman
(Mark 5.21-43; Luke 8.40-56)

18 While Jesus was still speaking, an official came and knelt in front of him. The man said, "My daughter has just now died! Please come and place your hand on her. Then she will live again."

19 Jesus and his disciples got up and went with the man.

20 A woman who had been bleeding for twelve years came up behind Jesus and barely touched his clothes. 21 She had said to herself, "If I can just touch his clothes, I will get well."

22 Jesus turned. He saw the woman and said, "Don't worry! You are now well because of your faith." At that moment she was healed.

23 When Jesus went into the home of the official and saw the musicians and the crowd of mourners,[u] 24 he said, "Get out of here! The little girl isn't dead. She is just asleep." Everyone started laughing at Jesus. 25 But after the crowd had been sent out of the house, Jesus went to the girl's bedside. He took her by the hand and helped her up.

26 News about this spread all over that part of the country.

Jesus Heals Two Blind Men

27 As Jesus was walking along, two blind men began following him and shouting, "Son of David,[v] have pity on us!"

28 After Jesus had gone indoors, the two blind men came up to him. He asked them, "Do you believe I can make you well?"

"Yes, Lord," they answered.

29 Jesus touched their eyes and said, "Because of your faith, you will be healed." 30 They were able to see, and Jesus strictly warned them not to tell anyone about him. 31 But they left and talked about him to everyone in that part of the country.

Jesus Heals a Man Who Could Not Talk

32 As Jesus and his disciples were on their way, some people brought to him a man who could not talk because a demon was in him. 33 After Jesus had forced the demon out, the man started talking. The crowds were so amazed that they began saying, "Nothing like this has ever happened in Israel!"

34 But the Pharisees said, "The leader of the demons gives him the power to force out demons."

Jesus Has Pity on People

35 Jesus went to every town and village. He taught in their meeting places and preached the good news about God's kingdom. Jesus also healed every kind of disease and sickness. 36 When he saw the crowds, he felt sorry for them. They were confused and helpless, like sheep without a shepherd. 37 He said to his disciples, "A large crop is in the fields, but there are only a few workers.

---

[q]9.9 *tax collector*: See the note at 5.46. [r]9.10 *Matthew's house*: Or "Jesus' house."
[s]9.14 *without eating*: See the note at 4.2. [t]9.17 *swell and burst the old skins*: While the juice from grapes was becoming wine, it would swell and stretch the skins in which it had been stored. If the skins were old and stiff, they would burst. [u]9.23 *the crowd of mourners*: The Jewish people often hired mourners for funerals. [v]9.27 *Son of David*: The Jewish people expected the Messiah to be from the family of King David, and for this reason the Messiah was often called the "Son of David."

³⁸Ask the Lord in charge of the harvest to send out workers to bring it in."

Jesus Chooses His Twelve Apostles
(Mark 3.13-19; Luke 6.12-16)

10 Jesus called together his twelve disciples. He gave them the power to force out evil spirits and to heal every kind of disease and sickness. ²The first of the twelve apostles was Simon, better known as Peter. His brother Andrew was an apostle, and so were James and John, the two sons of Zebedee. ³Philip, Bartholomew, Thomas, Matthew the tax collector,ʷ James the son of Alphaeus, and Thaddaeus were also apostles. ⁴The others were Simon, known as the Eager One,ˣ and Judas Iscariot,ʸ who later betrayed Jesus.

Instructions for the Twelve Apostles
(Mark 6.7-13; Luke 9.1-6)

⁵Jesus sent out the twelve apostles with these instructions:
Stay away from the Gentiles and don't go to any Samaritan town. ⁶Go only to the people of Israel, because they are like a flock of lost sheep. ⁷As you go, announce that the kingdom of heaven will soon be here.ᶻ ⁸Heal the sick, raise the dead to life, heal people who have leprosy,ᵃ and force out demons. You received without paying, now give without being paid. ⁹Don't take along any gold, silver, or copper coins. ¹⁰And don't carryᵇ a traveling bag or an extra shirt or sandals or a walking stick.
Workers deserve their food. ¹¹So when you go to a town or a village, find someone worthy enough to have you as their guest and stay with them until you leave. ¹²When you go to a home, give it your blessing of peace. ¹³If the home is deserving, let your blessing remain with them. But if the home isn't deserving, take back your blessing of peace. ¹⁴If someone won't welcome you or listen to your message, leave their home or town. And shake the dust from your feet at them.ᶜ ¹⁵I promise you that the day of judgment will be easier for the towns of Sodom and Gomorrahᵈ than for that town.

Warning about Trouble
(Mark 13.9-13; Luke 21.12-17)

¹⁶I am sending you like lambs into a pack of wolves. So be as wise as snakes and as innocent as doves. ¹⁷Watch out for people who will take you to court and have you beaten in their meeting places. ¹⁸Because of me, you will be dragged before rulers and kings to tell them and the Gentiles about your faith. ¹⁹But when someone arrests you, don't worry about what you will say or how you will say it. At that time you will be given the words to say. ²⁰But you will not really be the one speaking. The Spirit from your Father will tell you what to say.
²¹Brothers and sisters will betray one another and have each other put to death. Parents will betray their own children, and children will turn against their parents and have them killed. ²²Everyone will hate you because of me. But if you remain faithful until the end, you will be saved. ²³When people mistreat you in one town, hurry to another one. I promise you that before you have gone to all the towns of Israel, the Son of Man will come.
²⁴Disciples are not better than their teacher, and slaves are not better than their master. ²⁵It is enough for disciples to be like their teacher and for slaves to be like their master. If people call the head of the family Satan, what will they say about the rest of the family?

The One To Fear
(Luke 12.2-7)

²⁶Don't be afraid of anyone! Everything that is hidden will be found out, and every secret will be known. ²⁷Whatever I say to you in the dark, you must tell in the light. And you must announce from the housetops whatever I have whispered to you. ²⁸Don't be afraid of people. They can kill you, but they cannot harm your soul. Instead, you should fear God who can destroy both your body and your soul in hell. ²⁹Aren't two sparrows sold for only a penny? But your Father

---

ʷ10.3 *tax collector*: See the note at 5.46. ˣ10.4 *Eager One*: The Greek text has "Zealot," a name later given to the members of a Jewish group that resisted and fought against the Romans. ʸ10.4 *Iscariot*: This may mean "a man from Kerioth" (a place in Judea). But more probably it means "a man who was a liar" or "a man who was a betrayer." ᶻ10.7 *will soon be here*: Or "is already here." ᵃ10.8 *leprosy*: See the note at 8.2. ᵇ10.9,10 *Don't take along . . . don't carry*: Or "Don't accept . . . don't accept." ᶜ10.14 *shake the dust from your feet at them*: This was a way of showing rejection (see Acts 13.51). ᵈ10.15 *Sodom and Gomorrah*: During the time of Abraham the Lord destroyed these towns because the people there were so evil.

knows when any one of them falls to the ground. ³⁰Even the hairs on your head are counted. ³¹So don't be afraid! You are worth much more than many sparrows.

Telling Others about Christ
(Luke 12.8, 9)

³²If you tell others that you belong to me, I will tell my Father in heaven that you are my followers. ³³But if you reject me, I will tell my Father in heaven that you don't belong to me.

Not Peace, but Trouble
(Luke 12.51-53; 14.26, 27)

³⁴Don't think that I came to bring peace to the earth! I came to bring trouble, not peace. ³⁵I came to turn sons against their fathers, daughters against their mothers, and daughters-in-law against their mothers-in-law. ³⁶Your worst enemies will be in your own family.

³⁷If you love your father or mother or even your sons and daughters more than me, you are not fit to be my disciples. ³⁸And unless you are willing to take up your cross and come with me, you are not fit to be my disciples. ³⁹If you try to save your life, you will lose it. But if you give it up for me, you will surely find it.

Rewards
(Mark 9.41)

⁴⁰Anyone who welcomes you welcomes me. And anyone who welcomes me also welcomes the one who sent me. ⁴¹Anyone who welcomes a prophet, just because that person is a prophet, will be given the same reward as a prophet. Anyone who welcomes a good person, just because that person is good, will be given the same reward as a good person. ⁴²And anyone who gives one of my most humble followers a cup of cool water, just because that person is my follower, will surely be rewarded.

John the Baptist
(Luke 7.18-35)

11 After Jesus had finished instructing his twelve disciples, he left and began teaching and preaching in the towns.ᵉ

²John was in prison when he heard what Christ was doing. So John sent some of his followers ³to ask Jesus, "Are you the one we should be looking for? Or must we wait for someone else?"

⁴Jesus answered, "Go and tell John what you have heard and seen. ⁵The blind are now able to see, and the lame can walk. People with leprosyᶠ are being healed, and the deaf can hear. The dead are raised to life, and the poor are hearing the good news. ⁶God will bless everyone who doesn't reject me because of what I do."

⁷As John's followers were going away, Jesus spoke to the crowds about John:

What sort of person did you go out into the desert to see? Was he like tall grass blown about by the wind? ⁸What kind of man did you go out to see? Was he someone dressed in fine clothes? People who dress like that live in the king's palace. ⁹What did you really go out to see? Was he a prophet? He certainly was. I tell you that he was more than a prophet. ¹⁰In the Scriptures God says about him, "I am sending my messenger ahead of you to get things ready for you." ¹¹I tell you that no one ever born on this earth is greater than John the Baptist. But whoever is least in the kingdom of heaven is greater than John.

¹²From the time of John the Baptist until now, violent people have been trying to take over the kingdom of heaven by force. ¹³All the Books of the Prophets and the Law of Mosesᵍ told what was going to happen up to the time of John. ¹⁴And if you believe them, John is Elijah, the prophet you are waiting for. ¹⁵If you have ears, pay attention!

¹⁶You people are like children sitting in the market and shouting to each other,

¹⁷ "We played the flute,
  but you would not dance!
We sang a funeral song,
  but you would not mourn!"

¹⁸John the Baptist did not go around eating and drinking, and you said, "That man has a demon in him!" ¹⁹But the Son of Man goes around eating and drinking, and you say, "That man eats and drinks too much! He is even a friend of tax collectorsʰ and sinners." Yet Wisdom is shown to be right by what it does.

The Unbelieving Towns
(Luke 10.13-15)

²⁰In the towns where Jesus had worked most of his miracles, the people

---

ᵉ**11.1** *the towns*: The Greek text has "their towns," which may refer to the towns of Galilee or to the towns where Jesus' disciples had lived.   ᶠ**11.5** *leprosy*: See the note at 8.2.
ᵍ**11.13** *the Books of the Prophets and the Law of Moses*: The Jewish Scriptures, that is, the Old Testament.   ʰ**11.19** *tax collectors*: See the note at 5.46.

refused to turn to God. So Jesus was upset with them and said:

²¹You people of Chorazin are in for trouble! You people of Bethsaida are in for trouble too! If the miracles that took place in your towns had happened in Tyre and Sidon, the people there would have turned to God long ago. They would have dressed in sackcloth and put ashes on their heads.[i] ²²I tell you that on the day of judgment the people of Tyre and Sidon will get off easier than you will.

²³People of Capernaum, do you think you will be honored in heaven? You will go down to hell! If the miracles that took place in your town had happened in Sodom, that town would still be standing. ²⁴So I tell you that on the day of judgment the people of Sodom will get off easier than you.

Come to Me and Rest
(Luke 10.21, 22)

²⁵At that moment Jesus said:
My Father, Lord of heaven and earth, I am grateful that you hid all this from wise and educated people and showed it to ordinary people. ²⁶Yes, Father, that is what pleased you.

²⁷My Father has given me everything, and he is the only one who knows the Son. The only one who truly knows the Father is the Son. But the Son wants to tell others about the Father, so that they can know him too.

²⁸If you are tired from carrying heavy burdens, come to me and I will give you rest. ²⁹Take the yoke[j] I give you. Put it on your shoulders and learn from me. I am gentle and humble, and you will find rest. ³⁰This yoke is easy to bear, and this burden is light.

A Question about the Sabbath
(Mark 2.23-28; Luke 6.1-5)

12 One Sabbath, Jesus and his disciples were walking through some wheat fields.[k] His disciples were hungry and began picking and eating grains of wheat. ²Some Pharisees noticed this and said to Jesus, "Why are your disciples picking grain on the Sabbath? They are not supposed to do that!"

³Jesus answered:
You surely must have read what David did when he and his followers were hungry. ⁴He went into the house of God, and then they ate the sacred loaves of bread that only priests are supposed to eat. ⁵Haven't you read in the Law of Moses that the priests are allowed to work in the temple on the Sabbath? But no one says that they are guilty of breaking the law of the Sabbath. ⁶I tell you that there is something here greater than the temple. ⁷Don't you know what the Scriptures mean when they say, "Instead of offering sacrifices to me, I want you to be merciful to others?" If you knew what this means, you would not condemn these innocent disciples of mine. ⁸So the Son of Man is Lord over the Sabbath.

A Man with a Crippled Hand
(Mark 3.1-6; Luke 6.6-11)

⁹Jesus left and went into one of the Jewish meeting places, ¹⁰where there was a man whose hand was crippled. Some Pharisees wanted to accuse Jesus of doing something wrong, and they asked him, "Is it right to heal someone on the Sabbath?"

¹¹Jesus answered, "If you had a sheep that fell into a ditch on the Sabbath, wouldn't you lift it out? ¹²People are worth much more than sheep, and so it is right to do good on the Sabbath." ¹³Then Jesus told the man, "Hold out your hand." The man did, and it became as healthy as the other one.

¹⁴The Pharisees left and started making plans to kill Jesus.

God's Chosen Servant

¹⁵When Jesus found out what was happening, he left there and large crowds followed him. He healed all of their sick, ¹⁶but warned them not to tell anyone about him. ¹⁷So God's promise came true, just as Isaiah the prophet had said,

¹⁸ "Here is my chosen servant!
I love him,
    and he pleases me.
I will give him my Spirit,
    and he will bring justice
      to the nations.
¹⁹ He won't shout or yell
    or call out in the streets.
²⁰ He won't break off a bent reed
    or put out a dying flame,
but he will make sure
    that justice is done.

---

[i]11.21 *sackcloth . . . ashes on their heads*: This was one way that people showed how sorry they were for their sins. [j]11.29 *yoke*: Yokes were put on the necks of animals, so that they could pull a plow or wagon. A yoke was a symbol of obedience and hard work.
[k]12.1 *walking through some wheat fields*: It was the custom to let hungry travelers pick grains of wheat.

²¹ All nations will place
their hope in him."

Jesus and the Ruler of the Demons
(Mark 3.20-30; Luke 11.14-23; 12.10)

²²Some people brought to Jesus a man who was blind and could not talk because he had a demon in him. Jesus healed the man, and then he was able to talk and see. ²³The crowds were so amazed that they asked, "Could Jesus be the Son of David?"*l*

²⁴When the Pharisees heard this, they said, "He forces out demons by the power of Beelzebul, the ruler of the demons!"

²⁵Jesus knew what they were thinking, and he said to them:

Any kingdom where people fight each other will end up ruined. And a town or family that fights will soon destroy itself. ²⁶So if Satan fights against himself, how can his kingdom last? ²⁷If I use the power of Beelzebul to force out demons, whose power do your own followers use to force them out? Your followers are the ones who will judge you. ²⁸But when I force out demons by the power of God's Spirit, it proves that God's kingdom has already come to you. ²⁹How can anyone break into a strong man's house and steal his things, unless he first ties up the strong man? Then he can take everything.

³⁰If you are not on my side, you are against me. If you don't gather in the harvest with me, you scatter it. ³¹⁻³²I tell you that any sinful thing you do or say can be forgiven. Even if you speak against the Son of Man, you can be forgiven. But if you speak against the Holy Spirit, you can never be forgiven, either in this life or in the life to come.

A Tree and Its Fruit
(Luke 6.43-45)

³³A good tree produces only good fruit, and a bad tree produces bad fruit. You can tell what a tree is like by the fruit it produces. ³⁴You are a bunch of evil snakes, so how can you say anything good? Your words show what is in your hearts. ³⁵Good people bring good things out of their hearts, but evil people bring evil things out of their hearts. ³⁶I promise you that on the day of judgment, everyone will have to account for every careless word they have spoken. ³⁷On that day they will be told that they are either innocent or guilty because of the things they have said.

A Sign from Heaven
(Mark 8.11, 12; Luke 11.29-32)

³⁸Some Pharisees and teachers of the Law of Moses said, "Teacher, we want you to show us a sign from heaven."

³⁹But Jesus replied:

You want a sign because you are evil and won't believe! But the only sign you will get is the sign of the prophet Jonah. ⁴⁰He was in the stomach of a big fish for three days and nights, just as the Son of Man will be deep in the earth for three days and nights. ⁴¹On the day of judgment the people of Nineveh*m* will stand there with you and condemn you. They turned to God when Jonah preached, and yet here is something far greater than Jonah. ⁴²The Queen of the South*n* will also stand there with you and condemn you. She traveled a long way to hear Solomon's wisdom, and yet here is something much greater than Solomon.

Return of an Evil Spirit
(Luke 11.24-26)

⁴³When an evil spirit leaves a person, it travels through the desert, looking for a place to rest. But when the demon doesn't find a place, ⁴⁴it says, "I will go back to the home I left." When it gets there and finds the place empty, clean, and fixed up, ⁴⁵it goes off and finds seven other evil spirits even worse than itself. They all come and make their home there, and the person ends up in worse shape than before. That's how it will be with you evil people of today.

Jesus' Mother and Brothers
(Mark 3.31-35; Luke 8.19-21)

⁴⁶While Jesus was still speaking to the crowds, his mother and brothers came and stood outside because they wanted to talk with him. ⁴⁷Someone told Jesus, "Your mother and brothers are standing outside and want to talk with you."*o*

⁴⁸Jesus answered, "Who is my mother and who are my brothers?" ⁴⁹Then he pointed to his disciples and said, "These are my mother and my brothers! ⁵⁰Any-

---

*l***12.23** *Could Jesus be the Son of David*: Or "Does Jesus think he is the Son of David?" See the note at 9.27.   *m***12.41** *Nineveh*: During the time of Jonah this city was the capital of the Assyrian Empire, which was Israel's worst enemy. But Jonah was sent there to preach, so that the people would turn to the Lord and be saved.   *n***12.42** *Queen of the South*: Sheba, probably a country in southern Arabia.   *o***12.47** *with you*: Some manuscripts do not have verse 47.

one who obeys my Father in heaven is my brother or sister or mother."

A Story about a Farmer
(Mark 4.1-9; Luke 8.4-8)

13 That same day Jesus left the house and went out beside Lake Galilee, where he sat down to teach.[p] ²Such large crowds gathered around him that he had to sit in a boat, while the people stood on the shore. ³Then he taught them many things by using stories. He said:

A farmer went out to scatter seed in a field. ⁴While the farmer was scattering the seed, some of it fell along the road and was eaten by birds. ⁵Other seeds fell on thin, rocky ground and quickly started growing because the soil wasn't very deep. ⁶But when the sun came up, the plants were scorched and dried up, because they did not have enough roots. ⁷Some other seeds fell where thornbushes grew up and choked the plants. ⁸But a few seeds did fall on good ground where the plants produced a hundred or sixty or thirty times as much as was scattered. ⁹If you have ears, pay attention!

Why Jesus Used Stories
(Mark 4.10-12; Luke 8.9, 10)

¹⁰Jesus' disciples came to him and asked, "Why do you use nothing but stories when you speak to the people?"

¹¹Jesus answered:

I have explained the secrets about the kingdom of heaven to you, but not to others. ¹²Everyone who has something will be given more. But people who don't have anything will lose even what little they have. ¹³I use stories when I speak to them because when they look, they cannot see, and when they listen, they cannot hear or understand. ¹⁴So God's promise came true, just as the prophet Isaiah had said,

"These people will listen
and listen,
    but never understand.
They will look and look,
    but never see.
¹⁵ All of them have
    stubborn minds!
Their ears are stopped up,
    and their eyes are covered.
They cannot see or hear
    or understand.
If they could,
they would turn to me,
    and I would heal them."

¹⁶But God has blessed you, because your eyes can see and your ears can hear! ¹⁷Many prophets and good people were eager to see what you see and to hear what you hear. But I tell you that they did not see or hear.

Jesus Explains the Story about the Farmer
(Mark 4.13-20; Luke 8.11-15)

¹⁸Now listen to the meaning of the story about the farmer:

¹⁹The seeds that fell along the road are the people who hear the message about the kingdom, but don't understand it. Then the evil one comes and snatches the message from their hearts. ²⁰The seeds that fell on rocky ground are the people who gladly hear the message and accept it right away. ²¹But they don't have deep roots, and they don't last very long. As soon as life gets hard or the message gets them in trouble, they give up.

²²The seeds that fell among the thornbushes are also people who hear the message. But they start worrying about the needs of this life and are fooled by the desire to get rich. So the message gets choked out, and they never produce anything. ²³The seeds that fell on good ground are the people who hear and understand the message. They produce as much as a hundred or sixty or thirty times what was planted.

Weeds among the Wheat

²⁴Jesus then told them this story:

The kingdom of heaven is like what happened when a farmer scattered good seed in a field. ²⁵But while everyone was sleeping, an enemy came and scattered weed seeds in the field and then left.

²⁶When the plants came up and began to ripen, the farmer's servants could see the weeds. ²⁷The servants came and asked, "Sir, didn't you scatter good seed in your field? Where did these weeds come from?"

²⁸"An enemy did this," he replied.

His servants then asked, "Do you want us to go out and pull up the weeds?"

²⁹"No!" he answered. "You might also pull up the wheat. ³⁰Leave the weeds alone until harvest time. Then I'll tell my workers to gather the weeds and tie them up and burn them. But I'll have them store the wheat in my barn."

---

[p] 13.1 *sat down to teach*: Teachers in the ancient world, including Jewish teachers, usually sat down when they taught.

Stories about a Mustard Seed and Yeast
(Mark 4.30-32; Luke 13.18-21)

[31] Jesus told them another story:
The kingdom of heaven is like what happens when a farmer plants a mustard seed in a field. [32] Although it is the smallest of all seeds, it grows larger than any garden plant and becomes a tree. Birds even come and nest on its branches.
[33] Jesus also said:
The kingdom of heaven is like what happens when a woman mixes a little yeast into three big batches of flour. Finally, all the dough rises.

The Reason for Teaching with Stories
(Mark 4.33, 34)

[34] Jesus used stories when he spoke to the people. In fact, he did not tell them anything without using stories. [35] So God's promise came true, just as the prophet[q] had said,

"I will use stories
 to speak my message
and to explain things
 that have been hidden
since the creation
 of the world."

Jesus Explains the Story about the Weeds

[36] After Jesus left the crowd and went inside,[r] his disciples came to him and said, "Explain to us the story about the weeds in the wheat field."
[37] Jesus answered:
The one who scattered the good seed is the Son of Man. [38] The field is the world, and the good seeds are the people who belong to the kingdom. The weed seeds are those who belong to the evil one, [39] and the one who scattered them is the devil. The harvest is the end of time, and angels are the ones who bring in the harvest.
[40] Weeds are gathered and burned. That's how it will be at the end of time. [41] The Son of Man will send out his angels, and they will gather from his kingdom everyone who does wrong or causes others to sin. [42] Then he will throw them into a flaming furnace, where people will cry and grit their teeth in pain. [43] But everyone who has done right will shine like the sun in their Father's kingdom. If you have ears, pay attention!

A Hidden Treasure

[44] The kingdom of heaven is like what happens when someone finds treasure hidden in a field and buries it again. A person like that is happy and goes and sells everything in order to buy that field.

A Valuable Pearl

[45] The kingdom of heaven is like what happens when a shop owner is looking for fine pearls. [46] After finding a very valuable one, the owner goes and sells everything in order to buy that pearl.

A Fish Net

[47] The kingdom of heaven is like what happens when a net is thrown into a lake and catches all kinds of fish. [48] When the net is full, it is dragged to the shore, and the fishermen sit down to separate the fish. They keep the good ones, but throw the bad ones away. [49] That's how it will be at the end of time. Angels will come and separate the evil people from the ones who have done right. [50] Then those evil people will be thrown into a flaming furnace, where they will cry and grit their teeth in pain.

New and Old Treasures

[51] Jesus asked his disciples if they understood all these things. They said, "Yes, we do."
[52] So he told them, "Every student of the Scriptures who becomes a disciple in the kingdom of heaven is like someone who brings out new and old treasures from the storeroom."

The People of Nazareth Turn against Jesus
(Mark 6.1-6; Luke 4.16-30)

[53] When Jesus had finished telling these stories, he left [54] and went to his hometown. He taught in their meeting place, and the people were so amazed that they asked, "Where does he get all this wisdom and the power to work these miracles? [55] Isn't he the son of the carpenter? Isn't Mary his mother, and aren't James, Joseph, Simon, and Judas his brothers? [56] Don't his sisters still live here in our town? How can he do all this?" [57] So the people were very unhappy because of what he was doing.
But Jesus said, "Prophets are honored by everyone, except the people of their hometown and their own family." [58] And because the people did not have any faith, Jesus did not work many miracles there.

---

[q] 13.35 *the prophet*: Some manuscripts have "the prophet Isaiah." [r] 13.36 *went inside*: Or "went home."

The Death of John the Baptist
(Mark 6.14-29; Luke 9.7-9)

14 About this time Herod the ruler[s] heard the news about Jesus ²and told his officials, "This is John the Baptist! He has come back from death, and that's why he has the power to work these miracles."

³⁻⁴Herod had earlier arrested John and had him chained and put in prison. He did this because John had told him, "It isn't right for you to take Herodias, the wife of your brother Philip." ⁵Herod wanted to kill John. But the people thought John was a prophet, and Herod was afraid of what they might do.

⁶When Herod's birthday came, the daughter of Herodias danced for the guests. She pleased Herod ⁷so much that he swore to give her whatever she wanted. ⁸But the girl's mother told her to say, "Here on a platter I want the head of John the Baptist!"

⁹The king was sorry for what he had said. But he did not want to break the promise he had made in front of his guests. So he ordered a guard ¹⁰to go to the prison and cut off John's head. ¹¹It was taken on a platter to the girl, and she gave it to her mother. ¹²John's followers took his body and buried it. Then they told Jesus what had happened.

Jesus Feeds Five Thousand
(Mark 6.30-44; Luke 9.10-17; John 6.1-14)

¹³After Jesus heard about John, he crossed Lake Galilee[t] to go to some place where he could be alone. But the crowds found out and followed him on foot from the towns. ¹⁴When Jesus got out of the boat, he saw the large crowd. He felt sorry for them and healed everyone who was sick.

¹⁵That evening the disciples came to Jesus and said, "This place is like a desert, and it is already late. Let the crowds leave, so they can go to the villages and buy some food."

¹⁶Jesus replied, "They don't have to leave. Why don't you give them something to eat?"

¹⁷But they said, "We have only five small loaves of bread[u] and two fish."

¹⁸Jesus asked his disciples to bring the food to him, ¹⁹and he told the crowd to sit down on the grass. Jesus took the five loaves and the two fish. He looked up toward heaven and blessed the food. Then he broke the bread and handed it to his disciples, and they gave it to the people.

²⁰After everyone had eaten all they wanted, Jesus' disciples picked up twelve large baskets of leftovers.

²¹There were about five thousand men who ate, not counting the women and children.

Jesus Walks on the Water
(Mark 6.45-52; John 6.15-21)

²²Right away, Jesus made his disciples get into a boat and start back across the lake.[v] But he stayed until he had sent the crowds away. ²³Then he went up on a mountain where he could be alone and pray. Later that evening, he was still there.

²⁴By this time the boat was a long way from the shore. It was going against the wind and was being tossed around by the waves. ²⁵A little while before morning, Jesus came walking on the water toward his disciples. ²⁶When they saw him, they thought he was a ghost. They were terrified and started screaming.

²⁷At once, Jesus said to them, "Don't worry! I am Jesus. Don't be afraid."

²⁸Peter replied, "Lord, if it is really you, tell me to come to you on the water."

²⁹"Come on!" Jesus said. Peter then got out of the boat and started walking on the water toward him.

³⁰But when Peter saw how strong the wind was, he was afraid and started sinking. "Save me, Lord!" he shouted.

³¹Right away, Jesus reached out his hand. He helped Peter up and said, "You surely don't have much faith. Why do you doubt?"

³²When Jesus and Peter got into the boat, the wind died down. ³³The men in the boat worshiped Jesus and said, "You really are the Son of God!"

Jesus Heals Sick People in Gennesaret
(Mark 6.53-56)

³⁴Jesus and his disciples crossed the lake and came to shore near the town of Gennesaret. ³⁵The people found out that he was there, and they sent word to everyone who lived in that part of the country. So they brought all the sick people to Jesus. ³⁶They begged him just to let them touch his clothes, and everyone who did was healed.

The Teaching of the Ancestors
(Mark 7.1-13)

15 About this time some Pharisees and teachers of the Law of Moses came from Jerusalem. They asked Jesus, ²"Why don't your disciples obey what our ancestors taught us to do?

---

[s]14.1 *Herod the ruler*: Herod Antipas, the son of Herod the Great (see 2.1). [t]14.13 *crossed Lake Galilee*: To the east side. [u]14.17 *small loaves of bread*: These would have been flat and round or in the shape of a bun. [v]14.22 *back across the lake*: To the west side.

They don't even wash their hands[w] before they eat."

³Jesus answered:

Why do you disobey God and follow your own teaching? ⁴Didn't God command you to respect your father and mother? Didn't he tell you to put to death all who curse their parents? ⁵But you let people get by without helping their parents when they should. You let them say that what they have has been offered to God.[x] ⁶Is this any way to show respect to your parents? You ignore God's commands in order to follow your own teaching. ⁷And you are nothing but show-offs! Isaiah the prophet was right when he wrote that God had said,

⁸ "All of you praise me
    with your words,
   but you never really
    think about me.
⁹ It is useless for you
    to worship me,
   when you teach rules
    made up by humans."

What Really Makes People Unclean
(Mark 7.14-23)

¹⁰Jesus called the crowd together and said, "Pay attention and try to understand what I mean. ¹¹The food that you put into your mouth doesn't make you unclean and unfit to worship God. The bad words that come out of your mouth are what make you unclean."

¹²Then his disciples came over to him and asked, "Do you know that you insulted the Pharisees by what you said?"

¹³Jesus answered, "Every plant that my Father in heaven did not plant will be pulled up by the roots. ¹⁴Stay away from those Pharisees! They are like blind people leading other blind people, and all of them will fall into a ditch."

¹⁵Peter replied, "What did you mean when you talked about the things that make people unclean?"

¹⁶Jesus then said:

Don't any of you know what I am talking about by now? ¹⁷Don't you know that the food you put into your mouth goes into your stomach and then out of your body? ¹⁸But the words that come out of your mouth come from your heart. And they are what make you unfit to worship God. ¹⁹Out of your heart come evil thoughts, murder, unfaithfulness in marriage, vulgar deeds, stealing, telling lies, and insulting others. ²⁰These are what make you unclean. Eating without washing your hands will not make you unfit to worship God.

A Woman's Faith
(Mark 7.24-30)

²¹Jesus left and went to the territory near the cities of Tyre and Sidon. ²²Suddenly a Canaanite woman[y] from there came out shouting, "Lord and Son of David,[z] have pity on me! My daughter is full of demons." ²³Jesus did not say a word. But the woman kept following along and shouting, so his disciples came up and asked him to send her away.

²⁴Jesus said, "I was sent only to the people of Israel! They are like a flock of lost sheep."

²⁵The woman came closer. Then she knelt down and begged, "Please help me, Lord!"

²⁶Jesus replied, "It isn't right to take food away from children and feed it to dogs."[a]

²⁷"Lord, that's true," the woman said, "but even dogs get the crumbs that fall from their owner's table."

²⁸Jesus answered, "Dear woman, you really do have a lot of faith, and you will be given what you want." At that moment her daughter was healed.

Jesus Heals Many People

²⁹From there, Jesus went along Lake Galilee. Then he climbed a hill and sat down. ³⁰Large crowds came and brought many people who were crippled or blind or lame or unable to talk. They placed them, and many others, in front of Jesus, and he healed them all. ³¹Everyone was amazed at what they saw and heard. People who had never spoken could now speak. The lame were healed, the crippled could walk, and the blind were able to see. Everyone was praising the God of Israel.

Jesus Feeds Four Thousand
(Mark 8.1-10)

³²Jesus called his disciples together and told them, "I feel sorry for these people. They have been with me for three days, and they don't have anything to eat. I don't want to send them away hungry. They might faint on their way home."

---

[w]**15.2** *wash their hands*: The Jewish people had strict laws about washing their hands before eating, especially if they had been out in public.   [x]**15.5** *has been offered to God*: According to Jewish custom, when people said something was offered to God, it belonged to him and could not be used for anyone else, not even for their own parents.   [y]**15.22** *Canaanite woman*: This woman was not Jewish.   [z]**15.22** *Son of David*: See the note at 9.27.
[a]**15.26** *feed it to dogs*: The Jewish people sometimes referred to Gentiles as dogs.

[33] His disciples said, "This place is like a desert. Where can we find enough food to feed such a crowd?"

[34] Jesus asked them how much food they had. They replied, "Seven small loaves of bread[b] and a few little fish."

[35] After Jesus had told the people to sit down, [36] he took the seven loaves of bread and the fish and gave thanks. He then broke them and handed them to his disciples, who passed them around to the crowds.

[37] Everyone ate all they wanted, and the leftovers filled seven large baskets. [38] There were four thousand men who ate, not counting the women and children.

[39] After Jesus had sent the crowds away, he got into a boat and sailed across the lake. He came to shore near the town of Magadan.[c]

A Demand for a Sign from Heaven
(Mark 8.11-13; Luke 12.54-56)

16 The Pharisees and Sadducees came to Jesus and tried to test him by asking for a sign from heaven. [2] He told them:

If the sky is red in the evening, you say the weather will be good. [3] But if the sky is red and gloomy in the morning, you say it is going to rain. You can tell what the weather will be like by looking at the sky. But you don't understand what is happening now.[d] [4] You want a sign because you are evil and won't believe! But the only sign you will be given is what happened to Jonah.[e]

Then Jesus left.

The Yeast of the Pharisees and Sadducees
(Mark 8.14-21)

[5] The disciples had forgotten to bring any bread when they crossed the lake.[f] [6] Jesus then warned them, "Watch out! Guard against the yeast of the Pharisees and Sadducees."

[7] The disciples talked this over and said to each other, "He must be saying this because we didn't bring along any bread."

[8] Jesus knew what they were thinking and said:

You surely don't have much faith! Why are you talking about not having any bread? [9] Don't you understand? Have you forgotten about the five thousand people and all those baskets of leftovers from just five loaves of bread? [10] And what about the four thousand people and all those baskets of leftovers from only seven loaves of bread? [11] Don't you know by now that I am not talking to you about bread? Watch out for the yeast of the Pharisees and Sadducees!

[12] Finally, the disciples understood that Jesus wasn't talking about the yeast used to make bread, but about the teaching of the Pharisees and Sadducees.

Who Is Jesus?
(Mark 8.27-30; Luke 9.18-21)

[13] When Jesus and his disciples were near the town of Caesarea Philippi, he asked them, "What do people say about the Son of Man?"

[14] The disciples answered, "Some people say you are John the Baptist or maybe Elijah[g] or Jeremiah or some other prophet."

[15] Then Jesus asked them, "But who do you say I am?"

[16] Simon Peter spoke up, "You are the Messiah, the Son of the living God."

[17] Jesus told him:

Simon, son of Jonah, you are blessed! You didn't discover this on your own. It was shown to you by my Father in heaven. [18] So I will call you Peter, which means "a rock." On this rock I will build my church, and death itself will not have any power over it. [19] I will give you the keys to the kingdom of heaven, and God in heaven will allow whatever you allow on earth. But he will not allow anything that you don't allow.

[20] Jesus told his disciples not to tell anyone that he was the Messiah.

Jesus Speaks about His Suffering and Death
(Mark 8.31—9.1; Luke 9.22-27)

[21] From then on, Jesus began telling his disciples what would happen to him. He said, "I must go to Jerusalem. There the nation's leaders, the chief priests, and the teachers of the Law of Moses will make me suffer terribly. I will be killed, but three days later I will rise to life."

[22] Peter took Jesus aside and told him to stop talking like that. He said, "God would never let this happen to you, Lord!"

[23] Jesus turned to Peter and said, "Satan, get away from me! You're in my way

---

[b] *15.34 small loaves of bread*: See the note at 14.17.   [c] *15.39 Magadan*: The location is unknown.   [d] *16.2, 3 If the sky is red . . . what is happening now*: The words of Jesus in verses 2 and 3 are not in some manuscripts.   [e] *16.4 what happened to Jonah*: Jonah was in the stomach of a big fish for three days and nights (see 12.40).   [f] *16.5 crossed the lake*: To the east side.   [g] *16.14 Elijah*: Many of the Jewish people expected the prophet Elijah to come and prepare the way for the Messiah.

because you think like everyone else and not like God."

²⁴Then Jesus said to his disciples:
If any of you want to be my followers, you must forget about yourself. You must take up your cross and follow me. ²⁵If you want to save your life,*ʰ* you will destroy it. But if you give up your life for me, you will find it. ²⁶What will you gain, if you own the whole world but destroy yourself? What would you give to get back your soul? ²⁷The Son of Man will soon come in the glory of his Father and with his angels to reward all people for what they have done. ²⁸I promise you that some of those standing here will not die before they see the Son of Man coming with his kingdom.

The True Glory of Jesus
(Mark 9.2-13; Luke 9.28-36)

17 Six days later Jesus took Peter and the brothers James and John with him. They went up on a very high mountain where they could be alone. ²There in front of the disciples, Jesus was completely changed. His face was shining like the sun, and his clothes became white as light.

³All at once Moses and Elijah were there talking with Jesus. ⁴So Peter said to him, "Lord, it is good for us to be here! Let us make three shelters, one for you, one for Moses, and one for Elijah." ⁵While Peter was still speaking, the shadow of a bright cloud passed over them. From the cloud a voice said, "This is my own dear Son, and I am pleased with him. Listen to what he says!" ⁶When the disciples heard the voice, they were so afraid that they fell flat on the ground. ⁷But Jesus came over and touched them. He said, "Get up and don't be afraid!" ⁸When they opened their eyes, they saw only Jesus.

⁹On their way down from the mountain, Jesus warned his disciples not to tell anyone what they had seen until after the Son of Man had been raised from death.

¹⁰The disciples asked Jesus, "Don't the teachers of the Law of Moses say that Elijah must come before the Messiah does?"

¹¹Jesus told them, "Elijah certainly will come and get everything ready. ¹²In fact, he has already come. But the people did not recognize him and treated him just as they wanted to. They will soon make the Son of Man suffer in the same way." ¹³Then the disciples understood that Jesus was talking to them about John the Baptist.

Jesus Heals a Boy
(Mark 9.14-29; Luke 9.37-43a)

¹⁴Jesus and his disciples returned to the crowd. A man knelt in front of him ¹⁵and said, "Lord, have pity on my son! He has a bad case of epilepsy and often falls into a fire or into water. ¹⁶I brought him to your disciples, but none of them could heal him."

¹⁷Jesus said, "You people are too stubborn to have any faith! How much longer must I be with you? Why do I have to put up with you? Bring the boy here." ¹⁸Then Jesus spoke sternly to the demon. It went out of the boy, and right then he was healed.

¹⁹Later the disciples went to Jesus in private and asked him, "Why couldn't we force out the demon?"

²⁰⁻²¹Jesus replied:
It is because you don't have enough faith! But I can promise you this. If you had faith no larger than a mustard seed, you could tell this mountain to move from here to there. And it would. Everything would be possible for you.*ⁱ*

Jesus Again Speaks about His Death
(Mark 9.30-32; Luke 9.43b-45)

²²While Jesus and his disciples were going from place to place in Galilee, he told them, "The Son of Man will be handed over to people ²³who will kill him. But three days later he will rise to life." All of this made the disciples very sad.

Paying the Temple Tax

²⁴When Jesus and the others arrived in Capernaum, the collectors for the temple tax came to Peter and asked, "Does your teacher pay the temple tax?"

²⁵"Yes, he does," Peter answered.

After they had returned home, Jesus went up to Peter and asked him, "Simon, what do you think? Do the kings of this earth collect taxes and fees from their own people or from foreigners?"*ʲ*

²⁶Peter answered, "From foreigners."

Jesus replied, "Then their own people*ᵏ* don't have to pay. ²⁷But we don't want to cause trouble. So go cast a line into the lake and pull out the first fish you hook. Open its mouth, and you will find a coin. Use it to pay your taxes and mine."

ʰ **16.25** *life*: In verses 25 and 26 the same Greek word is translated "life," "yourself," and "soul."
ⁱ **17.20,21** *for you*: Some manuscripts add, "But the only way to force out that kind of demon is by praying and going without eating." *ʲ* **17.25** *from their own people or from foreigners*: Or "from their children or from others." *ᵏ* **17.26** *From foreigners . . . their own people*: Or "From other people . . . their children."

Who Is the Greatest?
(Mark 9.33-37; Luke 9.46-48)

18 About this time the disciples came to Jesus and asked him who would be the greatest in the kingdom of heaven. ²Jesus called a child over and had the child stand near him. ³Then he said:

I promise you this. If you don't change and become like a child, you will never get into the kingdom of heaven. ⁴But if you are as humble as this child, you are the greatest in the kingdom of heaven. ⁵And when you welcome one of these children because of me, you welcome me.

Temptations To Sin
(Mark 9.42-48; Luke 17.1, 2)

⁶It will be terrible for people who cause even one of my little followers to sin. Those people would be better off thrown into the deepest part of the ocean with a heavy stone tied around their necks! ⁷The world is in for trouble because of the way it causes people to sin. There will always be something to cause people to sin, but anyone who does this will be in for trouble.

⁸If your hand or foot causes you to sin, chop it off and throw it away! You would be better off to go into life crippled or lame than to have two hands or two feet and be thrown into the fire that never goes out. ⁹If your eye causes you to sin, poke it out and get rid of it. You would be better off to go into life with only one eye than to have two eyes and be thrown into the fires of hell.

The Lost Sheep
(Luke 15.3-7)

¹⁰⁻¹¹Don't be cruel to any of these little ones! I promise you that their angels are always with my Father in heaven.[l] ¹²Let me ask you this. What would you do if you had a hundred sheep and one of them wandered off? Wouldn't you leave the ninety-nine on the hillside and go look for the one that had wandered away? ¹³I am sure that finding it would make you happier than having the ninety-nine that never wandered off. ¹⁴That's how it is with your Father in heaven. He doesn't want any of these little ones to be lost.

When Someone Sins
(Luke 17.3)

¹⁵If one of my followers[m] sins against you, go and point out what was wrong. But do it in private, just between the two of you. If that person listens, you have won back a follower. ¹⁶But if that one refuses to listen, take along one or two others. The Scriptures teach that every complaint must be proven true by two or more witnesses. ¹⁷If the follower refuses to listen to them, report the matter to the church. Anyone who refuses to listen to the church must be treated like an unbeliever or a tax collector.[n]

Allowing and Not Allowing

¹⁸I promise you that God in heaven will allow whatever you allow on earth, but he will not allow anything you don't allow. ¹⁹I promise that when any two of you on earth agree about something you are praying for, my Father in heaven will do it for you. ²⁰Whenever two or three of you come together in my name,[o] I am there with you.

An Official Who Refused To Forgive

²¹Peter came up to the Lord and asked, "How many times should I forgive someone[p] who does something wrong to me? Is seven times enough?"

²²Jesus answered:

Not just seven times, but seventy-seven times![q] ²³This story will show you what the kingdom of heaven is like:

One day a king decided to call in his officials and ask them to give an account of what they owed him. ²⁴As he was doing this, one official was brought in who owed him fifty million silver coins. ²⁵But he didn't have any money to pay what he owed. The king ordered him to be sold, along with his wife and children and all he owned, in order to pay the debt.

²⁶The official got down on his knees and began begging, "Have pity on me, and I will pay you every cent I owe!" ²⁷The king felt sorry for him and let him go free. He even told the official that he did not have to pay back the money.

²⁸As the official was leaving, he happened to meet another official,

---

[l] *18.10,11 in heaven*: Some manuscripts add, "The Son of Man came to save people who were lost." [m] *18.15 followers*: The Greek text has "brother," which is used here and elsewhere in this chapter to refer to a follower of Christ. [n] *18.17 tax collector*: See the note at 5.46. [o] *18.20 in my name*: Or "as my followers." [p] *18.21 someone*: Or "a follower." See the note at 18.15. [q] *18.22 seventy-seven times*: Or "seventy times seven." The large number means that one follower should never stop forgiving another.

who owed him a hundred silver coins. So he grabbed the man by the throat. He started choking him and said, "Pay me what you owe!"

²⁹The man got down on his knees and began begging, "Have pity on me, and I will pay you back." ³⁰But the first official refused to have pity. Instead, he went and had the other official put in jail until he could pay what he owed.

³¹When some other officials found out what had happened, they felt sorry for the man who had been put in jail. Then they told the king what had happened. ³²The king called the first official back in and said, "You're an evil man! When you begged for mercy, I said you did not have to pay back a cent. ³³Don't you think you should show pity to someone else, as I did to you?" ³⁴The king was so angry that he ordered the official to be tortured until he could pay back everything he owed. ³⁵That is how my Father in heaven will treat you, if you don't forgive each of my followers with all your heart.

Teaching about Divorce
(Mark 10.1-12)

19 When Jesus finished teaching, he left Galilee and went to the part of Judea that is east of the Jordan River. ²Large crowds followed him, and he healed their sick people.

³Some Pharisees wanted to test Jesus. They came up to him and asked, "Is it right for a man to divorce his wife for just any reason?"

⁴Jesus answered, "Don't you know that in the beginning the Creator made a man and a woman? ⁵That's why a man leaves his father and mother and gets married. He becomes like one person with his wife. ⁶Then they are no longer two people, but one. And no one should separate a couple that God has joined together."

⁷The Pharisees asked Jesus, "Why did Moses say that a man could write out divorce papers and send his wife away?"

⁸Jesus replied, "You are so heartless! That's why Moses allowed you to divorce your wife. But from the beginning God did not intend it to be that way. ⁹I say that if your wife has not committed some terrible sexual sin,ʳ you must not divorce her to marry someone else. If you do, you are unfaithful."

¹⁰The disciples said, "If that's how it is between a man and a woman, it's better not to get married."

¹¹Jesus told them, "Only those people who have been given the gift of staying single can accept this teaching. ¹²Some people are unable to marry because of birth defects or because of what someone has done to their bodies. Others stay single for the sake of the kingdom of heaven. Anyone who can accept this teaching should do so."

Jesus Blesses Little Children
(Mark 10.13-16; Luke 18.15-17)

¹³Some people brought their children to Jesus, so that he could place his hands on them and pray for them. His disciples told the people to stop bothering him. ¹⁴But Jesus said, "Let the children come to me, and don't try to stop them! People who are like these children belong to God's kingdom."ˢ ¹⁵After Jesus had placed his hands on the children, he left.

A Rich Young Man
(Mark 10.17-31; Luke 18.18-30)

¹⁶A man came to Jesus and asked, "Teacher, what good thing must I do to have eternal life?"

¹⁷Jesus said to him, "Why do you ask me about what is good? Only God is good. If you want to have eternal life, you must obey his commandments."

¹⁸"Which ones?" the man asked.

Jesus answered, "Do not murder. Be faithful in marriage. Do not steal. Do not tell lies about others. ¹⁹Respect your father and mother. And love others as much as you love yourself." ²⁰The young man said, "I have obeyed all of these. What else must I do?"

²¹Jesus replied, "If you want to be perfect, go sell everything you own! Give the money to the poor, and you will have riches in heaven. Then come and be my follower." ²²When the young man heard this, he was sad, because he was very rich.

²³Jesus said to his disciples, "It's terribly hard for rich people to get into the kingdom of heaven! ²⁴In fact, it's easier for a camel to go through the eye of a needle than for a rich person to get into God's kingdom."

²⁵When the disciples heard this, they were greatly surprised and asked, "How can anyone ever be saved?"

²⁶Jesus looked straight at them and said, "There are some things that people cannot do, but God can do anything."

²⁷Peter replied, "Remember, we have left everything to be your followers! What will we get?"

²⁸Jesus answered:

Yes, all of you have become my

ʳ **19.9** *some terrible sexual sin*: See the note at 5.32. ˢ **19.14** *People who are like these children belong to God's kingdom*: Or "God's kingdom belongs to people who are like these children."

followers. And so in the future world, when the Son of Man sits on his glorious throne, I promise that you will sit on twelve thrones to judge the twelve tribes of Israel. ²⁹All who have given up home or brothers and sisters or father or mother or children or land for me will be given a hundred times as much. They will also have eternal life. ³⁰But many who are now first will be last, and many who are last will be first.

Workers in a Vineyard

20 As Jesus was telling what the kingdom of heaven would be like, he said:

Early one morning a man went out to hire some workers for his vineyard. ²After he had agreed to pay them the usual amount for a day's work, he sent them off to his vineyard.

³About nine that morning, the man saw some other people standing in the market with nothing to do. ⁴He said he would pay them what was fair, if they would work in his vineyard. ⁵So they went.

At noon and again about three in the afternoon he returned to the market. And each time he made the same agreement with others who were loafing around with nothing to do.

⁶Finally, about five in the afternoon the man went back and found some others standing there. He asked them, "Why have you been standing here all day long doing nothing?"

⁷"Because no one has hired us," they answered. Then he told them to go work in his vineyard.

⁸That evening the owner of the vineyard told the man in charge of the workers to call them in and give them their money. He also told the man to begin with the ones who were hired last. ⁹When the workers arrived, the ones who had been hired at five in the afternoon were given a full day's pay.

¹⁰The workers who had been hired first thought they would be given more than the others. But when they were given the same, ¹¹they began complaining to the owner of the vineyard. ¹²They said, "The ones who were hired last worked for only one hour. But you paid them the same that you did us. And we worked in the hot sun all day long!"

¹³The owner answered one of them, "Friend, I didn't cheat you. I paid you exactly what we agreed on. ¹⁴Take your money now and go! What business is it of yours if I want to pay them the same that I paid you? ¹⁵Don't I have the right to do what I want with my own money? Why should you be jealous, if I want to be generous?"

¹⁶Jesus then said, "So it is. Everyone who is now first will be last, and everyone who is last will be first."

Jesus Again Tells about His Death
(Mark 10.32-34; Luke 18.31-34)

¹⁷As Jesus was on his way to Jerusalem, he took his twelve disciples aside and told them in private:

¹⁸We are now on our way to Jerusalem, where the Son of Man will be handed over to the chief priests and the teachers of the Law of Moses. They will sentence him to death, ¹⁹and then they will hand him over to foreigners[t] who will make fun of him. They will beat him and nail him to a cross. But on the third day he will rise from death.

A Mother's Request
(Mark 10.35-45)

²⁰The mother of James and John[u] came to Jesus with her two sons. She knelt down and started begging him to do something for her. ²¹Jesus asked her what she wanted, and she said, "When you come into your kingdom, please let one of my sons sit at your right side and the other at your left."[v]

²²Jesus answered, "Not one of you knows what you are asking. Are you able to drink from the cup[w] that I must soon drink from?"

James and John said, "Yes, we are!"

²³Jesus replied, "You certainly will drink from my cup! But it isn't for me to say who will sit at my right side and at my left. That is for my Father to say."

²⁴When the ten other disciples heard this, they were angry with the two brothers. ²⁵But Jesus called the disciples together and said:

You know that foreign rulers like to order their people around. And their great leaders have full power over everyone they rule. ²⁶But don't act like them. If you want to be great, you must be the servant of all the others. ²⁷And if you want to be

---

[t]**20.19** *foreigners*: The Romans, who ruled Judea at this time.   [u]**20.20** *mother of James and John*: The Greek text has "mother of the sons of Zebedee" (see 26.37).   [v]**20.21** *right side . . . left*: The most powerful people in a kingdom sat at the right and left side of the king.   [w]**20.22** *drink from the cup*: In the Scriptures a cup is sometimes used as a symbol of suffering. To "drink from the cup" is to suffer.

first, you must be the slave of the rest. ²⁸The Son of Man did not come to be a slave master, but a slave who will give his life to rescue[x] many people.

Jesus Heals Two Blind Men
(Mark 10.46-52; Luke 18.35-43)

²⁹Jesus was followed by a large crowd as he and his disciples were leaving Jericho. ³⁰Two blind men were sitting beside the road. And when they heard that Jesus was coming their way, they shouted, "Lord and Son of David,[y] have pity on us!"

³¹The crowd told them to be quiet, but they shouted even louder, "Lord and Son of David, have pity on us!"

³²When Jesus heard them, he stopped and asked, "What do you want me to do for you?"

³³They answered, "Lord, we want to see!"

³⁴Jesus felt sorry for them and touched their eyes. Right away they could see, and they became his followers.

Jesus Enters Jerusalem
(Mark 11.1-11; Luke 19.28-38; John 12.12-19)

21 When Jesus and his disciples came near Jerusalem, he went to Bethphage on the Mount of Olives and sent two of them on ahead. ²He told them, "Go into the next village, where you will at once find a donkey and her colt. Untie the two donkeys and bring them to me. ³If anyone asks why you are doing that, just say, 'The Lord[z] needs them.' Right away he will let you have the donkeys."

⁴So God's promise came true, just as the prophet had said,

⁵ "Announce to the people
of Jerusalem:
'Your king is coming to you!
He is humble
and rides on a donkey.
He comes on the colt
of a donkey.'"

⁶The disciples left and did what Jesus had told them to do. ⁷They brought the donkey and its colt and laid some clothes on their backs. Then Jesus got on.

⁸Many people spread clothes in the road, while others put down branches[a] which they had cut from trees. ⁹Some people walked ahead of Jesus and others followed behind. They were all shouting,

"Hooray[b] for the Son of David![c]
God bless the one who comes
in the name of the Lord.
Hooray for God
in heaven above!"

¹⁰When Jesus came to Jerusalem, everyone in the city was excited and asked, "Who can this be?"

¹¹The crowd answered, "This is Jesus, the prophet from Nazareth in Galilee."

Jesus in the Temple
(Mark 11.15-19; Luke 19.45-48; John 2.13-22)

¹²Jesus went into the temple and chased out everyone who was selling or buying. He turned over the tables of the moneychangers and the benches of the ones who were selling doves. ¹³He told them, "The Scriptures say, 'My house should be called a place of worship.' But you have turned it into a place where robbers hide."

¹⁴Blind and lame people came to Jesus in the temple, and he healed them. ¹⁵But the chief priests and the teachers of the Law of Moses were angry when they saw his miracles and heard the children shouting praises to the Son of David.[c] ¹⁶The men said to Jesus, "Don't you hear what those children are saying?"

"Yes, I do!" Jesus answered. "Don't you know that the Scriptures say, 'Children and infants will sing praises'?"

¹⁷Then Jesus left the city and went out to the village of Bethany, where he spent the night.

Jesus Puts a Curse on a Fig Tree
(Mark 11.12-14, 20-24)

¹⁸When Jesus got up the next morning, he was hungry. He started out for the city, ¹⁹and along the way he saw a fig tree. But when he came to it, he found only leaves and no figs. So he told the tree, "You will never again grow any fruit!" Right then the fig tree dried up.

²⁰The disciples were shocked when they saw how quickly the tree had dried up. ²¹But Jesus said to them, "If you have faith and don't doubt, I promise that you can do what I did to this tree. And you will be able to do even more. You can tell this mountain to get up and jump into the sea, and it will. ²²If you

---

[x]**20.28** *rescue*: The Greek word often, though not always, means the payment of a price to free a slave or a prisoner. [y]**20.30** *Son of David*: See the note at 9.27. [z]**21.3** *The Lord*: Or "The master of the donkeys." [a]**21.8** *spread clothes . . . put down branches*: This was one way that the Jewish people welcomed a famous person. [b]**21.9** *Horray*: This translates a word that can mean "please save us." But it is most often used as a shout of praise to God. [c]**21.9,15** *Son of David*: See the note at 9.27.

have faith when you pray, you will be given whatever you ask for."

A Question about Jesus' Authority
(Mark 11.27-33; Luke 20.1-8)

23 Jesus had gone into the temple and was teaching when the chief priests and the leaders of the people came up to him. They asked, "What right do you have to do these things? Who gave you this authority?"
24 Jesus answered, "I have just one question to ask you. If you answer it, I will tell you where I got the right to do these things. 25 Who gave John the right to baptize? Was it God in heaven or merely some human being?"

They thought it over and said to each other, "We can't say that God gave John this right. Jesus will ask us why we didn't believe John. 26 On the other hand, these people think that John was a prophet, and we are afraid of what they might do to us. That's why we can't say that it was merely some human who gave John the right to baptize." 27 So they told Jesus, "We don't know."

Jesus said, "Then I won't tell you who gave me the right to do what I do."

A Story about Two Sons

28 Jesus said:

I will tell you a story about a man who had two sons. Then you can tell me what you think. The father went to the older son and said, "Go work in the vineyard today!" 29 His son told him that he would not do it, but later he changed his mind and went. 30 The man then told his younger son to go work in the vineyard. The boy said he would, but he didn't go.
31 Which one of the sons obeyed his father?

"The older one," the chief priests and leaders answered.

Then Jesus told them:

You can be sure that tax collectors[d] and prostitutes will get into the kingdom of God before you ever will! 32 When John the Baptist showed you how to do right, you would not believe him. But these evil people did believe. And even when you saw what they did, you still would not change your minds and believe.

Renters of a Vineyard
(Mark 12.1-12; Luke 20.9-19)

33 Jesus told the chief priests and leaders to listen to this story:

A land owner once planted a vineyard. He built a wall around it and dug a pit to crush the grapes in. He also built a lookout tower. Then he rented out his vineyard and left the country.
34 When it was harvest time, the owner sent some servants to get his share of the grapes. 35 But the renters grabbed those servants. They beat up one, killed one, and stoned one of them to death. 36 He then sent more servants than he did the first time. But the renters treated them in the same way.
37 Finally, the owner sent his own son to the renters, because he thought they would respect him. 38 But when they saw the man's son, they said, "Someday he will own the vineyard. Let's kill him! Then we can have it all for ourselves." 39 So they grabbed him, threw him out of the vineyard, and killed him.
40 Jesus asked, "When the owner of that vineyard comes, what do you suppose he will do to those renters?"
41 The chief priests and leaders answered, "He will kill them in some horrible way. Then he will rent out his vineyard to people who will give him his share of grapes at harvest time."
42 Jesus replied, "You surely know that the Scriptures say,

'The stone that the builders
  tossed aside
is now the most important
  stone of all.
This is something
  the Lord has done,
and it is amazing to us.'

43 I tell you that God's kingdom will be taken from you and given to people who will do what he demands. 44 Anyone who stumbles over this stone will be crushed, and anyone it falls on will be smashed to pieces."[e]
45 When the chief priests and the Pharisees heard these stories, they knew that Jesus was talking about them. 46 So they looked for a way to arrest Jesus. But they were afraid to, because the people thought he was a prophet.

The Great Banquet
(Luke 14.15-24)

22 Once again Jesus used stories to teach the people:
2 The kingdom of heaven is like what happened when a king gave a wedding banquet for his son. 3 The king sent some servants to tell the invited guests to come to the banquet, but the guests refused. 4 He sent other servants to say to the

---

[d]21.31 *tax collectors*: See the note at 5.46. manuscripts.

[e]21.44 *pieces*: Verse 44 is not in some

guests, "The banquet is ready! My cattle and prize calves have all been prepared. Everything is ready. Come to the banquet!"

⁵But the guests did not pay any attention. Some of them left for their farms, and some went to their places of business. ⁶Others grabbed the servants, then beat them up and killed them.

⁷This made the king so furious that he sent an army to kill those murderers and burn down their city. ⁸Then he said to the servants, "It is time for the wedding banquet, and the invited guests don't deserve to come. ⁹Go out to the street corners and tell everyone you meet to come to the banquet." ¹⁰They went out on the streets and brought in everyone they could find, good and bad alike. And the banquet room was filled with guests.

¹¹When the king went in to meet the guests, he found that one of them wasn't wearing the right kind of clothes for the wedding. ¹²The king asked, "Friend, why didn't you wear proper clothes for the wedding?" But the guest had no excuse. ¹³So the king gave orders for that person to be tied hand and foot and to be thrown outside into the dark. That's where people will cry and grit their teeth in pain. ¹⁴Many are invited, but only a few are chosen.

Paying Taxes
(Mark 12.13-17; Luke 20.20-26)

¹⁵The Pharisees got together and planned how they could trick Jesus into saying something wrong. ¹⁶They sent some of their followers and some of Herod's followers*ᶠ* to say to him, "Teacher, we know that you are honest. You teach the truth about what God wants people to do. And you treat everyone with the same respect, no matter who they are. ¹⁷Tell us what you think! Should we pay taxes to the Emperor or not?"

¹⁸Jesus knew their evil thoughts and said, "Why are you trying to test me? You show-offs! ¹⁹Let me see one of the coins used for paying taxes." They brought him a silver coin, ²⁰and he asked, "Whose picture and name are on it?"

²¹"The Emperor's," they answered.

Then Jesus told them, "Give the Emperor what belongs to him and give God what belongs to God." ²²His answer surprised them so much that they walked away.

Life in the Future World
(Mark 12.18-27; Luke 20.27-40)

²³The Sadducees did not believe that people would rise to life after death. So that same day some of the Sadducees came to Jesus and said:

²⁴Teacher, Moses wrote that if a married man dies and has no children, his brother should marry the widow. Their first son would then be thought of as the son of the dead brother.

²⁵Once there were seven brothers who lived here. The first one married, but died without having any children. So his wife was left to his brother. ²⁶The same thing happened to the second and third brothers and finally to all seven of them. ²⁷At last the woman died. ²⁸When God raises people from death, whose wife will this woman be? She had been married to all seven brothers.

²⁹Jesus answered:

You are completely wrong! You don't know what the Scriptures teach. And you don't know anything about the power of God. ³⁰When God raises people to life, they won't marry. They will be like the angels in heaven. ³¹And as for people being raised to life, God was speaking to you when he said, ³²"I am the God worshiped by Abraham, Isaac, and Jacob."*ᵍ* He isn't the God of the dead, but of the living.

³³The crowds were surprised to hear what Jesus was teaching.

The Most Important Commandment
(Mark 12.28-34; Luke 10.25-28)

³⁴After Jesus had made the Sadducees look foolish, the Pharisees heard about it and got together. ³⁵One of them was an expert in the Jewish Law. So he tried to test Jesus by asking, ³⁶"Teacher, what is the most important commandment in the Law?"

³⁷Jesus answered:

Love the Lord your God with all your heart, soul, and mind. ³⁸This is the first and most important commandment. ³⁹The second most important commandment is like this one. And it is, "Love others as much as you love yourself." ⁴⁰All the Law of Moses and the Books of the

---

*ᶠ*22.16 *Herod's followers*: People who were political followers of the family of Herod the Great (see 2.1) and his son Herod Antipas (see 14.1), and who wanted Herod to be king in Jerusalem.
*ᵍ*22.32 *I am the God worshiped by Abraham, Isaac, and Jacob*: Jesus argues that if God is worshiped by these three, they must still be alive, because he is the God of the living.

About David's Son
(Mark 12.35-37; Luke 20.41-44)

⁴¹While the Pharisees were still there, Jesus asked them, ⁴²"What do you think about the Messiah? Whose family will he come from?"

They answered, "He will be a son of King David."[i]

⁴³Jesus replied, "How then could the Spirit lead David to call the Messiah his Lord? David said,

⁴⁴ 'The Lord said to my Lord:
Sit at my right side[j]
until I make your enemies
into a footstool for you.'

⁴⁵If David called the Messiah his Lord, how can the Messiah be a son of King David?" ⁴⁶No one was able to give Jesus an answer, and from that day on, no one dared ask him any more questions.

Jesus Condemns the Pharisees and the Teachers of the Law of Moses
(Mark 12.38-40; Luke 11.37-52; 20.45-47)

23 Jesus said to the crowds and to his disciples:

²The Pharisees and the teachers of the Law are experts in the Law of Moses. ³So obey everything they teach you, but don't do as they do. After all, they say one thing and do something else.

⁴They pile heavy burdens on people's shoulders and won't lift a finger to help. ⁵Everything they do is just to show off in front of others. They even make a big show of wearing Scripture verses on their foreheads and arms, and they wear big tassels[k] for everyone to see. ⁶They love the best seats at banquets and the front seats in the meeting places. ⁷And when they are in the market, they like to have people greet them as their teachers.

⁸But none of you should be called a teacher. You have only one teacher, and all of you are like brothers and sisters. ⁹Don't call anyone on earth your father. All of you have the same Father in heaven. ¹⁰None of you should be called the leader. The Messiah is your only leader. ¹¹Whoever is the greatest should be the servant of the others. ¹²If you put yourself above others, you will be put down. But if you humble yourself, you will be honored.

¹³⁻¹⁴You Pharisees and teachers of the Law of Moses are in for trouble! You're nothing but show-offs. You lock people out of the kingdom of heaven. You won't go in yourselves, and you keep others from going in.[l]

¹⁵You Pharisees and teachers of the Law of Moses are in for trouble! You're nothing but show-offs. You travel over land and sea to win one follower. And when you have done so, you make that person twice as fit for hell as you are.

¹⁶You are in for trouble! You are supposed to lead others, but you are blind. You teach that it doesn't matter if a person swears by the temple. But you say that it does matter if someone swears by the gold in the temple. ¹⁷You blind fools! Which is greater, the gold or the temple that makes the gold sacred?

¹⁸You also teach that it doesn't matter if a person swears by the altar. But you say that it does matter if someone swears by the gift on the altar. ¹⁹Are you blind? Which is more important, the gift or the altar that makes the gift sacred? ²⁰Anyone who swears by the altar also swears by everything on it. ²¹And anyone who swears by the temple also swears by God, who lives there. ²²To swear by heaven is the same as swearing by God's throne and by the one who sits on that throne.

²³You Pharisees and teachers are show-offs, and you're in for trouble! You give God a tenth of the spices from your garden, such as mint, dill, and cumin. Yet you neglect the more important matters of the Law, such as justice, mercy, and faithfulness. These are the important things you should have done, though you should not have left the others undone either. ²⁴You blind leaders! You strain out a small fly but swallow a camel.

²⁵You Pharisees and teachers are show-offs, and you're in for trouble!

---

[h]**22.40** *the Law of Moses and the Books of the Prophets*: The Jewish Scriptures, that is, the Old Testament.   [i]**22.42** *son of King David*: See the note at 9.27.   [j]**22.44** *right side*: The place of power and honor.   [k]**23.5** *wearing Scripture verses on their foreheads and arms . . . tassels*: As a sign of their love for the Lord and his teachings, the Jewish people had wanted wearing Scripture verses in small leather boxes. But the Pharisees tried to show off by making the boxes bigger than necessary. The Jewish people were also taught to wear tassels on the four corners of their robes to show their love for God.   [l]**23.13,14** *from going in*: Some manuscripts add, "You Pharisees and teachers are in for trouble! And you're nothing but show-offs! You cheat widows out of their homes and then pray long prayers just to show off. So you will be punished most of all."

Matthew 23.26

You wash the outside of your cups and dishes, while inside there is nothing but greed and selfishness. [26]You blind Pharisee! First clean the inside of a cup, and then the outside will also be clean.

[27]You Pharisees and teachers are in for trouble! You're nothing but show-offs. You're like tombs that have been whitewashed.[m] On the outside they are beautiful, but inside they are full of bones and filth. [28]That's what you are like. Outside you look good, but inside you are evil and only pretend to be good.

[29]You Pharisees and teachers are nothing but show-offs, and you're in for trouble! You build monuments for the prophets and decorate the tombs of good people. [30]And you claim that you would not have taken part with your ancestors in killing the prophets. [31]But you prove that you really are the relatives of the ones who killed the prophets. [32]So keep on doing everything they did. [33]You are nothing but snakes and the children of snakes! How can you escape going to hell?

[34]I will send prophets and wise people and experts in the Law of Moses to you. But you will kill them or nail them to a cross or beat them in your meeting places or chase them from town to town. [35]That's why you will be held guilty for the murder of every good person, beginning with the good man Abel. This also includes Barachiah's son Zechariah,[n] the man you murdered between the temple and the altar. [36]I can promise that you people living today will be punished for all these things!

Jesus Loves Jerusalem
(Luke 13.34, 35)

[37]Jerusalem, Jerusalem! Your people have killed the prophets and have stoned the messengers who were sent to you. I have often wanted to gather your people, as a hen gathers her chicks under her wings. But you wouldn't let me. [38]And now your temple will be deserted. [39]You won't see me again until you say,

"Blessed is the one who comes
in the name of the Lord."

The Temple Will Be Destroyed
(Mark 13.1, 2; Luke 21.5, 6)

24 After Jesus left the temple, his disciples came over and said, "Look at all these buildings!"
[2]Jesus replied, "Do you see these buildings? They will certainly be torn down! Not one stone will be left in place."

Warning about Trouble
(Mark 13.3-13; Luke 21.7-19)

[3]Later, as Jesus was sitting on the Mount of Olives, his disciples came to him in private and asked, "When will this happen? What will be the sign of your coming and of the end of the world?"
[4]Jesus answered:

Don't let anyone fool you. [5]Many will come and claim to be me. They will say that they are the Messiah, and they will fool many people. [6]You will soon hear about wars and threats of wars, but don't be afraid. These things will have to happen first, but that isn't the end. [7]Nations and kingdoms will go to war against each other. People will starve to death, and in some places there will be earthquakes. [8]But this is just the beginning of troubles.

[9]You will be arrested, punished, and even killed. Because of me, you will be hated by people of all nations. [10]Many will give up and will betray and hate each other. [11]Many false prophets will come and fool a lot of people. [12]Evil will spread and cause many people to stop loving others. [13]But if you keep on being faithful right to the end, you will be saved. [14]When the good news about the kingdom has been preached all over the world and told to all nations, the end will come.

The Horrible Thing
(Mark 13.14-23; Luke 21.20-24)

[15]Someday you will see that "Horrible Thing" in the holy place, just as the prophet Daniel said. Everyone who reads this must try to understand! [16]If you are living in Judea at that time, run to the mountains. [17]If you are on the roof[o] of your house, don't go inside to get anything. [18]If you are out in the field, don't go back for your coat. [19]It will be a ter-

---

[m]**23.27** *whitewashed*: Tombs were whitewashed to keep anyone from accidentally touching them. A person who touched a dead body or a tomb was considered unclean and could not worship with the rest of the Jewish people. [n]**23.35** *Zechariah*: Genesis is the first book in the Jewish Scriptures, and it tells that Abel was the first person to be murdered. Second Chronicles is the last book in the Jewish Scriptures, and the last murder that it tells about is that of Zechariah. [o]**24.17** *roof*: In Palestine the houses usually had a flat roof. Stairs on the outside led up to the roof, which was made of beams and boards covered with packed earth.

rible time for women who are expecting babies or nursing young children. 20And pray that you won't have to escape in winter or on a Sabbath.p 21This will be the worst time of suffering since the beginning of the world, and nothing this terrible will ever happen again. 22If God doesn't make the time shorter, no one will be left alive. But because of God's chosen ones, he will make the time shorter.

23Someone may say, "Here is the Messiah!" or "There he is!" But don't believe it. 24False messiahs and false prophets will come and work great miracles and signs. They will even try to fool God's chosen ones. 25But I have warned you ahead of time. 26If you are told that the Messiah is out in the desert, don't go there! And if you are told that he is in some secret place, don't believe it! 27The coming of the Son of Man will be like lightning that can be seen from east to west. 28Where there is a corpse, there will always be buzzards.q

When the Son of Man Appears
(Mark 13.24-27; Luke 21.25-28)

29Right after those days of suffering,

"The sun will become dark,
and the moon
 will no longer shine.
The stars will fall,
and the powers in the skyr
 will be shaken."

30Then a sign will appear in the sky. And there will be the Son of Man.s All nations on earth will weep when they see the Son of Man coming on the clouds of heaven with power and great glory. 31At the sound of a loud trumpet, he will send his angels to bring his chosen ones together from all over the earth.

A Lesson from a Fig Tree
(Mark 13.28-31; Luke 21.29-33)

32Learn a lesson from a fig tree. When its branches sprout and start putting out leaves, you know that summer is near. 33So when you see all these things happening, you will know that the time has almost come.t 34I can promise you that some of the people of this generation will still be alive when all this happens. 35The sky and the earth won't last forever, but my words will.

No One Knows the Day or Time
(Mark 13.32-37; Luke 17.26-30, 34-36)

36No one knows the day or hour. The angels in heaven don't know, and the Son himself doesn't know.u Only the Father knows. 37When the Son of Man appears, things will be just as they were when Noah lived. 38People were eating, drinking, and getting married right up to the day that the flood came and Noah went into the big boat. 39They didn't know anything was happening until the flood came and swept them all away. That is how it will be when the Son of Man appears.

40Two men will be in the same field, but only one will be taken. The other will be left. 41Two women will be together grinding grain, but only one will be taken. The other will be left. 42So be on your guard! You don't know when your Lord will come. 43Homeowners never know when a thief is coming, and they are always on guard to keep one from breaking in. 44Always be ready! You don't know when the Son of Man will come.

Faithful and Unfaithful Servants
(Luke 12.35-48)

45Who are faithful and wise servants? Who are the ones the master will put in charge of giving the other servants their food supplies at the proper time? 46Servants are fortunate if their master comes and finds them doing their job. 47You may be sure that a servant who is always faithful will be put in charge of everything the master owns. 48But suppose one of the servants thinks that the master won't return until late. 49Suppose that evil servant

---

p**24.20** *in winter or on a Sabbath*: In Palestine the winters are cold and rainy and make travel difficult. The Jewish people were not allowed to travel much more than half a mile on the Sabbath. For these reasons it was hard for them to escape from their enemies in the winter or on a Sabbath. q**24.28** *Where there is a corpse, there will always be buzzards*: This saying may mean that when anything important happens, people soon know about it. Or the saying may mean that whenever something bad happens, curious people gather around and stare. But the word translated "buzzard" also means "eagle" and may refer to the Roman army, which had an eagle as its symbol. r**24.29** *the powers in the sky*: In ancient times people thought that the stars were spiritual powers. s**24.30** *And there will be the Son of Man*: Or "And it will be the Son of Man." t**24.33** *the time has almost come*: Or "he (that is, the Son of Man) will soon be here." u**24.36** *and the Son himself doesn't know*: These words are not in some manuscripts.

starts beating the other servants and eats and drinks with people who are drunk. ⁵⁰If that happens, the master will surely come on a day and at a time when the servant least expects him. ⁵¹That servant will then be punished and thrown out with the ones who only pretended to serve their master. There they will cry and grit their teeth in pain.

A Story about Ten Girls

25 The kingdom of heaven is like what happened one night when ten girls took their oil lamps and went to a wedding to meet the groom.ᵛ ²Five of the girls were foolish and five were wise. ³The foolish ones took their lamps, but no extra oil. ⁴The ones who were wise took along extra oil for their lamps.

⁵The groom was late arriving, and the girls became drowsy and fell asleep. ⁶Then in the middle of the night someone shouted, "Here's the groom! Come to meet him!"

⁷When the girls got up and started getting their lamps ready, ⁸the foolish ones said to the others, "Let us have some of your oil! Our lamps are going out."

⁹The girls who were wise answered, "There's not enough oil for all of us! Go and buy some for yourselves."

¹⁰While the foolish girls were on their way to get some oil, the groom arrived. The girls who were ready went into the wedding, and the doors were closed. ¹¹Later the other girls returned and shouted, "Sir, sir! Open the door for us!"

¹²But the groom replied, "I don't even know you!"

¹³So, my disciples, always be ready! You don't know the day or the time when all this will happen.

A Story about Three Servants
(Luke 19.11-27)

¹⁴The kingdom is also like what happened when a man went away and put his three servants in charge of all he owned. ¹⁵The man knew what each servant could do. So he handed five thousand coins to the first servant, two thousand to the second, and one thousand to the third. Then he left the country.

¹⁶As soon as the man had gone, the servant with the five thousand coins used them to earn five thousand more. ¹⁷The servant who had two thousand coins did the same with his money and earned two thousand more. ¹⁸But the servant with one thousand coins dug a hole and hid his master's money in the ground.

¹⁹Some time later the master of those servants returned. He called them in and asked what they had done with his money. ²⁰The servant who had been given five thousand coins brought them in with the five thousand that he had earned. He said, "Sir, you gave me five thousand coins, and I have earned five thousand more."

²¹"Wonderful!" his master replied. "You are a good and faithful servant. I left you in charge of only a little, but now I will put you in charge of much more. Come and share in my happiness!"

²²Next, the servant who had been given two thousand coins came in and said, "Sir, you gave me two thousand coins, and I have earned two thousand more."

²³"Wonderful!" his master replied. "You are a good and faithful servant. I left you in charge of only a little, but now I will put you in charge of much more. Come and share in my happiness!"

²⁴The servant who had been given one thousand coins then came in and said, "Sir, I know that you are hard to get along with. You harvest what you don't plant and gather crops where you haven't scattered seed. ²⁵I was frightened and went out and hid your money in the ground. Here is every single coin!"

²⁶The master of the servant told him, "You are lazy and good-for-nothing! You know that I harvest what I don't plant and gather crops where I haven't scattered seed. ²⁷You could have at least put my money in the bank, so that I could have earned interest on it."

²⁸Then the master said, "Now your money will be taken away and given to the servant with ten thousand coins! ²⁹Everyone who has something will be given more, and they will have more than enough. But everything will be taken from those who don't have anything. ³⁰You are a worthless servant, and you will be thrown out into the dark where people will cry and grit their teeth in pain."

ᵛ**25.1** *to meet the groom*: Some manuscripts add "and the bride." It was the custom for the groom to go to the home of the bride's parents to get his bride. Young girls and other guests would then go with them to the home of the groom's parents, where the wedding feast would take place.

The Final Judgment

31 When the Son of Man comes in his glory with all of his angels, he will sit on his royal throne. 32 The people of all nations will be brought before him, and he will separate them, as shepherds separate their sheep from their goats.

33 He will place the sheep on his right and the goats on his left. 34 Then the king will say to those on his right, "My father has blessed you! Come and receive the kingdom that was prepared for you before the world was created. 35 When I was hungry, you gave me something to eat, and when I was thirsty, you gave me something to drink. When I was a stranger, you welcomed me, 36 and when I was naked, you gave me clothes to wear. When I was sick, you took care of me, and when I was in jail, you visited me."

37 Then the ones who pleased the Lord will ask, "When did we give you something to eat or drink? 38 When did we welcome you as a stranger or give you clothes to wear 39 or visit you while you were sick or in jail?"

40 The king will answer, "Whenever you did it for any of my people, no matter how unimportant they seemed, you did it for me."

41 Then the king will say to those on his left, "Get away from me! You are under God's curse. Go into the everlasting fire prepared for the devil and his angels! 42 I was hungry, but you did not give me anything to eat, and I was thirsty, but you did not give me anything to drink. 43 I was a stranger, but you did not welcome me, and I was naked, but you did not give me any clothes to wear. I was sick and in jail, but you did not take care of me."

44 Then the people will ask, "Lord, when did we fail to help you when you were hungry or thirsty or a stranger or naked or sick or in jail?"

45 The king will say to them, "Whenever you failed to help any of my people, no matter how unimportant they seemed, you failed to do it for me."

46 Then Jesus said, "Those people will be punished forever. But the ones who pleased God will have eternal life."

The Plot To Kill Jesus
(Mark 14.1, 2; Luke 22.1, 2; John 11.45-53)

26 When Jesus had finished teaching, he told his disciples, 2 "You know that two days from now will be Passover. That is when the Son of Man will be handed over to his enemies and nailed to a cross."

3 At that time the chief priests and the nation's leaders were meeting at the home of Caiaphas the high priest. 4 They planned how they could sneak around and have Jesus arrested and put to death. 5 But they said, "We must not do it during Passover, because the people will riot."

At Bethany
(Mark 14.3-9; John 12.1-8)

6 Jesus was in the town of Bethany, eating at the home of Simon, who had leprosy.[w] 7 A woman came in with a bottle of expensive perfume and poured it on Jesus' head. 8 But when his disciples saw this, they became angry and complained, "Why such a waste? 9 We could have sold this perfume for a lot of money and given it to the poor."

10 Jesus knew what they were thinking, and he said:

Why are you bothering this woman? She has done a beautiful thing for me. 11 You will always have the poor with you, but you won't always have me. 12 She has poured perfume on my body to prepare it for burial.[x] 13 You may be sure that wherever the good news is told all over the world, people will remember what she has done. And they will tell others.

Judas and the Chief Priests
(Mark 14.10, 11; Luke 22.3-6)

14 Judas Iscariot[y] was one of the twelve disciples. He went to the chief priests 15 and asked, "How much will you give me if I help you arrest Jesus?" They paid Judas thirty silver coins, 16 and from then on he started looking for a good chance to betray Jesus.

Jesus Eats the Passover Meal with His Disciples
(Mark 14.12-21; Luke 22.7-13; John 13.21-30)

17 On the first day of the Festival of Thin Bread, Jesus' disciples came to him and asked, "Where do you want us to prepare the Passover meal?"

18 Jesus told them to go to a certain man in the city and tell him, "Our teacher says, 'My time has come! I want to eat the Passover meal with my disciples in your home.' " 19 They did as Jesus told them and prepared the meal.

20-21 When Jesus was eating with his twelve disciples that evening, he said, "One of you will surely hand me over to my enemies."

---

[w] **26.6** *leprosy*: See the note at 8.2. [x] **26.12** *poured perfume on my body to prepare it for burial*: The Jewish people taught that giving someone a proper burial was even more important than helping the poor. [y] **26.14** *Iscariot*: See the note at 10.4.

²²The disciples were very sad, and each one said to Jesus, "Lord, you can't mean me!"

²³He answered, "One of you men who has eaten with me from this dish will betray me. ²⁴The Son of Man will die, as the Scriptures say. But it's going to be terrible for the one who betrays me! That man would be better off if he had never been born."

²⁵Judas said, "Teacher, you surely don't mean me!"

"That's what you say!" Jesus replied. But later, Judas did betray him.

The Lord's Supper
(Mark 14.22-26; Luke 22.14-23; 1 Corinthians 11.23-25)

²⁶During the meal Jesus took some bread in his hands. He blessed the bread and broke it. Then he gave it to his disciples and said, "Take this and eat it. This is my body."

²⁷Jesus picked up a cup of wine and gave thanks to God. He then gave it to his disciples and said, "Take this and drink it. ²⁸This is my blood, and with it God makes his agreement with you. It will be poured out, so that many people will have their sins forgiven. ²⁹From now on I am not going to drink any wine, until I drink new wine with you in my Father's kingdom." ³⁰Then they sang a hymn and went out to the Mount of Olives.

Peter's Promise
(Mark 14.27-31; Luke 22.31-34; John 13.36-38)

³¹Jesus said to his disciples, "During this very night, all of you will reject me, as the Scriptures say,

'I will strike down
   the shepherd,
and the sheep
   will be scattered.'

³²But after I am raised to life, I will go to Galilee ahead of you."

³³Peter spoke up, "Even if all the others reject you, I never will!"

³⁴Jesus replied, "I promise you that before a rooster crows tonight, you will say three times that you don't know me." ³⁵But Peter said, "Even if I have to die with you, I will never say I don't know you."

All the others said the same thing.

Jesus Prays
(Mark 14.32-42; Luke 22.39-46)

³⁶Jesus went with his disciples to a place called Gethsemane. When they got there, he told them, "Sit here while I go over there and pray."

³⁷Jesus took along Peter and the two brothers, James and John.[z] He was very sad and troubled, ³⁸and he said to them, "I am so sad that I feel as if I am dying. Stay here and keep awake with me."

³⁹Jesus walked on a little way. Then he knelt with his face to the ground and prayed, "My Father, if it is possible, don't make me suffer by having me drink from this cup.[a] But do what you want, and not what I want."

⁴⁰He came back and found his disciples sleeping. So he said to Peter, "Can't any of you stay awake with me for just one hour? ⁴¹Stay awake and pray that you won't be tested. You want to do what is right, but you are weak."

⁴²Again Jesus went to pray and said, "My Father, if there is no other way, and I must suffer, I will still do what you want."

⁴³Jesus came back and found them sleeping again. They simply could not keep their eyes open. ⁴⁴He left them and prayed the same prayer once more.

⁴⁵Finally, Jesus returned to his disciples and said, "Are you still sleeping and resting?[b] The time has come for the Son of Man to be handed over to sinners. ⁴⁶Get up! Let's go. The one who will betray me is already here."

Jesus Is Arrested
(Mark 14.43-50; Luke 22.47-53; John 18.3-12)

⁴⁷Jesus was still speaking, when Judas the betrayer came up. He was one of the twelve disciples, and a large mob armed with swords and clubs was with him. They had been sent by the chief priests and the nation's leaders. ⁴⁸Judas had told them ahead of time, "Arrest the man I greet with a kiss."[c]

⁴⁹Judas walked right up to Jesus and said, "Hello, teacher." Then Judas kissed him.

⁵⁰Jesus replied, "My friend, why are you here?"[d]

The men grabbed Jesus and arrested him. ⁵¹One of Jesus' followers pulled out a sword. He struck the servant of the high priest and cut off his ear.

⁵²But Jesus told him, "Put your sword away. Anyone who lives by fighting will die by fighting. ⁵³Don't you know that I could ask my Father, and right away he would send me more than twelve armies of angels? ⁵⁴But then, how could the words of the Scriptures come true, which say that this must happen?"

---

[z]**26.37** *the two brothers, James and John*: The Greek text has "the two sons of Zebedee" (see 27.56).   [a]**26.39** *having me drink from this cup*: In the Scriptures "to drink from a cup" sometimes means to suffer (see the note at 20.22).   [b]**26.45** *Are you still sleeping and resting?*: Or "You may as well keep on sleeping and resting."   [c]**26.48** *the man I greet with a kiss*: It was the custom for people to greet each other with a kiss on the cheek.   [d]**26.50** *why are you here?*: Or "do what you came for."

⁵⁵Jesus said to the mob, "Why do you come with swords and clubs to arrest me like a criminal? Day after day I sat and taught in the temple, and you didn't arrest me. ⁵⁶But all this happened, so that what the prophets wrote would come true."

All of Jesus' disciples left him and ran away.

Jesus Is Questioned by the Council
(Mark 14.53-65; Luke 22.54, 55, 63-71; John 18.13, 14, 19-24)

⁵⁷After Jesus had been arrested, he was led off to the house of Caiaphas the high priest. The nation's leaders and the teachers of the Law of Moses were meeting there. ⁵⁸But Peter followed along at a distance and came to the courtyard of the high priest's palace. He went in and sat down with the guards to see what was going to happen.

⁵⁹The chief priests and the whole council wanted to put Jesus to death. So they tried to find some people who would tell lies about him in court.ᵉ ⁶⁰But they could not find any, even though many did come and tell lies. At last, two men came forward ⁶¹and said, "This man claimed that he would tear down God's temple and build it again in three days."

⁶²The high priest stood up and asked Jesus, "Why don't you say something in your own defense? Don't you hear the charges they are making against you?" ⁶³But Jesus did not answer. So the high priest said, "With the living God looking on, you must tell the truth. Tell us, are you the Messiah, the Son of God?"ᶠ

⁶⁴"That is what you say!" Jesus answered. "But I tell all of you,

'Soon you will see
    the Son of Man
sitting at the right sideᵍ
    of God All-Powerful
and coming on the clouds
    of heaven.'"

⁶⁵The high priest then tore his robe and said, "This man claims to be God! We don't need any more witnesses! You have heard what he said. ⁶⁶What do you think?"

They answered, "He is guilty and deserves to die!" ⁶⁷Then they spit in his face and hit him with their fists. Others slapped him ⁶⁸and said, "You think you are the Messiah! So tell us who hit you!"

Peter Says He Doesn't Know Jesus
(Mark 14.66-72; Luke 22.56-62; John 18.15-18, 25-27)

⁶⁹While Peter was sitting out in the courtyard, a servant girl came up to him and said, "You were with Jesus from Galilee."

⁷⁰But in front of everyone Peter said, "That isn't so! I don't know what you are talking about!"

⁷¹When Peter had gone out to the gate, another servant girl saw him and said to some people there, "This man was with Jesus from Nazareth."

⁷²Again Peter denied it, and this time he swore, "I don't even know that man!"

⁷³A little while later some people standing there walked over to Peter and said, "We know that you are one of them. We can tell it because you talk like someone from Galilee."

⁷⁴Peter began to curse and swear, "I don't know that man!"

Right then a rooster crowed, ⁷⁵and Peter remembered that Jesus had said, "Before a rooster crows, you will say three times that you don't know me." Then Peter went out and cried hard.

Jesus Is Taken to Pilate
(Mark 15.1; Luke 23.1, 2; John 18.28-32)

27 Early the next morning all the chief priests and the nation's leaders met and decided that Jesus should be put to death. ²They tied him up and led him away to Pilate the governor.

The Death of Judas
(Acts 1.18, 19)

³Judas had betrayed Jesus, but when he learned that Jesus had been sentenced to death, he was sorry for what he had done. He returned the thirty silver coins to the chief priests and leaders ⁴and said, "I have sinned by betraying a man who has never done anything wrong."

"So what? That's your problem," they replied. ⁵Judas threw the money into the temple and then went out and hanged himself.

⁶The chief priests picked up the money and said, "This money was paid to have a man killed. We can't put it in the temple treasury." ⁷Then they had a meeting and decided to buy a field that belonged to someone who made clay pots. They wanted to use it as a graveyard for foreigners. ⁸That's why people still call that place "Field of Blood." ⁹So the words of the prophet Jeremiah came true,

"They took
    the thirty silver coins,
the price of a person
    among the people of Israel.

ᵉ**26.59** *some people who would tell lies about him in court*: The Law of Moses taught that two witnesses were necessary before a person could be put to death (see verse 60).   ᶠ**26.63** *Son of God*: One of the titles used for the kings of Israel.   ᵍ**26.64** *right side*: See the note at 22.44.

¹⁰ They paid it
for a potter's field,ʰ
as the Lord
had commanded me."

Pilate Questions Jesus
(Mark 15.2-5; Luke 23.3-5; John 18.33-38)

¹¹Jesus was brought before Pilate the governor, who asked him, "Are you the king of the Jews?"

"Those are your words!" Jesus answered. ¹²And when the chief priests and leaders brought their charges against him, he did not say a thing.

¹³Pilate asked him, "Don't you hear what crimes they say you have done?" ¹⁴But Jesus did not say anything, and the governor was greatly amazed.

The Death Sentence
(Mark 15.6-15; Luke 23.13-26; John 18.39—19.16)

¹⁵During Passover the governor always freed a prisoner chosen by the people. ¹⁶At that time a well-known terrorist named Jesus Barabbasⁱ was in jail. ¹⁷So when the crowd came together, Pilate asked them, "Which prisoner do you want me to set free? Do you want Jesus Barabbas or Jesus who is called the Messiah?" ¹⁸Pilate knew that the leaders had brought Jesus to him because they were jealous.

¹⁹While Pilate was judging the case, his wife sent him a message. It said, "Don't have anything to do with that innocent man. I have had nightmares because of him."

²⁰But the chief priests and the leaders convinced the crowds to ask for Barabbas to be set free and for Jesus to be killed. ²¹Pilate asked the crowd again, "Which of these two men do you want me to set free?"

"Barabbas!" they replied.

²²Pilate asked them, "What am I to do with Jesus, who is called the Messiah?"

They all yelled, "Nail him to a cross!"

²³Pilate answered, "But what crime has he done?"

"Nail him to a cross!" they yelled even louder.

²⁴Pilate saw that there was nothing he could do and that the people were starting to riot. So he took some water and washed his handsʲ in front of them and said, "I won't have anything to do with killing this man. You are the ones doing it!"

²⁵Everyone answered, "We and our own families will take the blame for his death!"

²⁶Pilate set Barabbas free. Then he ordered his soldiers to beat Jesus with a whip and nail him to a cross.

Soldiers Make Fun of Jesus
(Mark 15.16-21; John 19.2, 3)

²⁷The governor's soldiers led Jesus into the fortressᵏ and brought together the rest of the troops. ²⁸They stripped off Jesus' clothes and put a scarlet robeˡ on him. ²⁹They made a crown out of thorn branches and placed it on his head, and they put a stick in his right hand. The soldiers knelt down and pretended to worship him. They made fun of him and shouted, "Hey, you king of the Jews!" ³⁰Then they spit on him. They took the stick from him and beat him on the head with it.

Jesus Is Nailed to a Cross
(Mark 15.22-32; Luke 23.27-43; John 19.17-27)

³¹When the soldiers had finished making fun of Jesus, they took off the robe. They put his own clothes back on him and led him off to be nailed to a cross. ³²On the way they met a man from Cyrene named Simon, and they forced him to carry Jesus' cross.

³³They came to a place named Golgotha, which means "Place of a Skull."ᵐ ³⁴There they gave Jesus some wine mixed with a drug to ease the pain. But when Jesus tasted what it was, he refused to drink it.

³⁵The soldiers nailed Jesus to a cross and gambled to see who would get his clothes. ³⁶Then they sat down to guard him. ³⁷Above his head they put a sign that told why he was nailed there. It read, "This is Jesus, the King of the Jews." ³⁸The soldiers also nailed two criminals on crosses, one to the right of Jesus and the other to his left.

³⁹People who passed by said terrible things about Jesus. They shook their heads and ⁴⁰shouted, "So you're the one who claimed you could tear down the temple and build it again in three days! If you are God's Son, save yourself and come down from the cross!"

⁴¹The chief priests, the leaders, and the teachers of the Law of Moses also

---

ʰ**27.10** *a potter's field*: Perhaps a field owned by someone who made clay pots. But it may have been a field where potters came to get clay or to make pots or to throw away their broken pieces of pottery.   ⁱ**27.16** *Jesus Barabbas*: Here and in verse 17 many manuscripts have "Barabbas."   ʲ**27.24** *washed his hands*: To show that he was innocent.   ᵏ**27.27** *fortress*: The place where the Roman governor stayed. It was probably at Herod's palace west of Jerusalem, though it may have been Fortress Antonia north of the temple, where the Roman troops were stationed.   ˡ**27.28** *scarlet robe*: This was probably a Roman soldier's robe.   ᵐ**27.33** *Place of a Skull*: The place was probably given this name because it was near a large rock in the shape of a human skull.

made fun of Jesus. They said, [42]"He saved others, but he can't save himself. If he is the king of Israel, he should come down from the cross! Then we will believe him. [43]He trusted God, so let God save him, if he wants to. He even said he was God's Son." [44]The two criminals also said cruel things to Jesus.

The Death of Jesus
(Mark 15.33-41; Luke 23.44-49; John 19.28-30)

[45]At noon the sky turned dark and stayed that way until three o'clock. [46]Then about that time Jesus shouted, "Eli, Eli, lema sabachthani?"[n] which means, "My God, my God, why have you deserted me?"
[47]Some of the people standing there heard Jesus and said, "He's calling for Elijah."[o] [48]One of them at once ran and grabbed a sponge. He soaked it in wine, then put it on a stick and held it up to Jesus.
[49]Others said, "Wait! Let's see if Elijah will come[p] and save him." [50]Once again Jesus shouted, and then he died.
[51]At once the curtain in the temple[q] was torn in two from top to bottom. The earth shook, and rocks split apart. [52]Graves opened, and many of God's people were raised to life. [53]Then after Jesus had risen to life, they came out of their graves and went into the holy city, where they were seen by many people.
[54]The officer and the soldiers guarding Jesus felt the earthquake and saw everything else that happened. They were frightened and said, "This man really was God's Son!"
[55]Many women had come with Jesus from Galilee to be of help to him, and they were there, looking on at a distance. [56]Mary Magdalene, Mary the mother of James and Joseph, and the mother of James and John[r] were some of these women.

Jesus Is Buried
(Mark 15.42-47; Luke 23.50-56; John 19.38-42)

[57]That evening a rich disciple named Joseph from the town of Arimathea [58]went and asked for Jesus' body. Pilate gave orders for it to be given to Joseph, [59]who took the body and wrapped it in a clean linen cloth. [60]Then Joseph put the body in his own tomb that had been cut into solid rock[s] and had never been used. He rolled a big stone against the entrance to the tomb and went away.
[61]All this time Mary Magdalene and the other Mary were sitting across from the tomb.
[62]On the next day, which was a Sabbath, the chief priests and the Pharisees went together to Pilate. [63]They said, "Sir, we remember what that liar said while he was still alive. He claimed that in three days he would come back from death. [64]So please order the tomb to be carefully guarded for three days. If you don't, his disciples may come and steal his body. They will tell the people that he has been raised to life, and this last lie will be worse than the first one."[t]
[65]Pilate said to them, "All right, take some of your soldiers and guard the tomb as well as you know how." [66]So they sealed it tight and placed soldiers there to guard it.

Jesus Is Alive
(Mark 16.1-8; Luke 24.1-12; John 20.1-10)

28 The Sabbath was over, and it was almost daybreak on Sunday when Mary Magdalene and the other Mary went to see the tomb. [2]Suddenly a strong earthquake struck, and the Lord's angel came down from heaven. He rolled away the stone and sat on it. [3]The angel looked as bright as lightning, and his clothes were white as snow. [4]The guards shook from fear and fell down, as though they were dead.
[5]The angel said to the women, "Don't be afraid! I know you are looking for Jesus, who was nailed to a cross. [6]He isn't here! God has raised him to life, just as Jesus said he would. Come, see the place where his body was lying. [7]Now hurry! Tell his disciples that he has been raised to life and is on his way to Galilee. Go there, and you will see him. That is what I came to tell you."
[8]The women were frightened and yet very happy, as they hurried from the tomb and ran to tell his disciples. [9]Suddenly Jesus met them and greeted them. They went near him, held on to his feet, and worshiped him. [10]Then Jesus said, "Don't be afraid! Tell my

---

[n]**27.46** *Eli . . . sabachthani*: These words are in Hebrew. [o]**27.47** *Elijah*: In Aramaic the name "Elijah" sounds like "Eli," which means "my God." [p]**27.49** *Elijah will come*: See the note at 16.14. [q]**27.51** *curtain in the temple*: There were two curtains in the temple. One was at the entrance, and the other separated the holy place from the most holy place that the Jewish people thought of as God's home on earth. The second curtain is probably the one that is meant. [r]**27.56** *of James and John*: The Greek text has "of Zebedee's sons" (see 26.37). [s]**27.60** *tomb . . . solid rock*: Some of the Jewish people buried their dead in rooms carved into solid rock. A heavy stone was rolled against the entrance. [t]**27.64** *the first one*: Probably the belief that Jesus is the Messiah.

Matthew 28.11 — 40

followers to go to Galilee. They will see me there."

Report of the Guard

¹¹While the women were on their way, some soldiers who had been guarding the tomb went into the city. They told the chief priests everything that had happened. ¹²So the chief priests met with the leaders and decided to bribe the soldiers with a lot of money. ¹³They said to the soldiers, "Tell everyone that Jesus' disciples came during the night and stole his body while you were asleep. ¹⁴If the governor[u] hears about this, we will talk to him. You won't have anything to worry about." ¹⁵The soldiers took the money and did what they were told. The people of Judea still tell each other this story.

[u]**28.14** *governor*: Pontius Pilate.

What Jesus' Followers Must Do
(Mark 16.14-18; Luke 24.36-49; John 20.19-23; Acts 1.6-8)

¹⁶Jesus' eleven disciples went to a mountain in Galilee, where Jesus had told them to meet him. ¹⁷They saw him and worshiped him, but some of them doubted.

¹⁸Jesus came to them and said:

I have been given all authority in heaven and on earth! ¹⁹Go to the people of all nations and make them my disciples. Baptize them in the name of the Father, the Son, and the Holy Spirit, ²⁰and teach them to do everything I have told you. I will be with you always, even until the end of the world.

MARK

ABOUT THIS BOOK

This is the shortest of the four New Testament books that tell about the life and teachings of Jesus, but it is also the most action-packed. From the very beginning of his ministry, Jesus worked mighty wonders. After choosing four followers (1.16-20), he immediately performed many miracles of healing. Among those healed were a man with an evil spirit in him (1.21-28), Simon's mother-in-law (1.30, 31), crowds of sick people (1.32-34), and a man with leprosy (1.40-45). Over and over Mark tells how Jesus healed people, but always in such a way as to show that he did these miracles by the power of God.

The religious leaders refused to accept Jesus. This led to conflicts (2.2—3.6) that finally made them start looking for a way to kill him (11.18). But the demons saw the power of Jesus, and they knew that he was the Son of God, although Jesus would not let them tell anyone.

This book is full of miracles that amazed the crowds and Jesus' followers. But, according to Mark, the most powerful miracle of Jesus is his suffering and death. The first person to understand this miracle was the Roman soldier who saw Jesus die on the cross and said, "This man really was the Son of God!" (15.39).

This Gospel is widely thought to be the first one written. The many explanations of Aramaic words and Jewish customs in Mark suggest that Mark wrote to Gentile or non-Jewish Christians. He wants to tell about Jesus and to encourage readers to believe in the power of Jesus to rescue them from sickness, demons, and death. He also wants to remind them that the new life of faith is not an easy life, and that they must follow Jesus by serving others and being ready to suffer as he did.

The first followers of Jesus to discover the empty tomb were three women, and the angel told them:

> Don't be alarmed! You are looking for Jesus from Nazareth, who was nailed to a cross. God has raised him to life, and he isn't here. (16.6)

A QUICK LOOK AT THIS BOOK

The Message of John the Baptist (1.1-8)
The Baptism and Temptation of Jesus (1.9-13)
Jesus in Galilee (1.14—9.50)
Jesus Goes from Galilee to Jerusalem (10.1-52)
Jesus' Last Week: His Trial and Death (11.1—15.47)
Jesus Is Alive (16.1-8)
Jesus Appears to His Followers (16.9-20)

The Preaching of John the Baptist
(Matthew 3.1-12; Luke 3.1-18; John 1.19-28)

1 This is the good news about Jesus Christ, the Son of God.[a] ²It began just as God had said in the book written by Isaiah the prophet,

"I am sending my messenger
  to get the way ready
    for you.
³ In the desert
  someone is shouting,
'Get the road ready
  for the Lord!

---

[a] 1.1 *the Son of God*: These words are not in some manuscripts.

Mark 1.4

Make a straight path for him.'"

[4] So John the Baptist showed up in the desert and told everyone, "Turn back to God and be baptized! Then your sins will be forgiven."

[5] From all Judea and Jerusalem crowds of people went to John. They told how sorry they were for their sins, and he baptized them in the Jordan River.

[6] John wore clothes made of camel's hair. He had a leather strap around his waist and ate grasshoppers and wild honey.

[7] John also told the people, "Someone more powerful is going to come. And I am not good enough even to stoop down and untie his sandals.[b] [8] I baptize you with water, but he will baptize you with the Holy Spirit!"

The Baptism of Jesus
(Matthew 3.13-17; Luke 3.21, 22)

[9] About that time Jesus came from Nazareth in Galilee, and John baptized him in the Jordan River. [10] As soon as Jesus came out of the water, he saw the sky open and the Holy Spirit coming down to him like a dove. [11] A voice from heaven said, "You are my own dear Son, and I am pleased with you."

Jesus and Satan
(Matthew 4.1-11; Luke 4.1-13)

[12] Right away God's Spirit made Jesus go into the desert. [13] He stayed there for forty days while Satan tested him. Jesus was with the wild animals, but angels took care of him.

Jesus Begins His Work
(Matthew 4.12-17; Luke 4.14, 15)

[14] After John was arrested, Jesus went to Galilee and told the good news that comes from God.[c] [15] He said, "The time has come! God's kingdom will soon be here.[d] Turn back to God and believe the good news!"

Jesus Chooses Four Fishermen
(Matthew 4.18-22; Luke 5.1-11)

[16] As Jesus was walking along the shore of Lake Galilee, he saw Simon and his brother Andrew. They were fishermen and were casting their nets into the lake. [17] Jesus said to them, "Come with me! I will teach you how to bring in people instead of fish." [18] Right then the two brothers dropped their nets and went with him.

[19] Jesus walked on and soon saw James and John, the sons of Zebedee. They were in a boat, mending their nets. [20] At once Jesus asked them to come with him. They left their father in the boat with the hired workers and went with him.

A Man with an Evil Spirit
(Luke 4.31-37)

[21] Jesus and his disciples went to the town of Capernaum. Then on the next Sabbath he went into the Jewish meeting place and started teaching. [22] Everyone was amazed at his teaching. He taught with authority, and not like the teachers of the Law of Moses. [23] Suddenly a man with an evil spirit[e] in him entered the meeting place and yelled, [24] "Jesus from Nazareth, what do you want with us? Have you come to destroy us? I know who you are! You are God's Holy One."

[25] Jesus told the evil spirit, "Be quiet and come out of the man!" [26] The spirit shook him. Then it gave a loud shout and left.

[27] Everyone was completely surprised and kept saying to each other, "What is this? It must be some new kind of powerful teaching! Even the evil spirits obey him." [28] News about Jesus quickly spread all over Galilee.

Jesus Heals Many People
(Matthew 8.14-17; Luke 4.38-41)

[29] As soon as Jesus left the meeting place with James and John, they went home with Simon and Andrew. [30] When they got there, Jesus was told that Simon's mother-in-law was sick in bed with fever. [31] Jesus went to her. He took hold of her hand and helped her up. The fever left her, and she served them a meal.

[32] That evening after sunset,[f] all who were sick or had demons in them were brought to Jesus. [33] In fact, the whole town gathered around the door of the house. [34] Jesus healed all kinds of terrible diseases and forced out a lot of demons. But the demons knew who he was, and he did not let them speak.

[35] Very early the next morning, Jesus got up and went to a place where he could be alone and pray. [36] Simon and the others started looking for him. [37] And when they found him, they said, "Everyone is looking for you!"

[38] Jesus replied, "We must go to the nearby towns, so that I can tell the good news to those people. This is why I have

---

[b] 1.7 *untie his sandals*: This was the duty of a slave.   [c] 1.14 *that comes from God*: Or "that is about God."   [d] 1.15 *will soon be here*: Or "is already here."   [e] 1.23 *evil spirit*: A Jewish person who had an evil spirit was considered "unclean" and was not allowed to eat or worship with other Jewish people.   [f] 1.32 *after sunset*: The Sabbath was over, and a new day began at sunset.

come." ³⁹Then Jesus went to Jewish meeting places everywhere in Galilee, where he preached and forced out demons.

Jesus Heals a Man
(Matthew 8.1-4; Luke 5.12-16)

⁴⁰A man with leprosy⁸ came to Jesus and knelt down.ʰ He begged, "You have the power to make me well, if only you wanted to."

⁴¹Jesus felt sorry forⁱ the man. So he put his hand on him and said, "I want to! Now you are well." ⁴²At once the man's leprosy disappeared, and he was well.

⁴³After Jesus strictly warned the man, he sent him on his way. ⁴⁴He said, "Don't tell anyone about this. Just go and show the priest that you are well. Then take a gift to the temple as Moses commanded, and everyone will know that you have been healed."ʲ

⁴⁵The man talked about it so much and told so many people, that Jesus could no longer go openly into a town. He had to stay away from the towns, but people still came to him from everywhere.

Jesus Heals a Crippled Man
(Matthew 9.1-8; Luke 5.17-26)

2 Jesus went back to Capernaum, and a few days later people heard that he was at home.ᵏ ²Then so many of them came to the house that there wasn't even standing room left in front of the door.

Jesus was still teaching ³when four people came up, carrying a crippled man on a mat. ⁴But because of the crowd, they could not get him to Jesus. So they made a hole in the roofˡ above him and let the man down in front of everyone.

⁵When Jesus saw how much faith they had, he said to the crippled man, "My friend, your sins are forgiven."

⁶Some of the teachers of the Law of Moses were sitting there. They started wondering, ⁷"Why would he say such a thing? He must think he is God! Only God can forgive sins."

⁸Right away, Jesus knew what they were thinking, and he said, "Why are you thinking such things? ⁹Is it easier for me to tell this crippled man that his sins are forgiven or to tell him to get up and pick up his mat and go on home? ¹⁰I will show you that the Son of Man has the right to forgive sins here on earth." So Jesus said to the man, ¹¹"Get up! Pick up your mat and go on home."

¹²The man got right up. He picked up his mat and went out while everyone watched in amazement. They praised God and said, "We have never seen anything like this!"

Jesus Chooses Levi
(Matthew 9.9-13; Luke 5.27-32)

¹³Once again, Jesus went to the shore of Lake Galilee. A large crowd gathered around him, and he taught them. ¹⁴As he walked along, he saw Levi, the son of Alphaeus. Levi was sitting at the place for paying taxes, and Jesus said to him, "Come with me!" So he got up and went with Jesus.

¹⁵Later, Jesus and his disciples were having dinner at Levi's house.ᵐ Many tax collectorsⁿ and other sinners had become followers of Jesus, and they were also guests at the dinner.

¹⁶Some of the teachers of the Law of Moses were Pharisees, and they saw that Jesus was eating with sinners and tax collectors. So they asked his disciples, "Why does he eat with tax collectors and sinners?"

¹⁷Jesus heard them and answered, "Healthy people don't need a doctor, but sick people do. I didn't come to invite good people to be my followers. I came to invite sinners."

People Ask about Going without Eating
(Matthew 9.14-17; Luke 5.33-39)

¹⁸The followers of John the Baptist and the Pharisees often went without eating.ᵒ Some people came and asked Jesus, "Why do the followers of John and those of the Pharisees often go without eating, while your disciples never do?"

¹⁹Jesus answered:

ᵍ1.40 *leprosy*: In biblical times the word "leprosy" was used for many different kinds of skin diseases. ʰ1.40 *and knelt down*: These words are not in some manuscripts. ⁱ1.41 *felt sorry for*: Some manuscripts have "was angry with." ʲ1.44 *everyone will know that you have been healed*: People with leprosy had to be examined by a priest and told that they were well (that is, "clean") before they could once again live a normal life in the Jewish community. The gift that Moses commanded was the sacrifice of some lambs together with flour mixed with olive oil. ᵏ2.1 *at home*: Or "in the house" (perhaps Simon Peter's home). ˡ2.4 *roof*: In Palestine the houses usually had a flat roof. Stairs on the outside led up to the roof that was made of beams and boards covered with packed earth. ᵐ2.15 *Levi's house*: Or "Jesus' house." ⁿ2.15 *tax collectors*: These were usually Jewish people who paid the Romans for the right to collect taxes. They were hated by other Jews who thought of them as traitors to their country and to their religion. ᵒ2.18 *without eating*: The Jewish people sometimes went without eating (also called "fasting") to show their love for God or to show sorrow for their sins.

The friends of a bridegroom don't go without eating while he is still with them. [20]But the time will come when he will be taken from them. Then they will go without eating.

[21]No one patches old clothes by sewing on a piece of new cloth. The new piece would shrink and tear a bigger hole.

[22]No one pours new wine into old wineskins. The wine would swell and burst the old skins.[p] Then the wine would be lost, and the skins would be ruined. New wine must be put into new wineskins.

A Question about the Sabbath
(Matthew 12.1-8; Luke 6.1-5)

[23]One Sabbath Jesus and his disciples were walking through some wheat fields. His disciples were picking grains of wheat as they went along.[q] [24]Some Pharisees asked Jesus, "Why are your disciples picking grain on the Sabbath? They are not supposed to do that!"

[25]Jesus answered, "Haven't you read what David did when he and his followers were hungry and in need? [26]It was during the time of Abiathar the high priest. David went into the house of God and ate the sacred loaves of bread that only priests are allowed to eat. He also gave some to his followers."

[27]Jesus finished by saying, "People were not made for the good of the Sabbath. The Sabbath was made for the good of people. [28]So the Son of Man is Lord over the Sabbath."

A Man with a Crippled Hand
(Matthew 12.9-14; Luke 6.6-11)

3 The next time that Jesus went into the meeting place, a man with a crippled hand was there. [2]The Pharisees[r] wanted to accuse Jesus of doing something wrong, and they kept watching to see if Jesus would heal him on the Sabbath.

[3]Jesus told the man to stand up where everyone could see him. [4]Then he asked, "On the Sabbath should we do good deeds or evil deeds? Should we save someone's life or destroy it?" But no one said a word.

[5]Jesus was angry as he looked around at the people. Yet he felt sorry for them because they were so stubborn. Then he told the man, "Stretch out your hand." He did, and his bad hand was healed.

[6]The Pharisees left. And right away they started making plans with Herod's followers[s] to kill Jesus.

Large Crowds Come to Jesus

[7]Jesus led his disciples down to the shore of the lake. Large crowds followed him from Galilee, Judea, [8]and Jerusalem. People came from Idumea, as well as other places east of the Jordan River. They also came from the region around the cities of Tyre and Sidon. All of these crowds came because they had heard what Jesus was doing. [9]He even had to tell his disciples to get a boat ready to keep him from being crushed by the crowds.

[10]After Jesus had healed many people, the other sick people begged him to let them touch him. [11]And whenever any evil spirits saw Jesus, they would fall to the ground and shout, "You are the Son of God!" [12]But Jesus warned the spirits not to tell who he was.

Jesus Chooses His Twelve Apostles
(Matthew 10.1-4; Luke 6.12-16)

[13]Jesus decided to ask some of his disciples to go up on a mountain with him, and they went. [14]Then he chose twelve of them to be his apostles,[t] so that they could be with him. He also wanted to send them out to preach [15]and to force out demons. [16]Simon was one of the twelve, and Jesus named him Peter. [17]There were also James and John, the two sons of Zebedee. Jesus called them Boanerges, which means "Thunderbolts." [18]Andrew, Philip, Bartholomew, Matthew, Thomas, James son of Alphaeus, and Thaddaeus were also apostles. The others were Simon, known as the Eager One,[u] [19]and Judas Iscariot,[v] who later betrayed Jesus.

Jesus and the Ruler of Demons
(Matthew 12.22-32; Luke 11.14-23; 12.10)

[20]Jesus went back home,[w] and once again such a large crowd gathered that

---

[p]2.22 *swell and burst the old skins*: While the juice from grapes was becoming wine, it would swell and stretch the skins in which it had been stored. If the skins were old and stiff, they would burst. [q]2.23 *went along*: It was the custom to let hungry travelers pick grains of wheat. [r]3.2 *Pharisees*: The Greek text has "they" (but see verse 6). [s]3.6 *Herod's followers*: People who were political followers of the family of Herod the Great and his son Herod Antipas. [t]3.14 *to be his apostles*: These words are not in some manuscripts. [u]3.18. *Eager One*: The Greek text has "Zealot," a name later given to the members of a Jewish group that resisted and fought against the Romans. [v]3.19 *Iscariot*: This may mean "a man from Kerioth" (a place in Judea). But more probably it means "a man who was a liar" or "a man who was a betrayer." [w]3.20 *went back home*: Or "entered a house" (perhaps the home of Simon Peter).

there was no chance even to eat. ²¹When Jesus' family heard what he was doing, they thought he was crazy and went to get him under control.

²²Some teachers of the Law of Moses came from Jerusalem and said, "This man is under the power of Beelzebul, the ruler of demons! He is even forcing out demons with the help of Beelzebul."

²³Jesus told the people to gather around him. Then he spoke to them in riddles and said:

How can Satan force himself out? ²⁴A nation whose people fight each other won't last very long. ²⁵And a family that fights won't last long either. ²⁶So if Satan fights against himself, that will be the end of him.

²⁷How can anyone break into the house of a strong man and steal his things, unless he first ties up the strong man? Then he can take everything.

²⁸I promise you that any of the sinful things you say or do can be forgiven, no matter how terrible those things are. ²⁹But if you speak against the Holy Spirit, you can never be forgiven. That sin will be held against you forever.

³⁰Jesus said this because the people were saying that he had an evil spirit in him.

Jesus' Mother and Brothers
(Matthew 12.46-50; Luke 8.19-21)

³¹Jesus' mother and brothers came and stood outside. Then they sent someone with a message for him to come out to them. ³²The crowd that was sitting around Jesus told him, "Your mother and your brothers and sisters˟ are outside and want to see you."

³³Jesus asked, "Who is my mother and who are my brothers?" ³⁴Then he looked at the people sitting around him and said, "Here are my mother and my brothers. ³⁵Anyone who obeys God is my brother or sister or mother."

A Story about a Farmer
(Matthew 13.1-9; Luke 8.4-8)

4 The next time Jesus taught beside Lake Galilee, a big crowd gathered. It was so large that he had to sit in a boat out on the lake, while the people stood on the shore. ²He used stories to teach them many things, and this is part of what he taught:

³Now listen! A farmer went out to scatter seed in a field. ⁴While the farmer was scattering the seed, some of it fell along the road and was eaten by birds. ⁵Other seeds fell on thin, rocky ground and quickly started growing because the soil wasn't very deep. ⁶But when the sun came up, the plants were scorched and dried up, because they did not have enough roots. ⁷Some other seeds fell where thornbushes grew up and choked out the plants. So they did not produce any grain. ⁸But a few seeds did fall on good ground where the plants grew and produced thirty or sixty or even a hundred times as much as was scattered.

⁹Then Jesus said, "If you have ears, pay attention."

Why Jesus Used Stories
(Matthew 13.10-17; Luke 8.9, 10)

¹⁰When Jesus was alone with the twelve apostles and some others, they asked him about these stories. ¹¹He answered:

I have explained the secret about God's kingdom to you, but for others I can use only stories. ¹²The reason is,

"These people will look
 and look, but never see.
They will listen and listen,
 but never understand.
If they did,
they would turn to God,
 and he would forgive them."

Jesus Explains the Story about the Farmer
(Matthew 13.18-23; Luke 8.11-15)

¹³Jesus told them:

If you don't understand this story, you won't understand any others. ¹⁴What the farmer is spreading is really the message about the kingdom. ¹⁵The seeds that fell along the road are the people who hear the message. But Satan soon comes and snatches it away from them. ¹⁶The seeds that fell on rocky ground are the people who gladly hear the message and accept it right away. ¹⁷But they don't have any roots, and they don't last very long. As soon as life gets hard or the message gets them in trouble, they give up.

¹⁸The seeds that fell among the thornbushes are also people who hear the message. ¹⁹But they start worrying about the needs of this life. They are fooled by the desire to get rich and to have all kinds of other things. So the message gets choked out, and they never produce anything. ²⁰The seeds that fell on good ground are the people who hear and welcome the message. They produce thirty or sixty or even a hundred times as much as was planted.

˟3.32 *and sisters*: These words are not in some manuscripts.

Light
(Luke 8.16-18)

²¹Jesus also said:

You don't light a lamp and put it under a clay pot or under a bed. Don't you put a lamp on a lampstand? ²²There is nothing hidden that will not be made public. There is no secret that will not be well known. ²³If you have ears, pay attention!

²⁴Listen carefully to what you hear! The way you treat others will be the way you will be treated—and even worse. ²⁵Everyone who has something will be given more. But people who don't have anything will lose what little they have.

Another Story about Seeds

²⁶Again Jesus said:

God's kingdom is like what happens when a farmer scatters seed in a field. ²⁷The farmer sleeps at night and is up and around during the day. Yet the seeds keep sprouting and growing, and he doesn't understand how. ²⁸It is the ground that makes the seeds sprout and grow into plants that produce grain. ²⁹Then when harvest season comes and the grain is ripe, the farmer cuts it with a sickle.ʸ

A Mustard Seed
(Matthew 13.31, 32; Luke 13.18, 19)

³⁰Finally, Jesus said:

What is God's kingdom like? What story can I use to explain it? ³¹It is like what happens when a mustard seed is planted in the ground. It is the smallest seed in all the world. ³²But once it is planted, it grows larger than any garden plant. It even puts out branches that are big enough for birds to nest in its shade.

The Reason for Teaching with Stories
(Matthew 13.34, 35)

³³Jesus used many other stories when he spoke to the people, and he taught them as much as they could understand. ³⁴He did not tell them anything without using stories. But when he was alone with his disciples, he explained everything to them.

A Storm
(Matthew 8.23-27; Luke 8.22-25)

³⁵That evening, Jesus said to his disciples, "Let's cross to the east side." ³⁶So they left the crowd, and his disciples started across the lake with him in the boat. Some other boats followed along. ³⁷Suddenly a windstorm struck the lake. Waves started splashing into the boat, and it was about to sink.

³⁸Jesus was in the back of the boat with his head on a pillow, and he was asleep. His disciples woke him and said, "Teacher, don't you care that we're about to drown?"

³⁹Jesus got up and ordered the wind and the waves to be quiet. The wind stopped, and everything was calm. ⁴⁰Jesus asked his disciples, "Why were you afraid? Don't you have any faith?"

⁴¹Now they were more afraid than ever and said to each other, "Who is this? Even the wind and the waves obey him!"

A Man with Evil Spirits
(Matthew 8.28-34; Luke 8.26-39)

5 Jesus and his disciples crossed Lake Galilee and came to shore near the town of Gerasa.ᶻ ²When he was getting out of the boat, a man with an evil spirit quickly ran to him ³from the graveyardᵃ where he had been living. No one was able to tie the man up anymore, not even with a chain. ⁴He had often been put in chains and leg irons, but he broke the chains and smashed the leg irons. No one could control him. ⁵Night and day he was in the graveyard or on the hills, yelling and cutting himself with stones.

⁶When the man saw Jesus in the distance, he ran up to him and knelt down. ⁷He shouted, "Jesus, Son of God in heaven, what do you want with me? Promise me in God's name that you won't torture me!" ⁸The man said this because Jesus had already told the evil spirit to come out of him.

⁹Jesus asked, "What is your name?"

The man answered, "My name is Lots, because I have 'lots' of evil spirits." ¹⁰He then begged Jesus not to send them away.

¹¹Over on the hillside a large herd of pigs was feeding. ¹²So the evil spirits begged Jesus, "Send us into those pigs! Let us go into them." ¹³Jesus let them go, and they went out of the man and into the pigs. The whole herd of about two thousand pigs rushed down the steep bank into the lake and drowned.

¹⁴The men taking care of the pigs ran to the town and the farms to spread the news. Then the people came out to see what had happened. ¹⁵When they came to Jesus, they saw the man who had once been full of demons. He was sitting there with his clothes on and in his right mind, and they were terrified.

ʸ4.29 *sickle*: A knife with a long curved blade, used to cut grain and other crops.
ᶻ5.1 *Gerasa*: Some manuscripts have "Gadara," and others have "Gergesa." ᵃ5.3 *graveyard*: It was thought that demons and evil spirits lived in graveyards.

¹⁶Everyone who had seen what had happened told about the man and the pigs. ¹⁷Then the people started begging Jesus to leave their part of the country. ¹⁸When Jesus was getting into the boat, the man begged to go with him. ¹⁹But Jesus would not let him. Instead, he said, "Go home to your family and tell them how much the Lord has done for you and how good he has been to you." ²⁰The man went away into the region near the ten cities known as Decapolis[b] and began telling everyone how much Jesus had done for him. Everyone who heard what had happened was amazed.

A Dying Girl and a Sick Woman
(Matthew 9.18-26; Luke 8.40-56)

²¹Once again Jesus got into the boat and crossed Lake Galilee.[c] Then as he stood on the shore, a large crowd gathered around him. ²²The person in charge of the Jewish meeting place was also there. His name was Jairus, and when he saw Jesus, he went over to him. He knelt at Jesus' feet ²³and started begging him for help. He said, "My daughter is about to die! Please come and touch her, so she will get well and live." ²⁴Jesus went with Jairus. Many people followed along and kept crowding around.

²⁵In the crowd was a woman who had been bleeding for twelve years. ²⁶She had gone to many doctors, and they had not done anything except cause her a lot of pain. She had paid them all the money she had. But instead of getting better, she only got worse.

²⁷The woman had heard about Jesus, so she came up behind him in the crowd and barely touched his clothes. ²⁸She had said to herself, "If I can just touch his clothes, I will get well." ²⁹As soon as she touched them, her bleeding stopped, and she knew she was well.

³⁰At that moment Jesus felt power go out from him. He turned to the crowd and asked, "Who touched my clothes?"

³¹His disciples said to him, "Look at all these people crowding around you! How can you ask who touched you?" ³²But Jesus turned to see who had touched him.

³³The woman knew what had happened to her. She came shaking with fear and knelt down in front of Jesus. Then she told him the whole story.

³⁴Jesus said to the woman, "You are now well because of your faith. May God give you peace! You are healed, and you will no longer be in pain."

³⁵While Jesus was still speaking, some men came from Jairus' home and said, "Your daughter has died! Why bother the teacher anymore?"

³⁶Jesus heard[d] what they said, and he said to Jairus, "Don't worry. Just have faith!"

³⁷Jesus did not let anyone go with him except Peter and the two brothers, James and John. ³⁸They went home with Jairus and saw the people crying and making a lot of noise.[e] ³⁹Then Jesus went inside and said to them, "Why are you crying and carrying on like this? The child isn't dead. She is just asleep." ⁴⁰But the people laughed at him.

After Jesus had sent them all out of the house, he took the girl's father and mother and his three disciples and went to where she was. ⁴¹⁻⁴²He took the twelve-year-old girl by the hand and said, "Talitha, koum!"[f] which means, "Little girl, get up!" The girl got right up and started walking around.

Everyone was greatly surprised. ⁴³But Jesus ordered them not to tell anyone what had happened. Then he said, "Give her something to eat."

The People of Nazareth Turn against Jesus
(Matthew 13.53-58; Luke 4.16-30)

6 Jesus left and returned to his hometown[g] with his disciples. ²The next Sabbath he taught in the Jewish meeting place. Many of the people who heard him were amazed and asked, "How can he do all this? Where did he get such wisdom and the power to work these miracles? ³Isn't he the carpenter,[h] the son of Mary? Aren't James, Joseph, Judas, and Simon his brothers? Don't his sisters still live here in our town?" The people were very unhappy because of what he was doing.

⁴But Jesus said, "Prophets are honored by everyone, except the people of their hometown and their relatives and their own family." ⁵Jesus could not work any miracles there, except to heal a few sick people by placing his hands on them. ⁶He was surprised that the people did not have any faith.

Instructions for the Twelve Apostles
(Matthew 10.5-15; Luke 9.1-6)

Jesus taught in all the neighboring villages. ⁷Then he called together his

---

[b]**5.20** *the ten cities known as Decapolis*: A group of ten cities east of Samaria and Galilee, where the people followed the Greek way of life.   [c]**5.21** *crossed Lake Galilee*: To the west side.   [d]**5.36** *heard*: Or "ignored."   [e]**5.38** *crying and making a lot of noise*: The Jewish people often hired mourners for funerals.   [f]**5.41,42** *Talitha, koum*: These words are in Aramaic, a language spoken in Palestine during the time of Jesus.   [g]**6.1** *hometown*: Nazareth.   [h]**6.3** *carpenter*: The Greek word may also mean someone who builds or works with stone or brick.

twelve apostles and sent them out two by two with power over evil spirits. ⁸He told them, "You may take along a walking stick. But don't carry food or a traveling bag or any money. ⁹It's all right to wear sandals, but don't take along a change of clothes. ¹⁰When you are welcomed into a home, stay there until you leave that town. ¹¹If any place won't welcome you or listen to your message, leave and shake the dust from your feet[i] as a warning to them."

¹²The apostles left and started telling everyone to turn to God. ¹³They forced out many demons and healed a lot of sick people by putting olive oil[j] on them.

The Death of John the Baptist
(Matthew 14.1-12; Luke 9.7-9)

¹⁴Jesus became so well-known that Herod the ruler[k] heard about him. Some people thought he was John the Baptist, who had come back to life with the power to work miracles. ¹⁵Others thought he was Elijah[l] or some other prophet who had lived long ago. ¹⁶But when Herod heard about Jesus, he said, "This must be John! I had his head cut off, and now he has come back to life."

¹⁷⁻¹⁸Herod had earlier married Herodias, the wife of his brother Philip. But John had told him, "It isn't right for you to take your brother's wife!" So, in order to please Herodias, Herod arrested John and put him in prison.

¹⁹Herodias had a grudge against John and wanted to kill him. But she could not do it ²⁰because Herod was afraid of John and protected him. He knew that John was a good and holy man. Even though Herod was confused by what John said,[m] he was glad to listen to him. And he often did.

²¹Finally, Herodias got her chance when Herod gave a great birthday celebration for himself and invited his officials, his army officers, and the leaders of Galilee. ²²The daughter of Herodias[n] came in and danced for Herod and his guests. She pleased them so much that Herod said, "Ask for anything, and it's yours! ²³I swear that I will give you as much as half of my kingdom, if you want it."

²⁴The girl left and asked her mother, "What do you think I should ask for?"

Her mother answered, "The head of John the Baptist!"

²⁵The girl hurried back and told Herod, "Right now on a platter I want the head of John the Baptist!"

²⁶The king was very sorry for what he had said. But he did not want to break the promise he had made in front of his guests. ²⁷At once he ordered a guard to cut off John's head there in prison. ²⁸The guard put the head on a platter and took it to the girl. Then she gave it to her mother.

²⁹When John's followers learned that he had been killed, they took his body and put it in a tomb.

Jesus Feeds Five Thousand
(Matthew 14.13-21; Luke 9.10-17; John 6.1-14)

³⁰After the apostles returned to Jesus,[o] they told him everything they had done and taught. ³¹But so many people were coming and going that Jesus and the apostles did not even have a chance to eat. Then Jesus said, "Let's go to a place[p] where we can be alone and get some rest." ³²They left in a boat for a place where they could be alone. ³³But many people saw them leave and figured out where they were going. So people from every town ran on ahead and got there first.

³⁴When Jesus got out of the boat, he saw the large crowd that was like sheep without a shepherd. He felt sorry for the people and started teaching them many things.

³⁵That evening the disciples came to Jesus and said, "This place is like a desert, and it is already late. ³⁶Let the crowds leave, so they can go to the farms and villages near here and buy something to eat."

³⁷Jesus replied, "You give them something to eat."

But they asked him, "Don't you know that it would take almost a year's wages[q] to buy all of these people something to eat?"

³⁸Then Jesus said, "How much bread do you have? Go and see!"

They found out and answered, "We have five small loaves of bread[r] and two fish." ³⁹Jesus told his disciples to have the people sit down on the green grass.

---

[i]**6.11** *shake the dust from your feet*: This was a way of showing rejection. [j]**6.13** *olive oil*: The Jewish people used olive oil as a way of healing people. Sometimes olive oil is a symbol for healing by means of a miracle (see James 5.14). [k]**6.14** *Herod the ruler*: Herod Antipas, the son of Herod the Great. [l]**6.15** *Elijah*: Many of the Jewish people expected the prophet Elijah to come and prepare the way for the Messiah. [m]**6.20** *was confused by what John said*: Some manuscripts have "did many things because of what John said." [n]**6.22** *Herodias*: Some manuscripts have "Herod." [o]**6.30** *the apostles returned to Jesus*: From the mission on which he had sent them (see 6.7, 12, 13). [p]**6.31** *a place*: This was probably northeast of Lake Galilee (see verse 45). [q]**6.37** *almost a year's wages*: The Greek text has "two hundred silver coins." Each coin was the average day's wage for a worker. [r]**6.38** *small loaves of bread*: These would have been flat and round or in the shape of a bun.

⁴⁰They sat down in groups of a hundred and groups of fifty. ⁴¹Jesus took the five loaves and the two fish. He looked up toward heaven and blessed the food. Then he broke the bread and handed it to his disciples to give to the people. He also divided the two fish, so that everyone could have some.

⁴²After everyone had eaten all they wanted, ⁴³Jesus' disciples picked up twelve large baskets of leftover bread and fish.

⁴⁴There were five thousand men who ate the food.

Jesus Walks on the Water
(Matthew 14.22-33; John 6.15-21)

⁴⁵Right away, Jesus made his disciples get into the boat and start back across to Bethsaida. But he stayed until he had sent the crowds away. ⁴⁶Then he told them good-by and went up on the side of a mountain to pray.

⁴⁷Later that evening he was still there by himself, and the boat was somewhere in the middle of the lake. ⁴⁸He could see that the disciples were struggling hard, because they were rowing against the wind. Not long before morning, Jesus came toward them. He was walking on the water and was about to pass the boat.

⁴⁹When the disciples saw Jesus walking on the water, they thought he was a ghost, and they started screaming. ⁵⁰All of them saw him and were terrified. But at that same time he said, "Don't worry! I am Jesus. Don't be afraid." ⁵¹He then got into the boat with them, and the wind died down. The disciples were completely confused. ⁵²Their minds were closed, and they could not understand the true meaning of the loaves of bread.

Jesus Heals Sick People in Gennesaret
(Matthew 14.34-36)

⁵³Jesus and his disciples crossed the lake and brought the boat to shore near the town of Gennesaret. ⁵⁴As soon as they got out of the boat, the people recognized Jesus. ⁵⁵So they ran all over that part of the country to bring their sick people to him on mats. They brought them each time they heard where he was. ⁵⁶In every village or farm or marketplace where Jesus went, the people brought their sick to him. They begged him to let them just touch his clothes, and everyone who did was healed.

The Teaching of the Ancestors
(Matthew 15.1-9)

7 Some Pharisees and several teachers of the Law of Moses from Jerusalem came and gathered around Jesus. ²They noticed that some of his disciples ate without first washing their hands.ˢ

³The Pharisees and many other Jewish people obey the teachings of their ancestors. They always wash their hands in the proper wayᵗ before eating. ⁴None of them will eat anything they buy in the market until it is washed. They also follow a lot of other teachings, such as washing cups, pitchers, and bowls.ᵘ

⁵The Pharisees and teachers asked Jesus, "Why don't your disciples obey what our ancestors taught us to do? Why do they eat without washing their hands?"

⁶Jesus replied:
You are nothing but show-offs! The prophet Isaiah was right when he wrote that God had said,

"All of you praise me
   with your words,
but you never really
   think about me.
⁷ It is useless for you
   to worship me,
when you teach rules
   made up by humans."

⁸You disobey God's commands in order to obey what humans have taught. ⁹You are good at rejecting God's commands so that you can follow your own teachings! ¹⁰Didn't Moses command you to respect your father and mother? Didn't he tell you to put to death all who curse their parents? ¹¹But you let people get by without helping their parents when they should. You let them say that what they own has been offered to God.ᵛ ¹²You won't let those people help their parents. ¹³And you ignore God's commands in order to follow your own teaching. You do a lot of other things that are just as bad.

What Really Makes People Unclean
(Matthew 15.10-20)

¹⁴Jesus called the crowd together again and said, "Pay attention and try to understand what I mean. ¹⁵⁻¹⁶The food that you put into your mouth doesn't

---

ˢ**7.2** *without first washing their hands*: The Jewish people had strict laws about washing their hands before eating, especially if they had been out in public.   ᵗ**7.3** *in the proper way*: The Greek text has "with the fist," but the exact meaning is not clear. It could mean "to the wrist" or "to the elbow."   ᵘ**7.4** *bowls*: Some manuscripts add "and sleeping mats."   ᵛ**7.11** *has been offered to God*: According to Jewish custom, when anything was offered to God, it could not be used for anyone else, not even for a person's parents.

make you unclean and unfit to worship God. The bad words that come out of your mouth are what make you unclean."[w]

[17]After Jesus and his disciples had left the crowd and had gone into the house, they asked him what these sayings meant. [18]He answered, "Don't you know what I am talking about by now? You surely know that the food you put into your mouth cannot make you unclean. [19]It doesn't go into your heart, but into your stomach, and then out of your body." By saying this, Jesus meant that all foods were fit to eat.

[20]Then Jesus said:

What comes from your heart is what makes you unclean. [21]Out of your heart come evil thoughts, vulgar deeds, stealing, murder, [22]unfaithfulness in marriage, greed, meanness, deceit, indecency, envy, insults, pride, and foolishness. [23]All of these come from your heart, and they are what make you unfit to worship God.

A Woman's Faith
(Matthew 15.21-28)

[24]Jesus left and went to the region near the city of Tyre, where he stayed in someone's home. He did not want people to know he was there, but they found out anyway. [25]A woman whose daughter had an evil spirit in her heard where Jesus was. And right away she came and knelt down at his feet. [26]The woman was Greek and had been born in the part of Syria known as Phoenicia. She begged Jesus to force the demon out of her daughter. [27]But Jesus said, "The children must first be fed! It isn't right to take away their food and feed it to dogs."[x]

[28]The woman replied, "Lord, even dogs eat the crumbs that children drop from the table."

[29]Jesus answered, "That's true! You may go now. The demon has left your daughter." [30]When the woman got back home, she found her child lying on the bed. The demon had gone.

Jesus Heals a Man Who Was Deaf and Could Hardly Talk

[31]Jesus left the region around Tyre and went by way of Sidon toward Lake Galilee. He went through the land near the ten cities known as Decapolis.[y] [32]Some people brought to him a man who was deaf and could hardly talk. They begged Jesus just to touch him.

[33]After Jesus had taken him aside from the crowd, he stuck his fingers in the man's ears. Then he spit and put it on the man's tongue. [34]Jesus looked up toward heaven, and with a groan he said, "Effatha!"[z] which means "Open up!" [35]At once the man could hear, and he had no more trouble talking clearly.

[36]Jesus told the people not to say anything about what he had done. But the more he told them, the more they talked about it. [37]They were completely amazed and said, "Everything he does is good! He even heals people who cannot hear or talk."

Jesus Feeds Four Thousand
(Matthew 15.32-39)

8 One day another large crowd gathered around Jesus. They had not brought along anything to eat. So Jesus called his disciples together and said, [2]"I feel sorry for these people. They have been with me for three days, and they don't have anything to eat. [3]Some of them live a long way from here. If I send them away hungry, they might faint on their way home."

[4]The disciples said, "This place is like a desert. Where can we find enough food to feed such a crowd?"

[5]Jesus asked them how much food they had. They replied, "Seven small loaves of bread."[a]

[6]After Jesus told the crowd to sit down, he took the seven loaves and blessed them. He then broke the loaves and handed them to his disciples, who passed them out to the crowd. [7]They also had a few little fish, and after Jesus had blessed these, he told the disciples to pass them around.

[8-9]The crowd of about four thousand people ate all they wanted, and the leftovers filled seven large baskets.

As soon as Jesus had sent the people away, [10]he got into the boat with the disciples and crossed to the territory near Dalmanutha.[b]

A Sign from Heaven
(Matthew 16.1-4)

[11]The Pharisees came out and started an argument with Jesus. They wanted to test him by asking for a sign from heaven. [12]Jesus groaned and said, "Why are you always looking for a sign? I can promise you that you will not be given one!" [13]Then he left them. He again got into a boat and crossed over to the other side of the lake.

---

[w] *7.15,16 unclean:* Some manuscripts add, "If you have ears, pay attention."   [x] *7.27 feed it to dogs:* The Jewish people often referred to Gentiles as dogs.   [y] *7.31 the ten cities known as Decapolis:* See the note at 5.20.   [z] *7.34 Effatha:* This word is in Aramaic, a language spoken in Palestine during the time of Jesus.   [a] *8.5 small loaves of bread:* See the note at 6.38.
[b] *8.10 Dalmanutha:* The place is unknown.

The Yeast of the Pharisees and of Herod
(Matthew 16.5-12)

[14] The disciples had forgotten to bring any bread, and they had only one loaf with them in the boat. [15] Jesus warned them, "Watch out! Guard against the yeast of the Pharisees and of Herod."[c]
[16] The disciples talked this over and said to each other, "He must be saying this because we don't have any bread."
[17] Jesus knew what they were thinking and asked, "Why are you talking about not having any bread? Don't you understand? Are your minds still closed? [18] Are your eyes blind and your ears deaf? Don't you remember [19] how many baskets of leftovers you picked up when I fed those five thousand people with only five small loaves of bread?"

"Yes," the disciples answered. "There were twelve baskets."

[20] Jesus then asked, "And how many baskets of leftovers did you pick up when I broke seven small loaves of bread for those four thousand people?"

"Seven," they answered.

[21] "Don't you know what I am talking about by now?" Jesus asked.

Jesus Heals a Blind Man at Bethsaida

[22] As Jesus and his disciples were going into Bethsaida, some people brought a blind man to him and begged him to touch the man. [23] Jesus took him by the hand and led him out of the village, where he spit into the man's eyes. He placed his hands on the blind man and asked him if he could see anything. [24] The man looked up and said, "I see people, but they look like trees walking around."

[25] Once again Jesus placed his hands on the man's eyes, and this time the man stared. His eyes were healed, and he saw everything clearly. [26] Jesus said to him, "You may return home now, but don't go into the village."

Who Is Jesus?
(Matthew 16.13-20; Luke 9.18-21)

[27] Jesus and his disciples went to the villages near the town of Caesarea Philippi. As they were walking along, he asked them, "What do people say about me?"

[28] The disciples answered, "Some say you are John the Baptist or maybe Elijah.[d] Others say you are one of the prophets."

[29] Then Jesus asked them, "But who do you say I am?"

"You are the Messiah!" Peter replied.

[30] Jesus warned the disciples not to tell anyone about him.

Jesus Speaks about His Suffering and Death
(Matthew 16.21-28; Luke 9.22-27)

[31] Jesus began telling his disciples what would happen to him. He said, "The nation's leaders, the chief priests, and the teachers of the Law of Moses will make the Son of Man suffer terribly. He will be rejected and killed, but three days later he will rise to life." [32] Then Jesus explained clearly what he meant.

Peter took Jesus aside and told him to stop talking like that. [33] But when Jesus turned and saw the disciples, he corrected Peter. He said to him, "Satan, get away from me! You are thinking like everyone else and not like God."

[34] Jesus then told the crowd and the disciples to come closer, and he said:

If any of you want to be my followers, you must forget about yourself. You must take up your cross and follow me. [35] If you want to save your life,[e] you will destroy it. But if you give up your life for me and for the good news, you will save it. [36] What will you gain, if you own the whole world but destroy yourself? [37] What could you give to get back your soul?

[38] Don't be ashamed of me and my message among these unfaithful and sinful people! If you are, the Son of Man will be ashamed of you when he comes in the glory of his Father with the holy angels.

9 I can assure you that some of the people standing here will not die before they see God's kingdom come with power.

The True Glory of Jesus
(Matthew 17.1-13; Luke 9.28-36)

[2] Six days later Jesus took Peter, James, and John with him. They went up on a high mountain, where they could be alone. There in front of the disciples, Jesus was completely changed. [3] And his clothes became much whiter than any bleach on earth could make them. [4] Then Moses and Elijah were there talking with Jesus.

[5] Peter said to Jesus, "Teacher, it is good for us to be here! Let us make three shelters, one for you, one for Moses, and one for Elijah." [6] But Peter and the others were terribly frightened, and he did not know what he was talking about.

[7] The shadow of a cloud passed over and covered them. From the cloud a voice said, "This is my Son, and I love him. Listen to what he says!" [8] At once

---

[c] **8.15** *Herod:* Herod Antipas, the son of Herod the Great.   [d] **8.28** *Elijah:* See the note at 6.15.
[e] **8.35** *life:* In verses 35-37 the same Greek word is translated "life," "yourself," and "soul."

the disciples looked around, but they saw only Jesus.

⁹As Jesus and his disciples were coming down the mountain, he told them not to say a word about what they had seen, until the Son of Man had been raised from death. ¹⁰So they kept it to themselves. But they wondered what he meant by the words "raised from death."

¹¹The disciples asked Jesus, "Don't the teachers of the Law of Moses say that Elijah must come before the Messiah does?"

¹²Jesus answered:

Elijah certainly will come[f] to get everything ready. But don't the Scriptures also say that the Son of Man must suffer terribly and be rejected? ¹³I can assure you that Elijah has already come. And people treated him just as they wanted to, as the Scriptures say they would.

Jesus Heals a Boy
(Matthew 17.14-20; Luke 9.37-43a)

¹⁴When Jesus and his three disciples came back down, they saw a large crowd around the other disciples. The teachers of the Law of Moses were arguing with them. ¹⁵The crowd was really surprised to see Jesus, and everyone hurried over to greet him.

¹⁶Jesus asked, "What are you arguing about?"

¹⁷Someone from the crowd answered, "Teacher, I brought my son to you. A demon keeps him from talking. ¹⁸Whenever the demon attacks my son, it throws him to the ground and makes him foam at the mouth and grit his teeth in pain. Then he becomes stiff. I asked your disciples to force out the demon, but they couldn't do it."

¹⁹Jesus said, "You people don't have any faith! How much longer must I be with you? Why do I have to put up with you? Bring the boy to me."

²⁰They brought the boy, and as soon as the demon saw Jesus, it made the boy shake all over. He fell down and began rolling on the ground and foaming at the mouth.

²¹Jesus asked the boy's father, "How long has he been like this?"

The man answered, "Ever since he was a child. ²²The demon has often tried to kill him by throwing him into a fire or into water. Please have pity and help us if you can!"

²³Jesus replied, "Why do you say 'if you can'? Anything is possible for someone who has faith!"

²⁴Right away the boy's father shouted, "I do have faith! Please help me to have even more."

²⁵When Jesus saw that a crowd was gathering fast, he spoke sternly to the evil spirit that had kept the boy from speaking or hearing. He said, "I order you to come out of the boy! Don't ever bother him again."

²⁶The spirit screamed and made the boy shake all over. Then it went out of him. The boy looked dead, and almost everyone said he was. ²⁷But Jesus took hold of his hand and helped him stand up.

²⁸After Jesus and the disciples had gone back home and were alone, they asked him, "Why couldn't we force out that demon?"

²⁹Jesus answered, "Only prayer can force out that kind of demon."

Jesus Again Speaks about His Death
(Matthew 17.22, 23; Luke 9.43b-45)

³⁰Jesus left with his disciples and started through Galilee. He did not want anyone to know about it, ³¹because he was teaching the disciples that the Son of Man would be handed over to people who would kill him. But three days later he would rise to life. ³²The disciples did not understand what Jesus meant, and they were afraid to ask.

Who Is the Greatest?
(Matthew 18.1-5; Luke 9.46-48)

³³Jesus and his disciples went to his home in Capernaum. After they were inside the house, Jesus asked them, "What were you arguing about along the way?" ³⁴They had been arguing about which one of them was the greatest, and so they did not answer.

³⁵After Jesus sat down and told the twelve disciples to gather around him, he said, "If you want the place of honor, you must become a slave and serve others!"

³⁶Then Jesus had a child stand near him. He put his arm around the child and said, ³⁷"When you welcome even a child because of me, you welcome me. And when you welcome me, you welcome the one who sent me."

For or against Jesus
(Luke 9.49, 50)

³⁸John said, "Teacher, we saw a man using your name to force demons out of people. But he wasn't one of us, and we told him to stop."

³⁹Jesus said to his disciples:

Don't stop him! No one who works miracles in my name will soon turn and say something bad about me. ⁴⁰Anyone who isn't against us is for us. ⁴¹And anyone who gives you a cup of water in my

---

[f]9.12 *Elijah certainly will come*: See the note at 6.15.

name, just because you belong to me, will surely be rewarded.

Temptations To Sin
(Matthew 18.6-9; Luke 17.1, 2)

⁴²It will be terrible for people who cause even one of my little followers to sin. Those people would be better off thrown into the ocean with a heavy stone tied around their necks. ⁴³⁻⁴⁴So if your hand causes you to sin, cut it off! You would be better off to go into life crippled than to have two hands and be thrown into the fires of hell that never go out.ᵍ ⁴⁵⁻⁴⁶If your foot causes you to sin, chop it off. You would be better off to go into life lame than to have two feet and be thrown into hell.ʰ ⁴⁷If your eye causes you to sin, get rid of it. You would be better off to go into God's kingdom with only one eye than to have two eyes and be thrown into hell. ⁴⁸The worms there never die, and the fire never stops burning.

⁴⁹Everyone must be salted with fire.ⁱ

⁵⁰Salt is good. But if it no longer tastes like salt, how can it be made salty again? Have salt among you and live at peace with each other.ʲ

Teaching about Divorce
(Matthew 19.1-12; Luke 16.18)

10 After Jesus left, he went to Judea and then on to the other side of the Jordan River. Once again large crowds came to him, and as usual, he taught them.

²Some Pharisees wanted to test Jesus. So they came up to him and asked if it was right for a man to divorce his wife. ³Jesus asked them, "What does the Law of Moses say about that?"

⁴They answered, "Moses allows a man to write out divorce papers and send his wife away."

⁵Jesus replied, "Moses gave you this law because you are so heartless. ⁶But in the beginning God made a man and a woman. ⁷That's why a man leaves his father and mother and gets married. ⁸He becomes like one person with his wife. Then they are no longer two people, but one. ⁹And no one should separate a couple that God has joined together."

¹⁰When Jesus and his disciples were back in the house, they asked him about what he had said. ¹¹He told them, "A man who divorces his wife and marries someone else is unfaithful to his wife. ¹²A woman who divorces her husbandᵏ and marries again is also unfaithful."

Jesus Blesses Little Children
(Matthew 19.13-15; Luke 18.15-17)

¹³Some people brought their children to Jesus so that he could bless them by placing his hands on them. But his disciples told the people to stop bothering him.

¹⁴When Jesus saw this, he became angry and said, "Let the children come to me! Don't try to stop them. People who are like these little children belong to the kingdom of God.ˡ ¹⁵I promise you that you cannot get into God's kingdom, unless you accept it the way a child does." ¹⁶Then Jesus took the children in his arms and blessed them by placing his hands on them.

A Rich Man
(Matthew 19.16-30; Luke 18.18-30)

¹⁷As Jesus was walking down a road, a man ran up to him. He knelt down, and asked, "Good teacher, what can I do to have eternal life?"

¹⁸Jesus replied, "Why do you call me good? Only God is good. ¹⁹You know the commandments. 'Do not murder. Be faithful in marriage. Do not steal. Do not tell lies about others. Do not cheat. Respect your father and mother.'"

²⁰The man answered, "Teacher, I have obeyed all these commandments since I was a young man."

²¹Jesus looked closely at the man. He liked him and said, "There's one thing you still need to do. Go sell everything you own. Give the money to the poor, and you will have riches in heaven. Then come with me."

²²When the man heard Jesus say this, he went away gloomy and sad because he was very rich.

²³Jesus looked around and said to his disciples, "It's hard for rich people to get into God's kingdom!" ²⁴The disciples were shocked to hear this. So Jesus told them again, "It's terribly hardᵐ to get

---

ᵍ **9.43,44** *never go out*: Some manuscripts add, "The worms there never die, and the fire never stops burning." ʰ **9.45,46** *thrown into hell*: Some manuscripts add, "The worms there never die, and the fire never stops burning." ⁱ **9.49** *salted with fire*: Some manuscripts add "and every sacrifice will be seasoned with salt." The verse may mean that Christ's followers must suffer because of their faith. ʲ **9.50** *Have salt among you and live at peace with each other*: This may mean that when Christ's followers have to suffer because of their faith, they must still try to live at peace with each other. ᵏ **10.12** *A woman who divorces her husband*: Roman law let a woman divorce her husband, but Jewish law did not let a woman do this. ˡ **10.14** *People who are like these little children belong to the kingdom of God*: Or "The kingdom of God belongs to people who are like these little children." ᵐ **10.24** *hard*: Some manuscripts add "for people who trust in their wealth." Others add "for the rich."

into God's kingdom! ²⁵In fact, it's easier for a camel to go through the eye of a needle than for a rich person to get into God's kingdom."

²⁶Jesus' disciples were even more amazed. They asked each other, "How can anyone ever be saved?"

²⁷Jesus looked at them and said, "There are some things that people cannot do, but God can do anything."

²⁸Peter replied, "Remember, we left everything to be your followers!"

²⁹Jesus told him:

You can be sure that anyone who gives up home or brothers or sisters or mother or father or children or land for me and for the good news ³⁰will be rewarded. In this world they will be given a hundred times as many houses and brothers and sisters and mothers and children and pieces of land, though they will also be mistreated. And in the world to come, they will have eternal life. ³¹But many who are now first will be last, and many who are now last will be first.

Jesus Again Tells about His Death
(Matthew 20.17-19; Luke 18.31-34)

³²The disciples were confused as Jesus led them toward Jerusalem, and his other followers were afraid. Once again, Jesus took the twelve disciples aside and told them what was going to happen to him. He said:

³³We are now on our way to Jerusalem where the Son of Man will be handed over to the chief priests and the teachers of the Law of Moses. They will sentence him to death and hand him over to foreigners,ⁿ ³⁴who will make fun of him and spit on him. They will beat him and kill him. But three days later he will rise to life.

The Request of James and John
(Matthew 20.20-28)

³⁵James and John, the sons of Zebedee, came up to Jesus and asked, "Teacher, will you do us a favor?"

³⁶Jesus asked them what they wanted, ³⁷and they answered, "When you come into your glory, please let one of us sit at your right side and the other at your left."ᵒ

³⁸Jesus told them, "You don't really know what you're asking! Are you able to drink from the cupᵖ that I must soon drink from or be baptized as I must be baptized?"ᵠ

³⁹"Yes, we are!" James and John answered.

Then Jesus replied, "You certainly will drink from the cup from which I must drink. And you will be baptized just as I must! ⁴⁰But it isn't for me to say who will sit at my right side and at my left. That is for God to decide."

⁴¹When the ten other disciples heard this, they were angry with James and John. ⁴²But Jesus called the disciples together and said:

You know that those foreigners who call themselves kings like to order their people around. And their great leaders have full power over the people they rule. ⁴³But don't act like them. If you want to be great, you must be the servant of all the others. ⁴⁴And if you want to be first, you must be everyone's slave. ⁴⁵The Son of Man did not come to be a slave master, but a slave who will give his life to rescueʳ many people.

Jesus Heals Blind Bartimaeus
(Matthew 20.29-34; Luke 18.35-43)

⁴⁶Jesus and his disciples went to Jericho. And as they were leaving, they were followed by a large crowd. A blind beggar by the name of Bartimaeus son of Timaeus was sitting beside the road. ⁴⁷When he heard that it was Jesus from Nazareth, he shouted, "Jesus, Son of David,ˢ have pity on me!" ⁴⁸Many people told the man to stop, but he shouted even louder, "Son of David, have pity on me!"

⁴⁹Jesus stopped and said, "Call him over!"

They called out to the blind man and said, "Don't be afraid! Come on! He is calling for you." ⁵⁰The man threw off his coat as he jumped up and ran to Jesus.

⁵¹Jesus asked, "What do you want me to do for you?"

The blind man answered, "Master,ᵗ I want to see!"

⁵²Jesus told him, "You may go. Your eyes are healed because of your faith."

Right away the man could see, and he went down the road with Jesus.

ⁿ **10.33** *foreigners*: The Romans who ruled Judea at this time.   ᵒ **10.37** *right side . . . left*: The most powerful people in a kingdom sat at the right and left side of the king.   ᵖ **10.38** *drink from the cup*: In the Scriptures a "cup" is sometimes used as a symbol of suffering. To "drink from the cup" would be to suffer.   ᵠ **10.38** *as I must be baptized*: Baptism is used with the same meaning that "cup" has in this verse.   ʳ **10.45** *rescue*: The Greek word often, though not always, means the payment of a price to free a slave or a prisoner.   ˢ **10.47** *Son of David*: The Jewish people expected the Messiah to be from the family of King David, and for this reason the Messiah was often called the "Son of David."   ᵗ **10.51** *Master*: A Hebrew word that may also mean "Teacher."

Jesus Enters Jerusalem
(Matthew 21.1-11; Luke 19.28-40; John 12.12-19)

11 Jesus and his disciples reached Bethphage and Bethany near the Mount of Olives. When they were getting close to Jerusalem, Jesus sent two of them on ahead. ²He told them, "Go into the next village. As soon as you enter it, you will find a young donkey that has never been ridden. Untie the donkey and bring it here. ³If anyone asks why you are doing that, say, 'The Lord ᵘ needs it and will soon bring it back.'"

⁴The disciples left and found the donkey tied near a door that faced the street. While they were untying it, ⁵some of the people standing there asked, "Why are you untying the donkey?" ⁶They told them what Jesus had said, and the people let them take it.

⁷The disciples led the donkey to Jesus. They put some of their clothes on its back, and Jesus got on. ⁸Many people spread clothes on the road, while others went to cut branches from the fields.ᵛ

⁹In front of Jesus and behind him, people went along shouting,

"Hooray!ʷ
God bless the one who comes
    in the name of the Lord!
¹⁰ God bless the coming kingdom
    of our ancestor David.
Hooray for God
    in heaven above!"

¹¹After Jesus had gone to Jerusalem, he went into the temple and looked around at everything. But since it was already late in the day, he went back to Bethany with the twelve disciples.

Jesus Puts a Curse on a Fig Tree
(Matthew 21.18, 19)

¹²When Jesus and his disciples left Bethany the next morning, he was hungry. ¹³From a distance Jesus saw a fig tree covered with leaves, and he went to see if there were any figs on the tree. But there were not any, because it wasn't the season for figs. ¹⁴So Jesus said to the tree, "Never again will anyone eat fruit from this tree!" The disciples heard him say this.

Jesus in the Temple
(Matthew 21.12-17; Luke 19.45-48; John 2.13-22)

¹⁵After Jesus and his disciples reached Jerusalem, he went into the temple and began chasing out everyone who was selling and buying. He turned over the tables of the moneychangers and the benches of those who were selling doves. ¹⁶Jesus would not let anyone carry things through the temple. ¹⁷Then he taught the people and said, "The Scriptures say, 'My house should be called a place of worship for all nations.' But you have made it a place where robbers hide!"

¹⁸The chief priests and the teachers of the Law of Moses heard what Jesus said, and they started looking for a way to kill him. They were afraid of him, because the crowds were completely amazed at his teaching.

¹⁹That evening, Jesus and the disciples went outside the city.

A Lesson from the Fig Tree
(Matthew 21.20-22)

²⁰As the disciples walked past the fig tree the next morning, they noticed that it was completely dried up, roots and all. ²¹Peter remembered what Jesus had said to the tree. Then Peter said, "Teacher, look! The tree you put a curse on has dried up."

²²Jesus told his disciples:

Have faith in God! ²³If you have faith in God and don't doubt, you can tell this mountain to get up and jump into the sea, and it will. ²⁴Everything you ask for in prayer will be yours, if you only have faith. ²⁵⁻²⁶Whenever you stand up to pray, you must forgive what others have done to you. Then your Father in heaven will forgive your sins.ˣ

A Question about Jesus' Authority
(Matthew 21.23-27; Luke 20.1-8)

²⁷Jesus and his disciples returned to Jerusalem. And as he was walking through the temple, the chief priests, the nation's leaders, and the teachers of the Law of Moses came over to him. ²⁸They asked, "What right do you have to do these things? Who gave you this authority?"

²⁹Jesus answered, "I have just one question to ask you. If you answer it, I will tell you where I got the right to do these things. ³⁰Who gave John the right to baptize? Was it God in heaven or merely some human being?"

³¹They thought it over and said to each other, "We can't say that God gave John this right. Jesus will ask us why we didn't believe John. ³²On the other hand, these people think that John was a prophet. So we can't say that it was

---

ᵘ**11.3** *The Lord*: Or "The master of the donkey." ᵛ**11.8** *spread . . . branches from the fields*: This was one way that the Jewish people welcomed a famous person. ʷ**11.9** *Hooray*: This translates a word that can mean "please save us." But it is most often used as a shout of praise to God. ˣ**11.25,26** *your sins*: Some manuscripts add, "But if you do not forgive others, God will not forgive you."

merely some human who gave John the right to baptize."

They were afraid of the crowd ³³and told Jesus, "We don't know."

Jesus replied, "Then I won't tell you who gave me the right to do what I do."

Renters of a Vineyard
(Matthew 21.33-46; Luke 20.9-19)

12 Jesus then told them this story:
A farmer once planted a vineyard. He built a wall around it and dug a pit to crush the grapes in. He also built a lookout tower. Then he rented out his vineyard and left the country. ²When it was harvest time, he sent a servant to get his share of the grapes. ³The renters grabbed the servant. They beat him up and sent him away without a thing.

⁴The owner sent another servant, but the renters beat him on the head and insulted him terribly. ⁵Then the man sent another servant, and they killed him. He kept sending servant after servant. They beat some of them and killed others.

⁶The owner had a son he loved very much. Finally, he sent his son to the renters because he thought they would respect him. ⁷But they said to themselves, "Someday he will own this vineyard. Let's kill him! That way we can have it all for ourselves." ⁸So they grabbed the owner's son and killed him. Then they threw his body out of the vineyard.

⁹Jesus asked, "What do you think the owner of the vineyard will do? He will come and kill those renters and let someone else have his vineyard. ¹⁰You surely know that the Scriptures say,

'The stone that the builders
    tossed aside
is now the most important
    stone of all.
¹¹ This is something
    the Lord has done,
and it is amazing to us.'"

¹²The leaders knew that Jesus was really talking about them, and they wanted to arrest him. But because they were afraid of the crowd, they let him alone and left.

Paying Taxes
(Matthew 22.15-22; Luke 20.20-26)

¹³The Pharisees got together with Herod's followers.ʸ Then they sent some men to trick Jesus into saying something wrong. ¹⁴They went to him and said, "Teacher, we know that you are honest. You treat everyone with the same respect, no matter who they are. And you teach the truth about what God wants people to do. Tell us, should we pay taxes to the Emperor or not?"

¹⁵Jesus knew what they were up to, and he said, "Why are you trying to test me? Show me a coin!"

¹⁶They brought him a silver coin, and he asked, "Whose picture and name are on it?"

"The Emperor's," they answered.

¹⁷Then Jesus told them, "Give the Emperor what belongs to him and give God what belongs to God." The men were amazed at Jesus.

Life in the Future World
(Matthew 22.23-33; Luke 20.27-40)

¹⁸The Sadducees did not believe that people would rise to life after death. So some of them came to Jesus and said:

¹⁹Teacher, Moses wrote that if a married man dies and has no children, his brother should marry the widow. Their first son would then be thought of as the son of the dead brother. ²⁰There were once seven brothers. The first one married, but died without having any children. ²¹The second brother married his brother's widow, and he also died without having children. The same thing happened to the third brother, ²²and finally to all seven brothers. At last the woman died. ²³When God raises people from death, whose wife will this woman be? After all, she had been married to all seven brothers.

²⁴Jesus answered:

You are completely wrong! You don't know what the Scriptures teach. And you don't know anything about the power of God. ²⁵When God raises people to life, they won't marry. They will be like the angels in heaven. ²⁶You surely know about people being raised to life. You know that in the story about Moses and the burning bush, God said, "I am the God worshiped by Abraham, Isaac, and Jacob."ᶻ ²⁷He isn't the God of the dead, but of the living. You Sadducees are all wrong.

The Most Important Commandment
(Matthew 22.34-40; Luke 10.25-28)

²⁸One of the teachers of the Law of Moses came up while Jesus and the Sadducees were arguing. When he heard

---

ʸ *12.13 Herod's followers*: People who were political followers of the family of Herod the Great and his son Herod Antipas.   ᶻ *12.26 "I am the God worshiped by Abraham, Isaac, and Jacob"*: Jesus argues that if God is worshiped by these three, they must still be alive, because he is the God of the living.

Jesus give a good answer, he asked him, "What is the most important commandment?"

29 Jesus answered, "The most important one says: 'People of Israel, you have only one Lord and God. 30 You must love him with all your heart, soul, mind, and strength.' 31 The second most important commandment says: 'Love others as much as you love yourself.' No other commandment is more important than these."

32 The man replied, "Teacher, you are certainly right to say there is only one God. 33 It is also true that we must love God with all our heart, mind, and strength, and that we must love others as much as we love ourselves. These commandments are more important than all the sacrifices and offerings that we could possibly make."

34 When Jesus saw that the man had given a sensible answer, he told him, "You are not far from God's kingdom." After this, no one dared ask Jesus any more questions.

About David's Son
(Matthew 22.41-46; Luke 20.41-44)

35 As Jesus was teaching in the temple, he said, "How can the teachers of the Law of Moses say that the Messiah will come from the family of King David? 36 The Holy Spirit led David to say,

'The Lord said to my Lord:
  Sit at my right side[a]
until I make your enemies
  into a footstool for you.'

37 If David called the Messiah his Lord, how can the Messiah be his son?"[b]

The large crowd enjoyed listening to Jesus teach.

Jesus Condemns the Pharisees and the Teachers of the Law of Moses
(Matthew 23.1-36; Luke 20.45-47)

38 As Jesus was teaching, he said:
Guard against the teachers of the Law of Moses! They love to walk around in long robes and be greeted in the market. 39 They like the front seats in the meeting places and the best seats at banquets. 40 But they cheat widows out of their homes and pray long prayers just to show off. They will be punished most of all.

A Widow's Offering
(Luke 21.1-4)

41 Jesus was sitting in the temple near the offering box and watching people put in their gifts. He noticed that many rich people were giving a lot of money. 42 Finally, a poor widow came up and put in two coins that were worth only a few pennies. 43 Jesus told his disciples to gather around him. Then he said:

I tell you that this poor widow has put in more than all the others. 44 Everyone else gave what they didn't need. But she is very poor and gave everything she had. Now she doesn't have a cent to live on.

The Temple Will Be Destroyed
(Matthew 24.1, 2; Luke 21.5, 6)

13 As Jesus was leaving the temple, one of his disciples said to him, "Teacher, look at these beautiful stones and wonderful buildings!"

2 Jesus replied, "Do you see these huge buildings? They will certainly be torn down! Not one stone will be left in place."

Warning about Trouble
(Matthew 24.3-14; Luke 21.7-19)

3 Later, as Jesus was sitting on the Mount of Olives across from the temple, Peter, James, John, and Andrew came to him in private. 4 They asked, "When will these things happen? What will be the sign that they are about to take place?"

5 Jesus answered:
Watch out and don't let anyone fool you! 6 Many will come and claim to be me. They will use my name and fool many people.

7 When you hear about wars and threats of wars, don't be afraid. These things will have to happen first, but that isn't the end. 8 Nations and kingdoms will go to war against each other. There will be earthquakes in many places, and people will starve to death. But this is just the beginning of troubles.

9 Be on your guard! You will be taken to courts and beaten with whips in their meeting places. And because of me, you will have to stand before rulers and kings to tell about your faith. 10 But before the end comes, the good news must be preached to all nations.

11 When you are arrested, don't worry about what you will say. You will be given the right words when the time comes. But you will not really be the ones speaking. Your words will come from the Holy Spirit.

12 Brothers and sisters will betray each other and have each other put to death. Parents will betray their own children, and children will turn against their parents and have them killed. 13 Everyone will hate you because of me. But if you keep on

---

[a] **12.36** *right side*: The place of power and honor. at 10.47.

[b] **12.37** *David . . . his son*: See the note

being faithful right to the end, you will be saved.

The Horrible Thing
(Matthew 24.15-21; Luke 21.20-24)

[14] Someday you will see that "Horrible Thing" where it should not be.[c] Everyone who reads this must try to understand! If you are living in Judea at that time, run to the mountains. [15] If you are on the roof[d] of your house, don't go inside to get anything. [16] If you are out in the field, don't go back for your coat. [17] It will be an awful time for women who are expecting babies or nursing young children. [18] Pray that it won't happen in winter.[e] [19] This will be the worst time of suffering since God created the world, and nothing this terrible will ever happen again. [20] If the Lord doesn't make the time shorter, no one will be left alive. But because of his chosen and special ones, he will make the time shorter.

[21] If someone should say, "Here is the Messiah!" or "There he is!" don't believe it. [22] False messiahs and false prophets will come and work miracles and signs. They will even try to fool God's chosen ones. [23] But be on your guard! That's why I am telling you these things now.

When the Son of Man Appears
(Matthew 24.29-31; Luke 21.25-28)

[24] In those days, right after that time of suffering,

"The sun will become dark,
  and the moon
    will no longer shine.
[25] The stars will fall,
  and the powers in the sky[f]
    will be shaken."

[26] Then the Son of Man will be seen coming in the clouds with great power and glory. [27] He will send his angels to gather his chosen ones from all over the earth.

A Lesson from a Fig Tree
(Matthew 24.32-35; Luke 21.29-33)

[28] Learn a lesson from a fig tree. When its branches sprout and start putting out leaves, you know summer is near. [29] So when you see all these things happening, you will know that the time has almost come.[g] [30] You can be sure that some of the people of this generation will still be alive when all this happens. [31] The sky and the earth will not last forever, but my words will.

No One Knows the Day or Time
(Matthew 24.36-44)

[32] No one knows the day or the time. The angels in heaven don't know, and the Son himself doesn't know. Only the Father knows. [33] So watch out and be ready! You don't know when the time will come. [34] It is like what happens when a man goes away for a while and places his servants in charge of everything. He tells each of them what to do, and he orders the guard to keep alert. [35] So be alert! You don't know when the master of the house will come back. It could be in the evening or at midnight or before dawn or in the morning. [36] But if he comes suddenly, don't let him find you asleep. [37] I tell everyone just what I have told you. Be alert!

A Plot To Kill Jesus
(Matthew 26.1-5; Luke 22.1, 2; John 11.45-53)

14 It was now two days before Passover and the Festival of Thin Bread. The chief priests and the teachers of the Law of Moses were planning how they could sneak around and have Jesus arrested and put to death. [2] They were saying, "We must not do it during the festival, because the people will riot."

At Bethany
(Matthew 26.6-13; John 12.1-8)

[3] Jesus was eating in Bethany at the home of Simon, who once had leprosy,[h] when a woman came in with a very expensive bottle of sweet-smelling perfume.[i] After breaking it open, she poured the perfume on Jesus' head. [4] This made some of the guests angry, and they complained, "Why such a waste? [5] We could have sold this perfume for more than three hundred silver coins and given the money to the poor!" So they started saying cruel things to the woman.

[6] But Jesus said:

Leave her alone! Why are you bothering her? She has done a beautiful thing for me. [7] You will always have the poor with you. And whenever you want to, you can give to

---

[c] **13.14** *where it should not be*: Probably the holy place in the temple.   [d] **13.15** *roof*: See the note at 2.4.   [e] **13.18** *in winter*: In Palestine the winters are cold and rainy and make travel difficult.   [f] **13.25** *the powers in the sky*: In ancient times people thought that the stars were spiritual powers.   [g] **13.29** *the time has almost come*: Or "he (that is, the Son of Man) will soon be here."   [h] **14.3** *leprosy*: In biblical times the word "leprosy" was used for many different skin diseases.   [i] **14.3** *sweet-smelling perfume*: The Greek text has "perfume made of pure spikenard," a plant used to make perfume.

them. But you won't always have me here with you. ⁸She has done all she could by pouring perfume on my body to prepare it for burial. ⁹You may be sure that wherever the good news is told all over the world, people will remember what she has done. And they will tell others.

Judas and the Chief Priests
(Matthew 26.14-16; Luke 22.3-6)

¹⁰Judas Iscariot^j was one of the twelve disciples. He went to the chief priests and offered to help them arrest Jesus. ¹¹They were glad to hear this, and they promised to pay him. So Judas started looking for a good chance to betray Jesus.

Jesus Eats with His Disciples
(Matthew 26.17-25; Luke 22.7-14, 21-23; John 13.21-30)

¹²It was the first day of the Festival of Thin Bread, and the Passover lambs were being killed. Jesus' disciples asked him, "Where do you want us to prepare the Passover meal?"
¹³Jesus said to two of the disciples, "Go into the city, where you will meet a man carrying a jar of water.^k Follow him, ¹⁴and when he goes into a house, say to the owner, 'Our teacher wants to know if you have a room where he can eat the Passover meal with his disciples.' ¹⁵The owner will take you upstairs and show you a large room furnished and ready for you to use. Prepare the meal there."
¹⁶The two disciples went into the city and found everything just as Jesus had told them. So they prepared the Passover meal.
¹⁷⁻¹⁸While Jesus and the twelve disciples were eating together that evening, he said, "The one who will betray me is now eating with me."
¹⁹This made the disciples sad, and one after another they said to Jesus, "You surely don't mean me!"
²⁰He answered, "It is one of you twelve men who is eating from this dish with me. ²¹The Son of Man will die, just as the Scriptures say. But it is going to be terrible for the one who betrays me. That man would be better off if he had never been born."

The Lord's Supper
(Matthew 26.26-30; Luke 22.14-23; 1 Corinthians 11.23-25)

²²During the meal Jesus took some bread in his hands. He blessed the bread and broke it. Then he gave it to his disciples and said, "Take this. It is my body."
²³Jesus picked up a cup of wine and gave thanks to God. He gave it to his disciples, and they all drank some. ²⁴Then he said, "This is my blood, which is poured out for many people, and with it God makes his agreement. ²⁵From now on I will not drink any wine, until I drink new wine in God's kingdom." ²⁶Then they sang a hymn and went out to the Mount of Olives.

Peter's Promise
(Matthew 26.31-35; Luke 22.31-34; John 13.36-38)

²⁷Jesus said to his disciples, "All of you will reject me, as the Scriptures say,

'I will strike down
    the shepherd,
and the sheep
    will be scattered.'

²⁸But after I am raised to life, I will go ahead of you to Galilee."
²⁹Peter spoke up, "Even if all the others reject you, I never will!"
³⁰Jesus replied, "This very night before a rooster crows twice, you will say three times that you don't know me."
³¹But Peter was so sure of himself that he said, "Even if I have to die with you, I will never say that I don't know you!"
All the others said the same thing.

Jesus Prays
(Matthew 26.36-46; Luke 22.39-46)

³²Jesus went with his disciples to a place called Gethsemane, and he told them, "Sit here while I pray."
³³Jesus took along Peter, James, and John. He was sad and troubled and ³⁴told them, "I am so sad that I feel as if I am dying. Stay here and keep awake with me."
³⁵⁻³⁶Jesus walked on a little way. Then he knelt down on the ground and prayed, "Father,^l if it is possible, don't let this happen to me! Father, you can do anything. Don't make me suffer by having me drink from this cup.^m But do what you want, and not what I want."
³⁷When Jesus came back and found the disciples sleeping, he said to Simon Peter, "Are you asleep? Can't you stay awake for just one hour? ³⁸Stay awake and pray that you won't be tested. You want to do what is right, but you are weak."
³⁹Jesus went back and prayed the same prayer. ⁴⁰But when he returned to the disciples, he found them sleeping again. They simply could not keep their

---

^j **14.10** *Iscariot*: See the note at 3.19. ^k **14.13** *a man carrying a jar of water*: A male slave carrying water could mean that the family was rich. ^l **14.35,36** *Father*: The Greek text has "Abba," which is an Aramaic word meaning "father." ^m **14.35,36** *by having me drink from this cup*: See the note at 10.38.

eyes open, and they did not know what to say. ⁴¹When Jesus returned to the disciples the third time, he said, "Are you still sleeping and resting?ⁿ Enough of that! The time has come for the Son of Man to be handed over to sinners. ⁴²Get up! Let's go. The one who will betray me is already here."

Jesus Is Arrested
(Matthew 26.47-56; Luke 22.47-53; John 18.3-12)

⁴³Jesus was still speaking, when Judas the betrayer came up. He was one of the twelve disciples, and a mob of men armed with swords and clubs were with him. They had been sent by the chief priests, the nation's leaders, and the teachers of the Law of Moses. ⁴⁴Judas had told them ahead of time, "Arrest the man I greet with a kiss.ᵒ Tie him up tight and lead him away."

⁴⁵Judas walked right up to Jesus and said, "Teacher!" Then Judas kissed him, ⁴⁶and the men grabbed Jesus and arrested him.

⁴⁷Someone standing there pulled out a sword. He struck the servant of the high priest and cut off his ear.

⁴⁸Jesus said to the mob, "Why do you come with swords and clubs to arrest me like a criminal? ⁴⁹Day after day I was with you and taught in the temple, and you didn't arrest me. But what the Scriptures say must come true."

⁵⁰All of Jesus' disciples ran off and left him. ⁵¹One of them was a young man who was wearing only a linen cloth. And when the men grabbed him, ⁵²he left the cloth behind and ran away naked.

Jesus Is Questioned by the Council
(Matthew 26.57-68; Luke 22.54, 55, 63-71; John 18.13, 14, 19-24)

⁵³Jesus was led off to the high priest. Then the chief priests, the nation's leaders, and the teachers of the Law of Moses all met together. ⁵⁴Peter had followed at a distance. And when he reached the courtyard of the high priest's house, he sat down with the guards to warm himself beside a fire.

⁵⁵The chief priests and the whole council tried to find someone to accuse Jesus of a crime, so they could put him to death. But they could not find anyone to accuse him. ⁵⁶Many people did tell lies against Jesus, but they did not agree on what they said. ⁵⁷Finally, some men stood up and lied about him. They said, ⁵⁸"We heard him say he would tear down this temple that we built. He also claimed that in three days he would build another one without any help." ⁵⁹But even then they did not agree on what they said.

⁶⁰The high priest stood up in the council and asked Jesus, "Why don't you say something in your own defense? Don't you hear the charges they are making against you?" ⁶¹But Jesus kept quiet and did not say a word. The high priest asked him another question, "Are you the Messiah, the Son of the glorious God?"ᵖ

⁶²"Yes, I am!" Jesus answered.

"Soon you will see
the Son of Man
sitting at the right sideᵠ
of God All-Powerful,
and coming with the clouds
of heaven."

⁶³At once the high priest ripped his robe apart and shouted, "Why do we need more witnesses? ⁶⁴You heard him claim to be God! What is your decision?" They all agreed that he should be put to death.

⁶⁵Some of the people started spitting on Jesus. They blindfolded him, hit him with their fists, and said, "Tell us who hit you!" Then the guards took charge of Jesus and beat him.

Peter Says He Doesn't Know Jesus
(Matthew 26.69-75; Luke 22.56-62; John 18.15-18, 25-27)

⁶⁶While Peter was still in the courtyard, a servant girl of the high priest came up ⁶⁷and saw Peter warming himself by the fire. She stared at him and said, "You were with Jesus from Nazareth!"

⁶⁸Peter replied, "That isn't true! I don't know what you're talking about. I don't have any idea what you mean." He went out to the gate, and a rooster crowed.ʳ

⁶⁹The servant girl saw Peter again and said to the people standing there, "This man is one of them!"

⁷⁰"No, I'm not!" Peter replied.

A little while later some of the people said to Peter, "You certainly are one of them. You're a Galilean!"

⁷¹This time Peter began to curse and swear, "I don't even know the man you're talking about!"

⁷²Right away the rooster crowed a second time. Then Peter remembered that Jesus had told him, "Before a rooster crows twice, you will say three

---

ⁿ**14.41** *Are you still sleeping and resting?*: Or "You may as well keep on sleeping and resting."
ᵒ**14.44** *greet with a kiss*: It was the custom for people to greet each other with a kiss on the cheek. ᵖ**14.61** *Son of the glorious God*: "Son of God" was one of the titles used for the kings of Israel. ᵠ**14.62** *right side*: See the note at 12.36. ʳ**14.68** *a rooster crowed*: These words are not in some manuscripts.

times that you don't know me." So Peter started crying.

Pilate Questions Jesus
(Matthew 27.1, 2, 11-14; Luke 23.1-5; John 18.28-38)

15 Early the next morning the chief priests, the nation's leaders, and the teachers of the Law of Moses met together with the whole Jewish council. They tied up Jesus and led him off to Pilate. ²He asked Jesus, "Are you the king of the Jews?"

"Those are your words," Jesus answered.

³The chief priests brought many charges against Jesus. ⁴Then Pilate questioned him again, "Don't you have anything to say? Don't you hear what crimes they say you have done?" ⁵But Jesus did not answer, and Pilate was amazed.

The Death Sentence
(Matthew 27.15-26; Luke 23.13-25; John 18.39—19.16)

⁶During Passover, Pilate always freed one prisoner chosen by the people. ⁷And at that time there was a prisoner named Barabbas. He and some others had been arrested for murder during a riot. ⁸The crowd now came and asked Pilate to set a prisoner free, just as he usually did.

⁹Pilate asked them, "Do you want me to free the king of the Jews?" ¹⁰Pilate knew that the chief priests had brought Jesus to him because they were jealous. ¹¹But the chief priests told the crowd to ask Pilate to free Barabbas.

¹²Then Pilate asked the crowd, "What do you want me to do with this man you say is*ˢ* the king of the Jews?"

¹³They yelled, "Nail him to a cross!"

¹⁴Pilate asked, "But what crime has he done?"

"Nail him to a cross!" they yelled even louder.

¹⁵Pilate wanted to please the crowd. So he set Barabbas free. Then he ordered his soldiers to beat Jesus with a whip and nail him to a cross.

Soldiers Make Fun of Jesus
(Matthew 27.27-30; John 19.2, 3)

¹⁶The soldiers led Jesus inside the courtyard of the fortress*ᵗ* and called together the rest of the troops. ¹⁷They put a purple robe*ᵘ* on him, and on his head they placed a crown that they had made out of thorn branches. ¹⁸They made fun of Jesus and shouted, "Hey, you king of the Jews!" ¹⁹Then they beat him on the head with a stick. They spit on him and knelt down and pretended to worship him.

²⁰When the soldiers had finished making fun of Jesus, they took off the purple robe. They put his own clothes back on him and led him off to be nailed to a cross. ²¹Simon from Cyrene happened to be coming in from a farm, and they forced him to carry Jesus' cross. Simon was the father of Alexander and Rufus.

Jesus Is Nailed to a Cross
(Matthew 27.31-44; Luke 23.27-43; John 19.17-27)

²²The soldiers took Jesus to Golgotha, which means "Place of a Skull."*ᵛ* ²³There they gave him some wine mixed with a drug to ease the pain, but he refused to drink it.

²⁴They nailed Jesus to a cross and gambled to see who would get his clothes. ²⁵It was about nine o'clock in the morning when they nailed him to the cross. ²⁶On it was a sign that told why he was nailed there. It read, "This is the King of the Jews." ²⁷⁻²⁸The soldiers also nailed two criminals on crosses, one to the right of Jesus and the other to his left.*ʷ*

²⁹People who passed by said terrible things about Jesus. They shook their heads and shouted, "Ha! So you're the one who claimed you could tear down the temple and build it again in three days. ³⁰Save yourself and come down from the cross!"

³¹The chief priests and the teachers of the Law of Moses also made fun of Jesus. They said to each other, "He saved others, but he can't save himself. ³²If he is the Messiah, the king of Israel, let him come down from the cross! Then we will see and believe." The two criminals also said cruel things to Jesus.

The Death of Jesus
(Matthew 27.45-56; Luke 23.44-49; John 19.28-30)

³³About noon the sky turned dark and stayed that way until around three o'clock. ³⁴Then about that time Jesus shouted, "Eloi, Eloi, lema sabachthani?"*ˣ* which means, "My God, my God, why have you deserted me?"

---

*ˢ***15.12** *this man you say is*: These words are not in some manuscripts. *ᵗ***15.16** *fortress*: The place where the Roman governor stayed. It was probably at Herod's palace west of Jerusalem, though it may have been Fortress Antonia, north of the temple, where the Roman troops were stationed. *ᵘ***15.17** *purple robe*: This was probably a Roman soldier's robe. *ᵛ***15.22** *Place of a Skull*: The place was probably given this name because it was near a large rock in the shape of a human skull. *ʷ***15.27-28** *left*: Some manuscripts add, "So the Scriptures came true which say, 'He was accused of being a criminal.'" *ˣ***15.34** *Eloi . . . sabachthani*: These words are in Aramaic, a language spoken in Palestine during the time of Jesus.

³⁵Some of the people standing there heard Jesus and said, "He is calling for Elijah."ʸ ³⁶One of them ran and grabbed a sponge. After he had soaked it in wine, he put it on a stick and held it up to Jesus. He said, "Let's wait and see if Elijah will comeᶻ and take him down!" ³⁷Jesus shouted and then died.

³⁸At once the curtain in the templeᵃ tore in two from top to bottom.

³⁹A Roman army officer was standing in front of Jesus. When the officer saw how Jesus died, he said, "This man really was the Son of God!"

⁴⁰⁻⁴¹Some women were looking on from a distance. They had come with Jesus to Jerusalem. But even before this they had been his followers and had helped him while he was in Galilee. Mary Magdalene and Mary the mother of the younger James and of Joseph were two of these women. Salome was also one of them.

Jesus Is Buried
(Matthew 27.57-61; Luke 23.50-56; John 19.38-42)

⁴²It was now the evening before the Sabbath, and the Jewish people were getting ready for that sacred day. ⁴³A man named Joseph from Arimathea was brave enough to ask Pilate for the body of Jesus. Joseph was a highly respected member of the Jewish council, and he was also waiting for God's kingdom to come.

⁴⁴Pilate was surprised to hear that Jesus was already dead, and he called in the army officer to find out if Jesus had been dead very long. ⁴⁵After the officer told him, Pilate let Joseph have Jesus' body.

⁴⁶Joseph bought a linen cloth and took the body down from the cross. He had it wrapped in the cloth, and he put it in a tomb that had been cut into solid rock. Then he rolled a big stone against the entrance to the tomb.

⁴⁷Mary Magdalene and Mary the mother of Joseph were watching and saw where the body was placed.

Jesus Is Alive
(Matthew 28.1-8; Luke 24.1-12; John 20.1-10)

16 After the Sabbath, Mary Magdalene, Salome, and Mary the mother of James bought some spices to put on Jesus' body. ²Very early on Sunday morning, just as the sun was coming up, they went to the tomb. ³On their way, they were asking one another, "Who will roll the stone away from the entrance for us?" ⁴But when they looked, they saw that the stone had already been rolled away. And it was a huge stone!

⁵The women went into the tomb, and on the right side they saw a young man in a white robe sitting there. They were alarmed.

⁶The man said, "Don't be alarmed! You are looking for Jesus from Nazareth, who was nailed to a cross. God has raised him to life, and he isn't here. You can see the place where they put his body. ⁷Now go and tell his disciples, and especially Peter, that he will go ahead of you to Galilee. You will see him there, just as he told you."

⁸When the women ran from the tomb, they were confused and shaking all over. They were too afraid to tell anyone what had happened.

ONE OLD ENDING TO MARK'S GOSPELᵇ

Jesus Appears to Mary Magdalene
(Matthew 28.9, 10; John 20.11-18)

⁹Very early on the first day of the week, after Jesus had risen to life, he appeared to Mary Magdalene. Earlier he had forced seven demons out of her. ¹⁰She left and told his friends, who were crying and mourning. ¹¹Even though they heard that Jesus was alive and that Mary had seen him, they would not believe it.

Jesus Appears to Two Disciples
(Luke 24.13-35)

¹²Later, Jesus appeared in another form to two disciples, as they were on their way out of the city. ¹³But when these disciples told what had happened, the others would not believe.

What Jesus' Followers Must Do
(Matthew 28.16-20; Luke 24.36-49; John 20.19-23; Acts 1.6-8)

¹⁴Afterwards, Jesus appeared to his eleven disciples as they were eating. He scolded them because they were too stubborn to believe the ones who had seen him after he had been raised to life. ¹⁵Then he told them:

Go and preach the good news to everyone in the world. ¹⁶Anyone who believes me and is baptized will be saved. But anyone who refuses to believe me will be condemned.

¹⁷Everyone who believes me will be

ʸ **15.35** *Elijah*: The name "Elijah" sounds something like "Eloi," which means "my God." ᶻ **15.36** *see if Elijah will come*: See the note at 6.15.   ᵃ **15.38** *curtain in the temple*: There were two curtains in the temple. One was at the entrance, and the other separated the holy place from the most holy place that the Jewish people thought of as God's home on earth. The second curtain is probably the one which is meant.   ᵇ **16.9** *One Old Ending to Mark's Gospel*: Verses 9-20 are not in some manuscripts.

able to do wonderful things. By using my name they will force out demons, and they will speak new languages. [18]They will handle snakes and will drink poison and not be hurt. They will also heal sick people by placing their hands on them.

Jesus Returns to Heaven
(Luke 24.50-53; Acts 1.9-11)

[19]After the Lord Jesus had said these things to the disciples, he was taken back up to heaven where he sat down at the right side[c] of God. [20]Then the disciples left and preached everywhere. The Lord was with them, and the miracles they worked proved that their message was true.

ANOTHER OLD ENDING TO MARK'S GOSPEL[d]

[9-10]The women quickly told Peter and his friends what had happened. Later, Jesus sent the disciples to the east and to the west with his sacred and everlasting message of how people can be saved forever.

---

[c]16.19 *right side*: See the note at 12.36.   [d]16.9,10 *Another Old Ending to Mark's Gospel*: Some manuscripts and early translations have both this shorter ending and the longer one (verses 9-20).

LUKE

ABOUT THIS BOOK

God's love is for everyone! Jesus came into the world to be the Savior of all people! These are two of the main thoughts in this book. Several of the best known stories that Jesus used for teaching about God's love are found only in Luke's Gospel: The Good Samaritan (10.25-37), A Lost Sheep (15.1-7), and A Lost Son (15.11-32). Only Luke tells how Jesus visited in the home of a hated tax collector (19.1-10) and promised life in paradise to a dying criminal (23.39-43).

Luke mentions God's Spirit more than any of the other New Testament writers. For example, the power of the Spirit was with John the Baptist from the time he was born (1.15). And the angel promised Mary, "The Holy Spirit will come down to you . . . So your child will be called the holy Son of God" (1.35). Jesus followed the Spirit (4.1, 14, 18; 10.21) and taught that the Spirit is God's greatest gift (11.13).

Luke shows how important prayer was to Jesus. Jesus prayed often: after being baptized (3.21), before choosing the disciples (6.12), before asking his disciples who they thought he was (9.18), and before giving up his life on the cross (23.34, 46). From Luke we learn of three stories that Jesus told to teach about prayer (11.5-9; 18.1-8, 9-14).

An important part of Luke's story is the way in which he shows the concern of Jesus for the poor: the good news is preached to them (4.18; 7.22), they receive God's blessings (6.20), they are invited to the great feast (14.13, 21), the poor man Lazarus is taken to heaven by angels (16.20, 22), and Jesus commands his disciples to sell what they have and give the money to the poor (12.33).

To make sure that readers would understand that Jesus was raised physically from death, Luke reports that the risen Jesus ate a piece of fish (24.42, 43). There could be no mistake about the risen Jesus: he was not a ghost. His being raised from death was real and not someone's imagination. Luke also wrote another book—the Acts of the Apostles—to show what happened to Jesus' followers after he was raised from death and taken up to heaven. No other Gospel has a second volume that continues the story.

Luke closes this first book that he wrote by telling that Jesus returned to heaven. But right before Jesus leaves, he tells his disciples:

The Scriptures say that the Messiah must suffer, then three days later he will rise from death. They also say that all people of every nation must be told in my name to turn to God, in order to be forgiven. So beginning in Jerusalem, you must tell everything that has happened. (24.46-48)

A QUICK LOOK AT THIS BOOK

Why Luke Wrote this Book (1.1-4)
The Births of John the Baptist and Jesus (1.5—2.52)
The Message of John the Baptist (3.1-20)
The Baptism and Temptation of Jesus (3.21—4.13)
Jesus' Ministry in Galilee (4.14—9.50)
Jesus Goes from Galilee to Jerusalem (9.51—19.27)
Jesus' Last Week: His Trial and Death (19.28—23.56)
Jesus Is Alive (24.1-12)
Jesus Appears. He Is Taken to Heaven (24.13-53)

1 Many people have tried to tell the story of what God has done among us. ²They wrote what we had been told by the ones who were there in the beginning and saw what happened. ³So I made a careful study[a] of everything and then decided to write and tell you exactly what took place. Honorable Theophilus, ⁴I have done this to let you know the truth about what you have heard.

An Angel Tells about the Birth of John

⁵When Herod was king of Judea, there was a priest by the name of Zechariah from the priestly group of Abijah. His wife Elizabeth was from the family of Aaron.[b] ⁶Both of them were good people and pleased the Lord God by obeying all that he had commanded. ⁷But they did not have children. Elizabeth could not have any, and both Zechariah and Elizabeth were already old.

⁸One day Zechariah's group of priests were on duty, and he was serving God as a priest. ⁹According to the custom of the priests, he had been chosen to go into the Lord's temple that day and to burn incense,[c] ¹⁰while the people stood outside praying.

¹¹All at once an angel from the Lord appeared to Zechariah at the right side of the altar. ¹²Zechariah was confused and afraid when he saw the angel. ¹³But the angel told him:

Don't be afraid, Zechariah! God has heard your prayers. Your wife Elizabeth will have a son, and you must name him John. ¹⁴His birth will make you very happy, and many people will be glad. ¹⁵Your son will be a great servant of the Lord. He must never drink wine or beer, and the power of the Holy Spirit will be with him from the time he is born.

¹⁶John will lead many people in Israel to turn back to the Lord their God. ¹⁷He will go ahead of the Lord with the same power and spirit that Elijah[d] had. And because of John, parents will be more thoughtful of their children. And people who now disobey God will begin to think as they ought to. That is how John will get people ready for the Lord.

¹⁸Zechariah said to the angel, "How will I know this is going to happen? My wife and I are both very old."

¹⁹The angel answered, "I am Gabriel, God's servant, and I was sent to tell you this good news. ²⁰You have not believed what I have said. So you will not be able to say a thing until all this happens. But everything will take place when it is supposed to."

²¹The crowd was waiting for Zechariah and kept wondering why he was staying so long in the temple. ²²When he did come out, he could not speak, and they knew he had seen a vision. He motioned to them with his hands, but did not say a thing.

²³When Zechariah's time of service in the temple was over, he went home. ²⁴Soon after that, his wife was expecting a baby, and for five months she did not leave the house. She said to herself, ²⁵"What the Lord has done for me will keep people from looking down on me."[e]

An Angel Tells about the Birth of Jesus

²⁶One month later God sent the angel Gabriel to the town of Nazareth in Galilee ²⁷with a message for a virgin named Mary. She was engaged to Joseph from the family of King David. ²⁸The angel greeted Mary and said, "You are truly blessed! The Lord is with you."

²⁹Mary was confused by the angel's words and wondered what they meant. ³⁰Then the angel told Mary, "Don't be afraid! God is pleased with you, ³¹and you will have a son. His name will be Jesus. ³²He will be great and will be called the Son of God Most High. The Lord God will make him king, as his ancestor David was. ³³He will rule the people of Israel forever, and his kingdom will never end."

³⁴Mary asked the angel, "How can this happen? I am not married!"

³⁵The angel answered, "The Holy Spirit will come down to you, and God's power will come over you. So your child will be called the holy Son of God. ³⁶Your relative Elizabeth is also going to have a son, even though she is old. No one thought she could ever have a baby, but in three months she will have a son. ³⁷Nothing is impossible for God!"

³⁸Mary said, "I am the Lord's servant! Let it happen as you have said." And the angel left her.

Mary Visits Elizabeth

³⁹A short time later Mary hurried to a town in the hill country of Judea. ⁴⁰She went into Zechariah's home, where she greeted Elizabeth. ⁴¹When Elizabeth heard Mary's greeting, her baby moved within her.

The Holy Spirit came upon Elizabeth. ⁴²Then in a loud voice she said to Mary:

---

[a] 1.3 *a careful study*: Or "a study from the beginning." [b] 1.5 *Aaron*: The brother of Moses and the first priest. [c] 1.9 *burn incense*: This was done twice a day, once in the morning and again in the late afternoon. [d] 1.17 *Elijah*: The prophet Elijah was known for his power to work miracles. [e] 1.25 *keep people from looking down on me*: When a married woman could not have children, it was thought that the Lord was punishing her.

God has blessed you more than any other woman! He has also blessed the child you will have. ⁴³Why should the mother of my Lord come to me? ⁴⁴As soon as I heard your greeting, my baby became happy and moved within me. ⁴⁵The Lord has blessed you because you believed that he will keep his promise.

Mary's Song of Praise

⁴⁶Mary said:

With all my heart
 I praise the Lord,
⁴⁷and I am glad
 because of God my Savior.
⁴⁸ He cares for me,
 his humble servant.
From now on,
 all people will say
 God has blessed me.
⁴⁹ God All-Powerful has done
 great things for me,
 and his name is holy.
⁵⁰ He always shows mercy
 to everyone
 who worships him.
⁵¹ The Lord has used
 his powerful arm
 to scatter those
 who are proud.
⁵² He drags strong rulers
 from their thrones
 and puts humble people
 in places of power.
⁵³ God gives the hungry
 good things to eat,
 and sends the rich away
 with nothing.
⁵⁴ He helps his servant Israel
 and is always merciful
 to his people.
⁵⁵ The Lord made this promise
 to our ancestors,
 to Abraham and his family
 forever!

⁵⁶Mary stayed with Elizabeth about three months. Then she went back home.

The Birth of John the Baptist

⁵⁷When Elizabeth's son was born, ⁵⁸her neighbors and relatives heard how kind the Lord had been to her, and they too were glad.

⁵⁹Eight days later they did for the child what the Law of Moses commands.ᶠ They were going to name him Zechariah, after his father. ⁶⁰But Elizabeth said, "No! His name is John."

⁶¹The people argued, "No one in your family has ever been named John." ⁶²So they motioned to Zechariah to find out what he wanted to name his son.

⁶³Zechariah asked for a writing tablet. Then he wrote, "His name is John." Everyone was amazed. ⁶⁴Right away, Zechariah started speaking and praising God.

⁶⁵All the neighbors were frightened because of what had happened, and everywhere in the hill country people kept talking about these things. ⁶⁶Everyone who heard about this wondered what this child would grow up to be. They knew that the Lord was with him.

Zechariah Praises the Lord

⁶⁷The Holy Spirit came upon Zechariah, and he began to speak:

⁶⁸ Praise the Lord,
 the God of Israel!
He has come
 to save his people.
⁶⁹ Our God has given us
 a mighty Saviorᵍ
 from the family
 of David his servant.
⁷⁰ Long ago the Lord promised
 by the words
 of his holy prophets
⁷¹ to save us from our enemies
 and from everyone
 who hates us.
⁷² God said he would be kind
 to our people and keep
 his sacred promise.
⁷³ He told our ancestor Abraham
⁷⁴ that he would rescue us
 from our enemies.
Then we could serve him
 without fear,
⁷⁵ by being holy and good
 as long as we live.
⁷⁶ You, my son, will be called
 a prophet of God
 in heaven above.
You will go ahead of the Lord
 to get everything ready
 for him.
⁷⁷ You will tell his people
 that they can be saved
 when their sins
 are forgiven.
⁷⁸ God's love and kindness
 will shine upon us
 like the sun that rises
 in the sky.ʰ
⁷⁹ On us who live
 in the dark shadow
 of death

ᶠ**1.59** *what the Law of Moses commands*: This refers to circumcision. It is the cutting off of skin from the private part of Jewish boys eight days after birth to show that they belong to the Lord.   ᵍ**1.69** *a mighty Savior*: The Greek text has "a horn of salvation." In the Scriptures animal horns are often a symbol of great strength.   ʰ**1.78** *like the sun that rises in the sky*: Or "like the Messiah coming from heaven."

this light will shine
to guide us
   into a life of peace.

⁸⁰As John grew up, God's Spirit gave him great power. John lived in the desert until the time he was sent to the people of Israel.

The Birth of Jesus
(Matthew 1.18-25)

2 About that time Emperor Augustus gave orders for the names of all the people to be listed in record books.ʲ ²These first records were made when Quirinius was governor of Syria.ʲ ³Everyone had to go to their own hometown to be listed. ⁴So Joseph had to leave Nazareth in Galilee and go to Bethlehem in Judea. Long ago Bethlehem had been King David's hometown, and Joseph went there because he was from David's family. ⁵Mary was engaged to Joseph and traveled with him to Bethlehem. She was soon going to have a baby, ⁶and while they were there, ⁷she gave birth to her first-bornᵏ son. She dressed him in baby clothesˡ and laid him on a bed of hay, because there was no room for them in the inn.

The Shepherds

⁸That night in the fields near Bethlehem some shepherds were guarding their sheep. ⁹All at once an angel came down to them from the Lord, and the brightness of the Lord's glory flashed around them. The shepherds were frightened. ¹⁰But the angel said, "Don't be afraid! I have good news for you, which will make everyone happy. ¹¹This very day in King David's hometown a Savior was born for you. He is Christ the Lord. ¹²You will know who he is, because you will find him dressed in baby clothes and lying on a bed of hay."

¹³Suddenly many other angels came down from heaven and joined in praising God. They said:

¹⁴ "Praise God in heaven!
   Peace on earth to everyone
      who pleases God."

¹⁵After the angels had left and gone back to heaven, the shepherds said to each other, "Let's go to Bethlehem and see what the Lord has told us about."

¹⁶They hurried off and found Mary and Joseph, and they saw the baby lying on a bed of hay. ¹⁷When the shepherds saw Jesus, they told his parents what the angel had said about him. ¹⁸Everyone listened and was surprised. ¹⁹But Mary kept thinking about all this and wondering what it meant.

²⁰As the shepherds returned to their sheep, they were praising God and saying wonderful things about him. Everything they had seen and heard was just as the angel had said.

²¹Eight days later Jesus' parents did for him what the Law of Moses commands.ᵐ And they named him Jesus, just as the angel had told Mary when he promised she would have a baby.

Simeon Praises the Lord

²²The time came for Mary and Joseph to do what the Law of Moses says a mother is supposed to do after her baby is born.ⁿ

They took Jesus to the temple in Jerusalem and presented him to the Lord, ²³just as the Law of the Lord says, "Each first-bornᵒ baby boy belongs to the Lord." ²⁴The Law of the Lord also says that parents have to offer a sacrifice, giving at least a pair of doves or two young pigeons. So that is what Mary and Joseph did.

²⁵At this time a man named Simeon was living in Jerusalem. Simeon was a good man. He loved God and was waiting for God to save the people of Israel. God's Spirit came to him ²⁶and told him that he would not die until he had seen Christ the Lord.

²⁷When Mary and Joseph brought Jesus to the temple to do what the Law of Moses says should be done for a new baby, the Spirit told Simeon to go into the temple. ²⁸Simeon took the baby Jesus in his arms and praised God,

²⁹ "Lord, I am your servant,
   and now I can die in peace,
because you have kept
   your promise to me.
³⁰ With my own eyes I have seen
   what you have done
      to save your people,
³¹ and foreign nations
   will also see this.

ⁱ2.1 *names . . . listed in record books*: This was done so that everyone could be made to pay taxes to the Emperor.   ʲ2.2 *Quirinius was governor of Syria*: It is known that Quirinius made a record of the people in A.D. 6 or 7. But the exact date of the record taking that Luke mentions is not known.   ᵏ2.7 *first-born*: The Jewish people said that the first-born son in each of their families belonged to the Lord.   ˡ2.7 *dressed him in baby clothes*: The Greek text has "wrapped him in wide strips of cloth," which was how young babies were dressed.
ᵐ2.21 *what the Law of Moses commands*: See the note at 1.59.   ⁿ2.22 *after her baby is born*: After a Jewish mother gave birth to a son, she was considered "unclean" and had to stay home until he was circumcised (see the note at 1.59). Then she had to stay home for another 33 days, before offering a sacrifice to the Lord.   ᵒ2.23 *first-born*: See the note at 2.7.

Luke 2.32

³² Your mighty power is a light
  for all nations,
and it will bring honor
  to your people Israel."

³³Jesus' parents were surprised at what Simeon had said. ³⁴Then he blessed them and told Mary, "This child of yours will cause many people in Israel to fall and others to stand. The child will be like a warning sign. Many people will reject him, ³⁵and you, Mary, will suffer as though you had been stabbed by a dagger. But all this will show what people are really thinking."

Anna Speaks about the Child Jesus

³⁶The prophet Anna was also there in the temple. She was the daughter of Phanuel from the tribe of Asher, and she was very old. In her youth she had been married for seven years, but her husband died. ³⁷And now she was eighty-four years old.ᵖ Night and day she served God in the temple by praying and often going without eating.ᵍ ³⁸At that time Anna came in and praised God. She spoke about the child Jesus to everyone who hoped for Jerusalem to be set free.

The Return to Nazareth

³⁹After Joseph and Mary had done everything that the Law of the Lord commands, they returned home to Nazareth in Galilee. ⁴⁰The child Jesus grew. He became strong and wise, and God blessed him.

The Boy Jesus in the Temple

⁴¹Every year Jesus' parents went to Jerusalem for Passover. ⁴²And when Jesus was twelve years old, they all went there as usual for the celebration. ⁴³After Passover his parents left, but they did not know that Jesus had stayed on in the city. ⁴⁴They thought he was traveling with some other people, and they went a whole day before they started looking for him. ⁴⁵When they could not find him with their relatives and friends, they went back to Jerusalem and started looking for him there.

⁴⁶Three days later they found Jesus sitting in the temple, listening to the teachers and asking them questions. ⁴⁷Everyone who heard him was surprised at how much he knew and at the answers he gave.

⁴⁸When his parents found him, they were amazed. His mother said, "Son, why have you done this to us? Your father and I have been very worried, and we have been searching for you!"

⁴⁹Jesus answered, "Why did you have to look for me? Didn't you know that I would be in my Father's house?"ʳ ⁵⁰But they did not understand what he meant.

⁵¹Jesus went back to Nazareth with his parents and obeyed them. His mother kept on thinking about all that had happened.

⁵²Jesus became wise, and he grew strong. God was pleased with him and so were the people.

The Preaching of John the Baptist
(Matthew 3.1-12; Mark 1.1-8; John 1.19-28)

3 For fifteen yearsˢ Emperor Tiberius had ruled that part of the world. Pontius Pilate was governor of Judea, and Herodᵗ was the ruler of Galilee. Herod's brother, Philip, was the ruler in the countries of Iturea and Trachonitis, and Lysanias was the ruler of Abilene. ²Annas and Caiaphas were the Jewish high priests.ᵘ

At that time God spoke to Zechariah's son John, who was living in the desert. ³So John went along the Jordan Valley, telling the people, "Turn back to God and be baptized! Then your sins will be forgiven." ⁴Isaiah the prophet wrote about John when he said,

"In the desert
  someone is shouting,
'Get the road ready
  for the Lord!
Make a straight path
  for him.
⁵ Fill up every valley
  and level every mountain
    and hill.
Straighten the crooked paths
  and smooth out
    the rough roads.
⁶ Then everyone will see
  the saving power of God.' "

⁷Crowds of people came out to be baptized, but John said to them, "You bunch of snakes! Who warned you to run from the coming judgment? ⁸Do something to show that you really have given up your sins. Don't start saying that you belong to Abraham's family. God can turn these stones into children for Abraham.ᵛ ⁹An ax is ready to cut the

---

ᵖ**2.37** *And now she was eighty-four years old*: Or "And now she had been a widow for eighty-four years." ᵍ**2.37** *without eating*: The Jewish people sometimes went without eating (also called "fasting") to show their love for God or to show sorrow for their sins. ʳ**2.49** *in my Father's house*: Or "doing my Father's work." ˢ**3.1** *For fifteen years*: This was either A.D. 28 or 29, and Jesus was about thirty years old (see 3.23). ᵗ**3.1** *Herod*: Herod Antipas, the son of Herod the Great. ᵘ**3.2** *Annas and Caiaphas . . . high priests*: Annas was high priest from A.D. 6 until 15. His son-in-law Caiaphas was high priest from A.D. 18 until 37. ᵛ**3.8** *children for Abraham*: The Jewish people thought they were God's chosen people because of God's promises to their ancestor Abraham.

trees down at their roots. Any tree that doesn't produce good fruit will be cut down and thrown into a fire."

[10] The crowds asked John, "What should we do?"

[11] John told them, "If you have two coats, give one to someone who doesn't have any. If you have food, share it with someone else."

[12] When tax collectors[w] came to be baptized, they asked John, "Teacher, what should we do?"

[13] John told them, "Don't make people pay more than they owe."

[14] Some soldiers asked him, "And what about us? What do we have to do?"

John told them, "Don't force people to pay money to make you leave them alone. Be satisfied with your pay."

[15] Everyone became excited and wondered, "Could John be the Messiah?"

[16] John said, "I am just baptizing with water. But someone more powerful is going to come, and I am not good enough even to untie his sandals.[x] He will baptize you with the Holy Spirit and with fire. [17] His threshing fork[y] is in his hand, and he is ready to separate the wheat from the husks. He will store the wheat in his barn and burn the husks with a fire that never goes out."

[18] In many different ways John preached the good news to the people. [19] But to Herod the ruler, he said, "It was wrong for you to take Herodias, your brother's wife." John also said that Herod had done many other bad things. [20] Finally, Herod put John in jail, and this was the worst thing he had done.

The Baptism of Jesus
(Matthew 3.13-17; Mark 1.9-11)

[21] While everyone else was being baptized, Jesus himself was baptized. Then as he prayed, the sky opened up, [22] and the Holy Spirit came down upon him in the form of a dove. A voice from heaven said, "You are my own dear Son, and I am pleased with you."

The Ancestors of Jesus
(Matthew 1.1-17)

[23] When Jesus began to preach, he was about thirty years old. Everyone thought he was the son of Joseph. But his family went back through Heli, [24] Matthat, Levi, Melchi, Jannai, Joseph, [25] Mattathias, Amos, Nahum, Esli, Naggai, [26] Maath, Mattathias, Semein, Josech, Joda; [27] Joanan, Rhesa, Zerubbabel, Shealtiel, Neri, [28] Melchi, Addi, Cosam, Elmadam, Er, [29] Joshua, Eliezer, Jorim, Matthat, Levi;

[30] Simeon, Judah, Joseph, Jonam, Eliakim, [31] Melea, Menna, Mattatha, Nathan, David, [32] Jesse, Obed, Boaz, Salmon, Nahshon;

[33] Amminadab, Admin, Arni, Hezron, Perez, Judah, [34] Jacob, Isaac, Abraham, Terah, Nahor, [35] Serug, Reu, Peleg, Eber, Shelah;

[36] Cainan, Arphaxad, Shem, Noah, Lamech, [37] Methuselah, Enoch, Jared, Mahalaleel, Kenan, [38] Enosh, and Seth.

The family of Jesus went all the way back to Adam and then to God.

Jesus and the Devil
(Matthew 4.1-11; Mark 1.12, 13)

4 When Jesus returned from the Jordan River, the power of the Holy Spirit was with him, and the Spirit led him into the desert. [2] For forty days Jesus was tested by the devil, and during that time he went without eating.[z] When it was all over, he was hungry.

[3] The devil said to Jesus, "If you are God's Son, tell this stone to turn into bread."

[4] Jesus answered, "The Scriptures say, 'No one can live only on food.' "

[5] Then the devil led Jesus up to a high place and quickly showed him all the nations on earth. [6] The devil said, "I will give all this power and glory to you. It has been given to me, and I can give it to anyone I want to. [7] Just worship me, and you can have it all."

[8] Jesus answered, "The Scriptures say:

'Worship the Lord your God
 and serve only him!' "

[9] Finally, the devil took Jesus to Jerusalem and had him stand on top of the temple. The devil said, "If you are God's Son, jump off. [10-11] The Scriptures say:

'God will tell his angels
 to take care of you.
They will catch you
 in their arms,
and you will not hurt
 your feet on the stones.' "

[12] Jesus answered, "The Scriptures also say, 'Don't try to test the Lord your God!' "

[13] After the devil had finished testing Jesus in every way possible, he left him for a while.

---

[w] 3.12 *tax collectors*: These were usually Jewish people who paid the Romans for the right to collect taxes. They were hated by other Jews who thought of them as traitors to their country and to their religion.   [x] 3.16 *untie his sandals*: This was the duty of a slave.
[y] 3.17 *threshing fork*: After Jewish farmers had trampled out the grain, they used a large fork to pitch the grain and the husks into the air. Wind would blow away the light husks, and the grain would fall back to the ground, where it could be gathered up.   [z] 4.2 *went without eating*: See the note at 2.37.

Jesus Begins His Work
(Matthew 4.12-17; Mark 1.14, 15)

¹⁴Jesus returned to Galilee with the power of the Spirit. News about him spread everywhere. ¹⁵He taught in the Jewish meeting places, and everyone praised him.

The People of Nazareth Turn against Jesus
(Matthew 13.53-58; Mark 6.1-6)

¹⁶Jesus went back to Nazareth, where he had been brought up, and as usual he went to the meeting place on the Sabbath. When he stood up to read from the Scriptures, ¹⁷he was given the book of Isaiah the prophet. He opened it and read,

¹⁸ "The Lord's Spirit
   has come to me,
because he has chosen me
   to tell the good news
      to the poor.
The Lord has sent me
   to announce freedom
      for prisoners,
to give sight to the blind,
to free everyone
   who suffers,
¹⁹ and to say, 'This is the year
   the Lord has chosen.' "

²⁰Jesus closed the book, then handed it back to the man in charge and sat down. Everyone in the meeting place looked straight at Jesus. ²¹Then Jesus said to them, "What you have just heard me read has come true today."

²²All the people started talking about Jesus and were amazed at the wonderful things he said. They kept on asking, "Isn't he Joseph's son?"

²³Jesus answered:

You will certainly want to tell me this saying, "Doctor, first make yourself well." You will tell me to do the same things here in my own hometown that you heard I did in Capernaum. ²⁴But you can be sure that no prophets are liked by the people of their own hometown.

²⁵Once during the time of Elijah there was no rain for three and a half years, and people everywhere were starving. There were many widows in Israel, ²⁶but Elijah was sent only to a widow in the town of Zarephath near the city of Sidon. ²⁷During the time of the prophet Elisha, many men in Israel had leprosy.[a] But no one was healed, except Naaman who lived in Syria.

²⁸When the people in the meeting place heard Jesus say this, they became so angry ²⁹that they got up and threw him out of town. They dragged him to the edge of the cliff on which the town was built, because they wanted to throw him down from there. ³⁰But Jesus slipped through the crowd and got away.

A Man with an Evil Spirit
(Mark 1.21-28)

³¹Jesus went to the town of Capernaum in Galilee and taught the people on the Sabbath. ³²His teaching amazed them because he spoke with power. ³³There in the Jewish meeting place was a man with an evil spirit. He yelled out, ³⁴"Hey, Jesus of Nazareth, what do you want with us? Are you here to get rid of us? I know who you are! You are God's Holy One."

³⁵Jesus ordered the evil spirit to be quiet and come out. The demon threw the man to the ground in front of everyone and left without harming him.

³⁶They all were amazed and kept saying to each other, "What kind of teaching is this? He has power to order evil spirits out of people!" ³⁷News about Jesus spread all over that part of the country.

Jesus Heals Many People
(Matthew 8.14-17; Mark 1.29-34)

³⁸Jesus left the meeting place and went to Simon's home. When Jesus got there, he was told that Simon's mother-in-law was sick with a high fever. ³⁹So Jesus went over to her and ordered the fever to go away. Right then she was able to get up and serve them a meal.

⁴⁰After the sun had set, people with all kinds of diseases were brought to Jesus. He put his hands on each one of them and healed them. ⁴¹Demons went out of many people and shouted, "You are the Son of God!" But Jesus ordered the demons not to speak because they knew he was the Messiah.

⁴²The next morning Jesus went out to a place where he could be alone, and crowds came looking for him. When they found him, they tried to stop him from leaving. ⁴³But Jesus said, "People in other towns must hear the good news about God's kingdom. That's why I was sent." ⁴⁴So he kept on preaching in the Jewish meeting places in Judea.[b]

Jesus Chooses His First Disciples
(Matthew 4.18-22; Mark 1.16-20)

5 Jesus was standing on the shore of Lake Gennesaret,[c] teaching the people as they crowded around him to hear

---

[a]4.27 *leprosy*: In biblical times the word "leprosy" was used for many different kinds of skin diseases. [b]4.44 *Judea*: Some manuscripts have "Galilee." [c]5.1 *Lake Gennesaret*: Another name for Lake Galilee.

God's message. ²Near the shore he saw two boats left there by some fishermen who had gone to wash their nets. ³Jesus got into the boat that belonged to Simon and asked him to row it out a little way from the shore. Then Jesus sat down[d] in the boat to teach the crowd.

⁴When Jesus had finished speaking, he told Simon, "Row the boat out into the deep water and let your nets down to catch some fish."

⁵"Master," Simon answered, "we have worked hard all night long and have not caught a thing. But if you tell me to, I will let the nets down." ⁶They did it and caught so many fish that their nets began ripping apart. ⁷Then they signaled for their partners in the other boat to come and help them. The men came, and together they filled the two boats so full that they both began to sink.

⁸When Simon Peter saw this happen, he knelt down in front of Jesus and said, "Lord, don't come near me! I am a sinner." ⁹Peter and everyone with him were completely surprised at all the fish they had caught. ¹⁰His partners James and John, the sons of Zebedee, were surprised too.

Jesus told Simon, "Don't be afraid! From now on you will bring in people instead of fish." ¹¹The men pulled their boats up on the shore. Then they left everything and went with Jesus.

Jesus Heals a Man
(Matthew 8.1-4; Mark 1.40-45)

¹²Jesus came to a town where there was a man who had leprosy.[e] When the man saw Jesus, he knelt down to the ground in front of Jesus and begged, "Lord, you have the power to make me well, if only you wanted to."

¹³Jesus put his hand on him and said, "I want to! Now you are well." At once the man's leprosy disappeared. ¹⁴Jesus told him, "Don't tell anyone about this, but go and show yourself to the priest. Offer a gift to the priest, just as Moses commanded, and everyone will know that you have been healed."[f]

¹⁵News about Jesus kept spreading. Large crowds came to listen to him teach and to be healed of their diseases. ¹⁶But Jesus would often go to some place where he could be alone and pray.

Jesus Heals a Crippled Man
(Matthew 9.1-8; Mark 2.1-12)

¹⁷One day some Pharisees and experts in the Law of Moses sat listening to Jesus teach. They had come from every village in Galilee and Judea and from Jerusalem.

God had given Jesus the power to heal the sick, ¹⁸and some people came carrying a crippled man on a mat. They tried to take him inside the house and put him in front of Jesus. ¹⁹But because of the crowd, they could not get him to Jesus. So they went up on the roof,[g] where they removed some tiles and let the mat down in the middle of the room.

²⁰When Jesus saw how much faith they had, he said to the crippled man, "My friend, your sins are forgiven."

²¹The Pharisees and the experts began arguing, "Jesus must think he is God! Only God can forgive sins."

²²Jesus knew what they were thinking, and he said, "Why are you thinking that? ²³Is it easier for me to tell this crippled man that his sins are forgiven or to tell him to get up and walk? ²⁴But now you will see that the Son of Man has the right to forgive sins here on earth." Jesus then said to the man, "Get up! Pick up your mat and walk home."

²⁵At once the man stood up in front of everyone. He picked up his mat and went home, giving thanks to God. ²⁶Everyone was amazed and praised God. What they saw surprised them, and they said, "We have seen a great miracle today!"

Jesus Chooses Levi
(Matthew 9.9-13; Mark 2.13-17)

²⁷Later, Jesus went out and saw a tax collector[h] named Levi sitting at the place for paying taxes. Jesus said to him, "Come with me." ²⁸Levi left everything and went with Jesus.

²⁹In his home Levi gave a big dinner for Jesus. Many tax collectors and other guests were also there.

³⁰The Pharisees and some of their teachers of the Law of Moses grumbled to Jesus' disciples, "Why do you eat and drink with those tax collectors and other sinners?"

³¹Jesus answered, "Healthy people don't need a doctor, but sick people do.

---

[d] **5.3** *sat down*: Teachers in the ancient world, including Jewish teachers, usually sat down when they taught. [e] **5.12** *leprosy*: See the note at 4.27. [f] **5.14** *everyone will know that you have been healed*: People with leprosy had to be examined by a priest and told that they were well (that is, "clean") before they could once again live a normal life in the Jewish community. The gift that Moses commanded was the sacrifice of some lambs together with flour mixed with olive oil. [g] **5.19** *roof*: In Palestine the houses usually had a flat roof. Stairs on the outside led up to the roof, which was made of beams and boards covered with packed earth. Luke says that the roof was made of (clay) tiles, which were also used for making roofs in New Testament times. [h] **5.27** *tax collector*: See the note at 3.12.

Luke 5.32

[32] I didn't come to invite good people to turn to God. I came to invite sinners."

People Ask about Going without Eating
(Matthew 9.14-17; Mark 2.18-22)

[33] Some people said to Jesus, "John's followers often pray and go without eating,[i] and so do the followers of the Pharisees. But your disciples never go without eating or drinking."

[34] Jesus told them, "The friends of a bridegroom don't go without eating while he is still with them. [35] But the time will come when he will be taken from them. Then they will go without eating."

[36] Jesus then told them these sayings:
No one uses a new piece of cloth to patch old clothes. The patch would shrink and make the hole even bigger.

[37] No one pours new wine into old wineskins. The new wine would swell and burst the old skins.[j] Then the wine would be lost, and the skins would be ruined. [38] New wine must be put only into new wineskins.

[39] No one wants new wine after drinking old wine. They say, "The old wine is better."

A Question about the Sabbath
(Matthew 12.1-8; Mark 2.23-28)

6 One Sabbath when Jesus and his disciples were walking through some wheat fields,[k] the disciples picked some wheat. They rubbed the husks off with their hands and started eating the grain. [2] Some Pharisees said, "Why are you picking grain on the Sabbath? You're not supposed to do that!"

[3] Jesus answered, "You surely have read what David did when he and his followers were hungry. [4] He went into the house of God and took the sacred loaves of bread that only priests were supposed to eat. He not only ate some himself, but even gave some to his followers."

[5] Jesus finished by saying, "The Son of Man is Lord over the Sabbath."

A Man with a Crippled Hand
(Matthew 12.9-14; Mark 3.1-6)

[6] On another Sabbath[l] Jesus was teaching in a Jewish meeting place, and a man with a crippled right hand was there. [7] Some Pharisees and teachers of the Law of Moses kept watching Jesus to see if he would heal the man. They did this because they wanted to accuse Jesus of doing something wrong.

[8] Jesus knew what they were thinking. So he told the man to stand up where everyone could see him. And the man stood up. [9] Then Jesus asked, "On the Sabbath should we do good deeds or evil deeds? Should we save someone's life or destroy it?"

[10] After he had looked around at everyone, he told the man, "Stretch out your hand." He did, and his bad hand became completely well.

[11] The teachers and the Pharisees were furious and started saying to each other, "What can we do about Jesus?"

Jesus Chooses His Twelve Apostles
(Matthew 10.1-4; Mark 3.13-19)

[12] About that time Jesus went off to a mountain to pray, and he spent the whole night there. [13] The next morning he called his disciples together and chose twelve of them to be his apostles. [14] One was Simon, and Jesus named him Peter. Another was Andrew, Peter's brother. There were also James, John, Philip, Bartholomew, [15] Matthew, Thomas, and James the son of Alphaeus. The rest of the apostles were Simon, known as the Eager One,[m] [16] Jude, who was the son of James, and Judas Iscariot,[n] who later betrayed Jesus.

Jesus Teaches, Preaches, and Heals
(Matthew 4.23-25)

[17] Jesus and his apostles went down from the mountain and came to some flat, level ground. Many other disciples were there to meet him. Large crowds of people from all over Judea, Jerusalem, and the coastal cities of Tyre and Sidon were there too. [18] These people had come to listen to Jesus and to be healed of their diseases. All who were troubled by evil spirits were also healed. [19] Everyone was trying to touch Jesus, because power was going out from him and healing them all.

Blessings and Troubles
(Matthew 5.1-12)

[20] Jesus looked at his disciples and said:

---

[i] **5.33** *without eating*: See the note at 2.37. [j] **5.37** *swell and burst the old skins*: While the juice from grapes was becoming wine, it would swell and stretch the skins in which it had been stored. If the skins were old and stiff, they would burst. [k] **6.1** *walking through some wheat fields*: It was the custom to let hungry travelers pick grains of wheat. [l] **6.6** *On another Sabbath*: Some manuscripts have a reading which may mean "the Sabbath after the next." [m] **6.15** *known as the Eager One*: The word "eager" translates the Greek word "zealot," which was a name later given to the members of a Jewish group that resisted and fought against the Romans. [n] **6.16** *Iscariot*: This may mean "a man from Kerioth" (a place in Judea). But more probably it means "a man who was a liar" or "a man who was a betrayer."

God will bless you people
who are poor.
    His kingdom belongs to you!
²¹ God will bless
    you hungry people.
You will have plenty
    to eat!
God will bless you people
who are crying.
    You will laugh!

²²God will bless you when others hate you and won't have anything to do with you. God will bless you when people insult you and say cruel things about you, all because you are a follower of the Son of Man. ²³Long ago your own people did these same things to the prophets. So when this happens to you, be happy and jump for joy! You will have a great reward in heaven.

²⁴ But you rich people
    are in for trouble.
You have already had
    an easy life!
²⁵ You well-fed people
    are in for trouble.
        You will go hungry!
You people
who are laughing now
    are in for trouble.
You are going to cry
    and weep!

²⁶You are in for trouble when everyone says good things about you. That is what your own people said about those prophets who told lies.

Love for Enemies
(Matthew 5.38-48; 7.12a)

²⁷This is what I say to all who will listen to me:
Love your enemies, and be good to everyone who hates you. ²⁸Ask God to bless anyone who curses you, and pray for everyone who is cruel to you. ²⁹If someone slaps you on one cheek, don't stop that person from slapping you on the other cheek. If someone wants to take your coat, don't try to keep back your shirt. ³⁰Give to everyone who asks and don't ask people to return what they have taken from you. ³¹Treat others just as you want to be treated.

³²If you love only someone who loves you, will God praise you for that? Even sinners love people who love them. ³³If you are kind only to someone who is kind to you, will God be pleased with you for that? Even sinners are kind to people who are kind to them. ³⁴If you lend money only to someone you think will pay you back, will God be pleased with you for that? Even sinners lend to sinners because they think they will get it all back.

³⁵But love your enemies and be good to them. Lend without expecting to be paid back.º Then you will get a great reward, and you will be the true children of God in heaven. He is good even to people who are unthankful and cruel. ³⁶Have pity on others, just as your Father has pity on you.

Judging Others
(Matthew 7.1-5)

³⁷Jesus said:
Don't judge others, and God won't judge you. Don't be hard on others, and God won't be hard on you. Forgive others, and God will forgive you. ³⁸If you give to others, you will be given a full amount in return. It will be packed down, shaken together, and spilling over into your lap. The way you treat others is the way you will be treated.

³⁹Jesus also used some sayings as he spoke to the people. He said:
Can one blind person lead another blind person? Won't they both fall into a ditch? ⁴⁰Are students better than their teacher? But when they are fully trained, they will be like their teacher.

⁴¹You can see the speck in your friend's eye. But you don't notice the log in your own eye. ⁴²How can you say, "My friend, let me take the speck out of your eye," when you don't see the log in your own eye? You show-offs! First, get the log out of your own eye. Then you can see how to take the speck out of your friend's eye.

A Tree and Its Fruit
(Matthew 7.17-20; 12.34b, 35)

⁴³A good tree cannot produce bad fruit, and a bad tree cannot produce good fruit. ⁴⁴You can tell what a tree is like by the fruit it produces. You cannot pick figs or grapes from thornbushes. ⁴⁵Good people do good things because of the good in their hearts. Bad people do bad things because of the evil in their hearts. Your words show what is in your heart.

Two Builders
(Matthew 7.24-27)

⁴⁶Why do you keep on saying that I am your Lord, when you refuse to

---

º**6.35** *without expecting to be paid back*: Some manuscripts have "without giving up on anyone."

do what I say? ⁴⁷Anyone who comes and listens to me and obeys me ⁴⁸is like someone who dug down deep and built a house on solid rock. When the flood came and the river rushed against the house, it was built so well that it didn't even shake. ⁴⁹But anyone who hears what I say and doesn't obey me is like someone whose house wasn't built on solid rock. As soon as the river rushed against that house, it was smashed to pieces!

Jesus Heals an Army Officer's Servant
(Matthew 8.5-13; John 4.43-54)

7 After Jesus had finished teaching the people, he went to Capernaum. ²In that town an army officer's servant was sick and about to die. The officer liked this servant very much. ³And when he heard about Jesus, he sent some Jewish leaders to ask him to come and heal the servant.

⁴The leaders went to Jesus and begged him to do something. They said, "This man deserves your help! ⁵He loves our nation and even built us a meeting place." ⁶So Jesus went with them.

When Jesus wasn't far from the house, the officer sent some friends to tell him, "Lord, don't go to any trouble for me! I am not good enough for you to come into my house. ⁷And I am certainly not worthy to come to you. Just say the word, and my servant will get well. ⁸I have officers who give orders to me, and I have soldiers who take orders from me. I can say to one of them, 'Go!' and he goes. I can say to another, 'Come!' and he comes. I can say to my servant, 'Do this!' and he will do it."

⁹When Jesus heard this, he was so surprised that he turned and said to the crowd following him, "In all of Israel I've never found anyone with this much faith!"

¹⁰The officer's friends returned and found the servant well.

A Widow's Son

¹¹Soon Jesus and his disciples were on their way to the town of Nain, and a big crowd was going along with them. ¹²As they came near the gate of the town, they saw people carrying out the body of a widow's only son. Many people from the town were walking along with her.

¹³When the Lord saw the woman, he felt sorry for her and said, "Don't cry!" ¹⁴Jesus went over and touched the stretcher on which the people were carrying the dead boy. They stopped, and Jesus said, "Young man, get up!" ¹⁵The boy sat up and began to speak. Jesus then gave him back to his mother.

¹⁶Everyone was frightened and praised God. They said, "A great prophet is here with us! God has come to his people."

¹⁷News about Jesus spread all over Judea and everywhere else in that part of the country.

John the Baptist
(Matthew 11.1-19)

¹⁸⁻¹⁹John's followers told John everything that was being said about Jesus. So he sent two of them to ask the Lord, "Are you the one we should be looking for? Or must we wait for someone else?"

²⁰When these messengers came to Jesus, they said, "John the Baptist sent us to ask, 'Are you the one we should be looking for? Or are we supposed to wait for someone else?' "

²¹At that time Jesus was healing many people who were sick or in pain or were troubled by evil spirits, and he was giving sight to a lot of blind people. ²²Jesus said to the messengers sent by John, "Go and tell John what you have seen and heard. Blind people are now able to see, and the lame can walk. People who have leprosy[p] are being healed, and the deaf can now hear. The dead are raised to life, and the poor are hearing the good news. ²³God will bless everyone who doesn't reject me because of what I do."

²⁴After John's messengers had gone, Jesus began speaking to the crowds about John:

What kind of person did you go out to the desert to see? Was he like tall grass blown about by the wind? ²⁵What kind of man did you really go out to see? Was he someone dressed in fine clothes? People who wear expensive clothes and live in luxury are in the king's palace. ²⁶What then did you go out to see? Was he a prophet? He certainly was! I tell you that he was more than a prophet. ²⁷In the Scriptures, God calls John his messenger and says, "I am sending my messenger ahead of you to get things ready for you." ²⁸No one ever born on this earth is greater than John. But whoever is least important in God's kingdom is greater than John.

²⁹Everyone had been listening to John. Even the tax collectors[q] had obeyed God and had done what was right by letting John baptize them. ³⁰But the Pharisees and the experts in the Law of Moses refused to obey God and be baptized by John.

³¹Jesus went on to say:

---

[p] 7.22 *leprosy*: See the note at 4.27.   [q] 7.29 *tax collectors*: See the note at 3.12.

What are you people like? What kind of people are you? ³²You are like children sitting in the market and shouting to each other,

"We played the flute,
 but you would not dance!
We sang a funeral song,
 but you would not cry!"

³³John the Baptist did not go around eating and drinking, and you said, "John has a demon in him!" ³⁴But because the Son of Man goes around eating and drinking, you say, "Jesus eats and drinks too much! He is even a friend of tax collectors and sinners." ³⁵Yet Wisdom is shown to be right by what its followers do.

Simon the Pharisee

³⁶A Pharisee invited Jesus to have dinner with him. So Jesus went to the Pharisee's home and got ready to eat.ʳ

³⁷When a sinful woman in that town found out that Jesus was there, she bought an expensive bottle of perfume. ³⁸Then she came and stood behind Jesus. She cried and started washing his feet with her tears and drying them with her hair. The woman kissed his feet and poured the perfume on them.

³⁹The Pharisee who had invited Jesus saw this and said to himself, "If this man really were a prophet, he would know what kind of woman is touching him! He would know that she is a sinner."

⁴⁰Jesus said to the Pharisee, "Simon, I have something to say to you."

"Teacher, what is it?" Simon replied.

⁴¹Jesus told him, "Two people were in debt to a moneylender. One of them owed him five hundred silver coins, and the other owed him fifty. ⁴²Since neither of them could pay him back, the moneylender said that they didn't have to pay him anything. Which one of them will like him more?"

⁴³Simon answered, "I suppose it would be the one who had owed more and didn't have to pay it back."

"You are right," Jesus said.

⁴⁴He turned toward the woman and said to Simon, "Have you noticed this woman? When I came into your home, you didn't give me any water so I could wash my feet. But she has washed my feet with her tears and dried them with her hair. ⁴⁵You didn't greet me with a kiss, but from the time I came in, she has not stopped kissing my feet. ⁴⁶You didn't even pour olive oil on my head,ˢ but she has poured expensive perfume on my feet. ⁴⁷So I tell you that all her sins are forgiven, and that is why she has shown great love. But anyone who has been forgiven for only a little will show only a little love."

⁴⁸Then Jesus said to the woman, "Your sins are forgiven."

⁴⁹Some other guests started saying to one another, "Who is this who dares to forgive sins?"

⁵⁰But Jesus told the woman, "Because of your faith, you are now saved.ᵗ May God give you peace!"

Women Who Helped Jesus

8 Soon after this, Jesus was going through towns and villages, telling the good news about God's kingdom. His twelve apostles were with him, ²and so were some women who had been healed of evil spirits and all sorts of diseases. One of the women was Mary Magdalene,ᵘ who once had seven demons in her. ³Joanna, Susanna, and many others had also used what they owned to help Jesusᵛ and his disciples. Joanna's husband Chuza was one of Herod's officials.ʷ

A Story about a Farmer
(Matthew 13.1-9; Mark 4.1-9)

⁴When a large crowd from several towns had gathered around Jesus, he told them this story:

⁵A farmer went out to scatter seed in a field. While the farmer was doing it, some of the seeds fell along the road and were stepped on or eaten by birds. ⁶Other seeds fell on rocky ground and started growing. But the plants did not have enough water and soon dried up. ⁷Some other seeds fell where thornbushes grew up and choked the plants. ⁸The rest of the seeds fell on good ground where they grew and produced a hundred times as many seeds.

ʳ*7.36 got ready to eat*: On special occasions the Jewish people often followed the Greek and Roman custom of lying down on their left side and leaning on their left elbow, while eating with their right hand. This is how the woman could come up behind Jesus and wash his feet (see verse 38). ˢ*7.44-46 washed my feet . . . greet me with a kiss . . . pour olive oil on my head*: Guests in a home were usually offered water so they could wash their feet, because most people either went barefoot or wore sandals and would come in the house with very dusty feet. Guests were also greeted with a kiss on the cheek, and special ones often had sweet-smelling olive oil poured on their head. ᵗ*7.50 saved*: Or "healed." The Greek word may have either meaning. ᵘ*8.2 Magdalene*: Meaning "from Magdala," a small town on the western shore of Lake Galilee. There is no hint that she is the sinful woman in 7.36-50. ᵛ*8.3 used what they owned to help Jesus*: Women often helped Jewish teachers by giving them money. ʷ*8.3 Herod's officials*: Herod Antipas, the son of Herod the Great.

When Jesus had finished speaking, he said, "If you have ears, pay attention!"

Why Jesus Used Stories
(Matthew 13.10-17; Mark 4.10-12)

[9]Jesus' disciples asked him what the story meant. [10]So he answered:

I have explained the secrets about God's kingdom to you, but for others I can only use stories. These people look, but they don't see, and they hear, but they don't understand.

Jesus Explains the Story about a Farmer
(Matthew 13.18-23; Mark 4.13-20)

[11]This is what the story means: The seed is God's message, [12]and the seeds that fell along the road are the people who hear the message. But the devil comes and snatches the message out of their hearts, so that they will not believe and be saved. [13]The seeds that fell on rocky ground are the people who gladly hear the message and accept it. But they don't have deep roots, and they believe only for a little while. As soon as life gets hard, they give up. [14]The seeds that fell among the thornbushes are also people who hear the message. But they are so eager for riches and pleasures that they never produce anything. [15]Those seeds that fell on good ground are the people who listen to the message and keep it in good and honest hearts. They last and produce a harvest.

Light
(Mark 4.21-25)

[16]No one lights a lamp and puts it under a bowl or under a bed. A lamp is always put on a lampstand, so that people who come into a house will see the light. [17]There is nothing hidden that will not be found. There is no secret that will not be well known. [18]Pay attention to how you listen! Everyone who has something will be given more, but people who have nothing will lose what little they think they have.

Jesus' Mother and Brothers
(Matthew 12.46-50; Mark 3.31-35)

[19]Jesus' mother and brothers went to see him, but because of the crowd they could not get near him. [20]Someone told Jesus, "Your mother and brothers are standing outside and want to see you."
[21]Jesus answered, "My mother and my brothers are those people who hear and obey God's message."

A Storm
(Matthew 8.23-27; Mark 4.35-41)

[22]One day, Jesus and his disciples got into a boat, and he said, "Let's cross the lake."[x] They started out, [23]and while they were sailing across, he went to sleep.

Suddenly a windstorm struck the lake, and the boat started sinking. They were in danger. [24]So they went to Jesus and woke him up, "Master, Master! We are about to drown!"

Jesus got up and ordered the wind and waves to stop. They obeyed, and everything was calm. [25]Then Jesus asked the disciples, "Don't you have any faith?"

But they were frightened and amazed. They said to each other, "Who is this? He can give orders to the wind and the waves, and they obey him!"

A Man with Demons in Him
(Matthew 8.28-34; Mark 5.1-20)

[26]Jesus and his disciples sailed across Lake Galilee and came to shore near the town of Gerasa.[y] [27]As Jesus was getting out of the boat, he was met by a man from that town. The man had demons in him. He had gone naked for a long time and no longer lived in a house, but in the graveyard.[z] [28]The man saw Jesus and screamed. He knelt down in front of him and shouted, "Jesus, Son of God in heaven, what do you want with me? I beg you not to torture me!" [29]He said this because Jesus had already told the evil spirit to go out of him.

The man had often been attacked by the demon. And even though he had been bound with chains and leg irons and kept under guard, he smashed whatever bound him. Then the demon would force him out into lonely places. [30]Jesus asked the man, "What is your name?"

He answered, "My name is Lots." He said this because there were 'lots' of demons in him. [31]They begged Jesus not to send them to the deep pit,[a] where they would be punished.

[32]A large herd of pigs was feeding there on the hillside. So the demons begged Jesus to let them go into the pigs, and Jesus let them go. [33]Then the demons left the man and went into the pigs. The whole herd rushed down the steep bank into the lake and drowned.

---

[x]**8.22** *cross the lake*: To the eastern shore of Lake Galilee, where most of the people were not Jewish.   [y]**8.26** *Gerasa*: Some manuscripts have "Gergesa."   [z]**8.27** *graveyard*: It was thought that demons and evil spirits lived in graveyards.   [a]**8.31** *deep pit*: The place where evil spirits are kept and punished.

³⁴When the men taking care of the pigs saw this, they ran to spread the news in the town and on the farms. ³⁵The people went out to see what had happened, and when they came to Jesus, they also found the man. The demons had gone out of him, and he was sitting there at the feet of Jesus. He had clothes on and was in his right mind. But the people were terrified.

³⁶Then all who had seen the man healed told about it. ³⁷Everyone from around Gerasaᵇ begged Jesus to leave, because they were so frightened.

When Jesus got into the boat to start back, ³⁸the man who had been healed begged to go with him. But Jesus sent him off and said, ³⁹"Go back home and tell everyone how much God has done for you." The man then went all over town, telling everything that Jesus had done for him.

A Dying Girl and a Sick Woman
(Matthew 9.18-26; Mark 5.21-43)

⁴⁰Everyone had been waiting for Jesus, and when he came back, a crowd was there to welcome him. ⁴¹Just then the man in charge of the Jewish meeting place came and knelt down in front of Jesus. His name was Jairus, and he begged Jesus to come to his home ⁴²because his twelve-year-old child was dying. She was his only daughter.

While Jesus was on his way, people were crowding all around him. ⁴³In the crowd was a woman who had been bleeding for twelve years. She had spent everything she had on doctors,ᶜ but none of them could make her well.

⁴⁴As soon as she came up behind Jesus and barely touched his clothes, her bleeding stopped.

⁴⁵"Who touched me?" Jesus asked.

While everyone was denying it, Peter said, "Master, people are crowding all around and pushing you from every side."ᵈ

⁴⁶But Jesus answered, "Someone touched me, because I felt power going out from me." ⁴⁷The woman knew that she could not hide, so she came trembling and knelt down in front of Jesus. She told everyone why she had touched him and that she had been healed right away.

⁴⁸Jesus said to the woman, "You are now well because of your faith. May God give you peace!"

⁴⁹While Jesus was speaking, someone came from Jairus' home and said, "Your daughter has died! Why bother the teacher anymore?"

⁵⁰When Jesus heard this, he told Jairus, "Don't worry! Have faith, and your daughter will get well."

⁵¹Jesus went into the house, but he did not let anyone else go with him, except Peter, John, James, and the girl's father and mother. ⁵²Everyone was crying and weeping for the girl. But Jesus said, "The child isn't dead. She is just asleep." ⁵³The people laughed at him because they knew she was dead.

⁵⁴Jesus took hold of the girl's hand and said, "Child, get up!" ⁵⁵She came back to life and got right up. Jesus told them to give her something to eat. ⁵⁶Her parents were surprised, but Jesus ordered them not to tell anyone what had happened.

Instructions for the Twelve Apostles
(Matthew 10.5-15; Mark 6.7-13)

9 Jesus called together his twelve apostles and gave them complete power over all demons and diseases. ²Then he sent them to tell about God's kingdom and to heal the sick. ³He told them, "Don't take anything with you! Don't take a walking stick or a traveling bag or food or money or even a change of clothes. ⁴When you are welcomed into a home, stay there until you leave that town. ⁵If people won't welcome you, leave the town and shake the dust from your feetᵉ as a warning to them."

⁶The apostles left and went from village to village, telling the good news and healing people everywhere.

Herod Is Worried
(Matthew 14.1-12; Mark 6.14-29)

⁷Herodᶠ the ruler heard about all that was happening, and he was worried. Some people were saying that John the Baptist had come back to life. ⁸Others were saying that Elijah had comeᵍ or that one of the prophets from long ago had come back to life. ⁹But Herod said, "I had John's head cut off! Who is this I hear so much about?" Herod was eager to meet Jesus.

Jesus Feeds Five Thousand
(Matthew 14.13-21; Mark 6.30-44; John 6.1-14)

¹⁰The apostles came back and told Jesus everything they had done. He then took them with him to the village of Bethsaida, where they could be alone. ¹¹But a lot of people found out about

---

ᵇ**8.37** *Gerasa*: See the note at 8.26. ᶜ**8.43** *She had spent everything she had on doctors*: Some manuscripts do not have these words. ᵈ**8.45** *from every side*: Some manuscripts add "and you ask, 'Who touched me?'" ᵉ**9.5** *shake the dust from your feet*: This was a way of showing rejection. ᶠ**9.7** *Herod*: Herod Antipas, the son of Herod the Great. ᵍ**9.8** *Elijah had come*: Many of the Jewish people expected the prophet Elijah to come and prepare the way for the Messiah.

this and followed him. Jesus welcomed them. He spoke to them about God's kingdom and healed everyone who was sick.

12 Late in the afternoon the twelve apostles came to Jesus and said, "Send the crowd to the villages and farms around here. They need to find a place to stay and something to eat. There is nothing in this place. It is like a desert!"

13 Jesus answered, "You give them something to eat."

But they replied, "We have only five small loaves of bread[h] and two fish. If we are going to feed all these people, we will have to go and buy food." 14 There were about five thousand men in the crowd.

Jesus said to his disciples, "Have the people sit in groups of fifty." 15 They did this, and all the people sat down. 16 Jesus took the five loaves and the two fish. He looked up toward heaven and blessed the food. Then he broke the bread and fish and handed them to his disciples to give to the people.

17 Everyone ate all they wanted. What was left over filled twelve baskets.

Who Is Jesus?
(Matthew 16.13-19; Mark 8.27-29)

18 When Jesus was alone praying, his disciples came to him, and he asked them, "What do people say about me?"

19 They answered, "Some say that you are John the Baptist or Elijah[i] or a prophet from long ago who has come back to life."

20 Jesus then asked them, "But who do you say I am?"

Peter answered, "You are the Messiah sent from God."

21 Jesus strictly warned his disciples not to tell anyone about this.

Jesus Speaks about His Suffering and Death
(Matthew 16.20-28; Mark 8.30—9.1)

22 Jesus told his disciples, "The nation's leaders, the chief priests, and the teachers of the Law of Moses will make the Son of Man suffer terribly. They will reject him and kill him, but three days later he will rise to life."

23 Then Jesus said to all the people:

If any of you want to be my followers, you must forget about yourself. You must take up your cross each day and follow me. 24 If you want to save your life,[j] you will destroy it. But if you give up your life for me, you will save it. 25 What will you gain, if you own the whole world but destroy yourself or waste your life? 26 If you are ashamed of me and my message, the Son of Man will be ashamed of you when he comes in his glory and in the glory of his Father and the holy angels. 27 You can be sure that some of the people standing here will not die before they see God's kingdom.

The True Glory of Jesus
(Matthew 17.1-8; Mark 9.2-8)

28 About eight days later Jesus took Peter, John, and James with him and went up on a mountain to pray. 29 While he was praying, his face changed, and his clothes became shining white. 30 Suddenly Moses and Elijah were there speaking with him. 31 They appeared in heavenly glory and talked about all that Jesus' death[k] in Jerusalem would mean.

32 Peter and the other two disciples had been sound asleep. All at once they woke up and saw how glorious Jesus was. They also saw the two men who were with him.

33 Moses and Elijah were about to leave, when Peter said to Jesus, "Master, it is good for us to be here! Let us make three shelters, one for you, one for Moses, and one for Elijah." But Peter did not know what he was talking about.

34 While Peter was still speaking, a shadow from a cloud passed over them, and they were frightened as the cloud covered them. 35 From the cloud a voice spoke, "This is my chosen Son. Listen to what he says!"

36 After the voice had spoken, Peter, John, and James saw only Jesus. For some time they kept quiet and did not say anything about what they had seen.

Jesus Heals a Boy
(Matthew 17.14-18; Mark 9.14-27)

37 The next day Jesus and his three disciples came down from the mountain and were met by a large crowd. 38 Just then someone in the crowd shouted, "Teacher, please do something for my son! He is my only child! 39 A demon often attacks him and makes him scream. It shakes him until he foams at the mouth, and it won't leave him until it has completely worn the boy out. 40 I begged your disciples to force out the demon, but they couldn't do it."

41 Jesus said to them, "You people are stubborn and don't have any faith! How much longer must I be with you? Why do I have to put up with you?"

Then Jesus said to the man, "Bring your son to me." 42 While the boy was

---

[h] 9.13 *small loaves of bread*: These would have been flat and round or in the shape of a bun.
[i] 9.19 *Elijah*: See the note at 9.8.   [j] 9.24 *life*: In verses 24, 25 a Greek word which often means "soul" is translated "life" and "yourself."   [k] 9.31 *Jesus' death*: In Greek this is "his departure," which probably includes his rising to life and his return to heaven.

being brought, the demon attacked him and made him shake all over. Jesus ordered the demon to stop. Then he healed the boy and gave him back to his father. ⁴³Everyone was amazed at God's great power.

Jesus Again Speaks about His Death
(Matthew 17.22, 23; Mark 9.30-32)

While everyone was still amazed at what Jesus was doing, he said to his disciples, ⁴⁴"Pay close attention to what I am telling you! The Son of Man will be handed over to his enemies." ⁴⁵But the disciples did not know what he meant. The meaning was hidden from them. They could not understand it, and they were afraid to ask.

Who Is the Greatest?
(Matthew 18.1-5; Mark 9.33-37)

⁴⁶Jesus' disciples were arguing about which one of them was the greatest. ⁴⁷Jesus knew what they were thinking, and he had a child stand there beside him. ⁴⁸Then he said to his disciples, "When you welcome even a child because of me, you welcome me. And when you welcome me, you welcome the one who sent me. Whichever one of you is the most humble is the greatest."

For or against Jesus
(Mark 9.38-40)

⁴⁹John said, "Master, we saw a man using your name to force demons out of people. But we told him to stop, because he isn't one of us."
⁵⁰"Don't stop him!" Jesus said. "Anyone who isn't against you is for you."

A Samaritan Village Refuses To Receive Jesus

⁵¹Not long before it was time for Jesus to be taken up to heaven, he made up his mind to go to Jerusalem. ⁵²He sent some messengers on ahead to a Samaritan village to get things ready for him. ⁵³But he was on his way to Jerusalem, so the people there refused to welcome him. ⁵⁴When the disciples James and John saw what was happening, they asked, "Lord, do you want us to call down fire from heaven to destroy these people?"*l*
⁵⁵But Jesus turned and corrected them for what they had said.*m* ⁵⁶Then they all went on to another village.

Three People Who Wanted To Be Followers
(Matthew 8.19-22)

⁵⁷Along the way someone said to Jesus, "I'll go anywhere with you!"
⁵⁸Jesus said, "Foxes have dens, and birds have nests, but the Son of Man doesn't have a place to call his own."
⁵⁹Jesus told someone else to come with him. But the man said, "Lord, let me wait until I bury my father."*n*
⁶⁰Jesus answered, "Let the dead take care of the dead, while you go and tell about God's kingdom."
⁶¹Then someone said to Jesus, "I want to go with you, Lord, but first let me go back and take care of things at home."
⁶²Jesus answered, "Anyone who starts plowing and keeps looking back isn't worth a thing to God's kingdom!"

The Work of the Seventy-Two Followers

10 Later the Lord chose seventy-two*o* other followers and sent them out two by two to every town and village where he was about to go. ²He said to them:
A large crop is in the fields, but there are only a few workers. Ask the Lord in charge of the harvest to send out workers to bring it in. ³Now go, but remember, I am sending you like lambs into a pack of wolves. ⁴Don't take along a moneybag or a traveling bag or sandals. And don't waste time greeting people on the road.*p* ⁵As soon as you enter a home, say, "God bless this home with peace." ⁶If the people living there are peace-loving, your prayer for peace will bless them. But if they are not peace-loving, your prayer will return to you. ⁷Stay with the same family, eating and drinking whatever they give you, because workers are worth what they earn. Don't move around from house to house.
⁸If the people of a town welcome you, eat whatever they offer. ⁹Heal their sick and say, "God's kingdom will soon be here!"*q*
¹⁰But if the people of a town refuse to welcome you, go out into the

---

*l*9.54 *to destroy these people*: Some manuscripts add "as Elijah did." *m*9.55 *what they had said*: Some manuscripts add, "and said, 'Don't you know what spirit you belong to? The Son of Man did not come to destroy people's lives, but to save them.'" *n*9.59 *bury my father*: The Jewish people taught that giving someone a proper burial was even more important than helping the poor. *o*10.1 *seventy-two*: Some manuscripts have "seventy." According to Jewish tradition, there were seventy nations on earth. But the ancient Greek translation of the Old Testament has "seventy-two" in place of "seventy." Jesus probably chose this number of followers to show that his message was for everyone in the world. *p*10.4 *waste time greeting people on the road*: In those days a polite greeting could take a long time. *q*10.9 *will soon be here*: Or "is already here."

street and say, [11]"We are shaking the dust from our feet[r] as a warning to you. And you can be sure that God's kingdom will soon be here!"[s] [12]I tell you that on the day of judgment the people of Sodom will get off easier than the people of that town!

The Unbelieving Towns
(Matthew 11.20-24)

[13]You people of Chorazin are in for trouble! You people of Bethsaida are also in for trouble! If the miracles that took place in your towns had happened in Tyre and Sidon, the people there would have turned to God long ago. They would have dressed in sackcloth and put ashes on their heads.[t] [14]On the day of judgment the people of Tyre and Sidon will get off easier than you will. [15]People of Capernaum, do you think you will be honored in heaven? Well, you will go down to hell!

[16]My followers, whoever listens to you is listening to me. Anyone who says "No" to you is saying "No" to me. And anyone who says "No" to me is really saying "No" to the one who sent me.

The Return of the Seventy-Two

[17]When the seventy-two[u] followers returned, they were excited and said, "Lord, even the demons obeyed when we spoke in your name!"

[18]Jesus told them:

I saw Satan fall from heaven like a flash of lightning. [19]I have given you the power to trample on snakes and scorpions and to defeat the power of your enemy Satan. Nothing can harm you. [20]But don't be happy because evil spirits obey you. Be happy that your names are written in heaven!

Jesus Thanks His Father
(Matthew 11.25-27; 13.16, 17)

[21]At that same time, Jesus felt the joy that comes from the Holy Spirit,[v] and he said:

My Father, Lord of heaven and earth, I am grateful that you hid all this from wise and educated people and showed it to ordinary people. Yes, Father, that is what pleased you. [22]My Father has given me everything, and he is the only one who knows the Son. The only one who really knows the Father is the Son. But the Son wants to tell others about the Father, so that they can know him too.

[23]Jesus then turned to his disciples and said to them in private, "You are really blessed to see what you see! [24]Many prophets and kings were eager to see what you see and to hear what you hear. But I tell you that they did not see or hear."

The Good Samaritan

[25]An expert in the Law of Moses stood up and asked Jesus a question to see what he would say. "Teacher," he asked, "what must I do to have eternal life?"

[26]Jesus answered, "What is written in the Scriptures? How do you understand them?"

[27]The man replied, "The Scriptures say, 'Love the Lord your God with all your heart, soul, strength, and mind.' They also say, 'Love your neighbors as much as you love yourself.' "

[28]Jesus said, "You have given the right answer. If you do this, you will have eternal life."

[29]But the man wanted to show that he knew what he was talking about. So he asked Jesus, "Who are my neighbors?"

[30]Jesus replied:

As a man was going down from Jerusalem to Jericho, robbers attacked him and grabbed everything he had. They beat him up and ran off, leaving him half dead.

[31]A priest happened to be going down the same road. But when he saw the man, he walked by on the other side. [32]Later a temple helper[w] came to the same place. But when he saw the man who had been beaten up, he also went by on the other side.

[33]A man from Samaria then came traveling along that road. When he saw the man, he felt sorry for him [34]and went over to him. He treated his wounds with olive oil and wine[x] and bandaged them. Then he put him on his own donkey and took him to an inn, where he took care of him. [35]The next morning he gave the innkeeper two silver coins and said, "Please take care of the man. If you spend more than this on him, I will pay you when I return."

[36]Then Jesus asked, "Which one of

---

[r]10.11 *shaking the dust from our feet*: This was a way of showing rejection.   [s]10.11 *will soon be here*: Or "is already here."   [t]10.13 *dressed in sackcloth . . . ashes on their heads*: This was one way that people showed how sorry they were for their sins.   [u]10.17 *seventy-two*: See the note at 10.1.   [v]10.21 *the Holy Spirit*: Some manuscripts have "his spirit."   [w]10.32 *temple helper*: A man from the tribe of Levi, whose job it was to work around the temple.   [x]10.34 *olive oil and wine*: In New Testament times these were used as medicine. Sometimes olive oil is a symbol for healing by means of a miracle (see James 5.14).

these three people was a real neighbor to the man who was beaten up by robbers?" ³⁷The teacher answered, "The one who showed pity."

Jesus said, "Go and do the same!"

Martha and Mary

³⁸The Lord and his disciples were traveling along and came to a village. When they got there, a woman named Martha welcomed him into her home. ³⁹She had a sister named Mary, who sat down in front of the Lord and was listening to what he said. ⁴⁰Martha was worried about all that had to be done. Finally, she went to Jesus and said, "Lord, doesn't it bother you that my sister has left me to do all the work by myself? Tell her to come and help me!"

⁴¹The Lord answered, "Martha, Martha! You are worried and upset about so many things, ⁴²but only one thing is necessary. Mary has chosen what is best, and it will not be taken away from her."

Prayer
(Matthew 6.9-13; 7.7-11)

11 When Jesus had finished praying, one of his disciples said to him, "Lord, teach us to pray, just as John taught his followers to pray."

²So Jesus told them, "Pray in this way:

'Father, help us
   to honor your name.
Come and set up
   your kingdom.
³ Give us each day
   the food we need.ʸ
⁴ Forgive our sins,
as we forgive everyone
   who has done wrong to us.
And keep us
   from being tempted.' "

⁵Then Jesus went on to say:

Suppose one of you goes to a friend in the middle of the night and says, "Let me borrow three loaves of bread. ⁶A friend of mine has dropped in, and I don't have a thing for him to eat." ⁷And suppose your friend answers, "Don't bother me! The door is bolted, and my children and I are in bed. I cannot get up to give you something."

⁸He may not get up and give you the bread, just because you are his friend. But he will get up and give you as much as you need, simply because you are not ashamed to keep on asking.

⁹So I tell you to ask and you will receive, search and you will find, knock and the door will be opened for you. ¹⁰Everyone who asks will receive, everyone who searches will find, and the door will be opened for everyone who knocks. ¹¹Which one of you fathers would give your hungry child a snake if the child asked for a fish? ¹²Which one of you would give your child a scorpion if the child asked for an egg? ¹³As bad as you are, you still know how to give good gifts to your children. But your heavenly Father is even more ready to give the Holy Spirit to anyone who asks.

Jesus and the Ruler of Demons
(Matthew 12.22-30; Mark 3.20-27)

¹⁴Jesus forced a demon out of a man who could not talk. And after the demon had gone out, the man started speaking, and the crowds were amazed. ¹⁵But some people said, "He forces out demons by the power of Beelzebul, the ruler of the demons!"

¹⁶Others wanted to put Jesus to the test. So they asked him to show them a sign from God. ¹⁷Jesus knew what they were thinking, and he said:

A kingdom where people fight each other will end up in ruin. And a family that fights will break up. ¹⁸If Satan fights against himself, how can his kingdom last? Yet you say that I force out demons by the power of Beelzebul. ¹⁹If I use his power to force out demons, whose power do your own followers use to force them out? They are the ones who will judge you. ²⁰But if I use God's power to force out demons, it proves that God's kingdom has already come to you.

²¹When a strong man arms himself and guards his home, everything he owns is safe. ²²But if a stronger man comes and defeats him, he will carry off the weapons in which the strong man trusted. Then he will divide with others what he has taken. ²³If you are not on my side, you are against me. If you don't gather in the crop with me, you scatter it.

Return of an Evil Spirit
(Matthew 12.43-45)

²⁴When an evil spirit leaves a person, it travels through the desert, looking for a place to rest. But when it doesn't find a place, it says, "I will go back to the home I left." ²⁵When it gets there and finds the place

---

ʸ**11.3** *the food we need*: Or "food for today" or "food for the coming day."

clean and fixed up, ²⁶it goes off and finds seven other evil spirits even worse than itself. They all come and make their home there, and that person ends up in worse shape than before.

Being Really Blessed

²⁷While Jesus was still talking, a woman in the crowd spoke up, "The woman who gave birth to you and nursed you is blessed!"
²⁸Jesus replied, "That's true, but the people who are really blessed are the ones who hear and obey God's message!"[z]

A Sign from God
(Matthew 12.38-42; Mark 8.12)

²⁹As crowds were gathering around Jesus, he said:
You people of today are evil! You keep looking for a sign from God. But what happened to Jonah[a] is the only sign you will be given. ³⁰Just as Jonah was a sign to the people of Nineveh, the Son of Man will be a sign to the people of today. ³¹When the judgment comes, the Queen of the South[b] will stand there with you and condemn you. She traveled a long way to hear Solomon's wisdom, and yet here is something far greater than Solomon. ³²The people of Nineveh will also stand there with you and condemn you. They turned to God when Jonah preached, and yet here is something far greater than Jonah.

Light
(Matthew 5.15; 6.22, 23)

³³No one lights a lamp and then hides it or puts it under a clay pot. A lamp is put on a lampstand, so that everyone who comes into the house can see the light. ³⁴Your eyes are the lamp for your body. When your eyes are good, you have all the light you need. But when your eyes are bad, everything is dark. ³⁵So be sure that your light isn't darkness. ³⁶If you have light, and nothing is dark, then light will be everywhere, as when a lamp shines brightly on you.

Jesus Condemns the Pharisees and Teachers of the Law of Moses
(Matthew 23.1-36; Mark 12.38-40; Luke 20.45-47)

³⁷When Jesus finished speaking, a Pharisee invited him home for a meal. Jesus went and sat down to eat.[c] ³⁸The Pharisee was surprised that he did not wash his hands[d] before eating. ³⁹So the Lord said to him:
You Pharisees clean the outside of cups and dishes, but on the inside you are greedy and evil. ⁴⁰You fools! Didn't God make both the outside and the inside?[e] ⁴¹If you would only give what you have to the poor, everything you do would please God.
⁴²You Pharisees are in for trouble! You give God a tenth of the spices from your gardens, such as mint and rue. But you cheat people, and you don't love God. You should be fair and kind to others and still give a tenth to God.
⁴³You Pharisees are in for trouble! You love the front seats in the meeting places, and you like to be greeted with honor in the market. ⁴⁴But you are in for trouble! You are like unmarked graves[f] that people walk on without even knowing it.
⁴⁵A teacher of the Law of Moses spoke up, "Teacher, you said cruel things about us."
⁴⁶Jesus replied:
You teachers are also in for trouble! You load people down with heavy burdens, but you won't lift a finger to help them carry the loads. ⁴⁷Yes, you are really in for trouble. You build monuments to honor the prophets your own people murdered long ago. ⁴⁸You must think that was the right thing for your people to do, or else you would not have built monuments for the prophets they murdered.
⁴⁹Because of your evil deeds, the Wisdom of God said, "I will send prophets and apostles to you. But you will murder some and mistreat others." ⁵⁰You people living today will be punished for all the prophets who have been murdered since the beginning of the world. ⁵¹This includes every prophet from the time

---

[z]11.28 *"That's true, but the people who are really blessed ... message"*: Or " 'That's not true, the people who are blessed ... message.' " [a]11.29 *what happened to Jonah*: Jonah was in the stomach of a big fish for three days and nights (see Matthew 12.40). [b]11.31 *Queen of the South*: Sheba, probably a country in southern Arabia. [c]11.37 *sat down to eat*: See the note at 7.36. [d]11.38 *did not wash his hands*: The Jewish people had strict laws about washing their hands before eating, especially if they had been out in public. [e]11.40 *Didn't God make both the outside and the inside?*: Or "Doesn't the person who washes the outside always wash the inside too?" [f]11.44 *unmarked graves*: Tombs were whitewashed to keep anyone from accidentally touching them. A person who touched a dead body or a tomb was considered unclean and could not worship with other Jewish people.

of Abel to the time of Zechariah,[g] who was murdered between the altar and the temple. You people will certainly be punished for all of this.

⁵²You teachers of the Law of Moses are really in for trouble! You carry the keys to the door of knowledge about God. But you never go in, and you keep others from going in.

⁵³Jesus was about to leave, but the teachers and the Pharisees wanted to get even with him. They tried to make him say what he thought about other things, ⁵⁴so that they could catch him saying something wrong.

Warnings

12 As thousands of people crowded around Jesus and were stepping on each other, he told his disciples:

Be sure to guard against the dishonest teaching[h] of the Pharisees! It is their way of fooling people. ²Everything that is hidden will be found out, and every secret will be known. ³Whatever you say in the dark will be heard when it is day. Whatever you whisper in a closed room will be shouted from the housetops.

The One To Fear
(Matthew 10.28-31)

⁴My friends, don't be afraid of people. They can kill you, but after that, there is nothing else they can do. ⁵God is the one you must fear. Not only can he take your life, but he can throw you into hell. God is certainly the one you should fear! ⁶Five sparrows are sold for just two pennies, but God doesn't forget a one of them. ⁷Even the hairs on your head are counted. So don't be afraid! You are worth much more than many sparrows.

Telling Others about Christ
(Matthew 10.32, 33; 12.32; 10.19, 20)

⁸If you tell others that you belong to me, the Son of Man will tell God's angels that you are my followers. ⁹But if you reject me, you will be rejected in front of them. ¹⁰If you speak against the Son of Man, you can be forgiven, but if you speak against the Holy Spirit, you cannot be forgiven. ¹¹When you are brought to trial in the Jewish meeting places or before rulers or officials, don't worry about how you will defend yourselves or what you will say. ¹²At that time the Holy Spirit will tell you what to say.

A Rich Fool

¹³A man in a crowd said to Jesus, "Teacher, tell my brother to give me my share of what our father left us when he died."

¹⁴Jesus answered, "Who gave me the right to settle arguments between you and your brother?"

¹⁵Then he said to the crowd, "Don't be greedy! Owning a lot of things won't make your life safe."

¹⁶So Jesus told them this story:

A rich man's farm produced a big crop, ¹⁷and he said to himself, "What can I do? I don't have a place large enough to store everything."

¹⁸Later, he said, "Now I know what I'll do. I'll tear down my barns and build bigger ones, where I can store all my grain and other goods. ¹⁹Then I'll say to myself, 'You have stored up enough good things to last for years to come. Live it up! Eat, drink, and enjoy yourself.'"

²⁰But God said to him, "You fool! Tonight you will die. Then who will get what you have stored up?"

²¹"This is what happens to people who store up everything for themselves, but are poor in the sight of God."

Worry
(Matthew 6.25-34)

²²Jesus said to his disciples:

I tell you not to worry about your life! Don't worry about having something to eat or wear. ²³Life is more than food or clothing. ²⁴Look at the crows! They don't plant or harvest, and they don't have storehouses or barns. But God takes care of them. You are much more important than any birds. ²⁵Can worry make you live longer?[i] ²⁶If you don't have power over small things, why worry about everything else?

²⁷Look how the wild flowers grow! They don't work hard to make their clothes. But I tell you that Solomon with all his wealth[j] wasn't as well clothed as one of these flowers. ²⁸God gives such beauty to everything that grows in the fields, even though it is here today and thrown

---

[g] 11.51 *from the time of Abel . . . Zechariah*: Genesis is the first book in the Jewish Scriptures, and it tells that Abel was the first person to be murdered. Second Chronicles is the last book in the Jewish Scriptures, and the last murder that it tells about is that of Zechariah.
[h] 12.1 *dishonest teaching*: The Greek text has "yeast," which is used here of a teaching that is not true (see Matthew 16.6, 12). [i] 12.25 *live longer*: Or "grow taller." [j] 12.27 *Solomon with all his wealth*: The Jewish people thought that Solomon was the richest person who had ever lived.

into a fire tomorrow. Won't he do even more for you? You have such little faith! ²⁹Don't keep worrying about having something to eat or drink. ³⁰Only people who don't know God are always worrying about such things. Your Father knows what you need. ³¹But put God's work first, and these things will be yours as well.

Treasures in Heaven
(Matthew 6.19-21)

³²My little group of disciples, don't be afraid! Your Father wants to give you the kingdom. ³³Sell what you have and give the money to the poor. Make yourselves moneybags that never wear out. Make sure your treasure is safe in heaven, where thieves cannot steal it and moths cannot destroy it. ³⁴Your heart will always be where your treasure is.

Faithful and Unfaithful Servants
(Matthew 24.45-51)

³⁵Be ready and keep your lamps burning ³⁶just like those servants who wait up for their master to return from a wedding feast. As soon as he comes and knocks, they open the door for him. ³⁷Servants are fortunate if their master finds them awake and ready when he comes! I promise you that he will get ready and have his servants sit down so he can serve them. ³⁸Those servants are really fortunate if their master finds them ready, even though he comes late at night or early in the morning. ³⁹You would surely not let a thief break into your home, if you knew when the thief was coming. ⁴⁰So always be ready! You don't know when the Son of Man will come.

⁴¹Peter asked Jesus, "Did you say this just for us or for everyone?"

⁴²The Lord answered:

Who are faithful and wise servants? Who are the ones the master will put in charge of giving the other servants their food supplies at the proper time? ⁴³Servants are fortunate if their master comes and finds them doing their job. ⁴⁴A servant who is always faithful will surely be put in charge of everything the master owns.

⁴⁵But suppose one of the servants thinks that the master won't return until late. Suppose that servant starts beating all the other servants and eats and drinks and gets drunk. ⁴⁶If that happens, the master will come on a day and at a time when the servant least expects him. That servant will then be punished and thrown out with the servants who cannot be trusted.

⁴⁷If servants are not ready or willing to do what their master wants them to do, they will be beaten hard. ⁴⁸But servants who don't know what their master wants them to do will not be beaten so hard for doing wrong. If God has been generous with you, he will expect you to serve him well. But if he has been more than generous, he will expect you to serve him even better.

Not Peace, but Trouble
(Matthew 10.34-36)

⁴⁹I came to set fire to the earth, and I wish it were already on fire! ⁵⁰I am going to be put to a hard test. And I will have to suffer a lot of pain until it is over. ⁵¹Do you think that I came to bring peace to earth? No indeed! I came to make people choose sides. ⁵²A family of five will be divided, with two of them against the other three. ⁵³Fathers and sons will turn against one another, and mothers and daughters will do the same. Mothers-in-law and daughters-in-law will also turn against each other.

Knowing What To Do
(Matthew 16.2, 3; 5.25, 26)

⁵⁴Jesus said to all the people:

As soon as you see a cloud coming up in the west, you say, "It's going to rain," and it does. ⁵⁵When the south wind blows, you say, "It's going to get hot," and it does. ⁵⁶Are you trying to fool someone? You can predict the weather by looking at the earth and sky, but you don't really know what's going on right now. ⁵⁷Why don't you understand the right thing to do? ⁵⁸When someone accuses you of something, try to settle things before you are taken to court. If you don't, you will be dragged before the judge. Then the judge will hand you over to the jailer, and you will be locked up. ⁵⁹You won't get out until you have paid the last cent you owe.

Turn Back to God

13 About this same time Jesus was told that Pilate had given orders for some people from Galilee to be killed while they were offering sacrifices. ²Jesus replied:

Do you think that these people were worse sinners than everyone else in Galilee just because of what happened to them? ³Not at all! But you can be sure that if you don't turn back to God, every one of you will also be killed. ⁴What about those eighteen people who died when the tower in Siloam fell on them? Do you think they were worse than everyone else in Jerusalem? ⁵Not at all! But you can be sure that if you don't turn back to God, every one of you will also die.

A Story about a Fig Tree

⁶Jesus then told them this story:
A man had a fig tree growing in his vineyard. One day he went out to pick some figs, but he didn't find any. ⁷So he said to the gardener, "For three years I have come looking for figs on this tree, and I haven't found any yet. Chop it down! Why should it take up space?"

⁸The gardener answered, "Master, leave it for another year. I'll dig around it and put some manure on it to make it grow. ⁹Maybe it will have figs on it next year. If it doesn't, you can have it cut down."

Healing a Woman on the Sabbath

¹⁰One Sabbath, Jesus was teaching in a Jewish meeting place, ¹¹and a woman was there who had been crippled by an evil spirit for eighteen years. She was completely bent over and could not straighten up. ¹²When Jesus saw the woman, he called her over and said, "You are now well." ¹³He placed his hands on her, and right away she stood up straight and praised God.

¹⁴The man in charge of the meeting place was angry because Jesus had healed someone on the Sabbath. So he said to the people, "Each week has six days when we can work. Come and be healed on one of those days, but not on the Sabbath."

¹⁵The Lord replied, "Are you trying to fool someone? Won't any one of you untie your ox or donkey and lead it out to drink on a Sabbath? ¹⁶This woman belongs to the family of Abraham, but Satan has kept her bound for eighteen years. Isn't it right to set her free on the Sabbath?" ¹⁷Jesus' words made his enemies ashamed. But everyone else in the crowd was happy about the wonderful things he was doing.

A Mustard Seed and Yeast
(Matthew 13.31-33; Mark 4.30-32)

¹⁸Jesus said, "What is God's kingdom like? What can I compare it with? ¹⁹It is like what happens when someone plants a mustard seed in a garden. The seed grows as big as a tree, and birds nest in its branches."

²⁰Then Jesus said, "What can I compare God's kingdom with? ²¹It is like what happens when a woman mixes yeast into three batches of flour. Finally, all the dough rises."

The Narrow Door
(Matthew 7.13, 14, 21-23)

²²As Jesus was on his way to Jerusalem, he taught the people in the towns and villages. ²³Someone asked him, "Lord, are only a few people going to be saved?"

Jesus answered:
²⁴Do all you can to go in by the narrow door! A lot of people will try to get in, but will not be able to. ²⁵Once the owner of the house gets up and locks the door, you will be left standing outside. You will knock on the door and say, "Sir, open the door for us!"

But the owner will answer, "I don't know a thing about you!"

²⁶Then you will start saying, "We dined with you, and you taught in our streets."

²⁷But he will say, "I really don't know who you are! Get away from me, you evil people!"

²⁸Then when you have been thrown outside, you will weep and grit your teeth because you will see Abraham, Isaac, Jacob, and all the prophets in God's kingdom. ²⁹People will come from all directions and sit down to feast in God's kingdom. ³⁰There the ones who are now least important will be the most important, and those who are now most important will be least important.

Jesus and Herod

³¹At that time some Pharisees came to Jesus and said, "You had better get away from here! Herod[k] wants to kill you."

³²Jesus said to them:
Go tell that fox, "I am going to force out demons and heal people today and tomorrow, and three days later I'll be through." ³³But I am going on my way today and tomorrow and the next day. After all, Jerusalem is the place where prophets are killed.

Jesus Loves Jerusalem
(Matthew 23.37-39)

³⁴Jerusalem, Jerusalem! Your people have killed the prophets and have stoned the messengers who were sent to you. I have often wanted to gather your people, as a hen gathers her chicks under her wings. But you wouldn't let me. ³⁵Now your temple will be deserted.

---

[k] 13.31 *Herod*: Herod Antipas, the son of Herod the Great.

You won't see me again until the time when you say,

"Blessed is the one who comes in the name of the Lord."

Jesus Heals a Sick Man

14 One Sabbath, Jesus was having dinner in the home of an important Pharisee, and everyone was carefully watching Jesus. ²All of a sudden a man with swollen legs stood up in front of him. ³Jesus turned and asked the Pharisees and the teachers of the Law of Moses, "Is it right to heal on the Sabbath?" ⁴But they did not say a word.

Jesus took hold of the man. Then he healed him and sent him away. ⁵Afterwards, Jesus asked the people, "If your son or ox falls into a well, wouldn't you pull him out right away, even on the Sabbath?" ⁶There was nothing they could say.

How To Be a Guest

⁷Jesus saw how the guests had tried to take the best seats. So he told them:

⁸When you are invited to a wedding feast, don't sit in the best place. Someone more important may have been invited. ⁹Then the one who invited you will come and say, "Give your place to this other guest!" You will be embarrassed and will have to sit in the worst place.

¹⁰When you are invited to be a guest, go and sit in the worst place. Then the one who invited you may come and say, "My friend, take a better seat!" You will then be honored in front of all the other guests. ¹¹If you put yourself above others, you will be put down. But if you humble yourself, you will be honored.

¹²Then Jesus said to the man who had invited him:

When you give a dinner or a banquet, don't invite your friends and family and relatives and rich neighbors. If you do, they will invite you in return, and you will be paid back. ¹³When you give a feast, invite the poor, the crippled, the lame, and the blind. ¹⁴They cannot pay you back. But God will bless you and reward you when his people rise from death.

The Great Banquet
(Matthew 22.1-10)

¹⁵After Jesus had finished speaking, one of the guests said, "The greatest blessing of all is to be at the banquet in God's kingdom!"

¹⁶Jesus told him:

A man once gave a great banquet and invited a lot of guests. ¹⁷When the banquet was ready, he sent a servant to tell the guests, "Everything is ready! Please come."

¹⁸One guest after another started making excuses. The first one said, "I bought some land, and I've got to look it over. Please excuse me."

¹⁹Another guest said, "I bought five teams of oxen, and I need to try them out. Please excuse me."

²⁰Still another guest said, "I have just gotten married, and I can't be there."

²¹The servant told his master what happened, and the master became so angry that he said, "Go as fast as you can to every street and alley in town! Bring in everyone who is poor or crippled or blind or lame."

²²When the servant returned, he said, "Master, I've done what you told me, and there is still plenty of room for more people."

²³His master then told him, "Go out along the back roads and fence rows and make people come in, so that my house will be full. ²⁴Not one of the guests I first invited will get even a bite of my food!"

Being a Disciple
(Matthew 10.37, 38)

²⁵Large crowds were walking along with Jesus, when he turned and said:

²⁶You cannot be my disciple, unless you love me more than you love your father and mother, your wife and children, and your brothers and sisters. You cannot come with me unless you love me more than you love your own life.

²⁷You cannot be my disciple unless you carry your own cross and come with me.

²⁸Suppose one of you wants to build a tower. What is the first thing you will do? Won't you sit down and figure out how much it will cost and if you have enough money to pay for it? ²⁹Otherwise, you will start building the tower, but not be able to finish. Then everyone who sees what is happening will laugh at you. ³⁰They will say, "You started building, but could not finish the job."

³¹What will a king do if he has only ten thousand soldiers to defend himself against a king who is about to attack him with twenty thousand soldiers? Before he goes out to battle, won't he first sit down and decide if he can win? ³²If he thinks he won't be able to defend himself, he will send messengers and ask for peace while the other king is still a long way off. ³³So then, you cannot be my disciple unless you give away everything you own.

Salt and Light
(Matthew 5.13; Mark 9.50)

³⁴Salt is good, but if it no longer tastes like salt, how can it be made to taste salty again? ³⁵It is no longer good for the soil or even for the manure pile. People simply throw it out. If you have ears, pay attention!

One Sheep
(Matthew 18.12-14)

15 Tax collectors[l] and sinners were all crowding around to listen to Jesus. ²So the Pharisees and the teachers of the Law of Moses started grumbling, "This man is friendly with sinners. He even eats with them."

³Then Jesus told them this story:

⁴If any of you has a hundred sheep, and one of them gets lost, what will you do? Won't you leave the ninety-nine in the field and go look for the lost sheep until you find it? ⁵And when you find it, you will be so glad that you will put it on your shoulder ⁶and carry it home. Then you will call in your friends and neighbors and say, "Let's celebrate! I've found my lost sheep."

⁷Jesus said, "In the same way there is more happiness in heaven because of one sinner who turns to God than over ninety-nine good people who don't need to."

One Coin

⁸Jesus told the people another story:

What will a woman do if she has ten silver coins and loses one of them? Won't she light a lamp, sweep the floor, and look carefully until she finds it? ⁹Then she will call in her friends and neighbors and say, "Let's celebrate! I've found the coin I lost."

¹⁰Jesus said, "In the same way God's angels are happy when even one person turns to him."

Two Sons

¹¹Jesus also told them another story: Once a man had two sons. ¹²The younger son said to his father, "Give me my share of the property." So the father divided his property between his two sons.

¹³Not long after that, the younger son packed up everything he owned and left for a foreign country, where he wasted all his money in wild living. ¹⁴He had spent everything, when a bad famine spread through that whole land. Soon he had nothing to eat.

¹⁵He went to work for a man in that country, and the man sent him out to take care of his pigs.[m] ¹⁶He would have been glad to eat what the pigs were eating,[n] but no one gave him a thing.

¹⁷Finally, he came to his senses and said, "My father's workers have plenty to eat, and here I am, starving to death! ¹⁸I will go to my father and say to him, 'Father, I have sinned against God in heaven and against you. ¹⁹I am no longer good enough to be called your son. Treat me like one of your workers.' "

²⁰The younger son got up and started back to his father. But when he was still a long way off, his father saw him and felt sorry for him. He ran to his son and hugged and kissed him.

²¹The son said, "Father, I have sinned against God in heaven and against you. I am no longer good enough to be called your son."

²²But his father said to the servants, "Hurry and bring the best clothes and put them on him. Give him a ring for his finger and sandals[o] for his feet. ²³Get the best calf and prepare it, so we can eat and celebrate. ²⁴This son of mine was dead, but has now come back to life. He was lost and has now been found." And they began to celebrate.

²⁵The older son had been out in the field. But when he came near the house, he heard the music and dancing. ²⁶So he called one of the servants over and asked, "What's going on here?"

²⁷The servant answered, "Your brother has come home safe and sound, and your father ordered us to kill the best calf." ²⁸The older brother got so angry that he would not even go into the house.

His father came out and begged him to go in. ²⁹But he said to his father, "For years I have worked for you like a slave and have always obeyed you. But you have never even given me a little goat, so that I could give a dinner for my friends. ³⁰This other son of yours wasted

---

[l]**15.1** *Tax collectors*: See the note at 3.12.   [m]**15.15** *pigs*: The Jewish religion taught that pigs were not fit to eat or even to touch. A Jewish man would have felt terribly insulted if he had to feed pigs, much less eat with them.   [n]**15.16** *what the pigs were eating*: The Greek text has "(bean) pods," which came from a tree in Palestine. These were used to feed animals. Poor people sometimes ate them too.   [o]**15.22** *ring . . . sandals*: These show that the young man's father fully accepted him as his son. A ring was a sign of high position in the family. Sandals showed that he was a son instead of a slave, since slaves did not usually wear sandals.

your money on prostitutes. And now that he has come home, you ordered the best calf to be killed for a feast."
³¹His father replied, "My son, you are always with me, and everything I have is yours. ³²But we should be glad and celebrate! Your brother was dead, but he is now alive. He was lost and has now been found."

A Dishonest Manager

16 Jesus said to his disciples: A rich man once had a manager to take care of his business. But he was told that his manager was wasting money. ²So the rich man called him in and said, "What is this I hear about you? Tell me what you have done! You are no longer going to work for me."

³The manager said to himself, "What shall I do now that my master is going to fire me? I can't dig ditches, and I'm ashamed to beg. ⁴I know what I'll do, so that people will welcome me into their homes after I've lost my job."

⁵Then one by one he called in the people who were in debt to his master. He asked the first one, "How much do you owe my master?"

⁶"A hundred barrels of olive oil," the man answered.

So the manager said, "Take your bill and sit down and quickly write 'fifty'."

⁷The manager asked someone else who was in debt to his master, "How much do you owe?"

"A thousand bushels*ᵖ* of wheat," the man replied.

The manager said, "Take your bill and write 'eight hundred'."

⁸The master praised his dishonest manager for looking out for himself so well. That's how it is! The people of this world look out for themselves better than the people who belong to the light.

⁹My disciples, I tell you to use wicked wealth to make friends for yourselves. Then when it is gone, you will be welcomed into an eternal home. ¹⁰Anyone who can be trusted in little matters can also be trusted in important matters. But anyone who is dishonest in little matters will be dishonest in important matters.

¹¹If you cannot be trusted with this wicked wealth, who will trust you with true wealth? ¹²And if you cannot be trusted with what belongs to someone else, who will give you something that will be your own? ¹³You cannot be the slave of two masters. You will like one more than the other or be more loyal to one than to the other. You cannot serve God and money.

Some Sayings of Jesus
(Matthew 11.12, 13; 5.31, 32; Mark 10.11, 12)

¹⁴The Pharisees really loved money. So when they heard what Jesus said, they made fun of him. ¹⁵But Jesus told them:

You are always making yourselves look good, but God sees what is in your heart. The things that most people think are important are worthless as far as God is concerned.

¹⁶Until the time of John the Baptist, people had to obey the Law of Moses and the Books of the Prophets.*ᵍ* But since God's kingdom has been preached, everyone is trying hard to get in. ¹⁷Heaven and earth will disappear before the smallest letter of the Law does.

¹⁸It is a terrible sin*ʳ* for a man to divorce his wife and marry another woman. It is also a terrible sin for a man to marry a divorced woman.

Lazarus and the Rich Man

¹⁹There was once a rich man who wore expensive clothes and every day ate the best food. ²⁰But a poor beggar named Lazarus was brought to the gate of the rich man's house. ²¹He was happy just to eat the scraps that fell from the rich man's table. His body was covered with sores, and dogs kept coming up to lick them. ²²The poor man died, and angels took him to the place of honor next to Abraham.*ˢ*

The rich man also died and was buried. ²³He went to hell*ᵗ* and was suffering terribly. When he looked up and saw Abraham far off and Lazarus at his side, ²⁴he said to Abraham, "Have pity on me! Send Lazarus to dip his finger in water and touch my tongue. I'm suffering terribly in this fire."

²⁵Abraham answered, "My friend,

---

*ᵖ***16.7** *A thousand bushels*: The Greek text has "A hundred measures," and each measure is about ten or twelve bushels.   *ᵍ***16.16** *the Law of Moses and the Books of the Prophets*: The Jewish Scriptures, that is, the Old Testament.   *ʳ***16.18** *a terrible sin*: The Greek text uses a word that means the sin of being unfaithful in marriage.   *ˢ***16.22** *the place of honor next to Abraham*: The Jewish people thought that heaven would be a banquet that God would give for them. Abraham would be the most important person there, and the guest of honor would sit next to him.   *ᵗ***16.23** *hell*: The Greek text has "hades," which the Jewish people often thought of as the place where the dead wait for the final judgment.

remember that while you lived, you had everything good, and Lazarus had everything bad. Now he is happy, and you are in pain. ²⁶And besides, there is a deep ditch between us, and no one from either side can cross over."

²⁷But the rich man said, "Abraham, then please send Lazarus to my father's home. ²⁸Let him warn my five brothers, so they won't come to this horrible place."

²⁹Abraham answered, "Your brothers can read what Moses and the prophets ᵘ wrote. They should pay attention to that."

³⁰Then the rich man said, "No, that's not enough! If only someone from the dead would go to them, they would listen and turn to God."

³¹So Abraham said, "If they won't pay attention to Moses and the prophets, they won't listen even to someone who comes back from the dead."

Faith and Service
(Matthew 18.6, 7, 21, 22; Mark 9.42)

17 Jesus said to his disciples: There will always be something that causes people to sin. But anyone who causes them to sin is in for trouble. A person who causes even one of my little followers to sin ²would be better off thrown into the ocean with a heavy stone tied around their neck. ³So be careful what you do.

Correct any followers ᵛ of mine who sin, and forgive the ones who say they are sorry. ⁴Even if one of them mistreats you seven times in one day and says, "I am sorry," you should still forgive that person.

⁵The apostles said to the Lord, "Make our faith stronger!"

⁶Jesus replied:

If you had faith no bigger than a tiny mustard seed, you could tell this mulberry tree to pull itself up, roots and all, and to plant itself in the ocean. And it would!

⁷If your servant comes in from plowing or from taking care of the sheep, would you say, "Welcome! Come on in and have something to eat"? ⁸No, you wouldn't say that. You would say, "Fix me something to eat. Get ready to serve me, so I can have my meal. Then later on you can eat and drink." ⁹Servants don't deserve special thanks for doing what they are supposed to do. ¹⁰And that's how it should be with you. When you've done all you should, then say, "We are merely servants, and we have simply done our duty."

Ten Men with Leprosy

¹¹On his way to Jerusalem, Jesus went along the border between Samaria and Galilee. ¹²As he was going into a village, ten men with leprosy ʷ came toward him. They stood at a distance ¹³and shouted, "Jesus, Master, have pity on us!"

¹⁴Jesus looked at them and said, "Go show yourselves to the priests." ˣ

On their way they were healed. ¹⁵When one of them discovered that he was healed, he came back, shouting praises to God. ¹⁶He bowed down at the feet of Jesus and thanked him. The man was from the country of Samaria.

¹⁷Jesus asked, "Weren't ten men healed? Where are the other nine? ¹⁸Why was this foreigner the only one who came back to thank God?" ¹⁹Then Jesus told the man, "You may get up and go. Your faith has made you well."

God's Kingdom
(Matthew 24.23-28, 37-41)

²⁰Some Pharisees asked Jesus when God's kingdom would come. He answered, "God's kingdom isn't something you can see. ²¹There is no use saying, 'Look! Here it is' or 'Look! There it is.' God's kingdom is here with you." ʸ

²²Jesus said to his disciples:

The time will come when you will long to see one of the days of the Son of Man, but you will not. ²³When people say to you, "Look there," or "Look here," don't go looking for him. ²⁴The day of the Son of Man will be like lightning flashing across the sky. ²⁵But first he must suffer terribly and be rejected by the people of today. ²⁶When the Son of Man comes, things will be just as they were when Noah lived. ²⁷People were eating, drinking, and getting married right up to the day when Noah went into the big boat. Then the flood came and drowned everyone on earth.

²⁸When Lot ᶻ lived, people were also eating and drinking. They were buying, selling, planting, and

---

ᵘ **16.29** *Moses and the prophets*: The Jewish Scriptures, that is, the Old Testament.
ᵛ **17.3** *followers*: The Greek text has "brothers," which is often used in the New Testament for followers of Jesus.   ʷ **17.12** *leprosy*: See the note at 4.27.   ˣ **17.14** *show yourselves to the priests*: See the note at 5.14.   ʸ **17.21** *here with you*: Or "in your hearts."   ᶻ **17.27,28** *Noah . . . Lot*: When God destroyed the earth by a flood, he saved Noah and his family. And when God destroyed the cities of Sodom and Gomorrah and the evil people who lived there, he rescued Lot and his family (see Genesis 19.1-29).

building. ²⁹But on the very day Lot left Sodom, fiery flames poured down from the sky and killed everyone. ³⁰The same will happen on the day when the Son of Man appears.

³¹At that time no one on a rooftop[a] should go down into the house to get anything. No one in a field should go back to the house for anything. ³²Remember what happened to Lot's wife.[b]

³³People who try to save their lives will lose them, and those who lose their lives will save them. ³⁴On that night two people will be sleeping in the same bed, but only one will be taken. The other will be left. ³⁵⁻³⁶Two women will be together grinding wheat, but only one will be taken. The other will be left.[c]

³⁷Then Jesus' disciples spoke up, "But where will this happen, Lord?"

Jesus said, "Where there is a corpse, there will always be buzzards."[d]

A Widow and a Judge

18 Jesus told his disciples a story about how they should keep on praying and never give up:

²In a town there was once a judge who didn't fear God or care about people. ³In that same town there was a widow who kept going to the judge and saying, "Make sure that I get fair treatment in court."

⁴For a while the judge refused to do anything. Finally, he said to himself, "Even though I don't fear God or care about people, ⁵I will help this widow because she keeps on bothering me. If I don't help her, she will wear me out."

⁶The Lord said:

Think about what that crooked judge said. ⁷Won't God protect his chosen ones who pray to him day and night? Won't he be concerned for them? ⁸He will surely hurry and help them. But when the Son of Man comes, will he find on this earth anyone with faith?

A Pharisee and a Tax Collector

⁹Jesus told a story to some people who thought they were better than others and who looked down on everyone else:

¹⁰Two men went into the temple to pray.[e] One was a Pharisee and the other a tax collector.[f] ¹¹The Pharisee stood over by himself and prayed,[g] "God, I thank you that I am not greedy, dishonest, and unfaithful in marriage like other people. And I am really glad that I am not like that tax collector over there. ¹²I go without eating[h] for two days a week, and I give you one tenth of all I earn."

¹³The tax collector stood off at a distance and did not think he was good enough even to look up toward heaven. He was so sorry for what he had done that he pounded his chest and prayed, "God, have pity on me! I am such a sinner."

¹⁴Then Jesus said, "When the two men went home, it was the tax collector and not the Pharisee who was pleasing to God. If you put yourself above others, you will be put down. But if you humble yourself, you will be honored."

Jesus Blesses Little Children
(Matthew 19.13-15; Mark 10.13-16)

¹⁵Some people brought their little children for Jesus to bless. But when his disciples saw them doing this, they told the people to stop bothering him. ¹⁶So Jesus called the children over to him and said, "Let the children come to me! Don't try to stop them. People who are like these children belong to God's kingdom.[i] ¹⁷You will never get into God's kingdom unless you enter it like a child!"

A Rich and Important Man
(Matthew 19.16-30; Mark 10.17-31)

¹⁸An important man asked Jesus, "Good Teacher, what must I do to have eternal life?"

¹⁹Jesus said, "Why do you call me good? Only God is good. ²⁰You know the commandments: 'Be faithful in marriage. Do not murder. Do not steal. Do not tell lies about others. Respect your father and mother.' "

²¹He told Jesus, "I have obeyed all these commandments since I was a young man."

---

[a] *17.31 rooftop*: See the note at 5.19.   [b] *17.32 what happened to Lot's wife*: She turned into a block of salt when she disobeyed God (see Genesis 19.26).   [c] *17.35,36 will be left*: Some manuscripts add, "Two men will be in the same field, but only one will be taken. The other will be left."   [d] *17.37 Where there is a corpse, there will always be buzzards*: This saying may mean that when anything important happens, people soon know about it. Or the saying may mean that whenever something bad happens, curious people gather around and stare. But the word translated "buzzard" also means "eagle" and may refer to the Roman army, which had an eagle as its symbol.   [e] *18.10 into the temple to pray*: Jewish people usually prayed there early in the morning and late in the afternoon.   [f] *18.10 tax collector*: See the note at 3.12.   [g] *18.11 stood over by himself and prayed*: Some manuscripts have "stood up and prayed to himself."   [h] *18.12 without eating*: See the note at 2.37.   [i] *18.16 People who are like these children belong to God's kingdom*: Or "God's kingdom belongs to people who are like these children."

²²When Jesus heard this, he said, "There is one thing you still need to do. Go and sell everything you own! Give the money to the poor, and you will have riches in heaven. Then come and be my follower." ²³When the man heard this, he was sad, because he was very rich.

²⁴Jesus saw how sad the man was. So he said, "It's terribly hard for rich people to get into God's kingdom! ²⁵In fact, it's easier for a camel to go through the eye of a needle than for a rich person to get into God's kingdom."

²⁶When the crowd heard this, they asked, "How can anyone ever be saved?"

²⁷Jesus replied, "There are some things that people cannot do, but God can do anything."

²⁸Peter said, "Remember, we left everything to be your followers!"

²⁹Jesus answered, "You can be sure that anyone who gives up home or wife or brothers or family or children because of God's kingdom ³⁰will be given much more in this life. And in the future world they will have eternal life."

Jesus Again Tells about His Death
(Matthew 20.17-19; Mark 10.32-34)

³¹Jesus took the twelve apostles aside and said:

We are now on our way to Jerusalem. Everything that the prophets wrote about the Son of Man will happen there. ³²He will be handed over to foreigners,ʲ who will make fun of him, mistreat him, and spit on him. ³³They will beat him and kill him, but three days later he will rise to life.

³⁴The apostles did not understand what Jesus was talking about. They could not understand, because the meaning of what he said was hidden from them.

Jesus Heals a Blind Beggar
(Matthew 20.29-34; Mark 10.46-52)

³⁵When Jesus was coming close to Jericho, a blind man sat begging beside the road. ³⁶The man heard the crowd walking by and asked what was happening. ³⁷Some people told him that Jesus from Nazareth was passing by. ³⁸So the blind man shouted, "Jesus, Son of David,ᵏ have pity on me!" ³⁹The people who were going along with Jesus told the man to be quiet. But he shouted even louder, "Son of David, have pity on me!"

⁴⁰Jesus stopped and told some people to bring the blind man over to him. When the blind man was getting near, Jesus asked, ⁴¹"What do you want me to do for you?"

"Lord, I want to see!" he answered.

⁴²Jesus replied, "Look and you will see! Your eyes are healed because of your faith." ⁴³Right away the man could see, and he went with Jesus and started thanking God. When the crowds saw what happened, they praised God.

Zacchaeus

19 Jesus was going through Jericho, ²where a man named Zacchaeus lived. He was in charge of collecting taxesˡ and was very rich. ³⁻⁴Jesus was heading his way, and Zacchaeus wanted to see what he was like. But Zacchaeus was a short man and could not see over the crowd. So he ran ahead and climbed up into a sycamore tree.

⁵When Jesus got there, he looked up and said, "Zacchaeus, hurry down! I want to stay with you today." ⁶Zacchaeus hurried down and gladly welcomed Jesus.

⁷Everyone who saw this started grumbling, "This man Zacchaeus is a sinner! And Jesus is going home to eat with him."

⁸Later that day Zacchaeus stood up and said to the Lord, "I will give half of my property to the poor. And I will now pay back four times as muchᵐ to everyone I have ever cheated."

⁹Jesus said to Zacchaeus, "Today you and your family have been saved,ⁿ because you are a true son of Abraham.ᵒ ¹⁰The Son of Man came to look for and to save people who are lost."

A Story about Ten Servants
(Matthew 25.14-30)

¹¹The crowd was still listening to Jesus as he was getting close to Jerusalem. Many of them thought that God's kingdom would soon appear, ¹²and Jesus told them this story:

A prince once went to a foreign country to be crowned king and then to return. ¹³But before leaving, he called in ten servants and gave

---

ʲ**18.32** *foreigners*: The Romans, who ruled Judea at this time. ᵏ**18.38** *Son of David*: The Jewish people expected the Messiah to be from the family of King David, and for this reason the Messiah was often called the "Son of David." ˡ**19.2** *in charge of collecting taxes*: See the note at 3.12. ᵐ**19.8** *pay back four times as much*: Both Jewish and Roman law said that a person must pay back four times the amount that was taken. ⁿ**19.9** *saved*: Zacchaeus was Jewish, but it is only now that he is rescued from sin and placed under God's care. ᵒ**19.9** *son of Abraham*: As used in this verse, the words mean that Zacchaeus is truly one of God's special people.

each of them some money. He told them, "Use this to earn more money until I get back."

¹⁴But the people of his country hated him, and they sent messengers to the foreign country to say, "We don't want this man to be our king."

¹⁵After the prince had been made king, he returned and called in his servants. He asked them how much they had earned with the money they had been given.

¹⁶The first servant came and said, "Sir, with the money you gave me I have earned ten times as much."

¹⁷"That's fine, my good servant!" the king said. "Since you have shown that you can be trusted with a small amount, you will be given ten cities to rule."

¹⁸The second one came and said, "Sir, with the money you gave me, I have earned five times as much."

¹⁹The king said, "You will be given five cities."

²⁰Another servant came and said, "Sir, here is your money. I kept it safe in a handkerchief. ²¹You are a hard man, and I was afraid of you. You take what isn't yours, and you harvest crops you didn't plant."

²²"You worthless servant!" the king told him. "You have condemned yourself by what you have just said. You knew that I am a hard man, taking what isn't mine and harvesting what I've not planted. ²³Why didn't you put my money in the bank? On my return, I could have had the money together with interest."

²⁴Then he said to some other servants standing there, "Take the money away from him and give it to the servant who earned ten times as much."

²⁵But they said, "Sir, he already has ten times as much!"

²⁶The king replied, "Those who have something will be given more. But everything will be taken away from those who don't have anything. ²⁷Now bring me the enemies who didn't want me to be their king. Kill them while I watch!"

Jesus Enters Jerusalem
(Matthew 21.1-11; Mark 11.1-11; John 12.12-19)

²⁸When Jesus had finished saying all this, he went on toward Jerusalem. ²⁹As he was getting near Bethphage and Bethany on the Mount of Olives, he sent two of his disciples on ahead. ³⁰He told them, "Go into the next village, where you will find a young donkey that has never been ridden. Untie the donkey and bring it here. ³¹If anyone asks why you are doing that, just say, 'The Lord*ᵖ* needs it.' "

³²They went off and found everything just as Jesus had said. ³³While they were untying the donkey, its owners asked, "Why are you doing that?"

³⁴They answered, "The Lord*ᵖ* needs it."

³⁵Then they led the donkey to Jesus. They put some of their clothes on its back and helped Jesus get on. ³⁶And as he rode along, the people spread clothes on the road*ᵍ* in front of him. ³⁷When Jesus was starting down the Mount of Olives, his large crowd of disciples were happy and praised God because of all the miracles they had seen. ³⁸They shouted,

"Blessed is the king who comes
in the name of the Lord!
Peace in heaven
and glory to God."

³⁹Some Pharisees in the crowd said to Jesus, "Teacher, make your disciples stop shouting!"

⁴⁰But Jesus answered, "If they keep quiet, these stones will start shouting."

⁴¹When Jesus came closer and could see Jerusalem, he cried ⁴²and said:

It is too bad that today your people don't know what will bring them peace! Now it is hidden from them. ⁴³Jerusalem, the time will come when your enemies will build walls around you to attack you. Armies will surround you and close in on you from every side. ⁴⁴They will level you to the ground and kill your people. Not one stone in your buildings will be left on top of another. This will happen because you did not see that God had come to save you.*ʳ*

Jesus in the Temple
(Matthew 21.12-17; Mark 11.15-19; John 2.13-22)

⁴⁵When Jesus entered the temple, he started chasing out the people who were selling things. ⁴⁶He told them, "The Scriptures say, 'My house should be a place of worship.' But you have made it a place where robbers hide!"

⁴⁷Each day, Jesus kept on teaching in the temple. So the chief priests, the teachers of the Law of Moses, and some

---

ᵖ19.31,34 The Lord: Or "The master of the donkey."   *ᵍ19.36 spread clothes on the road:* This was one way that Jewish people welcomed a famous person.   *ʳ19.44 that God had come to save you:* The Jewish people looked for the time when God would come and rescue them from their enemies. But when Jesus came, many of them refused to obey him.

other important people tried to have him killed. [48]But they could not find a way to do it, because everyone else was eager to listen to him.

A Question about Jesus' Authority
(Matthew 21.23-27; Mark 11.27-33)

20 One day, Jesus was teaching in the temple and telling the good news. So the chief priests, the teachers, and the nation's leaders [2]asked him, "What right do you have to do these things? Who gave you this authority?"

[3]Jesus replied, "I want to ask you a question. [4]Who gave John the right to baptize? Was it God in heaven or merely some human being?"

[5]They talked this over and said to each other, "We can't say that God gave John this right. Jesus will ask us why we didn't believe John. [6]And we can't say that it was merely some human who gave John the right to baptize. The crowd will stone us to death, because they think John was a prophet."

[7]So they told Jesus, "We don't know who gave John the right to baptize."

[8]Jesus replied, "Then I won't tell you who gave me the right to do what I do."

Renters of a Vineyard
(Matthew 21.33-46; Mark 12.1-12)

[9]Jesus told the people this story:

A man once planted a vineyard and rented it out. Then he left the country for a long time. [10]When it was time to harvest the crop, he sent a servant to ask the renters for his share of the grapes. But they beat up the servant and sent him away without anything. [11]So the owner sent another servant. The renters also beat him up. They insulted him terribly and sent him away without a thing. [12]The owner sent a third servant. He was also beaten terribly and thrown out of the vineyard.

[13]The owner then said to himself, "What am I going to do? I know what. I'll send my son, the one I love so much. They will surely respect him!"

[14]When the renters saw the owner's son, they said to one another, "Someday he will own the vineyard. Let's kill him! Then we can have it all for ourselves." [15]So they threw him out of the vineyard and killed him.

Jesus asked, "What do you think the owner of the vineyard will do? [16]I'll tell you what. He will come and kill those renters and let someone else have his vineyard."

When the people heard this, they said, "This must never happen!"

[17]But Jesus looked straight at them and said, "Then what do the Scriptures mean when they say, 'The stone that the builders tossed aside is now the most important stone of all'? [18]Anyone who stumbles over this stone will get hurt, and anyone it falls on will be smashed to pieces."

[19]The chief priests and the teachers of the Law of Moses knew that Jesus was talking about them when he was telling this story. They wanted to arrest him right then, but they were afraid of the people.

Paying Taxes
(Matthew 22.15-22; Mark 12.13-17)

[20]Jesus' enemies kept watching him closely, because they wanted to hand him over to the Roman governor. So they sent some men who pretended to be good. But they were really spies trying to catch Jesus saying something wrong. [21]The spies said to him, "Teacher, we know that you teach the truth about what God wants people to do. And you treat everyone with the same respect, no matter who they are. [22]Tell us, should we pay taxes to the Emperor or not?"

[23]Jesus knew that they were trying to trick him. So he told them, [24]"Show me a coin." Then he asked, "Whose picture and name are on it?"

"The Emperor's," they answered.

[25]Then he told them, "Give the Emperor what belongs to him and give God what belongs to God." [26]Jesus' enemies could not catch him saying anything wrong there in front of the people. They were amazed at his answer and kept quiet.

Life in the Future World
(Matthew 22.23-33; Mark 12.18-27)

[27]The Sadducees did not believe that people would rise to life after death. So some of them came to Jesus [28]and said:

Teacher, Moses wrote that if a married man dies and has no children, his brother should marry the widow. Their first son would then be thought of as the son of the dead brother.

[29]There were once seven brothers. The first one married, but died without having any children. [30]The second one married his brother's widow, and he also died without having any children. [31]The same thing happened to the third one. Finally, all seven brothers married that woman and died without having any children. [32]At last the woman died. [33]When God raises people from death, whose wife will this woman be? All seven brothers had married her.

Luke 20.34

34 Jesus answered:

The people in this world get married. **35** But in the future world no one who is worthy to rise from death will either marry **36** or die. They will be like the angels and will be God's children, because they have been raised to life.

37 In the story about the burning bush, Moses clearly shows that people will live again. He said, "The Lord is the God worshiped by Abraham, Isaac, and Jacob."[s] **38** So the Lord isn't the God of the dead, but of the living. This means that everyone is alive as far as God is concerned.

39 Some of the teachers of the Law of Moses said, "Teacher, you have given a good answer!" **40** From then on, no one dared to ask Jesus any questions.

About David's Son
(Matthew 22.41-46; Mark 12.35-37)

41 Jesus asked, "Why do people say that the Messiah will be the son of King David?[t] **42** In the book of Psalms, David himself says,

'The Lord said to my Lord,
   Sit at my right side[u]
43 until I make your enemies
   into a footstool for you.'

44 David spoke of the Messiah as his Lord, so how can the Messiah be his son?"

Jesus and the Teachers of the Law of Moses
(Matthew 23.1-36; Mark 12.38-40; Luke 11.37-54)

45 While everyone was listening to Jesus, he said to his disciples:

46 Guard against the teachers of the Law of Moses! They love to walk around in long robes, and they like to be greeted in the market. They want the front seats in the meeting places and the best seats at banquets. **47** But they cheat widows out of their homes and then pray long prayers just to show off. These teachers will be punished most of all.

A Widow's Offering
(Mark 12.41-44)

21 Jesus looked up and saw some rich people tossing their gifts into the offering box. **2** He also saw a poor widow putting in two pennies. **3** And he said, "I tell you that this poor woman has put in more than all the others. **4** Everyone else gave what they didn't need. But she is very poor and gave everything she had."

The Temple Will Be Destroyed
(Matthew 24.1, 2; Mark 13.1, 2)

5 Some people were talking about the beautiful stones used to build the temple and about the gifts that had been placed in it. Jesus said, **6** "Do you see these stones? The time is coming when not one of them will be left in place. They will all be knocked down."

Warning about Trouble
(Matthew 24.3-14; Mark 13.3-13)

7 Some people asked, "Teacher, when will all this happen? How can we know when these things are about to take place?"

8 Jesus replied:

Don't be fooled by those who will come and claim to be me. They will say, "I am Christ!" and "Now is the time!" But don't follow them. **9** When you hear about wars and riots, don't be afraid. These things will have to happen first, but that isn't the end. **10** Nations will go to war against one another, and kingdoms will attack each other. **11** There will be great earthquakes, and in many places people will starve to death and suffer terrible diseases. All sorts of frightening things will be seen in the sky.

12 Before all this happens, you will be arrested and punished. You will be tried in your meeting places and put in jail. Because of me you will be placed on trial before kings and governors. **13** But this will be your chance to tell about your faith.

14 Don't worry about what you will say to defend yourselves. **15** I will give you the wisdom to know what to say. None of your enemies will be able to oppose you or to say that you are wrong. **16** You will be betrayed by your own parents, brothers, family, and friends. Some of you will even be killed. **17** Because of me, you will be hated by everyone. **18** But don't worry![v] **19** You will be saved by being faithful to me.

Jerusalem Will Be Destroyed
(Matthew 24.15-21; Mark 13.14-19)

20 When you see Jerusalem surrounded by soldiers, you will know that it will soon be destroyed. **21** If you are living in Judea at that time, run to the mountains. If you are in

---

[s] **20.37** *"The Lord is the God worshiped by Abraham, Isaac, and Jacob"*: Jesus argues that if God is worshiped by these three, they must be alive, because he is the God of the living. [t] **20.41** *the son of King David*: See the note at 18.38. [u] **20.42** *right side*: The place of power and honor. [v] **21.18** *But don't worry*: The Greek text has "Not a hair of your head will be lost," which means, "There's no need to worry."

the city, leave it. And if you are out in the country, don't go back into the city. ²²This time of punishment is what is written about in the Scriptures. ²³It will be an awful time for women who are expecting babies or nursing young children! Everywhere in the land people will suffer horribly and be punished. ²⁴Some of them will be killed by swords. Others will be carried off to foreign countries. Jerusalem will be overrun by foreign nations until their time comes to an end.

When the Son of Man Appears
(Matthew 24.29-31; Mark 13.24-27)

²⁵Strange things will happen to the sun, moon, and stars. The nations on earth will be afraid of the roaring sea and tides, and they won't know what to do. ²⁶People will be so frightened that they will faint because of what is happening to the world. Every power in the sky will be shaken.ʷ ²⁷Then the Son of Man will be seen, coming in a cloud with great power and glory. ²⁸When all of this starts happening, stand up straight and be brave. You will soon be set free.

A Lesson from a Fig Tree
(Matthew 24.32-35; Mark 13.28-31)

²⁹Then Jesus told them a story:
When you see a fig tree or any other tree ³⁰putting out leaves, you know that summer will soon come. ³¹So, when you see these things happening, you know that God's kingdom will soon be here. ³²You can be sure that some of the people of this generation will still be alive when all of this takes place. ³³The sky and the earth won't last forever, but my words will.

A Warning

³⁴Don't spend all of your time thinking about eating or drinking or worrying about life. If you do, the final day will suddenly catch you ³⁵like a trap. That day will surprise everyone on earth. ³⁶Watch out and keep praying that you can escape all that is going to happen and that the Son of Man will be pleased with you.
³⁷Jesus taught in the temple each day, and he spent each night on the Mount of Olives. ³⁸Everyone got up early and came to the temple to hear him teach.

A Plot To Kill Jesus
(Matthew 26.1-5, 14, 16; Mark 14.1, 2, 10, 11; John 11.45-53)

22 The Festival of Thin Bread, also called Passover, was near. ²The chief priests and the teachers of the Law of Moses were looking for a way to get rid of Jesus, because they were afraid of what the people might do. ³Then Satan entered the heart of Judas Iscariot,ˣ who was one of the twelve apostles.
⁴Judas went to talk with the chief priests and the officers of the temple police about how he could help them arrest Jesus. ⁵They were very pleased and offered to pay Judas some money. ⁶He agreed and started looking for a good chance to betray Jesus when the crowds were not around.

Jesus Eats with His Disciples
(Matthew 26.17-25; Mark 14.12-21; John 13.21-30)

⁷The day had come for the Festival of Thin Bread, and it was time to kill the Passover lambs. ⁸So Jesus said to Peter and John, "Go and prepare the Passover meal for us to eat."
⁹But they asked, "Where do you want us to prepare it?"
¹⁰Jesus told them, "As you go into the city, you will meet a man carrying a jar of water.ʸ Follow him into the house ¹¹and say to the owner, 'Our teacher wants to know where he can eat the Passover meal with his disciples.' ¹²The owner will take you upstairs and show you a large room ready for you to use. Prepare the meal there."
¹³Peter and John left. They found everything just as Jesus had told them, and they prepared the Passover meal.

The Lord's Supper
(Matthew 26.26-30; Mark 14.22-26; 1 Corinthians 11.23-25)

¹⁴When the time came for Jesus and the apostles to eat, ¹⁵he said to them, "I have very much wanted to eat this Passover meal with you before I suffer. ¹⁶I tell you that I will not eat another Passover meal until it is finally eaten in God's kingdom."
¹⁷Jesus took a cup of wine in his hands and gave thanks to God. Then he told the apostles, "Take this wine and share it with each other. ¹⁸I tell you that I will not drink any more wine until God's kingdom comes."
¹⁹Jesus took some bread in his hands and gave thanks for it. He broke the

---

ʷ*21.26 Every power in the sky will be shaken*: In ancient times people thought that the stars were spiritual powers.   ˣ*22.3 Iscariot*: See the note at 6.16.   ʸ*22.10 a man carrying a jar of water*: A male slave carrying water would probably mean that the family was rich.

bread and handed it to his apostles. Then he said, "This is my body, which is given for you. Eat this as a way of remembering me!"
²⁰After the meal he took another cup of wine in his hands. Then he said, "This is my blood. It is poured out for you, and with it God makes his new agreement. ²¹The one who will betray me is here at the table with me! ²²The Son of Man will die in the way that has been decided for him, but it will be terrible for the one who betrays him!"
²³Then the apostles started arguing about who would ever do such a thing.

An Argument about Greatness

²⁴The apostles got into an argument about which one of them was the greatest. ²⁵So Jesus told them:
Foreign kings order their people around, and powerful rulers call themselves everyone's friends.ᶻ ²⁶But don't be like them. The most important one of you should be like the least important, and your leader should be like a servant. ²⁷Who do people think is the greatest, a person who is served or one who serves? Isn't it the one who is served? But I have been with you as a servant.
²⁸You have stayed with me in all my troubles. ²⁹So I will give you the right to rule as kings, just as my Father has given me the right to rule as a king. ³⁰You will eat and drink with me in my kingdom, and you will each sit on a throne to judge the twelve tribes of Israel.

Jesus' Disciples Will Be Tested
(Matthew 26.31-35; Mark 14.27-31; John 13.36-38)

³¹Jesus said, "Simon, listen to me! Satan has demanded the right to test each one of you, as a farmer does when he separates wheat from the husks.ᵃ ³²But Simon, I have prayed that your faith will be strong. And when you have come back to me, help the others."
³³Peter said, "Lord, I am ready to go with you to jail and even to die with you."
³⁴Jesus replied, "Peter, I tell you that before a rooster crows tomorrow morning, you will say three times that you don't know me."

Moneybags, Traveling Bags, and Swords

³⁵Jesus asked his disciples, "When I sent you out without a moneybag or a traveling bag or sandals, did you need anything?"
"No!" they answered.
³⁶Jesus told them, "But now, if you have a moneybag, take it with you. Also take a traveling bag, and if you don't have a sword,ᵇ sell some of your clothes and buy one. ³⁷Do this because the Scriptures say, 'He was considered a criminal.' This was written about me, and it will soon come true."
³⁸The disciples said, "Lord, here are two swords!"
"Enough of that!" Jesus replied.

Jesus Prays
(Matthew 26.36-46; Mark 14.32-42)

³⁹Jesus went out to the Mount of Olives, as he often did, and his disciples went with him. ⁴⁰When they got there, he told them, "Pray that you won't be tested."
⁴¹Jesus walked on a little way before he knelt down and prayed, ⁴²"Father, if you will, please don't make me suffer by having me drink from this cup.ᶜ But do what you want, and not what I want."
⁴³Then an angel from heaven came to help him. ⁴⁴Jesus was in great pain and prayed so sincerely that his sweat fell to the ground like drops of blood.ᵈ
⁴⁵Jesus got up from praying and went over to his disciples. They were asleep and worn out from being so sad. ⁴⁶He said to them, "Why are you asleep? Wake up and pray that you won't be tested."

Jesus Is Arrested
(Matthew 26.47-56; Mark 14.43-50; John 18.3-11)

⁴⁷While Jesus was still speaking, a crowd came up. It was led by Judas, one of the twelve apostles. He went over to Jesus and greeted him with a kiss.ᵉ
⁴⁸Jesus asked Judas, "Are you betraying the Son of Man with a kiss?"
⁴⁹When Jesus' disciples saw what was about to happen, they asked, "Lord, should we attack them with a sword?" ⁵⁰One of the disciples even struck at the high priest's servant with his sword and cut off the servant's right ear.
⁵¹"Enough of that!" Jesus said. Then

ᶻ**22.25** *everyone's friends*: This translates a Greek word that rulers sometimes used as a title for themselves or for special friends. ᵃ**22.31** *separates wheat from the husks*: See the note at 3.17. ᵇ**22.36** *moneybag . . . traveling bag . . . sword*: These were things that someone would take on a dangerous journey. Jesus was telling his disciples to be ready for anything that might happen. They seem to have understood what he meant (see 22.49-51). ᶜ**22.42** *having me drink from this cup*: In the Scriptures "to drink from a cup" sometimes means to suffer. ᵈ**22.43, 44** *Then an angel . . . like drops of blood*: Verses 43, 44 are not in some manuscripts. ᵉ**22.47** *greeted him with a kiss*: It was the custom for people to greet each other with a kiss on the cheek.

he touched the servant's ear and healed it. ⁵²Jesus spoke to the chief priests, the temple police, and the leaders who had come to arrest him. He said, "Why do you come out with swords and clubs and treat me like a criminal? ⁵³I was with you every day in the temple, and you didn't arrest me. But this is your time, and darkness*f* is in control."

Peter Says He Doesn't Know Jesus
(Matthew 26.57, 58, 67-75; Mark 14.53, 54, 66-72; John 18.12-18, 25-27)

⁵⁴Jesus was arrested and led away to the house of the high priest, while Peter followed at a distance. ⁵⁵Some people built a fire in the middle of the courtyard and were sitting around it. Peter sat there with them, ⁵⁶and a servant girl saw him. Then after she had looked at him carefully, she said, "This man was with Jesus!"

⁵⁷Peter said, "Woman, I don't even know that man!"

⁵⁸A little later someone else saw Peter and said, "You are one of them!"

"No, I'm not!" Peter replied.

⁵⁹About an hour later another man insisted, "This man must have been with Jesus. They both come from Galilee."

⁶⁰Peter replied, "I don't know what you are talking about!" Right then, while Peter was still speaking, a rooster crowed.

⁶¹The Lord turned and looked at Peter. And Peter remembered that the Lord had said, "Before a rooster crows tomorrow morning, you will say three times that you don't know me." ⁶²Then Peter went out and cried hard.

⁶³The men who were guarding Jesus made fun of him and beat him. ⁶⁴They put a blindfold on him and said, "Tell us who struck you!" ⁶⁵They kept on insulting Jesus in many other ways.

Jesus Is Questioned by the Council
(Matthew 26.59-66; Mark 14.55-64; John 18.19-24)

⁶⁶At daybreak the nation's leaders, the chief priests, and the teachers of the Law of Moses got together and brought Jesus before their council. ⁶⁷They said, "Tell us! Are you the Messiah?"

Jesus replied, "If I said so, you wouldn't believe me. ⁶⁸And if I asked you a question, you wouldn't answer. ⁶⁹But from now on, the Son of Man will be seated at the right side of God All-Powerful."

⁷⁰Then they asked, "Are you the Son of God?"*g*

Jesus answered, "You say I am!"*h*

⁷¹They replied, "Why do we need more witnesses? He said it himself!"

Pilate Questions Jesus
(Matthew 27.1, 2, 11-14; Mark 15.1-5; John 18.28-38)

23 Everyone in the council got up and led Jesus off to Pilate. ²They started accusing him and said, "We caught this man trying to get our people to riot and to stop paying taxes to the Emperor. He also claims that he is the Messiah, our king."

³Pilate asked Jesus, "Are you the king of the Jews?"

"Those are your words," Jesus answered.

⁴Pilate told the chief priests and the crowd, "I don't find him guilty of anything."

⁵But they all kept on saying, "He has been teaching and causing trouble all over Judea. He started in Galilee and has now come all the way here."

Jesus Is Brought before Herod

⁶When Pilate heard this, he asked, "Is this man from Galilee?" ⁷After Pilate learned that Jesus came from the region ruled by Herod,*i* he sent him to Herod, who was in Jerusalem at that time.

⁸For a long time Herod had wanted to see Jesus and was very happy because he finally had this chance. He had heard many things about Jesus and hoped to see him work a miracle.

⁹Herod asked him a lot of questions, but Jesus did not answer. ¹⁰Then the chief priests and the teachers of the Law of Moses stood up and accused him of all kinds of bad things.

¹¹Herod and his soldiers made fun of Jesus and insulted him. They put a fine robe on him and sent him back to Pilate. ¹²That same day Herod and Pilate became friends, even though they had been enemies before this.

The Death Sentence
(Matthew 27.15-26; Mark 15.6-15; John 18.39—19.16)

¹³Pilate called together the chief priests, the leaders, and the people. ¹⁴He told them, "You brought Jesus to me and said he was a troublemaker. But I have questioned him here in front of you, and I have not found him guilty of anything that you say he has done. ¹⁵Herod didn't find him guilty either and sent him back. This man doesn't deserve to be put to death! ¹⁶⁻¹⁷I will just

---

f **22.53** *darkness*: Darkness stands for the power of the devil.   *g* **22.70** *Son of God*: This was one of the titles used for the kings of Israel.   *h* **22.70** *You say I am*: Or "That's what you say."
i **23.7** *Herod*: Herod Antipas, the son of Herod the Great.

have him beaten with a whip and set free."*ʲ* ¹⁸But the whole crowd shouted, "Kill Jesus! Give us Barabbas!" ¹⁹Now Barabbas was in jail because he had started a riot in the city and had murdered someone.

²⁰Pilate wanted to set Jesus free, so he spoke again to the crowds. ²¹But they kept shouting, "Nail him to a cross! Nail him to a cross!"

²²Pilate spoke to them a third time, "But what crime has he done? I have not found him guilty of anything for which he should be put to death. I will have him beaten with a whip and set free."

²³The people kept on shouting as loud as they could for Jesus to be put to death. ²⁴Finally, Pilate gave in. ²⁵He freed the man who was in jail for rioting and murder, because he was the one the crowd wanted to be set free. Then Pilate handed Jesus over for them to do what they wanted with him.

Jesus Is Nailed to a Cross
(Matthew 27.31-44; Mark 15.21-32; John 19.17-27)

²⁶As Jesus was being led away, some soldiers grabbed hold of a man from Cyrene named Simon. He was coming in from the fields, but they put the cross on him and made him carry it behind Jesus.

²⁷A large crowd was following Jesus, and in the crowd a lot of women were crying and weeping for him. ²⁸Jesus turned to the women and said:

Women of Jerusalem, don't cry for me! Cry for yourselves and for your children. ²⁹Someday people will say, "Women who never had children are really fortunate!" ³⁰At that time everyone will say to the mountains, "Fall on us!" They will say to the hills, "Hide us!" ³¹If this can happen when the wood is green, what do you think will happen when it is dry?*ᵏ*

³²Two criminals were led out to be put to death with Jesus. ³³When the soldiers came to the place called "The Skull,"*ˡ* they nailed Jesus to a cross. They also nailed the two criminals to crosses, one on each side of Jesus.

³⁴⁻³⁵Jesus said, "Father, forgive these people! They don't know what they're doing."*ᵐ*

While the crowd stood there watching Jesus, the soldiers gambled for his clothes. The leaders insulted him by saying, "He saved others. Now he should save himself, if he really is God's chosen Messiah!"

³⁶The soldiers made fun of Jesus and brought him some wine. ³⁷They said, "If you are the king of the Jews, save yourself!"

³⁸Above him was a sign that said, "This is the King of the Jews."

³⁹One of the criminals hanging there also insulted Jesus by saying, "Aren't you the Messiah? Save yourself and save us!"

⁴⁰But the other criminal told the first one off, "Don't you fear God? Aren't you getting the same punishment as this man? ⁴¹We got what was coming to us, but he didn't do anything wrong." ⁴²Then he said to Jesus, "Remember me when you come into power!"

⁴³Jesus replied, "I promise that today you will be with me in paradise."*ⁿ*

The Death of Jesus
(Matthew 27.45-56; Mark 15.33-41; John 19.28-30)

⁴⁴Around noon the sky turned dark and stayed that way until the middle of the afternoon. ⁴⁵The sun stopped shining, and the curtain in the temple*ᵒ* split down the middle. ⁴⁶Jesus shouted, "Father, I put myself in your hands!" Then he died.

⁴⁷When the Roman officer saw what had happened, he praised God and said, "Jesus must really have been a good man!"

⁴⁸A crowd had gathered to see the terrible sight. Then after they had seen it, they felt brokenhearted and went home. ⁴⁹All of Jesus' close friends and the women who had come with him from Galilee stood at a distance and watched.

---

*ʲ*23.16,17 *set free*: Some manuscripts add, "Pilate said this, because at every Passover he was supposed to set one prisoner free for the Jewish people."   *ᵏ*23.31 *If this can happen when the wood is green, what do you think will happen when it is dry?*: This saying probably means, "If this can happen to an innocent person, what do you think will happen to one who is guilty?"   *ˡ*23.33 *"The Skull"*: The place was probably given this name because it was near a large rock in the shape of a human skull.   *ᵐ*23.34,35 *Jesus said, "Father, forgive these people! They don't know what they're doing."*: These words are not in some manuscripts.   *ⁿ*23.43 *paradise*: In the Greek translation of the Old Testament, this word is used for the Garden of Eden. In New Testament times it was sometimes used for the place where God's people are happy and at rest, as they wait for the final judgment.   *ᵒ*23.45 *curtain in the temple*: There were two curtains in the temple. One was at the entrance, and the other separated the holy place from the most holy place that the Jewish people thought of as God's home on earth. The second curtain is probably the one which is meant.

Jesus Is Buried
(Matthew 27.57-61; Mark 15.42-47; John 19.38-42)

50-51 There was a man named Joseph, who was from Arimathea in Judea. Joseph was a good and honest man, and he was eager for God's kingdom to come. He was also a member of the council, but he did not agree with what they had decided.

52 Joseph went to Pilate and asked for Jesus' body. 53 He took the body down from the cross and wrapped it in fine cloth. Then he put it in a tomb that had been cut out of solid rock and had never been used. 54 It was Friday, and the Sabbath was about to begin.[p]

55 The women who had come with Jesus from Galilee followed Joseph and watched how Jesus' body was placed in the tomb. 56 Then they went to prepare some sweet-smelling spices for his burial. But on the Sabbath they rested, as the Law of Moses commands.

Jesus Is Alive
(Matthew 28.1-10; Mark 16.1-8; John 20.1-10)

24 Very early on Sunday morning the women went to the tomb, carrying the spices that they had prepared. 2 When they found the stone rolled away from the entrance, 3 they went in. But they did not find the body of the Lord[q] Jesus, 4 and they did not know what to think.

Suddenly two men in shining white clothes stood beside them. 5 The women were afraid and bowed to the ground. But the men said, "Why are you looking in the place of the dead for someone who is alive? 6 Jesus isn't here! He has been raised from death. Remember that while he was still in Galilee, he told you, 7 'The Son of Man will be handed over to sinners who will nail him to a cross. But three days later he will rise to life.' " 8 Then they remembered what Jesus had said.

9-10 Mary Magdalene, Joanna, Mary the mother of James, and some other women were the ones who had gone to the tomb. When they returned, they told the eleven apostles and the others what had happened. 11 The apostles thought it was all nonsense, and they would not believe.

12 But Peter ran to the tomb. And when he stooped down and looked in, he saw only the burial clothes. Then he returned, wondering what had happened.[r]

Jesus Appears to Two Disciples
(Mark 16.12, 13)

13 That same day two of Jesus' disciples were going to the village of Emmaus, which was about seven miles from Jerusalem. 14 As they were talking and thinking about what had happened, 15 Jesus came near and started walking along beside them. 16 But they did not know who he was.

17 Jesus asked them, "What were you talking about as you walked along?"

The two of them stood there looking sad and gloomy. 18 Then the one named Cleopas asked Jesus, "Are you the only person from Jerusalem who didn't know what was happening there these last few days?"

19 "What do you mean?" Jesus asked. They answered:

Those things that happened to Jesus from Nazareth. By what he did and said he showed that he was a powerful prophet, who pleased God and all the people. 20 Then the chief priests and our leaders had him arrested and sentenced to die on a cross. 21 We had hoped that he would be the one to set Israel free! But it has already been three days since all this happened.

22 Some women in our group surprised us. They had gone to the tomb early in the morning, 23 but did not find the body of Jesus. They came back, saying that they had seen a vision of angels who told them that he is alive. 24 Some men from our group went to the tomb and found it just as the women had said. But they didn't see Jesus either.

25 Then Jesus asked the two disciples, "Why can't you understand? How can you be so slow to believe all that the prophets said? 26 Didn't you know that the Messiah would have to suffer before he was given his glory?" 27 Jesus then explained everything written about himself in the Scriptures, beginning with the Law of Moses and the Books of the Prophets.[s]

28 When the two of them came near the village where they were going, Jesus seemed to be going farther. 29 They begged him, "Stay with us! It's already late, and the sun is going down." So Jesus went into the house to stay with them.

30 After Jesus sat down to eat, he took some bread. He blessed it and broke it. Then he gave it to them. 31 At once they knew who he was, but he disappeared.

---

[p]**23.54** *the Sabbath was about to begin*: The Sabbath begins at sunset on Friday. [q]**24.3** *the Lord*: These words are not in some manuscripts. [r]**24.12** *what had happened*: Verse 12 is not in some manuscripts. [s]**24.27** *the Law of Moses and the Books of the Prophets*: See the note at 16.16.

³²They said to each other, "When he talked with us along the road and explained the Scriptures to us, didn't it warm our hearts?" ³³So they got right up and returned to Jerusalem.

The two disciples found the eleven apostles and the others gathered together. ³⁴And they learned from the group that the Lord was really alive and had appeared to Peter. ³⁵Then the disciples from Emmaus told what happened on the road and how they knew he was the Lord when he broke the bread.

What Jesus' Followers Must Do
(Matthew 28.16-20; Mark 16.14-18; John 20.19-23; Acts 1.6-8)

³⁶While Jesus' disciples were talking about what had happened, Jesus appeared and greeted them. ³⁷They were frightened and terrified because they thought they were seeing a ghost.

³⁸But Jesus said, "Why are you so frightened? Why do you doubt? ³⁹Look at my hands and my feet and see who I am! Touch me and find out for yourselves. Ghosts don't have flesh and bones as you see I have."

⁴⁰After Jesus said this, he showed them his hands and his feet. ⁴¹The disciples were so glad and amazed that they could not believe it. Jesus then asked them, "Do you have something to eat?" ⁴²They gave him a piece of baked fish. ⁴³He took it and ate it as they watched.

⁴⁴Jesus said to them, "While I was still with you, I told you that everything written about me in the Law of Moses, the Books of the Prophets, and in the Psalms*ᵗ* had to happen."

⁴⁵Then he helped them understand the Scriptures. ⁴⁶He told them:

The Scriptures say that the Messiah must suffer, then three days later he will rise from death. ⁴⁷They also say that all people of every nation must be told in my name to turn to God, in order to be forgiven. So beginning in Jerusalem, ⁴⁸you must tell everything that has happened. ⁴⁹I will send you the one my Father has promised,*ᵘ* but you must stay in the city until you are given power from heaven.

Jesus Returns to Heaven
(Mark 16.19, 20; Acts 1.9-11)

⁵⁰Jesus led his disciples out to Bethany, where he raised his hands and blessed them. ⁵¹As he was doing this, he left and was taken up to heaven.*ᵛ* ⁵²After his disciples had worshiped him,*ʷ* they returned to Jerusalem and were very happy. ⁵³They spent their time in the temple, praising God.

---

*ᵗ*24.44 *Psalms*: The Jewish Scriptures were made up of three parts: (1) the Law of Moses, (2) the Books of the Prophets, (3) and the Writings, which included the Psalms. Sometimes the Scriptures were just called the Law or the Law (of Moses) and the Books of the Prophets. *ᵘ*24.49 *the one my Father has promised*: Jesus means the Holy Spirit. *ᵛ*24.51 *and was taken up to heaven*: These words are not in some manuscripts. *ʷ*24.52 *After his disciples had worshiped him*: These words are not in some manuscripts.

JOHN

ABOUT THIS BOOK

Who is Jesus Christ? John answers this question in the first chapter of his Gospel. Using the words of an early Christian hymn, he calls Jesus the "Word" by which God created everything and by which he gave life to everyone (1.3, 4). He shows how John the Baptist announced Jesus' coming, "Here is the Lamb of God who takes away the sin of the world" (1.29). When Philip met Jesus he knew Jesus was "the one that Moses and the Prophets wrote about" (1.45). And, in the words of Nathanael, Jesus is "the Son of God and the King of Israel" (1.49).

In John's Gospel we learn a lot about who Jesus is by observing what he said and did when he was with other people. These include a Samaritan woman who received Jesus' offer of life-giving water, a woman who had been caught in sin, his friend Lazarus who was brought back to life by Jesus, and his follower Thomas who doubted that Jesus was raised from death. Jesus also refers to himself as "I am", a phrase which translates the most holy name for God in the Hebrew Scriptures. He uses this name for himself when he makes his claim to be the life-giving bread, the light of the world, the good shepherd, and the true vine.

Jesus performs seven miracles that are more than miracles. Each of them is a "sign" that tells us something about Jesus as the Son of God. For example, by healing a lame man (5.1-8), Jesus shows that he is just like his Father, who never stops working (5.17). This sign also teaches that the Son does only what he sees his Father doing (5.19), and that like the Father "the Son gives life to anyone he wants to" (5.21).

The way John tells the story of Jesus is quite different from the other three Gospels. Here, Jesus has long conversations with people about who he is and what God sent him to do. In these conversations he teaches many important things—for example, that he is the way, the truth and the life.

Why did John write? John himself tells us, "So that you will put your faith in Jesus as the Messiah and the Son of God" (20.31). How is this possible? Jesus answers that question in his words to Nicodemus:

> God loved the people of this world so much that he gave his only Son, so that everyone who has faith in him will have eternal life and never really die.   (3.16)

A QUICK LOOK AT THIS BOOK

A Hymn in Praise of the Word (1.1-18)
The Message of John the Baptist (1.19-34)
Jesus Chooses His First Disciples (1.35-51)
Jesus' Seven Special Miracles (2.1—12.50)
Jesus' Last Week: His Trial and Death (13.1—19.42)
Jesus Is Alive (20.1-10)
Jesus Appears to His Disciples (20.11—21.25)

The Word of Life

1 In the beginning was the one
  who is called the Word.
 The Word was with God
  and was truly God.
² From the very beginning
  the Word was with God.

³ And with this Word,
  God created all things.
 Nothing was made
  without the Word.
 Everything that was created
⁴ received its life from him,
 and his life gave light
  to everyone.
⁵ The light keeps shining
  in the dark,
 and darkness has never
  put it out.*a*
⁶ God sent a man named John,
⁷ who came to tell
  about the light
 and to lead all people
  to have faith.
⁸ John wasn't that light.
 He came only to tell
  about the light.

⁹ The true light that shines
  on everyone
  was coming into the world.
¹⁰ The Word was in the world,
 but no one knew him,
  though God had made the world
  with his Word.
¹¹ He came into his own world,
 but his own nation
  did not welcome him.
¹² Yet some people accepted him
  and put their faith in him.
 So he gave them the right
  to be the children of God.
¹³ They were not God's children
 by nature or because
  of any human desires.
 God himself was the one
  who made them his children.

¹⁴ The Word became
  a human being
  and lived here with us.
 We saw his true glory,
  the glory of the only Son
  of the Father.
 From him all the kindness
  and all the truth of God
  have come down to us.

¹⁵John spoke about him and shouted, "This is the one I told you would come! He is greater than I am, because he was alive before I was born."
¹⁶Because of all that the Son is, we have been given one blessing after another.*b* ¹⁷The Law was given by Moses, but Jesus Christ brought us undeserved kindness and truth. ¹⁸No one has ever seen God. The only Son, who is truly God and is closest to the Father, has shown us what God is like.

John the Baptist Tells about Jesus
(Matthew 3.1-12; Mark 1.1-8; Luke 3.15-17)

¹⁹⁻²⁰The Jewish leaders in Jerusalem sent priests and temple helpers to ask John who he was. He told them plainly, "I am not the Messiah." ²¹Then when they asked him if he were Elijah, he said, "No, I am not!" And when they asked if he were the Prophet,*c* he also said "No!"

²²Finally, they said, "Who are you then? We have to give an answer to the ones who sent us. Tell us who you are!"

²³John answered in the words of the prophet Isaiah, "I am only someone shouting in the desert, 'Get the road ready for the Lord!' "

²⁴Some Pharisees had also been sent to John. ²⁵They asked him, "Why are you baptizing people, if you are not the Messiah or Elijah or the Prophet?"

²⁶John told them, "I use water to baptize people. But here with you is someone you don't know. ²⁷Even though I came first, I am not good enough to untie his sandals." ²⁸John said this as he was baptizing east of the Jordan River in Bethany.*d*

The Lamb of God

²⁹The next day, John saw Jesus coming toward him and said:
  Here is the Lamb of God who takes away the sin of the world! ³⁰He is the one I told you about when I said, "Someone else will come. He is greater than I am, because he was alive before I was born." ³¹I didn't know who he was. But I came to baptize you with water, so that everyone in Israel would see him.

³²I was there and saw the Spirit come down on him like a dove from heaven. And the Spirit stayed on him. ³³Before this I didn't know who he was. But the one who sent me to baptize with water had told me, "You will see the Spirit come down and stay on someone. Then you will

---

a 1.5 *put it out*: Or "understood it."   *b* 1.16 *one blessing after another*: Or "one blessing in place of another."   *c* 1.21 *the Prophet*: Many of the Jewish people expected God to send them a prophet who would be like Moses, but with even greater power (see Deuteronomy 18.15, 18).   *d* 1.28 *Bethany*: An unknown village east of the Jordan with the same name as the village near Jerusalem.

know that he is the one who will baptize with the Holy Spirit." ³⁴I saw this happen, and I tell you that he is the Son of God.

The First Disciples of Jesus

³⁵The next day, John was there again, and two of his followers were with him. ³⁶When he saw Jesus walking by, he said, "Here is the Lamb of God!" ³⁷John's two followers heard him, and they went with Jesus.

³⁸When Jesus turned and saw them, he asked, "What do you want?"

They answered, "Rabbi, where do you live?" The Hebrew word "Rabbi" means "Teacher."

³⁹Jesus replied, "Come and see!" It was already about four o'clock in the afternoon when they went with him and saw where he lived. So they stayed on for the rest of the day.

⁴⁰One of the two men who had heard John and had gone with Jesus was Andrew, the brother of Simon Peter. ⁴¹The first thing Andrew did was to find his brother and tell him, "We have found the Messiah!" The Hebrew word "Messiah" means the same as the Greek word "Christ."

⁴²Andrew brought his brother to Jesus. And when Jesus saw him, he said, "Simon son of John, you will be called Cephas." This name can be translated as "Peter."[e]

Jesus Chooses Philip and Nathanael

⁴³⁻⁴⁴The next day Jesus decided to go to Galilee. There he met Philip, who was from Bethsaida, the hometown of Andrew and Peter. Jesus said to Philip, "Come with me."

⁴⁵Philip then found Nathanael and said, "We have found the one that Moses and the Prophets[f] wrote about. He is Jesus, the son of Joseph from Nazareth."

⁴⁶Nathanael asked, "Can anything good come from Nazareth?"

Philip answered, "Come and see."

⁴⁷When Jesus saw Nathanael coming toward him, he said, "Here is a true descendant of our ancestor Israel. And he isn't deceitful."[g]

⁴⁸"How do you know me?" Nathanael asked.

Jesus answered, "Before Philip called you, I saw you under the fig tree."

⁴⁹Nathanael said, "Rabbi, you are the Son of God and the King of Israel!"

⁵⁰Jesus answered, "Did you believe me just because I said that I saw you under the fig tree? You will see something even greater. ⁵¹I tell you for certain that you will see heaven open and God's angels going up and coming down on the Son of Man."[h]

Jesus at a Wedding in Cana

2 Three days later Mary, the mother of Jesus, was at a wedding feast in the village of Cana in Galilee. ²Jesus and his disciples had also been invited and were there.

³When the wine was all gone, Mary said to Jesus, "They don't have any more wine."

⁴Jesus replied, "Mother, my time hasn't yet come![i] You must not tell me what to do."

⁵Mary then said to the servants, "Do whatever Jesus tells you to do."

⁶At the feast there were six stone water jars that were used by the people for washing themselves in the way that their religion said they must. Each jar held about twenty or thirty gallons. ⁷Jesus told the servants to fill them to the top with water. Then after the jars had been filled, ⁸he said, "Now take some water and give it to the man in charge of the feast."

The servants did as Jesus told them, ⁹and the man in charge drank some of the water that had now turned into wine. He did not know where the wine had come from, but the servants did. He called the bridegroom over ¹⁰and said, "The best wine is always served first. Then after the guests have had plenty, the other wine is served. But you have kept the best until last!"

¹¹This was Jesus' first miracle,[j] and he did it in the village of Cana in Galilee. There Jesus showed his glory, and his disciples put their faith in him. ¹²After this, he went with his mother, his brothers, and his disciples to the town of Capernaum, where they stayed for a few days.

---

[e]**1.42** *Peter:* The Aramaic name "Cephas" and the Greek name "Peter" each mean "rock."

[f]**1.45** *Moses and the Prophets:* The Jewish Scriptures, that is, the Old Testament.

[g]**1.47** *Israel . . . isn't deceitful:* Israel (meaning "a man who wrestled with God" or "a prince of God") was the name that the Lord gave to Jacob (meaning "cheater" or "deceiver"), the famous ancestor of the Jewish people. [h]**1.51** *going up and coming down on the Son of Man:* When Jacob (see the note at verse 47) was running from his brother Esau, he had a dream in which he saw angels going up and down on a ladder from earth to heaven (see Genesis 32.22-32).

[i]**2.4** *my time hasn't yet come!:* The time when the true glory of Jesus would be seen, and he would be recognized as God's Son (see 12.23). [j]**2.11,18,23** *miracle:* The Greek text has "sign." In the Gospel of John the word "sign" is used for the miracle itself and as a way of pointing to Jesus as the Son of God.

Jesus in the Temple
(Matthew 21.12, 13; Mark 11.15-17; Luke 19.45, 46)

13 Not long before the Jewish festival of Passover, Jesus went to Jerusalem. 14 There he found people selling cattle, sheep, and doves in the temple. He also saw moneychangers sitting at their tables. 15 So he took some rope and made a whip. Then he chased everyone out of the temple, together with their sheep and cattle. He turned over the tables of the moneychangers and scattered their coins.

16 Jesus said to the people who had been selling doves, "Get those doves out of here! Don't make my Father's house a marketplace."

17 The disciples then remembered that the Scriptures say, "My love for your house burns in me like a fire."

18 The Jewish leaders asked Jesus, "What miracle[j] will you work to show us why you have done this?"

19 "Destroy this temple," Jesus answered, "and in three days I will build it again!"

20 The leaders replied, "It took forty-six years to build this temple. What makes you think you can rebuild it in three days?"

21 But Jesus was talking about his body as a temple. 22 And when he was raised from death, his disciples remembered what he had told them. Then they believed the Scriptures and the words of Jesus.

Jesus Knows What People Are Like

23 In Jerusalem during Passover many people put their faith in Jesus, because they saw him work miracles.[j] 24 But Jesus knew what was in their hearts, and he would not let them have power over him. 25 No one had to tell him what people were like. He already knew.

Jesus and Nicodemus

3 There was a man named Nicodemus who was a Pharisee and a Jewish leader. 2 One night he went to Jesus and said, "Sir, we know that God has sent you to teach us. You could not work these miracles, unless God were with you."

3 Jesus replied, "I tell you for certain that you must be born from above[k] before you can see God's kingdom!"

4 Nicodemus asked, "How can a grown man ever be born a second time?"

5 Jesus answered:

I tell you for certain that before you can get into God's kingdom, you must be born not only by water, but by the Spirit. 6 Humans give life to their children. Yet only God's Spirit can change you into a child of God. 7 Don't be surprised when I say that you must be born from above. 8 Only God's Spirit gives new life. The Spirit is like the wind that blows wherever it wants to. You can hear the wind, but you don't know where it comes from or where it is going.

9 "How can this be?" Nicodemus asked.

10 Jesus replied:

How can you be a teacher of Israel and not know these things? 11 I tell you for certain that we know what we are talking about because we have seen it ourselves. But none of you will accept what we say. 12 If you don't believe when I talk to you about things on earth, how can you possibly believe if I talk to you about things in heaven?

13 No one has gone up to heaven except the Son of Man, who came down from there. 14 And the Son of Man must be lifted up, just as that metal snake was lifted up by Moses in the desert.[l] 15 Then everyone who has faith in the Son of Man will have eternal life.

16 God loved the people of this world so much that he gave his only Son, so that everyone who has faith in him will have eternal life and never die. 17 God did not send his Son into the world to condemn its people. He sent him to save them! 18 No one who has faith in God's Son will be condemned. But everyone who doesn't have faith in him has already been condemned for not having faith in God's only Son.

19 The light has come into the world, and people who do evil things are judged guilty because they love the dark more than the light. 20 People who do evil hate the light and won't come to the light, because it clearly shows what they have done. 21 But everyone who lives by the truth will come to the light, because they want others to know that God is really the one doing what they do.

Jesus and John the Baptist

22 Later, Jesus and his disciples went to Judea, where he stayed with them for a while and was baptizing people.

23-24 John had not yet been put in jail.

---

[j]2.11,18,23 *miracle*: The Greek text has "sign." In the Gospel of John the word "sign" is used for the miracle itself and as a way of pointing to Jesus as the Son of God.   [k]3.3 *from above*: Or "in a new way." The same Greek word is used in verses 7, 31.   [l]3.14 *just as that metal snake was lifted up by Moses in the desert*: When the Lord punished the people of Israel by sending snakes to bite them, he told Moses to hold a metal snake up on a pole. Everyone who looked at the snake was cured of the snake bites (see Numbers 21.4-9).

He was at Aenon near Salim, where there was a lot of water, and people were coming there for John to baptize them.

²⁵John's followers got into an argument with a Jewish man[m] about a ceremony of washing.[n] ²⁶They went to John and said, "Rabbi, you spoke about a man when you were with him east of the Jordan. He is now baptizing people, and everyone is going to him."

²⁷John replied:

No one can do anything unless God in heaven allows it. ²⁸You surely remember how I told you that I am not the Messiah. I am only the one sent ahead of him.

²⁹At a wedding the groom is the one who gets married. The best man is glad just to be there and to hear the groom's voice. That's why I am so glad. ³⁰Jesus must become more important, while I become less important.

The One Who Comes from Heaven

³¹God's Son comes from heaven and is above all others. Everyone who comes from the earth belongs to the earth and speaks about earthly things. The one who comes from heaven is above all others. ³²He speaks about what he has seen and heard, and yet no one believes him. ³³But everyone who does believe him has shown that God is truthful. ³⁴The Son was sent to speak God's message, and he has been given the full power of God's Spirit.

³⁵The Father loves the Son and has given him everything. ³⁶Everyone who has faith in the Son has eternal life. But no one who rejects him will ever share in that life, and God will be angry with them forever.

4 Jesus knew that the Pharisees had heard that he was winning and baptizing more followers than John was. ²But Jesus' disciples were really the ones doing the baptizing, and not Jesus himself.

Jesus and the Samaritan Woman

³Jesus left Judea and started for Galilee again. ⁴This time he had to go through Samaria, ⁵and on his way he came to the town of Sychar. It was near the field that Jacob had long ago given to his son Joseph. ⁶⁻⁸The well that Jacob had dug was still there, and Jesus sat down beside it because he was tired from traveling. It was noon, and after Jesus' disciples had gone into town to buy some food, a Samaritan woman came to draw water from the well.

Jesus asked her, "Would you please give me a drink of water?"

⁹"You are a Jew," she replied, "and I am a Samaritan woman. How can you ask me for a drink of water when Jews and Samaritans won't have anything to do with each other?"[o]

¹⁰Jesus answered, "You don't know what God wants to give you, and you don't know who is asking you for a drink. If you did, you would ask me for the water that gives life."

¹¹"Sir," the woman said, "you don't even have a bucket, and the well is deep. Where are you going to get this life-giving water? ¹²Our ancestor Jacob dug this well for us, and his family and animals got water from it. Are you greater than Jacob?"

¹³Jesus answered, "Everyone who drinks this water will get thirsty again. ¹⁴But no one who drinks the water I give will ever be thirsty again. The water I give is like a flowing fountain that gives eternal life."

¹⁵The woman replied, "Sir, please give me a drink of that water! Then I won't get thirsty and have to come to this well again."

¹⁶Jesus told her, "Go and bring your husband."

¹⁷⁻¹⁸The woman answered, "I don't have a husband."

"That's right," Jesus replied, "you're telling the truth. You don't have a husband. You have already been married five times, and the man you are now living with isn't your husband."

¹⁹The woman said, "Sir, I can see that you are a prophet. ²⁰My ancestors worshiped on this mountain,[p] but you Jews say Jerusalem is the only place to worship."

²¹Jesus said to her:

Believe me, the time is coming when you won't worship the Father either on this mountain or in Jerusalem. ²²You Samaritans don't really know the one you worship. But we Jews do know the God we worship, and by using us, God will save the world. ²³But a time is coming, and it is already here! Even now the true worshipers are being led by the Spirit to worship the Father

---

[m]**3.25** *a Jewish man*: Some manuscripts have "some Jewish men." [n]**3.25** *about a ceremony of washing*: The Jewish people had many rules about washing themselves and their dishes, in order to make themselves fit to worship God. [o]**4.9** *won't have anything to do with each other*: Or "won't use the same cups." The Samaritans lived in the land between Judea and Galilee. They worshiped God differently from the Jews and did not get along with them. [p]**4.20** *this mountain*: Mount Gerizim, near the city of Shechem.

according to the truth. These are the ones the Father is seeking to worship him. ²⁴God is Spirit, and those who worship God must be led by the Spirit to worship him according to the truth.
²⁵The woman said, "I know that the Messiah will come. He is the one we call Christ. When he comes, he will explain everything to us."
²⁶"I am that one," Jesus told her, "and I am speaking to you now."
²⁷The disciples returned about this time and were surprised to find Jesus talking with a woman. But none of them asked him what he wanted or why he was talking with her.
²⁸The woman left her water jar and ran back into town. She said to the people, ²⁹"Come and see a man who told me everything I have ever done! Could he be the Messiah?" ³⁰Everyone in town went out to see Jesus.
³¹While this was happening, Jesus' disciples were saying to him, "Teacher, please eat something."
³²But Jesus told them, "I have food that you don't know anything about."
³³His disciples started asking each other, "Has someone brought him something to eat?"
³⁴Jesus said:
My food is to do what God wants! He is the one who sent me, and I must finish the work that he gave me to do. ³⁵You may say that there are still four months until harvest time. But I tell you to look, and you will see that the fields are ripe and ready to harvest.
³⁶Even now the harvest workers are receiving their reward by gathering a harvest that brings eternal life. Then everyone who planted the seed and everyone who harvests the crop will celebrate together. ³⁷So the saying proves true, "Some plant the seed, and others harvest the crop."
³⁸I am sending you to harvest crops in fields where others have done all the hard work.
³⁹A lot of Samaritans in that town put their faith in Jesus because the woman had said, "This man told me everything I have ever done." ⁴⁰They came and asked him to stay in their town, and he stayed on for two days.
⁴¹Many more Samaritans put their faith in Jesus because of what they heard him say. ⁴²They told the woman, "We no longer have faith in Jesus just because of what you told us. We have heard him ourselves, and we are certain that he is the Savior of the world!"

Jesus Heals an Official's Son
(Matthew 8.5-13; Luke 7.1-10)

⁴³⁻⁴⁴Jesus had said, "Prophets are honored everywhere, except in their own country." Then two days later he left ⁴⁵and went to Galilee. The people there welcomed him, because they had gone to the festival in Jerusalem and had seen everything he had done.
⁴⁶While Jesus was in Galilee, he returned to the village of Cana, where he had turned the water into wine. There was an official in Capernaum whose son was sick. ⁴⁷And when the man heard that Jesus had come from Judea, he went and begged him to keep his son from dying.
⁴⁸Jesus told the official, "You won't have faith unless you see miracles and wonders!"
⁴⁹The man replied, "Lord, please come before my son dies!"
⁵⁰Jesus then said, "Your son will live. Go on home to him." The man believed Jesus and started back home.
⁵¹Some of the official's servants met him along the road and told him, "Your son is better!" ⁵²He asked them when the boy got better, and they answered, "The fever left him yesterday at one o'clock."
⁵³The boy's father realized that at one o'clock the day before, Jesus had told him, "Your son will live!" So the man and everyone in his family put their faith in Jesus.
⁵⁴This was the second miracle*q* that Jesus worked after he left Judea and went to Galilee.

Jesus Heals a Sick Man

5 Later, Jesus went to Jerusalem for another Jewish festival.*r* ²In the city near the sheep gate was a pool with five porches, and its name in Hebrew was Bethzatha.*s*
³⁻⁴Many sick, blind, lame, and crippled people were lying close to the pool.*t*
⁵Beside the pool was a man who had been sick for thirty-eight years. ⁶When Jesus saw the man and realized that he had been crippled for a long time, he asked him, "Do you want to be healed?"
⁷The man answered, "Lord, I don't have anyone to put me in the pool when the water is stirred up. I try to get in, but someone else always gets there first."
⁸Jesus told him, "Pick up your mat

---

*q*4.54 *miracle*: See the note at 2.11.   *r*5.1 *another Jewish festival*: Either the Festival of Shelters or Passover.   *s*5.2 *Bethzatha*: Some manuscripts have "Bethesda" and others have "Bethsaida."   *t*5.3,4 *pool*: Some manuscripts add, "They were waiting for the water to be stirred, because an angel from the Lord would sometimes come down and stir it. The first person to get into the pool after that would be healed."

and walk!" ⁹Right then the man was healed. He picked up his mat and started walking around. The day on which this happened was a Sabbath.

¹⁰When the Jewish leaders saw the man carrying his mat, they said to him, "This is the Sabbath! No one is allowed to carry a mat on the Sabbath."

¹¹But he replied, "The man who healed me told me to pick up my mat and walk."

¹²They asked him, "Who is this man that told you to pick up your mat and walk?" ¹³But he did not know who Jesus was, and Jesus had left because of the crowd.

¹⁴Later, Jesus met the man in the temple and told him, "You are now well. But don't sin anymore or something worse might happen to you." ¹⁵The man left and told the leaders that Jesus was the one who had healed him. ¹⁶They started making a lot of trouble for Jesus because he did things like this on the Sabbath.

¹⁷But Jesus said, "My Father has never stopped working, and that is why I keep on working." ¹⁸Now the leaders wanted to kill Jesus for two reasons. First, he had broken the law of the Sabbath. But even worse, he had said that God was his Father, which made him equal with God.

The Son's Authority

¹⁹Jesus told the people:

I tell you for certain that the Son cannot do anything on his own. He can do only what he sees the Father doing, and he does exactly what he sees the Father do. ²⁰The Father loves the Son and has shown him everything he does. The Father will show him even greater things, and you will be amazed. ²¹Just as the Father raises the dead and gives life, so the Son gives life to anyone he wants to.

²²The Father doesn't judge anyone, but he has made his Son the judge of everyone. ²³The Father wants all people to honor the Son as much as they honor him. When anyone refuses to honor the Son, that is the same as refusing to honor the Father who sent him. ²⁴I tell you for certain that everyone who hears my message and has faith in the one who sent me has eternal life and will never be condemned. They have already gone from death to life.

²⁵I tell you for certain that the time will come, and it is already here, when all of the dead will hear the voice of the Son of God. And those who listen to it will live! ²⁶The Father has the power to give life, and he has given that same power to the Son. ²⁷And he has given his Son the right to judge everyone, because he is the Son of Man.

²⁸Don't be surprised! The time will come when all of the dead will hear the voice of the Son of Man, ²⁹and they will come out of their graves. Everyone who has done good things will rise to life, but everyone who has done evil things will rise and be condemned.

³⁰I cannot do anything on my own. The Father sent me, and he is the one who told me how to judge. I judge with fairness, because I obey him, and I don't just try to please myself.

Witnesses to Jesus

³¹If I speak for myself, there is no way to prove I am telling the truth. ³²But there is someone else who speaks for me, and I know what he says is true. ³³You sent messengers to John, and he told them the truth. ³⁴I don't depend on what people say about me, but I tell you these things so that you may be saved. ³⁵John was a lamp that gave a lot of light, and you were glad to enjoy his light for a while.

³⁶But something more important than John speaks for me. I mean the things that the Father has given me to do! All of these speak for me and prove that the Father sent me.

³⁷The Father who sent me also speaks for me, but you have never heard his voice or seen him face to face. ³⁸You have not believed his message, because you refused to have faith in the one he sent.

³⁹You search the Scriptures, because you think you will find eternal life in them. The Scriptures tell about me, ⁴⁰but you refuse to come to me for eternal life.

⁴¹I don't care about human praise, ⁴²but I do know that none of you love God. ⁴³I have come with my Father's authority, and you have not welcomed me. But you will welcome people who come on their own. ⁴⁴How could you possibly believe? You like to have your friends praise you, and you don't care about praise that the only God can give!

⁴⁵Don't think that I will be the one to accuse you to the Father. You have put your hope in Moses, yet he is the very one who will accuse you. ⁴⁶Moses wrote about me, and if you had believed Moses, you would have believed me. ⁴⁷But if you don't believe what Moses wrote, how can you believe what I say?

Feeding Five Thousand
(Matthew 14.13-21; Mark 6.30-44; Luke 9.10-17)

6 Jesus crossed Lake Galilee, which was also known as Lake Tiberias. ²A large crowd had seen him work miracles to heal the sick, and those people went with him. ³⁻⁴It was almost time for the Jewish festival of Passover, and Jesus went up on a mountain with his disciples and sat down.*ᵘ*

⁵When Jesus saw the large crowd coming toward him, he asked Philip, "Where will we get enough food to feed all these people?" ⁶He said this to test Philip, since he already knew what he was going to do.

⁷Philip answered, "Don't you know that it would take almost a year's wages*ᵛ* just to buy only a little bread for each of these people?"

⁸Andrew, the brother of Simon Peter, was one of the disciples. He spoke up and said, ⁹"There is a boy here who has five small loaves*ʷ* of barley bread and two fish. But what good is that with all these people?"

¹⁰The ground was covered with grass, and Jesus told his disciples to have everyone sit down. About five thousand men were in the crowd. ¹¹Jesus took the bread in his hands and gave thanks to God. Then he passed the bread to the people, and he did the same with the fish, until everyone had plenty to eat.

¹²The people ate all they wanted, and Jesus told his disciples to gather up the leftovers, so that nothing would be wasted. ¹³The disciples gathered them up and filled twelve large baskets with what was left over from the five barley loaves.

¹⁴After the people had seen Jesus work this miracle,*ˣ* they began saying, "This must be the Prophet*ʸ* who is to come into the world!" ¹⁵Jesus realized that they would try to force him to be their king. So he went up on a mountain, where he could be alone.

Jesus Walks on the Water
(Matthew 14.22-27; Mark 6.45-52)

¹⁶That evening, Jesus' disciples went down to the lake. ¹⁷They got into a boat and started across for Capernaum. Later that evening Jesus had still not come to them, ¹⁸and a strong wind was making the water rough.

¹⁹When the disciples had rowed for three or four miles, they saw Jesus walking on the water. He kept coming closer to the boat, and they were terrified. ²⁰But he said, "I am Jesus!*ᶻ* Don't be afraid!" ²¹The disciples wanted to take him into the boat, but suddenly the boat reached the shore where they were headed.

The Bread That Gives Life

²²The people who had stayed on the east side of the lake knew that only one boat had been there. They also knew that Jesus had not left in it with his disciples. But the next day ²³some boats from Tiberias sailed near the place where the crowd had eaten the bread for which the Lord had given thanks. ²⁴They saw that Jesus and his disciples had left. Then they got into the boats and went to Capernaum to look for Jesus. ²⁵They found him on the west side of the lake and asked, "Rabbi, when did you get here?"

²⁶Jesus answered, "I tell you for certain that you are not looking for me because you saw the miracles,*ᵃ* but because you ate all the food you wanted. ²⁷Don't work for food that spoils. Work for food that gives eternal life. The Son of Man will give you this food, because God the Father has given him the right to do so."

²⁸"What exactly does God want us to do?" the people asked.

²⁹Jesus answered, "God wants you to have faith in the one he sent."

³⁰They replied, "What miracle will you work, so that we can have faith in you? What will you do? ³¹For example, when our ancestors were in the desert, they were given manna*ᵇ* to eat. It happened just as the Scriptures say, 'God gave them bread from heaven to eat.'"

³²Jesus then told them, "I tell you for certain that Moses wasn't the one who gave you bread from heaven. My Father is the one who gives you the true bread from heaven. ³³And the bread that God gives is the one who came down from heaven to give life to the world."

³⁴The people said, "Lord, give us this bread and don't ever stop!"

³⁵Jesus replied:
I am the bread that gives life! No one who comes to me will ever be hungry. No one who has faith in me

---

ᵘ6.3,4 sat down: Possibly to teach. Teachers in the ancient world, including Jewish teachers, usually sat down to teach. *ᵛ6.7 almost a year's wages*: The Greek text has "two hundred silver coins." Each coin was worth the average day's wages for a worker. *ʷ6.9 small loaves*: These would have been flat and round or in the shape of a bun. *ˣ6.14 miracle*: See the note at 2.11. *ʸ6.14 the Prophet*: See the note at 1.21. *ᶻ6.20 I am Jesus*: The Greek text has "I am" (see the note at 8.24). *ᵃ6.26 miracles*: The Greek text has "signs" here and "sign" in verse 30 (see the note at 2.11). *ᵇ6.31 manna*: When the people of Israel were wandering through the desert, the Lord gave them a special kind of food to eat. It tasted like a wafer and was called "manna," which in Hebrew means, "What is this?"

will ever be thirsty. ³⁶I have told you already that you have seen me and still do not have faith in me. ³⁷Everything and everyone that the Father has given me will come to me, and I won't turn any of them away.

³⁸I didn't come from heaven to do what I want! I came to do what the Father wants me to do. He sent me, ³⁹and he wants to make certain that none of the ones he has given me will be lost. Instead, he wants me to raise them to life on the last day.ᶜ ⁴⁰My Father wants everyone who sees the Son to have faith in him and to have eternal life. Then I will raise them to life on the last day.

⁴¹The people started grumbling because Jesus had said he was the bread that had come down from heaven. ⁴²They were asking each other, "Isn't he Jesus, the son of Joseph? Don't we know his father and mother? How can he say that he has come down from heaven?"

⁴³Jesus told them:

Stop grumbling! ⁴⁴No one can come to me, unless the Father who sent me makes them want to come. But if they do come, I will raise them to life on the last day. ⁴⁵One of the prophets wrote, "God will teach all of them." And so everyone who listens to the Father and learns from him will come to me.

⁴⁶The only one who has seen the Father is the one who has come from him. No one else has ever seen the Father. ⁴⁷I tell you for certain that everyone who has faith in me has eternal life.

⁴⁸I am the bread that gives life! ⁴⁹Your ancestors ate mannaᵈ in the desert, and later they died. ⁵⁰But the bread from heaven has come down, so that no one who eats it will ever die. ⁵¹I am that bread from heaven! Everyone who eats it will live forever. My flesh is the life-giving bread that I give to the people of this world.

⁵²They started arguing with each other and asked, "How can he give us his flesh to eat?"

⁵³Jesus answered:

I tell you for certain that you won't live unless you eat the flesh and drink the blood of the Son of Man. ⁵⁴But if you do eat my flesh and drink my blood, you will have eternal life, and I will raise you to life on the last day. ⁵⁵My flesh is the true food, and my blood is the true drink. ⁵⁶If you eat my flesh and drink my blood, you are one with me, and I am one with you.

⁵⁷The living Father sent me, and I have life because of him. Now everyone who eats my flesh will live because of me. ⁵⁸The bread that comes down from heaven isn't like what your ancestors ate. They died, but whoever eats this bread will live forever.

⁵⁹Jesus was teaching in a Jewish place of worship in Capernaum when he said these things.

The Words of Eternal Life

⁶⁰Many of Jesus' disciples heard him and said, "This is too hard for anyone to understand."

⁶¹Jesus knew that his disciples were grumbling. So he asked, "Does this bother you? ⁶²What if you should see the Son of Man go up to heaven where he came from? ⁶³The Spirit is the one who gives life! Human strength can do nothing. The words that I have spoken to you are from that life-giving Spirit. ⁶⁴But some of you refuse to have faith in me." Jesus said this, because from the beginning he knew who would have faith in him. He also knew which one would betray him.

⁶⁵Then Jesus said, "You cannot come to me, unless the Father makes you want to come. That is why I have told these things to all of you."

⁶⁶Because of what Jesus said, many of his disciples turned their backs on him and stopped following him. ⁶⁷Jesus then asked his twelve disciples if they were going to leave him. ⁶⁸Simon Peter answered, "Lord, there is no one else that we can go to! Your words give eternal life. ⁶⁹We have faith in you, and we are sure that you are God's Holy One."

⁷⁰Jesus told his disciples, "I chose all twelve of you, but one of you is a demon!" ⁷¹Jesus was talking about Judas, the son of Simon Iscariot.ᵉ He would later betray Jesus, even though he was one of the twelve disciples.

Jesus' Brothers Don't Have Faith in Him

7 Jesus decided to leave Judea and to start going through Galilee because the Jewish leaders wanted to kill him. ²It was almost time for the Festival of Shelters, ³and Jesus' brothers said to him, "Why don't you go to Judea? Then your disciples can see what you are doing. ⁴No one does anything in secret, if they want others to know about them. So let the world know what you are

---

ᶜ**6.39** *the last day*: When God will judge all people.   ᵈ**6.49** *manna*: See the note at 6.31.
ᵉ**6.71** *Iscariot*: This may mean "a man from Kerioth" (a place in Judea). But more probably it means "a man who was a liar" or "a man who was a betrayer."

doing!" ⁵Even Jesus' own brothers had not yet become his followers.

⁶Jesus answered, "My time hasn't yet come,ᶠ but your time is always here. ⁷The people of this world cannot hate you. They hate me, because I tell them that they do evil things. ⁸Go on to the festival. My time hasn't yet come, and I am not going." ⁹Jesus said this and stayed on in Galilee.

Jesus at the Festival of Shelters

¹⁰After Jesus' brothers had gone to the festival, he went secretly, without telling anyone.

¹¹During the festival the Jewish leaders looked for Jesus and asked, "Where is he?" ¹²The crowds even got into an argument about him. Some were saying, "Jesus is a good man," while others were saying, "He is lying to everyone." ¹³But the people were afraid of their leaders, and none of them talked in public about him.

¹⁴When the festival was about half over, Jesus went into the temple and started teaching. ¹⁵The leaders were surprised and said, "How does this man know so much? He has never been taught!"

¹⁶Jesus replied:

I am not teaching something that I thought up. What I teach comes from the one who sent me. ¹⁷If you really want to obey God, you will know if what I teach comes from God or from me. ¹⁸If I wanted to bring honor to myself, I would speak for myself. But I want to honor the one who sent me. That is why I tell the truth and not a lie. ¹⁹Didn't Moses give you the Law? Yet none of you obey it! So why do you want to kill me?

²⁰The crowd replied, "You're crazy! What makes you think someone wants to kill you?"

²¹Jesus answered:

I worked one miracle,ᵍ and it amazed you. ²²Moses commanded you to circumcise your sons. But it wasn't really Moses who gave you this command. It was your ancestors, and even on the Sabbath you circumcise your sons ²³in order to obey the Law of Moses. Why are you angry with me for making someone completely well on the Sabbath? ²⁴Don't judge by appearances. Judge by what is right.

²⁵Some of the people from Jerusalem were saying, "Isn't this the man they want to kill? ²⁶Yet here he is, speaking for everyone to hear. And no one is arguing with him. Do you suppose the authorities know that he is the Messiah? ²⁷But how could that be? No one knows where the Messiah will come from, but we know where this man comes from."

²⁸As Jesus was teaching in the temple, he shouted, "Do you really think you know me and where I came from? I didn't come on my own! The one who sent me is truthful, and you don't know him. ²⁹But I know the one who sent me, because I came from him."

³⁰Some of the people wanted to arrest Jesus right then. But no one even laid a hand on him, because his time had not yet come.ʰ ³¹A lot of people in the crowd put their faith in him and said, "When the Messiah comes, he surely won't perform more miraclesⁱ than this man has done!"

Officers Sent To Arrest Jesus

³²When the Pharisees heard the crowd arguing about Jesus, they got together with the chief priests and sent some temple police to arrest him. ³³But Jesus told them, "I will be with you a little while longer, and then I will return to the one who sent me. ³⁴You will look for me, but you won't find me. You cannot go where I am going."

³⁵The Jewish leaders asked each other, "Where can he go to keep us from finding him? Is he going to some foreign country where our people live? Is he going there to teach the Greeks?ʲ ³⁶What did he mean by saying that we will look for him, but won't find him? Why can't we go where he is going?"

Streams of Life-Giving Water

³⁷On the last and most important day of the festival, Jesus stood up and shouted, "If you are thirsty, come to me and drink! ³⁸Have faith in me, and you will have life-giving water flowing from deep inside you, just as the Scriptures say." ³⁹Jesus was talking about the Holy Spirit, who would be given to everyone that had faith in him. The Spirit had not yet been given to anyone, since Jesus had not yet been given his full glory.ᵏ

The People Take Sides

⁴⁰When the crowd heard Jesus say this, some of them said, "He must be the Prophet!"ˡ ⁴¹Others said, "He is the Messiah!" Others even said, "Can the Mes-

---

ᶠ*7.6 My time hasn't yet come:* See the note at 2.4. ᵍ*7.21 one miracle:* The healing of the lame man (5.1-18; see also the note at 2.11). ʰ*7.30 his time had not yet come:* See the note at 2.4. ⁱ*7.31 miracles:* See the note at 2.11. ʲ*7.35 Greeks:* Perhaps Gentiles or Jews who followed Greek customs. ᵏ*7.39 had not yet been given his full glory:* In the Gospel of John, Jesus is given his full glory both when he is nailed to the cross and when he is raised from death to sit beside his Father in heaven. ˡ*7.40 the Prophet:* See the note at 1.21.

siah come from Galilee? ⁴²The Scriptures say that the Messiah will come from the family of King David. Doesn't this mean that he will be born in David's hometown of Bethlehem?" ⁴³The people started taking sides against each other because of Jesus. ⁴⁴Some of them wanted to arrest him, but no one laid a hand on him.

The Leaders Refuse To Have Faith in Jesus

⁴⁵When the temple police returned to the chief priests and Pharisees, they were asked, "Why didn't you bring Jesus here?"

⁴⁶They answered, "No one has ever spoken like that man!"

⁴⁷The Pharisees said to them, "Have you also been fooled? ⁴⁸Not one of the chief priests or the Pharisees has faith in him. ⁴⁹And these people who don't know the Law are under God's curse anyway."

⁵⁰Nicodemus was there at the time. He was a member of the council, and was the same one who had earlier come to see Jesus.ᵐ He said, ⁵¹"Our Law doesn't let us condemn people before we hear what they have to say. We cannot judge them before we know what they have done."

⁵²Then they said, "Nicodemus, you must be from Galilee! Read the Scriptures, and you will find that no prophet is to come from Galilee."

A Woman Caught in Sin

8 ⁵³Everyone else went home, ¹but Jesus walked out to the Mount of Olives. ²Then early the next morning he went to the temple. The people came to him, and he sat downⁿ and started teaching them.

³The Pharisees and the teachers of the Law of Moses brought in a woman who had been caught in bed with a man who wasn't her husband. They made her stand in the middle of the crowd. ⁴Then they said, "Teacher, this woman was caught sleeping with a man who isn't her husband. ⁵The Law of Moses teaches that a woman like this should be stoned to death! What do you say?"

⁶They asked Jesus this question, because they wanted to test him and bring some charge against him. But Jesus simply bent over and started writing on the ground with his finger.

⁷They kept on asking Jesus about the woman. Finally, he stood up and said, "If any of you have never sinned, then go ahead and throw the first stone at her!" ⁸Once again he bent over and began writing on the ground. ⁹The people left one by one, beginning with the oldest. Finally, Jesus and the woman were there alone.

¹⁰Jesus stood up and asked her, "Where is everyone? Isn't there anyone left to accuse you?"

¹¹"No sir," the woman answered.

Then Jesus told her, "I am not going to accuse you either. You may go now, but don't sin anymore."ᵒ

Jesus Is the Light for the World

¹²Once again Jesus spoke to the people. This time he said, "I am the light for the world! Follow me, and you won't be walking in the dark. You will have the light that gives life."

¹³The Pharisees objected, "You are the only one speaking for yourself, and what you say isn't true!"

¹⁴Jesus replied:

Even if I do speak for myself, what I say is true! I know where I came from and where I am going. But you don't know where I am from or where I am going. ¹⁵You judge in the same way that everyone else does, but I don't judge anyone. ¹⁶If I did judge, I would judge fairly, because I would not be doing it alone. The Father who sent me is here with me. ¹⁷Your Law requires two witnesses to prove that something is true. ¹⁸I am one of my witnesses, and the Father who sent me is the other one.

¹⁹"Where is your Father?" they asked.

"You don't know me or my Father!" Jesus answered. "If you knew me, you would know my Father."

²⁰Jesus said this while he was still teaching in the place where the temple treasures were stored. But no one arrested him, because his time had not yet come.ᵖ

You Cannot Go Where I Am Going

²¹Jesus also told them, "I am going away, and you will look for me. But you cannot go where I am going, and you will die with your sins unforgiven."

²²The Jewish leaders asked, "Does he intend to kill himself? Is that what he means by saying we cannot go where he is going?"

²³Jesus answered, "You are from below, but I am from above. You belong to this world, but I don't. ²⁴That is why I said you will die with your sins unforgiven. If you don't have faith in me for

---

ᵐ**7.50** *who had earlier come to see Jesus*: See 3.1-21.   ⁿ**8.2** *sat down*: See the note at 6.3, 4.
ᵒ**8.11** *don't sin anymore*: Verses 1-11 are not in some manuscripts. In other manuscripts these verses are placed after 7.36 or after 21.25 or after Luke 21.38, with some differences in the text.
ᵖ**8.20** *his time had not yet come*: See the note at 2.4.

who I am,[q] you will die, and your sins will not be forgiven."

²⁵"Who are you?" they asked Jesus.

Jesus answered, "I am exactly who I told you at the beginning. ²⁶There is a lot more I could say to condemn you. But the one who sent me is truthful, and I tell the people of this world only what I have heard from him."

²⁷No one understood that Jesus was talking to them about the Father.

²⁸Jesus went on to say, "When you have lifted up the Son of Man,[r] you will know who I am. You will also know that I don't do anything on my own. I say only what my Father taught me. ²⁹The one who sent me is with me. I always do what pleases him, and he will never leave me."

³⁰After Jesus said this, many of the people put their faith in him.

The Truth Will Set You Free

³¹Jesus told the people who had faith in him, "If you keep on obeying what I have said, you truly are my disciples. ³²You will know the truth, and the truth will set you free."

³³They answered, "We are Abraham's children! We have never been anyone's slaves. How can you say we will be set free?"

³⁴Jesus replied:

I tell you for certain that anyone who sins is a slave of sin! ³⁵And slaves don't stay in the family forever, though the Son will always remain in the family. ³⁶If the Son gives you freedom, you are free! ³⁷I know that you are from Abraham's family. Yet you want to kill me, because my message isn't really in your hearts. ³⁸I am telling you what my Father has shown me, just as you are doing what your father has taught you.

Your Father Is the Devil

³⁹The people said to Jesus, "Abraham is our father!"

Jesus replied, "If you were Abraham's children, you would do what Abraham did. ⁴⁰Instead, you want to kill me for telling you the truth that God gave me. Abraham never did anything like that. ⁴¹But you are doing exactly what your father does."

"Don't accuse us of having someone else as our father!" they said. "We just have one father, and he is God."

⁴²Jesus answered:

If God were your Father, you would love me, because I came from God and only from him. He sent me.

I did not come on my own. ⁴³Why can't you understand what I am talking about? Can't you stand to hear what I am saying? ⁴⁴Your father is the devil, and you do exactly what he wants. He has always been a murderer and a liar. There is nothing truthful about him. He speaks on his own, and everything he says is a lie. Not only is he a liar himself, but he is also the father of all lies.

⁴⁵Everything I have told you is true, and you still refuse to have faith in me. ⁴⁶Can any of you accuse me of sin? If you cannot, why won't you have faith in me? After all, I am telling you the truth. ⁴⁷Anyone who belongs to God will listen to his message. But you refuse to listen, because you don't belong to God.

Jesus and Abraham

⁴⁸The people told Jesus, "We were right to say that you are a Samaritan[s] and that you have a demon in you!"

⁴⁹Jesus answered, "I don't have a demon in me. I honor my Father, and you refuse to honor me. ⁵⁰I don't want honor for myself. But there is one who wants me to be honored, and he is also the one who judges. ⁵¹I tell you for certain that if you obey my words, you will never die."

⁵²Then the people said, "Now we are sure that you have a demon. Abraham is dead, and so are the prophets. How can you say that no one who obeys your words will ever die? ⁵³Are you greater than our father Abraham? He died, and so did the prophets. Who do you think you are?"

⁵⁴Jesus replied, "If I honored myself, it would mean nothing. My Father is the one who honors me. You claim that he is your God, ⁵⁵even though you don't really know him. If I said I didn't know him, I would be a liar, just like all of you. But I know him, and I do what he says. ⁵⁶Your father Abraham was really glad to see me."

⁵⁷"You are not even fifty years old!" they said. "How could you have seen Abraham?"

⁵⁸Jesus answered, "I tell you for certain that even before Abraham was, I was, and I am."[t] ⁵⁹The people picked up stones to kill Jesus, but he hid and left the temple.

Jesus Heals a Man Born Blind

9 As Jesus walked along, he saw a man who had been blind since birth. ²Jesus' disciples asked, "Teacher, why

---

[q]8.24 *I am*: For the Jewish people the most holy name of God is "Yahweh," which may be translated "I am." In the Gospel of John "I am" is sometimes used by Jesus to show that he is that one. [r]8.28 *lifted up the Son of Man*: See the note at 7.39. [s]8.48 *Samaritan*: See 4.9 and the note there. [t]8.58 *I am*: See the note at 8.24.

was this man born blind? Was it because he or his parents sinned?"

³"No, it wasn't!" Jesus answered. "But because of his blindness, you will see God work a miracle for him. ⁴As long as it is day, we must do what the one who sent me wants me to do. When night comes, no one can work. ⁵While I am in the world, I am the light for the world."

⁶After Jesus said this, he spit on the ground. He made some mud and smeared it on the man's eyes. ⁷Then he said, "Go and wash off the mud in Siloam Pool." The man went and washed in Siloam, which means "One Who Is Sent." When he had washed off the mud, he could see.

⁸The man's neighbors and the people who had seen him begging wondered if he really could be the same man. ⁹Some of them said he was the same beggar, while others said he only looked like him. But he told them, "I am that man."

¹⁰"Then how can you see?" they asked.

¹¹He answered, "Someone named Jesus made some mud and smeared it on my eyes. He told me to go and wash it off in Siloam Pool. When I did, I could see."

¹²"Where is he now?" they asked.

"I don't know," he answered.

The Pharisees Try To Find Out What Happened

¹³⁻¹⁴The day when Jesus made the mud and healed the man was a Sabbath. So the people took the man to the Pharisees. ¹⁵They asked him how he was able to see, and he answered, "Jesus made some mud and smeared it on my eyes. Then after I washed it off, I could see."

¹⁶Some of the Pharisees said, "This man Jesus doesn't come from God. If he did, he would not break the law of the Sabbath."

Others asked, "How could someone who is a sinner work such a miracle?"ᵘ

Since the Pharisees could not agree among themselves, ¹⁷they asked the man, "What do you say about this one who healed your eyes?"

"He is a prophet!" the man told them.

¹⁸But the Jewish leaders would not believe that the man had once been blind. They sent for his parents ¹⁹and asked them, "Is this the son that you said was born blind? How can he now see?"

²⁰The man's parents answered, "We are certain that he is our son, and we know that he was born blind. ²¹But we don't know how he got his sight or who gave it to him. Ask him! He is old enough to speak for himself."

²²⁻²³The man's parents said this because they were afraid of the Jewish leaders. The leaders had already agreed that no one was to have anything to do with anyone who said Jesus was the Messiah.

²⁴The leaders called the man back and said, "Swear by God to tell the truth! We know that Jesus is a sinner."

²⁵The man replied, "I don't know if he is a sinner or not. All I know is that I used to be blind, but now I can see!"

²⁶"What did he do to you?" the Jewish leaders asked. "How did he heal your eyes?"

²⁷The man answered, "I have already told you once, and you refused to listen. Why do you want me to tell you again? Do you also want to become his disciples?"

²⁸The leaders insulted the man and said, "You are his follower! We are followers of Moses. ²⁹We are sure that God spoke to Moses, but we don't even know where Jesus comes from."

³⁰"How strange!" the man replied. "He healed my eyes, and yet you don't know where he comes from. ³¹We know that God listens only to people who love and obey him. God doesn't listen to sinners. ³²And this is the first time in history that anyone has ever given sight to someone born blind. ³³Jesus could not do anything unless he came from God."

³⁴The leaders told the man, "You have been a sinner since the day you were born! Do you think you can teach us anything?" Then they said, "You can never come back into any of our meeting places!"

³⁵When Jesus heard what had happened, he went and found the man. Then Jesus asked, "Do you have faith in the Son of Man?"

³⁶He replied, "Sir, if you will tell me who he is, I will put my faith in him."

³⁷"You have already seen him," Jesus answered, "and right now he is talking with you."

³⁸The man said, "Lord, I put my faith in you!" Then he worshiped Jesus.

³⁹Jesus told him, "I came to judge the people of this world. I am here to give sight to the blind and to make blind everyone who can see."

⁴⁰When the Pharisees heard Jesus say this, they asked, "Are we blind?"

⁴¹Jesus answered, "If you were blind, you would not be guilty. But now that you claim to see, you will keep on being guilty."

A Story about Sheep

10 Jesus said:
I tell you for certain that only thieves and robbers climb over the fence instead of going in through the gate to the sheep pen. ²⁻³But the gatekeeper opens the gate for the

---
ᵘ9.16 *miracle*: See the note at 2.11.

shepherd, and he goes in through it. The sheep know their shepherd's voice. He calls each of them by name and leads them out. ⁴When he has led out all of his sheep, he walks in front of them, and they follow, because they know his voice. ⁵The sheep will not follow strangers. They don't recognize a stranger's voice, and they run away. ⁶Jesus told the people this story. But they did not understand what he was talking about.

Jesus Is the Good Shepherd

⁷Jesus said:

I tell you for certain that I am the gate for the sheep. ⁸Everyone who came before me was a thief or a robber, and the sheep did not listen to any of them. ⁹I am the gate. All who come in through me will be saved. Through me they will come and go and find pasture.

¹⁰A thief comes only to rob, kill, and destroy. I came so that everyone would have life, and have it in its fullest. ¹¹I am the good shepherd, and the good shepherd gives up his life for his sheep. ¹²Hired workers are not like the shepherd. They don't own the sheep, and when they see a wolf coming, they run off and leave the sheep. Then the wolf attacks and scatters the flock. ¹³Hired workers run away because they don't care about the sheep.

¹⁴I am the good shepherd. I know my sheep, and they know me. ¹⁵Just as the Father knows me, I know the Father, and I give up my life for my sheep. ¹⁶I have other sheep that are not in this sheep pen. I must bring them together too, when they hear my voice. Then there will be one flock of sheep and one shepherd.

¹⁷The Father loves me, because I give up my life, so that I may receive it back again. ¹⁸No one takes my life from me. I give it up willingly! I have the power to give it up and the power to receive it back again, just as my Father commanded me to do.

¹⁹The people took sides because of what Jesus had told them. ²⁰Many of them said, "He has a demon in him! He is crazy! Why listen to him?" ²¹But others said, "How could anyone with a demon in him say these things? No one like that could give sight to a blind person!"

Jesus Is Rejected

²²That winter, Jesus was in Jerusalem for the Temple Festival. ²³One day he was walking in that part of the temple known as Solomon's Porch,ᵛ ²⁴and the people gathered all around him. They said, "How long are you going to keep us guessing? If you are the Messiah, tell us plainly!"

²⁵Jesus answered:

I have told you, and you refused to believe me. The things I do by my Father's authority show who I am. ²⁶But since you are not my sheep, you don't believe me. ²⁷My sheep know my voice, and I know them. They follow me, ²⁸and I give them eternal life, so that they will never be lost. No one can snatch them out of my hand. ²⁹My Father gave them to me, and he is greater than all others.ʷ No one can snatch them from his hands, ³⁰and I am one with the Father.

³¹Once again the people picked up stones in order to kill Jesus. ³²But he said, "I have shown you many good things that my Father sent me to do. Which one are you going to stone me for?"

³³They answered, "We are not stoning you because of any good thing you did. We are stoning you because you did a terrible thing. You are just a man, and here you are claiming to be God!"

³⁴Jesus replied:

In your Scriptures doesn't God say, "You are gods"? ³⁵You can't argue with the Scriptures, and God spoke to those people and called them gods. ³⁶So why do you accuse me of a terrible sin for saying that I am the Son of God? After all, it is the Father who prepared me for this work. He is also the one who sent me into the world. ³⁷If I don't do as my Father does, you should not believe me. ³⁸But if I do what my Father does, you should believe because of that, even if you don't have faith in me. Then you will know for certain that the Father is one with me, and I am one with the Father.

³⁹Again they wanted to arrest Jesus. But he escaped ⁴⁰and crossed the Jordan to the place where John had earlier been baptizing. While Jesus was there, ⁴¹many people came to him. They were saying, "John didn't work any miracles, but everything he said about Jesus is true." ⁴²A lot of those people also put their faith in Jesus.

The Death of Lazarus

11 ¹⁻²A man by the name of Lazarus was sick in the village of Bethany. He had two sisters, Mary and Martha. This was the same Mary who later

---

ᵛ**10.23** *Solomon's Porch*: A public place with tall columns along the east side of the temple.
ʷ**10.29** *he is greater than all others*: Some manuscripts have "they are greater than all others."

poured perfume on the Lord's head and wiped his feet with her hair. ³The sisters sent a message to the Lord and told him that his good friend Lazarus was sick.

⁴When Jesus heard this, he said, "His sickness won't end in death. It will bring glory to God and his Son."

⁵Jesus loved Martha and her sister and brother. ⁶But he stayed where he was for two more days. ⁷Then he said to his disciples, "Now we will go back to Judea."

⁸"Teacher," they said, "the people there want to stone you to death! Why do you want to go back?"

⁹Jesus answered, "Aren't there twelve hours in each day? If you walk during the day, you will have light from the sun, and you won't stumble. ¹⁰But if you walk during the night, you will stumble, because you don't have any light." ¹¹Then he told them, "Our friend Lazarus is asleep, and I am going there to wake him up."

¹²They replied, "Lord, if he is asleep, he will get better." ¹³Jesus really meant that Lazarus was dead, but they thought he was talking only about sleep.

¹⁴Then Jesus told them plainly, "Lazarus is dead! ¹⁵I am glad that I wasn't there, because now you will have a chance to put your faith in me. Let's go to him."

¹⁶Thomas, whose nickname was "Twin," said to the other disciples, "Come on. Let's go, so we can die with him."

Jesus Brings Lazarus to Life

¹⁷When Jesus got to Bethany, he found that Lazarus had already been in the tomb four days. ¹⁸Bethany was only about two miles from Jerusalem, ¹⁹and many people had come from the city to comfort Martha and Mary because their brother had died.

²⁰When Martha heard that Jesus had arrived, she went out to meet him, but Mary stayed in the house. ²¹Martha said to Jesus, "Lord, if you had been here, my brother would not have died. ²²Yet even now I know that God will do anything you ask."

²³Jesus told her, "Your brother will live again!"

²⁴Martha answered, "I know that he will be raised to life on the last day,ˣ when all the dead are raised."

²⁵Jesus then said, "I am the one who raises the dead to life! Everyone who has faith in me will live, even if they die. ²⁶And everyone who lives because of faith in me will never really die. Do you believe this?"

²⁷"Yes, Lord!" she replied. "I believe that you are Christ, the Son of God. You are the one we hoped would come into the world."

²⁸After Martha said this, she went and privately said to her sister Mary, "The Teacher is here, and he wants to see you." ²⁹As soon as Mary heard this, she got up and went out to Jesus. ³⁰He was still outside the village where Martha had gone to meet him. ³¹Many people had come to comfort Mary, and when they saw her quickly leave the house, they thought she was going out to the tomb to cry. So they followed her.

³²Mary went to where Jesus was. Then as soon as she saw him, she knelt at his feet and said, "Lord, if you had been here, my brother would not have died."

³³When Jesus saw that Mary and the people with her were crying, he was terribly upset ³⁴and asked, "Where have you put his body?"

They replied, "Lord, come and you will see."

³⁵Jesus started crying, ³⁶and the people said, "See how much he loved Lazarus."

³⁷Some of them said, "He gives sight to the blind. Why couldn't he have kept Lazarus from dying?"

³⁸Jesus was still terribly upset. So he went to the tomb, which was a cave with a stone rolled against the entrance. ³⁹Then he told the people to roll the stone away. But Martha said, "Lord, you know that Lazarus has been dead four days, and there will be a bad smell."

⁴⁰Jesus replied, "Didn't I tell you that if you had faith, you would see the glory of God?"

⁴¹After the stone had been rolled aside, Jesus looked up toward heaven and prayed, "Father, I thank you for answering my prayer. ⁴²I know that you always answer my prayers. But I said this, so that the people here would believe that you sent me."

⁴³When Jesus had finished praying, he shouted, "Lazarus, come out!" ⁴⁴The man who had been dead came out. His hands and feet were wrapped with strips of burial cloth, and a cloth covered his face.

Jesus then told the people, "Untie him and let him go."

The Plot To Kill Jesus
(Matthew 26.1-5; Mark 14.1, 2; Luke 22.1, 2)

⁴⁵Many of the people who had come to visit Mary saw the things that Jesus did, and they put their faith in him. ⁴⁶Others went to the Pharisees and told what Jesus had done. ⁴⁷Then the chief priests and the Pharisees called the council together and said, "What should we do? This man is working a lot of miracles.ʸ ⁴⁸If we don't stop him now,

---

ˣ**11.24** *the last day*: When God will judge all people.   ʸ**11.47** *miracles*: See the note at 2.11.

everyone will put their faith in him. Then the Romans will come and destroy our temple and our nation."[z]

⁴⁹One of the council members was Caiaphas, who was also high priest that year. He spoke up and said, "You people don't have any sense at all! ⁵⁰Don't you know it is better for one person to die for the people than for the whole nation to be destroyed?" ⁵¹Caiaphas did not say this on his own. As high priest that year, he was prophesying that Jesus would die for the nation. ⁵²Yet Jesus would not die just for the Jewish nation. He would die to bring together all of God's scattered people. ⁵³From that day on, the council started making plans to put Jesus to death.

⁵⁴Because of this plot against him, Jesus stopped going around in public. He went to the town of Ephraim, which was near the desert, and he stayed there with his disciples.

⁵⁵It was almost time for Passover. Many of the Jewish people who lived out in the country had come to Jerusalem to get themselves ready[a] for the festival. ⁵⁶They looked around for Jesus. Then when they were in the temple, they asked each other, "You don't think he will come here for Passover, do you?" ⁵⁷The chief priests and the Pharisees told the people to let them know if any of them saw Jesus. That is how they hoped to arrest him.

At Bethany
(Matthew 26.6-13; Mark 14.3-9)

12 Six days before Passover Jesus went back to Bethany, where he had raised Lazarus from death. ²A meal had been prepared for Jesus. Martha was doing the serving, and Lazarus himself was there.

³Mary took a very expensive bottle of perfume[b] and poured it on Jesus' feet. She wiped them with her hair, and the sweet smell of the perfume filled the house.

⁴A disciple named Judas Iscariot[c] was there. He was the one who was going to betray Jesus, and he asked, ⁵"Why wasn't this perfume sold for three hundred silver coins and the money given to the poor?" ⁶Judas did not really care about the poor. He asked this because he carried the moneybag and sometimes would steal from it.

⁷Jesus replied, "Leave her alone! She has kept this perfume for the day of my burial. ⁸You will always have the poor with you, but you won't always have me."

A Plot To Kill Lazarus

⁹A lot of people came when they heard that Jesus was there. They also wanted to see Lazarus, because Jesus had raised him from death. ¹⁰So the chief priests made plans to kill Lazarus. ¹¹He was the reason that many of the Jewish people were turning from them and putting their faith in Jesus.

Jesus Enters Jerusalem
(Matthew 21.1-11; Mark 11.1-11; Luke 19.28-40)

¹²The next day a large crowd was in Jerusalem for Passover. When they heard that Jesus was coming for the festival, ¹³they took palm branches and went out to greet him.[d] They shouted,

"Hooray![e]
God bless the one who comes
  in the name of the Lord!
God bless the King
  of Israel!"

¹⁴Jesus found a donkey and rode on it, just as the Scriptures say,

¹⁵ "People of Jerusalem,
    don't be afraid!
  Your King is now coming,
    and he is riding
    on a donkey."

¹⁶At first, Jesus' disciples did not understand. But after he had been given his glory,[f] they remembered all this. Everything had happened exactly as the Scriptures said it would.

¹⁷⁻¹⁸A crowd had come to meet Jesus because they had seen him call Lazarus out of the tomb. They kept talking about him and this miracle.[g] ¹⁹But the Pharisees said to each other, "There is nothing that can be done! Everyone in the world is following Jesus."

Some Greeks Want To Meet Jesus

²⁰Some Greeks[h] had gone to Jerusalem to worship during Passover.

---

[z]11.48 *destroy our temple and our nation*: The Jewish leaders were afraid that Jesus would lead his followers to rebel against Rome and that the Roman army would then destroy their nation.   [a]11.55 *get themselves ready*: The Jewish people had to do certain things to prepare themselves to worship God.   [b]12.3 *very expensive bottle of perfume*: The Greek text has "expensive perfume made of pure spikenard," a plant used to make perfume.   [c]12.4 *Iscariot*: See the note at 6.71.   [d]12.13 *took palm branches and went out to greet him*: This was one way that the Jewish people welcomed a famous person.   [e]12.13 *Hooray*: This translates a word that can mean "please save us." But it is most often used as a shout of praise to God.   [f]12.16 *had been given his glory*: See the note at 7.39.   [g]12.17,18 *miracle*: See the note at 2.11.   [h]12.20 *Greeks*: Perhaps Gentiles who worshiped with the Jews. See the note at 7.35.

²¹Philip from Bethsaida in Galilee was there too. So they went to him and said, "Sir, we would like to meet Jesus." ²²Philip told Andrew. Then the two of them went to Jesus and told him.

The Son of Man Must Be Lifted Up

²³Jesus said:

The time has come for the Son of Man to be given his glory.*ⁱ* ²⁴I tell you for certain that a grain of wheat that falls on the ground will never be more than one grain unless it dies. But if it dies, it will produce lots of wheat. ²⁵If you love your life, you will lose it. If you give it up in this world, you will be given eternal life. ²⁶If you serve me, you must go with me. My servants will be with me wherever I am. If you serve me, my Father will honor you.

²⁷Now I am deeply troubled, and I don't know what to say. But I must not ask my Father to keep me from this time of suffering. In fact, I came into the world to suffer. ²⁸So Father, bring glory to yourself.

A voice from heaven then said, "I have already brought glory to myself, and I will do it again!" ²⁹When the crowd heard the voice, some of them thought it was thunder. Others thought an angel had spoken to Jesus.

³⁰Then Jesus told the crowd, "That voice spoke to help you, not me. ³¹This world's people are now being judged, and the ruler of this world*ʲ* is already being thrown out! ³²If I am lifted up above the earth, I will make everyone want to come to me." ³³Jesus was talking about the way he would be put to death.

³⁴The crowd said to Jesus, "The Scriptures teach that the Messiah will live forever. How can you say that the Son of Man must be lifted up? Who is this Son of Man?"

³⁵Jesus answered, "The light will be with you for only a little longer. Walk in the light while you can. Then you won't be caught walking blindly in the dark. ³⁶Have faith in the light while it is with you, and you will be children of the light."

The People Refuse To Have Faith in Jesus

After Jesus had said these things, he left and went into hiding. ³⁷He had worked a lot of miracles*ᵏ* among the people, but they were still not willing to have faith in him. ³⁸This happened so that what the prophet Isaiah had said would come true,

"Lord, who has believed
 our message?
And who has seen
 your mighty strength?"

³⁹The people could not have faith in Jesus, because Isaiah had also said,

⁴⁰ "The Lord has blinded
 the eyes of the people,
and he has made
 the people stubborn.
He did this so that they
 could not see
 or understand,
and so that they
 would not turn to the Lord
 and be healed."

⁴¹Isaiah said this, because he saw the glory of Jesus and spoke about him.*ˡ* ⁴²Even then, many of the leaders put their faith in Jesus, but they did not tell anyone about it. The Pharisees had already given orders for the people not to have anything to do with anyone who had faith in Jesus. ⁴³And besides, the leaders liked praise from others more than they liked praise from God.

Jesus Came To Save the World

⁴⁴In a loud voice Jesus said:

Everyone who has faith in me also has faith in the one who sent me. ⁴⁵And everyone who has seen me has seen the one who sent me. ⁴⁶I am the light that has come into the world. No one who has faith in me will stay in the dark.

⁴⁷I am not the one who will judge those who refuse to obey my teachings. I came to save the people of this world, not to be their judge. ⁴⁸But everyone who rejects me and my teachings will be judged on the last day*ᵐ* by what I have said. ⁴⁹I don't speak on my own. I say only what the Father who sent me has told me to say. ⁵⁰I know that his commands will bring eternal life. That is why I tell you exactly what the Father has told me.

Jesus Washes the Feet of His Disciples

13 It was before Passover, and Jesus knew that the time had come for him to leave this world and to return to the Father. He had always loved his followers in this world, and he loved them to the very end.

---

*ⁱ***12.23** *be given his glory*: See the note at 7.39.   *ʲ***12.31** *world*: In the Gospel of John "world" sometimes refers to the people who live in this world and to the evil forces that control their lives.   *ᵏ***12.37** *miracles*: See the note at 2.11.   *ˡ***12.41** *he saw the glory of Jesus and spoke about him*: Or "he saw the glory of God and spoke about Jesus."   *ᵐ***12.48** *the last day*: See the note at 6.39.

² Even before the evening meal started, the devil had made Judas, the son of Simon Iscariot,ⁿ decide to betray Jesus.

³ Jesus knew that he had come from God and would go back to God. He also knew that the Father had given him complete power. ⁴ So during the meal Jesus got up, removed his outer garment, and wrapped a towel around his waist. ⁵ He put some water into a large bowl. Then he began washing his disciples' feet and drying them with the towel he was wearing.

⁶ But when he came to Simon Peter, that disciple asked, "Lord, are you going to wash my feet?"

⁷ Jesus answered, "You don't really know what I am doing, but later you will understand."

⁸ "You will never wash my feet!" Peter replied.

"If I don't wash you," Jesus told him, "you don't really belong to me."

⁹ Peter said, "Lord, don't wash just my feet. Wash my hands and my head."

¹⁰ Jesus answered, "People who have bathed and are clean all over need to wash just their feet. And you, my disciples, are clean, except for one of you." ¹¹ Jesus knew who would betray him. That is why he said, "except for one of you."

¹² After Jesus had washed his disciples' feet and had put his outer garment back on, he sat down again.ᵒ Then he said:

Do you understand what I have done? ¹³ You call me your teacher and Lord, and you should, because that is who I am. ¹⁴ And if your Lord and teacher has washed your feet, you should do the same for each other. ¹⁵ I have set the example, and you should do for each other exactly what I have done for you. ¹⁶ I tell you for certain that servants are not greater than their master, and messengers are not greater than the one who sent them. ¹⁷ You know these things, and God will bless you, if you do them.

¹⁸ I am not talking about all of you. I know the ones I have chosen. But what the Scriptures say must come true. And they say, "The man who ate with me has turned against me!" ¹⁹ I am telling you this before it all happens. Then when it does happen, you will believe who I am.ᵖ ²⁰ I tell you for certain that anyone who welcomes my messengers also welcomes me, and anyone who welcomes me welcomes the one who sent me.

Jesus Tells What Will Happen to Him
(Matthew 26.20-25; Mark 14.17-21; Luke 22.21-23)

²¹ After Jesus had said these things, he was deeply troubled and told his disciples, "I tell you for certain that one of you will betray me." ²² They were confused about what he meant. And they just stared at each other.

²³ Jesus' favorite disciple was sitting next to him at the meal, ²⁴ and Simon motioned for that disciple to find out which one Jesus meant. ²⁵ So the disciple leaned toward Jesus and asked, "Lord, which one of us are you talking about?"

²⁶ Jesus answered, "I will dip this piece of bread in the sauce and give it to the one I was talking about."

Then Jesus dipped the bread and gave it to Judas, the son of Simon Iscariot.ᑫ ²⁷ Right then Satan took control of Judas.

Jesus said, "Judas, go quickly and do what you have to do." ²⁸ No one at the meal understood what Jesus meant. ²⁹ But because Judas was in charge of the money, some of them thought that Jesus had told him to buy something they needed for the festival. Others thought that Jesus had told him to give some money to the poor. ³⁰ Judas took the piece of bread and went out.

It was already night.

The New Command

³¹ After Judas had gone, Jesus said:

Now the Son of Man will be given glory, and he will bring glory to God. ³² Then, after God is given glory because of him, God will bring glory to him, and God will do it very soon.

³³ My children, I will be with you for a little while longer. Then you will look for me, but you won't find me. I tell you just as I told the people, "You cannot go where I am going." ³⁴ But I am giving you a new command. You must love each other, just as I have loved you. ³⁵ If you love each other, everyone will know that you are my disciples.

Peter's Promise
(Matthew 26.31-35; Mark 14.27-31; Luke 22.31-34)

³⁶ Simon Peter asked, "Lord, where are you going?"

Jesus answered, "You can't go with me now, but later on you will."

ⁿ**13.2** *Iscariot:* See the note at 6.71.   ᵒ**13.12** *sat down again:* On special occasions the Jewish people followed the Greek and Roman custom of lying down on their left side and leaning on their left elbow, while eating with their right hand.   ᵖ**13.19** *I am:* See the note at 8.24.   ᑫ**13.26** *Iscariot:* See the note at 6.71.

[37]Peter asked, "Lord, why can't I go with you now? I would die for you!"

[38]"Would you really die for me?" Jesus asked. "I tell you for certain that before a rooster crows, you will say three times that you don't even know me."

Jesus Is the Way to the Father

14 Jesus said to his disciples, "Don't be worried! Have faith in God and have faith in me.[r] [2]There are many rooms in my Father's house. I wouldn't tell you this, unless it was true. I am going there to prepare a place for each of you. [3]After I have done this, I will come back and take you with me. Then we will be together. [4]You know the way to where I am going."

[5]Thomas said, "Lord, we don't even know where you are going! How can we know the way?"

[6]"I am the way, the truth, and the life!" Jesus answered. "Without me, no one can go to the Father. [7]If you had known me, you would have known the Father. But from now on, you do know him, and you have seen him."

[8]Philip said, "Lord, show us the Father. That is all we need."

[9]Jesus replied:

Philip, I have been with you for a long time. Don't you know who I am? If you have seen me, you have seen the Father. How can you ask me to show you the Father? [10]Don't you believe that I am one with the Father and that the Father is one with me? What I say isn't said on my own. The Father who lives in me does these things.

[11]Have faith in me when I say that the Father is one with me and that I am one with the Father. Or else have faith in me simply because of the things I do. [12]I tell you for certain that if you have faith in me, you will do the same things that I am doing. You will do even greater things, now that I am going back to the Father. [13]Ask me, and I will do whatever you ask. This way the Son will bring honor to the Father. [14]I will do whatever you ask me to do.

The Holy Spirit Is Promised

[15]Jesus said to his disciples:

If you love me, you will do as I command. [16]Then I will ask the Father to send you the Holy Spirit who will help[s] you and always be with you. [17]The Spirit will show you what is true. The people of this world cannot accept the Spirit, because they don't see or know him. But you know the Spirit, who is with you and will keep on living in you.

[18]I won't leave you like orphans. I will come back to you. [19]In a little while the people of this world won't be able to see me, but you will see me. And because I live, you will live. [20]Then you will know that I am one with the Father. You will know that you are one with me, and I am one with you. [21]If you love me, you will do what I have said, and my Father will love you. I will also love you and show you what I am like.

[22]The other Judas, not Judas Iscariot,[t] then spoke up and asked, "Lord, what do you mean by saying that you will show us what you are like, but you will not show the people of this world?"

[23]Jesus replied:

If anyone loves me, they will obey me. Then my Father will love them, and we will come to them and live in them. [24]But anyone who doesn't love me, won't obey me. What they have heard me say doesn't really come from me, but from the Father who sent me.

[25]I have told you these things while I am still with you. [26]But the Holy Spirit will come and help[u] you, because the Father will send the Spirit to take my place. The Spirit will teach you everything and will remind you of what I said while I was with you.

[27]I give you peace, the kind of peace that only I can give. It isn't like the peace that this world can give. So don't be worried or afraid. [28]You have already heard me say that I am going and that I will also come back to you. If you really love me, you should be glad that I am going back to the Father, because he is greater than I am.

[29]I am telling you this before I leave, so that when it does happen, you will have faith in me. [30]I cannot speak with you much longer, because the ruler of this world is coming. But he has no power over me. [31]I obey my Father, so that everyone in the world might know that I love him.

It is time for us to go now.

Jesus Is the True Vine

15 Jesus said to his disciples:
I am the true vine, and my Father is the gardener. [2]He cuts away every branch of mine that

---

[r]14.1 *Have faith in God and have faith in me*: Or "You have faith in God, so have faith in me."
[s]14.16 *help*: The Greek word may mean "comfort," "encourage," or "defend."
[t]14.22 *Iscariot*: See the note at 6.71.   [u]14.26 *help*: See the note at 14.16.

doesn't produce fruit. But he trims clean every branch that does produce fruit, so that it will produce even more fruit. ³You are already clean because of what I have said to you.

⁴Stay joined to me, and I will stay joined to you. Just as a branch cannot produce fruit unless it stays joined to the vine, you cannot produce fruit unless you stay joined to me. ⁵I am the vine, and you are the branches. If you stay joined to me, and I stay joined to you, then you will produce lots of fruit. But you cannot do anything without me. ⁶If you don't stay joined to me, you will be thrown away. You will be like dry branches that are gathered up and burned in a fire.

⁷Stay joined to me and let my teachings become part of you. Then you can pray for whatever you want, and your prayer will be answered. ⁸When you become fruitful disciples of mine, my Father will be honored. ⁹I have loved you, just as my Father has loved me. So remain faithful to my love for you. ¹⁰If you obey me, I will keep loving you, just as my Father keeps loving me, because I have obeyed him.

¹¹I have told you this to make you as completely happy as I am. ¹²Now I tell you to love each other, as I have loved you. ¹³The greatest way to show love for friends is to die for them. ¹⁴And you are my friends, if you obey me. ¹⁵Servants don't know what their master is doing, and so I don't speak to you as my servants. I speak to you as my friends, and I have told you everything that my Father has told me.

¹⁶You did not choose me. I chose you and sent you out to produce fruit, the kind of fruit that will last. Then my Father will give you whatever you ask for in my name.ᵛ ¹⁷So I command you to love each other.

The World's Hatred

¹⁸If the people of this worldʷ hate you, just remember that they hated me first. ¹⁹If you belonged to the world, its people would love you. But you don't belong to the world. I have chosen you to leave the world behind, and that is why its people hate you. ²⁰Remember how I told you that servants are not greater than their master. So if people mistreat me, they will mistreat you. If they do what I say, they will do what you say.

²¹People will do to you exactly what they did to me. They will do it because you belong to me, and they don't know the one who sent me. ²²If I had not come and spoken to them, they would not be guilty of sin. But now they have no excuse for their sin. ²³Everyone who hates me also hates my Father. ²⁴I have done things that no one else has ever done. If they had not seen me do these things, they would not be guilty. But they did see me do these things, and they still hate me and my Father too. ²⁵That is why the Scriptures are true when they say, "People hated me for no reason."

²⁶I will send you the Spirit who comes from the Father and shows what is true. The Spirit will helpˣ you and will tell you about me. ²⁷Then you will also tell others about me, because you have been with me from the beginning.

16 I am telling you this to keep you from being afraid. ²You will be chased out of the Jewish meeting places. And the time will come when people will kill you and think they are doing God a favor. ³They will do these things because they don't know either the Father or me. ⁴I am saying this to you now, so that when the time comes, you will remember what I have said.

The Work of the Holy Spirit

I was with you at the first, and so I didn't tell you these things. ⁵But now I am going back to the Father who sent me, and none of you asks me where I am going. ⁶You are very sad from hearing all of this. ⁷But I tell you that I am going to do what is best for you. That is why I am going away. The Holy Spirit cannot come to helpˣ you until I leave. But after I am gone, I will send the Spirit to you.

⁸The Spirit will come and show the people of this world the truth about sin and God's justice and the judgment. ⁹The Spirit will show them that they are wrong about sin, because they didn't have faith in me. ¹⁰They are wrong about God's justice, because I am going to the Father, and you won't see me again. ¹¹And they are wrong about the judgment, because God has already judged the ruler of this world.

¹²I have much more to say to you,

ᵛ**15.16** *in my name*: Or "because you are my followers." ˣ**15.26; 16.7** *help*: See the note at 14.16.   ʷ**15.18** *world*: See the note at 12.31.

but right now it would be more than you could understand. ¹³The Spirit shows what is true and will come and guide you into the full truth. The Spirit doesn't speak on his own. He will tell you only what he has heard from me, and he will let you know what is going to happen. ¹⁴The Spirit will bring glory to me by taking my message and telling it to you. ¹⁵Everything that the Father has is mine. That is why I have said that the Spirit takes my message and tells it to you.

Sorrow Will Turn into Joy

¹⁶Jesus told his disciples, "For a little while you won't see me, but after a while you will see me."

¹⁷They said to each other, "What does Jesus mean by saying that for a little while we won't see him, but after a while we will see him? What does he mean by saying that he is going to the Father? ¹⁸What is this 'little while' that he is talking about? We don't know what he means."

¹⁹Jesus knew that they had some questions, so he said:

You are wondering what I meant when I said that for a little while you won't see me, but after a while you will see me. ²⁰I tell you for certain that you will cry and be sad, but the world will be happy. You will be sad, but later you will be happy.

²¹When a woman is about to give birth, she is in great pain. But after it is all over, she forgets the pain and is happy, because she has brought a child into the world. ²²You are now very sad. But later I will see you, and you will be so happy that no one will be able to change the way you feel. ²³When that time comes, you won't have to ask me about anything. I tell you for certain that the Father will give you whatever you ask for in my name. ²⁴You have not asked for anything in this way before, but now you must ask in my name.ʸ Then it will be given to you, so that you will be completely happy.

²⁵I have used examples to explain to you what I have been talking about. But the time will come when I will speak to you plainly about the Father and will no longer use examples like these. ²⁶You will ask the Father in my name,ᶻ and I won't have to ask him for you. ²⁷God the Father loves you because you love me, and you believe that I have come from him. ²⁸I came from the Father into the world, but I am leaving the world and returning to the Father.

²⁹The disciples said, "Now you are speaking plainly to us! You are not using examples. ³⁰At last we know that you understand everything, and we don't have any more questions. Now we believe that you truly have come from God."

³¹Jesus replied:

Do you really believe me? ³²The time will come and is already here when all of you will be scattered. Each of you will go back home and leave me by myself. But the Father will be with me, and I won't be alone. ³³I have told you this, so that you might have peace in your hearts because of me. While you are in the world, you will have to suffer. But cheer up! I have defeated the world.ᵃ

Jesus Prays

17 After Jesus had finished speaking to his disciples, he looked up toward heaven and prayed:

Father, the time has come for you to bring glory to your Son, in order that he may bring glory to you. ²And you gave him power over all people, so that he would give eternal life to everyone you give him. ³Eternal life is to know you, the only true God, and to know Jesus Christ, the one you sent. ⁴I have brought glory to you here on earth by doing everything you gave me to do. ⁵Now, Father, give me back the glory that I had with you before the world was created.

⁶You have given me some followers from this world, and I have shown them what you are like. They were yours, but you gave them to me, and they have obeyed you. ⁷They know that you gave me everything I have. ⁸I told my followers what you told me, and they accepted it. They know that I came from you, and they believe that you are the one who sent me. ⁹I am praying for them, but not for those who belong to this world.ᵃ My followers belong to you, and I am praying for them. ¹⁰All that I have is yours, and all that you have is mine, and they will bring glory to me.

¹¹Holy Father, I am no longer in the world. I am coming to you, but my followers are still in the world.

ʸ**16.23,24** *in my name . . . in my name*: Or "as my disciples . . . as my disciples." ᶻ**16.26** *in my name*: Or "because you are my followers." ᵃ**16.33; 17.9** *world*: See the note at 12.31.

So keep them safe by the power of the name that you have given me. Then they will be one with each other, just as you and I are one. ¹²While I was with them, I kept them safe by the power you have given me. I guarded them, and not one of them was lost, except the one who had to be lost. This happened so that what the Scriptures say would come true.

¹³I am on my way to you. But I say these things while I am still in the world, so that my followers will have the same complete joy that I do. ¹⁴I have told them your message. But the people of this world hate them, because they don't belong to this world, just as I don't.

¹⁵Father, I don't ask you to take my followers out of the world, but keep them safe from the evil one. ¹⁶They don't belong to this world, and neither do I. ¹⁷Your word is the truth. So let this truth make them completely yours. ¹⁸I am sending them into the world, just as you sent me. ¹⁹I have given myself completely for their sake, so that they may belong completely to the truth.

²⁰I am not praying just for these followers. I am also praying for everyone else who will have faith because of what my followers will say about me. ²¹I want all of them to be one with each other, just as I am one with you and you are one with me. I also want them to be one with us. Then the people of this world will believe that you sent me.

²²I have honored my followers in the same way that you honored me, in order that they may be one with each other, just as we are one. ²³I am one with them, and you are one with me, so that they may become completely one. Then this world's people will know that you sent me. They will know that you love my followers as much as you love me.

²⁴Father, I want everyone you have given me to be with me, wherever I am. Then they will see the glory that you have given me, because you loved me before the world was created. ²⁵Good Father, the people of this world don't know you. But I know you, and my followers know that you sent me. ²⁶I told them what you are like, and I will tell them even more. Then the love that you have for me will become part of them, and I will be one with them.

Jesus Is Betrayed and Arrested
(Matthew 26.47-56; Mark 14.43-50; Luke 22.47-53)

18 When Jesus had finished praying, he and his disciples crossed the Kidron Valley and went into a garden.[b] ²Jesus had often met there with his disciples, and Judas knew where the place was.

³⁻⁵Judas had promised to betray Jesus. So he went to the garden with some Roman soldiers and temple police, who had been sent by the chief priests and the Pharisees. They carried torches, lanterns, and weapons. Jesus already knew everything that was going to happen, but he asked, "Who are you looking for?"

They answered, "We are looking for Jesus from Nazareth!"

Jesus told them, "I am Jesus!"[c] ⁶At once they all backed away and fell to the ground.

⁷Jesus again asked, "Who are you looking for?"

"We are looking for Jesus from Nazareth," they answered.

⁸This time Jesus replied, "I have already told you that I am Jesus. If I am the one you are looking for, let these others go. ⁹Then everything will happen, just as I said, 'I did not lose anyone you gave me.'"

¹⁰Simon Peter had brought along a sword. He now pulled it out and struck at the servant of the high priest. The servant's name was Malchus, and Peter cut off his right ear. ¹¹Jesus told Peter, "Put your sword away. I must drink from the cup[d] that the Father has given me."

Jesus Is Brought to Annas
(Matthew 26.57, 58; Mark 14.53, 54; Luke 22.54)

¹²The Roman officer and his men, together with the temple police, arrested Jesus and tied him up. ¹³They took him first to Annas, who was the father-in-law of Caiaphas, the high priest that year. ¹⁴This was the same Caiaphas who had told the Jewish leaders, "It is better if one person dies for the people."

Peter Says He Doesn't Know Jesus
(Matthew 26.69, 70; Mark 14.66-68; Luke 22.55-57)

¹⁵Simon Peter and another disciple followed Jesus. That disciple knew the high priest, and he followed Jesus into the courtyard of the high priest's house. ¹⁶Peter stayed outside near the gate. But the other disciple came back out and

---

[b] 18.1 *garden*: The Greek word is usually translated "garden," but probably referred to an olive orchard. [c] 18.3-5 *I am Jesus*: The Greek text has "I am" (see the note at 8.24).
[d] 18.11 *drink from the cup*: In the Scriptures a cup is sometimes used as a symbol of suffering. To "drink from the cup" is to suffer.

spoke to the girl at the gate. She let Peter go in, ¹⁷but asked him, "Aren't you one of that man's followers?"

"No, I am not!" Peter answered.

¹⁸It was cold, and the servants and temple police had made a charcoal fire. They were warming themselves around it, when Peter went over and stood near the fire to warm himself.

Jesus Is Questioned by the High Priest
(Matthew 26.59-66; Mark 14.55-64; Luke 22.66-71)

¹⁹The high priest questioned Jesus about his followers and his teaching. ²⁰But Jesus told him, "I have spoken freely in front of everyone. And I have always taught in our meeting places and in the temple, where all of our people come together. I have not said anything in secret. ²¹Why are you questioning me? Why don't you ask the people who heard me? They know what I have said."

²²As soon as Jesus said this, one of the temple police hit him and said, "That's no way to talk to the high priest!"

²³Jesus answered, "If I have done something wrong, say so. But if not, why did you hit me?" ²⁴Jesus was still tied up, and Annas sent him to Caiaphas the high priest.

Peter Again Denies that He Knows Jesus
(Matthew 26.71-75; Mark 14.69-72; Luke 22.58-62)

²⁵While Simon Peter was standing there warming himself, someone asked him, "Aren't you one of Jesus' followers?"

Again Peter denied it and said, "No, I am not!"

²⁶One of the high priest's servants was there. He was a relative of the servant whose ear Peter had cut off, and he asked, "Didn't I see you in the garden with that man?"

²⁷Once more Peter denied it, and right then a rooster crowed.

Jesus Is Tried by Pilate
(Matthew 27.1, 2, 11-14; Mark 15.1-5; Luke 23.1-5)

²⁸It was early in the morning when Jesus was taken from Caiaphas to the building where the Roman governor stayed. But the crowd waited outside. Any of them who had gone inside would have become unclean and would not be allowed to eat the Passover meal.ᵉ

²⁹Pilate came out and asked, "What charges are you bringing against this man?"

³⁰They answered, "He is a criminal! That's why we brought him to you."

³¹Pilate told them, "Take him and judge him by your own laws."

The crowd replied, "We are not allowed to put anyone to death." ³²And so what Jesus said about his deathᶠ would soon come true.

³³Pilate then went back inside. He called Jesus over and asked, "Are you the king of the Jews?"

³⁴Jesus answered, "Are you asking this on your own or did someone tell you about me?"

³⁵"You know I'm not a Jew!" Pilate said. "Your own people and the chief priests brought you to me. What have you done?"

³⁶Jesus answered, "My kingdom doesn't belong to this world. If it did, my followers would have fought to keep me from being handed over to the Jewish leaders. No, my kingdom doesn't belong to this world."

³⁷"So you are a king," Pilate replied.

"You are saying that I am a king," Jesus told him. "I was born into this world to tell about the truth. And everyone who belongs to the truth knows my voice."

³⁸Pilate asked Jesus, "What is truth?"

Jesus Is Sentenced to Death
(Matthew 27.15-31; Mark 15.6-20; Luke 23.13-25)

Pilate went back out and said, "I don't find this man guilty of anything! ³⁹And since I usually set a prisoner free for you at Passover, would you like for me to set free the king of the Jews?"

⁴⁰They shouted, "No, not him! We want Barabbas." Now Barabbas was a terrorist.ᵍ

19 Pilate gave orders for Jesus to be beaten with a whip. ²The soldiers made a crown out of thorn branches and put it on Jesus. Then they put a purple robe on him. ³They came up to him and said, "Hey, you king of the Jews!" They also hit him with their fists.

⁴Once again Pilate went out. This time he said, "I will have Jesus brought out to you again. Then you can see for yourselves that I have not found him guilty."

⁵Jesus came out, wearing the crown of thorns and the purple robe. Pilate said, "Here is the man!"ʰ

ᵉ**18.28** *would have become unclean and would not be allowed to eat the Passover meal*: Jewish people who came in close contact with foreigners right before Passover were not allowed to eat the Passover meal. ᶠ**18.32** *about his death*: Jesus had said that he would die by being "lifted up," which meant that he would die on a cross. The Romans killed criminals by nailing them on a cross, but they did not let the Jews kill anyone in this way. ᵍ**18.40** *terrorist*: Someone who stirred up trouble against the Romans in the hope of gaining freedom for the Jewish people. ʰ**19.5** *"Here is the man!"*: Or "Look at the man!"

⁶When the chief priests and the temple police saw him, they yelled, "Nail him to a cross! Nail him to a cross!"

Pilate told them, "You take him and nail him to a cross! I don't find him guilty of anything."

⁷The crowd replied, "He claimed to be the Son of God! Our Jewish Law says that he must be put to death."

⁸When Pilate heard this, he was terrified. ⁹He went back inside and asked Jesus, "Where are you from?" But Jesus did not answer.

¹⁰"Why won't you answer my question?" Pilate asked. "Don't you know that I have the power to let you go free or to nail you to a cross?"

¹¹Jesus replied, "If God had not given you the power, you couldn't do anything at all to me. But the one who handed me over to you did something even worse."

¹²Then Pilate wanted to set Jesus free. But the crowd again yelled, "If you set this man free, you are no friend of the Emperor! Anyone who claims to be a king is an enemy of the Emperor."

¹³When Pilate heard this, he brought Jesus out. Then he sat down on the judge's bench at the place known as "The Stone Pavement." In Aramaic this pavement is called "Gabbatha." ¹⁴It was about noon on the day before Passover, and Pilate said to the crowd, "Look at your king!"

¹⁵"Kill him! Kill him!" they yelled. "Nail him to a cross!"

"So you want me to nail your king to a cross?" Pilate asked.

The chief priests replied, "The Emperor is our king!" ¹⁶Then Pilate handed Jesus over to be nailed to a cross.

Jesus Is Nailed to a Cross
(Matthew 27.32-44; Mark 15.21-32; Luke 23.26-43)

Jesus was taken away, ¹⁷and he carried his cross to a place known as "The Skull."*ⁱ* In Aramaic this place is called "Golgotha." ¹⁸There Jesus was nailed to the cross, and on each side of him a man was also nailed to a cross.

¹⁹Pilate ordered the charge against Jesus to be written on a board and put above the cross. It read, "Jesus of Nazareth, King of the Jews." ²⁰The words were written in Hebrew, Latin, and Greek.

The place where Jesus was taken wasn't far from the city, and many of the people read the charge against him. ²¹So the chief priests went to Pilate and said, "Why did you write that he is King of the Jews? You should have written, 'He claimed to be King of the Jews.' "

²²But Pilate told them, "What is written will not be changed!"

²³After the soldiers had nailed Jesus to the cross, they divided up his clothes into four parts, one for each of them. But his outer garment was made from a single piece of cloth, and it did not have any seams. ²⁴The soldiers said to each other, "Let's not rip it apart. We will gamble to see who gets it." This happened so that the Scriptures would come true, which say,

"They divided up my clothes
and gambled
   for my garments."

The soldiers then did what they had decided.

²⁵Jesus' mother stood beside his cross with her sister and Mary the wife of Clopas. Mary Magdalene was standing there too.*ʲ* ²⁶When Jesus saw his mother and his favorite disciple with her, he said to his mother, "This man is now your son." ²⁷Then he said to the disciple, "She is now your mother." From then on, that disciple took her into his own home.

The Death of Jesus
(Matthew 27.45-56; Mark 15.33-41; Luke 23.44-49)

²⁸Jesus knew that he had now finished his work. And in order to make the Scriptures come true, he said, "I am thirsty!" ²⁹A jar of cheap wine was there. Someone then soaked a sponge with the wine and held it up to Jesus' mouth on the stem of a hyssop plant. ³⁰After Jesus drank the wine, he said, "Everything is done!" He bowed his head and died.

A Spear Is Stuck in Jesus' Side

³¹The next day would be both a Sabbath and the Passover. It was a special day for the Jewish people,*ᵏ* and they did not want the bodies to stay on the crosses during that day. So they asked

---

*ⁱ***19.17** *The Skull*: The place was probably given this name because it was near a large rock in the shape of a human skull.   *ʲ***19.25** *Jesus' mother stood beside his cross with her sister and Mary the wife of Clopas. Mary Magdalene was standing there too*: The Greek text may also be understood to include only three women ("Jesus' mother stood beside the cross with her sister, Mary the mother of Clopas. Mary Magdalene was standing there too.") or merely two women ("Jesus' mother was standing there with her sister Mary of Clopas, that is, Mary Magdalene."). "Of Clopas" may mean "daughter of" or "mother of."   *ᵏ***19.31** *a special day for the Jewish people*: Passover could be any day of the week. But according to the Gospel of John, Passover was on a Sabbath in the year that Jesus was nailed to a cross.

Pilate to break the men's legs[l] and take their bodies down. ³²The soldiers first broke the legs of the other two men who were nailed there. ³³But when they came to Jesus, they saw that he was already dead, and they did not break his legs. ³⁴One of the soldiers stuck his spear into Jesus' side, and blood and water came out. ³⁵We know this is true, because it was told by someone who saw it happen. Now you can have faith too. ³⁶All this happened so that the Scriptures would come true, which say, "No bone of his body will be broken" ³⁷and, "They will see the one in whose side they stuck a spear."

Jesus Is Buried
(Matthew 27.57-61; Mark 15.42-47; Luke 23.50-56)

³⁸Joseph from Arimathea was one of Jesus' disciples. He had kept it secret though, because he was afraid of the Jewish leaders. But now he asked Pilate to let him have Jesus' body. Pilate gave him permission, and Joseph took it down from the cross. ³⁹Nicodemus also came with about seventy-five pounds of spices made from myrrh and aloes. This was the same Nicodemus who had visited Jesus one night.[m] ⁴⁰The two men wrapped the body in a linen cloth, together with the spices, which was how the Jewish people buried their dead. ⁴¹In the place where Jesus had been nailed to a cross, there was a garden with a tomb that had never been used. ⁴²The tomb was nearby, and since it was the time to prepare for the Sabbath, they were in a hurry to put Jesus' body there.

Jesus Is Alive
(Matthew 28.1-10; Mark 16.1-8; Luke 24.1-12)

20 On Sunday morning while it was still dark, Mary Magdalene went to the tomb and saw that the stone had been rolled away from the entrance. ²She ran to Simon Peter and to Jesus' favorite disciple and said, "They have taken the Lord from the tomb! We don't know where they have put him."

³Peter and the other disciple started for the tomb. ⁴They ran side by side, until the other disciple ran faster than Peter and got there first. ⁵He bent over and saw the strips of linen cloth lying inside the tomb, but he did not go in. ⁶When Simon Peter got there, he went into the tomb and saw the strips of cloth. ⁷He also saw the piece of cloth that had been used to cover Jesus' face. It was rolled up and in a place by itself. ⁸The disciple who got there first then went into the tomb, and when he saw it, he believed. ⁹At that time Peter and the other disciple did not know that the Scriptures said Jesus would rise to life. ¹⁰So the two of them went back to the other disciples.

Jesus Appears to Mary Magdalene
(Mark 16.9-11)

¹¹Mary Magdalene stood crying outside the tomb. She was still weeping, when she stooped down ¹²and saw two angels inside. They were dressed in white and were sitting where Jesus' body had been. One was at the head and the other was at the foot. ¹³The angels asked Mary, "Why are you crying?"

She answered, "They have taken away my Lord's body! I don't know where they have put him."

¹⁴As soon as Mary said this, she turned around and saw Jesus standing there. But she did not know who he was. ¹⁵Jesus asked her, "Why are you crying? Who are you looking for?"

She thought he was the gardener and said, "Sir, if you have taken his body away, please tell me, so I can go and get him."

¹⁶Then Jesus said to her, "Mary!"

She turned and said to him, "Rabboni." The Aramaic word "Rabboni" means "Teacher."

¹⁷Jesus told her, "Don't hold on to me! I have not yet gone to the Father. But tell my disciples that I am going to the one who is my Father and my God, as well as your Father and your God." ¹⁸Mary Magdalene then went and told the disciples that she had seen the Lord. She also told them what he had said to her.

Jesus Appears to His Disciples
(Matthew 28.16-20; Mark 16.14-18; Luke 24.36-49)

¹⁹The disciples were afraid of the Jewish leaders, and on the evening of that same Sunday they locked themselves in a room. Suddenly, Jesus appeared in the middle of the group. He greeted them ²⁰and showed them his hands and his side. When the disciples saw the Lord, they became very happy.

²¹After Jesus had greeted them again, he said, "I am sending you, just as the Father has sent me." ²²Then he breathed on them and said, "Receive the Holy Spirit. ²³If you forgive anyone's sins, they will be forgiven. But if you don't forgive their sins, they will not be forgiven."

---

[l] **19.31** *break the men's legs*: This was the way that the Romans sometimes speeded up the death of a person who had been nailed to a cross.   [m] **19.39** *Nicodemus who had visited Jesus one night*: See 3.1-21.

Jesus and Thomas

24 Although Thomas the Twin was one of the twelve disciples, he wasn't with the others when Jesus appeared to them. 25 So they told him, "We have seen the Lord!"

But Thomas said, "First, I must see the nail scars in his hands and touch them with my finger. I must put my hand where the spear went into his side. I won't believe unless I do this!"

26 A week later the disciples were together again. This time, Thomas was with them. Jesus came in while the doors were still locked and stood in the middle of the group. He greeted his disciples 27 and said to Thomas, "Put your finger here and look at my hands! Put your hand into my side. Stop doubting and have faith!"

28 Thomas replied, "You are my Lord and my God!"

29 Jesus said, "Thomas, do you have faith because you have seen me? The people who have faith in me without seeing me are the ones who are really blessed!"

Why John Wrote His Book

30 Jesus worked many other miracles[n] for his disciples, and not all of them are written in this book. 31 But these are written so that you will put your faith in Jesus as the Messiah and the Son of God. If you have faith in[o] him, you will have true life.

Jesus Appears to Seven Disciples

21 Jesus later appeared to his disciples along the shore of Lake Tiberias. 2 Simon Peter, Thomas the Twin, Nathanael from Cana in Galilee, and the brothers James and John,[p] were there, together with two other disciples. 3 Simon Peter said, "I'm going fishing!"

The others said, "We will go with you." They went out in their boat. But they didn't catch a thing that night.

4 Early the next morning Jesus stood on the shore, but the disciples did not realize who he was. 5 Jesus shouted, "Friends, have you caught anything?"

"No!" they answered.

6 So he told them, "Let your net down on the right side of your boat, and you will catch some fish."

They did, and the net was so full of fish that they could not drag it up into the boat.

7 Jesus' favorite disciple told Peter, "It's the Lord!" When Simon heard that it was the Lord, he put on the clothes that he had taken off while he was working. Then he jumped into the water. 8 The boat was only about a hundred yards from shore. So the other disciples stayed in the boat and dragged in the net full of fish.

9 When the disciples got out of the boat, they saw some bread and a charcoal fire with fish on it. 10 Jesus told his disciples, "Bring some of the fish you just caught." 11 Simon Peter got back into the boat and dragged the net to shore. In it were one hundred fifty-three large fish, but still the net did not rip.

12 Jesus said, "Come and eat!" But none of the disciples dared ask who he was. They knew he was the Lord. 13 Jesus took the bread in his hands and gave some of it to his disciples. He did the same with the fish. 14 This was the third time that Jesus appeared to his disciples after he was raised from death.

Jesus and Peter

15 When Jesus and his disciples had finished eating, he asked, "Simon son of John, do you love me more than the others do?"[q]

Simon Peter answered, "Yes, Lord, you know I do!"

"Then feed my lambs," Jesus said.

16 Jesus asked a second time, "Simon son of John, do you love me?"

Peter answered, "Yes, Lord, you know I love you!"

"Then take care of my sheep," Jesus told him.

17 Jesus asked a third time, "Simon son of John, do you love me?"

Peter was hurt because Jesus had asked him three times if he loved him. So he told Jesus, "Lord, you know everything. You know I love you."

Jesus replied, "Feed my sheep. 18 I tell you for certain that when you were a young man, you dressed yourself and went wherever you wanted to go. But when you are old, you will hold out your hands. Then others will wrap your belt around you and lead you where you don't want to go."

19 Jesus said this to tell how Peter would die and bring honor to God. Then he said to Peter, "Follow me!"

Jesus and His Favorite Disciple

20 Peter turned and saw Jesus' favorite disciple following them. He was the same one who had sat next to Jesus at the meal and had asked, "Lord, who is going to betray you?" 21 When Peter saw that disciple, he asked Jesus, "Lord, what about him?"

---

[n] 20.30 *miracles*: See the note at 2.11. [o] 20.31 *put your faith in . . . have faith in*: Some manuscripts have "keep on having faith in . . . keep on having faith in." [p] 21.2 *the brothers James and John*: Greek "the two sons of Zebedee." [q] 21.15 *more than the others do?*: Or "more than you love these things?"

²²Jesus answered, "What is it to you, if I want him to live until I return? You must follow me." ²³So the rumor spread among the other disciples that this disciple would not die. But Jesus did not say he would not die. He simply said, "What is it to you, if I want him to live until I return?"

²⁴This disciple is the one who told all of this. He wrote it, and we know he is telling the truth.

²⁵Jesus did many other things. If they were all written in books, I don't suppose there would be room enough in the whole world for all the books.

ACTS

ABOUT THIS BOOK

This is the second book written by Luke. His first one is commonly known as the Gospel of Luke. In it he told "all that Jesus did and taught from the very first until he was taken up to heaven" (1.1, 2). In this book Luke continues the story by describing some of the struggles the disciples faced as they tried to obey the command of Jesus: "You will tell everyone about me in Jerusalem, in all Judea, in Samaria, and everywhere in the world" (1.8).

So many different countries are mentioned in Acts that the book may seem to have been written only to tell about the spread of the Christian message. But that is only part of the story. After Jesus was taken up to heaven, one of the big problems for his followers was deciding who could belong to God's people. And since Jesus and his first followers were Jews, it was only natural for many of them to think that his message was only for Jews. But in Acts, the Spirit is always present to show that Jesus came to save both Jews and Gentiles, and that God wants followers from every nation and race to be part of his people.

The first conflict between Christians and Jews took place when some of the Jewish religious leaders rejected the message about Jesus (4.1-31; 7.1-59). But the most serious problems for the early church happened because the disciples at first failed to understand that anyone could become a follower of Jesus without first becoming a Jew. This began to change when Philip dared to take the message to the Samaritans (8.7-25), and when Peter went to the home of Cornelius, a captain in the Roman army (10.1-48).

Finally, Peter reported to the church in Jerusalem (11.1-18) and a meeting was held there (15.3-35) to discuss the question of who could become followers of Christ. Before the meeting was over, everyone agreed that the Spirit of God was leading them to reach out to Gentiles as well as Jews with the good news of Jesus.

The one who did the most for the spread of the faith was a man named Paul, and much of the book tells about his preaching among the Gentiles. Finally, he took the message to Rome, the world's most important city at that time (28.16-31). One of Luke's main reasons for writing was to show that nothing could keep the Christian message from spreading everywhere:

> *For two years Paul stayed in a rented house and welcomed everyone who came to see him. He bravely preached about God's kingdom and taught about the Lord Jesus Christ, and no one tried to stop him.* (28.30, 31)

A QUICK LOOK AT THIS BOOK

Telling the Good News in Jerusalem (1.1—8.3)
The Good News in Judea and Samaria (8.4—12.25)
Paul's First Journey to Tell the Good News (13.1—14.28)
An Important Decision in Jerusalem (15.1-35)
Paul's Second Journey to Tell the Good News (15.36—18.22)
Paul's Third Journey to Tell the Good News (18.23—21.16)
Paul's Arrest in Jerusalem (21.17—23.22)
Paul Is Taken to Caesarea (23.23—26.32)
Paul Is Taken to Rome (27.1—28.31)

1 Theophilus, I first wrote to you[a] about all that Jesus did and taught from the very first ²until he was taken up to heaven. But before he was taken up, he gave orders to the apostles he had chosen with the help of the Holy Spirit.

³For forty days after Jesus had suffered and died, he proved in many ways that he had been raised from death. He appeared to his apostles and spoke to them about God's kingdom. ⁴While he was still with them, he said:

Don't leave Jerusalem yet. Wait here for the Father to give you the Holy Spirit, just as I told you he has promised to do. ⁵John baptized with water, but in a few days you will be baptized with the Holy Spirit.

Jesus Is Taken to Heaven

⁶While the apostles were still with Jesus, they asked him, "Lord, are you now going to give Israel its own king again?"[b]

⁷Jesus said to them, "You don't need to know the time of those events that only the Father controls. ⁸But the Holy Spirit will come upon you and give you power. Then you will tell everyone about me in Jerusalem, in all Judea, in Samaria, and everywhere in the world." ⁹After Jesus had said this and while they were watching, he was taken up into a cloud. They could not see him, ¹⁰but as he went up, they kept looking up into the sky.

Suddenly two men dressed in white clothes were standing there beside them. ¹¹They said, "Why are you men from Galilee standing here and looking up into the sky? Jesus has been taken to heaven. But he will come back in the same way that you have seen him go."

Someone To Take the Place of Judas

¹²⁻¹³The Mount of Olives was about half a mile from Jerusalem. The apostles who had gone there were Peter, John, James, Andrew, Philip, Thomas, Bartholomew, Matthew, James the son of Alphaeus, Simon, known as the Eager One,[c] and Judas the son of James.

After the apostles returned to the city, they went upstairs to the room where they had been staying.

¹⁴The apostles often met together and prayed with a single purpose in mind.[d] The women and Mary the mother of Jesus would meet with them, and so would his brothers. ¹⁵One day there were about one hundred twenty of the Lord's followers meeting together, and Peter stood up to speak to them. ¹⁶⁻¹⁷He said:

My friends, long ago by the power of the Holy Spirit, David said something about Judas, and what he said has now happened. Judas was one of us and had worked with us, but he brought the mob to arrest Jesus. ¹⁸Then Judas bought some land with the money he was given for doing that evil thing. He fell headfirst into the field. His body burst open, and all his insides came out. ¹⁹When the people of Jerusalem found out about this, they called the place Akeldama, which in the local language means "Field of Blood."

²⁰In the book of Psalms it says,

"Leave his house empty,
and don't let anyone
live there."

It also says,

"Let someone else
have his job."

²¹⁻²²So we need someone else to help us tell others that Jesus has been raised from death. He must also be one of the men who was with us from the very beginning. He must have been with us from the time the Lord Jesus was baptized by John until the day he was taken to heaven.

²³Two men were suggested: One of them was Joseph Barsabbas, known as Justus, and the other was Matthias. ²⁴Then they all prayed, "Lord, you know what everyone is like! Show us the one you have chosen ²⁵to be an apostle and to serve in place of Judas, who got what he deserved." ²⁶They drew names, and Matthias was chosen to join the group of the eleven apostles.

The Coming of the Holy Spirit

2 On the day of Pentecost[e] all the Lord's followers were together in one place. ²Suddenly there was a noise from heaven like the sound of a mighty wind! It filled the house where they were meeting. ³Then they saw what looked like fiery tongues moving in all directions, and a tongue came and settled on each person there. ⁴The Holy

---

[a]1.1 *I first wrote to you*: The Gospel of Luke. [b]1.6 *are you now going to give Israel its own king again?*: Or "Are you now going to rule Israel as its king?" [c]1.12,13 *known as the Eager One*: The Greek text has "Zealot," a name later given to the members of a Jewish group that resisted and fought against the Romans. [d]1.14 *met together and prayed with a single purpose in mind*: Or "met together in a special place for prayer." [e]2.1 *Pentecost*: A Jewish festival that came fifty days after Passover and celebrated the wheat harvest. Jews later celebrated Pentecost as the time when they were given the Law of Moses.

Spirit took control of everyone, and they began speaking whatever languages the Spirit let them speak.

⁵Many religious Jews from every country in the world were living in Jerusalem. ⁶And when they heard this noise, a crowd gathered. But they were surprised, because they were hearing everything in their own languages. ⁷They were excited and amazed, and said:

Don't all these who are speaking come from Galilee? ⁸Then why do we hear them speaking our very own languages? ⁹Some of us are from Parthia, Media, and Elam. Others are from Mesopotamia, Judea, Cappadocia, Pontus, Asia, ¹⁰Phrygia, Pamphylia, Egypt, parts of Libya near Cyrene, Rome, ¹¹Crete, and Arabia. Some of us were born Jews, and others of us have chosen to be Jews. Yet we all hear them using our own languages to tell the wonderful things God has done.

¹²Everyone was excited and confused. Some of them even kept asking each other, "What does all this mean?"

¹³Others made fun of the Lord's followers and said, "They are drunk."

Peter Speaks to the Crowd

¹⁴Peter stood with the eleven apostles and spoke in a loud and clear voice to the crowd:

Friends and everyone else living in Jerusalem, listen carefully to what I have to say! ¹⁵You are wrong to think that these people are drunk. After all, it is only nine o'clock in the morning. ¹⁶But this is what God had the prophet Joel say,

¹⁷ "When the last days come,
 I will give my Spirit
  to everyone.
 Your sons and daughters
  will prophesy.
 Your young men
  will see visions,
 and your old men
  will have dreams.
¹⁸ In those days I will give
  my Spirit to my servants,
 both men and women,
  and they will prophesy.

¹⁹ I will work miracles
  in the sky above
 and wonders
  on the earth below.
 There will be blood and fire
  and clouds of smoke.
²⁰ The sun will turn dark,
  and the moon
  will be as red as blood
 before the great
  and wonderful day
  of the Lord appears.
²¹ Then the Lord
  will save everyone
  who asks for his help."

²²Now, listen to what I have to say about Jesus from Nazareth. God proved that he sent Jesus to you by having him work miracles, wonders, and signs. All of you know this. ²³God had already planned and decided that Jesus would be handed over to you. So you took him and had evil men put him to death on a cross. ²⁴But God set him free from death and raised him to life. Death could not hold him in its power. ²⁵What David said are really the words of Jesus,

"I always see the Lord
  near me,
 and I will not be afraid
  with him at my right side.
²⁶ Because of this,
  my heart will be glad,
 my words will be joyful,
  and I will live in hope.
²⁷ The Lord won't leave me
  in the grave.
 I am his holy one,
 and he won't let
  my body decay.
²⁸ He has shown me
  the path to life,
 and he makes me glad
  by being near me."

²⁹My friends, it is right for me to speak to you about our ancestor David. He died and was buried, and his tomb is still here. ³⁰But David was a prophet, and he knew that God had made a promise he would not break. He had told David that someone from his own family would someday be king.

³¹David knew this would happen, and so he told us that Christ would be raised to life. He said that God would not leave him in the grave or let his body decay. ³²All of us can tell you that God has raised Jesus to life!

³³Jesus was taken up to sit at the right side^f of God, and he was given the Holy Spirit, just as the Father had promised. Jesus is also the one who has given the Spirit to us, and that is what you are now seeing and hearing.

³⁴David didn't go up to heaven. So he wasn't talking about himself when he said, "The Lord told my Lord to sit at his right side, ³⁵until he made my Lord's enemies into a foot-

---

^f 2.33 *right side*: The place of honor and power.

stool for him." ³⁶Everyone in Israel should then know for certain that God has made Jesus both Lord and Christ, even though you put him to death on a cross.

³⁷When the people heard this, they were very upset. They asked Peter and the other apostles, "Friends, what shall we do?"

³⁸Peter said, "Turn back to God! Be baptized in the name of Jesus Christ, so that your sins will be forgiven. Then you will be given the Holy Spirit. ³⁹This promise is for you and your children. It is for everyone our Lord God will choose, no matter where they live."

⁴⁰Peter told them many other things as well. Then he said, "I beg you to save yourselves from what will happen to all these evil people." ⁴¹On that day about three thousand believed his message and were baptized. ⁴²They spent their time learning from the apostles, and they were like family to each other. They also broke bread[g] and prayed together.

Life among the Lord's Followers

⁴³Everyone was amazed by the many miracles and wonders that the apostles worked. ⁴⁴All the Lord's followers often met together, and they shared everything they had. ⁴⁵They would sell their property and possessions and give the money to whoever needed it. ⁴⁶Day after day they met together in the temple. They broke bread[g] together in different homes and shared their food happily and freely, ⁴⁷while praising God. Everyone liked them, and each day the Lord added to their group others who were being saved.

Peter and John Heal a Lame Man

3 The time of prayer[h] was about three o'clock in the afternoon, and Peter and John were going into the temple. ²A man who had been born lame was being carried to the temple door. Each day he was placed beside this door, known as the Beautiful Gate. He sat there and begged from the people who were going in.

³The man saw Peter and John entering the temple, and he asked them for money. ⁴But they looked straight at him and said, "Look up at us!"

⁵The man stared at them and thought he was going to get something. ⁶But Peter said, "I don't have any silver or gold! But I will give you what I do have. In the name of Jesus Christ from Nazareth, get up and start walking." ⁷Peter then took him by the right hand and helped him up.

At once the man's feet and ankles became strong, ⁸and he jumped up and started walking. He went with Peter and John into the temple, walking and jumping and praising God. ⁹Everyone saw him walking around and praising God. ¹⁰They knew that he was the beggar who had been lying beside the Beautiful Gate, and they were completely surprised. They could not imagine what had happened to the man.

Peter Speaks in the Temple

¹¹While the man kept holding on to Peter and John, the whole crowd ran to them in amazement at the place known as Solomon's Porch.[i] ¹²Peter saw that a crowd had gathered, and he said:

Friends, why are you surprised at what has happened? Why are you staring at us? Do you think we have some power of our own? Do you think we were able to make this man walk because we are so religious? ¹³The God that Abraham, Isaac, Jacob, and our other ancestors worshiped has brought honor to his Servant[j] Jesus. He is the one you betrayed. You turned against him when he was being tried by Pilate, even though Pilate wanted to set him free.

¹⁴You rejected Jesus, who was holy and good. You asked for a murderer to be set free, ¹⁵and you killed the one who leads people to life. But God raised him from death, and all of us can tell you what he has done. ¹⁶You see this man, and you know him. He put his faith in the name of Jesus and was made strong. Faith in Jesus made this man completely well while everyone was watching.

¹⁷My friends, I am sure that you and your leaders didn't know what you were doing. ¹⁸But God had his prophets tell that his Messiah would suffer, and now he has kept that promise. ¹⁹So turn to God! Give up your sins, and you will be forgiven. ²⁰Then that time will come when the Lord will give you fresh strength. He will send you Jesus, his chosen Messiah. ²¹But Jesus must stay in heaven until God makes all things new, just as his holy prophets promised long ago.

²²Moses said, "The Lord your God will choose one of your own people

---

[g]2.42,46 *broke bread*: They ate together and celebrated the Lord's Supper.   [h]3.1 *The time of prayer*: Many of the Jewish people prayed in their homes at regular times each day (see Daniel 6.11), and on special occasions they prayed in the temple.   [i]3.11 *Solomon's Porch*: A public place with tall columns along the east side of the temple.   [j]3.13 *Servant*: Or "Son."

to be a prophet, just as he chose me. Listen to everything he tells you. ²³No one who disobeys that prophet will be one of God's people any longer."

²⁴Samuel and all the other prophets who came later also spoke about what is now happening. ²⁵You are really the ones God told his prophets to speak to. And you were given the promise that God made to your ancestors. He said to Abraham, "All nations on earth will be blessed because of someone from your family." ²⁶God sent his chosen Son[k] to you first, because God wanted to bless you and make each one of you turn away from your sins.

Peter and John Are Brought in Front of the Council

4 The apostles were still talking to the people, when some priests, the captain of the temple guard, and some Sadducees arrived. ²These men were angry because the apostles were teaching the people that the dead would be raised from death, just as Jesus had been raised from death. ³It was already late in the afternoon, and they arrested Peter and John and put them in jail for the night. ⁴But a lot of people who had heard the message believed it. So by now there were about five thousand followers of the Lord.

⁵The next morning the leaders, the elders, and the teachers of the Law of Moses met in Jerusalem. ⁶The high priest Annas was there, as well as Caiaphas, John, Alexander, and other members of the high priest's family. ⁷They brought in Peter and John and made them stand in the middle while they questioned them. They asked, "By what power and in whose name have you done this?"

⁸Peter was filled with the Holy Spirit and told the nation's leaders and the elders:

⁹You are questioning us today about a kind deed in which a crippled man was healed. ¹⁰But there is something we must tell you and everyone else in Israel. This man is standing here completely well because of the power of Jesus Christ from Nazareth. You put Jesus to death on a cross, but God raised him to life. ¹¹He is the stone that you builders thought was worthless, and now he is the most important stone of all. ¹²Only Jesus has the power to save! His name is the only one in all the world that can save anyone.

¹³The officials were amazed to see how brave Peter and John were, and they knew that these two apostles were only ordinary men and not well educated. The officials were certain that these men had been with Jesus. ¹⁴But they could not deny what had happened. The man who had been healed was standing there with the apostles.

¹⁵The officials commanded them to leave the council room. Then the officials said to each other, ¹⁶"What can we do with these men? Everyone in Jerusalem knows about this miracle, and we cannot say it didn't happen. ¹⁷But to keep this thing from spreading, we will warn them never again to speak to anyone about the name of Jesus." ¹⁸So they called the two apostles back in and told them that they must never, for any reason, teach anything about the name of Jesus.

¹⁹Peter and John answered, "Do you think God wants us to obey you or to obey him? ²⁰We cannot keep quiet about what we have seen and heard."

²¹⁻²²The officials could not find any reason to punish Peter and John. So they threatened them and let them go. The man who was healed by this miracle was more than forty years old, and everyone was praising God for what had happened.

Peter and Others Pray for Courage

²³As soon as Peter and John had been set free, they went back and told the others everything that the chief priests and the leaders had said to them. ²⁴When the rest of the Lord's followers heard this, they prayed together and said:

Master, you created heaven and earth, the sea, and everything in them. ²⁵And by the Holy Spirit you spoke to our ancestor David. He was your servant, and you told him to say:

"Why are all the Gentiles
   so furious?
Why do people
   make foolish plans?
²⁶ The kings of earth
   prepare for war,
and the rulers
   join together
against the Lord
   and his Messiah."

²⁷Here in Jerusalem, Herod[l] and Pontius Pilate got together with the Gentiles and the people of Israel. Then they turned against your holy Servant[m] Jesus, your chosen Mes-

---

[k] 3.26 *Son:* Or "Servant."   [l] 4.27 *Herod:* Herod Antipas, the son of Herod the Great.
[m] 4.27,30 *Servant:* See the note at 3.13.

siah. [28]They did what you in your power and wisdom had already decided would happen. [29]Lord, listen to their threats! We are your servants. So make us brave enough to speak your message. [30]Show your mighty power, as we heal people and work miracles and wonders in the name of your holy Servant[m] Jesus. [31]After they had prayed, the meeting place shook. They were all filled with the Holy Spirit and bravely spoke God's message.

Sharing Possessions

[32]The group of followers all felt the same way about everything. None of them claimed that their possessions were their own, and they shared everything they had with each other. [33]In a powerful way the apostles told everyone that the Lord Jesus was now alive. God greatly blessed his followers,[n] [34]and no one went in need of anything. Everyone who owned land or houses would sell them and bring the money [35]to the apostles. Then they would give the money to anyone who needed it.

[36-37]Joseph was one of the followers who had sold a piece of property and brought the money to the apostles. He was a Levite from Cyprus, and the apostles called him Barnabas, which means "one who encourages others."

Peter Condemns Ananias and Sapphira

5 Ananias and his wife Sapphira also sold a piece of property. [2]But they agreed to cheat and keep some of the money for themselves.

So when Ananias took the rest of the money to the apostles, [3]Peter said, "Why has Satan made you keep back some of the money from the sale of the property? Why have you lied to the Holy Spirit? [4]The property was yours before you sold it, and even after you sold it, the money was still yours. What made you do such a thing? You didn't lie to people. You lied to God!"

[5]As soon as Ananias heard this, he dropped dead, and everyone who heard about it was frightened. [6]Some young men came in and wrapped up his body. Then they took it out and buried it.

[7]Three hours later Sapphira came in, but she did not know what had happened to her husband. [8]Peter asked her, "Tell me, did you sell the property for this amount?"

"Yes," she answered, "that's the amount."

[9]Then Peter said, "Why did the two of you agree to test the Lord's Spirit? The men who buried Ananias are by the door, and they will carry you out!" [10]At once she fell at Peter's feet and died.

When the young men came back in, they found Sapphira lying there dead. So they carried her out and buried her beside her husband. [11]The church members were afraid, and so was everyone else who heard what had happened.

Peter's Unusual Power

[12]The apostles worked many miracles and wonders among the people. All of the Lord's followers often met in the part of the temple known as Solomon's Porch.[o] [13]No one outside their group dared join them, even though everyone liked them very much.

[14]Many men and women started having faith in the Lord. [15]Then sick people were brought out to the road and placed on cots and mats. It was hoped that Peter would walk by, and his shadow would fall on them and heal them. [16]A lot of people living in the towns near Jerusalem brought those who were sick or troubled by evil spirits, and they were all healed.

Trouble for the Apostles

[17]The high priest and all the other Sadducees who were with him became jealous. [18]They arrested the apostles and put them in the city jail. [19]But that night an angel from the Lord opened the doors of the jail and led the apostles out. The angel said, [20]"Go to the temple and tell the people everything about this new life." [21]So they went into the temple before sunrise and started teaching.

The high priest and his men called together their council, which included all of Israel's leaders. Then they ordered the apostles to be brought to them from the jail. [22]The temple police who were sent to the jail did not find the apostles. They returned and said, [23]"We found the jail locked tight and the guards standing at the doors. But when we opened the doors and went in, we didn't find anyone there." [24]The captain of the temple police and the chief priests listened to their report, but they did not know what to think about it.

[25]Just then someone came in and said, "Right now those men you put in jail are in the temple, teaching the people!" [26]The captain went with some of the temple police and brought the apostles back. But they did not use force. They were afraid that the people might start throwing stones at them.

---

[m]4.27,30 *Servant*: See the note at 3.13. [n]4.33 *God greatly blessed his followers*: Or "Everyone highly respected his followers." [o]5.12 *Solomon's Porch*: See the note at 3.11.

27When the apostles were brought before the council, the high priest said to them, 28"We told you plainly not to teach in the name of Jesus. But look what you have done! You have been teaching all over Jerusalem, and you are trying to blame us for his death."

29Peter and the apostles replied:

We don't obey people. We obey God. 30You killed Jesus by nailing him to a cross. But the God our ancestors worshiped raised him to life 31and made him our Leader and Savior. Then God gave him a place at his right side,[p] so that the people of Israel would turn back to him and be forgiven. 32We are here to tell you about all this, and so is the Holy Spirit, who is God's gift to everyone who obeys God.

33When the council members heard this, they became so angry that they wanted to kill the apostles. 34But one of the members was the Pharisee Gamaliel, a highly respected teacher. He ordered the apostles to be taken out of the room for a little while. 35Then he said to the council:

People of Israel, be careful what you do with these men. 36Not long ago Theudas claimed to be someone important, and about four hundred men joined him. But he was killed. All his followers were scattered, and that was the end of that.

37Later, when the people of our nation were being counted, Judas from Galilee showed up. A lot of people followed him, but he was killed, and all his followers were scattered.

38So I advise you to stay away from these men. Leave them alone. If what they are planning is something of their own doing, it will fail. 39But if God is behind it, you cannot stop it anyway, unless you want to fight against God.

The council members agreed with what he said, 40and they called the apostles back in. They had them beaten with a whip and warned them not to speak in the name of Jesus. Then they let them go. 41The apostles left the council and were happy, because God had considered them worthy to suffer for the sake of Jesus. 42Every day they spent time in the temple and in one home after another. They never stopped teaching and telling the good news that Jesus is the Messiah.

Seven Leaders for the Church

6 A lot of people were now becoming followers of the Lord. But some of the ones who spoke Greek started complaining about the ones who spoke Aramaic. They complained that the Greek-speaking widows were not given their share when the food supplies were handed out each day.

2The twelve apostles called the whole group of followers together and said, "We should not give up preaching God's message in order to serve at tables.[q] 3My friends, choose seven men who are respected and wise and filled with God's Spirit. We will put them in charge of these things. 4We can spend our time praying and serving God by preaching."

5This suggestion pleased everyone, and they began by choosing Stephen. He had great faith and was filled with the Holy Spirit. Then they chose Philip, Prochorus, Nicanor, Timon, Parmenas, and also Nicolaus, who worshiped with the Jewish people[r] in Antioch. 6These men were brought to the apostles. Then the apostles prayed and placed their hands on the men to show that they had been chosen to do this work. 7God's message spread, and many more people in Jerusalem became followers. Even a large number of priests put their faith in the Lord.

Stephen Is Arrested

8God gave Stephen the power to work great miracles and wonders among the people. 9But some Jews from Cyrene and Alexandria were members of a group who called themselves "Free Men."[s] They started arguing with Stephen. Some others from Cilicia and Asia also argued with him. 10But they were no match for Stephen, who spoke with the great wisdom that the Spirit gave him. 11So they talked some men into saying, "We heard Stephen say terrible things against Moses and God!"

12They turned the people and their leaders and the teachers of the Law of Moses against Stephen. Then they all grabbed Stephen and dragged him in front of the council.

13Some men agreed to tell lies about Stephen, and they said, "This man keeps on saying terrible things about this holy temple and the Law of Moses. 14We have heard him claim that Jesus from Nazareth will destroy this place and change the customs that Moses gave us." 15Then all the council members

---

[p]5.31 *right side*: See the note at 2.33. [q]6.2 *to serve at tables*: This may mean either that they were in charge of handing out food to the widows or that they were in charge of the money, since the Greek word "table" may also mean "bank." [r]6.5 *worshiped with the Jewish people*: This translates the Greek word "proselyte" that means a Gentile who had accepted the Jewish religion. [s]6.9 *Free Men*: A group of Jewish men who had once been slaves, but had been freed.

stared at Stephen. They saw that his face looked like the face of an angel.

Stephen's Speech

7 The high priest asked Stephen, "Are they telling the truth about you?" ²Stephen answered:

Friends, listen to me. Our glorious God appeared to our ancestor Abraham while he was still in Mesopotamia, before he had moved to Haran. ³God told him, "Leave your country and your relatives and go to a land that I will show you." ⁴Then Abraham left the land of the Chaldeans and settled in Haran.

After his father died, Abraham came and settled in this land where you now live. ⁵God didn't give him any part of it, not even a square foot. But God did promise to give it to him and his family forever, even though Abraham didn't have any children. ⁶God said that Abraham's descendants would live for a while in a foreign land. There they would be slaves and would be mistreated four hundred years. ⁷But he also said, "I will punish the nation that makes them slaves. Then later they will come and worship me in this place."

⁸God said to Abraham, "Every son in each family must be circumcised to show that you have kept your agreement with me." So when Isaac was eight days old, Abraham circumcised him. Later, Isaac circumcised his son Jacob, and Jacob circumcised his twelve sons. ⁹ These men were our ancestors.

Joseph was also one of our famous ancestors. His brothers were jealous of him and sold him as a slave to be taken to Egypt. But God was with him ¹⁰and rescued him from all his troubles. God made him so wise that the Egyptian king Pharaoh[x] thought highly of him. The king even made Joseph governor over Egypt and put him in charge of everything he owned.

¹¹Everywhere in Egypt and Canaan the grain crops failed. There was terrible suffering, and our ancestors could not find enough to eat. ¹²But when Jacob heard that there was grain in Egypt, he sent our ancestors there for the first time. ¹³It was on their second trip that Joseph told his brothers who he was, and Pharaoh learned about Joseph's family.

¹⁴Joseph sent for his father and his relatives. In all, there were seventy-five of them. ¹⁵His father went to Egypt and died there, just as our ancestors did. ¹⁵Later their bodies were taken back to Shechem and placed in the tomb that Abraham had bought from the sons of Hamor.

¹⁷Finally, the time came for God to do what he had promised Abraham. By then the number of our people in Egypt had greatly increased. ¹⁸Another king was ruling Egypt, and he didn't know anything about Joseph. ¹⁹He tricked our ancestors and was cruel to them. He even made them leave their babies outside, so they would die.

²⁰During this time Moses was born. He was a very beautiful child, and for three months his parents took care of him in their home. ²¹Then when they were forced to leave him outside, the king's daughter found him and raised him as her own son. ²²Moses was given the best education in Egypt. He was a strong man and a powerful speaker.

²³When Moses was forty years old, he wanted to help the Israelites because they were his own people. ²⁴One day he saw an Egyptian mistreating one of them. So he rescued the man and killed the Egyptian. ²⁵Moses thought the rest of his people would realize that God was going to use him to set them free. But they didn't understand.

²⁶The next day Moses saw two of his own people fighting, and he tried to make them stop. He said, "Men, you are both Israelites. Why are you so cruel to each other?"

²⁷But the man who had started the fight pushed Moses aside and asked, "Who made you our ruler and judge? ²⁸Are you going to kill me, just as you killed that Egyptian yesterday?" ²⁹When Moses heard this, he ran away to live in the country of Midian. His two sons were born there.

³⁰Forty years later, an angel appeared to Moses from a burning bush in the desert near Mount Sinai. ³¹Moses was surprised by what he saw. He went closer to get a better look, and the Lord said, ³²"I am the God who was worshiped by your ancestors, Abraham, Isaac, and Jacob." Moses started shaking all over and didn't dare to look at the bush.

³³The Lord said to him, "Take off your sandals. The place where you are standing is holy. ³⁴With my own eyes I have seen the suffering of my people in Egypt. I have heard their groans and have come down to rescue them. Now I am sending you back to Egypt."

³⁵This was the same Moses that the people rejected by saying, "Who

---

[x]7.10 *Pharaoh*: A Hebrew word sometimes used for the title of the King of Egypt.

made you our leader and judge?" God's angel had spoken to Moses from the bush. And God had even sent the angel to help Moses rescue the people and be their leader.

³⁶In Egypt and at the Red Sea[t] and in the desert, Moses rescued the people by working miracles and wonders for forty years. ³⁷Moses is the one who told the people of Israel, "God will choose one of your people to be a prophet, just as he chose me." ³⁸Moses brought our people together in the desert, and the angel spoke to him on Mount Sinai. There he was given these life-giving words to pass on to us. ³⁹But our ancestors refused to obey Moses. They rejected him and wanted to go back to Egypt.

⁴⁰The people said to Aaron, "Make some gods to lead us! Moses led us out of Egypt, but we don't know what's happened to him now." ⁴¹Then they made an idol in the shape of a calf. They offered sacrifices to the idol and were pleased with what they had done.

⁴²God turned his back on his people and left them. Then they worshiped the stars in the sky, just as it says in the Book of the Prophets, "People of Israel, you didn't offer sacrifices and offerings to me during those forty years in the desert. ⁴³Instead, you carried the tent where the god Molech is worshiped, and you took along the star of your god Rephan. You made those idols and worshiped them. So now I will have you carried off beyond Babylonia."

⁴⁴The tent where our ancestors worshiped God was with them in the desert. This was the same tent that God had commanded Moses to make. And it was made like the model that Moses had seen. ⁴⁵Later it was given to our ancestors, and they took it with them when they went with Joshua. They carried the tent along as they took over the land from those people that God had chased out for them. Our ancestors used this tent until the time of King David. ⁴⁶ He pleased God and asked him if he could build a house of worship for the people[u] of Israel. ⁴⁷And it was finally King Solomon who built a house for God.[v]

⁴⁸But the Most High God doesn't live in houses made by humans. It is just as the prophet said, when he spoke for the Lord,

⁴⁹ "Heaven is my throne,
　　and the earth
　　　is my footstool.
　What kind of house
　　will you build for me?
　In what place will I rest?
⁵⁰　I have made everything."

⁵¹You stubborn and hardheaded people! You are always fighting against the Holy Spirit, just as your ancestors did. ⁵²Is there one prophet that your ancestors didn't mistreat? They killed the prophets who told about the coming of the One Who Obeys God.[w] And now you have turned against him and killed him. ⁵³Angels gave you God's Law, but you still don't obey it.

Stephen Is Stoned to Death

⁵⁴When the council members heard Stephen's speech, they were angry and furious. ⁵⁵But Stephen was filled with the Holy Spirit. He looked toward heaven, where he saw our glorious God and Jesus standing at his right side.[x] ⁵⁶Then Stephen said, "I see heaven open and the Son of Man standing at the right side of God!"

⁵⁷The council members shouted and covered their ears. At once they all attacked Stephen ⁵⁸and dragged him out of the city. Then they started throwing stones at him. The men who had brought charges against him put their coats at the feet of a young man named Saul.[y]

⁵⁹As Stephen was being stoned to death, he called out, "Lord Jesus, please welcome me!" ⁶⁰He knelt down and shouted, "Lord, don't blame them for what they have done." Then he died.

8 ¹⁻²Saul approved the stoning of Stephen. Some faithful followers of the Lord buried Stephen and mourned very much for him.

Saul Makes Trouble for the Church

At that time the church in Jerusalem suffered terribly. All of the Lord's followers, except the apostles, were scattered everywhere in Judea and Samaria. ³Saul started making a lot of trouble for the church. He went from house to

---

[t]7.36 *Red Sea*: This name comes from the Bible of the early Christians, a translation made into Greek about 200 B.C. It refers to the body of water that the Israelites crossed and was one of the marshes or fresh water lakes near the eastern part of the Nile Delta, where they lived and where the towns of Exodus 13.17—14.9 were located.　　[u]7.46 *the people*: Some manuscripts have "God."　　[v]7.47 *God*: Or "the people."　　[w]7.52 *One Who Obeys God*: That is, Jesus.
[x]7.55 *standing at his right side*: The "right side" is the place of honor and power. "Standing" may mean that Jesus is welcoming Stephen (see verse 59).　　[y]7.58 *Saul*: Better known as Paul, who became a famous follower of Jesus.

house, arresting men and women and putting them in jail.

The Good News Is Preached in Samaria

[4]The Lord's followers who had been scattered went from place to place, telling the good news. [5]Philip went to the city of Samaria and told the people about Christ. [6]They crowded around Philip because they were eager to hear what he was saying and to see him work miracles. [7]Many people with evil spirits were healed, and the spirits went out of them with a shout. A lot of crippled and lame people were also healed. [8]Everyone in that city was very glad because of what was happening.

[9]For some time a man named Simon had lived in the city of Samaria and had amazed the people. He practiced witchcraft and claimed to be somebody great. [10]Everyone, rich and poor, crowded around him. They said, "This man is the power of God called 'The Great Power.'" [11]For a long time, Simon had used witchcraft to amaze the people, and they kept crowding around him. [12]But when they believed what Philip was saying about God's kingdom and about the name of Jesus Christ, they were all baptized. [13]Even Simon believed and was baptized. He stayed close to Philip, because he marveled at all the miracles and wonders.

[14]The apostles in Jerusalem heard that some people in Samaria had accepted God's message, and they sent Peter and John. [15]When the two apostles arrived, they prayed that the people would be given the Holy Spirit. [16]Before this, the Holy Spirit had not been given to anyone in Samaria, though some of them had been baptized in the name of the Lord Jesus. [17]Peter and John then placed their hands on everyone who had faith in the Lord, and they were given the Holy Spirit.

[18]Simon noticed that the Spirit was given only when the apostles placed their hands on the people. So he brought money [19]and said to Peter and John, "Let me have this power too! Then anyone I place my hands on will also be given the Holy Spirit."

[20]Peter said to him, "You and your money will both end up in hell if you think you can buy God's gift! [21]You don't have any part in this, and God sees that your heart isn't right. [22]Get rid of these evil thoughts and ask God to forgive you. [23]I can see that you are jealous and bound by your evil ways."

[24]Simon said, "Please pray to the Lord, so that what you said won't happen to me."

[25]After Peter and John had preached about the Lord, they returned to Jerusalem. On their way they told the good news in many villages of Samaria.

Philip and an Ethiopian Official

[26]The Lord's angel said to Philip, "Go south[z] along the desert road that leads from Jerusalem to Gaza."[a] [27]So Philip left.

An important Ethiopian official happened to be going along that road in his chariot. He was the chief treasurer for Candace, the Queen of Ethiopia. The official had gone to Jerusalem to worship [28]and was now on his way home. He was sitting in his chariot, reading the book of the prophet Isaiah.

[29]The Spirit told Philip to catch up with the chariot. [30]Philip ran up close and heard the man reading aloud from the book of Isaiah. Philip asked him, "Do you understand what you are reading?"

[31]The official answered, "How can I understand unless someone helps me?" He then invited Philip to come up and sit beside him.

[32]The man was reading the passage that said,

"He was led like a sheep
   on its way to be killed.
He was silent as a lamb
   whose wool
     is being cut off,
and he did not say
   a word.
[33] He was treated like a nobody
   and did not receive
     a fair trial.
How can he have children,
   if his life
     is snatched away?"

[34]The official said to Philip, "Tell me, was the prophet talking about himself or about someone else?" [35]So Philip began at this place in the Scriptures and explained the good news about Jesus.

[36-37]As they were going along the road, they came to a place where there was some water. The official said, "Look! Here is some water. Why can't I be baptized?"[b] [38]He ordered the chariot to stop. Then they both went down into the water, and Philip baptized him.

[39]After they had come out of the water, the Lord's Spirit took Philip away. The official never saw him again, but he was very happy as he went on his way.

[40]Philip later appeared in Azotus. He

---

[z]**8.26** *Go south*: Or "About noon go."   [a]**8.26** *the desert road that leads from Jerusalem to Gaza*: Or "the road that leads from Jerusalem to Gaza in the desert."   [b]**8.36,37** *Why can't I be baptized*: Some manuscripts add, "Philip replied, 'You can, if you believe with all your heart.' "The official answered, 'I believe that Jesus Christ is the Son of God.'"

went from town to town, all the way to Caesarea, telling people about Jesus.

Saul Becomes a Follower of the Lord
(Acts 22.6-16; 26.12-18)

9 Saul kept on threatening to kill the Lord's followers. He even went to the high priest ²and asked for letters to the Jewish leaders in Damascus. He did this because he wanted to arrest and take to Jerusalem any man or woman who had accepted the Lord's Way.ᶜ ³When Saul had almost reached Damascus, a bright light from heaven suddenly flashed around him. ⁴He fell to the ground and heard a voice that said, "Saul! Saul! Why are you so cruel to me?"

⁵"Who are you?" Saul asked.

"I am Jesus," the Lord answered. "I am the one you are so cruel to. ⁶Now get up and go into the city, where you will be told what to do."

⁷The men with Saul stood there speechless. They had heard the voice, but they had not seen anyone. ⁸Saul got up from the ground, and when he opened his eyes, he could not see a thing. Someone then led him by the hand to Damascus, ⁹and for three days he was blind and did not eat or drink.

¹⁰A follower named Ananias lived in Damascus, and the Lord spoke to him in a vision. Ananias answered, "Lord, here I am."

¹¹The Lord said to him, "Get up and go to the house of Judas on Straight Street. When you get there, you will find a man named Saul from the city of Tarsus. Saul is praying, ¹²and he has seen a vision. He saw a man named Ananias coming to him and putting his hands on him, so that he could see again."

¹³Ananias replied, "Lord, a lot of people have told me about the terrible things this man has done to your followers in Jerusalem. ¹⁴Now the chief priests have given him the power to come here and arrest anyone who worships in your name."

¹⁵The Lord said to Ananias, "Go! I have chosen him to tell foreigners, kings, and the people of Israel about me. ¹⁶I will show him how much he must suffer for worshiping in my name."

¹⁷Ananias left and went into the house where Saul was staying. Ananias placed his hands on him and said, "Saul, the Lord Jesus has sent me. He is the same one who appeared to you along the road. He wants you to be able to see and to be filled with the Holy Spirit."

¹⁸Suddenly something like fish scales fell from Saul's eyes, and he could see. He got up and was baptized. ¹⁹Then he ate and felt much better.

Saul Preaches in Damascus

For several days Saul stayed with the Lord's followers in Damascus. ²⁰Soon he went to the Jewish meeting places and started telling people that Jesus is the Son of God. ²¹Everyone who heard Saul was amazed and said, "Isn't this the man who caused so much trouble for those people in Jerusalem who worship in the name of Jesus? Didn't he come here to arrest them and take them to the chief priests?"

²²Saul preached with such power that he completely confused the Jewish people in Damascus, as he tried to show them that Jesus is the Messiah.

²³Later some of them made plans to kill Saul, ²⁴but he found out about it. He learned that they were guarding the gates of the city day and night in order to kill him. ²⁵Then one night his followers let him down over the city wall in a large basket.

Saul in Jerusalem

²⁶When Saul arrived in Jerusalem, he tried to join the followers. But they were all afraid of him, because they did not believe he was a true follower. ²⁷Then Barnabas helped him by taking him to the apostles. He explained how Saul had seen the Lord and how the Lord had spoken to him. Barnabas also said that when Saul was in Damascus, he had spoken bravely in the name of Jesus.

²⁸Saul moved about freely with the followers in Jerusalem and told everyone about the Lord. ²⁹He was always arguing with the Jews who spoke Greek, and so they tried to kill him. ³⁰But the followers found out about this and took Saul to Caesarea. From there they sent him to the city of Tarsus.

³¹The church in Judea, Galilee, and Samaria now had a time of peace and kept on worshiping the Lord. The church became stronger, as the Holy Spirit encouraged it and helped it grow.

Peter Heals Aeneas

³²While Peter was traveling from place to place, he visited the Lord's followers who lived in the town of Lydda. ³³There he met a man named Aeneas, who for eight years had been sick in bed and could not move. ³⁴Peter said to Aeneas, "Jesus Christ has healed you! Get up and make up your bed."ᵈ Right away he stood up.

³⁵Many people in the towns of Lydda and Sharon saw Aeneas and became followers of the Lord.

ᶜ9.2 *accepted the Lord's Way*: In the book of Acts, this means to become a follower of the Lord Jesus.   ᵈ9.34 *and make up your bed*: Or "and fix something to eat."

Peter Brings Dorcas Back to Life

36 In Joppa there was a follower named Tabitha. Her Greek name was Dorcas, which means "deer." She was always doing good things for people and had given much to the poor. 37 But she got sick and died, and her body was washed and placed in an upstairs room. 38 Joppa wasn't far from Lydda, and the followers heard that Peter was there. They sent two men to say to him, "Please come with us as quickly as you can!" 39 Right away, Peter went with them.

The men took Peter upstairs into the room. Many widows were there crying. They showed him the coats and clothes that Dorcas had made while she was still alive. 40 After Peter had sent everyone out of the room, he knelt down and prayed. Then he turned to the body of Dorcas and said, "Tabitha, get up!" The woman opened her eyes, and when she saw Peter, she sat up. 41 He took her by the hand and helped her to her feet.

Peter called in the widows and the other followers and showed them that Dorcas had been raised from death. 42 Everyone in Joppa heard what had happened, and many of them put their faith in the Lord. 43 Peter stayed on for a while in Joppa in the house of a man named Simon, who made leather.

Peter and Cornelius

10 In Caesarea there was a man named Cornelius, who was the captain of a group of soldiers called "The Italian Unit." 2 Cornelius was a very religious man. He worshiped God, and so did everyone else who lived in his house. He had given a lot of money to the poor and was always praying to God.

3 One afternoon at about three o'clock,[e] Cornelius had a vision. He saw an angel from God coming to him and calling him by name. 4 Cornelius was surprised and stared at the angel. Then he asked, "What is this all about?"

The angel answered, "God has heard your prayers and knows about your gifts to the poor. 5 Now send some men to Joppa for a man named Simon Peter. 6 He is visiting with Simon the leather maker, who lives in a house near the sea." 7 After saying this, the angel left.

Cornelius called in two of his servants and one of his soldiers who worshiped God. 8 He explained everything to them and sent them off to Joppa.

9 The next day about noon these men were coming near Joppa. Peter went up on the roof[f] of the house to pray 10 and became very hungry. While the food was being prepared, he fell sound asleep and had a vision. 11 He saw heaven open, and something came down like a huge sheet held up by its four corners. 12 In it were all kinds of animals, snakes, and birds. 13 A voice said to him, "Peter, get up! Kill these and eat them."

14 But Peter said, "Lord, I can't do that! I've never eaten anything that is unclean and not fit to eat."[g]

15 The voice spoke to him again, "When God says that something can be used for food, don't say it isn't fit to eat."

16 This happened three times before the sheet was suddenly taken back to heaven.

17 Peter was still wondering what all of this meant, when the men sent by Cornelius came and stood at the gate. They had found their way to Simon's house 18 and were asking if Simon Peter was staying there.

19 While Peter was still thinking about the vision, the Holy Spirit said to him, "Three[h] men are here looking for you. 20 Hurry down and go with them. Don't worry, I sent them."

21 Peter went down and said to the men, "I am the one you are looking for. Why have you come?"

22 They answered, "Captain Cornelius sent us. He is a good man who worships God and is liked by the Jewish people. One of God's holy angels told Cornelius to send for you, so he could hear what you have to say." 23 Peter invited them to spend the night.

The next morning, Peter and some of the Lord's followers in Joppa left with the men who had come from Cornelius. 24 The next day they arrived in Caesarea where Cornelius was waiting for them. He had also invited his relatives and close friends.

25 When Peter arrived, Cornelius greeted him. Then he knelt at Peter's feet and started worshiping him. 26 But Peter took hold of him and said, "Stand up! I am nothing more than a human."

27 As Peter entered the house, he was still talking with Cornelius. Many people were there, 28 and Peter said to them, "You know that we Jews are not allowed to have anything to do with other people. But God has shown me that he doesn't think anyone is unclean or unfit. 29 I agreed to come here, but I want to know why you sent for me."

---

[e] **10.3** *at about three o'clock*: Probably while he was praying (see 3.1 and the note there).
[f] **10.9** *roof*: In Palestine the houses usually had a flat roof. Stairs on the outside led up to the roof, which was made of beams and boards covered with packed earth. [g] **10.14** *unclean and not fit to eat*: The Law of Moses taught that some foods were not fit to eat. [h] **10.19** *Three*: One manuscript has "two;" some manuscripts have "some."

³⁰Cornelius answered:
Four days ago at about three o'clock in the afternoon I was praying at home. Suddenly a man in bright clothes stood in front of me. ³¹He said, "Cornelius, God has heard your prayers, and he knows about your gifts to the poor. ³²Now send to Joppa for Simon Peter. He is visiting in the home of Simon the leather maker, who lives near the sea."

³³I sent for you right away, and you have been good enough to come. All of us are here in the presence of the Lord God, so that we can hear what he has to say.
³⁴Peter then said:
Now I am certain that God treats all people alike. ³⁵God is pleased with everyone who worships him and does right, no matter what nation they come from. ³⁶This is the same message that God gave to the people of Israel, when he sent Jesus Christ, the Lord of all, to offer peace to them.

³⁷You surely know what happened[i] everywhere in Judea. It all began in Galilee after John had told everyone to be baptized. ³⁸God gave the Holy Spirit and power to Jesus from Nazareth. He was with Jesus, as he went around doing good and healing everyone who was under the power of the devil. ³⁹We all saw what Jesus did both in Israel and in the city of Jerusalem.

Jesus was put to death on a cross. ⁴⁰But three days later, God raised him to life and let him be seen. ⁴¹Not everyone saw him. He was seen only by us, who ate and drank with him after he was raised from death. We were the ones God chose to tell others about him.

⁴²God told us to announce clearly to the people that Jesus is the one he has chosen to judge the living and the dead. ⁴³Every one of the prophets has said that all who have faith in Jesus will have their sins forgiven in his name.

⁴⁴While Peter was still speaking, the Holy Spirit took control of everyone who was listening. ⁴⁵Some Jewish followers of the Lord had come with Peter, and they were surprised that the Holy Spirit had been given to Gentiles. ⁴⁶Now they were hearing Gentiles speaking unknown languages and praising God.

Peter said, ⁴⁷"These Gentiles have been given the Holy Spirit, just as we have! I am certain that no one would dare stop us from baptizing them." ⁴⁸Peter ordered them to be baptized in the name of Jesus Christ, and they asked him to stay on for a few days.

Peter Reports to the Church in Jerusalem

11 The apostles and the followers in Judea heard that Gentiles had accepted God's message. ²So when Peter came to Jerusalem, some of the Jewish followers started arguing with him. They wanted Gentile followers to be circumcised, and ³they said, "You stayed in the homes of Gentiles, and you even ate with them!"
⁴Then Peter told them exactly what had happened:
⁵I was in the town of Joppa and was praying when I fell sound asleep and had a vision. I saw heaven open, and something like a huge sheet held by its four corners came down to me. ⁶When I looked in it, I saw animals, wild beasts, snakes, and birds. ⁷I heard a voice saying to me, "Peter, get up! Kill these and eat them."

⁸But I said, "Lord, I can't do that! I've never taken a bite of anything that is unclean and not fit to eat."[j]

⁹The voice from heaven spoke to me again, "When God says that something can be used for food, don't say it isn't fit to eat." ¹⁰This happened three times before it was all taken back into heaven.

¹¹Suddenly three men from Caesarea stood in front of the house where I was staying. ¹²The Holy Spirit told me to go with them and not to worry. Then six of the Lord's followers went with me to the home of a man ¹³who told us that an angel had appeared to him. The angel had ordered him to send to Joppa for someone named Simon Peter. ¹⁴Then Peter would tell him how he and everyone in his house could be saved.

¹⁵After I started speaking, the Holy Spirit was given to them, just as the Spirit had been given to us at the beginning. ¹⁶I remembered that the Lord had said, "John baptized with water, but you will be baptized with the Holy Spirit." ¹⁷God gave those Gentiles the same gift that he gave us when we put our faith in the Lord Jesus Christ. So how could I have gone against God?

¹⁸When they heard Peter say this, they stopped arguing and started praising God. They said, "God has now let Gentiles turn to him, and he has given life to them!"

---

[i] 10.37 *what happened*: Or "the message that went."
[j] 11.8 *unclean and not fit to eat*: See the note at 10.14.

The Church in Antioch

[19] Some of the Lord's followers had been scattered because of the terrible trouble that started when Stephen was killed. They went as far as Phoenicia, Cyprus, and Antioch, but they told the message only to the Jews.

[20] Some of the followers from Cyprus and Cyrene went to Antioch and started telling Gentiles[k] the good news about the Lord Jesus. [21] The Lord's power was with them, and many people turned to the Lord and put their faith in him. [22] News of what was happening reached the church in Jerusalem. Then they sent Barnabas to Antioch.

[23] When Barnabas got there and saw what God had been kind enough to do for them, he was very glad. So he begged them to remain faithful to the Lord with all their hearts. [24] Barnabas was a good man of great faith, and he was filled with the Holy Spirit. Many more people turned to the Lord.

[25] Barnabas went to Tarsus to look for Saul. [26] He found Saul and brought him to Antioch, where they met with the church for a whole year and taught many of its people. There in Antioch the Lord's followers were first called Christians.

[27] During this time some prophets from Jerusalem came to Antioch. [28] One of them was Agabus. Then with the help of the Spirit, he told that there would be a terrible famine everywhere in the world. And it happened when Claudius was Emperor.[l] [29] The followers in Antioch decided to send whatever help they could to the followers in Judea. [30] So they had Barnabas and Saul take their gifts to the church leaders in Jerusalem.

Herod Causes Trouble for the Church

12 At that time King Herod[m] caused terrible suffering for some members of the church. [2] He ordered soldiers to cut off the head of James, the brother of John. [3] When Herod saw that this pleased the Jewish people, he had Peter arrested during the Festival of Thin Bread. [4] He put Peter in jail and ordered four squads of soldiers to guard him. Herod planned to put him on trial in public after the festival.

[5] While Peter was being kept in jail, the church never stopped praying to God for him.

Peter Is Rescued

[6] The night before Peter was to be put on trial, he was asleep and bound by two chains. A soldier was guarding him on each side, and two other soldiers were guarding the entrance to the jail. [7] Suddenly an angel from the Lord appeared, and light flashed around in the cell. The angel poked Peter in the side and woke him up. Then he said, "Quick! Get up!"

The chains fell off his hands, [8] and the angel said, "Get dressed and put on your sandals." Peter did what he was told. Then the angel said, "Now put on your coat and follow me." [9] Peter left with the angel, but he thought everything was only a dream. [10] They went past the two groups of soldiers, and when they came to the iron gate to the city, it opened by itself. They went out and were going along the street, when all at once the angel disappeared.

[11] Peter now realized what had happened, and he said, "I am certain that the Lord sent his angel to rescue me from Herod and from everything the Jewish leaders planned to do to me." [12] Then Peter went to the house of Mary the mother of John whose other name was Mark. Many of the Lord's followers had come together there and were praying.

[13] Peter knocked on the gate, and a servant named Rhoda came to answer. [14] When she heard Peter's voice, she was too excited to open the gate. She ran back into the house and said that Peter was standing there.

[15] "You are crazy!" everyone told her. But she kept saying that it was Peter. Then they said, "It must be his angel."[n] [16] But Peter kept on knocking, until finally they opened the gate. They saw him and were completely amazed.

[17] Peter motioned for them to keep quiet. Then he told how the Lord had led him out of jail. He also said, "Tell James[o] and the others what has happened." After that, he left and went somewhere else.

[18] The next morning the soldiers who had been on guard were terribly worried and wondered what had happened to Peter. [19] Herod ordered his own soldiers to search for him, but they could not find him. Then he questioned the guards and had them put to death. After this, Herod left Judea to stay in Caesarea for a while.

---

[k] 11.20 *Gentiles*: This translates a Greek word that may mean "people who speak Greek" or "people who live as Greeks do." Here the word seems to mean "people who are not Jews." Some manuscripts have "Greeks," which also seems to mean "people who are not Jews."
[l] 11.28 *when Claudius was Emperor*: A.D. 41-54.   [m] 12.1 *Herod*: Herod Agrippa I, the grandson of Herod the Great.   [n] 12.15 *his angel*: Probably meaning "his guardian angel."
[o] 12.17 *James*: The brother of the Lord.

Herod Dies

[20] Herod and the people of Tyre and Sidon were very angry with each other. But their country got its food supply from the region that he ruled. So a group of them went to see Blastus, who was one of Herod's high officials. They convinced Blastus that they wanted to make peace between their cities and Herod, [21] and a day was set for them to meet with him.

Herod came dressed in his royal robes. He sat down on his throne and made a speech. [22] The people shouted, "You speak more like a god than a man!" [23] At once an angel from the Lord struck him down because he took the honor that belonged to God. Later, Herod was eaten by worms and died.

[24] God's message kept spreading. [25] And after Barnabas and Saul had done the work they were sent to do, they went back to Jerusalem[p] with John, whose other name was Mark.

Barnabas and Saul Are Chosen and Sent

13 The church at Antioch had several prophets and teachers. They were Barnabas, Simeon, also called Niger, Lucius from Cyrene, Manaen, who was Herod's[q] close friend, and Saul. [2] While they were worshiping the Lord and going without eating,[r] the Holy Spirit told them, "Appoint Barnabas and Saul to do the work for which I have chosen them." [3] Everyone prayed and went without eating for a while longer. Next, they placed their hands on Barnabas and Saul to show that they had been appointed to do this work. Then everyone sent them on their way.

Barnabas and Saul in Cyprus

[4] After Barnabas and Saul had been sent by the Holy Spirit, they went to Seleucia. From there they sailed to the island of Cyprus. [5] They arrived at Salamis and began to preach God's message in the Jewish meeting places. They also had John[s] as a helper.

[6] Barnabas and Saul went all the way to the city of Paphos on the other end of the island, where they met a Jewish man named Bar-Jesus. He practiced witchcraft and was a false prophet. [7] He also worked for Sergius Paulus, who was very smart and was the governor of the island. Sergius Paulus wanted to hear God's message, and he sent for Barnabas and Saul. [8] But Bar-Jesus, whose other name was Elymas, was against them. He even tried to keep the governor from having faith in the Lord.

[9] Then Saul, better known as Paul, was filled with the Holy Spirit. He looked straight at Elymas [10] and said, "You son of the devil! You are a liar, a crook, and an enemy of everything that is right. When will you stop speaking against the true ways of the Lord? [11] The Lord is going to punish you by making you completely blind for a while."

Suddenly the man's eyes were covered by a dark mist, and he went around trying to get someone to lead him by the hand. [12] When the governor saw what had happened, he was amazed at this teaching about the Lord. So he put his faith in the Lord.

Paul and Barnabas in Antioch of Pisidia

[13] Paul and the others left Paphos and sailed to Perga in Pamphylia. But John[s] left them and went back to Jerusalem. [14] The rest of them went on from Perga to Antioch in Pisidia. Then on the Sabbath they went to the Jewish meeting place and sat down.

[15] After the reading of the Law and the Prophets,[t] the leaders sent someone over to tell Paul and Barnabas, "Friends, if you have anything to say that will help the people, please say it."

[16] Paul got up. He motioned with his hand and said:

People of Israel, and everyone else who worships God, listen! [17] The God of Israel chose our ancestors, and he let our people prosper while they were living in Egypt. Then with his mighty power he led them out, [18] and for about forty years he took care of[u] them in the desert. [19] He destroyed seven nations in the land of Canaan and gave their land to our people. [20] All this happened in about 450 years.

Then God gave our people judges until the time of the prophet Samuel, [21] but the people demanded a king. So for forty years God gave them King Saul, the son of Kish from the tribe of Benjamin. [22] Later, God removed Saul and let David rule in his place. God said about him, "David the son of Jesse is the kind of person who pleases me most! He does everything I want him to do."

[23] God promised that someone

---

[p]12.25 *went back to Jerusalem*: Some manuscripts have "left Jerusalem," and others have "went to Antioch."   [q]13.1 *Herod's*: Herod Antipas, the son of Herod the Great.   [r]13.2 *going without eating*: The Jews often went without eating as a way of showing how much they loved God. This is also called "fasting."   [s]13.5,13 *John*: Whose other name was Mark (see 12.12, 25).   [t]13.15 *the Law and the Prophets*: The Jewish Scriptures, that is, the Old Testament.   [u]13.18 *took care of*: Some manuscripts have "put up with."

from David's family would come to save the people of Israel, and that one is Jesus. ²⁴But before Jesus came, John was telling everyone in Israel to turn back to God and be baptized. ²⁵Then, when John's work was almost done, he said, "Who do you people think I am? Do you think I am the Promised One? He will come later, and I am not good enough to untie his sandals."

²⁶Now listen, you descendants of Abraham! Pay attention, all of you Gentiles who are here to worship God! Listen to this message about how to be saved, because it is for everyone. ²⁷The people of Jerusalem and their leaders didn't realize who Jesus was. And they didn't understand the words of the prophets that they read each Sabbath. So they condemned Jesus just as the prophets had said.

²⁸⁻²⁹They did exactly what the Scriptures said they would. Even though they couldn't find any reason to put Jesus to death, they still asked Pilate to have him killed.

After Jesus had been put to death, he was taken down from the cross[v] and placed in a tomb. ³⁰But God raised him from death! ³¹Then for many days Jesus appeared to his followers who had gone with him from Galilee to Jerusalem. Now they are telling our people about him.

³²God made a promise to our ancestors. And we are here to tell you the good news ³³that he has kept this promise to us. It is just as the second Psalm says about Jesus,

"You are my son because today
   I have become your Father."

³⁴God raised Jesus from death and will never let his body decay. It is just as God said,

"I will make to you
the same holy promise
   that I made to David."

³⁵And in another psalm it says, "God will never let the body of his Holy One decay."

³⁶When David was alive, he obeyed God. Then after he died, he was buried in the family grave, and his body decayed. ³⁷But God raised Jesus from death, and his body did not decay.

³⁸My friends, the message is that Jesus can forgive your sins! The Law of Moses could not set you free from all your sins. ³⁹But everyone who has faith in Jesus is set free. ⁴⁰Make sure that what the prophets have said doesn't happen to you. They said,

⁴¹ "Look, you people
   who make fun of God!
Be amazed
   and disappear.
I will do something today
   that you won't believe,
even if someone
   tells you about it!"

⁴²As Paul and Barnabas were leaving the meeting, the people begged them to say more about these same things on the next Sabbath. ⁴³After the service, many Jews and a lot of Gentiles who worshiped God went with them. Paul and Barnabas begged them all to remain faithful to God, who had been so kind to them.

⁴⁴The next Sabbath almost everyone in town came to hear the message about the Lord.[w] ⁴⁵When the Jewish people saw the crowds, they were very jealous. They insulted Paul and spoke against everything he said.

⁴⁶But Paul and Barnabas bravely said:
We had to tell God's message to you before we told it to anyone else. But you rejected the message! This proves that you don't deserve eternal life. Now we are going to the Gentiles. ⁴⁷The Lord has given us this command,

"I have placed you here
as a light
   for the Gentiles.
You are to take
   the saving power of God
to people everywhere on earth."

⁴⁸This message made the Gentiles glad, and they praised what they had heard about the Lord.[w] Everyone who had been chosen for eternal life then put their faith in the Lord.

⁴⁹The message about the Lord spread all over that region. ⁵⁰But the Jewish leaders went to some of the important men in the town and to some respected women who were religious. They turned them against Paul and Barnabas and started making trouble for them. They even chased them out of that part of the country.

⁵¹Paul and Barnabas shook the dust from that place off their feet[x] and went on to the city of Iconium.

⁵²But the Lord's followers in Antioch

---

[v]**13.28,29** *cross:* This translates a Greek word that means "wood," "pole," or "tree."
[w]**13.44,48** *the Lord:* Some manuscripts have "God."   [x]**13.51** *shook the dust from that place off their feet:* This was a way of showing rejection.

were very happy and were filled with the Holy Spirit.

Paul and Barnabas in Iconium

14 Paul and Barnabas spoke in the Jewish meeting place in Iconium, just as they had done at Antioch, and many Jews and Gentiles[y] put their faith in the Lord. [2]But the Jews who did not have faith in him made the other Gentiles angry and turned them against the Lord's followers.

[3]Paul and Barnabas stayed there for a while, having faith in the Lord and bravely speaking his message. The Lord gave them the power to work miracles and wonders, and he showed that their message about his great kindness was true.

[4]The people of Iconium did not know what to think. Some of them believed the Jewish group, and others believed the apostles. [5]Finally, some Gentiles and Jews, together with their leaders, decided to make trouble for Paul and Barnabas and to stone them to death.

[6-7]But when the two apostles found out what was happening, they escaped to the region of Lycaonia. They preached the good news there in the towns of Lystra and Derbe and in the nearby countryside.

Paul and Barnabas in Lystra

[8]In Lystra there was a man who had been born with crippled feet and had never been able to walk. [9]The man was listening to Paul speak, when Paul saw that he had faith in Jesus and could be healed. So he looked straight at the man [10]and shouted, "Stand up!" The man jumped up and started walking around.

[11]When the crowd saw what Paul had done, they yelled out in the language of Lycaonia, "The gods have turned into humans and have come down to us!" [12]The people then gave Barnabas the name Zeus, and they gave Paul the name Hermes,[z] because he did the talking.

[13]The temple of Zeus was near the entrance to the city. Its priest and the crowds wanted to offer a sacrifice to Barnabas and Paul. So the priest brought some bulls and flowers to the city gates. [14]When the two apostles found out about this, they tore their clothes in horror and ran to the crowd, shouting:

[15]Why are you doing this? We are humans just like you. Please give up all this foolishness. Turn to the living God, who made the sky, the earth, the sea, and everything in them. [16]In times past, God let each nation go its own way. [17]But he showed that he was there by the good things he did. God sends rain from heaven and makes your crops grow. He gives food to you and makes your hearts glad.

[18]Even after Paul and Barnabas had said all this, they could hardly keep the people from offering a sacrifice to them.

[19]Some Jewish leaders from Antioch and Iconium came and turned the crowds against Paul. They hit him with stones and dragged him out of the city, thinking he was dead. [20]But when the Lord's followers gathered around Paul, he stood up and went back into the city. The next day he and Barnabas went to Derbe.

Paul and Barnabas Return to Antioch in Syria

[21]Paul and Barnabas preached the good news in Derbe and won some people to the Lord. Then they went back to Lystra, Iconium, and Antioch in Pisidia. [22]They encouraged the followers and begged them to remain faithful. They told them, "We have to suffer a lot before we can get into God's kingdom." [23]Paul and Barnabas chose some leaders for each of the churches. Then they went without eating[a] and prayed that the Lord would take good care of these leaders.

[24]Paul and Barnabas went on through Pisidia to Pamphylia, [25]where they preached in the town of Perga. Then they went down to Attalia [26]and sailed to Antioch in Syria. It was there that they had been placed in God's care for the work they had now completed.[b]

[27]After arriving in Antioch, they called the church together. They told the people what God had helped them do and how he had made it possible for the Gentiles to believe. [28]Then they stayed there with the followers for a long time.

15 Some people came from Judea and started teaching the Lord's followers that they could not be saved, unless they were circumcised as Moses had taught. [2]This caused trouble, and Paul and Barnabas argued with them about this teaching. So it was decided to send Paul and Barnabas and a few others to Jerusalem to discuss this problem with the apostles and the church leaders.

---

[y]14.1 *Gentiles*: The Greek text has "Greeks," which probably means people who were not Jews. But it may mean Gentiles who worshiped with the Jews.   [z]14.12 *Hermes*: The Greeks thought of Hermes as the messenger of the other gods, especially of Zeus, their chief god.
[a]14.23 *went without eating*: See the note at 13.2.   [b]14.26 *the work they had now completed*: See 13.1-3.

The Church Leaders Meet in Jerusalem

³The men who were sent by the church went through Phoenicia and Samaria, telling how the Gentiles had turned to God. This news made the Lord's followers very happy. ⁴When the men arrived in Jerusalem, they were welcomed by the church, including the apostles and the leaders. They told them everything God had helped them do. ⁵But some Pharisees had become followers of the Lord. They stood up and said, "Gentiles who have faith in the Lord must be circumcised and told to obey the Law of Moses."

⁶The apostles and church leaders met to discuss this problem about Gentiles. ⁷They had talked it over for a long time, when Peter got up and said:

My friends, you know that God decided long ago to let me be the one from your group to preach the good news to the Gentiles. God did this so that they would hear and obey him. ⁸He knows what is in everyone's heart. And he showed that he had chosen the Gentiles, when he gave them the Holy Spirit, just as he had given his Spirit to us. ⁹God treated them in the same way that he treated us. They put their faith in him, and he made their hearts pure.

¹⁰Now why are you trying to make God angry by placing a heavy burden on these followers? This burden was too heavy for us or our ancestors. ¹¹But our Lord Jesus was kind to us, and we are saved by faith in him, just as the Gentiles are.

¹²Everyone kept quiet and listened as Barnabas and Paul told how God had given them the power to work a lot of miracles and wonders for the Gentiles. ¹³After they had finished speaking, James[c] said:

My friends, listen to me! ¹⁴Simon Peter[d] has told how God first came to the Gentiles and made some of them his own people. ¹⁵This agrees with what the prophets wrote,

¹⁶ "I, the Lord, will return
    and rebuild
        David's fallen house.
I will build it from its ruins
    and set it up again.
¹⁷ Then other nations
    will turn to me
        and be my chosen ones.
    I, the Lord, say this.
¹⁸   I promised it long ago."

¹⁹And so, my friends, I don't think we should place burdens on the Gentiles who are turning to God. ²⁰We should simply write and tell them not to eat anything that has been offered to idols. They should be told not to eat the meat of any animal that has been strangled or that still has blood in it. They must also not commit any terrible sexual sins.[e]

²¹We must remember that the Law of Moses has been preached in city after city for many years, and every Sabbath it is read when we Jews meet.

A Letter to Gentiles Who Had Faith in the Lord

²²The apostles, the leaders, and all the church members decided to send some men to Antioch along with Paul and Barnabas. They chose Silas and Judas Barsabbas,[f] who were two leaders of the Lord's followers. ²³They wrote a letter that said:

We apostles and leaders send friendly greetings to all of you Gentiles who are followers of the Lord in Antioch, Syria, and Cilicia. ²⁴We have heard that some people from here have terribly upset you by what they said. But we did not send them! ²⁵So we met together and decided to choose some men and to send them to you along with our good friends Barnabas and Paul. ²⁶These men have risked their lives for our Lord Jesus Christ. ²⁷We are also sending Judas and Silas, who will tell you in person the same things that we are writing.

²⁸The Holy Spirit has shown us that we should not place any extra burden on you. ²⁹But you should not eat anything offered to idols. You should not eat any meat that still has the blood in it or any meat of any animal that has been strangled. You must also not commit any terrible sexual sins. If you follow these instructions, you will do well.

We send our best wishes.

³⁰The four men left Jerusalem and went to Antioch. Then they called the church members together and gave them the letter. ³¹When the letter was read, everyone was pleased and greatly encouraged. ³²Judas and Silas were prophets, and they spoke a long time, encouraging and helping the Lord's followers.

³³The men from Jerusalem stayed on

---

[c] *15.13 James*: The Lord's brother.   [d] *15.14 Simon Peter*: The Greek text has "Simeon," which is another form of the name "Simon." The apostle Peter is meant.   [e] *15.20 not commit any terrible sexual sins*: This probably refers to the laws about the wrong kind of marriages that are forbidden in Leviticus 18.6-18 or to some serious sexual sin.   [f] *15.22 Judas Barsabbas*: He may have been a brother of Joseph Barsabbas (see 1.23), but the name "Barsabbas" was often used by the Jewish people.

Acts 15.34-35

in Antioch for a while. And when they left to return to the ones who had sent them, the followers wished them well. ³⁴⁻³⁵But Paul and Barnabas stayed on in Antioch, where they and many others taught and preached about the Lord.ᵍ

Paul and Barnabas Go Their Separate Ways

³⁶Sometime later Paul said to Barnabas, "Let's go back and visit the Lord's followers in the cities where we preached his message. Then we will know how they are doing." ³⁷Barnabas wanted to take along John, whose other name was Mark. ³⁸But Paul did not want to, because Mark had left them in Pamphylia and had stopped working with them.

³⁹Paul and Barnabas argued, then each of them went his own way. Barnabas took Mark and sailed to Cyprus, ⁴⁰but Paul took Silas and left after the followers had placed them in God's care. ⁴¹They traveled through Syria and Cilicia, encouraging the churches.

Timothy Works with Paul and Silas

16 Paul and Silas went back to Derbe and Lystra, where there was a follower named Timothy. His mother was also a follower. She was Jewish, and his father was Greek. ²The Lord's followers in Lystra and Iconium said good things about Timothy, ³and Paul wanted him to go with them. But Paul first had him circumcised, because all the Jewish people around there knew that Timothy's father was Greek.ʰ

⁴As Paul and the others went from city to city, they told the followers what the apostles and leaders in Jerusalem had decided, and they urged them to follow these instructions. ⁵The churches became stronger in their faith, and each day more people put their faith in the Lord.

Paul's Vision in Troas

⁶Paul and his friends went through Phrygia and Galatia, but the Holy Spirit would not let them preach in Asia. ⁷After they arrived in Mysia, they tried to go into Bithynia, but the Spirit of Jesus would not let them. ⁸So they went on throughⁱ Mysia until they came to Troas. ⁹During the night, Paul had a vision of someone from Macedonia who was standing there and begging him, "Come over to Macedonia and help us!" ¹⁰After Paul had seen the vision, we began looking for a way to go to Macedonia. We were sure that God had called us to preach the good news there.

Lydia Becomes a Follower of the Lord

¹¹We sailed straight from Troas to Samothrace, and the next day we arrived in Neapolis. ¹²From there we went to Philippi, which is a Roman colony in the first district of Macedonia.ʲ

We spent several days in Philippi. ¹³Then on the Sabbath we went outside the city gate to a place by the river, where we thought there would be a Jewish meeting place for prayer. We sat down and talked with the women who came. ¹⁴One of them was Lydia, who was from the city of Thyatira and sold expensive purple cloth. She was a worshiper of the Lord God, and he made her willing to accept what Paul was saying. ¹⁵Then after she and her family were baptized, she kept on begging us, "If you think I really do have faith in the Lord, come stay in my home." Finally, we accepted her invitation.

Paul and Silas Are Put in Jail

¹⁶One day on our way to the place of prayer, we were met by a slave girl. She had a spirit in her that gave her the power to tell the future. By doing this she made a lot of money for her owners. ¹⁷The girl followed Paul and the rest of us and kept yelling, "These men are servants of the Most High God! They are telling you how to be saved."

¹⁸This went on for several days. Finally, Paul got so upset that he turned and said to the spirit, "In the name of Jesus Christ, I order you to leave this girl alone!" At once the evil spirit left her.

¹⁹When the girl's owners realized that they had lost all chances for making more money, they grabbed Paul and Silas and dragged them into court. ²⁰They told the officials, "These Jews are upsetting our city! ²¹They are telling us to do things we Romans are not allowed to do."

²²The crowd joined in the attack on Paul and Silas. Then the officials tore the clothes off the two men and ordered them to be beaten with a whip. ²³After they had been badly beaten, they were put in jail, and the jailer was told to guard them carefully. ²⁴The jailer did as he was told. He put them deep inside the jail and chained their feet to heavy blocks of wood.

²⁵About midnight Paul and Silas were praying and singing praises to God, while the other prisoners listened.

ᵍ**15.34,35** Verse 34, which says that Silas decided to stay on in Antioch, is not in some manuscripts.   ʰ**16.3** *had him circumcised . . . Timothy's father was Greek*: Timothy would not have been acceptable to the Jews unless he had been circumcised, and Greeks did not circumcise their sons.   ⁱ**16.8** *went on through*: Or "passed by."   ʲ**16.12** *in the first district of Macedonia*: Some manuscripts have "and the leading city of Macedonia."

²⁶Suddenly a strong earthquake shook the jail to its foundations. The doors opened, and the chains fell from all the prisoners.

²⁷When the jailer woke up and saw that the doors were open, he thought that the prisoners had escaped. He pulled out his sword and was about to kill himself. ²⁸But Paul shouted, "Don't harm yourself! No one has escaped."

²⁹The jailer asked for a torch and went into the jail. He was shaking all over as he knelt down in front of Paul and Silas. ³⁰After he had led them out of the jail, he asked, "What must I do to be saved?"

³¹They replied, "Have faith in the Lord Jesus and you will be saved! This is also true for everyone who lives in your home."

³²Then Paul and Silas told him and everyone else in his house about the Lord. ³³While it was still night, the jailer took them to a place where he could wash their cuts and bruises. Then he and everyone in his home were baptized. ³⁴They were very glad that they had put their faith in God. After this, the jailer took Paul and Silas to his home and gave them something to eat.

³⁵The next morning the officials sent some police with orders for the jailer to let Paul and Silas go. ³⁶The jailer told Paul, "The officials have ordered me to set you free. Now you can leave in peace."

³⁷But Paul told the police, "We are Roman citizens,[k] and the Roman officials had us beaten in public without giving us a trial. They threw us into jail. Now do they think they can secretly send us away? No, they cannot! They will have to come here themselves and let us out."

³⁸When the police told the officials that Paul and Silas were Roman citizens, the officials were afraid. ³⁹So they came and apologized. They led them out of the jail and asked them to please leave town. ⁴⁰But Paul and Silas went straight to the home of Lydia, where they saw the Lord's followers and encouraged them. Then they left.

Trouble in Thessalonica

17 After Paul and his friends had traveled through Amphipolis and Apollonia, they went on to Thessalonica. A Jewish meeting place was in that city. ²So as usual, Paul went there to worship, and on three Sabbaths he spoke to the people. He used the Scriptures ³to show them that the Messiah had to suffer, but that he would rise from death. Paul also told them that Jesus is the Messiah he was preaching about. ⁴Some of them believed what Paul had said, and they became followers with Paul and Silas. Some Gentiles[l] and many important women also believed the message.

⁵The Jewish leaders were jealous and got some worthless bums who hung around the marketplace to start a riot in the city. They wanted to drag Paul and Silas out to the mob, and so they went straight to Jason's home. ⁶But when they did not find them there, they dragged out Jason and some of the Lord's followers. They took them to the city authorities and shouted, "Paul and Silas have been upsetting things everywhere. Now they have come here, ⁷and Jason has welcomed them into his home. All of them break the laws of the Roman Emperor by claiming that someone named Jesus is king."

⁸The officials and the people were upset when they heard this. ⁹So they made Jason and the other followers pay bail before letting them go.

People in Berea Welcome the Message

¹⁰That same night the Lord's followers sent Paul and Silas on to Berea, and after they arrived, they went to the Jewish meeting place. ¹¹The people in Berea were much nicer than those in Thessalonica, and they gladly accepted the message. Day after day they studied the Scriptures to see if these things were true. ¹²Many of them put their faith in the Lord, including some important Greek women and several men.

¹³When the Jewish leaders in Thessalonica heard that Paul had been preaching God's message in Berea, they went there and caused trouble by turning the crowds against Paul.

¹⁴Right away the followers sent Paul down to the coast, but Silas and Timothy stayed in Berea. ¹⁵Some men went with Paul as far as Athens, and then returned with instructions for Silas and Timothy to join him as soon as possible.

Paul in Athens

¹⁶While Paul was waiting in Athens, he was upset to see all the idols in the city. ¹⁷He went to the Jewish meeting place to speak to the Jews and to anyone who worshiped with them. Day after day he also spoke to everyone he met in the market. ¹⁸Some of them were Epicureans[m] and some were

---

[k] 16.37 *Roman citizens*: Only a small number of the people living in the Roman Empire were citizens, and they had special rights and privileges.   [l] 17.4 *Gentiles*: See the note at 14.1.
[m] 17.18 *Epicureans*: People who followed the teaching of a man named Epicurus, who taught that happiness should be the main goal in life.

Stoics,[n] and they started arguing with him.

People were asking, "What is this know-it-all trying to say?"

Some even said, "Paul must be preaching about foreign gods! That's what he means when he talks about Jesus and about people rising from death."[o]

[19] They brought Paul before a council called the Areopagus, and said, "Tell us what your new teaching is all about. [20] We have heard you say some strange things, and we want to know what you mean."

[21] More than anything else the people of Athens and the foreigners living there loved to hear and to talk about anything new. [22] So Paul stood up in front of the council and said:

People of Athens, I see that you are very religious. [23] As I was going through your city and looking at the things you worship, I found an altar with the words, "To an Unknown God." You worship this God, but you don't really know him. So I want to tell you about him. [24] This God made the world and everything in it. He is Lord of heaven and earth, and he doesn't live in temples built by human hands. [25] He doesn't need help from anyone. He gives life, breath, and everything else to all people. [26] From one person God made all nations who live on earth, and he decided when and where every nation would be.

[27] God has done all this, so that we will look for him and reach out and find him. He isn't far from any of us, [28] and he gives us the power to live, to move, and to be who we are. "We are his children," just as some of your poets have said.

[29] Since we are God's children, we must not think that he is like an idol made out of gold or silver or stone. He isn't like anything that humans have thought up and made. [30] In the past, God forgave all this because people did not know what they were doing. But now he says that everyone everywhere must turn to him. [31] He has set a day when he will judge the world's people with fairness. And he has chosen the man Jesus to do the judging for him. God has given proof of this to all of us by raising Jesus from death.

[32] As soon as the people heard Paul say that a man had been raised from death, some of them started laughing. Others said, "We will hear you talk about this some other time." [33] When Paul left the council meeting, [34] some of the men put their faith in the Lord and went with Paul. One of them was a council member named Dionysius. A woman named Damaris and several others also put their faith in the Lord.

Paul in Corinth

18 Paul left Athens and went to Corinth, [2] where he met Aquila, a Jewish man from Pontus. Not long before this, Aquila had come from Italy with his wife Priscilla, because Emperor Claudius had ordered the Jewish people to leave Rome.[p] Paul went to see Aquila and Priscilla [3] and found out that they were tent makers. Paul was a tent maker too. So he stayed with them, and they worked together.

[4] Every Sabbath, Paul went to the Jewish meeting place. He spoke to Jews and Gentiles[q] and tried to win them over. [5] But after Silas and Timothy came from Macedonia, he spent all his time preaching to the Jews about Jesus the Messiah. [6] Finally, they turned against him and insulted him. So he shook the dust from his clothes[r] and told them, "Whatever happens to you will be your own fault! I am not to blame. From now on I am going to preach to the Gentiles."

[7] Paul then moved into the house of a man named Titius Justus, who worshiped God and lived next door to the Jewish meeting place. [8] Crispus was the leader of the meeting place. He and everyone in his family put their faith in the Lord. Many others in Corinth also heard the message, and all the people who had faith in the Lord were baptized.

[9] One night, Paul had a vision, and in it the Lord said, "Don't be afraid to keep on preaching. Don't stop! [10] I am with you, and you won't be harmed. Many people in this city belong to me." [11] Paul stayed on in Corinth for a year and a half, teaching God's message to the people.

[12] While Gallio was governor of Achaia, some of the Jewish leaders got together and grabbed Paul. They brought him into court [13] and said, "This man is trying to make our people worship God in a way that is against our Law!"

[14] Even before Paul could speak, Gallio said, "If you were charging this man

---

[n] **17.18** *Stoics*: Followers of a man named Zeno, who taught that people should learn self-control and be guided by their consciences. [o] **17.18** *people rising from death*: Or "a goddess named 'Rising from Death.'" [p] **18.2** *Emperor Claudius had ordered all the Jewish people to leave Rome*: Probably A.D. 49, though it may have been A.D. 41. [q] **18.4** *Gentiles*: Here the word is "Greeks." But see the note at 14.1. [r] **18.6** *shook the dust from his clothes*: This means the same as shaking dust from the feet (see the note at 13.51).

with a crime or some other wrong, I would have to listen to you. ¹⁵But since this concerns only words, names, and your own law, you will have to take care of it. I refuse to judge such matters." ¹⁶Then he sent them out of the court. ¹⁷The crowd grabbed Sosthenes, the Jewish leader, and beat him up in front of the court. But none of this mattered to Gallio.

Paul Returns to Antioch in Syria

¹⁸After Paul had stayed for a while with the Lord's followers in Corinth, he told them good-by and sailed on to Syria with Aquila and Priscilla. But before he left, he had his head shaved*s* at Cenchreae because he had made a promise to God.

¹⁹The three of them arrived in Ephesus, where Paul left Priscilla and Aquila. He then went into the Jewish meeting place to talk with the people there. ²⁰They asked him to stay longer, but he refused. ²¹He told them good-by and said, "If God lets me, I will come back."

²²Paul sailed to Caesarea, where he greeted the church. Then he went on to Antioch. ²³After staying there for a while, he left and visited several places in Galatia and Phrygia. He helped the followers there to become stronger in their faith.

Apollos in Ephesus

²⁴A Jewish man named Apollos came to Ephesus. Apollos had been born in the city of Alexandria. He was a very good speaker and knew a lot about the Scriptures. ²⁵He also knew much about the Lord's Way,*t* and he spoke about it with great excitement. What he taught about Jesus was right, but all he knew was John's message about baptism.

²⁶Apollos started speaking bravely in the Jewish meeting place. But when Priscilla and Aquila heard him, they took him to their home and helped him understand God's Way even better.

²⁷Apollos decided to travel through Achaia. So the Lord's followers wrote letters, encouraging the followers there to welcome him. After Apollos arrived in Achaia, he was a great help to everyone who had put their faith in the Lord Jesus because of God's kindness. ²⁸He got into fierce arguments with the Jewish people, and in public he used the Scriptures to prove that Jesus is the Messiah.

Paul in Ephesus

19 While Apollos was in Corinth, Paul traveled across the hill country to Ephesus, where he met some of the Lord's followers. ²He asked them, "When you put your faith in Jesus, were you given the Holy Spirit?"

"No!" they answered. "We have never even heard of the Holy Spirit."

³"Then why were you baptized?" Paul asked.

They answered, "Because of what John taught."*u*

⁴Paul replied, "John baptized people so that they would turn to God. But he also told them that someone else was coming, and that they should put their faith in him. Jesus is the one that John was talking about." ⁵After the people heard Paul say this, they were baptized in the name of the Lord Jesus. ⁶Then Paul placed his hands on them. The Holy Spirit was given to them, and they spoke unknown languages and prophesied. ⁷There were about twelve men in this group.

⁸For three months Paul went to the Jewish meeting place and talked bravely with the people about God's kingdom. He tried to win them over, ⁹but some of them were stubborn and refused to believe. In front of everyone they said terrible things about God's Way. Paul left and took the followers with him to the lecture hall of Tyrannus. He spoke there every day ¹⁰for two years, until every Jew and Gentile*v* in Asia had heard the Lord's message.

The Sons of Sceva

¹¹God gave Paul the power to work great miracles. ¹²People even took handkerchiefs and aprons that had touched Paul's body, and they carried them to everyone who was sick. All of the sick people were healed, and the evil spirits went out.

¹³Some Jewish men started going around trying to force out evil spirits by using the name of the Lord Jesus. They said to the spirits, "Come out in the name of that same Jesus that Paul preaches about!"

¹⁴Seven sons of a Jewish high priest named Sceva were doing this, ¹⁵when an evil spirit said to them, "I know Jesus! And I have heard about Paul. But who are you?" ¹⁶Then the man with the evil spirit jumped on them and beat them up. They ran out of the house, naked and bruised.

---

*s***18.18** *he had his head shaved*: Paul had promised to be a "Nazirite" for a while. This meant that for the time of the promise, he could not cut his hair or drink wine. When the time was over, he would have to cut his hair and offer a sacrifice to God.   *t***18.25** *the Lord's Way*: See the note at 9.2.   *u***19.3** *Then why were you baptized? . . . Because of what John taught*: Or "In whose name were you baptized? . . . We were baptized in John's name."
*v***19.10,17** *Gentile(s)*: The text has "Greek(s)" (see the note at 14.1).

[17] When the Jews and Gentiles[v] in Ephesus heard about this, they were so frightened that they praised the name of the Lord Jesus. [18] Many who were followers now started telling everyone about the evil things they had been doing. [19] Some who had been practicing witchcraft even brought their books and burned them in public. These books were worth about fifty thousand silver coins. [20] So the Lord's message spread and became even more powerful.

The Riot in Ephesus

[21] After all of this had happened, Paul decided[w] to visit Macedonia and Achaia on his way to Jerusalem. Paul had said, "From there I will go on to Rome." [22] So he sent his two helpers, Timothy and Erastus, to Macedonia. But he stayed on in Asia for a while.

[23] At that time there was serious trouble because of the Lord's Way.[x] [24] A silversmith named Demetrius had a business that made silver models of the temple of the goddess Artemis. Those who worked for him earned a lot of money. [25] Demetrius brought together everyone who was in the same business and said:

Friends, you know that we make a good living at this. [26] But you have surely seen and heard how this man Paul is upsetting a lot of people, not only in Ephesus, but almost everywhere in Asia. He claims that the gods we humans make are not really gods at all. [27] Everyone will start saying terrible things about our business. They will stop respecting the temple of the goddess Artemis, who is worshiped in Asia and all over the world. Our great goddess will be forgotten!

[28] When the workers heard this, they got angry and started shouting, "Great is Artemis, the goddess of the Ephesians!" [29] Soon the whole city was in a riot, and some men grabbed Gaius and Aristarchus, who had come from Macedonia with Paul. Then everyone in the crowd rushed to the place where the town meetings were held.

[30] Paul wanted to go out and speak to the people, but the Lord's followers would not let him. [31] A few of the local officials were friendly to Paul, and they sent someone to warn him not to go.

[32] Some of the people in the meeting were shouting one thing, and others were shouting something else. Everyone was completely confused, and most of them did not even know why they were there.

[33] Several of the Jewish leaders pushed a man named Alexander to the front of the crowd and started telling him what to say. He motioned with his hand and tried to explain what was going on. [34] But when the crowd saw that he was Jewish, they all shouted for two hours, "Great is Artemis, the goddess of the Ephesians!"

[35] Finally, a town official made the crowd be quiet. Then he said:

People of Ephesus, who in the world doesn't know that our city is the center for worshiping the great goddess Artemis? Who doesn't know that her image which fell from heaven is right here? [36] No one can deny this, and so you should calm down and not do anything foolish. [37] You have brought men in here who have not robbed temples or spoken against our goddess.

[38] If Demetrius and his workers have a case against these men, we have courts and judges. Let them take their complaints there. [39] But if you want to do more than that, the matter will have to be brought before the city council. [40] We could easily be accused of starting a riot today. There is no excuse for it! We cannot even give a reason for this uproar.

[41] After saying this, he told the people to leave.

Paul Goes through Macedonia and Greece

20 When the riot was over, Paul sent for the followers and encouraged them. He then told them good-by and left for Macedonia. [2] As he traveled from place to place, he encouraged the followers with many messages. Finally, he went to Greece[y] [3] and stayed there for three months.

Paul was about to sail to Syria. But some of the Jewish leaders plotted against him, so he decided to return by way of Macedonia. [4] With him were Sopater, son of Pyrrhus from Berea, and Aristarchus and Secundus from Thessalonica. Gaius from Derbe was also with him, and so were Timothy and the two Asians, Tychicus and Trophimus. [5] They went on ahead to Troas and waited for us there. [6] After the Festival of Thin Bread, we sailed from Philippi. Five days later we met them in Troas and stayed there for a week.

---

[v] **19.10,17** *Gentile(s)*: The text has "Greek(s)" (see the note at 14.1).   [w] **19.21** *Paul decided*: Or "Paul was led by the Holy Spirit."   [x] **19.23** *the Lord's Way*: See the note at 9.2.
[y] **20.2** *Greece*: Probably Corinth.

Paul's Last Visit to Troas

⁷On the first day of the week[z] we met to break bread together.[a] Paul spoke to the people until midnight because he was leaving the next morning. ⁸In the upstairs room where we were meeting, there were a lot of lamps. ⁹A young man by the name of Eutychus was sitting on a window sill. While Paul was speaking, the young man got very sleepy. Finally, he went to sleep and fell three floors all the way down to the ground. When they picked him up, he was dead.

¹⁰Paul went down and bent over Eutychus. He took him in his arms and said, "Don't worry! He's alive." ¹¹After Paul had gone back upstairs, he broke bread, and ate with us. He then spoke until dawn and left. ¹²Then the followers took the young man home alive and were very happy.

The Voyage from Troas to Miletus

¹³Paul decided to travel by land to Assos. The rest of us went on ahead by ship, and we were to take him aboard there. ¹⁴When he met us in Assos, he came aboard, and we sailed on to Mitylene. ¹⁵The next day we came to a place near Chios, and the following day we reached Samos. The day after that we sailed to Miletus. ¹⁶Paul had decided to sail on past Ephesus, because he did not want to spend too much time in Asia. He was in a hurry and wanted to be in Jerusalem in time for Pentecost.[b]

Paul Says Good-By to the Church Leaders of Ephesus

¹⁷From Miletus, Paul sent a message for the church leaders at Ephesus to come and meet with him. ¹⁸When they got there, he said:

You know everything I did during the time I was with you when I first came to Asia. ¹⁹Some of the Jews plotted against me and caused me a lot of sorrow and trouble. But I served the Lord and was humble. ²⁰When I preached in public or taught in your homes, I didn't hold back from telling anything that would help you. ²¹I told Jews and Gentiles to turn to God and have faith in our Lord Jesus.

²²I don't know what will happen to me in Jerusalem, but I must obey God's Spirit and go there. ²³In every city I visit, I am told by the Holy Spirit that I will be put in jail and will be in trouble in Jerusalem. ²⁴But I don't care what happens to me, as long as I finish the work that the Lord Jesus gave me to do. And that work is to tell the good news about God's great kindness.

²⁵I have gone from place to place, preaching to you about God's kingdom, but now I know that none of you will ever see me again. ²⁶I tell you today that I am no longer responsible for any of you! ²⁷I have told you everything God wants you to know. ²⁸Look after yourselves and everyone the Holy Spirit has placed in your care. Be like shepherds to God's church. It is the flock that he bought with the blood of his own Son.[c]

²⁹I know that after I am gone, others will come like fierce wolves to attack you. ³⁰Some of your own people will tell lies to win over the Lord's followers. ³¹Be on your guard! Remember how day and night for three years I kept warning you with tears in my eyes.

³²I now place you in God's care. Remember the message about his great kindness! This message can help you and give you what belongs to you as God's people. ³³I have never wanted anyone's money or clothes. ³⁴You know how I have worked with my own hands to make a living for myself and my friends. ³⁵By everything I did, I showed how you should work to help everyone who is weak. Remember that our Lord Jesus said, "More blessings come from giving than from receiving."

³⁶After Paul had finished speaking, he knelt down with all of them and prayed. ³⁷Everyone cried and hugged and kissed him. ³⁸They were especially sad because Paul had told them, "You will never see me again."

Then they went with him to the ship.

Paul Goes to Jerusalem

21 After saying good-by, we sailed straight to Cos. The next day we reached Rhodes and from there sailed on to Patara. ²We found a ship going to Phoenicia, so we got on board and sailed off.

³We came within sight of Cyprus and then sailed south of it on to the port of Tyre in Syria, where the ship was going to unload its cargo. ⁴We looked up the Lord's followers and stayed with them for a week. The Holy Spirit had told them to warn Paul not to go on to Jerusalem. ⁵But when the week was

---

[z]**20.7** *On the first day of the week*: Since the Jewish day began at sunset, the meeting would have begun in the evening.   [a]**20.7** *break bread together*: See the note at 2.46.   [b]**20.16** *in time for Pentecost*: The Jewish people liked to be in Jerusalem for this festival (see the note at 2.1).   [c]**20.28** *the blood of his own Son*: Or "his own blood."

over, we started on our way again. All the men, together with their wives and children, walked with us from the town to the seashore. We knelt on the beach and prayed. ⁶Then after saying good-by to each other, we got into the ship, and they went back home.

⁷We sailed from Tyre to Ptolemais, where we greeted the followers and stayed with them for a day. ⁸The next day we went to Caesarea and stayed with Philip, the preacher. He was one of the seven men who helped the apostles, ⁹and he had four unmarried*ᵈ* daughters who prophesied.

¹⁰We had been in Caesarea for several days, when the prophet Agabus came to us from Judea. ¹¹He took Paul's belt, and with it he tied up his own hands and feet. Then he told us, "The Holy Spirit says that some of the Jewish leaders in Jerusalem will tie up the man who owns this belt. They will also hand him over to the Gentiles." ¹²After Agabus said this, we and the followers living there begged Paul not to go to Jerusalem.

¹³But Paul answered, "Why are you crying and breaking my heart? I am not only willing to be put in jail for the Lord Jesus. I am even willing to die for him in Jerusalem!"

¹⁴Since we could not get Paul to change his mind, we gave up and prayed, "Lord, please make us willing to do what you want."

¹⁵Then we got ready to go to Jerusalem. ¹⁶Some of the followers from Caesarea went with us and took us to stay in the home of Mnason. He was from Cyprus and had been a follower from the beginning.

Paul Visits James

¹⁷When we arrived in Jerusalem, the Lord's followers gladly welcomed us. ¹⁸Paul went with us to see James*ᵉ* the next day, and all the church leaders were present. ¹⁹Paul greeted them and told how God had used him to help the Gentiles. ²⁰Everyone who heard this praised God and said to Paul:

My friend, you can see how many tens of thousands of the Jewish people have become followers! And all of them are eager to obey the Law of Moses. ²¹But they have been told that you are teaching those who live among the Gentiles to disobey this Law. They claim that you are telling them not to circumcise their sons or to follow Jewish customs.

²²What should we do now that our people have heard that you are here? ²³Please do what we ask, because four of our men have made special promises to God. ²⁴Join with them and prepare yourself for the ceremony that goes with the promises. Pay the cost for their heads to be shaved. Then everyone will learn that the reports about you are not true. They will know that you do obey the Law of Moses.

²⁵Some while ago we told the Gentile followers what we think they should do. We instructed them not to eat anything offered to idols. They were told not to eat any meat with blood still in it or the meat of an animal that has been strangled. They were also told not to commit any terrible sexual sins.*ᶠ*

²⁶The next day Paul took the four men with him and got himself ready at the same time they did. Then he went into the temple and told when the final ceremony would take place and when an offering would be made for each of them.

Paul Is Arrested

²⁷When the period of seven days for the ceremony was almost over, some of the Jewish people from Asia saw Paul in the temple. They got a large crowd together and started attacking him. ²⁸They were shouting, "Friends, help us! This man goes around everywhere, saying bad things about our nation and about the Law of Moses and about this temple. He has even brought shame to this holy temple by bringing in Gentiles." ²⁹Some of them thought that Paul had brought Trophimus from Ephesus into the temple, because they had seen them together in the city.

³⁰The whole city was in an uproar, and the people turned into a mob. They grabbed Paul and dragged him out of the temple. Then suddenly the doors were shut. ³¹The people were about to kill Paul when the Roman army commander heard that all Jerusalem was starting to riot. ³²So he quickly took some soldiers and officers and ran to where the crowd had gathered.

As soon as the mob saw the commander and soldiers, they stopped beating Paul. ³³The army commander went over and arrested him and had him bound with two chains. Then he tried to find out who Paul was and what he had done. ³⁴Part of the crowd shouted one thing, and part of them shouted something else. But they were making so much noise that the commander could not find out a thing. Then he ordered Paul to be taken into the fortress. ³⁵As they reached the steps, the crowd became so wild that the soldiers had to lift Paul up and carry him. ³⁶The crowd fol-

---

ᵈ21.9 unmarried: Or "virgin." *ᵉ21.18 James*: The Lord's brother. *ᶠ21.25 not to commit any terrible sexual sins*: See the note at 15.20.

lowed and kept shouting, "Kill him! Kill him!"

Paul Speaks to the Crowd

[37]When Paul was about to be taken into the fortress, he asked the commander, "Can I say something to you?"

"How do you know Greek?" the commander asked. [38]"Aren't you that Egyptian who started a riot not long ago and led four thousand terrorists into the desert?"

[39]"No!" Paul replied. "I am a Jew from Tarsus, an important city in Cilicia. Please let me speak to the crowd."

[40]The commander told him he could speak, so Paul stood on the steps and motioned to the people. When they were quiet, he spoke to them in Aramaic:

22 "My friends and leaders of our nation, listen as I explain what happened!" [2]When the crowd heard Paul speak to them in Aramaic, they became even quieter. Then Paul said:

[3]I am a Jew, born and raised in the city of Tarsus in Cilicia. I was a student of Gamaliel and was taught to follow every single law of our ancestors. In fact, I was just as eager to obey God as any of you are today.

[4]I made trouble for everyone who followed the Lord's Way,[g] and I even had some of them killed. I had others arrested and put in jail. I didn't care if they were men or women. [5]The high priest and all the council members can tell you that this is true. They even gave me letters to the Jewish leaders in Damascus, so that I could arrest people there and bring them to Jerusalem to be punished.

[6]One day about noon I was getting close to Damascus, when a bright light from heaven suddenly flashed around me. [7]I fell to the ground and heard a voice asking, "Saul, Saul, why are you so cruel to me?"

[8]"Who are you?" I answered.

The Lord replied, "I am Jesus from Nazareth! I am the one you are so cruel to." [9]The men who were traveling with me saw the light, but did not hear the voice.

[10]I asked, "Lord, what do you want me to do?"

Then he told me, "Get up and go to Damascus. When you get there, you will be told what to do." [11]The light had been so bright that I couldn't see. And the other men had to lead me by the hand to Damascus.

[12]In that city there was a man named Ananias, who faithfully obeyed the Law of Moses and was well liked by all the Jewish people living there. [13]He came to me and said, "Saul, my friend, you can now see again!"

At once I could see. [14]Then Ananias told me, "The God that our ancestors worshiped has chosen you to know what he wants done. He has chosen you to see the One Who Obeys God[h] and to hear his voice. [15]You must tell everyone what you have seen and heard. [16]What are you waiting for? Get up! Be baptized, and wash away your sins by praying to the Lord."

[17]After this I returned to Jerusalem and went to the temple to pray. There I had a vision [18]of the Lord who said to me, "Hurry and leave Jerusalem! The people won't listen to what you say about me."

[19]I replied, "Lord, they know that in many of our meeting places I arrested and beat people who had faith in you. [20]Stephen was killed because he spoke for you, and I stood there and cheered them on. I even guarded the clothes of the men who murdered him."

[21]But the Lord told me to go, and he promised to send me far away to the Gentiles.

[22]The crowd listened until Paul said this. Then they started shouting, "Get rid of this man! He doesn't deserve to live." [23]They kept shouting. They waved their clothes around and threw dust into the air.

Paul and the Roman Army Commander

[24]The Roman commander ordered Paul to be taken into the fortress and beaten with a whip. He did this to find out why the people were screaming at Paul.

[25]While the soldiers were tying Paul up to be beaten, he asked the officer standing there, "Is it legal to beat a Roman citizen before he has been tried in court?"

[26]When the officer heard this, he went to the commander and said, "What are you doing? This man is a Roman citizen!"

[27]The commander went to Paul and asked, "Tell me, are you a Roman citizen?"

"Yes," Paul answered.

[28]The commander then said, "I paid a lot of money to become a Roman citizen."[i]

But Paul replied, "I was born a Roman citizen."

[29]The men who were about to beat and question Paul quickly backed off.

---

[g]**22.4** *followed the Lord's Way*: See the note at 9.2.   [h]**22.14** *One Who Obeys God*: See the note at 7.52.   [i]**22.28** *Roman citizen*: See the note at 16.37.

And the commander himself was frightened when he realized that he had put a Roman citizen in chains.

Paul Is Tried by the Council

[30] The next day the commander wanted to know the real reason why the Jewish leaders had brought charges against Paul. So he had Paul's chains removed, and he ordered the chief priests and the whole council to meet. Then he had Paul led in and made him stand in front of them.

23 Paul looked straight at the council members and said, "My friends, to this day I have served God with a clear conscience!" [2] Then Ananias the high priest ordered the men standing beside Paul to hit him on the mouth. [3] Paul turned to the high priest and said, "You whitewashed wall![j] God will hit you. You sit there to judge me by the Law of Moses. But at the same time you order men to break the Law by hitting me."

[4] The men standing beside Paul asked, "Don't you know you are insulting God's high priest?"

[5] Paul replied, "Oh! I didn't know he was the high priest. The Scriptures do tell us not to speak evil about a leader of our people."

[6] When Paul saw that some of the council members were Sadducees and others were Pharisees, he shouted, "My friends, I am a Pharisee and the son of a Pharisee. I am on trial simply because I believe that the dead will be raised to life."

[7] As soon as Paul said this, the Pharisees and the Sadducees got into a big argument, and the council members started taking sides. [8] The Sadducees do not believe in angels or spirits or that the dead will rise to life. But the Pharisees believe in all of these, [9] and so there was a lot of shouting. Some of the teachers of the Law of Moses were Pharisees. Finally, they became angry and said, "We don't find anything wrong with this man. Maybe a spirit or an angel really did speak to him."

[10] The argument became fierce, and the commander was afraid that Paul would be pulled apart. So he ordered the soldiers to go in and rescue Paul. Then they took him back into the fortress.

[11] That night the Lord stood beside Paul and said, "Don't worry! Just as you have told others about me in Jerusalem, you must also tell about me in Rome."

A Plot To Kill Paul

[12-13] The next morning more than forty Jewish men got together and vowed that they would not eat or drink anything until they had killed Paul. [14] Then some of them went to the chief priests and the nation's leaders and said, "We have promised God that we would not eat a thing until we have killed Paul. [15] You and everyone in the council must go to the commander and pretend that you want to find out more about the charges against Paul. Ask for him to be brought before your court. Meanwhile, we will be waiting to kill him before he gets there."

[16] When Paul's nephew heard about the plot, he went to the fortress and told Paul about it. [17] So Paul said to one of the army officers, "Take this young man to the commander. He has something to tell him."

[18] The officer took him to the commander and said, "The prisoner named Paul asked me to bring this young man to you, because he has something to tell you."

[19] The commander took the young man aside and asked him in private, "What do you want to tell me?"

[20] He answered, "Some men are planning to ask you to bring Paul down to the Jewish council tomorrow. They will claim that they want to find out more about him. [21] But please don't do what they say. More than forty men are going to attack Paul. They have made a vow not to eat or drink anything until they have killed him. Even now they are waiting to hear what you decide."

[22] The commander sent the young man away after saying to him, "Don't let anyone know that you told me this."

Paul Is Sent to Felix the Governor

[23] The commander called in two of his officers and told them, "By nine o'clock tonight have two hundred soldiers ready to go to Caesarea. Take along seventy men on horseback and two hundred foot soldiers with spears. [24] Get a horse ready for Paul and make sure that he gets safely through to Felix the governor."

[25] The commander wrote a letter that said:

[26] Greetings from Claudius Lysias to the Honorable Governor Felix:

[27] Some Jews grabbed this man and were about to kill him. But when I found out that he was a Roman citizen, I took some soldiers and rescued him.

[28] I wanted to find out what they had against him. So I brought him before their council [29] and learned that the charges concern only their religious laws. This man isn't guilty of anything for which he should die or even be put in jail.

---

[j] 23.3 *whitewashed wall*: Someone who pretends to be good, but really isn't.

[30] As soon as I learned that there was a plot against him, I sent him to you and told their leaders to bring charges against him in your court.

[31] The soldiers obeyed the commander's orders, and that same night they took Paul to the city of Antipatris. [32] The next day the foot soldiers returned to the fortress and let the soldiers on horseback take him the rest of the way. [33] When they came to Caesarea, they gave the letter to the governor and handed Paul over to him.

[34] The governor read the letter. Then he asked Paul and found out that he was from Cilicia. [35] The governor said, "I will listen to your case as soon as the people come to bring their charges against you." After saying this, he gave orders for Paul to be kept as a prisoner in Herod's palace.[k]

Paul Is Accused in the Court of Felix

24 Five days later Ananias the high priest, together with some of their leaders and a lawyer named Tertullus, went to the governor to present their case against Paul. [2] So Paul was called in, and Tertullus stated the case against him:[l]

Honorable Felix, you have brought our people a long period of peace, and because of your concern our nation is much better off. [3] All of us are always grateful for what you have done. [4] I don't want to bother you, but please be patient with us and listen to me for just a few minutes.

[5] This man has been found to be a real pest and troublemaker for Jews all over the world. He is also a leader of a group called Nazarenes. [6-8] When he tried to disgrace the temple, we arrested him.[m] If you question him, you will find out for yourself that our charges are true.

[9] The Jewish crowd spoke up and agreed with what Tertullus had said.

Paul Defends Himself

[10] The governor motioned for Paul to speak, and he began:

I know that you have judged the people of our nation for many years, and I am glad to defend myself in your court.

[11] It was no more than twelve days ago that I went to worship in Jerusalem. You can find this out easily enough. [12] Never once did the Jews find me arguing with anyone in the temple. I didn't cause trouble in the Jewish meeting places or in the city itself. [13] There is no way that they can prove these charges that they are now bringing against me.

[14] I admit that their leaders think that the Lord's Way[n] which I follow is based on wrong beliefs. But I still worship the same God that my ancestors worshiped. And I believe everything written in the Law of Moses and in the Prophets.[o] [15] I am just as sure as these people are that God will raise from death everyone who is good or evil. [16] And because I am sure, I try my best to have a clear conscience in whatever I do for God or for people.

[17] After being away for several years, I returned here to bring gifts for the poor people of my nation and to offer sacrifices. [18] This is what I was doing when I was found going through a ceremony in the temple. I wasn't with a crowd, and there was no uproar.

[19] Some Jews from Asia were there at that time, and if they have anything to say against me, they should be here now. [20] Or ask the ones who are here. They can tell you that they didn't find me guilty of anything when I was tried by their own council. [21] The only charge they can bring against me is what I shouted out in court, when I said, "I am on trial today because I believe that the dead will be raised to life!"

[22] Felix knew a lot about the Lord's Way.[p] But he brought the trial to an end and said, "I will make my decision after Lysias the commander arrives." [23] He then ordered the army officer to keep Paul under guard, but not to lock him up or to stop his friends from helping him.

Paul Is Kept under Guard

[24] Several days later Felix and his wife Drusilla, who was Jewish, went to the place where Paul was kept under guard. They sent for Paul and listened while he spoke to them about having faith in Christ Jesus. [25] But Felix was frightened when Paul started talking to them about doing right, about self-control, and about the coming judgment. So he said to Paul, "That's enough for now. You may go. But when I have time I will send

---

[k] 23.35 *Herod's palace*: The palace built by Herod the Great and used by the Roman governors of Palestine. [l] 24.2 *Paul was called in, and Tertullus stated the case against him*: Or "Tertullus was called in and stated the case against Paul." [m] 24.6-8 *we arrested him*: Some manuscripts add, "We wanted to judge him by our own laws. But Lysias the commander took him away from us by force. Then Lysias ordered us to bring our charges against this man in your court." [n] 24.14 *the Lord's Way*: See the note at 9.2. [o] 24.14 *Law of Moses . . . the Prophets*: The Jewish Scriptures, that is, the Old Testament. [p] 24.22 *the Lord's Way*: See the note at 9.2.

for you." ²⁶After this, Felix often sent for Paul and talked with him, because he hoped that Paul would offer him a bribe.
²⁷Two years later Porcius Festus became governor in place of Felix. But since Felix wanted to do the Jewish leaders a favor, he kept Paul in jail.

Paul Asks To Be Tried by the Roman Emperor

25 Three days after Festus had become governor, he went from Caesarea to Jerusalem. ²There the chief priests and some Jewish leaders told him about their charges against Paul. They also asked Festus ³if he would be willing to bring Paul to Jerusalem. They begged him to do this because they were planning to attack and kill Paul on the way. ⁴But Festus told them, "Paul will be kept in Caesarea, and I am soon going there myself. ⁵If he has done anything wrong, let your leaders go with me and bring charges against him there."

⁶Festus stayed in Jerusalem for eight or ten more days before going to Caesarea. Then the next day he took his place as judge and had Paul brought into court. ⁷As soon as Paul came in, the Jewish leaders from Jerusalem crowded around him and said he was guilty of many serious crimes. But they could not prove anything. ⁸Then Paul spoke in his own defense, "I have not broken the Law of my people. And I have not done anything against either the temple or the Emperor."

⁹Festus wanted to please the leaders. So he asked Paul, "Are you willing to go to Jerusalem and be tried by me on these charges?"

¹⁰Paul replied, "I am on trial in the Emperor's court, and that's where I should be tried. You know very well that I have not done anything to harm the Jewish nation. ¹¹If I had done something deserving death, I would not ask to escape the death penalty. But I am not guilty of any of these crimes, and no one has the right to hand me over to these people. I now ask to be tried by the Emperor himself."

¹²After Festus had talked this over with members of his council, he told Paul, "You have asked to be tried by the Emperor, and to the Emperor you will go!"

Paul Speaks to Agrippa and Bernice

¹³A few days later King Agrippa and Bernice came to Caesarea to visit Festus. ¹⁴They had been there for several days, when Festus told the king about the charges against Paul. He said:

Felix left a man here in jail, ¹⁵and when I went to Jerusalem, the chief priests and the Jewish leaders came and asked me to find him guilty. ¹⁶I told them that it isn't the Roman custom to hand a man over to people who are bringing charges against him. He must first have the chance to meet them face to face and to defend himself against their charges.

¹⁷So when they came here with me, I wasted no time. On the very next day I took my place on the judge's bench and ordered him to be brought in. ¹⁸But when the men stood up to make their charges against him, they did not accuse him of any of the crimes that I thought they would. ¹⁹Instead, they argued with him about some of their beliefs and about a dead man named Jesus, who Paul said was alive.

²⁰Since I did not know how to find out the truth about all this, I asked Paul if he would be willing to go to Jerusalem and be put on trial there. ²¹But Paul asked to be kept in jail until the Emperor could decide his case. So I ordered him to be kept here until I could send him to the Emperor.

²²Then Agrippa said to Festus, "I would also like to hear what this man has to say."

Festus answered, "You can hear him tomorrow."

²³The next day Agrippa and Bernice made a big show as they came into the meeting room. High ranking army officers and leading citizens of the town were also there. Festus then ordered Paul to be brought in ²⁴and said:

King Agrippa and other guests, look at this man! Every Jew from Jerusalem and Caesarea has come to me, demanding for him to be put to death. ²⁵I have not found him guilty of any crime deserving death. But because he has asked to be judged by the Emperor, I have decided to send him to Rome.

²⁶I have to write some facts about this man to the Emperor. So I have brought him before all of you, but especially before you, King Agrippa. After we have talked about his case, I will then have something to write. ²⁷It makes no sense to send a prisoner to the Emperor without stating the charges against him.

Paul's Defense before Agrippa

26 Agrippa told Paul, "You may now speak for yourself."
Paul stretched out his hand and said:
²King Agrippa, I am glad for this chance to defend myself before you today on all these charges that my own people have brought against

me. ³You know a lot about our religious customs and the beliefs that divide us. So I ask you to listen patiently to me.

⁴⁻⁵All the Jews have known me since I was a child. They know what kind of life I have lived in my own country and in Jerusalem. And if they were willing, they could tell you that I was a Pharisee, a member of a group that is stricter than any other. ⁶Now I am on trial because I believe the promise God made to our people long ago.

⁷Day and night our twelve tribes have earnestly served God, waiting for his promised blessings. King Agrippa, because of this hope, the Jewish leaders have brought charges against me. ⁸Why should any of you doubt that God raises the dead to life?

⁹I once thought that I should do everything I could to oppose Jesus from Nazareth. ¹⁰I did this first in Jerusalem, and with the authority of the chief priests I put many of God's people in jail. I even voted for them to be killed. ¹¹I often had them punished in our meeting places, and I tried to make them give up their faith. In fact, I was so angry with them, that I went looking for them in foreign cities.

¹²King Agrippa, one day I was on my way to Damascus with the authority and permission of the chief priests. ¹³About noon I saw a light brighter than the sun. It flashed from heaven on me and on everyone traveling with me. ¹⁴We all fell to the ground. Then I heard a voice say to me in Aramaic, "Saul, Saul, why are you so cruel to me? It's foolish to fight against me!"

¹⁵"Who are you?" I asked.

Then the Lord answered, "I am Jesus! I am the one you are so cruel to. ¹⁶Now stand up. I have appeared to you, because I have chosen you to be my servant. You are to tell others what you have learned about me and what I will show you later."

¹⁷The Lord also said, "I will protect you from the Jews and from the Gentiles that I am sending you to. ¹⁸I want you to open their eyes, so that they will turn from darkness to light and from the power of Satan to God. Then their sins will be forgiven, and by faith in me they will become part of God's holy people."

¹⁹King Agrippa, I obeyed this vision from heaven. ²⁰First I preached to the people in Damascus, and then I went to Jerusalem and all over Judea. Finally, I went to the Gentiles and said, "Stop sinning and turn to God! Then prove what you have done by the way you live."

²¹That is why some men grabbed me in the temple and tried to kill me. ²²But all this time God has helped me, and I have preached both to the rich and to the poor. I have told them only what the prophets and Moses said would happen. ²³I told them how the Messiah would suffer and be the first to be raised from death, so that he could bring light to his own people and to the Gentiles.

²⁴Before Paul finished defending himself, Festus shouted, "Paul, you're crazy! Too much learning has driven you out of your mind."

²⁵But Paul replied, "Honorable Festus, I am not crazy. What I am saying is true, and it makes sense. ²⁶None of these things happened off in a corner somewhere. I am sure that King Agrippa knows what I am talking about. That's why I can speak so plainly to him."

²⁷Then Paul said to Agrippa, "Do you believe what the prophets said? I know you do."

²⁸Agrippa asked Paul, "In such a short time do you think you can talk me into being a Christian?"

²⁹Paul answered, "Whether it takes a short time or a long time, I wish you and everyone else who hears me today would become just like me! Except, of course, for these chains."

³⁰Then King Agrippa, Governor Festus, Bernice, and everyone who was with them got up. ³¹But before they left, they said, "This man isn't guilty of anything. He doesn't deserve to die or to be put in jail."

³²Agrippa told Festus, "Paul could have been set free, if he had not asked to be tried by the Roman Emperor."

Paul Is Taken to Rome

27 When it was time for us to sail to Rome, Captain Julius from the Emperor's special troops was put in charge of Paul and the other prisoners. ²We went aboard a ship from Adramyttium that was about to sail to some ports along the coast of Asia. Aristarchus from Thessalonica in Macedonia sailed on the ship with us.

³The next day we came to shore at Sidon. Captain Julius was very kind to Paul. He even let him visit his friends, so they could give him whatever he needed. ⁴When we left Sidon, the winds were blowing against us, and we sailed close to the island of Cyprus to be safe from the wind. ⁵Then we sailed south of Cilicia and Pamphylia until we came to the port of Myra in Lycia. ⁶There the army captain found a ship

from Alexandria that was going to Italy. So he ordered us to board that ship.

⁷We sailed along slowly for several days and had a hard time reaching Cnidus. The wind would not let us go any farther in that direction, so we sailed past Cape Salmone, where the island of Crete would protect us from the wind. ⁸We went slowly along the coast and finally reached a place called Fair Havens, not far from the town of Lasea.

⁹By now we had already lost a lot of time, and sailing was no longer safe. In fact, even the Great Day of Forgiveness[a] was past. ¹⁰Then Paul spoke to the crew of the ship, "Men, listen to me! If we sail now, our ship and its cargo will be badly damaged, and many lives will be lost." ¹¹But Julius listened to the captain of the ship and its owner, rather than to Paul.

¹²The harbor at Fair Havens wasn't a good place to spend the winter. Because of this, almost everyone agreed that we should at least try to sail along the coast of Crete as far as Phoenix. It had a harbor that opened toward the southwest and northwest,[r] and we could spend the winter there.

The Storm at Sea

¹³When a gentle wind from the south started blowing, the men thought it was a good time to do what they had planned. So they pulled up the anchor, and we sailed along the coast of Crete. ¹⁴But soon a strong wind called "The Northeaster" blew against us from the island. ¹⁵The wind struck the ship, and we could not sail against it. So we let the wind carry the ship.

¹⁶We went along the island of Cauda on the side that was protected from the wind. We had a hard time holding the lifeboat in place, ¹⁷but finally we got it where it belonged. Then the sailors wrapped ropes around the ship to hold it together. They lowered the sail and let the ship drift along, because they were afraid it might hit the sandbanks in the gulf of Syrtis.

¹⁸The storm was so fierce that the next day they threw some of the ship's cargo overboard. ¹⁹Then on the third day, with their bare hands they threw overboard some of the ship's gear. ²⁰For several days we could not see either the sun or the stars. A strong wind kept blowing, and we finally gave up all hope of being saved.

²¹Since none of us had eaten anything for a long time, Paul stood up and told the men:

You should have listened to me! If you had stayed on in Crete, you would not have had this damage and loss. ²²But now I beg you to cheer up, because you will be safe. Only the ship will be lost.

²³I belong to God, and I worship him. Last night he sent an angel ²⁴to tell me, "Paul, don't be afraid! You will stand trial before the Emperor. And because of you, God will save the lives of everyone on the ship." ²⁵Cheer up! I am sure that God will do exactly what he promised. ²⁶But we will first be shipwrecked on some island.

²⁷For fourteen days and nights we had been blown around over the Mediterranean Sea. But about midnight the sailors realized that we were getting near land. ²⁸They measured and found that the water was about one hundred twenty feet deep. A little later they measured again and found it was only about ninety feet. ²⁹The sailors were afraid that we might hit some rocks, and they let down four anchors from the back of the ship. Then they prayed for daylight.

³⁰The sailors wanted to escape from the ship. So they lowered the lifeboat into the water, pretending that they were letting down an anchor from the front of the ship. ³¹But Paul said to Captain Julius and the soldiers, "If the sailors don't stay on the ship, you won't have any chance to save your lives." ³²The soldiers then cut the ropes that held the lifeboat and let it fall into the sea.

³³Just before daylight Paul begged the people to eat something. He told them, "For fourteen days you have been so worried that you haven't eaten a thing. ³⁴I beg you to eat something. Your lives depend on it. Do this and not one of you will be hurt."

³⁵After Paul had said this, he took a piece of bread and gave thanks to God. Then in front of everyone, he broke the bread and ate some. ³⁶They all felt encouraged, and each of them ate something. ³⁷There were 276 people on the ship, ³⁸and after everyone had eaten, they threw the cargo of wheat into the sea to make the ship lighter.

The Shipwreck

³⁹Morning came, and the ship's crew saw a coast that they did not recognize. But they did see a cove with a beach. So they decided to try to run the ship aground on the beach. ⁴⁰They cut the anchors loose and let them sink into the

---

[a]27.9 *Great Day of Forgiveness*: This Jewish festival took place near the end of September. The sailing season was dangerous after the middle of September, and it was stopped completely between the middle of November and the middle of March. [r]27.12 *southwest and northwest*: Or "northeast and southeast."

sea. At the same time they untied the ropes that were holding the rudders. Next, they raised the sail at the front of the ship and let the wind carry the ship toward the beach. ⁴¹But it ran aground on a sandbank. The front of the ship stuck firmly in the sand, and the rear was being smashed by the force of the waves.

⁴²The soldiers decided to kill the prisoners to keep them from swimming away and escaping. ⁴³But Captain Julius wanted to save Paul's life, and he did not let the soldiers do what they had planned. Instead, he ordered everyone who could swim to dive into the water and head for shore. ⁴⁴Then he told the others to hold on to planks of wood or parts of the ship. At last, everyone safely reached shore.

On the Island of Malta

28 When we came ashore, we learned that the island was called Malta. ²The local people were very friendly, and they welcomed us by building a fire, because it was rainy and cold.

³After Paul had gathered some wood and had put it on the fire, the heat caused a snake to crawl out, and it bit him on the hand. ⁴When the local people saw the snake hanging from Paul's hand, they said to each other, "This man must be a murderer! He didn't drown in the sea, but the goddess of justice will kill him anyway."

⁵Paul shook the snake off into the fire and wasn't harmed. ⁶The people kept thinking that Paul would either swell up or suddenly drop dead. They watched him for a long time, and when nothing happened to him, they changed their minds and said, "This man is a god."

⁷The governor of the island was named Publius, and he owned some of the land around there. Publius was very friendly and welcomed us into his home for three days. ⁸His father was in bed, sick with fever and stomach trouble, and Paul went to visit him. Paul healed the man by praying and placing his hands on him.

⁹After this happened, everyone on the island brought their sick people to Paul, and they were all healed. ¹⁰The people were very respectful to us, and when we sailed, they gave us everything we needed.

From Malta to Rome

¹¹Three months later we sailed in a ship that had been docked at Malta for the winter. The ship was from Alexandria in Egypt and was known as "The Twin Gods."ˢ ¹²We arrived in Syracuse and stayed for three days. ¹³From there we sailed to Rhegium. The next day a south wind began to blow, and two days later we arrived in Puteoli. ¹⁴There we found some of the Lord's followers, who begged us to stay with them. A week later we left for the city of Rome.

¹⁵Some of the followers in Rome heard about us and came to meet us at the Market of Appius and at the Three Inns. When Paul saw them, he thanked God and was encouraged.

Paul in Rome

¹⁶We arrived in Rome, and Paul was allowed to live in a house by himself with a soldier to guard him.

¹⁷Three days after we got there, Paul called together some of the Jewish leaders and said:

My friends, I have never done anything to hurt our people, and I have never gone against the customs of our ancestors. But in Jerusalem I was handed over as a prisoner to the Romans. ¹⁸They looked into the charges against me and wanted to release me. They found that I had not done anything deserving death. ¹⁹The Jewish leaders disagreed, so I asked to be tried by the Emperor.

But I don't have anything to say against my own nation. ²⁰I am bound by these chains because of what we people of Israel hope for. That's why I have called you here to talk about this hope of ours.

²¹The leaders replied, "No one from Judea has written us a letter about you. And not one of them has come here to report on you or to say anything against you. ²²But we would like to hear what you have to say. We understand that people everywhere are against this new group."

²³They agreed on a time to meet with Paul, and many of them came to his house. From early morning until late in the afternoon, Paul talked to them about God's kingdom. He used the Law of Moses and the Books of the Prophetsᵗ to try to win them over to Jesus.

²⁴Some of the leaders agreed with what Paul said, but others did not. ²⁵Since they could not agree among themselves, they started leaving. But Paul said, "The Holy Spirit said the right thing when he sent Isaiah the prophet ²⁶to tell our ancestors,

'Go to these people
    and tell them:

ˢ**28.11** *known as "The Twin Gods"*: Or "carried on its bow a wooden carving of the Twin Gods." These gods were Castor and Pollux, two of the favorite gods among sailors. ᵗ**28.23** *Law of Moses and the Books of the Prophets*: The Jewish Bible, that is, the Old Testament.

You will listen and listen,
  but never understand.
You will look and look,
  but never see.
²⁷ All of you
  have stubborn hearts.
Your ears are stopped up,
  and your eyes are covered.
You cannot see or hear
  or understand.
If you could,
  you would turn to me,
  and I would heal you.' "

²⁸⁻²⁹Paul said, "You may be sure that God wants to save the Gentiles! And they will listen."ᵘ

³⁰For two years Paul stayed in a rented house and welcomed everyone who came to see him. ³¹He bravely preached about God's kingdom and taught about the Lord Jesus Christ, and no one tried to stop him.

ᵘ**28.28,29** *And they will listen*: Some manuscripts add, "After Paul said this, the people left, but they got into a fierce argument among themselves."

ROMANS

ABOUT THIS BOOK

Paul wrote this letter to introduce himself and his message to the church at Rome. He had never been to this important city, although he knew the names of many Christians there and hoped to visit them soon (15.22—16.21). Paul tells them that he is an apostle, chosen to preach the good news (1.1). And the message he proclaims "is God's powerful way of saving all people who have faith, whether they are Jews or Gentiles" (1.16).

Paul reminds his readers, "All of us have sinned and fallen short of God's glory" (3.23). But how can we be made acceptable to God? This is the main question that Paul answers in this letter. He begins by showing how everyone has failed to do what God requires. The Jews have not obeyed the Law of Moses, and the Gentiles have refused even to think about God, although God has spoken to them in many different ways (1.18—3.20).

> Now we see how God does make us acceptable to him. . . . He accepts people only because they have faith in Jesus Christ . . . God treats us much better than we deserve, and because of Christ Jesus, he freely accepts us and sets us free from our sins. (3.21a-24)
>
> God gave Jesus to die for our sins, and he raised him to life, so that we would be made acceptable to God. (4.25)

A QUICK LOOK AT THIS LETTER

Paul and His Message of Good News (1.1-17)
Everyone Is Guilty (1.18—3.20)
God's Way of Accepting People (3.21—4.25)
A New Life for God's People (5.1—8.39)
What about the People of Israel? (9.1—11.36)
How to Live the New Life of Love (12.1—15.13)
Paul's Plans and Personal Greetings (15.14—16.27)

---

1 From Paul, a servant of Christ Jesus.

God chose me to be an apostle, and he appointed me to preach the good news ²that he promised long ago by what his prophets said in the holy Scriptures. ³⁻⁴This good news is about his Son, our Lord Jesus Christ! As a human, he was from the family of David. But the Holy Spirit[a] proved that Jesus is the powerful Son of God,[b] because he was raised from death.

⁵Jesus was kind to me and chose me to be an apostle,[c] so that people of all nations would obey and have faith. ⁶You are some of those people chosen by Jesus Christ.

⁷This letter is to all of you in Rome. God loves you and has chosen you to be his very own people.

I pray that God our Father and our Lord Jesus Christ will be kind to you and will bless you with peace!

---

[a] 1.4 *the Holy Spirit*: Or "his own spirit of holiness." [b] 1.4 *proved that Jesus is the powerful Son of God*: Or "proved in a powerful way that Jesus is the Son of God." [c] 1.5 *Jesus was kind to me and chose me to be an apostle*: Or "Jesus was kind to us and chose us to be his apostles."

A Prayer of Thanks

⁸First, I thank God in the name of Jesus Christ for all of you. I do this because people everywhere in the world are talking about your faith. ⁹God has seen how I never stop praying for you, while I serve him with all my heart and tell the good news about his Son.

¹⁰In all my prayers, I ask God to make it possible for me to visit you. ¹¹I want to see you and share with you the same blessings that God's Spirit has given me. Then you will grow stronger in your faith. ¹²What I am saying is that we can encourage each other by the faith that is ours.

¹³My friends, I want you to know that I have often planned to come for a visit. But something has always kept me from doing it. I want to win followers to Christ in Rome, as I have done in many other places. ¹⁴⁻¹⁵It doesn't matter if people are civilized and educated, or if they are uncivilized and uneducated. I must tell the good news to everyone. That's why I am eager to visit all of you in Rome.

The Power of the Good News

¹⁶I am proud of the good news! It is God's powerful way of saving all people who have faith, whether they are Jews or Gentiles. ¹⁷The good news tells how God accepts everyone who has faith, but only those who have faith.ᵈ It is just as the Scriptures say, "The people God accepts because of their faith will live."ᵉ

Everyone Is Guilty

¹⁸From heaven God shows how angry he is with all the wicked and evil things that sinful people do to crush the truth. ¹⁹They know everything that can be known about God, because God has shown it all to them. ²⁰God's eternal power and character cannot be seen. But from the beginning of creation, God has shown what these are like by all he has made. That's why those people don't have any excuse. ²¹They know about God, but they don't honor him or even thank him. Their thoughts are useless, and their stupid minds are in the dark. ²²They claim to be wise, but they are fools. ²³They don't worship the glorious and eternal God. Instead, they worship idols that are made to look like humans who cannot live forever, and like birds, animals, and reptiles.

²⁴So God let these people go their own way. They did what they wanted to do, and their filthy thoughts made them do shameful things with their bodies. ²⁵They gave up the truth about God for a lie, and they worshiped God's creation instead of God, who will be praised forever. Amen.

²⁶God let them follow their own evil desires. Women no longer wanted to have sex in a natural way, and they did things with each other that were not natural. ²⁷Men behaved in the same way. They stopped wanting to have sex with women and had strong desires for sex with other men. They did shameful things with each other, and what has happened to them is punishment for their foolish deeds.

²⁸Since these people refused even to think about God, he let their useless minds rule over them. That's why they do all sorts of indecent things. ²⁹They are evil, wicked, and greedy, as well as mean in every possible way. They want what others have, and they murder, argue, cheat, and are hard to get along with. They gossip, ³⁰say cruel things about others, and hate God. They are proud, conceited, and boastful, always thinking up new ways to do evil.

These people don't respect their parents. ³¹They are stupid, unreliable, and don't have any love or pity for others. ³²They know God has said that anyone who acts this way deserves to die. But they keep on doing evil things, and they even encourage others to do them.

God's Judgment Is Fair

2 Some of you accuse others of doing wrong. But there is no excuse for what you do. When you judge others, you condemn yourselves, because you are guilty of doing the very same things. ²We know that God is right to judge everyone who behaves in this way. ³Do you really think God won't punish you, when you behave exactly like the people you accuse? ⁴You surely don't think much of God's wonderful goodness or of his patience and willingness to put up with you. Don't you know that the reason God is good to you is because he wants you to turn to him?

⁵But you are stubborn and refuse to turn to God. So you are making things even worse for yourselves on that day when he will show how angry he is and will judge the world with fairness. ⁶God will reward each of us for what we have done. ⁷He will give eternal life to everyone who has patiently done what is good in the hope of receiving glory, honor, and life that lasts forever. ⁸But he will show how angry and furious he can be with every selfish person who rejects the truth and wants to do evil. ⁹All who

---

ᵈ **1.17** *but only those who have faith*: Or "and faith is all that matters."   ᵉ **1.17** *The people God accepts because of their faith will live*: Or "The people God accepts will live because of their faith."

are wicked will be punished with trouble and suffering. It doesn't matter if they are Jews or Gentiles. ¹⁰But all who do right will be rewarded with glory, honor, and peace, whether they are Jews or Gentiles. ¹¹God doesn't have any favorites!

¹²Those people who don't know about God's Law will still be punished for what they do wrong. And the Law will be used to judge everyone who knows what it says. ¹³God accepts those who obey his Law, but not those who simply hear it.

¹⁴Some people naturally obey the Law's commands, even though they don't have the Law. ¹⁵This proves that the conscience is like a law written in the human heart. And it will show whether we are forgiven or condemned, ¹⁶when God appoints Jesus Christ to judge everyone's secret thoughts, just as my message says.

The Jews and the Law

¹⁷Some of you call yourselves Jews. You trust in the Law and take pride in God. ¹⁸By reading the Scriptures you learn how God wants you to behave, and you discover what is right. ¹⁹You are sure that you are a guide for the blind and a light for all who are in the dark. ²⁰And since there is knowledge and truth in God's Law, you think you can instruct fools and teach young people.

²¹But how can you teach others when you refuse to learn? You preach that it is wrong to steal. But do you steal? ²²You say people should be faithful in marriage. But are you faithful? You hate idols, yet you rob their temples. ²³You take pride in the Law, but you disobey the Law and bring shame to God. ²⁴It is just as the Scriptures tell us, "You have made foreigners say insulting things about God."

²⁵Being circumcised is worthwhile, if you obey the Law. But if you don't obey the Law, you are no better off than people who are not circumcised. ²⁶In fact, if they obey the Law, they are as good as anyone who is circumcised. ²⁷So everyone who obeys the Law, but has never been circumcised, will condemn you. Even though you are circumcised and have the Law, you still don't obey its teachings.

²⁸Just because you live like a Jew and are circumcised doesn't make you a real Jew. ²⁹To be a real Jew you must obey the Law. True circumcision is something that happens deep in your heart, not something done to your body. And besides, you should want praise from God and not from humans.

3 What good is it to be a Jew? What good is it to be circumcised? ²It is good in a lot of ways! First of all, God's messages were spoken to the Jews. ³It is true that some of them did not believe the message. But does this mean that God cannot be trusted, just because they did not have faith? ⁴No, indeed! God tells the truth, even if everyone else is a liar. The Scriptures say about God,

> "Your words
> will be proven true,
> and in court
> you will win your case."

⁵If our evil deeds show how right God is, then what can we say? Is it wrong for God to become angry and punish us? What a foolish thing to ask. ⁶But the answer is, "No." Otherwise, how could God judge the world? ⁷Since your lies bring great honor to God by showing how truthful he is, you may ask why God still says you are a sinner. ⁸You might as well say, "Let's do something evil, so that something good will come of it!" Some people even claim that we are saying this. But God is fair and will judge them as well.

No One Is Good

⁹What does all this mean? Does it mean that we Jews are better off^f than the Gentiles? No, it doesn't! Jews, as well as Gentiles, are ruled by sin, just as I have said. ¹⁰The Scriptures tell us,

> "No one is acceptable to God!
> ¹¹ Not one of them understands
> or even searches for God.
> ¹² They have all turned away
> and are worthless.
> There isn't one person
> who does right.
> ¹³ Their words are like
> an open pit,
> and their tongues are good
> only for telling lies.
> Each word is as deadly
> as the fangs of a snake,
> ¹⁴ and they say nothing
> but bitter curses.
> ¹⁵ These people quickly
> become violent.
> ¹⁶ Wherever they go,
> they leave ruin
> and destruction.
> ¹⁷ They don't know how
> to live in peace.
> ¹⁸   They don't even fear God."

¹⁹We know that everything in the Law was written for those who are under its power. The Law says these things to stop anyone from making excuses and to let God show that the whole world is

---

^f 3.9 *better off*: Or "worse off."

guilty. ²⁰God doesn't accept people simply because they obey the Law. No, indeed! All the Law does is to point out our sin.

God's Way of Accepting People

²¹Now we see how God does make us acceptable to him. The Law and the Prophets[g] tell how we become acceptable, and it isn't by obeying the Law of Moses. ²²God treats everyone alike. He accepts people only because they have faith in Jesus Christ. ²³All of us have sinned and fallen short of God's glory. ²⁴But God treats us much better than we deserve,[h] and because of Christ Jesus, he freely accepts us and sets us free from our sins. ²⁵⁻²⁶God sent Christ to be our sacrifice. Christ offered his life's blood, so that by faith in him we could come to God. And God did this to show that in the past he was right to be patient and forgive sinners. This also shows that God is right when he accepts people who have faith in Jesus.

²⁷What is left for us to brag about? Not a thing! Is it because we obeyed some law? No! It is because of faith. ²⁸We see that people are acceptable to God because they have faith, and not because they obey the Law. ²⁹Does God belong only to the Jews? Isn't he also the God of the Gentiles? Yes, he is! ³⁰There is only one God, and he accepts Gentiles as well as Jews, simply because of their faith. ³¹Do we destroy the Law by our faith? Not at all! We make it even more powerful.

The Example of Abraham

4 Well then, what can we say about our ancestor Abraham? ²If he became acceptable to God because of what he did, then he would have something to brag about. But he would never be able to brag about it to God. ³The Scriptures say, "God accepted Abraham because Abraham had faith in him."

⁴Money paid to workers isn't a gift. It is something they earn by working. ⁵But you cannot make God accept you because of something you do. God accepts sinners only because they have faith in him. ⁶In the Scriptures David talks about the blessings that come to people who are acceptable to God, even though they don't do anything to deserve these blessings. David says,

⁷ "God blesses people
　　whose sins are forgiven
　　and whose evil deeds
　　　are forgotten.

⁸ The Lord blesses people
　　whose sins are erased
　　　from his book."

⁹Are these blessings meant for circumcised people or for those who are not circumcised? Well, the Scriptures say that God accepted Abraham because Abraham had faith in him. ¹⁰But when did this happen? Was it before or after Abraham was circumcised? Of course, it was before.

¹¹Abraham let himself be circumcised to show that he had been accepted because of his faith even before he was circumcised. This makes Abraham the father of all who are acceptable to God because of their faith, even though they are not circumcised. ¹²This also makes Abraham the father of everyone who is circumcised and has faith in God, as Abraham did before he was circumcised.

The Promise Is for All Who Have Faith

¹³God promised Abraham and his descendants that he would give them the world. This promise wasn't made because Abraham had obeyed a law, but because his faith in God made him acceptable. ¹⁴If Abraham and his descendants were given this promise because they had obeyed a law, then faith would mean nothing, and the promise would be worthless.

¹⁵God becomes angry when his Law is broken. But where there isn't a law, it cannot be broken. ¹⁶Everything depends on having faith in God, so that God's promise is assured by his great kindness. This promise isn't only for Abraham's descendants who have the Law. It is for all who are Abraham's descendants because they have faith, just as he did. Abraham is the ancestor of us all. ¹⁷The Scriptures say that Abraham would become the ancestor of many nations. This promise was made to Abraham because he had faith in God, who raises the dead to life and creates new things.

¹⁸God promised Abraham a lot of descendants. And when it all seemed hopeless, Abraham still had faith in God and became the ancestor of many nations. ¹⁹Abraham's faith never became weak, not even when he was nearly a hundred years old. He knew that he was almost dead and that his wife Sarah could not have children. ²⁰But Abraham never doubted or questioned God's promise. His faith made him strong, and he gave all the credit to God.

---

[g]3.21 *The Law and the Prophets*: The Jewish Scriptures, that is, the Old Testament.
[h]3.24 *treats us much better than we deserve*: The Greek word *charis*, traditionally rendered "grace," is translated here and other places in the CEV to express the overwhelming kindness of God.

²¹Abraham was certain that God could do what he had promised. ²²So God accepted him, ²³just as we read in the Scriptures. But these words were not written only for Abraham. ²⁴They were written for us, since we will also be accepted because of our faith in God, who raised our Lord Jesus to life. ²⁵God gave Jesus to die for our sins, and he raised him to life, so that we would be made acceptable to God.

What It Means To Be Acceptable to God

5 By faith we have been made acceptable to God. And now, because of our Lord Jesus Christ, we live at peace[i] with God. ²Christ has also introduced us[j] to God's undeserved kindness on which we take our stand. So we are happy, as we look forward to sharing in the glory of God. ³But that's not all! We gladly suffer,[k] because we know that suffering helps us to endure. ⁴And endurance builds character, which gives us a hope ⁵that will never disappoint us. All of this happens because God has given us the Holy Spirit, who fills our hearts with his love.

⁶Christ died for us at a time when we were helpless and sinful. ⁷No one is really willing to die for an honest person, though someone might be willing to die for a truly good person. ⁸But God showed how much he loved us by having Christ die for us, even though we were sinful.

⁹But there is more! Now that God has accepted us because Christ sacrificed his life's blood, we will also be kept safe from God's anger. ¹⁰Even when we were God's enemies, he made peace with us, because his Son died for us. Yet something even greater than friendship is ours. Now that we are at peace with God, we will be saved by his Son's life. ¹¹And in addition to everything else, we are happy because God sent our Lord Jesus Christ to make peace with us.

Adam and Christ

¹²Adam sinned, and that sin brought death into the world. Now everyone has sinned, and so everyone must die. ¹³Sin was in the world before the Law came. But no record of sin was kept, because there was no Law. ¹⁴Yet death still had power over all who lived from the time of Adam to the time of Moses. This happened, though not everyone disobeyed a direct command from God, as Adam did.

In some ways Adam is like Christ who came later. ¹⁵But the gift that God was kind enough to give was very different from Adam's sin. That one sin brought death to many others. Yet in an even greater way, Jesus Christ alone brought God's gift of kindness to many people.

¹⁶There is a lot of difference between Adam's sin and God's gift. That one sin led to punishment. But God's gift made it possible for us to be acceptable to him, even though we have sinned many times. ¹⁷Death ruled like a king because Adam had sinned. But that cannot compare with what Jesus Christ has done. God has been so kind to us, and he has accepted us because of Jesus. And so we will live and rule like kings.

¹⁸Everyone was going to be punished because Adam sinned. But because of the good thing that Christ has done, God accepts us and gives us the gift of life. ¹⁹Adam disobeyed God and caused many others to be sinners. But Jesus obeyed him and will make many people acceptable to God.

²⁰The Law came, so that the full power of sin could be seen. Yet where sin was powerful, God's kindness was even more powerful. ²¹Sin ruled by means of death. But God's kindness now rules, and God has accepted us because of Jesus Christ our Lord. This means that we will have eternal life.

Dead to Sin but Alive because of Christ

6 What should we say? Should we keep on sinning, so that God's wonderful kindness will show up even better? ²No, we should not! If we are dead to sin, how can we go on sinning? ³Don't you know that all who share in Christ Jesus by being baptized also share in his death? ⁴When we were baptized, we died and were buried with Christ. We were baptized, so that we would live a new life, as Christ was raised to life by the glory of God the Father.

⁵If we shared in Jesus' death by being baptized, we will be raised to life with him. ⁶We know that the persons we used to be were nailed to the cross with Jesus. This was done, so that our sinful bodies would no longer be the slaves of sin. ⁷We know that sin doesn't have power over dead people.

⁸As surely as we died with Christ, we believe we will also live with him. ⁹We know that death no longer has any power over Christ. He died and was raised to life, never again to die. ¹⁰When Christ died, he died for sin once and for all. But now he is alive, and he lives only for God. ¹¹In the same way, you must think of yourselves as dead to the power of sin. But Christ Jesus has given life to you, and you live for God.

¹²Don't let sin rule your body. After all, your body is bound to die, so don't

---

[i]5.1 *we live at peace*: Some manuscripts have "let us live at peace."   [j]5.2 *introduced us*: Some manuscripts add "by faith."   [k]5.3 *We gladly suffer*: Or "Let us gladly suffer."

obey its desires ¹³or let any part of it become a slave of evil. Give yourselves to God, as people who have been raised from death to life. Make every part of your body a slave that pleases God. ¹⁴Don't let sin keep ruling your lives. You are ruled by God's kindness and not by the Law.

Slaves Who Do What Pleases God

¹⁵What does all this mean? Does it mean we are free to sin, because we are ruled by God's wonderful kindness and not by the Law? Certainly not! ¹⁶Don't you know that you are slaves of anyone you obey? You can be slaves of sin and die, or you can be obedient slaves of God and be acceptable to him. ¹⁷You used to be slaves of sin. But I thank God that with all your heart you obeyed the teaching you received from me. ¹⁸Now you are set free from sin and are slaves who please God.

¹⁹I am using these everyday examples, because in some ways you are still weak. You used to let the different parts of your body be slaves of your evil thoughts. But now you must make every part of your body serve God, so that you will belong completely to him.

²⁰When you were slaves of sin, you didn't have to please God. ²¹But what good did you receive from the things you did? All you have to show for them is your shame, and they lead to death. ²²Now you have been set free from sin, and you are God's slaves. This will make you holy and will lead you to eternal life. ²³Sin pays off with death. But God's gift is eternal life given by Jesus Christ our Lord.

An Example from Marriage

7 My friends, you surely understand enough about law to know that laws only have power over people who are alive. ²For example, the Law says that a man's wife must remain his wife as long as he lives. But once her husband is dead, she is free ³to marry someone else. However, if she goes off with another man while her husband is still alive, she is said to be unfaithful.

⁴That is how it is with you, my friends. You are now part of the body of Christ and are dead to the power of the Law. You are free to belong to Christ, who was raised to life so that we could serve God. ⁵When we thought only of ourselves, the Law made us have sinful desires. It made every part of our bodies into slaves who are doomed to die. ⁶But the Law no longer rules over us. We are like dead people, and it cannot have any power over us. Now we can serve God in a new way by obeying his Spirit, and not in the old way by obeying the written Law.

The Battle with Sin

⁷Does this mean that the Law is sinful? Certainly not! But if it had not been for the Law, I would not have known what sin is really like. For example, I would not have known what it means to want something that belongs to someone else, unless the Law had told me not to do that. ⁸It was sin that used this command as a way of making me have all kinds of desires. But without the Law, sin is dead.

⁹Before I knew about the Law, I was alive. But as soon as I heard that command, sin came to life, ¹⁰and I died. The very command that was supposed to bring life to me, instead brought death. ¹¹Sin used this command to trick me, and because of it I died. ¹²Still, the Law and its commands are holy and correct and good.

¹³Am I saying that something good caused my death? Certainly not! It was sin that killed me by using something good. Now we can see how terrible and evil sin really is. ¹⁴We know that the Law is spiritual. But I am merely a human, and I have been sold as a slave to sin. ¹⁵In fact, I don't understand why I act the way I do. I don't do what I know is right. I do the things I hate. ¹⁶Although I don't do what I know is right, I agree that the Law is good. ¹⁷So I am not the one doing these evil things. The sin that lives in me is what does them.

¹⁸I know that my selfish desires won't let me do anything that is good. Even when I want to do right, I cannot. ¹⁹Instead of doing what I know is right, I do wrong. ²⁰And so, if I don't do what I know is right, I am no longer the one doing these evil things. The sin that lives in me is what does them.

²¹The Law has shown me that something in me keeps me from doing what I know is right. ²²With my whole heart I agree with the Law of God. ²³But in every part of me I discover something fighting against my mind, and it makes me a prisoner of sin that controls everything I do. ²⁴What a miserable person I am. Who will rescue me from this body that is doomed to die? ²⁵Thank God! Jesus Christ will rescue me.

So with my mind I serve the Law of God, although my selfish desires make me serve the law of sin.

Living by the Power of God's Spirit

8 If you belong to Christ Jesus, you won't be punished. ²The Holy Spirit will give you life that comes from Christ Jesus and will set you¹ free from sin and

---

¹8.2 *you*: Some manuscripts have "me."

death. ³The Law of Moses cannot do this, because our selfish desires make the Law weak. But God set you free when he sent his own Son to be like us sinners and to be a sacrifice for our sin. God used Christ's body to condemn sin. ⁴He did this, so that we would do what the Law commands by obeying the Spirit instead of our own desires.

⁵People who are ruled by their desires think only of themselves. Everyone who is ruled by the Holy Spirit thinks about spiritual things. ⁶If our minds are ruled by our desires, we will die. But if our minds are ruled by the Spirit, we will have life and peace. ⁷Our desires fight against God, because they do not and cannot obey God's laws. ⁸If we follow our desires, we cannot please God.

⁹You are no longer ruled by your desires, but by God's Spirit, who lives in you. People who don't have the Spirit of Christ in them don't belong to him. ¹⁰But Christ lives in you. So you are alive because God has accepted you, even though your bodies must die because of your sins. ¹¹Yet God raised Jesus to life! God's Spirit now lives in you, and he will raise you to life by his Spirit.

¹²My dear friends, we must not live to satisfy our desires. ¹³If you do, you will die. But you will live, if by the help of God's Spirit you say "No" to your desires. ¹⁴Only those people who are led by God's Spirit are his children. ¹⁵God's Spirit doesn't make us slaves who are afraid of him. Instead, we become his children and call him our Father.ᵐ ¹⁶God's Spirit makes us sure that we are his children. ¹⁷His Spirit lets us know that together with Christ we will be given what God has promised. We will also share in the glory of Christ, because we have suffered with him.

A Wonderful Future for God's People

¹⁸I am sure that what we are suffering now cannot compare with the glory that will be shown to us. ¹⁹In fact, all creation is eagerly waiting for God to show who his children are. ²⁰Meanwhile, creation is confused, but not because it wants to be confused. God made it this way in the hope ²¹that creation would be set free from decay and would share in the glorious freedom of his children. ²²We know that all creation is still groaning and is in pain, like a woman about to give birth.

²³The Spirit makes us sure about what we will be in the future. But now we groan silently, while we wait for God to show that we are his children.ⁿ This means that our bodies will also be set free. ²⁴And this hope is what saves us. But if we already have what we hope for, there is no need to keep on hoping. ²⁵However, we hope for something we have not yet seen, and we patiently wait for it.

²⁶In certain ways we are weak, but the Spirit is here to help us. For example, when we don't know what to pray for, the Spirit prays for us in ways that cannot be put into words. ²⁷All of our thoughts are known to God. He can understand what is in the mind of the Spirit, as the Spirit prays for God's people. ²⁸We know that God is always at work for the good of everyone who loves him.ᵒ They are the ones God has chosen for his purpose, ²⁹and he has always known who his chosen ones would be. He had decided to let them become like his own Son, so that his Son would be the first of many children. ³⁰God then accepted the people he had already decided to choose, and he has shared his glory with them.

God's Love

³¹What can we say about all this? If God is on our side, can anyone be against us? ³²God did not keep back his own Son, but he gave him for us. If God did this, won't he freely give us everything else? ³³If God says his chosen ones are acceptable to him, can anyone bring charges against them? ³⁴Or can anyone condemn them? No indeed! Christ died and was raised to life, and now he is at God's right side,ᵖ speaking to him for us. ³⁵Can anything separate us from the love of Christ? Can trouble, suffering, and hard times, or hunger and nakedness, or danger and death? ³⁶It is exactly as the Scriptures say,

"For you we face death
 all day long.
We are like sheep
 on their way
 to be butchered."

³⁷In everything we have won more than a victory because of Christ who loves us. ³⁸I am sure that nothing can separate us from God's love—not life or death, not angels or spirits, not the present or the future, ³⁹and not powers above or powers below. Nothing in all creation

---

ᵐ**8.15** *our Father*: The Greek text uses the Aramaic word "Abba" (meaning "father"), which shows the close relation between the children and their father.   ⁿ**8.23** *to show that we are his children*: These words are not in some manuscripts. The translation of the remainder of the verse would then read, "while we wait for God to set our bodies free."   ᵒ**8.28** *God is always at work for the good of everyone who loves him*: Or "All things work for the good of everyone who loves God" or "God's Spirit always works for the good of everyone who loves God."   ᵖ**8.34** *right side*: The place of power and honor.

can separate us from God's love for us in Christ Jesus our Lord!

God's Choice of Israel

9 I am a follower of Christ, and the Holy Spirit is a witness to my conscience. So I tell the truth and I am not lying when I say ²my heart is broken and I am in great sorrow. ³I would gladly be placed under God's curse and be separated from Christ for the good of my own people. ⁴They are the descendants of Israel, and they are also God's chosen people. God showed them his glory. He made agreements with them and gave them his Law. The temple is theirs and so are the promises that God made to them. ⁵They have those famous ancestors, who were also the ancestors of Jesus Christ. I pray that God, who rules over all, will be praised forever!*q* Amen.

⁶It cannot be said that God broke his promise. After all, not all of the people of Israel are the true people of God. ⁷⁻⁸In fact, when God made the promise to Abraham, he meant only Abraham's descendants by his son Isaac. God was talking only about Isaac when he promised ⁹Sarah, "At this time next year I will return, and you will already have a son."

¹⁰Don't forget what happened to the twin sons of Isaac and Rebekah. ¹¹⁻¹²Even before they were born or had done anything good or bad, the Lord told Rebekah that her older son would serve the younger one. The Lord said this to show that he makes his own choices and that it wasn't because of anything either of them had done. ¹³That's why the Scriptures say that the Lord liked Jacob more than Esau.

¹⁴Are we saying that God is unfair? Certainly not! ¹⁵The Lord told Moses that he has pity and mercy on anyone he wants to. ¹⁶Everything then depends on God's mercy and not on what people want or do. ¹⁷In the Scriptures the Lord says to the king of Egypt, "I let you become king, so that I could show you my power and be praised by all people on earth." ¹⁸Everything depends on what God decides to do, and he can either have pity on people or make them stubborn.

God's Anger and Mercy

¹⁹Someone may ask, "How can God blame us, if he makes us behave in the way he wants us to?" ²⁰But, my friend, I ask, "Who do you think you are to question God? Does the clay have the right to ask the potter why he shaped it the way he did? ²¹Doesn't a potter have the right to make a fancy bowl and a plain bowl out of the same lump of clay?"

²²God wanted to show his anger and reveal his power against everyone who deserved to be destroyed. But instead, he patiently put up with them. ²³He did this by showing how glorious he is when he has pity on the people he has chosen to share in his glory. ²⁴Whether Jews or Gentiles, we are those chosen ones, ²⁵just as the Lord says in the book of Hosea,

"Although they are not
my people,
I will make them my people.
I will treat with love
those nations
that have never been loved.

²⁶ "Once they were told,
'You are not my people.'
But in that very place
they will be called
children of the living God."

²⁷And this is what the prophet Isaiah said about the people of Israel,

"The people of Israel
are as many
as the grains of sand
along the beach.
But only a few who are left
will be saved.
²⁸ The Lord will be quick
and sure to do on earth
what he has warned
he will do."

²⁹Isaiah also said,

"If the Lord All-Powerful
had not spared some
of our descendants,
we would have been destroyed
like the cities of Sodom
and Gomorrah."*r*

Israel and the Good News

³⁰What does all of this mean? It means that the Gentiles were not trying to be acceptable to God, but they found that he would accept them if they had faith. ³¹⁻³²It also means that the people of Israel were not acceptable to God. And why not? It was because they were trying*s* to be acceptable by obeying the Law instead of by having faith in God. The people of Israel fell over the stone that makes people stumble, ³³just as God says in the Scriptures,

---

*q*9.5 *Christ. I pray that God, who rules over all, will be praised forever*: Or "Christ, who rules over all. I pray that God will be praised forever" or "Christ. And I pray that Christ, who is God and rules over all, will be praised forever."   *r*9.29 *Sodom and Gomorrah*: During the time of Abraham the Lord destroyed these two cities because their people were so sinful.   *s*9.31 *because they were trying*: Or "while they were trying" or "even though they were trying."

"Look! I am placing in Zion
a stone to make people
stumble and fall.
But those who have faith
in that one will never
be disappointed."

10 Dear friends, my greatest wish and my prayer to God is for the people of Israel to be saved. ²I know they love God, but they don't understand ³what makes people acceptable to him. So they refuse to trust God, and they try to be acceptable by obeying the Law. ⁴But Christ makes the Law no longer necessary[t] for those who become acceptable to God by faith.

Anyone Can Be Saved

⁵Moses said that a person could become acceptable to God by obeying the Law. He did this when he wrote, "If you want to live, you must do all that the Law commands." ⁶But people whose faith makes them acceptable to God will never ask, "Who will go up to heaven to bring Christ down?" ⁷Neither will they ask, "Who will go down into the world of the dead to raise him to life?"

⁸All who are acceptable because of their faith simply say, "The message is as near as your mouth or your heart." And this is the same message we preach about faith. ⁹So you will be saved, if you honestly say, "Jesus is Lord," and if you believe with all your heart that God raised him from death. ¹⁰God will accept you and save you, if you truly believe this and tell it to others.

¹¹The Scriptures say that no one who has faith will be disappointed, ¹²no matter if that person is a Jew or a Gentile. There is only one Lord, and he is generous to everyone who asks for his help. ¹³All who call out to the Lord will be saved.

¹⁴How can people have faith in the Lord and ask him to save them, if they have never heard about him? And how can they hear, unless someone tells them? ¹⁵And how can anyone tell them without being sent by the Lord? The Scriptures say it is a beautiful sight to see even the feet of someone coming to preach the good news. ¹⁶Yet not everyone has believed the message. For example, the prophet Isaiah asked, "Lord, has anyone believed what we said?"

¹⁷No one can have faith without hearing the message about Christ. ¹⁸But am I saying that the people of Israel did not hear? No, I am not! The Scriptures say,

"The message was told
everywhere on earth.

It was announced
all over the world."

¹⁹Did the people of Israel understand or not? Moses answered this question when he told that the Lord had said,

"I will make Israel jealous
of people
who are a nation
of nobodies.
I will make them angry
at people
who don't understand
a thing."

²⁰Isaiah was fearless enough to tell that the Lord had said,

"I was found by people
who were not looking
for me.
I appeared to the ones
who were not asking
about me."

²¹And Isaiah said about the people of Israel,

"All day long the Lord
has reached out
to people who are stubborn
and refuse to obey."

God Has Not Rejected His People

11 Am I saying that God has turned his back on his people? Certainly not! I am one of the people of Israel, and I myself am a descendant of Abraham from the tribe of Benjamin. ²God did not turn his back on his chosen people. Don't you remember reading in the Scriptures how Elijah complained to God about the people of Israel? ³He said, "Lord, they killed your prophets and destroyed your altars. I am the only one left, and now they want to kill me." ⁴But the Lord told Elijah, "I still have seven thousand followers who have not worshiped Baal." ⁵It is the same way now. God was kind to the people of Israel, and so a few of them are still his followers. ⁶This happened because of God's undeserved kindness and not because of anything they have done. It could not have happened except for God's kindness.

⁷This means that only a chosen few of the people of Israel found what all of them were searching for. And the rest of them were stubborn, ⁸just as the Scriptures say,

"God made them so stupid
that their eyes are blind,
and their ears
are still deaf."

⁹Then David said,

---

[t] **10.4** *But Christ makes the Law no longer necessary*: Or "But Christ gives the full meaning to the Law."

"Turn their meals
 into bait for a trap,
so that they will stumble
 and be given
 what they deserve.
¹⁰ Blindfold their eyes!
 Don't let them see.
Bend their backs
 beneath a burden
 that will never be lifted."

Gentiles Will Be Saved

¹¹Do I mean that the people of Israel fell, never to get up again? Certainly not! Their failure made it possible for the Gentiles to be saved, and this will make the people of Israel jealous. ¹²But if the rest of the world's people were helped so much by Israel's sin and loss, they will be helped even more by their full return.

¹³I am now speaking to you Gentiles, and as long as I am an apostle to you, I will take pride in my work. ¹⁴I hope in this way to make some of my own people jealous enough to be saved. ¹⁵When Israel rejected God,[u] the rest of the people in the world were able to turn to him. So when God makes friends with Israel, it will be like bringing the dead back to life. ¹⁶If part of a batch of dough is made holy by being offered to God, then all of the dough is holy. If the roots of a tree are holy, the rest of the tree is holy too.

¹⁷You Gentiles are like branches of a wild olive tree that were made to be part of a cultivated olive tree. You have taken the place of some branches that were cut away from it. And because of this, you enjoy the blessings that come from being part of that cultivated tree. ¹⁸But don't think you are better than the branches that were cut away. Just remember that you are not supporting the roots of that tree. Its roots are supporting you.

¹⁹Maybe you think those branches were cut away, so that you could be put in their place. ²⁰That's true enough. But they were cut away because they did not have faith, and you are where you are because you do have faith. So don't be proud, but be afraid. ²¹If God cut away those natural branches, couldn't he do the same to you?

²²Now you see both how kind and how hard God can be. He was hard on those who fell, but he was kind to you. And he will keep on being kind to you, if you keep on trusting in his kindness. Otherwise, you will be cut away too.

²³If those other branches will start having faith, they will be made a part of that tree again. God has the power to put them back. ²⁴After all, it wasn't natural for branches to be cut from a wild olive tree and to be made part of a cultivated olive tree. So it is much more likely that God will join the natural branches back to the cultivated olive tree.

The People of Israel Will Be Brought Back

²⁵My friends, I don't want you Gentiles to be too proud of yourselves. So I will explain the mystery of what has happened to the people of Israel. Some of them have become stubborn, and they will stay like that until the complete number of you Gentiles has come in. ²⁶In this way all of Israel will be saved, as the Scriptures say,

"From Zion someone will come
 to rescue us.
Then Jacob's descendants
 will stop being evil.
²⁷ This is what the Lord
 has promised to do
when he forgives their sins."

²⁸The people of Israel are treated as God's enemies, so that the good news can come to you Gentiles. But they are still the chosen ones, and God loves them because of their famous ancestors. ²⁹God doesn't take back the gifts he has given or forget about the people he has chosen.

³⁰At one time you Gentiles rejected God. But now Israel has rejected God, and you have been shown mercy. ³¹And because of the mercy shown to you, they will also be shown mercy. ³²All people have disobeyed God, and that's why he treats them as prisoners. But he does this, so that he can have mercy on all of them.

³³Who can measure the wealth and wisdom and knowledge of God? Who can understand his decisions or explain what he does?

³⁴ "Has anyone known
 the thoughts of the Lord
 or given him advice?
³⁵ Has anyone loaned
 something to the Lord
 that must be repaid?"

³⁶Everything comes from the Lord. All things were made because of him and will return to him. Praise the Lord forever! Amen.

Christ Brings New Life

12 Dear friends, God is good. So I beg you to offer your bodies to him as a living sacrifice, pure and pleasing. That's the most sensible way to serve God. ²Don't be like the people of this world, but let God change the way

---

[u] 11.15 *When Israel rejected God*: Or "When Israel was rejected."

you think. Then you will know how to do everything that is good and pleasing to him.

³I realize how kind God has been to me, and so I tell each of you not to think you are better than you really are. Use good sense and measure yourself by the amount of faith that God has given you. ⁴A body is made up of many parts, and each of them has its own use. ⁵That's how it is with us. There are many of us, but we each are part of the body of Christ, as well as part of one another.

⁶God has also given each of us different gifts to use. If we can prophesy, we should do it according to the amount of faith we have. ⁷If we can serve others, we should serve. If we can teach, we should teach. ⁸If we can encourage others, we should encourage them. If we can give, we should be generous. If we are leaders, we should do our best. If we are good to others, we should do it cheerfully.

Rules for Christian Living

⁹Be sincere in your love for others. Hate everything that is evil and hold tight to everything that is good. ¹⁰Love each other as brothers and sisters and honor others more than you do yourself. ¹¹Never give up. Eagerly follow the Holy Spirit and serve the Lord. ¹²Let your hope make you glad. Be patient in time of trouble and never stop praying. ¹³Take care of God's needy people and welcome strangers into your home.

¹⁴Ask God to bless everyone who mistreats you. Ask him to bless them and not to curse them. ¹⁵When others are happy, be happy with them, and when they are sad, be sad. ¹⁶Be friendly with everyone. Don't be proud and feel that you are smarter than others. Make friends with ordinary people.ᵛ ¹⁷Don't mistreat someone who has mistreated you. But try to earn the respect of others, ¹⁸and do your best to live at peace with everyone.

¹⁹Dear friends, don't try to get even. Let God take revenge. In the Scriptures the Lord says,

"I am the one to take revenge
  and pay them back."

²⁰The Scriptures also say,

"If your enemies are hungry,
  give them something to eat.
And if they are thirsty,
  give them something
    to drink.
This will be the same
  as piling burning coals
    on their heads."

²¹Don't let evil defeat you, but defeat evil with good.

Obey Rulers

13 Obey the rulers who have authority over you. Only God can give authority to anyone, and he puts these rulers in their places of power. ²People who oppose the authorities are opposing what God has done, and they will be punished. ³Rulers are a threat to evil people, not to good people. There is no need to be afraid of the authorities. Just do right, and they will praise you for it. ⁴After all, they are God's servants, and it is their duty to help you.

If you do something wrong, you ought to be afraid, because these rulers have the right to punish you. They are God's servants who punish criminals to show how angry God is. ⁵But you should obey the rulers because you know it is the right thing to do, and not just because of God's anger.

⁶You must also pay your taxes. The authorities are God's servants, and it is their duty to take care of these matters. ⁷Pay all that you owe, whether it is taxes and fees or respect and honor.

Love

⁸Let love be your only debt! If you love others, you have done all that the Law demands. ⁹In the Law there are many commands, such as, "Be faithful in marriage. Do not murder. Do not steal. Do not want what belongs to others." But all of these are summed up in the command that says, "Love others as much as you love yourself." ¹⁰No one who loves others will harm them. So love is all that the Law demands.

The Day When Christ Returns

¹¹You know what sort of times we live in, and so you should live properly. It is time to wake up. You know that the day when we will be saved is nearer now than when we first put our faith in the Lord. ¹²Night is almost over, and day will soon appear. We must stop behaving as people do in the dark and be ready to live in the light. ¹³So behave properly, as people do in the day. Don't go to wild parties or get drunk or be vulgar or indecent. Don't quarrel or be jealous. ¹⁴Let the Lord Jesus Christ be as near to you as the clothes you wear. Then you won't try to satisfy your selfish desires.

Don't Criticize Others

14 Welcome all the Lord's followers, even those whose faith is weak. Don't criticize them for having beliefs

---

ᵛ**12.16** *Make friends with ordinary people*: Or "Do ordinary jobs."

that are different from yours. ²Some think it is all right to eat anything, while those whose faith is weak will eat only vegetables. ³But you should not criticize others for eating or for not eating. After all, God welcomes everyone. ⁴What right do you have to criticize someone else's servants? Only their Lord can decide if they are doing right, and the Lord will make sure that they do right.

⁵Some of the Lord's followers think one day is more important than another. Others think all days are the same. But each of you should make up your own mind. ⁶Any followers who count one day more important than another day do it to honor their Lord. And any followers who eat meat give thanks to God, just like the ones who don't eat meat.

⁷Whether we live or die, it must be for God, rather than for ourselves. ⁸Whether we live or die, it must be for the Lord. Alive or dead, we still belong to the Lord. ⁹This is because Christ died and rose to life, so that he would be the Lord of the dead and of the living. ¹⁰Why do you criticize other followers of the Lord? Why do you look down on them? The day is coming when God will judge all of us. ¹¹In the Scriptures God says,

"I swear by my very life
that everyone will kneel down
and praise my name!"

¹²And so, each of us must give an account to God for what we do.

Don't Cause Problems for Others

¹³We must stop judging others. We must also make up our minds not to upset anyone's faith. ¹⁴The Lord Jesus has made it clear to me that God considers all foods fit to eat. But if you think some foods are unfit to eat, then for you they are not fit.

¹⁵If you are hurting others by the foods you eat, you are not guided by love. Don't let your appetite destroy someone Christ died for. ¹⁶Don't let your right to eat bring shame to Christ. ¹⁷God's kingdom isn't about eating and drinking. It is about pleasing God, about living in peace, and about true happiness. All this comes from the Holy Spirit. ¹⁸If you serve Christ in this way, you will please God and be respected by people. ¹⁹We should try*ʷ* to live at peace and help each other have a strong faith.

²⁰Don't let your appetite destroy what God has done. All foods are fit to eat, but it is wrong to cause problems for others by what you eat. ²¹It is best not to eat meat or drink wine or do anything else that causes problems for other followers of the Lord. ²²What you believe about these things should be kept between you and God. You are fortunate, if your actions don't make you have doubts. ²³But if you do have doubts about what you eat, you are going against your beliefs. And you know that is wrong, because anything you do against your beliefs is sin.

Please Others and Not Yourself

15 If our faith is strong, we should be patient with the Lord's followers whose faith is weak. We should try to please them instead of ourselves. ²We should think of their good and try to help them by doing what pleases them. ³Even Christ did not try to please himself. But as the Scriptures say, "The people who insulted you also insulted me." ⁴And the Scriptures were written to teach and encourage us by giving us hope. ⁵God is the one who makes us patient and cheerful. I pray that he will help you live at peace with each other, as you follow Christ. ⁶Then all of you together will praise God, the Father of our Lord Jesus Christ.

The Good News Is for Jews and Gentiles

⁷Honor God by accepting each other, as Christ has accepted you. ⁸I tell you that Christ came as a servant of the Jews to show that God has kept the promises he made to their famous ancestors. Christ also came, ⁹so that the Gentiles would praise God for being kind to them. It is just as the Scriptures say,

"I will tell the nations
about you,
and I will sing praises
to your name."

¹⁰The Scriptures also say to the Gentiles, "Come and celebrate with God's people."

¹¹Again the Scriptures say,

"Praise the Lord,
all you Gentiles.
All you nations, come
and worship him."

¹²Isaiah says,

"Someone from David's family
will come to power.
He will rule the nations,
and they will put their hope
in him."

¹³I pray that God, who gives hope, will bless you with complete happiness and peace because of your faith. And may the power of the Holy Spirit fill you with hope.

ʷ **14.19** *We should try*: Some manuscripts have "We try."

Paul's Work as a Missionary

¹⁴My friends, I am sure that you are very good and that you have all the knowledge you need to teach each other. ¹⁵But I have spoken to you plainly and have tried to remind you of some things. God was so kind to me! ¹⁶He chose me to be a servant of Christ Jesus for the Gentiles and to do the work of a priest in the service of his good news. God did this so that the Holy Spirit could make the Gentiles into a holy offering, pleasing to him.

¹⁷Because of Christ Jesus, I can take pride in my service for God. ¹⁸In fact, all I will talk about is how Christ let me speak and work, so that the Gentiles would obey him. ¹⁹Indeed, I will tell how Christ worked miracles and wonders by the power of the Holy Spirit. I have preached the good news about him all the way from Jerusalem to Illyricum. ²⁰But I have always tried to preach where people have never heard about Christ. I am like a builder who doesn't build on anyone else's foundation. ²¹It is just as the Scriptures say,

"All who haven't been told
about him
  will see him,
and those who haven't heard
about him
  will understand."

Paul's Plan To Visit Rome

²²My work has always kept me from coming to see you. ²³Now there is nothing left for me to do in this part of the world, and for years I have wanted to visit you. ²⁴So I plan to stop off on my way to Spain. Then after a short, but refreshing, visit with you, I hope you will quickly send me on.

²⁵⁻²⁶I am now on my way to Jerusalem to deliver the money that the Lord's followers in Macedonia and Achaia collected for God's needy people. ²⁷This is something they really wanted to do. But sharing their money with the Jews was also like paying back a debt, because the Jews had already shared their spiritual blessings with the Gentiles. ²⁸After I have safely delivered this money, I will visit you and then go on to Spain. ²⁹And when I do arrive in Rome, I know it will be with the full blessings of Christ.

³⁰My friends, by the power of the Lord Jesus Christ and by the love that comes from the Holy Spirit, I beg you to pray sincerely with me and for me. ³¹Pray that God will protect me from the unbelievers in Judea, and that his people in Jerusalem will be pleased with what I am doing. ³²Ask God to let me come to you and have a pleasant and refreshing visit. ³³I pray that God, who gives peace, will be with all of you. Amen.

Personal Greetings

16 I have good things to say about Phoebe, who is a leader in the church at Cenchreae. ²Welcome her in a way that is proper for someone who has faith in the Lord and is one of God's own people. Help her in any way you can. After all, she has proved to be a respected leader for many others, including me.

³Give my greetings to Priscilla and Aquila. They have not only served Christ Jesus together with me, ⁴but they have even risked their lives for me. I am grateful for them and so are all the Gentile churches. ⁵Greet the church that meets in their home.

Greet my dear friend Epaenetus, who was the first person in Asia to have faith in Christ.

⁶Greet Mary, who has worked so hard for you.

⁷Greet my relatives[x] Andronicus and Junias,[y] who were in jail with me. They are highly respected by the apostles and were followers of Christ before I was.

⁸Greet Ampliatus, my dear friend whose faith is in the Lord.

⁹Greet Urbanus, who serves Christ along with us.

Greet my dear friend Stachys.

¹⁰Greet Apelles, a faithful servant of Christ.

Greet Aristobulus and his family.

¹¹Greet Herodion, who is a relative[z] of mine.

Greet Narcissus and the others in his family, who have faith in the Lord.

¹²Greet Tryphaena and Tryphosa, who work hard for the Lord.

Greet my dear friend Persis. She also works hard for the Lord.

¹³Greet Rufus, that special servant of the Lord, and greet his mother, who has been like a mother to me.

¹⁴Greet Asyncritus, Phlegon, Hermes, Patrobas, and Hermas, as well as our friends who are with them.

¹⁵Greet Philologus, Julia, Nereus and his sister, and Olympas, and all of God's people who are with them.

¹⁶Be sure to give each other a warm greeting.

All of Christ's churches greet you.

¹⁷My friends, I beg you to watch out for anyone who causes trouble and divides the church by refusing to do what all of you were taught. Stay away from them! ¹⁸They want to serve themselves and not Christ the Lord. Their flattery and fancy talk fool people who don't know any better. ¹⁹I am glad that

---

[x]**16.7** *relatives*: Or "Jewish friends." [y]**16.7** *Junias*: Or Junia. Some manuscripts have Julia.
[z]**16.11, 21** *relative(s)*: See the note at verse 7.

everyone knows how well you obey the Lord. But still, I want you to understand what is good and not have anything to do with evil. ²⁰Then God, who gives peace, will soon crush Satan under your feet. I pray that our Lord Jesus will be kind to you.

²¹Timothy, who works with me, sends his greetings, and so do my relatives,ᶻ Lucius, Jason, and Sosipater.

²²I, Tertius, also send my greetings. I am a follower of the Lord, and I wrote this letter.ᵃ

²³⁻²⁴Gaius welcomes me and the whole church into his home, and he sends his greetings.

Erastus, the city treasurer, and our dear friend Quartus send their greetings too.ᵇ

Paul's Closing Prayer

²⁵Praise God! He can make you strong by means of my good news, which is the message aboutᶜ Jesus Christ. For ages and ages this message was kept secret, ²⁶but now at last it has been told. The eternal God commanded his prophets to write about the good news, so that all nations would obey and have faith. ²⁷And now, because of Jesus Christ, we can praise the only wise God forever! Amen.ᵈ

ᶻ**16.11,21** *relative(s)*: See the note at verse 7.   ᵃ**16.22** *I wrote this letter*: Paul probably dictated this letter to Tertius.   ᵇ**16.23,24** *send their greetings too*: Some manuscripts add, "I pray that our Lord Jesus Christ will always be kind to you. Amen."   ᶜ**16.25** *about*: Or "from."   ᵈ**16.27** *Amen*: Some manuscripts have verses 25-27 after 14.23. Others have the verses here and after 14.23, and one manuscript has them after 15.33.

1 CORINTHIANS

ABOUT THIS LETTER

Although this letter is called the First Letter to the Corinthians, it is not really the first one that Paul wrote to this church. We know this because he mentions in this letter that he had written one before (5.9). The Christians in Corinth had also written to him (7.1), and part of First Corinthians contains Paul's answers to questions they had asked.

Corinth is a large port city in southern Greece. Paul began his work there in a Jewish meeting place, but he had to move next door to the home of a Gentile who had become a follower of Jesus (Acts 18.1-17). Most of the followers in Corinth were poor people (1 Corinthians 1.26-29), though some of them were wealthy (1 Corinthians 11.18-21), and one was even the city treasurer (Romans 16.23). While he was in Corinth, Paul worked as a tentmaker to earn a living (Acts 18.3; 1 Corinthians 4.12; 9.1-18).

Paul was especially concerned about the way the Corinthian Christians were always arguing and dividing themselves into groups (1.10—4.21) and about the way they treated one another (5.1—6.20). These are two of Paul's main concerns as he writes this letter. But he also wants to answer the questions they asked him about marriage (7.1-40) and food offered to idols (8.1-13). Paul encourages them to worship God the right way (10.1—14.40) and to be firm in their belief that God has given them victory over death (15.1-58).

Love, Paul tells them, is even more important than faith or hope. All of the problems in the church could be solved, if all the members would love one another, as Christians should:

> *Love is kind and patient,*
> *never jealous, boastful,*
> *proud, or rude.*
> *Love rejoices in the truth,*
> *but not in evil.*
> *Love is always supportive,*
> *loyal, hopeful,*
> *and trusting.*
> *Love never fails!*
> *(13.4, 5a, 6-8a)*

A QUICK LOOK AT THIS LETTER

Paul's Greeting and Prayer (1.1-9)
A Call for Unity (1.10—4.21)
Problems in Relationships (5.1—7.40)
Honoring God Instead of Idols (8.1—11.1)
Guidance for Worship and Church Life (11.2—14.40)
Christ's Victory Over Death (15.1-58)
An Offering for the Poor (16.1-4)
Paul's Travel Plans (16.5-12)
Personal Concerns and Greetings (16.13-24)

1 Corinthians 1.1

1 From Paul, chosen by God to be an apostle of Christ Jesus, and from Sosthenes, who is also a follower.

²To God's church in Corinth. Christ Jesus chose you to be his very own people, and you worship in his name, as we and all others do who call him Lord.

³My prayer is that God our Father and the Lord Jesus Christ will be kind to you and will bless you with peace!

⁴I never stop thanking my God for being kind enough to give you Christ Jesus, ⁵who helps you speak and understand so well. ⁶Now you are certain that everything we told you about our Lord Christ Jesus is true. ⁷You are not missing out on any blessings, as you wait for him to return. ⁸And until the day Christ does return, he will keep you completely innocent. ⁹God can be trusted, and he chose you to be partners with his Son, our Lord Jesus Christ.

Taking Sides

¹⁰My dear friends, as a follower of our Lord Jesus Christ, I beg you to get along with each other. Don't take sides. Always try to agree in what you think. ¹¹Several people from Chloe's family[a] have already reported to me that you keep arguing with each other. ¹²They have said that some of you claim to follow me, while others claim to follow Apollos or Peter[b] or Christ.

¹³Has Christ been divided up? Was I nailed to a cross for you? Were you baptized in my name? ¹⁴I thank God[c] that I didn't baptize any of you except Crispus and Gaius. ¹⁵Not one of you can say that you were baptized in my name. ¹⁶I did baptize the family[d] of Stephanas, but I don't remember if I baptized anyone else. ¹⁷Christ did not send me to baptize. He sent me to tell the good news without using big words that would make the cross of Christ lose its power.

Christ Is God's Power and Wisdom

¹⁸The message about the cross doesn't make any sense to lost people. But for those of us who are being saved, it is God's power at work. ¹⁹As God says in the Scriptures,

"I will destroy the wisdom
of all who claim
   to be wise.
I will confuse those
who think they know
   so much."

²⁰What happened to those wise people? What happened to those experts in the Scriptures? What happened to the ones who think they have all the answers? Didn't God show that the wisdom of this world is foolish? ²¹God was wise and decided not to let the people of this world use their wisdom to learn about him.

Instead, God chose to save only those who believe the foolish message we preach. ²²Jews ask for miracles, and Greeks want something that sounds wise. ²³But we preach that Christ was nailed to a cross. Most Jews have problems with this, and most Gentiles think it is foolish. ²⁴Our message is God's power and wisdom for the Jews and the Greeks that he has chosen. ²⁵Even when God is foolish, he is wiser than everyone else, and even when God is weak, he is stronger than everyone else.

²⁶My dear friends, remember what you were when God chose you. The people of this world didn't think that many of you were wise. Only a few of you were in places of power, and not many of you came from important families. ²⁷But God chose the foolish things of this world to put the wise to shame. He chose the weak things of this world to put the powerful to shame.

²⁸What the world thinks is worthless, useless, and nothing at all is what God has used to destroy what the world considers important. ²⁹God did all this to keep anyone from bragging to him. ³⁰You are God's children. He sent Christ Jesus to save us and to make us wise, acceptable, and holy. ³¹So if you want to brag, do what the Scriptures say and brag about the Lord.

Telling about Christ and the Cross

2 Friends, when I came and told you the mystery[e] that God had shared with us, I didn't use big words or try to sound wise. ²In fact, while I was with you, I made up my mind to speak only about Jesus Christ, who had been nailed to a cross.

³At first, I was weak and trembling with fear. ⁴When I talked with you or preached, I didn't try to prove anything by sounding wise. I simply let God's Spirit show his power. ⁵That way you would have faith because of God's power and not because of human wisdom.

⁶We do use wisdom when speaking to people who are mature in their faith. But it isn't the wisdom of this world or of its rulers, who will soon disappear. ⁷We speak of God's hidden and mysteri-

---

[a]1.11 *family*: Family members and possibly slaves and others who may have lived in the house. [b]1.12 *Peter*: The Greek text has "Cephas," which is an Aramaic name meaning "rock." Peter is the Greek name with the same meaning. [c]1.14 *I thank God*: Some manuscripts have "I thank my God." [d]1.16 *family*: See the note at 1.11. [e]2.1 *mystery*: Some manuscripts have "testimony."

ous wisdom that God decided to use for our glory long before the world began. [8]The rulers of this world didn't know anything about this wisdom. If they had known about it, they would not have nailed the glorious Lord to a cross. [9]But it is just as the Scriptures say,

"What God has planned
  for people who love him
is more than eyes have seen
  or ears have heard.
It has never even
  entered our minds!"

[10]God's Spirit has shown you everything. His Spirit finds out everything, even what is deep in the mind of God. [11]You are the only one who knows what is in your own mind, and God's Spirit is the only one who knows what is in God's mind. [12]But God has given us his Spirit. That's why we don't think the same way that the people of this world think. That's also why we can recognize the blessings that God has given us.

[13]Every word we speak was taught to us by God's Spirit, not by human wisdom. And this same Spirit helps us teach spiritual things to spiritual people.[f] [14]That's why only someone who has God's Spirit can understand spiritual blessings. Anyone who doesn't have God's Spirit thinks these blessings are foolish. [15]People who are guided by the Spirit can make all kinds of judgments, but they cannot be judged by others. [16]The Scriptures ask,

"Has anyone ever known
  the thoughts of the Lord
  or given him advice?"

But we understand what Christ is thinking.[g]

Working Together for God

3 My friends, you are acting like the people of this world. That's why I could not speak to you as spiritual people. You are like babies as far as your faith in Christ is concerned. [2]So I had to treat you like babies and feed you milk. You could not take solid food, and you still cannot, [3]because you are not yet spiritual. You are jealous and argue with each other. This proves that you are not spiritual and that you are acting like the people of this world.

[4]Some of you say that you follow me, and others claim to follow Apollos. Isn't that how ordinary people behave? [5]Apollos and I are merely servants who helped you to have faith. It was the Lord who made it all happen. [6]I planted the seeds, Apollos watered them, but God made them sprout and grow. [7]What matters isn't those who planted or watered, but God who made the plants grow. [8]The one who plants is just as important as the one who waters. And each one will be paid for what they do. [9]Apollos and I work together for God, and you are God's garden and God's building.

Only One Foundation

[10]God was kind and let me become an expert builder. I laid a foundation on which others have built. But we must each be careful how we build, [11]because Christ is the only foundation. [12-13]Whatever we build on that foundation will be tested by fire on the day of judgment. Then everyone will find out if we have used gold, silver, and precious stones, or wood, hay, and straw. [14]We will be rewarded if our building is left standing. [15]But if it is destroyed by the fire, we will lose everything. Yet we ourselves will be saved, like someone escaping from flames.

[16]All of you surely know that you are God's temple and that his Spirit lives in you. [17]Together you are God's holy temple, and God will destroy anyone who destroys his temple.

[18]Don't fool yourselves! If any of you think you are wise in the things of this world, you will have to become foolish before you can be truly wise. [19]This is because God considers the wisdom of this world to be foolish. It is just as the Scriptures say, "God catches the wise when they try to outsmart him." [20]The Scriptures also say, "The Lord knows that the plans made by wise people are useless." [21-22]So stop bragging about what anyone has done. Paul and Apollos and Peter[h] all belong to you. In fact, everything is yours, including the world, life, death, the present, and the future. Everything belongs to you, [23]and you belong to Christ, and Christ belongs to God.

The Work of the Apostles

4 Think of us as servants of Christ who have been given the work of explaining God's mysterious ways. [2]And since our first duty is to be faithful to the one we work for, [3]it doesn't matter to me if I am judged by you or even by a court of law. In fact, I don't judge myself. [4]I don't know of anything against me, but that doesn't prove that I am right. The Lord is my judge. [5]So don't judge anyone until the Lord returns. He will show what is hidden in the dark and what is in everyone's heart. Then

---

[f]**2.13** *teach spiritual things to spiritual people*: Or "compare spiritual things with spiritual things."   [g]**2.16** *we understand what Christ is thinking*: Or "we think as Christ does."
[h]**3.21,22** *Peter*: See the note at 1.12.

God will be the one who praises each of us.

⁶Friends, I have used Apollos and myself as examples to teach you the meaning of the saying, "Follow the rules." I want you to stop saying that one of us is better than the other. ⁷What is so special about you? What do you have that you were not given? And if it was given to you, how can you brag? ⁸Are you already satisfied? Are you now rich? Have you become kings while we are still nobodies? I wish you were kings. Then we could have a share in your kingdom.

⁹It seems to me that God has put us apostles in the worst possible place. We are like prisoners on their way to death. Angels and the people of this world just laugh at us. ¹⁰Because of Christ we are thought of as fools, but Christ has made you wise. We are weak and hated, but you are powerful and respected. ¹¹Even today we go hungry and thirsty and don't have anything to wear except rags. We are mistreated and don't have a place to live. ¹²We work hard with our own hands, and when people abuse us, we wish them well. When we suffer, we are patient. ¹³When someone curses us, we answer with kind words. Until now we are thought of as nothing more than the trash and garbage of this world.

¹⁴I am not writing to embarrass you. I want to help you, just as parents help their own dear children. ¹⁵Ten thousand people may teach you about Christ, but I am your only father. You became my children when I told you about Christ Jesus, ¹⁶and I want you to be like me. ¹⁷That's why I sent Timothy to you. I love him like a son, and he is a faithful servant of the Lord. Timothy will tell you what I do to follow Christ and how it agrees with what I always teach about Christ in every church.

¹⁸Some of you think I am not coming for a visit, and so you are bragging. ¹⁹But if the Lord lets me come, I will soon be there. Then I will find out if the ones who are doing all this bragging really have any power. ²⁰God's kingdom isn't just a lot of words. It is power. ²¹What do you want me to do when I arrive? Do you want me to be hard on you or to be kind and gentle?

Immoral Followers

5 I have heard terrible things about some of you. In fact, you are behaving worse than the Gentiles. A man is even sleeping with his own stepmother.[i] ²You are proud, when you ought to feel bad enough to chase away anyone who acts like that.

³⁻⁴I am with you only in my thoughts. But in the name of our Lord Jesus I have already judged this man, as though I were with you in person. So when you meet together and the power of the Lord Jesus is with you, I will be there too. ⁵You must then hand that man over to Satan. His body will be destroyed, but his spirit will be saved when the Lord Jesus returns.

⁶Stop being proud! Don't you know how a little yeast can spread through the whole batch of dough? ⁷Get rid of the old yeast! Then you will be like fresh bread made without yeast, and that is what you are. Our Passover lamb is Christ, who has already been sacrificed. ⁸So don't celebrate the festival by being evil and sinful, which is like serving bread made with yeast. Be pure and truthful and celebrate by using bread made without yeast.

⁹In my other letter[j] I told you not to have anything to do with immoral people. ¹⁰But I wasn't talking about the people of this world. You would have to leave this world to get away from everyone who is immoral or greedy or who cheats or worships idols. ¹¹I was talking about your own people who are immoral or greedy or worship idols or curse others or get drunk or cheat. Don't even eat with them! ¹²Why should I judge outsiders? Aren't we supposed to judge only church members? ¹³God judges everyone else. The Scriptures say, "Chase away any of your own people who are evil."

Taking Each Other to Court

6 When one of you has a complaint against another, do you take your complaint to a court of sinners? Or do you take it to God's people? ²Don't you know that God's people will judge the world? And if you are going to judge the world, can't you settle small problems? ³Don't you know that we will judge angels? And if that is so, we can surely judge everyday matters. ⁴Why do you take everyday complaints to judges who are not respected by the church? ⁵I say this to your shame. Aren't any of you wise enough to act as a judge between one follower and another? ⁶Why should one of you take another to be tried by unbelievers?

⁷When one of you takes another to court, all of you lose. It would be better to let yourselves be cheated and robbed. ⁸But instead, you cheat and rob other followers.

⁹Don't you know that evil people won't have a share in the blessings of

---

[i]5.1 *is even sleeping with his own stepmother*: Or "has even married his own stepmother."
[j]5.9 *other letter*: An unknown letter that Paul wrote to the Christians at Corinth before he wrote this one.

God's kingdom? Don't fool yourselves! No one who is immoral or worships idols or is unfaithful in marriage or is a pervert or behaves like a homosexual ¹⁰will share in God's kingdom. Neither will any thief or greedy person or drunkard or anyone who curses and cheats others. ¹¹Some of you used to be like that. But now the name of our Lord Jesus Christ and the power of God's Spirit have washed you and made you holy and acceptable to God.

Honor God with Your Body

¹²Some of you say, "We can do anything we want to." But I tell you that not everything is good for us. So I refuse to let anything have power over me. ¹³You also say, "Food is meant for our bodies, and our bodies are meant for food." But I tell you that God will destroy them both. We are not supposed to do indecent things with our bodies. We are to use them for the Lord who is in charge of our bodies. ¹⁴God will raise us from death by the same power that he used when he raised our Lord to life.

¹⁵Don't you know that your bodies are part of the body of Christ? Is it right for me to join part of the body of Christ to a prostitute? No, it isn't! ¹⁶Don't you know that a man who does that becomes part of her body? The Scriptures say, "The two of them will be like one person." ¹⁷But anyone who is joined to the Lord is one in spirit with him.

¹⁸Don't be immoral in matters of sex. That is a sin against your own body in a way that no other sin is. ¹⁹You surely know that your body is a temple where the Holy Spirit lives. The Spirit is in you and is a gift from God. You are no longer your own. ²⁰God paid a great price for you. So use your body to honor God.

Questions about Marriage

7 Now I will answer the questions that you asked in your letter. You asked, "Is it best for people not to marry?"ᵏ ²Well, having your own husband or wife should keep you from doing something immoral. ³Husbands and wives should be fair with each other about having sex. ⁴A wife belongs to her husband instead of to herself, and a husband belongs to his wife instead of to himself. ⁵So don't refuse sex to each other, unless you agree not to have sex for a little while, in order to spend time in prayer. Then Satan won't be able to tempt you because of your lack of self-control. ⁶In my opinion that is what should be done, though I don't know of anything the Lord said about this matter. ⁷I wish that all of you were like me, but God has given different gifts to each of us.

⁸Here is my advice for people who have never been married and for widows. You should stay single, just as I am. ⁹But if you don't have enough self-control, then go ahead and get married. After all, it is better to marry than to burn with desire.ˡ

¹⁰I instruct married couples to stay together, and this is exactly what the Lord himself taught. A wife who leaves her husband ¹¹should either stay single or go back to her husband. And a husband should not leave his wife.

¹²I don't know of anything else the Lord said about marriage. All I can do is to give you my own advice. If your wife isn't a follower of the Lord, but is willing to stay with you, don't divorce her. ¹³If your husband isn't a follower, but is willing to stay with you, don't divorce him. ¹⁴Your husband or wife who isn't a follower is made holy by having you as a mate. This also makes your children holy and keeps them from being unclean in God's sight.

¹⁵If your husband or wife isn't a follower of the Lord and decides to divorce you, then you should agree to it. You are no longer bound to that person. After all, God chose you and wants you to live at peace. ¹⁶And besides, how do you know if you will be able to save your husband or wife who isn't a follower?

Obeying the Lord at All Times

¹⁷In every church I tell the people to stay as they were when the Lord Jesus chose them and God called them to be his own. Now I say the same thing to you. ¹⁸If you are already circumcised, don't try to change it. If you are not circumcised, don't get circumcised. ¹⁹Being circumcised or uncircumcised isn't really what matters. The important thing is to obey God's commands. ²⁰So don't try to change what you were when God chose you. ²¹Are you a slave? Don't let that bother you. But if you can win your freedom, you should. ²²When the Lord chooses slaves, they become his free people. And when he chooses free people, they become slaves of Christ. ²³God paid a great price for you. So don't become slaves of anyone else. ²⁴Stay what you were when God chose you.

Unmarried People

²⁵I don't know of anything that the Lord said about people who have never been married.ᵐ But I will tell you what I think. And you can trust me, because the Lord has treated me with kindness.

ᵏ*7.1 people not to marry*: Or "married couples not to have sex." ˡ*7.9 with desire*: Or "in the flames of hell." ᵐ*7.25 people who have never been married*: Or "virgins."

²⁶We are now going through hard times, and I think it is best for you to stay as you are. ²⁷If you are married, stay married. If you are not married, don't try to get married. ²⁸It isn't wrong to marry, even if you have never been married before. But those who marry will have a lot of trouble, and I want to protect you from that.

²⁹My friends, what I mean is that the Lord will soon come,ⁿ and it won't matter if you are married or not. ³⁰It will be all the same if you are crying or laughing, or if you are buying or are completely broke. ³¹It won't make any difference how much good you are getting from this world or how much you like it. This world as we know it is now passing away.

³²I want all of you to be free from worry. An unmarried man worries about how to please the Lord. ³³But a married man has more worries. He must worry about the things of this world, because he wants to please his wife. ³⁴So he is pulled in two directions. Unmarried women and women who have never been married° worry only about pleasing the Lord, and they keep their bodies and minds pure. But a married woman worries about the things of this world, because she wants to please her husband. ³⁵What I am saying is for your own good—it isn't to limit your freedom. I want to help you to live right and to love the Lord above all else.

³⁶But suppose you are engaged to someone old enough to be married, and you want her so much that all you can think about is getting married. Then go ahead and marry.ᵖ There is nothing wrong with that. ³⁷But it is better to have self-control and to make up your mind not to marry. ³⁸It is perfectly all right to marry, but it is better not to get married at all.

³⁹A wife should stay married to her husband until he dies. Then she is free to marry again, but only to a man who is a follower of the Lord. ⁴⁰However, I think I am obeying God's Spirit when I say she would be happier to stay single.

Food Offered to Idols

8 In your letter you asked me about food offered to idols. All of us know something about this subject. But knowledge makes us proud of ourselves, while love makes us helpful to others. ²In fact, people who think they know so much don't know anything at all. ³But God has no doubts about who loves him.

⁴Even though food is offered to idols, we know that none of the idols in this world are alive. After all, there is only one God. ⁵Many things in heaven and on earth are called gods and lords, but none of them really are gods or lords. ⁶We have only one God, and he is the Father. He created everything, and we live for him. Jesus Christ is our only Lord. Everything was made by him, and by him life was given to us.

⁷Not everyone knows these things. In fact, many people have grown up with the belief that idols have life in them. So when they eat meat offered to idols, they are bothered by a weak conscience. ⁸But food doesn't bring us any closer to God. We are no worse off if we don't eat, and we are no better off if we do.

⁹Don't cause problems for someone with a weak conscience, just because you have the right to eat anything. ¹⁰You know all this, and so it doesn't bother you to eat in the temple of an idol. But suppose a person with a weak conscience sees you and decides to eat food that has been offered to idols. ¹¹Then what you know has destroyed someone Christ died for. ¹²When you sin by hurting a follower with a weak conscience, you sin against Christ. ¹³So if I hurt one of the Lord's followers by what I eat, I will never eat meat as long as I live.

The Rights of an Apostle

9 I am free. I am an apostle. I have seen the Lord Jesus and have led you to have faith in him. ²Others may think that I am not an apostle, but you are proof that I am an apostle to you.

³When people question me, I tell them ⁴that Barnabas and I have the right to our food and drink. ⁵We each have the right to marry one of the Lord's followers and to take her along with us, just as the other apostles and the Lord's brothers and Peterᑫ do. ⁶Are we the only ones who have to support ourselves by working at another job? ⁷Do soldiers pay their own salaries? Don't people who raise grapes eat some of what they grow? Don't shepherds get milk from their own goats?

⁸⁻⁹I am not saying this on my own authority. The Law of Moses tells us not to muzzle an ox when it is grinding grain. But was God concerned only about an

---

ⁿ**7.29** *the Lord will soon come:* Or "there's not much time left" or "the time for decision comes quickly." °**7.34** *women who have never been married:* Or "virgins." ᵖ**7.36** *But suppose you are engaged . . . go ahead and marry:* Verses 36-38 may also be translated: "³⁶"If you feel that you are not treating your grown daughter right by keeping her from getting married, then let her marry. You won't be doing anything wrong. ³⁷But it is better to have self-control and make up your mind not to let your daughter get married. ³⁸It is all right for you to let her marry. But it is better if you don't let her marry at all." ᑫ**9.5** *Peter:* See the note at 1.12.

ox? ¹⁰No, he wasn't! He was talking about us. This was written in the Scriptures so that all who plow and all who grind the grain will look forward to sharing in the harvest.

¹¹When we told the message to you, it was like planting spiritual seed. So we have the right to accept material things as our harvest from you. ¹²If others have the right to do this, we have an even greater right. But we haven't used this right of ours. We are willing to put up with anything to keep from causing trouble for the message about Christ.

¹³Don't you know that people who work in the temple make their living from what is brought to the temple? Don't you know that a person who serves at the altar is given part of what is offered? ¹⁴In the same way, the Lord wants everyone who preaches the good news to make a living from preaching this message.

¹⁵But I have never used these privileges of mine, and I am not writing this because I want to start now. I would rather die than have someone rob me of the right to take pride in this. ¹⁶I don't have any reason to brag about preaching the good news. Preaching is something God told me to do, and if I don't do it, I am doomed. ¹⁷If I preach because I want to, I will be paid. But even if I don't want to, it is still something God has sent me to do. ¹⁸What pay am I given? It is the chance to preach the good news free of charge and not to use the privileges that are mine because I am a preacher.

¹⁹I am not anyone's slave. But I have become a slave to everyone, so that I can win as many people as possible. ²⁰When I am with the Jews, I live like a Jew to win Jews. They are ruled by the Law of Moses, and I am not. But I live by the Law to win them. ²¹And when I am with people who are not ruled by the Law, I forget about the Law to win them. Of course, I never really forget about the law of God. In fact, I am ruled by the law of Christ. ²²When I am with people whose faith is weak, I live as they do to win them. I do everything I can to win everyone I possibly can. ²³I do all this for the good news, because I want to share in its blessings.

A Race and a Fight

²⁴You know that many runners enter a race, and only one of them wins the prize. So run to win! ²⁵Athletes work hard to win a crown that cannot last, but we do it for a crown that will last forever. ²⁶I don't run without a goal. And I don't box by beating my fists in the air. ²⁷I keep my body under control and make it my slave, so I won't lose out after telling the good news to others.

Don't Worship Idols

10 Friends, I want to remind you that all of our ancestors walked under the cloud and went through the sea. ²This was like being baptized and becoming followers of Moses. ³All of them also ate the same spiritual food ⁴and drank the same spiritual drink, which flowed from the spiritual rock that followed them. That rock was Christ. ⁵But most of them did not please God. So they died, and their bodies were scattered all over the desert.

⁶What happened to them is a warning to keep us from wanting to do the same evil things. ⁷They worshiped idols, just as the Scriptures say, "The people sat down to eat and drink. Then they got up to dance around." So don't worship idols. ⁸Some of those people did shameful things, and in a single day about twenty-three thousand of them died. Don't do shameful things as they did. ⁹And don't try to test Christ,ʳ as some of them did and were later bitten by poisonous snakes. ¹⁰Don't even grumble, as some of them did and were killed by the destroying angel. ¹¹These things happened to them as a warning to us. All this was written in the Scriptures to teach us who live in these last days.

¹²Even if you think you can stand up to temptation, be careful not to fall. ¹³You are tempted in the same way that everyone else is tempted. But God can be trusted not to let you be tempted too much, and he will show you how to escape from your temptations.

¹⁴My friends, you must keep away from idols. ¹⁵I am speaking to you as people who have enough sense to know what I am talking about. ¹⁶When we drink from the cup that we ask God to bless, isn't that sharing in the blood of Christ? When we eat the bread that we break, isn't that sharing in the body of Christ? ¹⁷By sharing in the same loaf of bread, we become one body, even though there are many of us.

¹⁸Aren't the people of Israel sharing in the worship when they gather around the altar and eat the sacrifices offered there? ¹⁹Am I saying that either the idols or the food sacrificed to them is anything at all? ²⁰No, I am not! That food is really sacrificed to demons and not to God. I don't want you to have anything to do with demons. ²¹You cannot drink from the cup of demons and still drink from the Lord's cup. You cannot eat at the table of demons and still eat at the Lord's table. ²²We would make

---

ʳ10.9 *Christ*: Some manuscripts have "the Lord."

Always Honor God

²³Some of you say, "We can do whatever we want to!" But I tell you that not everything may be good or helpful. ²⁴We should think about others and not about ourselves. ²⁵However, when you buy meat in the market, go ahead and eat it. Keep your conscience clear by not asking where the meat came from. ²⁶The Scriptures say, "The earth and everything in it belong to the Lord."

²⁷If an unbeliever invites you to dinner, and you want to go, then go. Eat whatever you are served. Don't cause a problem for someone's conscience by asking where the food came from. ²⁸⁻²⁹But if you are told that it has been sacrificed to idols, don't cause a problem by eating it. I don't mean a problem for yourself, but for the one who told you. Why should my freedom be limited by someone else's conscience? ³⁰If I give thanks for what I eat, why should anyone accuse me of doing wrong?

³¹When you eat or drink or do anything else, always do it to honor God. ³²Don't cause problems for Jews or Greeks or anyone else who belongs to God's church. ³³I always try to please others instead of myself, in the hope that many of them will be saved. 11 ¹You must follow my example, as I follow the example of Christ.

Rules for Worship

²I am proud of you, because you always remember me and obey the teachings I gave you. ³Now I want you to know that Christ is the head over all men, and a man is the head over a woman. But God is the head over Christ. ⁴This means that any man who prays or prophesies with something on his head brings shame to his head.

⁵But any woman who prays or prophesies without something on her head brings shame to her head. In fact, she may as well shave her head.ˢ ⁶A woman should wear something on her head. It is a disgrace for a woman to shave her head or cut her hair. But if she refuses to wear something on her head, let her cut off her hair.

⁷Men were created to be like God and to bring honor to God. This means that a man should not wear anything on his head. Women were created to bring honor to men. ⁸It was the woman who was made from a man, and not the man who was made from a woman. ⁹He wasn't created for her. She was created for him. ¹⁰And so, because of this, and also because of the angels, a woman ought to wear something on her head, as a sign of her authority.ᵗ

¹¹As far as the Lord is concerned, men and women need each other. ¹²It is true that the first woman came from a man, but all other men have been given birth by women. Yet God is the one who created everything. ¹³Ask yourselves if it is proper for a woman to pray without something on her head. ¹⁴Isn't it unnatural and disgraceful for men to have long hair? ¹⁵But long hair is a beautiful way for a woman to cover her head. ¹⁶This is how things are done in all of God's churches,ᵘ and that's why none of you should argue about what I have said.

Rules for the Lord's Supper

¹⁷Your worship services do you more harm than good. I am certainly not going to praise you for this. ¹⁸I am told that you can't get along with each other when you worship, and I am sure that some of what I have heard is true. ¹⁹You are bound to argue with each other, but it is easy to see which of you have God's approval.

²⁰When you meet together, you don't really celebrate the Lord's Supper. ²¹You even start eating before everyone gets to the meeting, and some of you go hungry, while others get drunk. ²²Don't you have homes where you can eat and drink? Do you hate God's church? Do you want to embarrass people who don't have anything? What can I say to you? I certainly cannot praise you.

The Lord's Supper
(Matthew 26.26-29; Mark 14.22-25; Luke 22.14-20)

²³I have already told you what the Lord Jesus did on the night he was betrayed. And it came from the Lord himself.

He took some bread in his hands. ²⁴Then after he had given thanks, he broke it and said, "This is my body, which is given for you. Eat this and remember me."

²⁵After the meal, Jesus took a cup of wine in his hands and said, "This is my blood, and with it God makes his new agreement with you. Drink this and remember me."

²⁶The Lord meant that when you eat this bread and drink from this cup, you tell about his death until he comes.

ˢ**11.5** *she may as well shave her head*: A woman's hair was a mark of beauty, and it was shameful for a woman to cut her hair short or to shave her head, so that she looked like a man.
ᵗ**11.10** *as a sign of her authority*: Or "as a sign that she is under someone's authority."
ᵘ**11.16** *This is how things are done in all of God's churches*: Or "There is no set rule for this in any of God's churches."

²⁷But if you eat the bread and drink the wine in a way that isn't worthy of the Lord, you sin against his body and blood. ²⁸That's why you must examine the way you eat and drink. ²⁹If you fail to understand that you are the body of the Lord, you will condemn yourselves by the way you eat and drink. ³⁰That's why many of you are sick and weak and why a lot of others have died. ³¹If we carefully judge ourselves, we won't be punished. ³²But when the Lord judges and punishes us, he does it to keep us from being condemned with the rest of the world.

³³My dear friends, you should wait until everyone gets there before you start eating. If you really are hungry, you can eat at home. Then you won't condemn yourselves when you meet together.

After I arrive, I will instruct you about the other matters.

Spiritual Gifts

12 My friends, you asked me about spiritual gifts. ²I want you to remember that before you became followers of the Lord, you were led in all the wrong ways by idols that cannot even talk. ³Now I want you to know that if you are led by God's Spirit, you will say that Jesus is Lord, and you will never curse Jesus.

⁴There are different kinds of spiritual gifts, but they all come from the same Spirit. ⁵There are different ways to serve the same Lord, ⁶and we can each do different things. Yet the same God works in all of us and helps us in everything we do.

⁷The Spirit has given each of us a special way of serving others. ⁸Some of us can speak with wisdom, while others can speak with knowledge, but these gifts come from the same Spirit. ⁹To others the Spirit has given great faith or the power to heal the sick ¹⁰or the power to work mighty miracles. Some of us are prophets, and some of us recognize when God's Spirit is present.ᵛ Others can speak different kinds of languages, and still others can tell what these languages mean. ¹¹But it is the Spirit who does all this and decides which gifts to give to each of us.

One Body with Many Parts

¹²The body of Christ has many different parts, just as any other body does. ¹³Some of us are Jews, and others are Gentiles. Some of us are slaves, and others are free. But God's Spirit baptized each of us and made us part of the body of Christ. Now we each drink from that same Spirit.ʷ

¹⁴Our bodies don't have just one part. They have many parts. ¹⁵Suppose a foot says, "I'm not a hand, and so I'm not part of the body." Wouldn't the foot still belong to the body? ¹⁶Or suppose an ear says, "I'm not an eye, and so I'm not part of the body." Wouldn't the ear still belong to the body? ¹⁷If our bodies were only an eye, we couldn't hear a thing. And if they were only an ear, we couldn't smell a thing. ¹⁸But God has put all parts of our body together in the way that he decided is best.

¹⁹A body isn't really a body, unless there is more than one part. ²⁰It takes many parts to make a single body. ²¹That's why the eyes cannot say they don't need the hands. That's also why the head cannot say it doesn't need the feet. ²²In fact, we cannot get along without the parts of the body that seem to be the weakest. ²³We take special care to dress up some parts of our bodies. We are modest about our personal parts, ²⁴but we don't have to be modest about other parts.

God put our bodies together in such a way that even the parts that seem the least important are valuable. ²⁵He did this to make all parts of the body work together smoothly, with each part caring about the others. ²⁶If one part of our body hurts, we hurt all over. If one part of our body is honored, the whole body will be happy.

²⁷Together you are the body of Christ. Each one of you is part of his body. ²⁸First, God chose some people to be apostles and prophets and teachers for the church. But he also chose some to work miracles or heal the sick or help others or be leaders or speak different kinds of languages. ²⁹Not everyone is an apostle. Not everyone is a prophet. Not everyone is a teacher. Not everyone can work miracles. ³⁰Not everyone can heal the sick. Not everyone can speak different kinds of languages. Not everyone can tell what these languages mean. ³¹I want you to desire the best gifts.ˣ So I will show you a much better way.

Love

13 What if I could speak all languages of humans and of angels?

ᵛ**12.10** *and some of us . . . present*: Or "and some of us recognize the difference between God's Spirit and other spirits." ʷ**12.13** *Some of us are Jews . . . that same Spirit*: Verse 13 may also be translated, "God's Spirit is inside each of us, and all around us as well. So it doesn't matter that some of us are Jews and others are Gentiles and that some are slaves and others are free. Together we are one body." ˣ**12.31** *I want you to desire the best gifts*: Or "You desire the best gifts."

If I did not love others,
   I would be nothing more
than a noisy gong
   or a clanging cymbal.
² What if I could prophesy
   and understand all secrets
      and all knowledge?
And what if I had faith
   that moved mountains?
I would be nothing,
   unless I loved others.
³ What if I gave away all
      that I owned
   and let myself
      be burned alive?ʸ
I would gain nothing,
   unless I loved others.
⁴ Love is kind and patient,
never jealous, boastful,
   proud, or ⁵rude.
Love isn't selfish
   or quick tempered.
It doesn't keep a record
   of wrongs that others do.
⁶ Love rejoices in the truth,
   but not in evil.
⁷ Love is always supportive,
   loyal, hopeful,
      and trusting.
⁸ Love never fails!

Everyone who prophesies
      will stop,
   and unknown languages
      will no longer
         be spoken.
   All that we know
      will be forgotten.
⁹ We don't know everything,
   and our prophecies
      are not complete.
¹⁰ But what is perfect
      will someday appear,
   and what isn't perfect
      will then disappear.

¹¹ When we were children,
   we thought and reasoned
      as children do.
But when we grew up,
   we quit our childish ways.
¹² Now all we can see of God
   is like a cloudy picture
      in a mirror.
Later we will see him
   face to face.
We don't know everything,
   but then we will,
just as God completely
   understands us.
¹³ For now there are faith,
   hope, and love.
But of these three,
   the greatest is love.

Speaking Unknown Languages and Prophesying

14 Love should be your guide. Be eager to have the gifts that come from the Holy Spirit, especially the gift of prophecy. ²If you speak languages that others don't know, God will understand what you are saying, though no one else will know what you mean. You will be talking about mysteries that only the Spirit understands. ³But when you prophesy, you will be understood, and others will be helped. They will be encouraged and made to feel better.

⁴By speaking languages that others don't know, you help only yourself. But by prophesying you help everyone in the church. ⁵I am glad for you to speak unknown languages, although I had rather for you to prophesy. In fact, prophesying does much more good than speaking unknown languages, unless someone can help the church by explaining what you mean.

⁶My friends, what good would it do, if I came and spoke unknown languages to you and didn't explain what I meant? How would I help you, unless I told you what God had shown me or gave you some knowledge or prophecy or teaching? ⁷If all musical instruments sounded alike, how would you know the difference between a flute and a harp? ⁸If a bugle call isn't clear, how would you know to get ready for battle?

⁹That's how it is when you speak unknown languages. If no one can understand what you are talking about, you will only be talking to the wind. ¹⁰There are many different languages in this world, and all of them make sense. ¹¹But if I don't understand the language that someone is using, we will be like foreigners to each other. ¹²If you really want spiritual gifts, choose the ones that will be most helpful to the church.

¹³When we speak languages that others don't know, we should pray for the power to explain what we mean. ¹⁴For example, if I use an unknown language in my prayers, my spirit prays but my mind is useless. ¹⁵Then what should I do? There are times when I should pray with my spirit, and times when I should pray with my mind. Sometimes I should sing with my spirit, and at other times I should sing with my mind.

¹⁶Suppose some strangers are in your worship service, when you are praising God with your spirit. If they don't understand you, how will they know to say, "Amen"? ¹⁷You may be worshiping God in a wonderful way, but no one else will be helped. ¹⁸I thank God that I

ʸ **13.3** *and let myself be burned alive:* Some manuscripts have "so that I could brag."

speak unknown languages more than any of you. [19]But words that make sense can help the church. That's why in church I had rather speak five words that make sense than to speak ten thousand words in a language that others don't know.

[20]My friends, stop thinking like children. Think like mature people and be as innocent as tiny babies. [21]In the Scriptures the Lord says,

"I will use strangers
  who speak unknown languages
    to talk to my people.
They will speak to them
    in foreign languages,
but still my people
    won't listen to me."

[22]Languages that others don't know may mean something to unbelievers, but not to the Lord's followers. Prophecy, on the other hand, is for followers, not for unbelievers. [23]Suppose everyone in your worship service started speaking unknown languages, and some outsiders or some unbelievers come in. Won't they think you are crazy? [24]But suppose all of you are prophesying when those unbelievers and outsiders come in. They will realize that they are sinners, and they will want to change their ways because of what you are saying. [25]They will tell what is hidden in their hearts. Then they will kneel down and say to God, "We are certain that you are with these people."

Worship Must Be Orderly

[26]My friends, when you meet to worship, you must do everything for the good of everyone there. That's how it should be when someone sings or teaches or tells what God has said or speaks an unknown language or explains what the language means. [27]No more than two or three of you should speak unknown languages during the meeting. You must take turns, and someone should always be there to explain what you mean. [28]If no one can explain, you must keep silent in church and speak only to yourself and to God.

[29]Two or three persons may prophesy, and everyone else must listen carefully. [30]If someone sitting there receives a message from God, the speaker must stop and let the other person speak. [31]Let only one person speak at a time, then all of you will learn something and be encouraged. [32]A prophet should be willing to stop and let someone else speak. [33]God wants everything to be done peacefully and in order.

When God's people meet in church, [34]the women must not be allowed to speak. They must keep quiet and listen, as the Law of Moses teaches. [35]If there is something they want to know, they can ask their husbands when they get home. It is disgraceful for women to speak in church. [36]God's message did not start with you people, and you are not the only ones it has reached.

[37]If you think of yourself as a prophet or a spiritual person, you will know that I am writing only what the Lord has commanded. [38]So don't pay attention to anyone who ignores what I am writing. [39]My friends, be eager to prophesy and don't stop anyone from speaking languages that others don't know. [40]But do everything properly and in order.

Christ Was Raised to Life

15 My friends, I want you to remember the message that I preached and that you believed and trusted. [2]You will be saved by this message, if you hold firmly to it. But if you don't, your faith was all for nothing.

[3]I told you the most important part of the message exactly as it was told to me. That part is:

Christ died for our sins,
    as the Scriptures say.
[4] He was buried,
    and three days later
he was raised to life,
    as the Scriptures say.
[5] Christ appeared to Peter,[z]
    then to the twelve.
[6] After this, he appeared
    to more than five hundred
        other followers.
Most of them are still alive,
    but some have died.
[7] He also appeared to James,
    and then to all
        of the apostles.

[8]Finally, he appeared to me, even though I am like someone who was born at the wrong time.[a]

[9]I am the least important of all the apostles. In fact, I caused so much trouble for God's church that I don't even deserve to be called an apostle. [10]But God was kind! He made me what I am, and his wonderful kindness wasn't wasted. I worked much harder than any of the other apostles, although it was really God's kindness at work and not me. [11]But it doesn't matter if I preached or if they preached. All of you believed the message just the same.

God's People Will Be Raised to Life

[12]If we preach that Christ was raised from death, how can some of you say

---

[z]**15.5** *Peter*: See the note at 1.12.   [a]**15.8** *who was born at the wrong time*: The meaning of these words in Greek is not clear.

that the dead will not be raised to life? ¹³If they won't be raised to life, Christ himself wasn't raised to life. ¹⁴And if Christ wasn't raised to life, our message is worthless, and so is your faith. ¹⁵If the dead won't be raised to life, we have told lies about God by saying that he raised Christ to life, when he really did not. ¹⁶So if the dead won't be raised to life, Christ wasn't raised to life. ¹⁷Unless Christ was raised to life, your faith is useless, and you are still living in your sins. ¹⁸And those people who died after putting their faith in him are completely lost. ¹⁹If our hope in Christ is good only for this life, we are worse off than anyone else.

²⁰But Christ has been raised to life! And he makes us certain that others will also be raised to life. ²¹Just as we will die because of Adam, we will be raised to life because of Christ. ²²Adam brought death to all of us, and Christ will bring life to all of us. ²³But we must each wait our turn. Christ was the first to be raised to life, and his people will be raised to life when he returns. ²⁴Then after Christ has destroyed all powers and forces, the end will come, and he will give the kingdom to God the Father. ²⁵Christ will rule until he puts all his enemies under his power, ²⁶and the last enemy he destroys will be death. ²⁷When the Scriptures say that he will put everything under his power, they don't include God. It was God who put everything under the power of Christ. ²⁸After everything is under the power of God's Son, he will put himself under the power of God, who put everything under his Son's power. Then God will mean everything to everyone.

²⁹If the dead are not going to be raised to life, what will people do who are being baptized for them? Why are they being baptized for those dead people? ³⁰And why do we always risk our lives ³¹and face death every day? The pride that I have in you because of Christ Jesus our Lord is what makes me say this. ³²What do you think I gained by fighting wild animals in Ephesus? If the dead are not raised to life,

"Let's eat and drink.
Tomorrow we die."

³³Don't fool yourselves. Bad friends will destroy you. ³⁴Be sensible and stop sinning. You should be embarrassed that some people still don't know about God.

What Our Bodies Will Be Like

³⁵Some of you have asked, "How will the dead be raised to life? What kind of bodies will they have?" ³⁶Don't be foolish. A seed must die before it can sprout from the ground. ³⁷Wheat seeds and all other seeds look different from the sprouts that come up. ³⁸This is because God gives everything the kind of body he wants it to have. ³⁹People, animals, birds, and fish are each made of flesh, but none of them are alike. ⁴⁰Everything in the heavens has a body, and so does everything on earth. But each one is very different from all the others. ⁴¹The sun isn't like the moon, the moon isn't like the stars, and each star is different.

⁴²That's how it will be when our bodies are raised to life. These bodies will die, but the bodies that are raised will live forever. ⁴³These ugly and weak bodies will become beautiful and strong. ⁴⁴As surely as there are physical bodies, there are spiritual bodies. And our physical bodies will be changed into spiritual bodies.

⁴⁵The first man was named Adam, and the Scriptures tell us that he was a living person. But Jesus, who may be called the last Adam, is a life-giving spirit. ⁴⁶We see that the one with a spiritual body did not come first. He came after the one who had a physical body. ⁴⁷The first man was made from the dust of the earth, but the second man came from heaven. ⁴⁸Everyone on earth has a body like the body of the one who was made from the dust of the earth. And everyone in heaven has a body like the body of the one who came from heaven. ⁴⁹Just as we are like the one who was made out of earth, we will be like the one who came from heaven.

⁵⁰My friends, I want you to know that our bodies of flesh and blood will decay. This means that they cannot share in God's kingdom, which lasts forever. ⁵¹I will explain a mystery to you. Not every one of us will die, but we will all be changed. ⁵²It will happen suddenly, quicker than the blink of an eye. At the sound of the last trumpet the dead will be raised. We will all be changed, so that we will never die again. ⁵³Our dead and decaying bodies will be changed into bodies that won't die or decay. ⁵⁴The bodies we now have are weak and can die. But they will be changed into bodies that are eternal. Then the Scriptures will come true,

"Death has lost the battle!
⁵⁵ Where is its victory?
Where is its sting?"

⁵⁶Sin is what gives death its sting, and the Law is the power behind sin. ⁵⁷But thank God for letting our Lord Jesus Christ give us the victory!

⁵⁸My dear friends, stand firm and don't be shaken. Always keep busy working for the Lord. You know that everything you do for him is worthwhile.

A Collection for God's People

16 When you collect money for God's people, I want you to do exactly what I told the churches in Galatia to do. ²That is, each Sunday each of you must put aside part of what you have earned. If you do this, you won't have to take up a collection when I come. ³Choose some followers to take the money to Jerusalem. I will send them on with the money and with letters which show that you approve of them. ⁴If you think I should go along, they can go with me.

Paul's Travel Plans

⁵After I have gone through Macedonia, I hope to see you ⁶and visit with you for a while. I may even stay all winter, so that you can help me on my way to wherever I will be going next. ⁷If the Lord lets me, I would rather come later for a longer visit than to stop off now for only a short visit. ⁸I will stay in Ephesus until Pentecost, ⁹because there is a wonderful opportunity for me to do some work here. But there are also many people who are against me.

¹⁰When Timothy arrives, give him a friendly welcome. He is doing the Lord's work, just as I am. ¹¹Don't let anyone mistreat him. I am looking for him to return to me together with the other followers. So when he leaves, send him off with your blessings.

¹²I have tried hard to get our friend Apollos to visit you with the other followers. He doesn't want to come just now, but he will come when he can.

Personal Concerns and Greetings

¹³Keep alert. Be firm in your faith. Stay brave and strong. ¹⁴Show love in everything you do.

¹⁵You know that Stephanas and his family were the first in Achaia to have faith in the Lord. They have done all they can for God's people. My friends, I ask you ¹⁶to obey leaders like them and to do the same for all others who work hard with you.

¹⁷I was glad to see Stephanas and Fortunatus and Achaicus. Having them here was like having you. ¹⁸They made me feel much better, just as they made you feel better. You should appreciate people like them.

¹⁹Greetings from the churches in Asia.

Aquila and Priscilla, together with the church that meets in their house, send greetings in the name of the Lord.

²⁰All of the Lord's followers send their greetings.

Give each other a warm greeting.

²¹I am signing this letter myself: PAUL.

²²I pray that God will put a curse on everyone who doesn't love the Lord. And may the Lord come soon.

²³I pray that the Lord Jesus will be kind to you.

²⁴I love everyone who belongs to Christ Jesus.

2 CORINTHIANS

ABOUT THIS LETTER

In the beginning of this letter Paul answers the concerns of the Christians in Corinth who accused him of not living up to his promise to visit them. Paul had changed his mind for a good reason. He had stayed away from Corinth so that he would not seem to be too hard and demanding (1.23). He also wanted to see if they would follow his instructions about forgiving and comforting people who had sinned (2.5-11).

Paul reminds the Corinthians that God is generous and wants them to be just as generous in their giving to help God's people in Jerusalem and Judea (8.1—9.15).

Paul is a servant of God's new agreement (3.1-17). He is faithful in trying to bring people to God, even if it means terrible suffering for himself (4.1—6.13; 10.1—12.10). And what has God done to make it possible for us to come to him?

God has done it all! He sent Christ to make peace between himself and us, and he has given us the work of making peace between himself and others.

What we mean is that God was in Christ, offering peace and forgiveness to the people of this world. And he has given us the work of sharing his message about peace. (5.18, 19)

A QUICK LOOK AT THIS LETTER

Paul Gives Thanks to God (1.1-11)
The Work of an Apostle for God's People (1.12—2.17)
Guided by the Love of Christ (3.1—7.16)
Gifts for the Poor (8.1—9.15)
Paul Is a True Apostle (10.1—13.10)
Final Greetings (13.11-13)

---

1 From Paul, chosen by God to be an apostle of Jesus Christ, and from Timothy, who is also a follower.

To God's church in Corinth and to all of God's people in Achaia.

²I pray that God our Father and the Lord Jesus Christ will be kind to you and will bless you with peace!

Paul Gives Thanks

³Praise God, the Father of our Lord Jesus Christ! The Father is a merciful God, who always gives us comfort. ⁴He comforts us when we are in trouble, so that we can share that same comfort with others in trouble. ⁵We share in the terrible sufferings of Christ, but also in the wonderful comfort he gives. ⁶We suffer in the hope that you will be comforted and saved. And because we are comforted, you will also be comforted, as you patiently endure suffering like ours. ⁷You never disappoint us. You suffered as much as we did, and we know that you will be comforted as we were.

⁸My friends, I want you to know what a hard time we had in Asia. Our sufferings were so horrible and so unbearable that death seemed certain. ⁹In fact, we felt sure that we were going to die. But this made us stop trusting in ourselves and start trusting God, who raises the dead to life. ¹⁰God saved us from the threat of death,[a] and we are sure that he will do it again and again. ¹¹Please help us by praying for us. Then many people will give thanks for the blessings we receive in answer to all these prayers.

---

[a] 1.10 *the threat of death*: Some manuscripts have "many threats of death."

Paul's Change of Plans

¹²We can be proud of our clear conscience. We have always lived honestly and sincerely, especially when we were with you. And we were guided by God's wonderful kindness instead of by the wisdom of this world. ¹³I am not writing anything you cannot read and understand. I hope you will understand it completely, ¹⁴just as you already partly understand us. Then when our Lord Jesus returns, you can be as proud of us as we are of you.

¹⁵I was so sure of your pride in us that I had planned to visit you first of all. In this way you would have the blessing of two visits from me. ¹⁶Once on my way to Macedonia and again on my return from there. Then you could send me on to Judea. ¹⁷Do you think I couldn't make up my mind about what to do? Or do I seem like someone who says "Yes" or "No" simply to please others? ¹⁸God can be trusted, and so can I, when I say that our answer to you has always been "Yes" and never "No." ¹⁹This is because Jesus Christ the Son of God is always "Yes" and never "No." And he is the one that Silas,*ᵇ* Timothy, and I told you about.

²⁰Christ says "Yes" to all of God's promises. That's why we have Christ to say "Amen"*ᶜ* for us to the glory of God. ²¹And so God makes it possible for you and us to stand firmly together with Christ. God is also the one who chose us ²²and put his Spirit in our hearts to show that we belong only to him.

²³God is my witness that I stayed away from Corinth, just to keep from being hard on you. ²⁴We are not bosses who tell you what to believe. We are working with you to make you glad, because your faith is strong.

2 I have decided not to make my next visit with you so painful. ²If I make you feel bad, who would be left to cheer me up, except the people I had made to feel bad? ³The reason I want to be happy is to make you happy. I wrote as I did because I didn't want to visit you and be made to feel bad, when you should make me feel happy. ⁴At the time I wrote, I was suffering terribly. My eyes were full of tears, and my heart was broken. But I didn't want to make you feel bad. I only wanted to let you know how much I cared for you.

Forgiveness

⁵I don't want to be hard on you. But if one of you has made someone feel bad, I am not really the one who has been made to feel bad. Some of you are the ones. ⁶Most of you have already pointed out the wrong that person did, and that is punishment enough for what was done.

⁷When people sin, you should forgive and comfort them, so they won't give up in despair. ⁸You should make them sure of your love for them.

⁹I also wrote because I wanted to test you and find out if you would follow my instructions. ¹⁰I will forgive anyone you forgive. Yes, for your sake and with Christ as my witness, I have forgiven whatever needed to be forgiven. ¹¹I have done this to keep Satan from getting the better of us. We all know what goes on in his mind.

¹²When I went to Troas to preach the good news about Christ, I found that the Lord had already prepared the way. ¹³But I was worried when I didn't find my friend Titus there. So I left the other followers and went on to Macedonia.

¹⁴I am grateful that God always makes it possible for Christ to lead us to victory. God also helps us spread the knowledge about Christ everywhere, and this knowledge is like the smell of perfume. ¹⁵⁻¹⁶In fact, God thinks of us as a perfume that brings Christ to everyone. For people who are being saved, this perfume has a sweet smell and leads them to a better life. But for people who are lost, it has a bad smell and leads them to a horrible death.

No one really has what it takes to do this work. ¹⁷A lot of people try to get rich from preaching God's message. But we are God's sincere messengers, and by the power of Christ we speak our message with God as our witness.

God's New Agreement

3 Are we once again bragging about ourselves? Do we need letters to you or from you to tell others about us? Some people do need letters that tell about them. ²But you are our letter, and you are in our*ᵈ* hearts for everyone to read and understand. ³You are like a letter written by Christ and delivered by us. But you are not written with pen and ink or on tablets made of stone. You are written in our hearts by the Spirit of the living God.

⁴We are sure about all this. Christ makes us sure in the very presence of God. ⁵We don't have the right to claim that we have done anything on our own. God gives us what it takes to do all that we do. ⁶He makes us worthy to be the servants of his new agreement that comes from the Holy Spirit and not from a written Law. After all, the Law brings death, but the Spirit brings life.

---

*ᵇ***1.19** *Silas*: The Greek text has "Silvanus," which is another form of the name Silas.
*ᶜ***1.20** *Amen*: The word "amen" is used here with the meaning of "yes." *ᵈ***3.2** *our*: Some manuscripts have "your."

⁷The Law of Moses brought only the promise of death, even though it was carved on stones and given in a wonderful way. Still the Law made Moses' face shine so brightly that the people of Israel could not look at it, even though it was a fading glory. ⁸So won't the agreement that the Spirit brings to us be even more wonderful? ⁹If something that brings the death sentence is glorious, won't something that makes us acceptable to God be even more glorious? ¹⁰In fact, the new agreement is so wonderful that the Law is no longer glorious at all. ¹¹The Law was given with a glory that faded away. But the glory of the new agreement is much greater, because it will never fade away.

¹²This wonderful hope makes us feel like speaking freely. ¹³We are not like Moses. His face was shining, but he covered it to keep the people of Israel from seeing the brightness fade away. ¹⁴The people were stubborn, and something still keeps them from seeing the truth when the Law is read. Only Christ can take away the covering that keeps them from seeing.

¹⁵When the Law of Moses is read, they have their minds covered over ¹⁶with a covering that is removed only for those who turn to the Lord. ¹⁷The Lord and the Spirit are one and the same, and the Lord's Spirit sets us free. ¹⁸So our faces are not covered. They show the bright glory of the Lord, as the Lord's Spirit makes us more and more like our glorious Lord.

Treasure in Clay Jars

4 God has been kind enough to trust us with this work. That's why we never give up. ²We don't do shameful things that must be kept secret. And we don't try to fool anyone or twist God's message around. God is our witness that we speak only the truth, so others will be sure that we can be trusted. ³If there is anything hidden about our message, it is hidden only to someone who is lost.

⁴The god who rules this world has blinded the minds of unbelievers. They cannot see the light, which is the good news about our glorious Christ, who shows what God is like. ⁵We are not preaching about ourselves. Our message is that Jesus Christ is Lord. He also sent us to be your servants. ⁶The Scriptures say, "God commanded light to shine in the dark." Now God is shining in our hearts to let you know that his glory is seen in Jesus Christ.

⁷We are like clay jars in which this treasure is stored. The real power comes from God and not from us. ⁸We often suffer, but we are never crushed. Even when we don't know what to do, we never give up. ⁹In times of trouble, God is with us, and when we are knocked down, we get up again. ¹⁰⁻¹¹We face death every day because of Jesus. Our bodies show what his death was like, so that his life can also be seen in us. ¹²This means that death is working in us, but life is working in you.

¹³In the Scriptures it says, "I spoke because I had faith." We have that same kind of faith. So we speak ¹⁴because we know that God raised the Lord Jesus to life. And just as God raised Jesus, he will also raise us to life. Then he will bring us into his presence together with you. ¹⁵All of this has been done for you, so that more and more people will know how kind God is and will praise and honor him.

Faith in the Lord

¹⁶We never give up. Our bodies are gradually dying, but we ourselves are being made stronger each day. ¹⁷These little troubles are getting us ready for an eternal glory that will make all our troubles seem like nothing. ¹⁸Things that are seen don't last forever, but things that are not seen are eternal. That's why we keep our minds on the things that cannot be seen.

5 Our bodies are like tents that we live in here on earth. But when these tents are destroyed, we know that God will give each of us a place to live. These homes will not be buildings that someone has made, but they are in heaven and will last forever. ²While we are here on earth, we sigh because we want to live in that heavenly home. ³We want to put it on like clothes and not be naked.

⁴These tents we now live in are like a heavy burden, and we groan. But we don't do this just because we want to leave these bodies that will die. It is because we want to change them for bodies that will never die. ⁵God is the one who makes all of this possible. He has given us his Spirit to make us certain that he will do it. ⁶So always be cheerful!

As long as we are in these bodies, we are away from the Lord. ⁷But we live by faith, not by what we see. ⁸We should be cheerful, because we would rather leave these bodies and be at home with the Lord. ⁹But whether we are at home with the Lord or away from him, we still try our best to please him. ¹⁰After all, Christ will judge each of us for the good or the bad that we do while living in these bodies.

Bringing People to God

¹¹We know what it means to respect the Lord, and we encourage everyone to turn to him. God himself knows what

we are like, and I hope you also know what kind of people we are. ¹²We are not trying once more to brag about ourselves. But we want you to be proud of us, when you are with those who are not sincere and brag about what others think of them.

¹³If we seem out of our minds, it is between God and us. But if we are in our right minds, it is for your good. ¹⁴We are ruled by Christ's love for us. We are certain that if one person died for everyone else, then all of us have died. ¹⁵And Christ did die for all of us. He died so we would no longer live for ourselves, but for the one who died and was raised to life for us.

¹⁶We are careful not to judge people by what they seem to be, though we once judged Christ in that way. ¹⁷Anyone who belongs to Christ is a new person. The past is forgotten, and everything is new. ¹⁸God has done it all! He sent Christ to make peace between himself and us, and he has given us the work of making peace between himself and others.

¹⁹What we mean is that God was in Christ, offering peace and forgiveness to the people of this world. And he has given us the work of sharing his message about peace. ²⁰We were sent to speak for Christ, and God is begging you to listen to our message. We speak for Christ and sincerely ask you to make peace with God. ²¹Christ never sinned! But God treated him as a sinner, so that Christ could make us acceptable to God.

6 We work together with God, and we beg you to make good use of God's kindness to you. ²In the Scriptures God says,

"When the time came,
 I listened to you,
and when you needed help,
 I came to save you."

That time has come. This is the day for you to be saved.

³We don't want anyone to find fault with our work, and so we try hard not to cause problems. ⁴But in everything and in every way we show that we truly are God's servants. We have always been patient, though we have had a lot of trouble, suffering, and hard times. ⁵We have been beaten, put in jail, and hurt in riots. We have worked hard and have gone without sleep or food. ⁶But we have kept ourselves pure and have been understanding, patient, and kind. The Holy Spirit has been with us, and our love has been real. ⁷We have spoken the truth, and God's power has worked in us. In all our struggles we have said and done only what is right.

⁸Whether we were honored or dishonored or praised or cursed, we always told the truth about ourselves. But some people said we did not. ⁹We are unknown to others, but well known to you. We seem to be dying, and yet we are still alive. We have been punished, but never killed, ¹⁰and we are always happy, even in times of suffering. Although we are poor, we have made many people rich. And though we own nothing, everything is ours.

¹¹Friends in Corinth, we are telling the truth when we say that there is room in our hearts for you. ¹²We are not holding back on our love for you, but you are holding back on your love for us. ¹³I speak to you as I would speak to my own children. Please make room in your hearts for us.

The Temple of the Living God

¹⁴Stay away from people who are not followers of the Lord! Can someone who is good get along with someone who is evil? Are light and darkness the same? ¹⁵Is Christ a friend of Satan?ᵉ Can people who follow the Lord have anything in common with those who don't? ¹⁶Do idols belong in the temple of God? We are the temple of the living God, as God himself says,

"I will live with these people
 and walk among them.
I will be their God,
and they will be
 my people."

¹⁷The Lord also says,

"Leave them and stay away!
Don't touch anything
 that isn't clean.
Then I will welcome you
¹⁸ and be your Father.
You will be my sons
 and my daughters,
as surely as I am God,
 the All-Powerful."

7 My friends, God has made us these promises. So we should stay away from everything that keeps our bodies and spirits from being clean. We should honor God and try to be completely like him.

The Church Makes Paul Happy

²Make a place for us in your hearts! We haven't mistreated or hurt anyone. We haven't cheated anyone. ³I am not saying this to be hard on you. But, as I have said before, you will always be in our thoughts, whether we live or die.

ᵉ**6.15** *Satan*: The Greek text has "Beliar," which is another form of the Hebrew word "Belial," meaning "wicked" or "useless." The Jewish people sometimes used this as a name for Satan.

⁴I trust you completely.ᶠ I am always proud of you, and I am greatly encouraged. In all my trouble I am still very happy.

⁵After we came to Macedonia, we didn't have any chance to rest. We were faced with all kinds of problems. We were troubled by enemies and troubled by fears. ⁶But God cheers up people in need, and that is what he did when he sent Titus to us. ⁷Of course, we were glad to see Titus, but what really made us glad is the way you cheered him up. He told how sorry you were and how concerned you were about me. And this made me even happier.

⁸I don't feel bad anymore, even though my letterᵍ hurt your feelings. I did feel bad at first, but I don't now. I know that the letter hurt you for a while. ⁹Now I am happy, but not because I hurt your feelings. It is because God used your hurt feelings to make you turn back to him, and none of you were harmed by us. ¹⁰When God makes you feel sorry enough to turn to him and be saved, you don't have anything to feel bad about. But when this world makes you feel sorry, it can cause your death.

¹¹Just look what God has done by making you feel sorry! You sincerely want to prove that you are innocent. You are angry. You are shocked. You are eager to see that justice is done. You have proved that you were completely right in this matter. ¹²When I wrote you, it wasn't to accuse the one who was wrong or to take up for the one who was hurt. I wrote, so that God would show you how much you do care for us. ¹³And we were greatly encouraged.

Although we were encouraged, we felt even better when we saw how happy Titus was, because you had shown that he had nothing to worry about. ¹⁴We had told him how much we thought of you, and you did not disappoint us. Just as we have always told you the truth, so everything we told him about you has also proved to be true. ¹⁵Titus loves all of you very much, especially when he remembers how you obeyed him and how you trembled with fear when you welcomed him. ¹⁶It makes me really glad to know that I can depend on you.

Generous Giving

8 My friends, we want you to know that the churches in Macedoniaʰ have shown others how kind God is. ²Although they were going through hard times and were very poor, they were glad to give generously. ³They gave as much as they could afford and even more, simply because they wanted to. ⁴They even asked and begged us to let them have the joy of giving their money for God's people. ⁵And they did more than we had hoped. They gave themselves first to the Lord and then to us, just as God wanted them to do.

⁶Titus was the one who got you started doing this good thing, so we begged him to have you finish what you had begun. ⁷You do everything better than anyone else. You have stronger faith. You speak better and know more. You are eager to give, and you love us better.ⁱ Now you must give more generously than anyone else.

⁸I am not ordering you to do this. I am simply testing how real your love is by comparing it with the concern that others have shown. ⁹You know that our Lord Jesus Christ was kind enough to give up all his riches and become poor, so that you could become rich.

¹⁰A year ago you were the first ones to give, and you gave because you wanted to. So listen to my advice. ¹¹I think you should finish what you started. If you give according to what you have, you will prove that you are as eager to give as you were to think about giving. ¹²It doesn't matter how much you have. What matters is how much you are willing to give from what you have.

¹³I am not trying to make life easier for others by making life harder for you. But it is only fair ¹⁴for you to share with them when you have so much, and they have so little. Later, when they have more than enough, and you are in need, they can share with you. Then everyone will have a fair share, ¹⁵just as the Scriptures say,

> "Those who gathered
> too much
>   had nothing left.
> Those who gathered
> only a little
>   had all they needed."

Titus and His Friends

¹⁶I am grateful that God made Titus care as much about you as we do. ¹⁷When we begged Titus to visit you, he said he would. He wanted to because he cared so much for you. ¹⁸With Titus we are also sending one of the Lord's followers who is well known in every church for spreading the good news. ¹⁹The churches chose this follower to

---

ᶠ 7.4 *I trust you completely:* Or "I have always spoken the truth to you" or "I can speak freely to you."   ᵍ 7.8 *my letter:* There is no copy of this letter that Paul wrote to the church at Corinth.   ʰ 8.1 *churches in Macedonia:* The churches that Paul had started in Philippi and Thessalonica. The church in Berea is probably also meant.   ⁱ 8.7 *you love us better:* Some manuscripts have "we love you better."

travel with us while we carry this gift that will bring praise to the Lord and show how much we hope to help. ²⁰We don't want anyone to find fault with the way we handle your generous gift. ²¹But we want to do what pleases the Lord and what people think is right.

²²We are also sending someone else with Titus and the other follower. We approve of this man. In fact, he has already shown us many times that he wants to help. And now he wants to help even more than ever, because he trusts you so much. ²³Titus is my partner, who works with me to serve you. The other two followers are sent by the churches, and they bring honor to Christ. ²⁴Treat them in such a way that the churches will see your love and will know why we bragged about you.

The Money for God's People

9 I don't need to write you about the money you plan to give for God's people. ²I know how eager you are to give. And I have proudly told the Lord's followers in Macedonia that you people in Achaia have been ready for a whole year. Now your desire to give has made them want to give. ³That's why I am sending Titus and the two others to you. I want you to be ready, just as I promised. This will prove that we were not wrong to brag about you.

⁴Some followers from Macedonia may come with me, and I want them to find that you have the money ready. If you don't, I would be embarrassed for trusting you to do this. But you would be embarrassed even more. ⁵So I have decided to ask Titus and the others to spend some time with you before I arrive. This way they can arrange to collect the money you have promised. Then you will have the chance to give because you want to, and not because you feel forced to.

⁶Remember this saying,

"A few seeds make
 a small harvest,
but a lot of seeds make
 a big harvest."

⁷Each of you must make up your own mind about how much to give. But don't feel sorry that you must give and don't feel that you are forced to give. God loves people who love to give. ⁸God can bless you with everything you need, and you will always have more than enough to do all kinds of good things for others. ⁹The Scriptures say,

"God freely gives his gifts
 to the poor,
and always does right."

¹⁰God gives seed to farmers and provides everyone with food. He will increase what you have, so that you can give even more to those in need. ¹¹You will be blessed in every way, and you will be able to keep on being generous. Then many people will thank God when we deliver your gift.

¹²What you are doing is much more than a service that supplies God's people with what they need. It is something that will make many others thank God. ¹³The way in which you have proved yourselves by this service will bring honor and praise to God. You believed the message about Christ, and you obeyed it by sharing generously with God's people and with everyone else. ¹⁴Now they are praying for you and want to see you, because God used you to bless them so very much. ¹⁵Thank God for his gift that is too wonderful for words!

Paul Defends His Work for Christ

10 Do you think I am a coward when I am with you and brave when I am far away? Well, I ask you to listen, because Christ himself was humble and gentle. ²Some people have said that we act like the people of this world. So when I arrive, I expect I will have to be firm and forceful in what I say to them. Please don't make me treat you that way. ³We live in this world, but we don't act like its people ⁴or fight our battles with the weapons of this world. Instead, we use God's power that can destroy fortresses. We destroy arguments ⁵and every bit of pride that keeps anyone from knowing God. We capture people's thoughts and make them obey Christ. ⁶And when you completely obey him, we will punish anyone who refuses to obey.

⁷You judge by appearances.ʲ If any of you think you are the only ones who belong to Christ, then think again. We belong to Christ as much as you do. ⁸Maybe I brag a little too much about the authority that the Lord gave me to help you and not to hurt you. Yet I am not embarrassed to brag. ⁹And I am not trying to scare you with my letters. ¹⁰Some of you are saying, "Paul's letters are harsh and powerful. But in person, he is a weakling and has nothing worth saying." ¹¹Those people had better understand that when I am with you, I will do exactly what I say in my letters.

¹²We won't dare compare ourselves with those who think so much of themselves. But they are foolish to compare themselves with themselves. ¹³We won't brag about something we don't have a right to brag about. We will only brag

---

ʲ**10.7** *You judge by appearances*: Or "Take a close look at yourselves."

about the work that God has sent us to do, and you are part of that work. ¹⁴We are not bragging more than we should. After all, we did bring the message about Christ to you.

¹⁵We don't brag about what others have done, as if we had done those things ourselves. But I hope that as you become stronger in your faith, we will be able to reach many more of the people around you.ᵏ That has always been our goal. ¹⁶Then we will be able to preach the good news in other lands where we cannot take credit for work someone else has already done. ¹⁷The Scriptures say, "If you want to brag, then brag about the Lord." ¹⁸You may brag about yourself, but the only approval that counts is the Lord's approval.

Paul and the False Apostles

11 Please put up with a little of my foolishness. ²I am as concerned about you as God is. You were like a virgin bride I had chosen only for Christ. ³But now I fear that you will be tricked, just as Eve was tricked by that lying snake. I am afraid that you might stop thinking about Christ in an honest and sincere way. ⁴We told you about Jesus, and you received the Holy Spirit and accepted our message. But you let some people tell you about another Jesus. Now you are ready to receive another spirit and accept a different message. ⁵I think I am as good as any of those super apostles. ⁶I may not speak as well as they do, but I know as much. And this has already been made perfectly clear to you.

⁷Was it wrong for me to lower myself and honor you by preaching God's message free of charge? ⁸I robbed other churches by taking money from them to serve you. ⁹Even when I was in need, I still didn't bother you. In fact, some of the Lord's followers from Macedonia brought me what I needed. I have not been a burden to you in the past, and I will never be a burden. ¹⁰As surely as I speak the truth about Christ, no one in Achaia can stop me from bragging about this. ¹¹And it isn't because I don't love you. God himself knows how much I do love you.

¹²I plan to go on doing just what I have always done. Then those people won't be able to brag about doing the same things we are doing. ¹³Anyway, they are no more than false apostles and dishonest workers. They only pretend to be apostles of Christ. ¹⁴And it is no wonder. Even Satan tries to make himself look like an angel of light. ¹⁵So why does it seem strange for Satan's servants to pretend to do what is right? Someday they will get exactly what they deserve.

Paul's Sufferings for Christ

¹⁶I don't want any of you to think that I am a fool. But if you do, then let me be a fool and brag a little. ¹⁷When I do all this bragging, I do it as a fool and not for the Lord. ¹⁸Yet if others want to brag about what they have done, so will I. ¹⁹And since you are so smart, you will gladly put up with a fool. ²⁰In fact, you let people make slaves of you and cheat you and steal from you. Why, you even let them strut around and slap you in the face. ²¹I am ashamed to say that we are too weak to behave in such a way.

If they can brag, so can I, but it is a foolish thing to do. ²²Are they Hebrews? So am I. Are they Jews? So am I. Are they from the family of Abraham? Well, so am I. ²³Are they servants of Christ? I am a fool to talk this way, but I serve him better than they do. I have worked harder and have been put in jail more times. I have been beaten with whips more and have been in danger of death more often.

²⁴Five times the Jews gave me thirty-nine lashes with a whip. ²⁵Three times the Romans beat me with a big stick, and once my enemies stoned me. I have been shipwrecked three times, and I even had to spend a night and a day in the sea. ²⁶During my many travels, I have been in danger from rivers, robbers, my own people, and foreigners. My life has been in danger in cities, in deserts, at sea, and with people who only pretended to be the Lord's followers.

²⁷I have worked and struggled and spent many sleepless nights. I have gone hungry and thirsty and often had nothing to eat. I have been cold from not having enough clothes to keep me warm, ²⁸Besides everything else, each day I am burdened down, worrying about all the churches. ²⁹When others are weak, I am weak too. When others are tricked into sin, I get angry.ˡ

³⁰If I have to brag, I will brag about how weak I am. ³¹God, the Father of our Lord Jesus, knows I am not lying. And God is to be praised forever! ³²The governor of Damascus at the time of King Aretas had the city gates guarded, so that he could capture me. ³³But I escaped by being let down in a basket through a window in the city wall.

ᵏ*10.15 we will be able to reach many more of the people around you:* Or "you will praise us even more because of our work among you." ˡ*11.29 When others are tricked into sin, I get angry:* Or "When others stumble into sin, I hurt for them."

Visions from the Lord

12 I have to brag. There is nothing to be gained by it, but I must brag about the visions and other things that the Lord has shown me. ²I know about one of Christ's followers who was taken up into the third heaven fourteen years ago. I don't know if the man was still in his body when it happened, but God certainly knows.

³As I said, only God really knows if this man was in his body at the time. ⁴But he was taken up into paradise,*ᵐ* where he heard things that are too wonderful to tell. ⁵I will brag about that man, but not about myself, except to say how weak I am.

⁶Yet even if I did brag, I would not be foolish. I would simply be speaking the truth. But I will try not to say too much. That way, none of you will think more highly of me than you should because of what you have seen me do and say. ⁷Of course, I am now referring to the wonderful things I saw. One of Satan's angels was sent to make me suffer terribly, so that I would not feel too proud.*ⁿ*

⁸Three times I begged the Lord to make this suffering go away. ⁹But he replied, "My kindness is all you need. My power is strongest when you are weak." So if Christ keeps giving me his power, I will gladly brag about how weak I am. ¹⁰Yes, I am glad to be weak or insulted or mistreated or to have troubles and sufferings, if it is for Christ. Because when I am weak, I am strong.

Paul's Concern for the Lord's Followers at Corinth

¹¹I have been making a fool of myself. But you forced me to do it, when you should have been speaking up for me. I may be nothing at all, but I am as good as those super apostles. ¹²When I was with you, I was patient and worked all the powerful miracles and signs and wonders of a true apostle. ¹³You missed out on only one blessing that the other churches received. That is, you didn't have to support me. Forgive me for doing you wrong.

¹⁴I am planning to visit you for the third time. But I still won't make a burden of myself. What I really want is you, and not what you have. Children are not supposed to save up for their parents, but parents are supposed to take care of their children. ¹⁵So I will gladly give all that I have and all that I am. Will you love me less for loving you too much?

¹⁶You agree that I wasn't a burden to you. Maybe that's because I was trying to catch you off guard and trick you. ¹⁷Were you cheated by any of those I sent to you? ¹⁸I urged Titus to visit you, and I sent another follower with him. But Titus didn't cheat you, and we felt and behaved the same way he did.

¹⁹Have you been thinking all along that we have been defending ourselves to you? Actually, we have been speaking to God as followers of Christ. But, my friends, we did it all for your good.

²⁰I am afraid that when I come, we won't be pleased with each other. I fear that some of you may be arguing or jealous or angry or selfish or gossiping or insulting each other. I even fear that you may be proud and acting like a mob. ²¹I am afraid God will make me ashamed when I visit you again. I will feel like crying because many of you have never given up your old sins. You are still doing things that are immoral, indecent, and shameful.

Final Warnings and Greetings

13 I am on my way to visit you for the third time. And as the Scriptures say, "Any charges must be proved true by at least two or three witnesses." ²During my second visit I warned you that I would punish you and anyone else who doesn't stop sinning. I am far away from you now, but I give you the same warning. ³This should prove to you that I am speaking for Christ. When he corrects you, he won't be weak. He will be powerful! ⁴Although he was weak when he was nailed to the cross, he now lives by the power of God. We are weak, just as Christ was. But you will see that we will live by the power of God, just as Christ does.

⁵Test yourselves and find out if you really are true to your faith. If you pass the test, you will discover that Christ is living in you. But if Christ isn't living in you, you have failed. ⁶I hope you will discover that we have not failed. ⁷We pray that you will stop doing evil things. We don't pray like this to make ourselves look good, but to get you to do right, even if we are failures.

⁸All we can do is to follow the truth and not fight against it. ⁹Even though we are weak, we are glad that you are strong, and we pray that you will do even better. ¹⁰I am writing these things to you before I arrive. This way I won't have to be hard on you when I use the authority that the Lord has given me. I

ᵐ12.4 paradise: In the Greek translation of the Old Testament, this word is used for the Garden of Eden. In New Testament times it was sometimes used for the place where God's people are happy and at rest, as they wait for the final judgment. *ⁿ12.7 Of course . . . too proud:* Or "Because of the wonderful things that I saw, one of Satan's angels was sent to make me suffer terribly, so that I would not feel too proud."

2 Corinthians 13.11

was given this authority, so that I could help you and not destroy you.

[11] Good-by, my friends. Do better and pay attention to what I have said. Try to get along and live peacefully with each other.

Now I pray that God, who gives love and peace, will be with you. [12] Give each other a warm greeting. All of God's people send their greetings.

[13] I pray that the Lord Jesus Christ will bless you and be kind to you! May God bless you with his love, and may the Holy Spirit join all your hearts together.

GALATIANS

ABOUT THIS LETTER

From the very beginning of this letter to the churches in the region of Galatia (in central Asia Minor), Paul makes two things clear to his readers: he is a true apostle, and his message is the only true message (1.1-10). These statements were very important, because some people claimed that Paul was a false apostle with a false message.

Paul was indeed a true apostle, and his mission to the Gentiles was given to him by the Lord and approved by the apostles in Jerusalem (1.18—2.10). Paul had even corrected the apostle Peter, when he had stopped eating with Gentile followers who were not obeying the Law of Moses (2.1-18).

Faith is the only way to be saved. Paul insists that this was true already for Abraham, who had received God's promise by faith. And Paul leaves no doubt about what his own faith means to him:

I have been nailed to the cross with Christ. I have died, but Christ lives in me. And I now live by faith in the Son of God, who loved me and gave his life for me.

(2.19b, 20)

A QUICK LOOK AT THIS LETTER

A True Apostle and the True Message (1.1-10)
God Chose Paul To Be an Apostle (1.11-24)
Paul Defends His Message (2.1-21)
Faith Is the Only Way To Be Saved (3.1—4.31)
Guided by the Spirit and Love (5.1—6.10)
Final Warnings (6.11-18)

---

1 ¹⁻²From the apostle Paul and from all the Lord's followers with me.

I was chosen to be an apostle by Jesus Christ and by God the Father, who raised him from death. No mere human chose or appointed me to this work.

To the churches in Galatia.

³I pray that God the Father and our Lord Jesus Christ will be kind to you and will bless you with peace! ⁴Christ obeyed God our Father and gave himself as a sacrifice for our sins to rescue us from this evil world. ⁵God will be given glory forever and ever. Amen.

The Only True Message

⁶I am shocked that you have so quickly turned from God, who chose you because of his wonderful kindness.[a] You have believed another message, ⁷when there is really only one true message. But some people are causing you trouble and want to make you turn away from the good news about Christ. ⁸I pray that God will punish anyone who preaches anything different from our message to you! It doesn't matter if that person is one of us or an angel from heaven. ⁹I have said it before, and I will say it again. I hope God will punish anyone who preaches anything different from what you have already believed.

¹⁰I am not trying to please people. I want to please God. Do you think I am trying to please people? If I were doing that, I would not be a servant of Christ.

How Paul Became an Apostle

¹¹My friends, I want you to know that no one made up the message I preach. ¹²It wasn't given or taught to me by some mere human. My message came

---

[a] 1.6 *his wonderful kindness*: Some manuscripts have "the wonderful kindness of Christ."

directly from Jesus Christ when he appeared to me.

[13] You know how I used to live as a Jew. I was cruel to God's church and even tried to destroy it. [14] I was a much better Jew than anyone else my own age, and I obeyed every law that our ancestors had given us. [15] But even before I was born, God had chosen me. He was kind and had decided [16] to show me his Son, so that I would announce his message to the Gentiles. I didn't talk this over with anyone. [17] I didn't say a word, not even to the men in Jerusalem who were apostles before I was. Instead, I went at once to Arabia, and afterwards I returned to Damascus.

[18] Three years later I went to visit Peter[b] in Jerusalem and stayed with him for fifteen days. [19] The only other apostle I saw was James, the Lord's brother. [20] And in the presence of God I swear I am telling the truth.

[21] Later, I went to the regions of Syria and Cilicia. [22] But no one who belonged to Christ's churches in Judea had ever seen me in person. [23] They had only heard that the one who had been cruel to them was now preaching the message that he had once tried to destroy. [24] And because of me, they praised God.

2 Fourteen years later I went to Jerusalem with Barnabas. I also took along Titus. [2] But I went there because God had told me to go, and I explained the good news that I had been preaching to the Gentiles. Then I met privately with the ones who seemed to be the most important leaders. I wanted to make sure that my work in the past and my future work would not be for nothing.

[3] Titus went to Jerusalem with me. He was a Greek, but still he wasn't forced to be circumcised. [4] We went there because of those who pretended to be followers and had sneaked in among us as spies. They had come to take away the freedom that Christ Jesus had given us, and they were trying to make us their slaves. [5] But we wanted you to have the true message. That's why we didn't give in to them, not even for a second.

[6] Some of them were supposed to be important leaders, but I didn't care who they were. God doesn't have any favorites! None of these so-called special leaders added anything to my message. [7] They realized that God had sent me with the good news for Gentiles, and that he had sent Peter with the same message for Jews. [8] God, who had sent Peter on a mission to the Jews, was now using me to preach to the Gentiles.

[9] James, Peter,[b] and John realized that God had given me the message about his undeserved kindness. And these men are supposed to be the backbone of the church. They even gave Barnabas and me a friendly handshake. This was to show that we would work with Gentiles and that they would work with Jews. [10] They only asked us to remember the poor, and that was something I had always been eager to do.

Paul Corrects Peter at Antioch

[11] When Peter came to Antioch, I told him face to face that he was wrong. [12] He used to eat with Gentile followers of the Lord, until James sent some Jewish followers. Peter was afraid of the Jews and soon stopped eating with Gentiles. [13] He and the other Jews hid their true feelings so well that even Barnabas was fooled. [14] But when I saw that they were not really obeying the truth that is in the good news, I corrected Peter in front of everyone and said:

Peter, you are a Jew, but you live like a Gentile. So how can you force Gentiles to live like Jews?

[15] We are Jews by birth and are not sinners like Gentiles. [16] But we know that God accepts only those who have faith in Jesus Christ. No one can please God by simply obeying the Law. So we put our faith in Christ Jesus, and God accepted us because of our faith.

[17] When we Jews started looking for a way to please God, we discovered that we are sinners too. Does this mean that Christ is the one who makes us sinners? No, it doesn't! [18] But if I tear down something and then build it again, I prove that I was wrong at first. [19] It was the Law itself that killed me and freed me from its power, so that I could live for God.

I have been nailed to the cross with Christ. [20] I have died, but Christ lives in me. And I now live by faith in the Son of God, who loved me and gave his life for me. [21] I don't turn my back on God's undeserved kindness. If we can be acceptable to God by obeying the Law, it was useless for Christ to die.

Faith Is the Only Way

3 You stupid Galatians! I told you exactly how Jesus Christ was nailed to a cross. Has someone now put an evil spell on you? [2] I want to know only one thing. How were you given God's Spirit? Was it by obeying the Law of Moses or by hearing about Christ and having

---

[b]1.18;2.9 *Peter*: The Greek text has "Cephas," which is an Aramaic name meaning "rock." Peter is the Greek name with the same meaning.

faith in him? ³How can you be so stupid? Do you think that by yourself you can complete what God's Spirit started in you? ⁴Have you gone through all of this for nothing? Is it all really for nothing? ⁵God gives you his Spirit and works miracles in you. But does he do this because you obey the Law of Moses or because you have heard about Christ and have faith in him?

⁶The Scriptures say that God accepted Abraham because Abraham had faith. ⁷And so, you should understand that everyone who has faith is a child of Abraham.ᶜ ⁸Long ago the Scriptures said that God would accept the Gentiles because of their faith. That's why God told Abraham the good news that all nations would be blessed because of him. ⁹This means that everyone who has faith will share in the blessings that were given to Abraham because of his faith.

¹⁰Anyone who tries to please God by obeying the Law is under a curse. The Scriptures say, "Everyone who doesn't obey everything in the Law is under a curse." ¹¹No one can please God by obeying the Law. The Scriptures also say, "The people God accepts because of their faith will live."ᵈ

¹²The Law isn't based on faith. It promises life only to people who obey its commands. ¹³But Christ rescued us from the Law's curse, when he became a curse in our place. This is because the Scriptures say that anyone who is nailed to a tree is under a curse. ¹⁴And because of what Jesus Christ has done, the blessing that was promised to Abraham was taken to the Gentiles. This happened so that by faith we would be given the promised Holy Spirit.

The Law and the Promise

¹⁵My friends, I will use an everyday example to explain what I mean. Once someone agrees to something, no one else can change or cancel the agreement.ᵉ ¹⁶That is how it is with the promises God made to Abraham and his descendant.ᶠ The promises were not made to many descendants, but only to one, and that one is Christ. ¹⁷What I am saying is that the Law cannot change or cancel God's promise that was made 430 years before the Law was given. ¹⁸If we have to obey the Law in order to receive God's blessings, those blessings don't really come to us because of God's promise. But God was kind to Abraham and made him a promise.

¹⁹What is the use of the Law? It was given later to show that we sin. But it was only supposed to last until the coming of that descendantᵍ who was given the promise. In fact, angels gave the Law to Moses, and he gave it to the people. ²⁰There is only one God, and the Law did not come directly from him.

Slaves and Children

²¹Does the Law disagree with God's promises? No, it doesn't! If any law could give life to us, we could become acceptable to God by obeying that law. ²²But the Scriptures say that sin controls everyone, so that God's promises will be for anyone who has faith in Jesus Christ.

²³The Law controlled us and kept us under its power until the time came when we would have faith. ²⁴In fact, the Law was our teacher. It was supposed to teach us until we had faith and were acceptable to God. ²⁵But once a person has learned to have faith, there is no more need to have the Law as a teacher.

²⁶All of you are God's children because of your faith in Christ Jesus. ²⁷And when you were baptized, it was as though you had put on Christ in the same way you put on new clothes. ²⁸Faith in Christ Jesus is what makes each of you equal with each other, whether you are a Jew or a Greek, a slave or a free person, a man or a woman. ²⁹So if you belong to Christ, you are now part of Abraham's family,ʰ and you will be given what God has promised. ¹Children who are under age are no better off than slaves, even though everything their parents own will someday be theirs. ²This is because children are placed in the care of guardians and teachers until the time their parents have set. ³That is how it was with us. We were like children ruled by the powers of this world.

⁴But when the time was right, God sent his Son, and a woman gave birth to him. His Son obeyed the Law, ⁵so he could set us free from the Law, and we could become God's children. ⁶Now that we are his children, God has sent the Spirit of his Son into our hearts. And his

---

ᶜ**3.7** *a child of Abraham*: God chose Abraham, and so it was believed that anyone who was a child of Abraham was also a child of God (see the note at 3.29). ᵈ**3.11** *The people God accepts because of their faith will live*: Or "The people God accepts will live because of their faith." ᵉ**3.15** *Once someone . . . cancel the agreement*: Or "Once a person makes out a will, no one can change or cancel it." ᶠ**3.16** *descendant*: The Greek text has "seed," which may mean one or many descendants. In this verse Paul says it means Christ. ᵍ**3.19** *that descendant*: Jesus. ʰ**3.29** *you are now part of Abraham's family*: Paul tells the Galatians that faith in Jesus Christ is what makes someone a true child of Abraham and of God (see the note at 3.7).

Spirit tells us that God is our Father. [7]You are no longer slaves. You are God's children, and you will be given what he has promised.

Paul's Concern for the Galatians

[8]Before you knew God, you were slaves of gods that are not real. [9]But now you know God, or better still, God knows you. How can you turn back and become the slaves of those weak and pitiful powers?[i] [10]You even celebrate certain days, months, seasons, and years. [11]I am afraid I have wasted my time working with you.

[12]My friends, I beg you to be like me, just as I once tried to be like you. Did you mistreat me [13]when I first preached to you? No you didn't, even though you knew I had come there because I was sick. [14]My illness must have caused you some trouble, but you didn't hate me or turn me away because of it. You welcomed me as though I were one of God's angels or even Christ Jesus himself. [15]Where is that good feeling now? I am sure that if it had been possible, you would have taken out your own eyes and given them to me. [16]Am I now your enemy, just because I told you the truth?

[17]Those people may be paying you a lot of attention, but it isn't for your good. They only want to keep you away from me, so you will pay them a lot of attention. [18]It is always good to give your attention to something worthwhile, even when I am not with you. [19]My children, I am in terrible pain until Christ may be seen living in you. [20]I wish I were with you now. Then I would not have to talk this way. You really have me puzzled.

Hagar and Sarah

[21]Some of you would like to be under the rule of the Law of Moses. But do you know what the Law says? [22]In the Scriptures we learn that Abraham had two sons. The mother of one of them was a slave, while the mother of the other one had always been free. [23]The son of the slave woman was born in the usual way. But the son of the free woman was born because of God's promise.

[24]All of this has another meaning as well. Each of the two women stands for one of the agreements God made with his people. Hagar, the slave woman, stands for the agreement that was made at Mount Sinai. Everyone born into her family is a slave. [25]Hagar also stands for Mount Sinai in Arabia[j] and for the present city of Jerusalem. She[k] and her children are slaves.

[26]But our mother is the city of Jerusalem in heaven above, and she isn't a slave. [27]The Scriptures say about her,

"You have never had children,
  but now you can be glad.
You have never given birth,
  but now you can shout.
Once you had no children,
  but now you will have
more children than a woman
  who has been married
  for a long time."

[28]My friends, you were born because of this promise, just as Isaac was. [29]But the child who was born in the natural way made trouble for the child who was born because of the Spirit. The same thing is happening today. [30]The Scriptures say, "Get rid of the slave woman and her son! He won't be given anything. The son of the free woman will receive everything." [31]My friends, we are children of the free woman and not of the slave.

Christ Gives Freedom

5 Christ has set us free! This means we are really free. Now hold on to your freedom and don't ever become slaves of the Law again.

[2]I, Paul, promise you that Christ won't do you any good if you get circumcised. [3]If you do, you must obey the whole Law. [4]And if you try to please God by obeying the Law, you have cut yourself off from Christ and his wonderful kindness. [5]But the Spirit makes us sure that God will accept us because of our faith in Christ. [6]If you are a follower of Christ Jesus, it makes no difference whether you are circumcised or not. All that matters is your faith that makes you love others.

[7]You were doing so well until someone made you turn from the truth. [8]And that person was certainly not sent by the one who chose you. [9]A little yeast can change a whole batch of dough, [10]but you belong to the Lord. That makes me certain that you will do what I say, instead of what someone else tells you to do. Whoever is causing trouble for you will be punished.

[11]My friends, if I still preach that people need to be circumcised, why am I in so much trouble? The message about the cross would no longer be a problem, if I told people to be circumcised. [12]I wish that everyone who is upsetting you

---

[i]**4.9** *powers*: Spirits were thought to control human lives and were believed to be connected with the movements of the stars.   [j]**4.25** *Hagar also stands for Mount Sinai in Arabia*: Some manuscripts have "Sinai is a mountain in Arabia." This sentence would then be translated: "Sinai is a mountain in Arabia, and Hagar stands for the present city of Jerusalem."
[k]**4.25** *She*: "Hagar" or "Jerusalem."

would not only get circumcised, but would cut off much more!

¹³My friends, you were chosen to be free. So don't use your freedom as an excuse to do anything you want. Use it as an opportunity to serve each other with love. ¹⁴All that the Law says can be summed up in the command to love others as much as you love yourself. ¹⁵But if you keep attacking each other like wild animals, you had better watch out or you will destroy yourselves.

God's Spirit and Our Own Desires

¹⁶If you are guided by the Spirit, you won't obey your selfish desires. ¹⁷The Spirit and your desires are enemies of each other. They are always fighting each other and keeping you from doing what you feel you should. ¹⁸But if you obey the Spirit, the Law of Moses has no control over you.

¹⁹People's desires make them give in to immoral ways, filthy thoughts, and shameful deeds. ²⁰They worship idols, practice witchcraft, hate others, and are hard to get along with. People become jealous, angry, and selfish. They not only argue and cause trouble, but they are ²¹envious. They get drunk, carry on at wild parties, and do other evil things as well. I told you before, and I am telling you again: No one who does these things will share in the blessings of God's kingdom.

²²God's Spirit makes us loving, happy, peaceful, patient, kind, good, faithful, ²³gentle, and self-controlled. There is no law against behaving in any of these ways. ²⁴And because we belong to Christ Jesus, we have killed our selfish feelings and desires. ²⁵God's Spirit has given us life, and so we should follow the Spirit. ²⁶But don't be conceited or make others jealous by claiming to be better than they are.

Help Each Other

6 My friends, you are spiritual. So if someone is trapped in sin, you should gently lead that person back to the right path. But watch out, and don't be tempted yourself. ²You obey the law of Christ when you offer each other a helping hand.

³If you think you are better than others, when you really aren't, you are wrong. ⁴Do your own work well, and then you will have something to be proud of. But don't compare yourself with others. ⁵We each must carry our own load.

⁶Share every good thing you have with anyone who teaches you what God has said.

⁷You cannot fool God, so don't make a fool of yourself! You will harvest what you plant. ⁸If you follow your selfish desires, you will harvest destruction, but if you follow the Spirit, you will harvest eternal life. ⁹Don't get tired of helping others. You will be rewarded when the time is right, if you don't give up. ¹⁰We should help people whenever we can, especially if they are followers of the Lord.

Final Warnings

¹¹You can see what big letters I make when I write with my own hand.

¹²Those people who are telling you to get circumcised are only trying to show how important they are. And they don't want to get into trouble for preaching about the cross of Christ. ¹³They are circumcised, but they don't obey the Law of Moses. All they want is to brag about having you circumcised. ¹⁴But I will never brag about anything except the cross of our Lord Jesus Christ. Because of his cross, the world is dead as far as I am concerned, and I am dead as far as the world is concerned.

¹⁵It doesn't matter if you are circumcised or not. All that matters is that you are a new person.

¹⁶If you follow this rule, you will belong to God's true people. God will treat you with undeserved kindness and will bless you with peace.

¹⁷On my own body are scars that prove I belong to Christ Jesus. So I don't want anyone to bother me anymore.

¹⁸My friends, I pray that the Lord Jesus Christ will be kind to you! Amen.

EPHESIANS

ABOUT THIS LETTER

"Praise the God and Father of our Lord Jesus Christ for the spiritual blessings that Christ has brought us from heaven!" (1.3). Paul begins his letter to the Christians in Ephesus with a powerful reminder of the main theme of his message. Christ died on the cross to set us free (1.7, 8). But God raised Christ from death, and he now sits at God's right side in heaven, where he rules over this world. And he will rule over the future world as well (1.20, 21).

Christ brought Jews and Gentiles together by "breaking down the wall of hatred" that separated them (2.14) and he united them all as part of that holy temple where God's Spirit lives (2.22). This was according to God's eternal plan (3.11).

There is only one Lord, one Spirit of God, and one God, who is the Father of all people (4.4, 5). This means that Christians must let the Spirit keep their hearts united, so they can live at peace with each other (4.3). The idea of all Christians being one with Christ is so central to this letter that it occurs twenty times. There is one faith and one baptism by which believers become one body.

Ephesus was a port city on the western shore of Asia Minor (modern-day Turkey). In Paul's time this was the fourth largest city in the Roman Empire. It was also an ancient center of nature religion where the goddess Artemis was widely worshiped (Acts 19).

Paul lets the Ephesians know that much is expected of people who are called to a new life (4.17—5.20). Followers of the Lord are God's dear children, and they must do as God does (5.1). They used to live in the dark, but they must now live in the light and make their light shine (5.8, 9).

Paul then teaches husbands and wives, children and parents, and slaves and masters how to live as Christians (5.21—6.9).

Paul never forgets how kind God is:

God was merciful! We were dead because of our sins, but God loved us so much that he made us alive with Christ, and God's wonderful kindness is what saves you.
(2.4, 5)

You were saved by faith in God, who treats us much better than we deserve. This is God's gift to you, and not anything you have done on your own. *(2.8)*

A QUICK LOOK AT THIS LETTER

Greetings (1.1, 2)
Christ Brings Spiritual Blessings (1.3—3.21)
A New Life in Unity with Christ (4.1—6.20)
Final Greetings (6.21-24)

---

1 From Paul, chosen by God to be an apostle of Christ Jesus.

To God's people who live in Ephesus and[a] are faithful followers of Christ Jesus.

² I pray that God our Father and our Lord Jesus Christ will be kind to you and will bless you with peace!

Christ Brings Spiritual Blessings

³ Praise the God and Father of our Lord Jesus Christ for the spiritual bless-

---
[a] 1.1 *live in Ephesus and*: Some manuscripts do not have these words.

ings that Christ has brought us from heaven! ⁴Before the world was created, God had Christ choose us to live with him and to be his holy and innocent and loving people. ⁵God was kind[b] and decided that Christ would choose us to be God's own adopted children. ⁶God was very kind to us because of the Son he dearly loves, and so we should praise God.

⁷⁻⁸Christ sacrificed his life's blood to set us free, which means that our sins are now forgiven. Christ did this because God was so kind to us. God has great wisdom and understanding, ⁹and by what Christ has done, God has shown us his own mysterious ways. ¹⁰Then when the time is right, God will do all that he has planned, and Christ will bring together everything in heaven and on earth.

¹¹God always does what he plans, and that's why he appointed Christ to choose us. ¹²He did this so that we Jews would bring honor to him and be the first ones to have hope because of him. ¹³Christ also brought you the truth, which is the good news about how you can be saved. You put your faith in Christ and were given the promised Holy Spirit to show that you belong to God. ¹⁴The Spirit also makes us sure that we will be given what God has stored up for his people. Then we will be set free, and God will be honored and praised.

Paul's Prayer

¹⁵I have heard about your faith in the Lord Jesus and your love for all of God's people. ¹⁶So I never stop being grateful for you, as I mention you in my prayers. ¹⁷I ask the glorious Father and God of our Lord Jesus Christ to give you his Spirit. The Spirit will make you wise and let you understand what it means to know God. ¹⁸My prayer is that light will flood your hearts and that you will understand the hope that was given to you when God chose you. Then you will discover the glorious blessings that will be yours together with all of God's people.

¹⁹I want you to know about the great and mighty power that God has for us followers. It is the same wonderful power he used ²⁰when he raised Christ from death and let him sit at his right side[c] in heaven. ²¹There Christ rules over all forces, authorities, powers, and rulers. He rules over all beings in this world and will rule in the future world as well. ²²God has put all things under the power of Christ, and for the good of the church he has made him the head of everything. ²³The church is Christ's body and is filled with Christ who completely fills everything.[d]

From Death to Life

2 In the past you were dead because you sinned and fought against God. ²You followed the ways of this world and obeyed the devil. He rules the world, and his spirit has power over everyone who doesn't obey God. ³Once we were also ruled by the selfish desires of our bodies and minds. We had made God angry, and we were going to be punished like everyone else.

⁴⁻⁵But God was merciful! We were dead because of our sins, but God loved us so much that he made us alive with Christ, and God's wonderful kindness is what saves you. ⁶God raised us from death to life with Christ Jesus, and he has given us a place beside Christ in heaven. ⁷God did this so that in the future world he could show how truly good and kind he is to us because of what Christ Jesus has done. ⁸You were saved by faith in God, who treats us much better than we deserve.[e] This is God's gift to you, and not anything you have done on your own. ⁹It isn't something you have earned, so there is nothing you can brag about. ¹⁰God planned for us to do good things and to live as he has always wanted us to live. That's why he sent Christ to make us what we are.

United by Christ

¹¹Don't forget that you are Gentiles. In fact, you used to be called "uncircumcised" by those who take pride in being circumcised. ¹²At that time you did not know about Christ. You were foreigners to the people of Israel, and you had no part in the promises that God had made to them. You were living in this world without hope and without God, ¹³and you were far from God. But Christ offered his life's blood as a sacrifice and brought you near God.

¹⁴Christ has made peace between Jews and Gentiles, and he has united us by breaking down the wall of hatred that separated us. Christ gave his own body ¹⁵to destroy the Law of Moses with all its rules and commands. He even brought Jews and Gentiles together as though we were only one person, when he united us in peace. ¹⁶On the cross

---

[b]**1.4,5** *holy and innocent and loving people.* ⁵*God was kind*: Or "holy and innocent people. God was loving ⁵and kind." [c]**1.20** *right side*: The place of power and honor. [d]**1.23** *and is filled with Christ who completely fills everything*: Or "which completely fills Christ and fully completes his work." [e]**2.8** *treats us much better than we deserve*: The Greek word *charis*, traditionally rendered "grace," is translated here and other places in the CEV to express the overwhelming kindness of God.

Christ did away with our hatred for each other. He also made peace[f] between us and God by uniting Jews and Gentiles in one body. [17]Christ came and preached peace to you Gentiles, who were far from God, and peace to us Jews, who were near God. [18]And because of Christ, all of us can come to the Father by the same Spirit.

[19]You Gentiles are no longer strangers and foreigners. You are citizens with everyone else who belongs to the family of God. [20]You are like a building with the apostles and prophets as the foundation and with Christ as the most important stone. [21]Christ is the one who holds the building together and makes it grow into a holy temple for the Lord. [22]And you are part of that building Christ has built as a place for God's own Spirit to live.

Paul's Mission to the Gentiles

3 Christ Jesus made me his prisoner, so that I could help you Gentiles. [2]You have surely heard about God's kindness in choosing me to help you. [3]In fact, this letter tells you a little about how God has shown me his mysterious ways. [4]As you read the letter, you will also find out how well I really do understand the mystery about Christ. [5]No one knew about this mystery until God's Spirit told it to his holy apostles and prophets. [6]And the mystery is this: Because of Christ Jesus, the good news has given the Gentiles a share in the promises that God gave to the Jews. God has also let the Gentiles be part of the same body.

[7]God treated me with kindness. His power worked in me, and it became my job to spread the good news. [8]I am the least important of all God's people. But God was kind and chose me to tell the Gentiles that because of Christ there are blessings that cannot be measured. [9]God, who created everything, wanted me to help everyone understand the mysterious plan that had always been hidden in his mind. [10]Then God would use the church to show the powers and authorities in the spiritual world that he has many different kinds of wisdom.

[11]God did this according to his eternal plan. And he was able to do what he had planned because of all that Christ Jesus our Lord had done. [12]Christ now gives us courage and confidence, so that we can come to God by faith. [13]That's why you should not be discouraged when I suffer for you. After all, it will bring honor to you.

Christ's Love for Us

[14]I kneel in prayer to the Father. [15]All beings in heaven and on earth receive their life from him.[g] [16]God is wonderful and glorious. I pray that his Spirit will make you become strong followers [17]and that Christ will live in your hearts because of your faith. Stand firm and be deeply rooted in his love. [18]I pray that you and all of God's people will understand what is called wide or long or high or deep.[h] [19]I want you to know all about Christ's love, although it is too wonderful to be measured. Then your lives will be filled with all that God is.

[20-21]I pray that Christ Jesus and the church will forever bring praise to God. His power at work in us can do far more than we dare ask or imagine. Amen.

Unity with Christ

4 As a prisoner of the Lord, I beg you to live in a way that is worthy of the people God has chosen to be his own. [2]Always be humble and gentle. Patiently put up with each other and love each other. [3]Try your best to let God's Spirit keep your hearts united. Do this by living at peace. [4]All of you are part of the same body. There is only one Spirit of God, just as you were given one hope when you were chosen to be God's people. [5]We have only one Lord, one faith, and one baptism. [6]There is one God who is the Father of all people. Not only is God above all others, but he works by using all of us, and he lives in all of us.

[7]Christ has generously divided out his gifts to us. [8]As the Scriptures say,

"When he went up
  to the highest place,
he led away many prisoners
  and gave gifts to people."

[9]When it says, "he went up," it means that Christ had been deep in the earth. [10]This also means that the one who went deep into the earth is the same one who went into the highest heaven, so that he would fill the whole universe.

[11]Christ chose some of us to be apostles, prophets, missionaries, pastors, and teachers, [12]so that his people would learn to serve and his body would grow strong. [13]This will continue until we are united by our faith and by our understanding of the Son of God. Then we will be mature, just as Christ is, and we will be completely like him.[i]

---

[f]*2.16 He also made peace:* Or "The cross also made peace." [g]*3.15 receive their life from him:* Or "know who they really are because of him." [h]*3.18 what is called wide or long or high or deep:* This may refer to the heavenly Jerusalem or to God's love or wisdom or to the meaning of the cross. [i]*4.13 and we will be completely like him:* Or "and he is completely perfect."

¹⁴We must stop acting like children. We must not let deceitful people trick us by their false teachings, which are like winds that toss us around from place to place. ¹⁵Love should always make us tell the truth. Then we will grow in every way and be more like Christ, the head ¹⁶of the body. Christ holds it together and makes all of its parts work perfectly, as it grows and becomes strong because of love.

The Old Life and the New Life

¹⁷As a follower of the Lord, I order you to stop living like stupid, godless people. ¹⁸Their minds are in the dark, and they are stubborn and ignorant and have missed out on the life that comes from God. They no longer have any feelings about what is right, ¹⁹and they are so greedy that they do all kinds of indecent things.

²⁰⁻²¹But that isn't what you were taught about Jesus Christ. He is the truth, and you heard about him and learned about him. ²²You were told that your foolish desires will destroy you and that you must give up your old way of life with all its bad habits. ²³Let the Spirit change your way of thinking ²⁴and make you into a new person. You were created to be like God, and so you must please him and be truly holy.

Rules for the New Life

²⁵We are part of the same body. Stop lying and start telling each other the truth. ²⁶Don't get so angry that you sin. Don't go to bed angry ²⁷and don't give the devil a chance.

²⁸If you are a thief, quit stealing. Be honest and work hard, so you will have something to give to people in need.

²⁹Stop all your dirty talk. Say the right thing at the right time and help others by what you say.

³⁰Don't make God's Spirit sad. The Spirit makes you sure that someday you will be free from your sins.

³¹Stop being bitter and angry and mad at others. Don't yell at one another or curse each other or ever be rude. ³²Instead, be kind and merciful, and forgive others, just as God forgave you because of Christ.

5 Do as God does. After all, you are his dear children. ²Let love be your guide. Christ loved us[j] and offered his life for us as a sacrifice that pleases God.

³You are God's people, so don't let it be said that any of you are immoral or indecent or greedy. ⁴Don't use dirty or foolish or filthy words. Instead, say how thankful you are. ⁵Being greedy, indecent, or immoral is just another way of worshiping idols. You can be sure that people who behave in this way will never be part of the kingdom that belongs to Christ and to God.

Living as People of Light

⁶Don't let anyone trick you with foolish talk. God punishes everyone who disobeys him and says[k] foolish things. ⁷So don't have anything to do with anyone like that.

⁸You used to be like people living in the dark, but now you are people of the light because you belong to the Lord. So act like people of the light ⁹and make your light shine. Be good and honest and truthful, ¹⁰as you try to please the Lord. ¹¹Don't take part in doing those worthless things that are done in the dark. Instead, show how wrong they are. ¹²It is disgusting even to talk about what is done in the dark. ¹³But the light will show what these things are really like. ¹⁴Light shows up everything,[l] just as the Scriptures say,

"Wake up from your sleep
    and rise from death.
Then Christ will shine on you."

¹⁵Act like people with good sense and not like fools. ¹⁶These are evil times, so make every minute count. ¹⁷Don't be stupid. Instead, find out what the Lord wants you to do. ¹⁸Don't destroy yourself by getting drunk, but let the Spirit fill your life. ¹⁹When you meet together, sing psalms, hymns, and spiritual songs, as you praise the Lord with all your heart. ²⁰Always use the name of our Lord Jesus Christ to thank God the Father for everything.

Wives and Husbands

²¹Honor Christ and put others first. ²²A wife should put her husband first, as she does the Lord. ²³A husband is the head of his wife, as Christ is the head and the Savior of the church, which is his own body. ²⁴Wives should always put their husbands first, as the church puts Christ first.

²⁵A husband should love his wife as much as Christ loved the church and gave his life for it. ²⁶He made the church holy by the power of his word, and he made it pure by washing it with water. ²⁷Christ did this, so that he would have a glorious and holy church, without faults or spots or wrinkles or any other flaws.

²⁸In the same way, a husband should love his wife as much as he loves himself. A husband who loves his wife shows that he loves himself. ²⁹None of us hate our own bodies. We provide for

---

[j]5.2 *us*: Some manuscripts have "you."   [k]5.6 *says*: Or "does."   [l]5.14 *Light shows up everything*: Or "Everything that is seen in the light becomes light itself."

them and take good care of them, just as Christ does for the church, ³⁰because we are each part of his body. ³¹As the Scriptures say, "A man leaves his father and mother to get married, and he becomes like one person with his wife." ³²This is a great mystery, but I understand it to mean Christ and his church. ³³So each husband should love his wife as much as he loves himself, and each wife should respect her husband.

Children and Parents

6 Children, you belong to the Lord, and you do the right thing when you obey your parents. The first commandment with a promise says, ²"Obey your father and your mother, ³and you will have a long and happy life."

⁴Parents, don't be hard on your children. Raise them properly. Teach them and instruct them about the Lord.

Slaves and Masters

⁵Slaves, you must obey your earthly masters. Show them great respect and be as loyal to them as you are to Christ. ⁶Try to please them at all times, and not just when you think they are watching. You are slaves of Christ, so with your whole heart you must do what God wants you to do. ⁷Gladly serve your masters, as though they were the Lord himself, and not simply people. ⁸You know that you will be rewarded for any good things you do, whether you are slaves or free.

⁹Slave owners, you must treat your slaves with this same respect. Don't threaten them. They have the same Master in heaven that you do, and he doesn't have any favorites.

The Fight against Evil

¹⁰Finally, let the mighty strength of the Lord make you strong. ¹¹Put on all the armor that God gives, so you can defend yourself against the devil's tricks. ¹²We are not fighting against humans. We are fighting against forces and authorities and against rulers of darkness and powers in the spiritual world. ¹³So put on all the armor that God gives. Then when that evil day[m] comes, you will be able to defend yourself. And when the battle is over, you will still be standing firm.

¹⁴Be ready! Let the truth be like a belt around your waist, and let God's justice protect you like armor. ¹⁵Your desire to tell the good news about peace should be like shoes on your feet. ¹⁶Let your faith be like a shield, and you will be able to stop all the flaming arrows of the evil one. ¹⁷Let God's saving power be like a helmet, and for a sword use God's message that comes from the Spirit.

¹⁸Never stop praying, especially for others. Always pray by the power of the Spirit. Stay alert and keep praying for God's people. ¹⁹Pray that I will be given the message to speak and that I may fearlessly explain the mystery about the good news. ²⁰I was sent to do this work, and that's the reason I am in jail. So pray that I will be brave and will speak as I should.

Final Greetings

²¹⁻²²I want you to know how I am getting along and what I am doing. That's why I am sending Tychicus to you. He is a dear friend, as well as a faithful servant of the Lord. He will tell you how I am doing, and he will cheer you up.

²³I pray that God the Father and the Lord Jesus Christ will give peace, love, and faith to every follower! ²⁴May God be kind to everyone who keeps on loving our Lord Jesus Christ.

---

[m] 6.13 *that evil day*: Either the present (see 5.16) or "the day of death" or "the day of judgment."

PHILIPPIANS

ABOUT THIS LETTER

Paul wrote this letter from jail (1.7) to thank the Lord's followers at Philippi for helping him with their gifts and prayers (1.5; 4.10-19). He hopes to be set free, so that he can continue preaching the good news (3.17-19). But he knows that he might be put to death (1.21; 2.17; 3.10).

The city of Philippi is in the part of northern Greece known as Macedonia. It was at Philippi that Paul had entered Europe for the first time, and there he preached the good news and began a church (Acts 16). He now warns the Christians at Philippi that they may have to suffer, just as Christ suffered and Paul is now suffering. If this happens, the Philippians should count it a blessing that comes from having faith in Christ (1.28-30).

There were problems in the church at Philippi, because some of the members claimed that people must obey the law of Moses, or they could not be saved. But Paul has no patience with such members and warns the church, "Watch out for those people who behave like dogs!" (3.2-11). This letter is also filled with joy. Even in jail, Paul is happy because he has discovered how to make the best of a bad situation and because he remembers all the kindness shown to him by the people in the church at Philippi.

Paul reminds them that God's people are to live in harmony (2.2; 4.2, 3) and to think the same way that Christ Jesus did:

> *Christ was truly God.*
> *But he did not try to remain*
>   *equal with God.*
> *He gave up everything*
>   *and became a slave,*
> *when he became*
>   *like one of us.* (2.6, 7)

A QUICK LOOK AT THIS LETTER

Greetings and a Prayer (1.1-11)
What Life Means to Paul (1.12-30)
Christ's Example of True Humility (2.1-18)
News about Paul's Friends (2.19-30)
Being Acceptable to God (3.1—4.9)
Paul Thanks the Philippians (4.10-20)
Final Greetings (4.21-23)

---

1 From Paul and Timothy, servants of Christ Jesus.

To all of God's people who belong to Christ Jesus at Philippi and to all of your church officials and officers.[a]

²I pray that God our Father and the Lord Jesus Christ will be kind to you and will bless you with peace!

Paul's Prayer for the Church in Philippi

³Every time I think of you, I thank my God. ⁴And whenever I mention you in my prayers, it makes me happy. ⁵This is because you have taken part with me in spreading the good news from the first day you heard about it. ⁶God is the one

---

[a] 1.1 *church officials and officers*: Or "bishops and deacons."

Philippians 1.7

who began this good work in you, and I am certain that he won't stop before it is complete on the day that Christ Jesus returns.

⁷You have a special place in my heart. So it is only natural for me to feel the way I do. All of you have helped in the work that God has given me, as I defend the good news and tell about it here in jail. ⁸God himself knows how much I want to see you. He knows that I care for you in the same way that Christ Jesus does.

⁹I pray that your love will keep on growing and that you will fully know and understand ¹⁰how to make the right choices. Then you will still be pure and innocent when Christ returns. And until that day, ¹¹Jesus Christ will keep you busy doing good deeds that bring glory and praise to God.

What Life Means to Paul

¹²My dear friends, I want you to know that what has happened to me has helped to spread the good news. ¹³The Roman guards and all the others know that I am here in jail because I serve Christ. ¹⁴Now most of the Lord's followers have become brave and are fearlessly telling the message.[b]

¹⁵Some are preaching about Christ because they are jealous and envious of us. Others are preaching because they want to help. ¹⁶They love Christ and know that I am here to defend the good news about him. ¹⁷But the ones who are jealous of us are not sincere. They just want to cause trouble for me while I am in jail. ¹⁸But that doesn't matter. All that matters is that people are telling about Christ, whether they are sincere or not. That is what makes me glad.

I will keep on being glad, ¹⁹because I know that your prayers and the help that comes from the Spirit of Christ Jesus will keep me safe. ²⁰I honestly expect and hope that I will never do anything to be ashamed of. Whether I live or die, I always want to be as brave as I am now and bring honor to Christ.

²¹If I live, it will be for Christ, and if I die, I will gain even more. ²²I don't know what to choose. I could keep on living and doing something useful. ²³It is a hard choice to make. I want to die and be with Christ, because that would be much better. ²⁴⁻²⁵But I know that all of you still need me. That's why I am sure I will stay on to help you grow and be happy in your faith. ²⁶Then, when I visit you again, you will have good reason to take great pride in Christ Jesus because of me.[c]

²⁷Above all else, you must live in a way that brings honor to the good news about Christ. Then, whether I visit you or not, I will hear that all of you think alike. I will know that you are working together and that you are struggling side by side to get others to believe the good news.

²⁸Be brave when you face your enemies. Your courage will show them that they are going to be destroyed, and it will show you that you will be saved. God will make all of this happen, ²⁹and he has blessed you. Not only do you have faith in Christ, but you suffer for him. ³⁰You saw me suffer, and you still hear about my troubles. Now you must suffer in the same way.

True Humility

2 Christ encourages you, and his love comforts you. God's Spirit unites you, and you are concerned for others. ²Now make me completely happy! Live in harmony by showing love for each other. Be united in what you think, as if you were only one person. ³Don't be jealous or proud, but be humble and consider others more important than yourselves. ⁴Care about them as much as you care about yourselves ⁵and think the same way that Christ Jesus thought:[d]

⁶ Christ was truly God.
  But he did not try to remain[e]
    equal with God.
⁷ Instead he gave up everything[f]
    and became a slave,
  when he became
    like one of us.

⁸ Christ was humble.
  He obeyed God and even died
    on a cross.
⁹ Then God gave Christ
    the highest place
  and honored his name
    above all others.
¹⁰ So at the name of Jesus
    everyone will bow down,
  those in heaven, on earth,
    and under the earth.
¹¹ And to the glory
    of God the Father
  everyone will openly agree,
    "Jesus Christ is Lord!"

Lights in the World

¹²My dear friends, you always obeyed when I was with you. Now that I am

---

[b] 1.14 *the message*: Some manuscripts have "the Lord's message," and others have "God's message." [c] 1.26 *take great pride in Christ Jesus because of me*: Or "take great pride in me because of Christ Jesus." [d] 2.5 *think the same way that Christ Jesus thought*: Or "think the way you should because you belong to Christ Jesus." [e] 2.6 *remain*: Or "become."
[f] 2.7 *He gave up everything*: Greek, "He emptied himself."

away, you should obey even more. So work with fear and trembling to discover what it really means to be saved. [13]God is working in you to make you willing and able to obey him.

[14]Do everything without grumbling or arguing. [15]Then you will be the pure and innocent children of God. You live among people who are crooked and evil, but you must not do anything that they can say is wrong. Try to shine as lights among the people of this world, [16]as you hold firmly to[g] the message that gives life. Then on the day when Christ returns, I can take pride in you. I can also know that my work and efforts were not useless.

[17]Your faith in the Lord and your service are like a sacrifice offered to him. And my own blood may have to be poured out with the sacrifice.[h] If this happens, I will be glad and rejoice with you. [18]In the same way, you should be glad and rejoice with me.

Timothy and Epaphroditus

[19]I want to be encouraged by news about you. So I hope the Lord Jesus will soon let me send Timothy to you. [20]I don't have anyone else who cares about you as much as he does. [21]The others think only about what interests them and not about what concerns Christ Jesus. [22]But you know what kind of person Timothy is. He has worked with me like a son in spreading the good news. [23]I hope to send him to you, as soon as I find out what is going to happen to me. [24]And I feel sure that the Lord will also let me come soon.

[25]I think I ought to send my dear friend Epaphroditus back to you. He is a follower and a worker and a soldier of the Lord, just as I am. You sent him to look after me, [26]but now he is eager to see you. He is worried, because you heard he was sick. [27]In fact, he was very sick and almost died. But God was kind to him, and also to me, and he kept me from being burdened down with sorrow.

[28]Now I am more eager than ever to send Epaphroditus back again. You will be glad to see him, and I won't have to worry any longer. [29]Be sure to give him a cheerful welcome, just as people who serve the Lord deserve. [30]He almost died working for Christ, and he risked his own life to do for me what you could not.

Being Acceptable to God

3 Finally, my dear friends, be glad that you belong to the Lord. It doesn't bother me to write the same things to you that I have written before. In fact, it is for your own good.

[2]Watch out for those people who behave like dogs! They are evil and want to do more than just circumcise you. [3]But we are the ones who are truly circumcised, because we worship by the power of God's Spirit[i] and take pride in Christ Jesus. We don't brag about what we have done, [4]although I could. Others may brag about themselves, but I have more reason to brag than anyone else. [5]I was circumcised when I was eight days old,[j] and I am from the nation of Israel and the tribe of Benjamin. I am a true Hebrew. As a Pharisee, I strictly obeyed the Law of Moses. [6]And I was so eager that I even made trouble for the church. I did everything the Law demands in order to please God.

[7]But Christ has shown me that what I once thought was valuable is worthless. [8]Nothing is as wonderful as knowing Christ Jesus my Lord. I have given up everything else and count it all as garbage. All I want is Christ [9]and to know that I belong to him. I could not make myself acceptable to God by obeying the Law of Moses. God accepted me simply because of my faith in Christ. [10]All I want is to know Christ and the power that raised him to life. I want to suffer and die as he did, [11]so that somehow I also may be raised to life.

Running toward the Goal

[12]I have not yet reached my goal, and I am not perfect. But Christ has taken hold of me. So I keep on running and struggling to take hold of the prize. [13]My friends, I don't feel that I have already arrived. But I forget what is behind, and I struggle for what is ahead. [14]I run toward the goal, so that I can win the prize of being called to heaven. This is the prize that God offers because of what Christ Jesus has done. [15]All of us who are mature should think in this same way. And if any of you think differently, God will make it clear to you. [16]But we must keep going in the direction that we are now headed.

[17]My friends, I want you to follow my example and learn from others who closely follow the example we set for you. [18]I often warned you that many people are living as enemies of the cross of Christ. And now with tears in my eyes, I warn you again [19]that they are headed for hell! They worship their stomachs and brag about the disgusting things they do. All they can think about are the things of this world.

---

[g]2.16 *hold firmly to*: Or "offer them." [h]2.17 *my own blood may have to be poured out with the sacrifice*: Offerings of water or wine were sometimes poured out when animals were sacrificed on the altar. [i]3.3 *by the power of God's Spirit*: Some manuscripts have "sincerely." [j]3.5 *when I was eight days old*: Jewish boys are circumcised eight days after birth.

²⁰But we are citizens of heaven and are eagerly waiting for our Savior to come from there. Our Lord Jesus Christ ²¹has power over everything, and he will make these poor bodies of ours like his own glorious body.

4 Dear friends, I love you and long to see you. Please keep on being faithful to the Lord. You are my pride and joy.

Paul Encourages the Lord's Followers

²Euodia and Syntyche, you belong to the Lord, so I beg you to stop arguing with each other. ³And, my true partner,*ᵏ* I ask you to help them. These women have worked together with me and with Clement and with the others in spreading the good news. Their names are now written in the book of life.*ˡ*

⁴Always be glad because of the Lord! I will say it again: Be glad. ⁵Always be gentle with others. The Lord will soon be here. ⁶Don't worry about anything, but pray about everything. With thankful hearts offer up your prayers and requests to God. ⁷Then, because you belong to Christ Jesus, God will bless you with peace that no one can completely understand. And this peace will control the way you think and feel.

⁸Finally, my friends, keep your minds on whatever is true, pure, right, holy, friendly, and proper. Don't ever stop thinking about what is truly worthwhile and worthy of praise. ⁹You know the teachings I gave you, and you know what you heard me say and saw me do. So follow my example. And God, who gives peace, will be with you.

Paul Gives Thanks for the Gifts He Was Given

¹⁰The Lord has made me very grateful that at last you have thought about me once again. Actually, you were thinking about me all along, but you didn't have any chance to show it. ¹¹I am not complaining about having too little. I have learned to be satisfied with*ᵐ* whatever I have. ¹²I know what it is to be poor or to have plenty, and I have lived under all kinds of conditions. I know what it means to be full or to be hungry, to have too much or too little. ¹³Christ gives me the strength to face anything.

¹⁴It was good of you to help me when I was having such a hard time. ¹⁵My friends at Philippi, you remember what it was like when I started preaching the good news in Macedonia.*ⁿ* After I left there, you were the only church that became my partner by giving blessings and by receiving them in return. ¹⁶Even when I was in Thessalonica, you helped me more than once. ¹⁷I am not trying to get something from you, but I want you to receive the blessings that come from giving.

¹⁸I have been paid back everything, and with interest. I am completely satisfied with the gifts that you had Epaphroditus bring me. They are like a sweet-smelling offering or like the right kind of sacrifice that pleases God. ¹⁹I pray that God will take care of all your needs with the wonderful blessings that come from Christ Jesus! ²⁰May God our Father be praised forever and ever. Amen.

Final Greetings

²¹Give my greetings to all who are God's people because of Christ Jesus. The Lord's followers here with me send you their greetings.

²²All of God's people send their greetings, especially those in the service of the Emperor.

²³I pray that our Lord Jesus Christ will be kind to you and will bless your life!

---

*ᵏ*4.3 *partner*: Or "Syzygus," a person's name. *ˡ*4.3 *the book of life*: A book in which the names of God's people are written. *ᵐ*4.11 *be satisfied with*: Or "get by on." *ⁿ*4.15 *when I started preaching the good news in Macedonia*: Paul is talking about his first visit to Philippi (see Acts 16.12-40).

COLOSSIANS

✝

ABOUT THIS LETTER

Colossae was an important city in western Asia Minor, about 100 miles east of the port city of Ephesus. Paul had never been to Colossae, but he was pleased to learn that the Christians there were strong in their faith (1.3-7; 2.6, 7). They had heard the good news from a man named Epaphras who had lived there (1.7; 4.12, 13), but was in jail with Paul (Philemon 23) at the time that Paul wrote this letter (1.14; 4.3, 10, 18).

Many of the church members in Colossae were Gentiles (1.27), and some of them were influenced by strange religious ideas and practices (2.16-23). They thought that to obey God fully they must give up certain physical desires and worship angels and other spiritual powers. But Paul wanted them to know that Christ was with God in heaven, ruling over all powers in the universe (3.1). And so, their worship should be directed to Christ.

Paul quotes a beautiful hymn that explains who Christ is:

> Christ is exactly like God,
> who cannot be seen.
> He is the first-born Son,
> superior to all creation.
>
> God himself was pleased
> to live fully in his Son.
> And God was pleased
> for him to make peace
> by sacrificing his blood
> on the cross.
> (1.15, 19, 20a)

A QUICK LOOK AT THIS LETTER

Greetings (1.1, 2)
A Prayer of Thanks (1.3-8)
The Person and Work of Christ (1.9—2.19)
New Life with Christ (2.20—4.6)
Final Greetings (4.7-18)

---

1 From Paul, chosen by God to be an apostle of Christ Jesus, and from Timothy, who is also a follower.

²To God's people who live in Colossae and are faithful followers of Christ.

I pray that God our Father will be kind to you and will bless you with peace!

A Prayer of Thanks

³Each time we pray for you, we thank God, the Father of our Lord Jesus Christ. ⁴We have heard of your faith in Christ and of your love for all of God's people, ⁵because what you hope for is kept safe for you in heaven. You first heard about this hope when you believed the true message, which is the good news.

⁶The good news is spreading all over the world with great success. It has spread in that same way among you, ever since the first day you learned the truth about God's wonderful kindness ⁷from our good friend Epaphras. He works together with us for Christ and is

Colossians 1.8

a faithful worker for you.[a] [8]He is also the one who told us about the love that God's Spirit has given you.

The Person and Work of Christ

[9]We have not stopped praying for you since the first day we heard about you. In fact, we always pray that God will show you everything he wants you to do and that you may have all the wisdom and understanding that his Spirit gives. [10]Then you will live a life that honors the Lord, and you will always please him by doing good deeds. You will come to know God even better. [11]His glorious power will make you patient and strong enough to endure anything, and you will be truly happy.

[12]I pray that you will be grateful to God for letting you[a] have part in what he has promised his people in the kingdom of light. [13]God rescued us from the dark power of Satan and brought us into the kingdom of his dear Son, [14]who forgives our sins and sets us free.

[15] Christ is exactly like God,
    who cannot be seen.
He is the first-born Son,
    superior to all creation.
[16] Everything was created by him,
    everything in heaven
        and on earth,
    everything seen and unseen,
    including all forces
        and powers,
    and all rulers
        and authorities.
All things were created
    by God's Son,
and everything was made
    for him.

[17] God's Son was before all else,
    and by him everything
        is held together.
[18] He is the head of his body,
    which is the church.
He is the very beginning,
    the first to be raised
        from death,
    so that he would be
        above all others.

[19] God himself was pleased
    to live fully in his Son.
[20] And God was pleased
    for him to make peace
    by sacrificing his blood
        on the cross,
    so that all beings in heaven
        and on earth
    would be brought back to God.

[21]You used to be far from God. Your thoughts made you his enemies, and you did evil things. [22]But his Son became a human and died. So God made peace with you, and now he lets you stand in his presence as people who are holy and faultless and innocent. [23]But you must stay deeply rooted and firm in your faith. You must not give up the hope you received when you heard the good news. It was preached to everyone on earth, and I myself have become a servant of this message.

Paul's Service to the Church

[24]I am glad that I can suffer for you. I am pleased also that in my own body I can continue[b] the suffering of Christ for his body, the church. [25]God's plan was to make me a servant of his church and to send me to preach his complete message to you. [26]For ages and ages this message was kept secret from everyone, but now it has been explained to God's people. [27]God did this because he wanted you Gentiles to understand his wonderful and glorious mystery. And the mystery is that Christ lives in you, and he is your hope of sharing in God's glory.

[28]We announce the message about Christ, and we use all our wisdom to warn and teach everyone, so that all of Christ's followers will grow and become mature. [29]That's why I work so hard and use the mighty power he gives me.

2 I want you to know what a struggle I am going through for you, for God's people at Laodicea, and for all of those followers who have never met me. [2]I do it to encourage them. Then as their hearts are joined together in love, they will be wonderfully blessed with complete understanding. And they will truly know Christ. Not only is he the key to God's mystery, [3]but all wisdom and knowledge are hidden away in him. [4]I tell you these things to keep you from being fooled by fancy talk. [5]Even though I am not with you, I keep thinking about you. I am glad to know that you are living as you should and that your faith in Christ is strong.

Christ Brings Real Life

[6]You have accepted Christ Jesus as your Lord. Now keep on following him. [7]Plant your roots in Christ and let him be the foundation for your life. Be strong in your faith, just as you were taught. And be grateful.

[8]Don't let anyone fool you by using senseless arguments. These arguments may sound wise, but they are only human teachings. They come from the

---

[a]1.7,12 *you*: Some manuscripts have "us."   [b]1.24 *continue*: Or "complete."

powers of this world[c] and not from Christ.

⁹God lives fully in Christ. ¹⁰And you are fully grown because you belong to Christ, who is over every power and authority. ¹¹Christ has also taken away your selfish desires, just as circumcision removes flesh from the body. ¹²And when you were baptized, it was the same as being buried with Christ. Then you were raised to life because you had faith in the power of God, who raised Christ from death. ¹³You were dead, because you were sinful and were not God's people. But God let Christ make you[d] alive, when he forgave all our sins.

¹⁴God wiped out the charges that were against us for disobeying the Law of Moses. He took them away and nailed them to the cross. ¹⁵There Christ defeated all powers and forces. He let the whole world see them being led away as prisoners when he celebrated his victory.

¹⁶Don't let anyone tell you what you must eat or drink. Don't let them say that you must celebrate the New Moon festival, the Sabbath, or any other festival. ¹⁷These things are only a shadow of what was to come. But Christ is real!

¹⁸Don't be cheated by people who make a show of acting humble and who worship angels.[e] They brag about seeing visions. But it is all nonsense, because their minds are filled with selfish desires. ¹⁹They are no longer part of Christ, who is the head of the whole body. Christ gives the body its strength, and he uses its joints and muscles to hold it together, as it grows by the power of God.

Christ Brings New Life

²⁰You died with Christ. Now the forces of the universe[f] don't have any power over you. Why do you live as if you had to obey such rules as, ²¹"Don't handle this. Don't taste that. Don't touch this."? ²²After these things are used, they are no longer good for anything. So why be bothered with the rules that humans have made up? ²³Obeying these rules may seem to be the smart thing to do. They appear to make you love God more and to be very humble and to have control over your body. But they don't really have any power over our desires.

3 You have been raised to life with Christ. Now set your heart on what is in heaven, where Christ rules at God's right side.[g] ²Think about what is up there, not about what is here on earth. ³You died, which means that your life is hidden with Christ, who sits beside God. ⁴Christ gives meaning to your[h] life, and when he appears, you will also appear with him in glory.

⁵Don't be controlled by your body. Kill every desire for the wrong kind of sex. Don't be immoral or indecent or have evil thoughts. Don't be greedy, which is the same as worshiping idols. ⁶God is angry with people who disobey him by doing[i] these things. ⁷And that is exactly what you did, when you lived among people who behaved in this way. ⁸But now you must stop doing such things. You must quit being angry, hateful, and evil. You must no longer say insulting or cruel things about others. ⁹And stop lying to each other. You have given up your old way of life with its habits.

¹⁰Each of you is now a new person. You are becoming more and more like your Creator, and you will understand him better. ¹¹It doesn't matter if you are a Greek or a Jew, or if you are circumcised or not. You may even be a barbarian or a Scythian,[j] and you may be a slave or a free person. Yet Christ is all that matters, and he lives in all of us.

¹²God loves you and has chosen you as his own special people. So be gentle, kind, humble, meek, and patient. ¹³Put up with each other, and forgive anyone who does you wrong, just as Christ has forgiven you. ¹⁴Love is more important than anything else. It is what ties everything completely together.

¹⁵Each one of you is part of the body of Christ, and you were chosen to live together in peace. So let the peace that comes from Christ control your thoughts. And be grateful. ¹⁶Let the message about Christ completely fill your lives, while you use all your wisdom to teach and instruct each other. With thankful hearts, sing psalms, hymns, and spiritual songs to God. ¹⁷Whatever you say or do should be done in the name of the Lord Jesus, as you give thanks to God the Father because of him.

Some Rules for Christian Living

¹⁸A wife must put her husband first. This is her duty as a follower of the Lord.

---

[c]**2.8** *powers of this world:* Spirits and unseen forces were thought to control human lives and were believed to be connected with the movements of the stars.   [d]**2.13** *you:* See the note at 1.7.   [e]**2.18** *worship angels:* Or "worship with angels (in visions of heaven)."   [f]**2.20** *forces of the universe:* See the note at 2.8.   [g]**3.1** *right side:* The place of power and honor.   [h]**3.4** *your:* Some manuscripts have "our." [i]**3.6** *people who disobey him by doing:* Some manuscripts do not have these words.   [j]**3.11** *a barbarian or a Scythian:* Barbarians were people who could not speak Greek and would be in the lower class of society. Scythians were people who were known for their cruelty.

19A husband must love his wife and not abuse her.

20Children must always obey their parents. This pleases the Lord.

21Parents, don't be hard on your children. If you are, they might give up.

22Slaves, you must always obey your earthly masters. Try to please them at all times, and not just when you think they are watching. Honor the Lord and serve your masters with your whole heart. **23**Do your work willingly, as though you were serving the Lord himself, and not just your earthly master. **24**In fact, the Lord Christ is the one you are really serving, and you know that he will reward you. **25**But Christ has no favorites! He will punish evil people, just as they deserve.

4 Slave owners, be fair and honest with your slaves. Don't forget that you have a Master in heaven.

2Never give up praying. And when you pray, keep alert and be thankful. **3**Be sure to pray that God will make a way for us to spread his message and explain the mystery about Christ, even though I am in jail for doing this. **4**Please pray that I will make the message as clear as possible.

5When you are with unbelievers, always make good use of the time. **6**Be pleasant and hold their interest when you speak the message. Choose your words carefully and be ready to give answers to anyone who asks questions.

Final Greetings

7Tychicus is the dear friend, who faithfully works and serves the Lord with us, and he will give you the news about me. **8**I am sending him to cheer you up by telling you how we are getting along. **9**Onesimus, that dear and faithful follower from your own group, is coming with him. The two of them will tell you everything that has happened here.

10Aristarchus is in jail with me. He sends greetings to you, and so does Mark, the cousin of Barnabas. You have already been told to welcome Mark, if he visits you. **11**Jesus, who is known as Justus, sends his greetings. These three men are the only Jewish followers who have worked with me for the kingdom of God. They have given me much comfort.

12Your own Epaphras, who serves Christ Jesus, sends his greetings. He always prays hard that you may fully know what the Lord wants you to do and that you may do it completely. **13**I have seen how much trouble he has gone through for you and for the followers in Laodicea and Hierapolis.

14Our dear doctor Luke sends you his greetings, and so does Demas.

15Give my greetings to the followers at Laodicea, especially to Nympha and the church that meets in her home.

16After this letter has been read to your people, be sure to have it read in the church at Laodicea. And you should read the letter that I have sent to them.[k]

17Remind Archippus to do the work that the Lord has given him to do.

18I am signing this letter myself: PAUL.

Don't forget that I am in jail.
I pray that God will be kind to you.

---

[k] **4.16** *the letter that I have sent to them*: This is the only mention of the letter to the church at Laodicea.

1 THESSALONIANS

ABOUT THIS LETTER

Paul started the church in Thessalonica (2.13, 14), while working hard to support himself (2.9). In this important city of northern Greece, many of the followers had worshiped idols before becoming Christians (1.9). But they were faithful to the Lord, and because of them the Lord's message had spread everywhere in that region (1.8). This letter may have been the first one that Paul wrote, and maybe even the first of all the New Testament writings.

Some people in Thessalonica began to oppose Paul, and he had to escape to Athens. But he sent his young friend Timothy to find out how the Christians were doing (3.1-5). When Timothy returned, he gave Paul good reports of their faith and love (3.6-10).

The church itself had problems. Some of its members had quit working, since they thought that the Lord would soon return (4.11, 12). Others were worried because relatives and friends had already died before Christ's return. So Paul tried to explain to them more clearly what would happen when the Lord returns (4.13-15), and then told them how they should live in the meanwhile (5.1-11).

Paul's final instructions are well worth remembering:

Always be joyful and never stop praying. Whatever happens, keep thanking God because of Jesus Christ. This is what God wants you to do. (5.16-18)

A QUICK LOOK AT THIS LETTER

Greetings (1.1-3)
The Thessalonians' Faith and Example (1.4—3.13)
A Life That Pleases God (4.1-12)
What to Expect When the Lord Returns (4.13—5.11)
Final Instructions and Greetings (5.12-28)

---

1 From Paul, Silas,[a] and Timothy.
To the church in Thessalonica, the people of God the Father and of the Lord Jesus Christ.

I pray that God will be kind to you and will bless you with peace!

²We thank God for you and always mention you in our prayers. Each time we pray, ³we tell God our Father about your faith and loving work and about your firm hope in our Lord Jesus Christ.

The Thessalonians' Faith and Example

⁴My dear friends, God loves you, and we know he has chosen you to be his people. ⁵When we told you the good news, it was with the power and assurance that come from the Holy Spirit, and not simply with words. You knew what kind of people we were and how we helped you. ⁶So, when you accepted the message, you followed our example and the example of the Lord. You suffered, but the Holy Spirit made you glad.

⁷You became an example for all the Lord's followers in Macedonia and Achaia. ⁸And because of you, the Lord's message has spread everywhere in those regions. Now the news of your faith in God is known all over the world, and we don't have to say a thing about it. ⁹Everyone is talking about how you welcomed us and how you turned away from idols to serve the true and living God. ¹⁰They also tell how you are waiting for his Son Jesus to come from heaven. God raised him from death, and

---

[a] 1.1 *Silas*: The Greek text has "Silvanus," another form of the name Silas.

on the day of judgment Jesus will save us from God's anger.

Paul's Work in Thessalonica

2 My friends, you know that our time with you wasn't wasted. [2]As you remember, we had been mistreated and insulted at Philippi. But God gave us the courage to tell you the good news about him, even though many people caused us trouble. [3]We didn't have any hidden motives when we won you over, and we didn't try to fool or trick anyone. [4]God was pleased to trust us with his message. We didn't speak to please people, but to please God who knows our motives.

[5]You also know that we didn't try to flatter anyone. God himself knows that what we did wasn't a cover-up for greed. [6]We were not trying to get you or anyone else to praise us. [7]But as apostles, we could have demanded help from you. After all, Christ is the one who sent us. We chose to be like children or like a mother[b] nursing her baby. [8]We cared so much for you, and you became so dear to us, that we were willing to give our lives for you when we gave you God's message.

[9]My dear friends, you surely haven't forgotten our hard work and hardships. You remember how night and day we struggled to make a living, so that we could tell you God's message without being a burden to anyone. [10]Both you and God are witnesses that we were pure and honest and innocent in our dealings with you followers of the Lord. [11]You also know we did everything for you that parents would do for their own children. [12]We begged, encouraged, and urged each of you to live in a way that would honor God. He is the one who chose you to share in his own kingdom and glory.

[13]We always thank God that you believed the message we preached. It came from him, and it isn't something made up by humans. You accepted it as God's message, and now he is working in you. [14]My friends, you did just like God's churches in Judea and like the other followers of Christ Jesus there. And so, you were mistreated by your own people, in the same way they were mistreated by their people.

[15]Those Jews killed the Lord Jesus and the prophets, and they even chased us away. God doesn't like what they do and neither does anyone else. [16]They keep us from speaking his message to the Gentiles and from leading them to be saved. The Jews have always gone too far with their sins. Now God has finally become angry and will punish them.

Paul Wants To Visit the Church Again

[17]My friends, we were kept from coming to you for a while, but we never stopped thinking about you. We were eager to see you and tried our best to visit you in person. [18]We really wanted to come. I myself tried several times, but Satan always stopped us. [19]After all, when the Lord Jesus appears, who else but you will give us hope and joy and be like a glorious crown for us? [20]You alone are our glory and joy!

3 Finally, we couldn't stand it any longer. We decided to stay in Athens by ourselves [2]and send our friend Timothy to you. He works with us as God's servant and preaches the good news about Christ. We wanted him to make you strong in your faith and to encourage you. [3]We didn't want any of you to be discouraged by all these troubles. You knew we would have to suffer, [4]because when we were with you, we told you this would happen. And we did suffer, as you well know. [5]At last, when I could not wait any longer, I sent Timothy to find out about your faith. I hoped that Satan had not tempted you and made all our work useless.

[6]Timothy has come back from his visit with you and has told us about your faith and love. He also said that you always have happy memories of us and that you want to see us as much as we want to see you.

[7]My friends, even though we have a lot of trouble and suffering, your faith makes us feel better about you. [8]Your strong faith in the Lord is like a breath of new life. [9]How can we possibly thank God enough for all the happiness you have brought us? [10]Day and night we sincerely pray that we will see you again and help you to have an even stronger faith.

[11]We pray that God our Father and our Lord Jesus will let us visit you. [12]May the Lord make your love for each other and for everyone else grow by leaps and bounds. That's how our love for you has grown. [13]And when our Lord comes with all of his people, I pray that he will make your hearts pure and innocent in the sight of God the Father.

A Life That Pleases God

4 Finally, my dear friends, since you belong to the Lord Jesus, we beg and urge you to live as we taught you. Then you will please God. You are already living that way, but try even harder. [2]Remember the instructions we

---

[b]2.7 *like children or like a mother*: Some manuscripts have "as gentle as a mother."

gave you as followers of the Lord Jesus. ³God wants you to be holy, so don't be immoral in matters of sex. ⁴Respect and honor your wife.ᶜ ⁵Don't be a slave of your desires or live like people who don't know God. ⁶You must not cheat any of the Lord's followers in matters of sex.ᵈ Remember, we warned you that he punishes everyone who does such things. ⁷God didn't choose you to be filthy, but to be pure. ⁸So if you don't obey these rules, you are not really disobeying us. You are disobeying God, who gives you his Holy Spirit.

⁹We don't have to write you about the need to love each other. God has taught you to do this, ¹⁰and you already have shown your love for all of his people in Macedonia. But, my dear friends, we ask you to do even more. ¹¹Try your best to live quietly, to mind your own business, and to work hard, just as we taught you to do. ¹²Then you will be respected by people who are not followers of the Lord, and you won't have to depend on anyone.

The Lord's Coming

¹³My friends, we want you to understand how it will be for those followers who have already died. Then you won't grieve over them and be like people who don't have any hope. ¹⁴We believe that Jesus died and was raised to life. We also believe that when God brings Jesus back again, he will bring with him all who had faith in Jesus before they died. ¹⁵Our Lord Jesus told us that when he comes, we won't go up to meet him ahead of his followers who have already died.

¹⁶With a loud command and with the shout of the chief angel and a blast of God's trumpet, the Lord will return from heaven. Then those who had faith in Christ before they died will be raised to life. ¹⁷Next, all of us who are still alive will be taken up into the clouds together with them to meet the Lord in the sky. From that time on we will all be with the Lord forever. ¹⁸Encourage each other with these words.

5 I don't need to write you about the time or date when all this will happen. ²You surely know that the Lord's returnᵉ will be as a thief coming at night. ³People will think they are safe and secure. But destruction will suddenly strike them like the pains of a woman about to give birth. And they won't escape.

⁴My dear friends, you don't live in darkness, and so that day won't surprise you like a thief. ⁵You belong to the light and live in the day. We don't live in the night or belong to the dark. ⁶Others may sleep, but we should stay awake and be alert. ⁷People sleep during the night, and some even get drunk. ⁸But we belong to the day. So we must stay sober and let our faith and love be like a suit of armor. Our firm hope that we will be saved is our helmet.

⁹God doesn't intend to punish us, but wants us to be saved by our Lord Jesus Christ. ¹⁰Christ died for us, so that we could live with him, whether we are alive or dead when he comes. ¹¹That's why you must encourage and help each other, just as you are already doing.

Final Instructions and Greetings

¹²My friends, we ask you to be thoughtful of your leaders who work hard and tell you how to live for the Lord. ¹³Show them great respect and love because of their work. Try to get along with each other. ¹⁴My friends, we beg you to warn anyone who isn't living right. Encourage anyone who feels left out, help all who are weak, and be patient with everyone. ¹⁵Don't be hateful to people, just because they are hateful to you. Rather, be good to each other and to everyone else.

¹⁶Always be joyful ¹⁷and never stop praying. ¹⁸Whatever happens, keep thanking God because of Jesus Christ. This is what God wants you to do.

¹⁹Don't turn away God's Spirit ²⁰or ignore prophecies. ²¹Put everything to the test. Accept what is good ²²and don't have anything to do with evil.

²³I pray that God, who gives peace, will make you completely holy. And may your spirit, soul, and body be kept healthy and faultless until our Lord Jesus Christ returns. ²⁴The one who chose you can be trusted, and he will do this.

²⁵Friends, please pray for us.

²⁶Give the Lord's followers a warm greeting.

²⁷In the name of the Lord I beg you to read this letter to all his followers.

²⁸I pray that our Lord Jesus Christ will be kind to you!

ᶜ**4.4** *your wife*: Or "your body." ᵈ**4.6** *in matters of sex*: Or "in business." ᵉ**5.2** *the Lord's return*: The Greek text has "the day of the Lord."

2 THESSALONIANS

ABOUT THIS LETTER

In this letter to the believers in Thessalonica, Paul begins by thanking God that their faith and love keep growing all the time (1.3). They were going through a lot of troubles, but Paul insists that this is God's way of testing their faith, not a way of punishing them (1.4, 5).

Someone in Thessalonica claimed to have a letter from Paul, saying that the Lord had already returned (2.2). But Paul warns the church not to be fooled! The Lord will not return until after the "wicked one" has appeared (2.3).

Paul also warns against laziness (3.6-10), and he tells the church to guard against any followers who refuse to obey what he has written in this letter.

The letter closes with a prayer:

I pray that the Lord, who gives peace, will always bless you with peace. May the Lord be with all of you. (3.16)

A QUICK LOOK AT THIS LETTER

Greetings (1.1, 2)
The Lord's Return Will Bring Justice (1.3-12)
The Lord Has Not Returned Yet (2.1-12)
Be Faithful (2.13-17)
Pray and Work (3.1-15)
A Final Prayer (3.16-18)

---

1 From Paul, Silas,[a] and Timothy. To the church in Thessalonica, the people of God our Father and of the Lord Jesus Christ.

² I pray that God our Father and the Lord Jesus Christ will be kind to you and will bless you with peace!

When Christ Returns

³ My dear friends, we always have good reason to thank God for you, because your faith in God and your love for each other keep growing all the time. ⁴ That's why we brag about you to all of God's churches. We tell them how patient you are and how you keep on having faith, even though you are going through a lot of trouble and suffering.

⁵ All of this shows that God judges fairly and that he is making you fit to share in his kingdom for which you are suffering. ⁶ It is only right for God to punish everyone who is causing you trouble, ⁷ but he will give you relief from your troubles. He will do the same for us, when the Lord Jesus comes from heaven with his powerful angels ⁸ and with a flaming fire.

Our Lord Jesus will punish anyone who doesn't know God and won't obey his message. ⁹ Their punishment will be eternal destruction, and they will be kept far from the presence of our Lord and his glorious strength. ¹⁰ This will happen on that day when the Lord returns to be praised and honored by all who have faith in him and belong to him. This includes you, because you believed what we said.

¹¹ God chose you, and we keep praying that God will make you worthy of being his people. We pray for God's power to help you do all the good things that you hope to do and that your faith makes you want to do. ¹² Then, because God and our Lord Jesus Christ are so kind, you will bring honor to the name of our

---

[a] 1.1 *Silas:* The Greek text has "Silvanus," which is another form of the name Silas.

Lord Jesus, and he will bring honor to you.

The Lord's Return

2 When our Lord Jesus returns, we will be gathered up to meet him. So I ask you, my friends, ²not to be easily upset or disturbed by people who claim that the Lord[b] has already come. They may say that they heard this directly from the Holy Spirit, or from someone else, or even that they read it in one of our letters. ³But don't be fooled! People will rebel against God. Then before the Lord returns, the wicked[c] one who is doomed to be destroyed will appear. ⁴He will brag and oppose everything that is holy or sacred. He will even sit in God's temple and claim to be God. ⁵Don't you remember that I told you this while I was still with you?

⁶You already know what is holding this wicked one back until it is time for him to come. ⁷His mysterious power is already at work, but someone is holding him back. And the wicked one won't appear until that someone is out of the way. ⁸Then he will appear, but the Lord Jesus will kill him simply by breathing on him. He will be completely destroyed by the Lord's glorious return.

⁹When the wicked one appears, Satan will pretend to work all kinds of miracles, wonders, and signs. ¹⁰Lost people will be fooled by his evil deeds. They could be saved, but they will refuse to love the truth and accept it. ¹¹So God will make sure that they are fooled into believing a lie. ¹²All of them will be punished, because they would rather do evil than believe the truth.

Be Faithful

¹³My friends, the Lord loves you, and it is only natural for us to thank God for you. God chose you to be the first ones to be saved.[d] His Spirit made you holy, and you put your faith in the truth. ¹⁴God used our preaching as his way of inviting you to share in the glory of our Lord Jesus Christ. ¹⁵My friends, that's why you must remain faithful and follow closely what we taught you in person and by our letters.

¹⁶God our Father loves us. He is kind and has given us eternal comfort and a wonderful hope. We pray that our Lord Jesus Christ and God our Father ¹⁷will encourage you and help you always to do and say the right thing.

Pray for Us

3 Finally, our friends, please pray for us. This will help the message about the Lord to spread quickly, and others will respect it, just as you do. ²Pray that we may be kept safe from worthless and evil people. After all, not everyone has faith. ³But the Lord can be trusted to make you strong and protect you from harm. ⁴He has made us sure that you are obeying what we taught you and that you will keep on obeying. ⁵I pray that the Lord will guide you to be as loving as God and as patient as Christ.

Warnings against Laziness

⁶My dear friends, in the name of[e] the Lord Jesus, I beg you not to have anything to do with any of your people who loaf around and refuse to obey the instructions we gave you. ⁷You surely know that you should follow our example. We didn't waste our time loafing, ⁸and we didn't accept food from anyone without paying for it. We didn't want to be a burden to any of you, so night and day we worked as hard as we could.

⁹We had the right not to work, but we wanted to set an example for you. ¹⁰We also gave you the rule that if you don't work, you don't eat. ¹¹Now we learn that some of you just loaf around and won't do any work, except the work of a busybody. ¹²So, for the sake of our Lord Jesus Christ, we ask and beg these people to settle down and start working for a living. ¹³Dear friends, you must never become tired of doing right.

¹⁴Be on your guard against any followers who refuse to obey what we have written in this letter. Put them to shame by not having anything to do with them. ¹⁵Don't consider them your enemies, but speak kindly to them as you would to any other follower.

Final Prayer

¹⁶I pray that the Lord, who gives peace, will always bless you with peace. May the Lord be with all of you.

¹⁷I always sign my letters as I am now doing: PAUL.

¹⁸I pray that our Lord Jesus Christ will be kind to all of you.

---

[b]2.2 *Lord*: The Greek text has "day of the Lord." [c]2.3 *wicked*: Some manuscripts have "sinful." [d]2.13 *God chose you to be the first ones to be saved*: Some manuscripts have "From the beginning God chose you to be saved." [e]3.6 *in the name of*: Or "as a follower of."

1 TIMOTHY

ABOUT THIS LETTER

Timothy traveled and worked with Paul (Romans 16.21; 1 Corinthians 16.10; Philippians 2.19), and because of their shared faith, Timothy was like a son to Paul (1.2). Timothy became one of Paul's most faithful co-workers, and Paul mentions Timothy in five of his letters.

Although this letter is addressed to Timothy personally, it actually addresses many of the concerns Paul had with the life of the entire church. Guidelines are given for choosing church officials (3.1-7), officers (3.8-13), and leaders (5.17-20).

Christians are to pray for everyone and to remember:

> There is only one God,
> and Christ Jesus
> is the only one
> who can bring us
> to God.   (2.5)

A QUICK LOOK AT THIS LETTER

Greetings (1.1, 2)
Instructions for Church Life (1.3—3.13)
The Mystery of Our Religion (3.14—4.5)
Paul's Advice to Timothy (4.6—6.21)

---

1 From Paul.
God our Savior and Christ Jesus commanded me to be an apostle of Christ Jesus, who gives us hope.

²Timothy, because of our faith, you are like a son to me. I pray that God our Father and our Lord Jesus Christ will be kind and merciful to you. May they bless you with peace!

Warning against False Teaching

³When I was leaving for Macedonia, I asked you to stay on in Ephesus and warn certain people there to stop spreading their false teachings. ⁴You needed to warn them to stop wasting their time on senseless stories and endless lists of ancestors. Such things only cause arguments. They don't help anyone to do God's work that can only be done by faith.

⁵You must teach people to have genuine love, as well as a good conscience and true faith. ⁶There are some who have given up these for nothing but empty talk. ⁷They want to be teachers of the Law of Moses. But they don't know what they are talking about, even though they think they do.

⁸We know that the Law is good, if it is used in the right way. ⁹We also understand that it wasn't given to control people who please God, but to control lawbreakers, criminals, godless people, and sinners. It is for wicked and evil people, and for murderers, who would even kill their own parents. ¹⁰The Law was written for people who are sexual perverts or who live as homosexuals or are kidnappers or liars or won't tell the truth in court. It is for anything else that opposes the correct teaching ¹¹of the good news that the glorious and wonderful God has given me.

Being Thankful for God's Kindness

¹²I thank Christ Jesus our Lord. He has given me the strength for my work because he knew that he could trust me. ¹³I used to say terrible and insulting

things about him, and I was cruel. But he had mercy on me because I didn't know what I was doing, and I had not yet put my faith in him. ¹⁴Christ Jesus our Lord was very kind to me. He has greatly blessed my life with faith and love just like his own.

¹⁵"Christ Jesus came into the world to save sinners." This saying is true, and it can be trusted. I was the worst sinner of all! ¹⁶But since I was worse than anyone else, God had mercy on me and let me be an example of the endless patience of Christ Jesus. He did this so that others would put their faith in Christ and have eternal life. ¹⁷I pray that honor and glory will always be given to the only God, who lives forever and is the invisible and eternal King! Amen.

¹⁸Timothy, my son, the instructions I am giving you are based on what some prophets*ᵃ* once said about you. If you follow these instructions, you will fight like a good soldier. ¹⁹You will be faithful and have a clear conscience. Some people have made a mess of their faith because they didn't listen to their consciences. ²⁰Two of them are Hymenaeus and Alexander. I have given these men over to the power of Satan, so they will learn not to oppose God.

How To Pray

2 First of all, I ask you to pray for everyone. Ask God to help and bless them all, and tell God how thankful you are for each of them. ²Pray for kings and others in power, so that we may live quiet and peaceful lives as we worship and honor God. ³This kind of prayer is good, and it pleases God our Savior. ⁴God wants everyone to be saved and to know the whole truth, which is,

⁵ There is only one God,
  and Christ Jesus
    is the only one
  who can bring us
    to God.
  Jesus was truly human,
    and he gave himself
      to rescue all of us.
⁶ God showed us this
    at the right time.

⁷This is why God chose me to be a preacher and an apostle of the good news. I am telling the truth. I am not lying. God sent me to teach the Gentiles about faith and truth.

⁸I want everyone everywhere to lift innocent hands toward heaven and pray, without being angry or arguing with each other.

⁹I would like for women to wear modest and sensible clothes. They should not have fancy hairdos, or wear expensive clothes, or put on jewelry made of gold or pearls. ¹⁰Women who claim to love God should do helpful things for others, ¹¹and they should learn by being quiet and paying attention. ¹²They should be silent and not be allowed to teach or to tell men what to do. ¹³After all, Adam was created before Eve, ¹⁴and the man Adam wasn't the one who was fooled. It was the woman Eve who was completely fooled and sinned. ¹⁵But women will be saved by having children,*ᵇ* if they stay faithful, loving, holy, and modest.

Church Officials

3 It is true that*ᶜ* anyone who desires to be a church official*ᵈ* wants to be something worthwhile. ²That's why officials must have a good reputation and be faithful in marriage.*ᵉ* They must be self-controlled, sensible, well-behaved, friendly to strangers, and able to teach. ³They must not be heavy drinkers or troublemakers. Instead, they must be kind and gentle and not love money.

⁴Church officials must be in control of their own families, and they must see that their children are obedient and always respectful. ⁵If they don't know how to control their own families, how can they look after God's people?

⁶They must not be new followers of the Lord. If they are, they might become proud and be doomed along with the devil. ⁷Finally, they must be well-respected by people who are not followers. Then they won't be trapped and disgraced by the devil.

Church Officers

⁸Church officers*ᶠ* should be serious. They must not be liars, heavy drinkers, or greedy for money. ⁹And they must have a clear conscience and hold firmly to what God has shown us about our faith. ¹⁰They must first prove themselves. Then if no one has anything against them, they can serve as officers.

¹¹Women*ᵍ* must also be serious. They must not gossip or be heavy drinkers,

---

*ᵃ***1.18** *prophets*: Probably the Christian prophets referred to in 4.14.   *ᵇ***2.15** *saved by having children*: Or "brought safely through childbirth" or "saved by the birth of a child" (that is, by the birth of Jesus) or "saved by being good mothers."   *ᶜ***3.1** *It is true that*: These words may be taken with 2.15. If so, that verse would be translated: "It is true that women will be saved . . . holy, and modest." And 3.1 would be translated, "Anyone who desires . . . something worthwhile."   *ᵈ***3.1** *church official*: Or "bishop."   *ᵉ***3.2** *be faithful in marriage*: Or "be the husband of only one wife" or "have never been divorced."   *ᶠ***3.8** *Church officers*: Or "Deacons."   *ᵍ***3.11** *Women*: Either church officers or the wives of church officers.

and they must be faithful in everything they do. [12]Church officers must be faithful in marriage.[h] They must be in full control of their children and everyone else in their home. [13]Those who serve well as officers will earn a good reputation and will be highly respected for their faith in Christ Jesus.

The Mystery of Our Religion

[14]I hope to visit you soon. But I am writing these instructions, [15]so that if I am delayed, you will know how everyone who belongs to God's family ought to behave. After all, the church of the living God is the strong foundation of truth.

[16]Here is the great mystery of our religion:

Christ[i] came as a human.
The Spirit proved
   that he pleased God,
and he was seen by angels.

Christ was preached
   to the nations.
People in this world
   put their faith in him,
and he was taken up to glory.

People Will Turn from Their Faith

4 God's Spirit clearly says that in the last days many people will turn from their faith. They will be fooled by evil spirits and by teachings that come from demons. [2]They will also be fooled by the false claims of liars whose consciences have lost all feeling. These liars [3]will forbid people to marry or to eat certain foods. But God created these foods to be eaten with thankful hearts by his followers who know the truth. [4]Everything God created is good. And if you give thanks, you may eat anything. [5]What God has said and your prayer will make it fit to eat.

Paul's Advice to Timothy

[6]If you teach these things to other followers, you will be a good servant of Christ Jesus. You will show that you have grown up on the teachings about our faith and on the good instructions you have obeyed. [7]Don't have anything to do with worthless, senseless stories. Work hard to be truly religious. [8-9]As the saying goes,

"Exercise is good
   for your body,
but religion helps you
   in every way.
It promises life
   now and forever."

These words are worthwhile and should not be forgotten. [10]We have put our hope in the living God, who is the Savior of everyone, but especially of those who have faith. That's why we work and struggle so hard.[j] [11]Teach these things and tell everyone to do what you say. [12]Don't let anyone make fun of you, just because you are young. Set an example for other followers by what you say and do, as well as by your love, faith, and purity.

[13]Until I arrive, be sure to keep on reading the Scriptures in worship, and don't stop preaching and teaching. [14]Use the gift you were given when the prophets spoke and the group of church leaders[k] blessed you by placing their hands on you. [15]Remember these things and think about them, so everyone can see how well you are doing. [16]Be careful about the way you live and about what you teach. Keep on doing this, and you will save not only yourself, but the people who hear you.

How To Act toward Others

5 Don't correct an older man. Encourage him, as you would your own father. Treat younger men as you would your own brother, [2]and treat older women as you would your own mother. Show the same respect to younger women that you would to your sister.

[3]Take care of any widow who is really in need. [4]But if a widow has children or grandchildren, they should learn to serve God by taking care of her, as she once took care of them. This is what God wants them to do. [5]A widow who is really in need is one who doesn't have any relatives. She has faith in God, and she keeps praying to him night and day, asking for his help.

[6]A widow who thinks only about having a good time is already dead, even though she is still alive.

[7]Tell all of this to everyone, so they will do the right thing. [8]People who don't take care of their relatives, and especially their own families, have given up their faith. They are worse than someone who doesn't have faith in the Lord.

[9]For a widow to be put on the list of widows, she must be at least sixty years old, and she must have been faithful in

---

[h]**3.12** *be faithful in marriage*: See the note at 3.2.   [i]**3.16** *Christ*: The Greek text has "he," probably meaning "Christ." Some manuscripts have "God."   [j]**4.10** *struggle so hard*: Some manuscripts have "are treated so badly."   [k]**4.14** *group of church leaders*: Or "group of elders" or "group of presbyters" or "group of priests." This translates one Greek word, and it is related to the one used in 5.17, 19.

marriage.^l ^10She must also be well-known for doing all sorts of good things, such as raising children, giving food to strangers, welcoming God's people into her home,^m helping people in need, and always making herself useful.

^11Don't put young widows on the list. They may later have a strong desire to get married. Then they will turn away from Christ ^12and become guilty of breaking their promise to him. ^13Besides, they will become lazy and get into the habit of going from house to house. Next, they will start gossiping and become busybodies, talking about things that are none of their business.

^14I would prefer that young widows get married, have children, and look after their families. Then the enemy won't have any reason to say insulting things about us. ^15Look what's already happened to some of the young widows! They have turned away to follow Satan.

^16If a woman who is a follower has any widows in her family, she^n should help them. This will keep the church from having that burden, and then the church can help widows who are really in need.

Church Leaders

^17Church leaders^o who do their job well deserve to be paid^p twice as much, especially if they work hard at preaching and teaching. ^18It is just as the Scriptures say, "Don't muzzle an ox when you are using it to grind grain." You also know the saying, "Workers are worth their pay."

^19Don't listen to any charge against a church leader, unless at least two or three people bring the same charges. ^20But if any of the leaders should keep on sinning, they must be corrected in front of the whole group, as a warning to everyone else.

^21In the presence of God and Christ Jesus and their chosen angels, I order you to follow my instructions! Be fair with everyone, and don't have any favorites.

^22Don't be too quick to accept people into the service of the Lord^q by placing your hands on them.

Don't sin because others do, but stay close to God.

^23Stop drinking only water. Take a little wine to help your stomach trouble and the other illnesses you always have.

^24Some people get caught in their sins right away, even before the time of judgment. But other people's sins don't show up until later. ^25It is the same with good deeds. Some are easily seen, but none of them can be hidden.

6 If you are a slave, you should respect and honor your owner. This will keep people from saying bad things about God and about our teaching. ^2If any of you slaves have owners who are followers, you should show them respect. After all, they are also followers of Christ, and he loves them. So you should serve and help them the best you can.

False Teaching and True Wealth

These are the things you must teach and tell the people to do. ^3Anyone who teaches something different disagrees with the correct and godly teaching of our Lord Jesus Christ. ^4Those people who disagree are proud of themselves, but they don't really know a thing. Their minds are sick, and they like to argue over words. They cause jealousy, disagreements, unkind words, evil suspicions, ^5and nasty quarrels. They have wicked minds and have missed out on the truth.

These people think religion is supposed to make you rich. ^6And religion does make your life rich, by making you content with what you have. ^7We didn't bring anything into this world, and we won't^r take anything with us when we leave. ^8So we should be satisfied just to have food and clothes. ^9People who want to be rich fall into all sorts of temptations and traps. They are caught by foolish and harmful desires that drag them down and destroy them. ^10The love of money causes all kinds of trouble. Some people want money so much that they have given up their faith and caused themselves a lot of pain.

Fighting a Good Fight for the Faith

^11Timothy, you belong to God, so keep away from all these evil things. Try your best to please God and to be like him. Be faithful, loving, dependable, and gentle. ^12Fight a good fight for the faith and claim eternal life. God offered it to you when you clearly told about your faith,

---

^l *5.9 been faithful in marriage*: Or "been the wife of only one husband" or "never been divorced."   ^m *5.10 welcoming God's people into her home*: The Greek text has "washing the feet of God's people." In New Testament times most people either went barefoot or wore sandals, and a host would often wash the feet of special guests.   ^n *5.16 woman ... she*: Some manuscripts have "man or woman ... that person."   ^o *5.17 leaders*: Or "elders" or "presbyters" or "priests."   ^p *5.17 paid*: Or "honored" or "respected."   ^q *5.22 to accept people into the service of the Lord*: Or "to forgive people."   ^r *6.7 we won't*: Some manuscripts have "we surely won't."

while so many people listened. ¹³Now I ask you to make a promise. Make it in the presence of God, who gives life to all, and in the presence of Jesus Christ, who openly told Pontius Pilate about his faith. ¹⁴Promise to obey completely and fully all that you have been told until our Lord Jesus Christ returns.

¹⁵ The glorious God
>   is the only Ruler,
>   the King of kings
>   and Lord of lords.
> At the time that God
>   has already decided,
> he will send Jesus Christ
>   back again.

¹⁶ Only God lives forever!
> And he lives in light
>   that no one can come near.
> No human has ever seen God
>   or ever can see him.

> God will be honored,
> and his power
>   will last forever. Amen.

¹⁷Warn the rich people of this world not to be proud or to trust in wealth that is easily lost. Tell them to have faith in God, who is rich and blesses us with everything we need to enjoy life. ¹⁸Instruct them to do as many good deeds as they can and to help everyone. Remind the rich to be generous and share what they have. ¹⁹This will lay a solid foundation for the future, so that they will know what true life is like.

²⁰Timothy, guard what God has placed in your care! Don't pay any attention to that godless and stupid talk that sounds smart but really isn't. ²¹Some people have even lost their faith by believing this talk.

I pray that the Lord will be kind to all of you!

2 TIMOTHY

ABOUT THIS LETTER

In his second letter to Timothy, Paul is more personal than in his first one. Timothy is like a "dear child" to Paul, and Paul always mentions him in his prayers (1.2, 3) because he wants Timothy to be a "good soldier" of Christ Jesus and to learn to endure suffering (2.1, 3). Paul mentions Timothy's mother and grandmother by name in this letter and reminds Timothy how he had placed his hands on him as a special sign that the Spirit was guiding his work.

Some who claimed to be followers of the Lord had already been trapped by the devil, and Paul warns Timothy to run from those temptations that often catch young people (2.20-26; 3.1-9). He tells Timothy to keep preaching God's message, even if it is not the popular thing to do (4.2). He should also beware of false teachers.

Paul knows that he will soon die for his faith, but he will be rewarded for his faithfulness (4.6-8), and he reminds Timothy of the true message:

> If we died with Christ,
>   we will live with him.
> If we don't give up,
>   we will rule with him.
>   (2.11, 12a)

A QUICK LOOK AT THIS LETTER

Greetings and Prayer for Timothy (1.1, 2)
Do Not Be Ashamed of the Lord (1.3-18)
How To Be a Good Soldier of Christ (2.1-26)
What People Will Be Like in the Last Days (3.1-9)
Keep Being Faithful (3.10—4.8)
Personal Instructions and Final Greetings (4.9-22)

---

1 From Paul, an apostle of Christ Jesus.

God himself chose me to be an apostle, and he gave me the promised life that Jesus Christ makes possible.
²Timothy, you are like a dear child to me. I pray that God our Father and our Lord Christ Jesus will be kind and merciful to you and will bless you with peace!

Do Not Be Ashamed of the Lord

³Night and day I mention you in my prayers. I am always grateful for you, as I pray to the God my ancestors and I have served with a clear conscience. ⁴I remember how you cried, and I want to see you, because that will make me truly happy. ⁵I also remember the genuine faith of your mother Eunice. Your grandmother Lois had the same sort of faith, and I am sure that you have it as well. ⁶So I ask you to make full use of the gift that God gave you when I placed my hands on you.[a] Use it well. ⁷God's Spirit[b] doesn't make cowards out of us. The Spirit gives us power, love, and self-control.

⁸Don't be ashamed to speak for our Lord. And don't be ashamed of me, just because I am in jail for serving him. Use the power that comes from God and join

---

[a] 1.6 *when I placed my hands on you*: Church leaders placed their hands on people who were being appointed to preach or teach (see 1 Timothy 4.14).   [b] 1.7 *God's Spirit*: Or "God."

with me in suffering for telling the good news.

⁹ God saved us and chose us
    to be his holy people.
We did nothing
    to deserve this,
but God planned it
    because he is so kind.
Even before time began
God planned for Christ Jesus
    to show kindness to us.

¹⁰ Now Christ Jesus has come
    to show us the kindness
      of God.
Christ our Savior defeated death
    and brought us
      the good news.
It shines like a light
and offers life
    that never ends.

¹¹My work is to be a preacher, an apostle, and a teacher.[c] ¹²That's why I am suffering now. But I am not ashamed! I know the one I have faith in, and I am sure that he can guard until the last day what he has trusted me with.[d] ¹³Now follow the example of the correct teaching I gave you, and let the faith and love of Christ Jesus be your model. ¹⁴You have been trusted with a wonderful treasure. Guard it with the help of the Holy Spirit, who lives within you.

¹⁵You know that everyone in Asia has turned against me, especially Phygelus and Hermogenes.

¹⁶I pray that the Lord will be kind to the family of Onesiphorus. He often cheered me up and wasn't ashamed of me when I was put in jail. ¹⁷Then after he arrived in Rome, he searched everywhere until he found me. ¹⁸I pray that the Lord Jesus will ask God to show mercy to Onesiphorus on the day of judgment. You know how much he helped me in Ephesus.

A Good Soldier of Christ Jesus

2 Timothy, my child, Christ Jesus is kind, and you must let him make you strong. ²You have often heard me teach. Now I want you to tell these same things to followers who can be trusted to tell others.

³As a good soldier of Christ Jesus you must endure your share of suffering. ⁴Soldiers on duty don't work at outside jobs. They try only to please their commanding officer. ⁵No one wins an athletic contest without obeying the rules. ⁶And farmers who work hard are the first to eat what grows in their field. ⁷If you keep in mind what I have told you, the Lord will help you understand completely.

⁸Keep your mind on Jesus Christ! He was from the family of David and was raised from death, just as my good news says. ⁹And because of this message, I am locked up in jail and treated like a criminal. But God's good news isn't locked in jail, ¹⁰and so I am willing to put up with anything. Then God's special people will be saved. They will be given eternal glory because they belong to Christ Jesus. ¹¹Here is a true message:

"If we died with Christ,
    we will live with him.
¹² If we don't give up,
    we will rule with him.
If we deny
    that we know him,
he will deny
    that he knows us.
¹³ If we are not faithful,
    he will still be faithful.
Christ cannot deny
    who he is."

An Approved Worker

¹⁴Don't let anyone forget these things. And with God[e] as your witness, you must warn them not to argue about words. These arguments don't help anyone. In fact, they ruin everyone who listens to them. ¹⁵Do your best to win God's approval as a worker who doesn't need to be ashamed and who teaches only the true message.

¹⁶Keep away from worthless and useless talk. It only leads people farther away from God. ¹⁷That sort of talk is like a sore that won't heal. And Hymenaeus and Philetus have been talking this way ¹⁸by teaching that the dead have already been raised to life. This is far from the truth, and it is destroying the faith of some people.

¹⁹But the foundation that God has laid is solid. On it is written, "The Lord knows who his people are. So everyone who worships the Lord must turn away from evil."

²⁰In a large house some dishes are made of gold or silver, while others are made of wood or clay. Some of these are special, and others are not. ²¹That's also how it is with people. The ones who stop doing evil and make themselves pure will become special. Their lives will be holy and pleasing to their Master, and they will be able to do all kinds of good deeds.

²²Run from temptations that capture

---

[c]**1.11** *teacher*: Some manuscripts add "of the Gentiles."   [d]**1.12** *what he has trusted me with*: Or "what I have trusted him with."   [e]**2.14** *God*: Some manuscripts have "the Lord," and others have "Christ."

young people. Always do the right thing. Be faithful, loving, and easy to get along with. Worship with people whose hearts are pure. [23]Stay away from stupid and senseless arguments. These only lead to trouble, [24]and God's servants must not be troublemakers. They must be kind to everyone, and they must be good teachers and very patient.

[25]Be humble when you correct people who oppose you. Maybe God will lead them to turn to him and learn the truth. [26]They have been trapped by the devil, and he makes them obey him, but God may help them escape.

What People Will Be Like in the Last Days

3 You can be certain that in the last days there will be some very hard times. [2]People will love only themselves and money. They will be proud, stuck-up, rude, and disobedient to their parents. They will also be ungrateful, godless, [3]heartless, and hateful. Their words will be cruel, and they will have no self-control or pity. These people will hate everything that is good. [4]They will be sneaky, reckless, and puffed up with pride. Instead of loving God, they will love pleasure. [5]Even though they will make a show of being religious, their religion won't be real. Don't have anything to do with such people.

[6]Some men fool whole families, just to get power over those women who are slaves of sin and are controlled by all sorts of desires. [7]These women always want to learn something new, but they never can discover the truth. [8]Just as Jannes and Jambres[f] opposed Moses, these people are enemies of the truth. Their minds are sick, and their faith isn't real. [9]But they won't get very far with their foolishness. Soon everyone will know the truth about them, just as Jannes and Jambres were found out.

Paul's Last Instructions to Timothy

[10]Timothy, you know what I teach and how I live. You know what I want to do and what I believe. You have seen how patient and loving I am, and how in the past I put up with [11]trouble and suffering in the cities of Antioch, Iconium, and Lystra. Yet the Lord rescued me from all those terrible troubles. [12]Anyone who belongs to Christ Jesus and wants to live right will have trouble from others. [13]But evil people who pretend to be what they are not will become worse than ever, as they fool others and are fooled themselves.

[14]Keep on being faithful to what you were taught and to what you believed. After all, you know who taught you these things. [15]Since childhood, you have known the Holy Scriptures that are able to make you wise enough to have faith in Christ Jesus and be saved. [16]Everything in the Scriptures is God's Word. All of it is useful for teaching and helping people and for correcting them and showing them how to live. [17]The Scriptures train God's servants to do all kinds of good deeds.

4 When Christ Jesus comes as king, he will be the judge of everyone, whether they are living or dead. So with God and Christ as witnesses, I command you [2]to preach God's message. Do it willingly, even if it isn't the popular thing to do. You must correct people and point out their sins. But also cheer them up, and when you instruct them, always be patient. [3]The time is coming when people won't listen to good teaching. Instead, they will look for teachers who will please them by telling them only what they are itching to hear. [4]They will turn from the truth and eagerly listen to senseless stories. [5]But you must stay calm and be willing to suffer. You must work hard to tell the good news and to do your job well.

[6]Now the time has come for me to die. My life is like a drink offering[g] being poured out on the altar. [7]I have fought well. I have finished the race, and I have been faithful. [8]So a crown will be given to me for pleasing the Lord. He judges fairly, and on the day of judgment he will give a crown to me and to everyone else who wants him to appear with power.

Personal Instructions

[9]Come to see me as soon as you can. [10]Demas loves the things of this world so much that he left me and went to Thessalonica. Crescens has gone to Galatia, and Titus has gone to Dalmatia. [11]Only Luke has stayed with me.

Mark can be very helpful to me, so please find him and bring him with you. [12]I sent Tychicus to Ephesus.

[13]When you come, bring the coat I left at Troas with Carpus. Don't forget to bring the scrolls, especially the ones made of leather.[h]

[14]Alexander, the metalworker, has hurt me in many ways. But the Lord will

---

[f]3.8 *Jannes and Jambres*: These names are not found in the Old Testament. But many believe these were the names of the two Egyptian magicians who opposed Moses when he wanted to lead the people of Israel out of Egypt (see Exodus 7.11, 22).   [g]4.6 *drink offering*: Water or wine was sometimes poured out as an offering when an animal sacrifice was made.
[h]4.13 *the ones made of leather*: A scroll was a kind of rolled up book, and it could be made out of paper (called "papyrus") or leather (that is, animal skin) or even copper.

pay him back for what he has done. ¹⁵Alexander opposes what we preach. You had better watch out for him.

¹⁶When I was first put on trial, no one helped me. In fact, everyone deserted me. I hope it won't be held against them. ¹⁷But the Lord stood beside me. He gave me the strength to tell his full message, so that all Gentiles would hear it. And I was kept safe from hungry lions. ¹⁸The Lord will always keep me from being harmed by evil, and he will bring me safely into his heavenly kingdom. Praise him forever and ever! Amen.

Final Greetings

¹⁹Give my greetings to Priscilla and Aquila and to the family of Onesiphorus.

²⁰Erastus stayed at Corinth. Trophimus was sick when I left him at Miletus.

²¹Do your best to come before winter. Eubulus, Pudens, Linus, and Claudia send you their greetings, and so do the rest of the Lord's followers.

²²I pray that the Lord will bless your life and will be kind to you.

TITUS

ABOUT THIS LETTER

Paul mentions Titus several times in his letters as someone who worked with him in Asia Minor and Greece (2 Corinthians 2.13; 7.6, 13; 8.6, 16, 23; 12.18; Galatians 2.3). He is told by Paul to appoint church leaders and officials in Crete.

Paul instructs Titus to make sure that church leaders and officials have good reputations (1.5-9) and that all of the Lord's followers keep themselves pure and avoid arguments (1.10—2.9).

Paul includes special instructions for the different groups within the church in Crete. He reminds Titus that a new way of life is possible because of what God has done by sending Jesus Christ: God has saved them, washed them by the power of the Holy Spirit, and given them a fresh start and the hope of eternal life.

Paul also tells how we are saved:

> *God our Savior showed us*
> *how good and kind he is.*
> *He saved us because*
> *of his mercy,*
> *and not because*
> *of any good things*
> *that we have done.*
>
> *(3.4, 5)*

A QUICK LOOK AT THIS LETTER

Greetings and a Prayer for Titus (1.1-4)
Instructions for Church Officials (1.5-16)
Instructions for Church People (2.1—3.11)
Personal Advice and Final Greetings (3.12-15)

---

1 From Paul, a servant of God and an apostle of Jesus Christ.

I encourage God's own people to have more faith and to understand the truth about religion. ²Then they will have the hope of eternal life that God promised long ago. And God never tells a lie! ³So, at the proper time, God our Savior gave this message and told me to announce what he had said.

⁴Titus, because of our faith, you are like a son to me. I pray that God our Father and Christ Jesus our Savior will be kind to you and will bless you with peace!

What Titus Was To Do in Crete

⁵I left you in Crete to do what had been left undone and to appoint leaders*ᵃ* for the churches in each town. As I told you, ⁶they must have a good reputation and be faithful in marriage.*ᵇ* Their children must be followers of the Lord and not have a reputation for being wild and disobedient.

⁷Church officials*ᶜ* are in charge of

---

*ᵃ***1.5** *leaders*: Or "elders" or "presbyters" or "priests."   *ᵇ***1.6** *be faithful in marriage*: Or "be the husband of only one wife" or "have never been divorced."   *ᶜ***1.7** *Church officials*: Or "Bishops."

God's work, and so they must also have a good reputation. They must not be bossy, quick-tempered, heavy drinkers, bullies, or dishonest in business. [8]Instead, they must be friendly to strangers and enjoy doing good things. They must also be sensible, fair, pure, and self-controlled. [9]They must stick to the true message they were taught, so that their good teaching can help others and correct everyone who opposes it.

[10]There are many who don't respect authority, and they fool others by talking nonsense. This is especially true of some Jewish followers. [11]But you must make them be quiet. They are after money, and they upset whole families by teaching what they should not. [12]It is like one of their own prophets once said,

"The people of Crete
   always tell lies.
They are greedy and lazy
   like wild animals."

[13]That surely is a true saying. And you should be hard on such people, so you can help them grow stronger in their faith. [14]Don't pay any attention to any of those senseless Jewish stories and human commands. These are made up by people who won't obey the truth.

[15]Everything is pure for someone whose heart is pure. But nothing is pure for an unbeliever with a dirty mind. That person's mind and conscience are destroyed. [16]Such people claim to know God, but their actions prove that they really don't. They are disgusting. They won't obey God, and they are too worthless to do anything good.

Instructions for Different Groups of People

2 Titus, you must teach only what is correct. [2]Tell the older men to have self-control and to be serious and sensible. Their faith, love, and patience must never fail.

[3]Tell the older women to behave as those who love the Lord should. They must not gossip about others or be slaves of wine. They must teach what is proper, [4]so the younger women will be loving wives and mothers. [5]Each of the younger women must be sensible and kind, as well as a good homemaker, who puts her own husband first. Then no one can say insulting things about God's message.

[6]Tell the young men to have self-control in everything.

[7]Always set a good example for others. Be sincere and serious when you teach. [8]Use clean language that no one can criticize. Do this, and your enemies will be too ashamed to say anything against you.

[9]Tell slaves always to please their owners by obeying them in everything. Slaves must not talk back to their owners [10]or steal from them. They must be completely honest and trustworthy. Then everyone will show great respect for what is taught about God our Savior.

God's Kindness and the New Life

[11]God has shown us how kind he is by coming to save all people. [12]He taught us to give up our wicked ways and our worldly desires and to live decent and honest lives in this world. [13]We are filled with hope, as we wait for the glorious return of our great God and Savior Jesus Christ.[d] [14]He gave himself to rescue us from everything that is evil and to make our hearts pure. He wanted us to be his own people and to be eager to do right.

[15]Teach these things, as you use your full authority to encourage and correct people. Make sure you earn everyone's respect.

Doing Helpful Things

3 Remind your people to obey the rulers and authorities and not to be rebellious. They must always be ready to do something helpful [2]and not say cruel things or argue. They should be gentle and kind to everyone. [3]We used to be stupid, disobedient, and foolish, as well as slaves of all sorts of desires and pleasures. We were evil and jealous. Everyone hated us, and we hated everyone.

[4] God our Savior showed us
   how good and kind he is.
[5] He saved us because
   of his mercy,
and not because
   of any good things
     that we have done.

God washed us by the power
   of the Holy Spirit.
He gave us new birth
   and a fresh beginning.
[6] God sent Jesus Christ
our Savior
   to give us his Spirit.

[7] Jesus treated us much better
   than we deserve.

---

[d]**2.13** *the glorious return of our great God and Savior Jesus Christ*: Or "the glorious return of our great God and our Savior Jesus Christ" or "the return of Jesus Christ, who is the glory of our great God and Savior."

He made us acceptable to God and gave us the hope of eternal life.

⁸This message is certainly true.

These teachings are useful and helpful for everyone. I want you to insist that the people follow them, so that all who have faith in God will be sure to do good deeds. ⁹But don't have anything to do with stupid arguments about ancestors. And stay away from disagreements and quarrels about the Law of Moses. Such arguments are useless and senseless.

¹⁰Warn troublemakers once or twice. Then don't have anything else to do with them. ¹¹You know that their minds are twisted, and their own sins show how guilty they are.

Personal Instructions and Greetings

¹²I plan to send Artemas or Tychicus to you. After he arrives, please try your best to meet me at Nicopolis. I have decided to spend the winter there.

¹³When Zenas the lawyer and Apollos get ready to leave, help them as much as you can, so they won't have need of anything.

¹⁴Our people should learn to spend their time doing something useful and worthwhile.

¹⁵Greetings to you from everyone here. Greet all of our friends who share in our faith.

I pray that the Lord will be kind to all of you!

PHILEMON

ABOUT THIS LETTER

Philemon was a wealthy man who owned slaves and who used his large house for church meetings (2). He probably lived in Colossae, since Paul's letter to the Colossians mentions Onesimus, a slave of Philemon, and Archippus (Colossians 4.9, 17).

Paul is writing from jail on behalf of Onesimus, a runaway slave owned by Philemon. Onesimus had become a follower of the Lord and a valuable friend to Paul, and Paul is writing to encourage Philemon to accept Onesimus also as a friend and follower of the Lord.

This letter is an excellent example of the art of letter-writing in the Roman world, and it is the most personal of all Paul's letters. The way the letter is written suggests that Paul and Philemon were close friends.

A QUICK LOOK AT THIS LETTER

Greetings to Philemon (1-3)
Paul Speaks to Philemon about Onesimus (4-22)
Final Greetings and a Prayer (23-25)

---

¹From Paul, who is in jail for serving Christ Jesus, and from Timothy, who is like a brother because of our faith.

Philemon, you work with us and are very dear to us. This letter is to you ²and to the church that meets in your home. It is also to our dear friend Apphia and to Archippus, who serves the Lord as we do.

³I pray that God our Father and our Lord Jesus Christ will be kind to you and will bless you with peace!

Philemon's Love and Faith

⁴Philemon, each time I mention you in my prayers, I thank God. ⁵I hear about your faith in our Lord Jesus and about your love for all of God's people. ⁶As you share your faith with others, I pray that they may come to know all the blessings Christ has given us. ⁷My friend, your love has made me happy and has greatly encouraged me. It has also cheered the hearts of God's people.

Paul Speaks to Philemon about Onesimus

⁸Christ gives me the courage to tell you what to do. ⁹But I would rather ask you to do it simply because of love. Yes, as someone[a] in jail for Christ, ¹⁰I beg you to help Onesimus![b] He is like a son to me because I led him to Christ here in jail. ¹¹Before this, he was useless to you, but now he is useful both to you and to me.

¹²Sending Onesimus back to you makes me very sad. ¹³I would like to keep him here with me, where he could take your place in helping me while I am here in prison for preaching the good news. ¹⁴But I won't do anything unless you agree to it first. I want your act of kindness to come from your heart, and not be something you feel forced to do.

¹⁵Perhaps Onesimus was taken from you for a little while so that you could have him back for good, ¹⁶but not as a slave. Onesimus is much more than a slave. To me he is a dear friend, but to you he is even more, both as a person and as a follower of the Lord.

¹⁷If you consider me a friend because of Christ, then welcome Onesimus as you would welcome me. ¹⁸If he has cheated you or owes you anything, charge it to my account. ¹⁹With my own

---

[a] 9 *someone*: Greek "a messenger" or "an old man." [b] 10 *Onesimus*: In Greek this name means "useful."

hand I write: I, PAUL, WILL PAY YOU BACK. But don't forget that you owe me your life. ²⁰My dear friend and follower of Christ our Lord, please cheer me up by doing this for me.

²¹I am sure you will do all I have asked, and even more. ²²Please get a room ready for me. I hope your prayers will be answered, and I can visit you.

²³Epaphras is also here in jail for being a follower of Christ Jesus. He sends his greetings, ²⁴and so do Mark, Aristarchus, Demas, and Luke, who work together with me.

²⁵I pray that the Lord Jesus Christ will be kind to you!

HEBREWS

ABOUT THIS LETTER

Many religious people in the first century after Jesus' birth, both Jews and Gentiles, had questions about the religion of the early Christians. They were looking for evidence that this new faith was genuine. Jews had the miracle of crossing the Red Sea and the agreement made with God at Mount Sinai to support their faith. But what miracles did Christians have? Jews had beautiful worship ceremonies and a high priest who offered sacrifices in the temple so that the people would be forgiven. But what did Christians have? How could this new Christian faith, centered in Jesus, offer forgiveness of sins and friendship with God?

The letter to the Hebrews was written to answer exactly these kinds of questions. In it the author tells the readers how important Jesus really is. He is greater than any of God's angels (1.5-14), greater than any prophet, and greater even than Moses and Joshua (2.1—4.14). Jesus is the perfect high priest because he never sinned, and by offering his own life he has made the perfect sacrifice for sin once for all time (9.23—10.18). By his death and return from death he has opened the way for all people to come to God (4.14—5.10; 7.1—8.13).

This letter has much to say about the importance of faith. The writer points out that what Jesus offers comes only by faith. And this faith makes his followers sure of what they hope for and gives them proof of things that cannot be seen. The writer praises God's faithful people of the past (11.1-40) and encourages those who follow Jesus now to keep their eyes on him as they run the race (12.1-3).

What does it mean to have a high priest like Jesus?

Jesus understands every weakness of ours, because he was tempted in every way that we are. But he did not sin! So whenever we are in need, we should come bravely before the throne of our merciful God. There we will be treated with undeserved kindness, and we will find help. (4.15, 16)

A QUICK LOOK AT THIS LETTER

The Greatness of God's Son (1.1-4)
Jesus Is Greater than Angels (1.5—2.18)
Jesus Is Greater than Moses and Joshua (3.1—4.13)
Jesus Is the Great High Priest (4.14—7.28)
Jesus Brings a Better Agreement (8.1—9.22)
Jesus' Sacrifice Is Once and for All (9.23—10.31)
Some of God's People Who Had Great Faith (11.1-40)
Follow the Example of Jesus (12.1—13.19)
Final Prayers and Greetings (13.20-25)

---

1 Long ago in many ways and at many times God's prophets spoke his message to our ancestors. ²But now at last, God sent his Son to bring his message to us. God created the universe by his Son, and everything will someday belong to the Son. ³God's Son has all the brightness of God's own glory and is like him in every way. By his own mighty word, he holds the universe together.

After the Son had washed away our

sins, he sat down at the right side^a of the glorious God in heaven. ⁴He had become much greater than the angels, and the name he was given is far greater than any of theirs.

God's Son Is Greater than Angels

⁵ God has never said
    to any of the angels,
"You are my Son, because today
    I have become your Father!"
Neither has God said
    to any of them,
"I will be his Father,
    and he will be my Son!"

⁶When God brings his first-born Son^b into the world, he commands all of his angels to worship him. ⁷And when God speaks about the angels, he says,

"I change my angels into wind
    and my servants
        into flaming fire."

⁸But God says about his Son,

"You are God,
    and you will rule
        as King forever!
Your^c royal power
    brings about justice.
⁹ You loved justice
    and hated evil,
and so I, your God,
    have chosen you.
I appointed you
    and made you happier
        than any of your friends."

¹⁰The Scriptures also say,

"In the beginning, Lord,
    you were the one
who laid the foundation
    of the earth
        and created the heavens.
¹¹ They will all disappear
    and wear out like clothes,
        but you will last forever.
¹² You will roll them up
    like a robe
and change them
    like a garment.
But you are always the same,
    and you will live forever."

¹³ God never said to any
    of the angels,
"Sit at my right side
    until I make your enemies
        into a footstool for you!"

¹⁴Angels are merely spirits sent to serve people who are going to be saved.

This Great Way of Being Saved

2 We must give our full attention to what we were told, so that we won't drift away. ²The message spoken by angels proved to be true, and all who disobeyed or rejected it were punished as they deserved. ³So if we refuse this great way of being saved, how can we hope to escape? The Lord himself was the first to tell about it, and people who heard the message proved to us that it was true. ⁴God himself showed that his message was true by working all kinds of powerful miracles and wonders. He also gave his Holy Spirit to anyone he chose to.

The One Who Leads Us To Be Saved

⁵We know that God did not put the future world under the power of angels. ⁶Somewhere in the Scriptures someone says to God,

"What makes you care
    about us humans?
Why are you concerned
    for weaklings such as we?
⁷ You made us lower
    than the angels
        for a while.
Yet you have crowned us
    with glory and honor.^d
⁸ And you have put everything
    under our power!"

God has put everything under our power and has not left anything out of our power. But we still don't see it all under our power. ⁹What we do see is Jesus, who for a little while was made lower than the angels. Because of God's wonderful kindness, Jesus died for everyone. And now that Jesus has suffered and died, he is crowned with glory and honor!

¹⁰Everything belongs to God, and all things were created by his power. So God did the right thing when he made Jesus perfect by suffering, as Jesus led many of God's children to be saved and to share in his glory. ¹¹Jesus and the people he makes holy all belong to the same family. That is why he isn't ashamed to call them his brothers and sisters. ¹²He even said to God,

"I will tell them your name
    and sing your praises
when they come together
    to worship."

¹³He also said,

"I will trust God."

Then he said,

---

^a**1.3** *right side*: The place of honor and power.   ^b**1.6** *first-born Son*: The first son born into a family had certain privileges that the other children did not have. In 12.23 "first-born" refers to God's special people.   ^c**1.8** *Your*: Some manuscripts have "His."   ^d**2.7** *and honor*: Some manuscripts add "and you have placed us in charge of all you created."

"Here I am with the children
God has given me."

¹⁴We are people of flesh and blood. That is why Jesus became one of us. He died to destroy the devil, who had power over death. ¹⁵But he also died to rescue all of us who live each day in fear of dying. ¹⁶Jesus clearly did not come to help angels, but he did come to help Abraham's descendants. ¹⁷He had to be one of us, so that he could serve God as our merciful and faithful high priest and sacrifice himself for the forgiveness of our sins. ¹⁸And now that Jesus has suffered and was tempted, he can help anyone else who is tempted.

Jesus Is Greater than Moses

3 My friends, God has chosen you to be his holy people. So think about Jesus, the one we call our apostle and high priest! ²Jesus was faithful to God, who appointed him, just as Moses was faithful in serving all of ᵉ God's people. ³But Jesus deserves more honor than Moses, just as the builder of a house deserves more honor than the house. ⁴Of course, every house is built by someone, and God is really the one who built everything.

⁵Moses was a faithful servant and told God's people what would be said in the future. ⁶But Christ is the Son in charge of God's people. And we are those people, if we keep on being brave and don't lose hope.

A Rest for God's People

⁷It is just as the Holy Spirit says,

"If you hear God's voice today,
⁸ don't be stubborn!
Don't rebel like those people
  who were tested
    in the desert.
*⁹ For forty years your ancestors
    tested God and saw
      the things he did.
¹⁰ "Then God got tired of them
      and said,
  'You people never
      show good sense,
  and you don't understand
      what I want you to do.'
¹¹ God became angry
      and told the people,
  'You will never enter
      my place of rest!' "

¹²My friends, watch out! Don't let evil thoughts or doubts make any of you turn from the living God. ¹³You must encourage one another each day. And you must keep on while there is still a time that can be called "today." If you don't, then sin may fool some of you and make you stubborn. ¹⁴We were sure about Christ when we first became his people. So let's hold tightly to our faith until the end. ¹⁵The Scriptures say,

"If you hear his voice today,
  don't be stubborn
    like those who rebelled."

¹⁶Who were those people that heard God's voice and rebelled? Weren't they the same ones that came out of Egypt with Moses? ¹⁷Who were the people that made God angry for forty years? Weren't they the ones that sinned and died in the desert? ¹⁸And who did God say would never enter his place of rest? Weren't they the ones that disobeyed him? ¹⁹We see that those people did not enter the place of rest because they did not have faith.

4 The promise to enter the place of rest is still good, and we must take care that none of you miss out. ²We have heard the message, just as they did. But they failed to believe what they heard, and the message did not do them any good. ³Only people who have faith will enter the place of rest. It is just as the Scriptures say,

"God became angry
  and told the people,
'You will never enter
  my place of rest!' "

God said this, even though everything has been ready from the time of creation. ⁴In fact, somewhere the Scriptures say that by the seventh day, God had finished his work, and so he rested. ⁵We also read that he later said, "You people will never enter my place of rest!" ⁶This means that the promise to enter is still good, because those who first heard about it disobeyed and did not enter. ⁷Much later God told David to make the promise again, just as I have already said,

"If you hear his voice today,
  don't be stubborn!"

⁸If Joshua had really given the people rest, there would not be any need for God to talk about another day of rest. ⁹But God has promised us a Sabbath when we will rest, even though it has not yet come. ¹⁰On that day God's people will rest from their work, just as God rested from his work.

¹¹We should do our best to enter that place of rest, so that none of us will disobey and miss going there, as they did. ¹²What God has said isn't only alive and active! It is sharper than any double-edged sword. His word can cut through our spirits and souls and through our joints and marrow, until it discovers the

---

ᵉ3.2 *all of*: Some manuscripts do not have these words.

desires and thoughts of our hearts. ¹³Nothing is hidden from God! He sees through everything, and we will have to tell him the truth.

Jesus Is the Great High Priest

¹⁴We have a great high priest, who has gone into heaven, and he is Jesus the Son of God. That is why we must hold on to what we have said about him. ¹⁵Jesus understands every weakness of ours, because he was tempted in every way that we are. But he did not sin! ¹⁶So whenever we are in need, we should come bravely before the throne of our merciful God. There we will be treated with undeserved kindness, and we will find help.

5 Every high priest is appointed to help others by offering gifts and sacrifices to God because of their sins. ²A high priest has weaknesses of his own, and he feels sorry for foolish and sinful people. ³That is why he must offer sacrifices for his own sins and for the sins of others. ⁴But no one can have the honor of being a high priest simply by wanting to be one. Only God can choose a priest, and God is the one who chose Aaron.

⁵That is how it was with Christ. He became a high priest, but not just because he wanted the honor of being one. It was God who told him,

"You are my Son, because today
I have become your Father!"

⁶In another place, God says,

"You are a priest forever
just like Melchizedek."ᶠ

⁷God had the power to save Jesus from death. And while Jesus was on earth, he begged God with loud crying and tears to save him. He truly worshiped God, and God listened to his prayers. ⁸Jesus is God's own Son, but still he had to suffer before he could learn what it really means to obey God. ⁹Suffering made Jesus perfect, and now he can save forever all who obey him. ¹⁰This is because God chose him to be a high priest like Melchizedek.

Warning against Turning Away

¹¹Much more could be said about this subject. But it is hard to explain, and all of you are slow to understand. ¹²By now you should have been teachers, but once again you need to be taught the simplest things about what God has said. You need milk instead of solid food. ¹³People who live on milk are like babies who don't really know what is right. ¹⁴Solid food is for mature people who have been trained to know right from wrong.

6 We must try to become mature and start thinking about more than just the basic things we were taught about Christ. We shouldn't need to keep talking about why we ought to turn from deeds that bring death and why we ought to have faith in God. ²And we shouldn't need to keep teaching about baptismsᵍ or about the laying on of handsʰ or about people being raised from death and the future judgment. ³Let's grow up, if God is willing.

⁴⁻⁶But what about people who turn away after they have already seen the light and have received the gift from heaven and have shared in the Holy Spirit? What about those who turn away after they have received the good message of God and the powers of the future world? There is no way to bring them back. What they are doing is the same as nailing the Son of God to a cross and insulting him in public!

⁷A field is useful to farmers, if there is enough rain to make good crops grow. In fact, God will bless that field. ⁸But land that produces only thornbushes is worthless. It is likely to fall under God's curse, and in the end it will be set on fire.

⁹My friends, we are talking this way. But we are sure that you are doing those really good things that people do when they are being saved. ¹⁰God is always fair. He will remember how you helped his people in the past and how you are still helping them. You belong to God, and he won't forget the love you have shown his people. ¹¹We wish that each of you would always be eager to show how strong and lasting your hope really is. ¹²Then you would never be lazy. You would be following the example of those who had faith and were patient until God kept his promise to them.

God's Promise Is Sure

¹³No one is greater than God. So he made a promise in his own name when he said to Abraham, ¹⁴"I, the Lord, will bless you with many descendants!" ¹⁵Then after Abraham had been very patient, he was given what God had promised. ¹⁶When anyone wants to settle an argument, they make a vow by using the name of someone or something greater than themselves. ¹⁷So when God wanted to prove for certain that his

---

ᶠ5.6 *Melchizedek*: When Melchizedek is mentioned in the Old Testament, he is described as a priest who lived before Aaron. Nothing is said about his ancestors or his death (see 7.3 and Genesis 14.17-20).   ᵍ6.2 *baptisms*: Or "ceremonies of washing."   ʰ6.2 *laying on of hands*: This was a ceremony in which church leaders and others put their hands on people to show that those people were chosen to do some special kind of work.

promise to his people could not be broken, he made a vow. [18]God cannot tell lies! And so his promises and vows are two things that can never be changed.

We have run to God for safety. Now his promises should greatly encourage us to take hold of the hope that is right in front of us. [19]This hope is like a firm and steady anchor for our souls. In fact, hope reaches behind the curtain[i] and into the most holy place. [20]Jesus has gone there ahead of us, and he is our high priest forever, just like Melchizedek.[j]

The Priestly Family of Melchizedek

7 Melchizedek was both king of Salem and priest of God Most High. He was the one who went out and gave Abraham his blessing, when Abraham returned from killing the kings. [2]Then Abraham gave him a tenth of everything he had.

The meaning of the name Melchizedek is "King of Justice." But since Salem means "peace," he is also "King of Peace." [3]We are not told that he had a father or mother or ancestors or beginning or end. He is like the Son of God and will be a priest forever.[k]

[4]Notice how great Melchizedek is! Our famous ancestor Abraham gave him a tenth of what he had taken from his enemies. [5]The Law teaches that even Abraham's descendants must give a tenth of what they possess. And they are to give this to their own relatives, who are the descendants of Levi and are priests. [6]Although Melchizedek wasn't a descendant of Levi, Abraham gave him a tenth of what he had. Then Melchizedek blessed Abraham, who had been given God's promise. [7]Everyone agrees that a person who gives a blessing is greater than the one who receives the blessing.

[8]Priests are given a tenth of what people earn. But all priests die, except Melchizedek, and the Scriptures teach that he is alive. [9]Levi's descendants are now the ones who receive a tenth from people. We could even say that when Abraham gave Melchizedek a tenth, Levi also gave him a tenth. [10]This is because Levi was born later into the family of Abraham, who gave a tenth to Melchizedek.

[11]Even though the Law of Moses says that the priests must be descendants of Levi, those priests cannot make anyone perfect. So there needs to be a priest like Melchizedek, rather than one from the priestly family of Aaron.[l] [12]And when the rules for selecting a priest are changed, the Law must also be changed.

[13]The person we are talking about is our Lord, who came from a tribe that had never had anyone to serve as a priest at the altar. [14]Everyone knows he came from the tribe of Judah, and Moses never said that priests would come from that tribe.

[15]All of this becomes clearer, when someone who is like Melchizedek is appointed to be a priest. [16]That person wasn't appointed because of his ancestors, but because his role can never end. [17]The Scriptures say about him,

"You are a priest forever,
just like Melchizedek."

[18]In this way a weak and useless command was put aside, [19]because the Law cannot make anything perfect. At the same time, we are given a much better hope, and it can bring us close to God.

[20-21]God himself made a promise when this priest was appointed. But he did not make a promise like this when the other priests were appointed. The promise he made is,

"I, the Lord, promise that you
will be a priest forever!
And I will never
change my mind!"

[22]This means that Jesus guarantees us a better agreement with God. [23]There have been a lot of other priests, and all of them have died. [24]But Jesus will never die, and so he will be a priest forever! [25]He is forever able to save[m] the people he leads to God, because he always lives to speak to God for them.

[26]Jesus is the high priest we need. He is holy and innocent and faultless, and not at all like us sinners. Jesus is honored above all beings in heaven, [27]and he is better than any other high priest. Jesus doesn't need to offer sacrifices each day for his own sins and then for the sins of the people. He offered a sacrifice once for all, when he gave himself. [28]The Law appoints priests who have weaknesses. But God's promise, which came later than the Law, appoints his Son. And he is the perfect high priest forever.

A Better Promise

8 What I mean is that we have a high priest who sits at the right side[n] of God's great throne in heaven. [2]He also

---

[i]*6.19 behind the curtain*: In the tent that was used for worship, a curtain separated the "holy place" from the "most holy place," which only the high priest could enter. [j]*6.20 Melchizedek*: See the note at 5.6. [k]*7.3 will be a priest forever*: See the note at 5.6. [l]*7.11 descendants of Levi . . . from the priestly family of Aaron*: Levi was the ancestor of the tribe from which priests and their helpers (called "Levites") were chosen. Aaron was the first high priest. [m]*7.25 forever able to save*: Or "able to save forever." [n]*8.1 right side*: See the note at 1.3.

serves as the priest in the most holy place*o* inside the real tent there in heaven. This tent of worship was set up by the Lord, not by humans.

³Since all priests must offer gifts and sacrifices, Christ also needed to have something to offer. ⁴If he were here on earth, he would not be a priest at all, because here the Law appoints other priests to offer sacrifices. ⁵But the tent where they serve is just a copy and a shadow of the real one in heaven. Before Moses made the tent, he was told, "Be sure to make it exactly like the pattern you were shown on the mountain!" ⁶Now Christ has been appointed to serve as a priest in a much better way, and he has given us much assurance of a better agreement.

⁷If the first agreement with God had been all right, there would not have been any need for another one. ⁸But the Lord found fault with it and said,

"I tell you the time will come,
when I will make
    a new agreement
with the people of Israel
    and the people of Judah.
⁹ It won't be like the agreement
    that I made
    with their ancestors,
when I took them by the hand
    and led them out of Egypt.
They broke their agreement
    with me,
and I stopped caring
    about them!

¹⁰ "But now I tell the people
    of Israel
    this is my new agreement:
'The time will come
    when I, the Lord,
will write my laws
    on their minds and hearts.
I will be their God,
and they will be
    my people.
¹¹ Not one of them
will have to teach another
    to know me, their Lord.'

"All of them will know me,
    no matter who they are.
¹² I will treat them with kindness,
    even though they are wicked.
    I will forget their sins."

¹³When the Lord talks about a new agreement, he means that the first one is out of date. And anything that is old and useless will soon disappear.

The Tent in Heaven

9 The first promise that was made included rules for worship and a tent for worship here on earth. ²The first part of the tent was called the holy place, and a lampstand, a table, and the sacred loaves of bread were kept there.

³Behind the curtain was the most holy place. ⁴The gold altar that was used for burning incense was in this holy place. The gold-covered sacred chest was also there, and inside it were three things. First, there was a gold jar filled with manna.*p* Then there was Aaron's walking stick that sprouted.*q* Finally, there were the flat stones with the Ten Commandments written on them. ⁵On top of the chest were the glorious creatures with wings*r* opened out above the place of mercy.*s*

Now isn't the time to go into detail about these things. ⁶But this is how everything was when the priests went each day into the first part of the tent to do their duties. ⁷However, only the high priest could go into the second part of the tent, and he went in only once a year. Each time he carried blood to offer for his sins and for any sins that the people had committed without meaning to.

⁸All of this is the Holy Spirit's way of saying that no one could enter the most holy place while the tent was still the place of worship. ⁹This also has a meaning for today. It shows that we cannot make our consciences clear by offering gifts and sacrifices. ¹⁰These rules are merely about such things as eating and drinking and ceremonies for washing ourselves. And rules about physical things will last only until the time comes to change them for something better.

¹¹Christ came as the high priest of the good things that are now here.*t* He also went into a much better tent that wasn't made by humans and that doesn't belong to this world. ¹²Then Christ went once for all into the most holy place and freed us from sin forever. He did this by offering his own blood instead of the blood of goats and bulls.

---

*o*8.2 *most holy place*: See the note at 6.19.   *p*9.4 *manna*: When the people of Israel were wandering through the desert, the Lord provided them with food that could be made into thin wafers. This food was called manna, which in Hebrew means "What is it?"   *q*9.4 *Aaron's walking stick that sprouted*: According to Numbers 17.1-11, Aaron's walking stick sprouted and produced almonds to show that the Lord was pleased with him and Moses.
*r*9.5 *glorious creatures with wings*: Two of these creatures (called "cherubim" in Hebrew and Greek) with outspread wings were on top of the sacred chest and were symbols of God's throne.   *s*9.5 *place of mercy*: The lid of the sacred chest, which was thought to be God's throne on earth.   *t*9.11 *that are now here*: Some manuscripts have "that were coming."

[13] According to the Law of Moses, those people who become unclean are not fit to worship God. Yet they will be considered clean, if they are sprinkled with the blood of goats and bulls and with the ashes of a sacrificed calf. [14] But Christ was sinless, and he offered himself as an eternal and spiritual sacrifice to God. That's why his blood is much more powerful and makes our[u] consciences clear. Now we can serve the living God and no longer do things that lead to death.

[15] Christ died to rescue those who had sinned and broken the old agreement. Now he brings his chosen ones a new agreement with its guarantee of God's eternal blessings! [16] In fact, making an agreement of this kind is like writing a will. This is because the one who makes the will must die before it is of any use. [17] In other words, a will doesn't go into effect as long as the one who made it is still alive.

[18] Blood was also used[v] to put the first agreement into effect. [19] Moses told the people all that the Law said they must do. Then he used red wool and a hyssop plant to sprinkle the people and the book of the Law with the blood of bulls and goats[w] and with water. [20] He told the people, "With this blood God makes his agreement with you." [21] Moses also sprinkled blood on the tent and on everything else that was used in worship. [22] The Law says that almost everything must be sprinkled with blood, and no sins can be forgiven unless blood is offered.

Christ's Great Sacrifice

[23] These things are only copies of what is in heaven, and so they had to be made holy by these ceremonies. But the real things in heaven must be made holy by something better. [24] This is why Christ did not go into a tent that had been made by humans and was only a copy of the real one. Instead, he went into heaven and is now there with God to help us.

[25] Christ did not have to offer himself many times. He wasn't like a high priest who goes into the most holy place each year to offer the blood of an animal. [26] If he had offered himself every year, he would have suffered many times since the creation of the world. But instead, near the end of time he offered himself once and for all, so that he could be a sacrifice that does away with sin.

[27] We die only once, and then we are judged. [28] So Christ died only once to take away the sins of many people. But when he comes again, it will not be to take away sin. He will come to save everyone who is waiting for him.

10

The Law of Moses is like a shadow of the good things to come. This shadow isn't the good things themselves, because it cannot free people from sin by the sacrifices that are offered year after year. [2] If there were worshipers who already have their sins washed away and their consciences made clear, there would not be any need to go on offering sacrifices. [3-4] But the blood of bulls and goats cannot take away sins. It only reminds people of their sins from one year to the next.

[5] When Christ came into the world, he said to God,

"Sacrifices and offerings
 are not what you want,
but you have given me
 my body.
[6] No, you are not pleased
 with animal sacrifices
 and offerings for sin."

[7] Then Christ said,

"And so, my God,
 I have come to do
what you want,
 as the Scriptures say."

[8] The Law teaches that offerings and sacrifices must be made because of sin. But why did Christ mention these things and say that God did not want them? [9] Well, it was to do away with offerings and sacrifices and to replace them. That is what he meant by saying to God, "I have come to do what you want." [10] So we are made holy because Christ obeyed God and offered himself once for all.

[11] The priests do their work each day, and they keep on offering sacrifices that can never take away sins. [12] But Christ offered himself as a sacrifice that is good forever. Now he is sitting at God's right side,[x] [13] and he will stay there until his enemies are put under his power. [14] By his one sacrifice he has forever set free from sin the people he brings to God.

[15] The Holy Spirit also speaks of this by telling us that the Lord said,

[16] "When the time comes,
 I will make an agreement
 with them.
I will write my laws
 on their minds and hearts.
[17] Then I will forget
 about their sins
 and no longer remember
 their evil deeds."

---

[u] **9.14** *our*: Some manuscripts have "your," and others have "their."   [v] **9.18** *Blood was also used*: Or "There also had to be a death."   [w] **9.19** *blood of bulls and goats*: Some manuscripts do not have "and goats."   [x] **10.12** *right side*: See the note at 1.3.

¹⁸When sins are forgiven, there is no more need to offer sacrifices.

Encouragement and Warning

¹⁹My friends, the blood of Jesus gives us courage to enter the most holy place ²⁰by a new way that leads to life! And this way takes us through the curtain that is Christ himself.

²¹We have a great high priest who is in charge of God's house. ²²So let's come near God with pure hearts and a confidence that comes from having faith. Let's keep our hearts pure, our consciences free from evil, and our bodies washed with clean water. ²³We must hold tightly to the hope that we say is ours. After all, we can trust the one who made the agreement with us. ²⁴We should keep on encouraging each other to be thoughtful and to do helpful things. ²⁵Some people have gotten out of the habit of meeting for worship, but we must not do that. We should keep on encouraging each other, especially since you know that the day of the Lord's coming is getting closer.

²⁶No sacrifices can be made for people who decide to sin after they find out about the truth. ²⁷They are God's enemies, and all they can look forward to is a terrible judgment and a furious fire. ²⁸If two or more witnesses accused someone of breaking the Law of Moses, that person could be put to death. ²⁹But it is much worse to dishonor God's Son and to disgrace the blood of the promise that made us holy. And it is just as bad to insult the Holy Spirit, who shows us mercy. ³⁰We know that God has said he will punish and take revenge. We also know that the Scriptures say the Lord will judge his people. ³¹It is a terrible thing to fall into the hands of the living God!

³²Don't forget all the hard times you went through when you first received the light. ³³Sometimes you were abused and mistreated in public, and at other times you shared in the sufferings of others. ³⁴You were kind to people in jail. And you gladly let your possessions be taken away, because you knew you had something better, something that would last forever.

³⁵Keep on being brave! It will bring you great rewards. ³⁶Learn to be patient, so that you will please God and be given what he has promised. ³⁷As the Scriptures say,

"God is coming soon!
  It won't be very long.
³⁸ The people God accepts
  will live because
    of their faith."ʸ

But he isn't pleased
  with anyone
    who turns back."

³⁹We are not like those people who turn back and get destroyed. We will keep on having faith until we are saved.

The Great Faith of God's People

11 Faith makes us sure of what we hope for and gives us proof of what we cannot see. ²It was their faith that made our ancestors pleasing to God.

³Because of our faith, we know that the world was made at God's command. We also know that what can be seen was made out of what cannot be seen.

⁴Because Abel had faith, he offered God a better sacrifice than Cain did. God was pleased with him and his gift, and even though Abel is now dead, his faith still speaks for him.

⁵Enoch had faith and did not die. He pleased God, and God took him up to heaven. That's why his body was never found. ⁶But without faith no one can please God. We must believe that God is real and that he rewards everyone who searches for him.

⁷Because Noah had faith, he was warned about something that had not yet happened. He obeyed and built a boat that saved him and his family. In this way the people of the world were judged, and Noah was given the blessings that come to everyone who pleases God.

⁸Abraham had faith and obeyed God. He was told to go to the land that God had said would be his, and he left for a country he had never seen. ⁹Because Abraham had faith, he lived as a stranger in the promised land. He lived there in a tent, and so did Isaac and Jacob, who were later given the same promise. ¹⁰Abraham did this, because he was waiting for the eternal city that God had planned and built.

¹¹Even when Sarah was too old to have children, she had faith that God would do what he had promised, and she had a son. ¹²Her husband Abraham was almost dead, but he became the ancestor of many people. In fact, there are as many of them as there are stars in the sky or grains of sand along the beach.

¹³Every one of those people died. But they still had faith, even though they had not received what they had been promised. They were glad just to see these things from far away, and they agreed that they were only strangers and foreigners on this earth. ¹⁴When

---

ʸ **10.38** *The people God accepts will live because of their faith*: Or "The people God accepts because of their faith will live."

people talk this way, it is clear that they are looking for a place to call their own. ¹⁵If they had been talking about the land where they had once lived, they could have gone back at any time. ¹⁶But they were looking forward to a better home in heaven. That's why God wasn't ashamed for them to call him their God. He even built a city for them.

¹⁷⁻¹⁸Abraham had been promised that Isaac, his only son,ᶻ would continue his family. But when Abraham was tested, he had faith and was willing to sacrifice Isaac, ¹⁹because he was sure that God could raise people to life. This was just like getting Isaac back from death.

²⁰Isaac had faith, and he promised blessings to Jacob and Esau. ²¹Later, when Jacob was about to die, he leaned on his walking stick and worshiped. Then because of his faith he blessed each of Joseph's sons. ²²And right before Joseph died, he had faith that God would lead the people of Israel out of Egypt. So he told them to take his bones with them.

²³Because Moses' parents had faith, they kept him hidden until he was three months old. They saw that he was a beautiful child, and they were not afraid to disobey the king's orders.ᵃ ²⁴Then after Moses grew up, his faith made him refuse to be called the king's grandson. ²⁵He chose to be mistreated with God's people instead of having the good time that sin could bring for a little while. ²⁶Moses knew that the treasures of Egypt were not as wonderful as what he would receive from suffering for the Messiah,ᵇ and he looked forward to his reward.

²⁷Because of his faith, Moses left Egypt. Moses had seen the invisible God and wasn't afraid of the king's anger. ²⁸His faith also made him celebrate Passover. He sprinkled the blood of animals on the doorposts, so that the firstborn sons of the people of Israel would not be killed by the destroying angel.

²⁹Because of their faith, the people walked through the Red Seaᶜ on dry land. But when the Egyptians tried to do it, they were drowned.

³⁰God's people had faith, and when they had walked around the city of Jericho for seven days, its walls fell down.

³¹Rahab had been a prostitute, but she had faith and welcomed the spies. So she wasn't killed with the people who disobeyed.

³²What else can I say? There isn't enough time to tell about Gideon, Barak, Samson, Jephthah, David, Samuel, and the prophets. ³³Their faith helped them conquer kingdoms, and because they did right, God made promises to them. They closed the jaws of lions ³⁴and put out raging fires and escaped from the swords of their enemies. Although they were weak, they were given the strength and power to chase foreign armies away.

³⁵Some women received their loved ones back from death. Many of these people were tortured, but they refused to be released. They were sure that they would get a better reward when the dead are raised to life. ³⁶Others were made fun of and beaten with whips, and some were chained in jail. ³⁷Still others were stoned to death or sawed in twoᵈ or killed with swords. Some had nothing but sheep skins or goat skins to wear. They were poor, mistreated, and tortured. ³⁸The world did not deserve these good people, who had to wander in deserts and on mountains and had to live in caves and holes in the ground.

³⁹All of them pleased God because of their faith! But still they died without being given what had been promised. ⁴⁰This was because God had something better in store for us. And he did not want them to reach the goal of their faith without us.

A Large Crowd of Witnesses

12 Such a large crowd of witnesses is all around us! So we must get rid of everything that slows us down, especially the sin that just won't let go. And we must be determined to run the race that is ahead of us. ²We must keep our eyes on Jesus, who leads us and makes our faith complete. He endured the shame of being nailed to a cross, because he knew that later on he would be glad he did. Now he is seated at the right sideᵉ of God's throne! ³So keep your mind on Jesus, who put up with many insults from sinners. Then you won't get discouraged and give up.

⁴None of you have yet been hurtᶠ in your battle against sin. ⁵But you have

---

ᶻ**11.17,18** *his only son:* Although Abraham had a son by a slave woman, his son Isaac was considered his only son, because he was born as a result of God's promise to Abraham.
ᵃ**11.23** *the king's orders:* The king of Egypt ordered all Israelite baby boys to be left outside of their homes, so they would die or be killed.   ᵇ**11.26** *the Messiah:* Or "Christ."
ᶜ**11.29** *Red Sea:* This name comes from the Bible of the early Christians, a translation made into Greek about 200 B.C. It refers to the body of water that the Israelites crossed and was one of the marshes or fresh water lakes near the eastern part of the Nile Delta, where they lived and where the towns of Exodus 13.17—14.9 were located.   ᵈ**11.37** *sawed in two:* Some manuscripts have "tested" or "tempted."   ᵉ**12.2** *right side:* See the note at 1.3.   ᶠ**12.4** *hurt:* Or "killed."

forgotten that the Scriptures say to God's children,

> "When the Lord punishes you,
> don't make light of it,
> and when he corrects you,
> don't be discouraged.
> 6 The Lord corrects the people
> he loves
> and disciplines those
> he calls his own."

⁷Be patient when you are being corrected! This is how God treats his children. Don't all parents correct their children? ⁸God corrects all of his children, and if he doesn't correct you, then you don't really belong to him. ⁹Our earthly fathers correct us, and we still respect them. Isn't it even better to be given true life by letting our spiritual Father correct us?

¹⁰Our human fathers correct us for a short time, and they do it as they think best. But God corrects us for our own good, because he wants us to be holy, as he is. ¹¹It is never fun to be corrected. In fact, at the time it is always painful. But if we learn to obey by being corrected, we will do right and live at peace.

¹²Now stand up straight! Stop your knees from shaking ¹³and walk a straight path. Then lame people will be healed, instead of getting worse.

Warning against Turning from God

¹⁴Try to live at peace with everyone! Live a clean life. If you don't, you will never see the Lord. ¹⁵Make sure that no one misses out on God's wonderful kindness. Don't let anyone become bitter and cause trouble for the rest of you. ¹⁶Watch out for immoral and ungodly people like Esau, who sold his future blessing⁹ for only one meal. ¹⁷You know how he later wanted it back. But there was nothing he could do to change things, even though he begged his father and cried.

¹⁸You have not come to a place like Mount Sinaiʰ that can be seen and touched. There is no flaming fire or dark cloud or storm ¹⁹or trumpet sound. The people of Israel heard a voice speak. But they begged it to stop, ²⁰because they could not obey its commands. They were even told to kill any animal that touched the mountain. ²¹The sight was so frightening that Moses said he shook with fear.

²²You have now come to Mount Zion and to the heavenly Jerusalem. This is the city of the living God, where thousands and thousands of angels have come to celebrate. ²³Here you will find all of God's dearest children,ⁱ whose names are written in heaven. And you will find God himself, who judges everyone. Here also are the spirits of those good people who have been made perfect. ²⁴And Jesus is here! He is the one who makes God's new agreement with us, and his sprinkled blood says much better things than the blood of Abel.ʲ

²⁵Make sure that you obey the one who speaks to you. The people did not escape, when they refused to obey the one who spoke to them at Mount Sinai. Do you think you can possibly escape, if you refuse to obey the one who speaks to you from heaven? ²⁶When God spoke the first time, his voice shook only the earth. This time he has promised to shake the earth once again, and heaven too.

²⁷The words "once again" mean that these created things will someday be shaken and removed. Then what cannot be shaken will last. ²⁸We should be grateful that we were given a kingdom that cannot be shaken. And in this kingdom we please God by worshiping him and by showing him great honor and respect. ²⁹Our God is like a destructive fire!

Service That Pleases God

13 Keep being concerned about each other as the Lord's followers should.

²Be sure to welcome strangers into your home. By doing this, some people have welcomed angels as guests, without even knowing it.

³Remember the Lord's people who are in jail and be concerned for them. Don't forget those who are suffering, but imagine that you are there with them.

⁴Have respect for marriage. Always be faithful to your partner, because God will punish anyone who is immoral or unfaithful in marriage.

⁵Don't fall in love with money. Be satisfied with what you have. The Lord has promised that he will not leave us or desert us. ⁶That should make you feel like saying,

> "The Lord helps me!
> Why should I be afraid
> of what people
> can do to me?"

⁷Don't forget about your leaders who taught you God's message. Remember

---

ᵍ **12.16** *sold his future blessing*: As the first-born son, Esau had certain privileges that were known as a "birthright." ʰ **12.18** *a place like Mount Sinai*: The Greek text has "a place," but the writer is referring to the time that the Lord spoke to the people of Israel from Mount Sinai (see Exodus 19.16-25). ⁱ **12.23** *all of God's dearest children*: The Greek text has "the gathering of the first-born children" (see the note at 1.6). ʲ **12.24** *blood of Abel*: Cain and Abel were the two sons of Adam and Eve. Cain murdered Abel (see Genesis 4.1-16).

what kind of lives they lived and try to have faith like theirs.

⁸Jesus Christ never changes! He is the same yesterday, today, and forever. ⁹Don't be fooled by any kind of strange teachings. It is better to receive strength from God's undeserved kindness than to depend on certain foods. After all, these foods don't really help the people who eat them. ¹⁰But we have an altar where even the priests who serve in the place of worship have no right to eat.

¹¹After the high priest offers the blood of animals as a sin offering, the bodies of those animals are burned outside the camp. ¹²Jesus himself suffered outside the city gate, so that his blood would make people holy. ¹³That's why we should go outside the camp to Jesus and share in his disgrace. ¹⁴On this earth we don't have a city that lasts forever, but we are waiting for such a city.

¹⁵Our sacrifice is to keep offering praise to God in the name of Jesus. ¹⁶But don't forget to help others and to share your possessions with them. This too is like offering a sacrifice that pleases God.

¹⁷Obey your leaders and do what they say. They are watching over you, and they must answer to God. So don't make them sad as they do their work. Make them happy. Otherwise, they won't be able to help you at all.

¹⁸Pray for us. Our consciences are clear, and we always try to live right. ¹⁹I especially want you to pray that I can visit you again soon.

Final Prayers and Greetings

²⁰God gives peace, and he raised our Lord Jesus Christ from death. Now Jesus is like a Great Shepherd whose blood was used to make God's eternal agreement with his flock.[k] ²¹I pray that God will make you ready to obey him and that you will always be eager to do right. May Jesus help you do what pleases God. To Jesus Christ be glory forever and ever! Amen.

²²My friends, I have written only a short letter to encourage you, and I beg you to pay close attention to what I have said.

²³By now you surely must know that our friend Timothy is out of jail. If he gets here in time, I will bring him with me when I come to visit you.

²⁴Please give my greetings to your leaders and to the rest of the Lord's people.

His followers from Italy send you their greetings.

²⁵I pray that God will be kind to all of you![l]

---

[k] 13.20 *whose blood was used to make God's eternal agreement with his flock*: See 9.18-22.
[l] 13.25 *to all of you!*: Some manuscripts add "Amen."

JAMES

ABOUT THIS LETTER

This is a good example of a general letter, because it is addressed to Christians scattered throughout the Roman Empire. Though written as a letter, it is more like a short book of instructions for daily living.

For James faith means action! In fact, the entire book is a series of examples that show faith in action in wise and practical ways.

His advice was clear and to the point: If you are poor, don't despair! Don't give up when your faith is being tested. Don't get angry quickly. Don't favor the rich over the poor. Do good things for others. Control your tongue and desires. Surrender to God and rely on his wisdom. Resist the devil. Don't brag about what you are going to do. If you are rich, use your money to help the poor. Be patient and kind, and pray for those who need God's help.

A QUICK LOOK AT THIS LETTER

Greetings (1.1)
A Life of Faith and Wisdom (1.2-18)
Hearing and Obeying God's Message (1.19-27)
Don't Favor the Rich and Powerful (2.1-13)
Faith and Works (2.14-26)
Wisdom and Words (3.1-18)
Warning against Friendship with the World (4.1—5.6)
Patience, Kindness, and Prayer (5.7-20)

---

1 From James, a servant of God and of our Lord Jesus Christ.

Greetings to the twelve tribes scattered all over the world.[a]

Faith and Wisdom

² My friends, be glad, even if you have a lot of trouble. ³ You know that you learn to endure by having your faith tested. ⁴ But you must learn to endure everything, so that you will be completely mature and not lacking in anything.

⁵ If any of you need wisdom, you should ask God, and it will be given to you. God is generous and won't correct you for asking. ⁶ But when you ask for something, you must have faith and not doubt. Anyone who doubts is like an ocean wave tossed around in a storm. ⁷⁻⁸ If you are that kind of person, you can't make up your mind, and you surely can't be trusted. So don't expect the Lord to give you anything at all.

Poor People and Rich People

⁹ Any of God's people who are poor should be glad that he thinks so highly of them. ¹⁰ But any who are rich should be glad when God makes them humble. Rich people will disappear like wild flowers ¹¹ scorched by the burning heat of the sun. The flowers lose their blossoms, and their beauty is destroyed. That is how the rich will disappear, as they go about their business.

Trials and Temptations

¹² God will bless you, if you don't give up when your faith is being tested. He will reward you with a glorious life,[b] just as he rewards everyone who loves him.

¹³ Don't blame God when you are

---

[a] 1.1 *twelve tribes scattered all over the world*: James is saying that the Lord's followers are like the tribes of Israel that were scattered everywhere by their enemies.   [b] 1.12 *a glorious life*: The Greek text has "the crown of life." In ancient times an athlete who had won a contest was rewarded with a crown of flowers as a sign of victory.

tempted! God cannot be tempted by evil, and he doesn't use evil to tempt others. [14]We are tempted by our own desires that drag us off and trap us. [15]Our desires make us sin, and when sin is finished with us, it leaves us dead.

[16]Don't be fooled, my dear friends. [17]Every good and perfect gift comes down from the Father who created all the lights in the heavens. He is always the same and never makes dark shadows by changing. [18]He wanted us to be his own special people,[c] and so he sent the true message to give us new birth.

Hearing and Obeying

[19]My dear friends, you should be quick to listen and slow to speak or to get angry. [20]If you are angry, you cannot do any of the good things that God wants done. [21]You must stop doing anything immoral or evil. Instead be humble and accept the message that is planted in you to save you.

[22]Obey God's message! Don't fool yourselves by just listening to it. [23]If you hear the message and don't obey it, you are like people who stare at themselves in a mirror [24]and forget what they look like as soon as they leave. [25]But you must never stop looking at the perfect law that sets you free. God will bless you in everything you do, if you listen and obey, and don't just hear and forget.

[26]If you think you are being religious, but can't control your tongue, you are fooling yourself, and everything you do is useless. [27]Religion that pleases God the Father must be pure and spotless. You must help needy orphans and widows and not let this world make you evil.

Warning against Having Favorites

2 My friends, if you have faith in our glorious Lord Jesus Christ, you won't treat some people better than others. [2]Suppose a rich person wearing fancy clothes and a gold ring comes to one of your meetings. And suppose a poor person dressed in worn-out clothes also comes. [3]You must not give the best seat to the one in fancy clothes and tell the one who is poor to stand at the side or sit on the floor. [4]That is the same as saying that some people are better than others, and you would be acting like a crooked judge.

[5]My dear friends, pay attention. God has given a lot of faith to the poor people in this world. He has also promised them a share in his kingdom that he will give to everyone who loves him. [6]You mistreat the poor. But isn't it the rich who boss you around and drag you off to court? [7]Aren't they the ones who make fun of your Lord?

[8]You will do all right, if you obey the most important law[d] in the Scriptures. It is the law that commands us to love others as much as we love ourselves. [9]But if you treat some people better than others, you have done wrong, and the Scriptures teach that you have sinned.

[10]If you obey every law except one, you are still guilty of breaking them all. [11]The same God who told us to be faithful in marriage also told us not to murder. So even if you are faithful in marriage, but murder someone, you still have broken God's Law.

[12]Speak and act like people who will be judged by the law that sets us free. [13]Do this, because on the day of judgment there will be no pity for those who have not had pity on others. But even in judgment, God is merciful![e]

Faith and Works

[14]My friends, what good is it to say you have faith, when you don't do anything to show that you really do have faith? Can that kind of faith save you? [15]If you know someone who doesn't have any clothes or food, [16]you shouldn't just say, "I hope all goes well for you. I hope you will be warm and have plenty to eat." What good is it to say this, unless you do something to help? [17]Faith that doesn't lead us to do good deeds is all alone and dead!

[18]Suppose someone disagrees and says, "It is possible to have faith without doing kind deeds."

I would answer, "Prove that you have faith without doing kind deeds, and I will prove that I have faith by doing them." [19]You surely believe there is only one God. That's fine. Even demons believe this, and it makes them shake with fear.

[20]Does some stupid person want proof that faith without deeds is useless? [21]Well, our ancestor Abraham pleased God by putting his son Isaac on the altar to sacrifice him. [22]Now you see how Abraham's faith and deeds worked together. He proved that his faith was real by what he did. [23]This is what the Scriptures mean by saying, "Abraham had faith in God, and God was pleased with him." That's how Abraham became God's friend.

[24]You can now see that we please God

---

[c]**1.18** *his own special people*: The Greek text has "the first of his creatures." The Law of Moses taught that the first-born of all animals and the first part of the harvest were special and belonged to the Lord. [d]**2.8** *most important law*: The Greek text has "royal law," meaning the one given by the king (that is, God). [e]**2.13** *But even in judgment, God is merciful!*: Or "So be merciful, and you will be shown mercy on the day of judgment."

by what we do and not only by what we believe. ²⁵For example, Rahab had been a prostitute. But she pleased God when she welcomed the spies and sent them home by another way.

²⁶Anyone who doesn't breathe is dead, and faith that doesn't do anything is just as dead!

The Tongue

3 My friends, we should not all try to become teachers. In fact, teachers will be judged more strictly than others. ²All of us do many wrong things. But if you can control your tongue, you are mature and able to control your whole body.

³By putting a bit into the mouth of a horse, we can turn the horse in different directions. ⁴It takes strong winds to move a large sailing ship, but the captain uses only a small rudder to make it go in any direction. ⁵Our tongues are small too, and yet they brag about big things.

It takes only a spark to start a forest fire! ⁶The tongue is like a spark. It is an evil power that dirties the rest of the body and sets a person's entire life on fire with flames that come from hell itself. ⁷All kinds of animals, birds, reptiles, and sea creatures can be tamed and have been tamed. ⁸But our tongues get out of control. They are restless and evil, and always spreading deadly poison.

⁹⁻¹⁰My dear friends, with our tongues we speak both praises and curses. We praise our Lord and Father, and we curse people who were created to be like God, and this isn't right. ¹¹Can clean water and dirty water both flow from the same spring? ¹²Can a fig tree produce olives or a grapevine produce figs? Does fresh water come from a well full of salt water?

Wisdom from Above

¹³Are any of you wise or sensible? Then show it by living right and by being humble and wise in everything you do. ¹⁴But if your heart is full of bitter jealousy and selfishness, don't brag or lie to cover up the truth. ¹⁵That kind of wisdom doesn't come from above. It is earthly and selfish and comes from the devil himself. ¹⁶Whenever people are jealous or selfish, they cause trouble and do all sorts of cruel things. ¹⁷But the wisdom that comes from above leads us to be pure, friendly, gentle, sensible, kind, helpful, genuine, and sincere. ¹⁸When peacemakers plant seeds of peace, they will harvest justice.

Friendship with the World

4 Why do you fight and argue with each other? Isn't it because you are full of selfish desires that fight to control your body? ²You want something you don't have, and you will do anything to get it. You will even kill! But you still cannot get what you want, and you won't get it by fighting and arguing. You should pray for it. ³Yet even when you do pray, your prayers are not answered, because you pray just for selfish reasons.

⁴You people aren't faithful to God! Don't you know that if you love the world, you are God's enemies? And if you decide to be a friend of the world, you make yourself an enemy of God. ⁵Do you doubt the Scriptures that say, "God truly cares about the Spirit he has put in us"?^f ⁶In fact, God treats us with even greater kindness, just as the Scriptures say,

"God opposes everyone
  who is proud,
but he is kind to everyone
  who is humble."

⁷Surrender to God! Resist the devil, and he will run from you. ⁸Come near to God, and he will come near to you. Clean up your lives, you sinners. Purify your hearts, you people who can't make up your mind. ⁹Be sad and sorry and weep. Stop laughing and start crying. Be gloomy instead of glad. ¹⁰Be humble in the Lord's presence, and he will honor you.

Saying Cruel Things about Others

¹¹My friends, don't say cruel things about others! If you do, or if you condemn others, you are condemning God's Law. And if you condemn the Law, you put yourself above the Law and refuse to obey either it ¹²or God who gave it. God is our judge, and he can save or destroy us. What right do you have to condemn anyone?

Warning against Bragging

¹³You should know better than to say, "Today or tomorrow we will go to the city. We will do business there for a year and make a lot of money!" ¹⁴What do you know about tomorrow? How can you be so sure about your life? It is nothing more than mist that appears for only a little while before it disappears. ¹⁵You should say, "If the Lord lets us live, we will do these things." ¹⁶Yet you are stupid enough to brag, and it is wrong to be so proud. ¹⁷If you don't do what you know is right, you have sinned.

---

^f4.5 *God truly cares about the Spirit he has put in us*: One possible meaning for the difficult Greek text; other translations are possible, such as, "the Spirit that God put in us truly cares."

Warning to the Rich

5 You rich people should cry and weep! Terrible things are going to happen to you. [2] Your treasures have already rotted, and moths have eaten your clothes. [3] Your money has rusted, and the rust will be evidence against you, as it burns your body like fire. Yet you keep on storing up wealth in these last days. [4] You refused to pay the people who worked in your fields, and now their unpaid wages are shouting out against you. The Lord All-Powerful has surely heard the cries of the workers who harvested your crops.

[5] While here on earth, you have thought only of filling your own stomachs and having a good time. But now you are like fat cattle on their way to be butchered. [6] You have condemned and murdered innocent people, who couldn't even fight back.

Be Patient and Kind

[7] My friends, be patient until the Lord returns. Think of farmers who wait patiently for the spring and summer rains to make their valuable crops grow. [8] Be patient like those farmers and don't give up. The Lord will soon be here! [9] Don't grumble about each other or you will be judged, and the judge is right outside the door.

[10] My friends, follow the example of the prophets who spoke for the Lord. They were patient, even when they had to suffer. [11] In fact, we praise the ones who endured the most. You remember how patient Job was and how the Lord finally helped him. The Lord did this because he is so merciful and kind.

[12] My friends, above all else, don't take an oath. You must not swear by heaven or by earth or by anything else. "Yes" or "No" is all you need to say. If you say anything more, you will be condemned.

[13] If you are having trouble, you should pray. And if you are feeling good, you should sing praises. [14] If you are sick, ask the church leaders[g] to come and pray for you. Ask them to put olive oil[h] on you in the name of the Lord. [15] If you have faith when you pray for sick people, they will get well. The Lord will heal them, and if they have sinned, he will forgive them.

[16] If you have sinned, you should tell each other what you have done. Then you can pray for one another and be healed. The prayer of an innocent person is powerful, and it can help a lot. [17] Elijah was just as human as we are, and for three and a half years his prayers kept the rain from falling. [18] But when he did pray for rain, it fell from the skies and made the crops grow.

[19] My friends, if any followers have wandered away from the truth, you should try to lead them back. [20] If you turn sinners from the wrong way, you will save them from death, and many of their sins will be forgiven.

---

[g] 5.14 *church leaders*: Or "elders" or "presbyters" or "priests."

[h] 5.14 *olive oil*: The Jewish people used olive oil for healing.

1 PETER

ABOUT THIS LETTER

In this letter Peter has much to say about suffering. He shows how it can be a way of serving the Lord, of sharing the faith, and of being tested. The letter was written to Christians scattered all over the northern part of Asia Minor. In this part of the Roman Empire many Christians had already suffered unfair treatment from people who did not believe in Jesus. And they could expect to suffer even more.

Peter was quick to offer encouragement. His letter reminds the readers that some of the Lord's followers may have to go through times of hard testing. But this should make them glad, Peter declares, because it will strengthen their faith and bring them honor on the day when Jesus Christ returns (1.6, 7).

Peter reminds them that Christ suffered here on earth, and when his followers suffer for doing right they are sharing his sufferings (2.18-25; 4.12-17). In fact, Christians should expect to suffer for their faith (3.8—4.19).

But because of who God is and because of what God has done by raising Jesus Christ from death, Christians can have hope in the future. Just as Christ suffered before he received honor from God, so will Christians be tested by suffering before they receive honor when the Lord returns. Peter uses poetic language to remind his readers of what Christ has done:

> *Christ died once for our sins.*
> *An innocent person died*
>   *for those who are guilty.*
> *Christ did this*
>   *to bring you to God,*
> *when his body*
>   *was put to death*
> *and his spirit*
>   *was made alive.* (3.18)

A QUICK LOOK AT THIS LETTER

Greetings and Prayer (1.1, 2)
A Real Reason for Hope (1.3-12)
Living as God's Holy People (1.13—2.17)
The Example of Christ's Suffering (2.18-25)
Being a Christian and Suffering (3.1—4.19)
Advice for Church Leaders (5.1-11)
Final Greetings (5.12-14)

---

1 From Peter, an apostle of Jesus Christ. To God's people who are scattered like foreigners in Pontus, Galatia, Cappadocia, Asia, and Bithynia. ²God the Father decided to choose you as his people, and his Spirit has made you holy. You have obeyed Jesus Christ and are sprinkled with his blood.[a]

---

[a] **1.2** *sprinkled with his blood*: According to Exodus 24.3-8 the people of Israel were sprinkled with the blood of cows to show they would keep their agreement with God. Peter says that it is the blood of Jesus that seals the agreement between God and his people (see Hebrews 9.18-21).

I pray that God will be kind to you and will keep on giving you peace!

A Real Reason for Hope

³Praise God, the Father of our Lord Jesus Christ. God is so good, and by raising Jesus from death, he has given us new life and a hope that lives on. ⁴God has something stored up for you in heaven, where it will never decay or be ruined or disappear.

⁵You have faith in God, whose power will protect you until the last day.ᵇ Then he will save you, just as he has always planned to do. ⁶On that day you will be glad, even if you have to go through many hard trials for a while. ⁷Your faith will be like gold that has been tested in a fire. And these trials will prove that your faith is worth much more than gold that can be destroyed. They will show that you will be given praise and honor and glory when Jesus Christ returns.

⁸You have never seen Jesus, and you don't see him now. But still you love him and have faith in him, and no words can tell how glad and happy ⁹you are to be saved. That's why you have faith.

¹⁰Some prophets told how kind God would be to you, and they searched hard to find out more about the way you would be saved. ¹¹The Spirit of Christ was in them and was telling them how Christ would suffer and would then be given great honor. So they searched to find out exactly who Christ would be and when this would happen. ¹²But they were told that they were serving you and not themselves. They preached to you by the power of the Holy Spirit, who was sent from heaven. And their message was only for you, even though angels would like to know more about it.

Chosen To Live a Holy Life

¹³Be alert and think straight. Put all your hope in how kind God will be to you when Jesus Christ appears. ¹⁴Behave like obedient children. Don't let your lives be controlled by your desires, as they used to be. ¹⁵Always live as God's holy people should, because God is the one who chose you, and he is holy. ¹⁶That's why the Scriptures say, "I am the holy God, and you must be holy too."

¹⁷You say that God is your Father, but God doesn't have favorites! He judges all people by what they do. So you must honor God while you live as strangers here on earth. ¹⁸You were rescuedᶜ from the useless way of life that you learned from your ancestors. But you know that you were not rescued by such things as silver or gold that don't last forever. ¹⁹You were rescued by the precious blood of Christ, that spotless and innocent lamb. ²⁰Christ was chosen even before the world was created, but because of you, he did not come until these last days. ²¹And when he did come, it was to lead you to have faith in God, who raised him from death and honored him in a glorious way. That's why you have put your faith and hope in God.

²²You obeyed the truth,ᵈ and your souls were made pure. Now you sincerely love each other. But you must keep on loving with all your heart. ²³Do this because God has given you new birth by his message that lives on forever. ²⁴The Scriptures say,

"Humans wither like grass,
and their glory fades
like wild flowers.
Grass dries up,
and flowers fall
to the ground.
²⁵ But what the Lord has said
will stand forever."

Our good news to you is what the Lord has said.

A Living Stone and a Holy Nation

2 Stop being hateful! Quit trying to fool people, and start being sincere. Don't be jealous or say cruel things about others. ²Be like newborn babies who are thirsty for the pure spiritual milk that will help you grow and be saved. ³You have already found out how good the Lord really is.

⁴Come to Jesus Christ. He is the living stone that people have rejected, but which God has chosen and highly honored. ⁵And now you are living stones that are being used to build a spiritual house. You are also a group of holy priests, and with the help of Jesus Christ you will offer sacrifices that please God. ⁶It is just as God says in the Scriptures,

"Look! I am placing in Zion
a choice and precious
cornerstone.
No one who has faith
in that one
will be disappointed."

⁷You are followers of the Lord, and that stone is precious to you. But it isn't precious to those who refuse to follow

---

ᵇ**1.5** *the last day*: When God will judge all people. ᶜ**1.18** *rescued*: The Greek word often, though not always, means payment of a price to free a slave or prisoner. ᵈ**1.22** *You obeyed the truth*: Some manuscripts add "by the power of the Spirit."

him. They are the builders who tossed aside the stone that turned out to be the most important one of all. ⁸They disobeyed the message and stumbled and fell over that stone, because they were doomed.

⁹But you are God's chosen and special people. You are a group of royal priests and a holy nation. God has brought you out of darkness into his marvelous light. Now you must tell all the wonderful things that he has done. The Scriptures say,

¹⁰ "Once you were nobody.
Now you are God's people.
At one time no one
had pity on you.
Now God has treated you
with kindness.

Live as God's Servants Should

¹¹Dear friends, you are foreigners and strangers on this earth. So I beg you not to surrender to those desires that fight against you. ¹²Always let others see you behaving properly, even though they may still accuse you of doing wrong. Then on the day of judgment, they will honor God by telling the good things they saw you do.

¹³The Lord wants you to obey all human authorities, especially the Emperor, who rules over everyone. ¹⁴You must also obey governors, because they are sent by the Emperor to punish criminals and to praise good citizens. ¹⁵God wants you to silence stupid and ignorant people by doing right. ¹⁶You are free, but still you are God's servants, and you must not use your freedom as an excuse for doing wrong. ¹⁷Respect everyone and show special love for God's people. Honor God and respect the Emperor.

The Example of Christ's Suffering

¹⁸Servants, you must obey your masters and always show respect to them. Do this, not only to those who are kind and thoughtful, but also to those who are cruel. ¹⁹God will bless you, even if others treat you unfairly for being loyal to him. ²⁰You don't gain anything by being punished for some wrong you have done. But God will bless you, if you have to suffer for doing something good. ²¹After all, God chose you to suffer as you follow in the footsteps of Christ, who set an example by suffering for you.

²² Christ did not sin
or ever tell a lie.
²³ Although he was abused,
he never tried to get even.
And when he suffered,
he made no threats.
Instead, he had faith in God,
who judges fairly.
²⁴ Christ carried the burden
of our sins.
He was nailed to the cross,
so that we would stop sinning
and start living right.
By his cuts and bruises
you are healed.
²⁵ You had wandered away
like sheep.
Now you have returned
to the one
who is your shepherd
and protector.

Wives and Husbands

3 If you are a wife, you must put your husband first. Even if he opposes our message, you will win him over by what you do. No one else will have to say anything to him, ²because he will see how you honor God and live a pure life. ³Don't depend on things like fancy hairdos or gold jewelry or expensive clothes to make you look beautiful. ⁴Be beautiful in your heart by being gentle and quiet. This kind of beauty will last, and God considers it very special.

⁵Long ago those women who worshiped God and put their hope in him made themselves beautiful by putting their husbands first. ⁶For example, Sarah obeyed Abraham and called him her master. You are her true children, if you do right and don't let anything frighten you.

⁷If you are a husband, you should be thoughtful of your wife. Treat her with honor, because she isn't as strong as you are, and she shares with you in the gift of life. Then nothing will stand in the way of your prayers.

Suffering for Doing Right

⁸Finally, all of you should agree and have concern and love for each other. You should also be kind and humble. ⁹Don't be hateful and insult people just because they are hateful and insult you. Instead, treat everyone with kindness. You are God's chosen ones, and he will bless you. The Scriptures say,

¹⁰ "Do you really love life?
Do you want to be happy?
Then stop saying cruel things
and quit telling lies.
¹¹ Give up your evil ways
and do right,
as you find and follow
the road that leads
to peace.
¹² The Lord watches over
everyone who obeys him,
and he listens
to their prayers.
But he opposes everyone
who does evil."

1 Peter 3.13

¹³Can anyone really harm you for being eager to do good deeds? ¹⁴Even if you have to suffer for doing good things, God will bless you. So stop being afraid and don't worry about what people might do. ¹⁵Honor Christ and let him be the Lord of your life.

Always be ready to give an answer when someone asks you about your hope. ¹⁶Give a kind and respectful answer and keep your conscience clear. This way you will make people ashamed for saying bad things about your good conduct as a follower of Christ. ¹⁷You are better off to obey God and suffer for doing right than to suffer for doing wrong.

¹⁸ Christ died once for our sins.
An innocent person died
for those who are guilty.
Christ did this
to bring you to God,
when his body
was put to death
and his spirit
was made alive.

¹⁹Christ then preached to the spirits that were being kept in prison. ²⁰They had disobeyed God while Noah was building the boat, but God had been patient with them. Eight people went into that boat and were brought safely through the flood. ²¹Those flood waters were like baptism that now saves you. But baptism is more than just washing your body. It means turning to God with a clear conscience, because Jesus Christ was raised from death. ²²Christ is now in heaven, where he sits at the right side*ᵉ* of God. All angels, authorities, and powers are under his control.

Being Faithful to God

4 Christ suffered here on earth. Now you must be ready to suffer as he did, because suffering shows that you have stopped sinning. ²It means you have turned from your own desires and want to obey God for the rest of your life. ³You have already lived long enough like people who don't know God. You were immoral and followed your evil desires. You went around drinking and partying and carrying on. In fact, you even worshiped disgusting idols. ⁴Now your former friends wonder why you have stopped running around with them, and they curse you for it. ⁵But they will have to answer to God, who judges the living and the dead. ⁶The good news has even been preached to the dead,*ᶠ* so that after they have been judged for what they have done in this life, their spirits will live with God.

⁷Everything will soon come to an end. So be serious and be sensible enough to pray.

⁸Most important of all, you must sincerely love each other, because love wipes away many sins.

⁹Welcome people into your home and don't grumble about it.

¹⁰Each of you has been blessed with one of God's many wonderful gifts to be used in the service of others. So use your gift well. ¹¹If you have the gift of speaking, preach God's message. If you have the gift of helping others, do it with the strength that God supplies. Everything should be done in a way that will bring honor to God because of Jesus Christ, who is glorious and powerful forever. Amen.

Suffering for Being a Christian

¹²Dear friends, don't be surprised or shocked that you are going through testing that is like walking through fire. ¹³Be glad for the chance to suffer as Christ suffered. It will prepare you for even greater happiness when he makes his glorious return.

¹⁴Count it a blessing when you suffer for being a Christian. This shows that God's glorious Spirit is with you. ¹⁵But you deserve to suffer if you are a murderer, a thief, a crook, or a busybody. ¹⁶Don't be ashamed to suffer for being a Christian. Praise God that you belong to him. ¹⁷God has already begun judging his own people. And if his judgment begins with us, imagine how terrible it will be for those who refuse to obey his message. The Scriptures say,

¹⁸ "If good people barely escape,
what will happen to sinners
and to others
who don't respect God?"

¹⁹If you suffer for obeying God, you must have complete faith in your faithful Creator and keep on doing right.

Helping Christian Leaders

5 Church leaders,*ᵍ* I am writing to encourage you. I too am a leader, as well as a witness to Christ's suffering, and I will share in his glory when it is shown to us.

²Just as shepherds watch over their sheep, you must watch over everyone God has placed in your care. Do it willingly in order to please God, and not simply because you think you must. Let it be something you want to do, instead of something you do merely to make

---

*ᵉ*3.22 *right side*: The place of honor and power. *ᶠ*4.6 *the dead*: Either people who died after becoming followers of Christ or the people of Noah's day (see 3.19). *ᵍ*5.1 *Church leaders*: Or "Elders" or "Presbyters" or "Priests."

money. ³Don't be bossy to those people who are in your care, but set an example for them. ⁴Then when Christ the Chief Shepherd returns, you will be given a crown that will never lose its glory.

⁵All of you young people should obey your elders. In fact, everyone should be humble toward everyone else. The Scriptures say,

"God opposes proud people,
but he helps everyone
who is humble."

⁶Be humble in the presence of God's mighty power, and he will honor you when the time comes. ⁷God cares for you, so turn all your worries over to him.

⁸Be on your guard and stay awake. Your enemy, the devil, is like a roaring lion, sneaking around to find someone to attack. ⁹But you must resist the devil and stay strong in your faith. You know that all over the world the Lord's followers are suffering just as you are. ¹⁰But God shows undeserved kindness to everyone. That's why he appointed Christ Jesus to choose you to share in his eternal glory. You will suffer for a while, but God will make you complete, steady, strong, and firm. ¹¹God will be in control forever! Amen.

Final Greetings

¹²Silvanus helped me write this short letter, and I consider him a faithful follower of the Lord. I wanted to encourage you and tell you how kind God really is, so that you will keep on having faith in him.

¹³Greetings from the Lord's followers in Babylon.[h] They are God's chosen ones.

Mark, who is like a son to me, sends his greetings too.

¹⁴Give each other a warm greeting. I pray that God will give peace to everyone who belongs to Christ.[i]

---

[h]**5.13** *Babylon*: This may be a secret name for the city of Rome.   [i]**5.14** *Christ*: Some manuscripts add "Amen."

2 PETER

ABOUT THIS LETTER

The writer of this letter wants the readers to know that Christians must live in a way that pleases God (1.3) and hold firmly to the truth they were given (1.12).

He warns them that false prophets and teachers had entered the Christian community and were trying to lead the Lord's followers away from the truth. But they will be punished for their evil deeds (2.1-22). When false teachers are at work, Christians must stick to their faith and be examples for others of right living. They must have understanding, self-control and patience, and they should show love for God and all people.

The readers must never forget that the Lord's return is certain, no matter what others may say (3.1-18):

> Don't forget that for the Lord one day is the same as a thousand years, and a thousand years is the same as one day. The Lord isn't slow about keeping his promises, as some people think he is. In fact, God is patient, because he wants everyone to turn from sin and no one to be lost.
> (3.8, 9)

A QUICK LOOK AT THIS LETTER

Greetings and Prayer (1.1, 2)
How the Lord's Followers Should Live (1.3-15)
The Glory of Christ (1.16-21)
False Prophets and Teachers (2.1-22)
The Lord's Return Is Certain (3.1-18)

---

1 From Simon Peter, a servant and an apostle of Jesus Christ.

To everyone who shares with us in the privilege of believing that our God and Savior Jesus Christ will do what is just and fair.[a]

2 I pray that God will be kind to you and will let you live in perfect peace! May you keep learning more and more about God and our Lord Jesus.

Living as the Lord's Followers

3 We have everything we need to live a life that pleases God. It was all given to us by God's own power, when we learned that he had invited us to share in his wonderful goodness. 4 God made great and marvelous promises, so that his nature would become part of us. Then we could escape our evil desires and the corrupt influences of this world.

5 Do your best to improve your faith. You can do this by adding goodness, understanding, 6 self-control, patience, devotion to God, 7 concern for others, and love. 8 If you keep growing in this way, it will show that what you know about our Lord Jesus Christ has made your lives useful and meaningful. 9 But if you don't grow, you are like someone who is nearsighted or blind, and you have forgotten that your past sins are forgiven.

10 My friends, you must do all you can to show that God has really chosen and selected you. If you keep on doing this, you won't stumble and fall. 11 Then our Lord and Savior Jesus Christ will give you a glorious welcome into his kingdom that will last forever.

12 You are holding firmly to the truth

---

[a] 1.1 *To everyone who ... just and fair*: Or "To everyone whose faith in the justice and fairness of our God and Savior Jesus Christ is as precious as our own faith."

that you were given. But I am still going to remind you of these things. ¹³In fact, I think I should keep on reminding you until I leave this body. ¹⁴And our Lord Jesus Christ has already told me that I will soon leave it behind. ¹⁵That is why I am doing my best to make sure that each of you remembers all of this after I am gone.

The Message about the Glory of Christ

¹⁶When we told you about the power and the return of our Lord Jesus Christ, we were not telling clever stories that someone had made up. But with our own eyes we saw his true greatness. ¹⁷God, our great and wonderful Father, truly honored him by saying, "This is my own dear Son, and I am pleased with him." ¹⁸We were there with Jesus on the holy mountain and heard this voice speak from heaven.

¹⁹All of this makes us even more certain that what the prophets said is true. So you should pay close attention to their message, as you would to a lamp shining in some dark place. You must keep on paying attention until daylight comes and the morning star rises in your hearts. ²⁰But you need to realize that no one alone can understand any of the prophecies in the Scriptures. ²¹The prophets did not think these things up on their own, but they were guided by the Spirit of God.

False Prophets and Teachers

2 Sometimes false prophets spoke to the people of Israel. False teachers will also sneak in and speak harmful lies to you. But these teachers don't really belong to the Master who paid a great price for them, and they will quickly destroy themselves. ²Many people will follow their evil ways and cause others to tell lies about the true way. ³They will be greedy and cheat you with smooth talk. But long ago God decided to punish them, and God doesn't sleep. ⁴God did not have pity on the angels that sinned. He had them tied up and thrown into the dark pits of hell until the time of judgment. ⁵And during Noah's time, God did not have pity on the ungodly people of the world. He destroyed them with a flood, though he did save eight people, including Noah, who preached the truth.

⁶God punished the cities of Sodom and Gomorrah[b] by burning them to ashes, and this is a warning to anyone else who wants to sin.

⁷⁻⁸Lot lived right and was greatly troubled by the terrible way those wicked people were living. He was a good man, and day after day he suffered because of the evil things he saw and heard. So the Lord rescued him. ⁹This shows that the Lord knows how to rescue godly people from their sufferings and to punish evil people while they wait for the day of judgment.

¹⁰The Lord is especially hard on people who disobey him and don't think of anything except their own filthy desires. They are reckless and proud and are not afraid of cursing the glorious beings in heaven. ¹¹Although angels are more powerful than these evil beings,[c] even the angels don't dare to accuse them to the Lord.

¹²These people are no better than senseless animals that live by their feelings and are born to be caught and killed. They speak evil of things they don't know anything about. But their own corrupt deeds will destroy them. ¹³They have done evil, and they will be rewarded with evil.

They think it is fun to have wild parties during the day. They are immoral, and the meals they eat with you are spoiled by the shameful and selfish way they carry on.[d] ¹⁴All they think about is having sex with someone else's husband or wife. There is no end to their wicked deeds. They trick people who are easily fooled, and their minds are filled with greedy thoughts. But they are headed for trouble!

¹⁵They have left the true road and have gone down the wrong path by following the example of the prophet Balaam. He was the son of Beor and loved what he got from being a crook. ¹⁶But a donkey corrected him for this evil deed. It spoke to him with a human voice and made him stop his foolishness.

¹⁷These people are like dried up water holes and clouds blown by a windstorm. The darkest part of hell is waiting for them. ¹⁸They brag out loud about their stupid nonsense. And by being vulgar and crude, they trap people who have barely escaped from living the wrong kind of life. ¹⁹They promise freedom to everyone. But they are merely slaves of filthy living, because people are slaves of whatever controls them.

²⁰When they learned about our Lord and Savior Jesus Christ, they escaped from the filthy things of this world. But they are again caught up and controlled by these filthy things, and now they are

---

[b]**2.6** *Sodom and Gomorrah*: During the time of Abraham the Lord destroyed these cities because the people there were so evil (see Genesis 19.24).   [c]**2.11** *evil beings*: Or "evil teachers."   [d]**2.13** *and the meals they eat with you are spoiled by the shameful and selfish way they carry on*: Some manuscripts have "and the meals they eat with you are spoiled by the shameful way they carry on during your feasts of Christian love."

in worse shape than they were at first. ²¹They would have been better off if they had never known about the right way. Even after they knew what was right, they turned their backs on the holy commandments that they were given. ²²What happened to them is just like the true saying,

"A dog will come back
   to lick up its own vomit.
A pig that has been washed
   will roll in the mud."

The Lord Will Return

3 My dear friends, this is the second letter I have written to encourage you to do some honest thinking. I don't want you to forget ²what God's prophets said would happen. You must never forget what the holy prophets taught in the past. And you must remember what the apostles told you our Lord and Savior has commanded us to do.

³But first you must realize that in the last days some people won't think about anything except their own selfish desires. They will make fun of you ⁴and say, "Didn't your Lord promise to come back? Yet the first leaders have already died, and the world hasn't changed a bit."

⁵They will say this because they want to forget that long ago the heavens and the earth were made at God's command. The earth came out of water and was made from water. ⁶Later it was destroyed by the waters of a mighty flood. ⁷But God has commanded the present heavens and earth to remain until the day of judgment. Then they will be set on fire, and ungodly people will be destroyed.

⁸Dear friends, don't forget that for the Lord one day is the same as a thousand years, and a thousand years is the same as one day. ⁹The Lord isn't slow about keeping his promises, as some people think he is. In fact, God is patient, because he wants everyone to turn from sin and no one to be lost.

¹⁰The day of the Lord's return will surprise us like a thief. The heavens will disappear with a loud noise, and the heat will melt the whole universe.ᵉ Then the earth and everything on it will be seen for what they are.ᶠ

¹¹Everything will be destroyed. So you should serve and honor God by the way you live. ¹²You should look forward to the day when God judges everyone, and you should try to make it come soon.ᵍ On that day the heavens will be destroyed by fire, and everything else will melt in the heat. ¹³But God has promised us a new heaven and a new earth, where justice will rule. We are really looking forward to that!

¹⁴My friends, while you are waiting, you should make certain that the Lord finds you pure, spotless, and living at peace. ¹⁵Don't forget that the Lord is patient because he wants people to be saved. This is also what our dear friend Paul said when he wrote you with the wisdom that God had given him. ¹⁶Paul talks about these same things in all his letters, but part of what he says is hard to understand. Some ignorant and unsteady people even destroy themselves by twisting what he said. They do the same thing with other Scriptures too.

¹⁷My dear friends, you have been warned ahead of time! So don't let the errors of evil people lead you down the wrong path and make you lose your balance. ¹⁸Let the wonderful kindness and the understanding that come from our Lord and Savior Jesus Christ help you to keep on growing. Praise Jesus now and forever! Amen.ʰ

ᵉ**3.10** *the whole universe*: Probably the sun, moon, and stars, or the elements that everything in the universe is made of.   ᶠ**3.10** *will be seen for what they are*: Some manuscripts have "will go up in flames."   ᵍ**3.12** *and you should try to make it come soon*: Or "and you should eagerly desire for that day to come."   ʰ**3.18** *Amen*: Some manuscripts do not have "Amen."

1 JOHN

ABOUT THIS LETTER

John wants Christian believers to know that when we tell God about our sins, God will forgive us and take them away (1.9).

The true test of faith is love for each other (3.11-24). Because God is love, his people must be like him (4.1-21). For a complete victory over sin, we must not only love others, but we must believe that Jesus, the Son of God, is truly Christ, and that his death for us was real (5.1-12).

Remember:

> The Word that gives life
> was from the beginning,
> and this is the one
> our message is about.
> (1.1a)

A QUICK LOOK AT THIS LETTER

The Word that Gives Life (1.1-4)
God Is Light and Christ Is Our Example (1.5—2.6)
The New Commandment (2.7-17)
The Enemies of Christ and God's Children (2.18—3.10)
God's Love and Our Love (3.11—4.21)
Victory Over the World (5.1-21)

---

1 The Word that gives life
was from the beginning,
and this is the one
our message is about.

Our ears have heard,
our own eyes have seen,
and our hands touched
this Word.

²The one who gives life appeared! We saw it happen, and we are witnesses to what we have seen. Now we are telling you about this eternal life that was with the Father and appeared to us. ³We are telling you what we have seen and heard, so that you may share in this life with us. And we share in it with the Father and with his Son Jesus Christ. ⁴We are writing to tell you these things, because this makes us[a] truly happy.

God Is Light

⁵Jesus told us that God is light and doesn't have any darkness in him. Now we are telling you.

⁶If we say that we share in life with God and keep on living in the dark, we are lying and are not living by the truth. ⁷But if we live in the light, as God does, we share in life with each other. And the blood of his Son Jesus washes all our sins away. ⁸If we say that we have not sinned, we are fooling ourselves, and the truth isn't in our hearts. ⁹But if we confess our sins to God, he can always be trusted to forgive us and take our sins away.

---

[a] 1.4 *us*: Some manuscripts have "you."

¹⁰If we say that we have not sinned, we make God a liar, and his message isn't in our hearts.ᵇ

Christ Helps Us

2 My children, I am writing this so that you won't sin. But if you do sin, Jesus Christ always does the right thing, and he will speak to the Father for us. ²Christ is the sacrifice that takes away our sins and the sins of all the world's people.

³When we obey God, we are sure that we know him. ⁴But if we claim to know him and don't obey him, we are lying and the truth isn't in our hearts. ⁵We truly love God only when we obey him as we should, and then we know that we belong to him. ⁶If we say we are his, we must follow the example of Christ.

The New Commandment

⁷My dear friends, I am not writing to give you a new commandment. It is the same one that you were first given, and it is the message you heard. ⁸But it really is a new commandment, and you know its true meaning, just as Christ does. You can see the darkness fading away and the true light already shining.

⁹If we claim to be in the light and hate someone, we are still in the dark. ¹⁰But if we love others, we are in the light, and we don't cause problems for them.ᶜ ¹¹If we hate others, we are living and walking in the dark. We don't know where we are going, because we can't see in the dark.

¹² Children, I am writing you,
because your sins
have been forgiven
in the name of Christ.
¹³ Parents, I am writing you,
because you have known
the one who was there
from the beginning.
Young people, I am writing you,
because you have defeated
the evil one.
¹⁴ Children, I am writing you,
because you have known
the Father.
Parents, I am writing you,
because you have known
the one who was there
from the beginning.
Young people, I am writing you,
because you are strong.
God's message is firm
in your hearts,
and you have defeated
the evil one.

¹⁵Don't love the world or anything that belongs to the world. If you love the world, you cannot love the Father. ¹⁶Our foolish pride comes from this world, and so do our selfish desires and our desire to have everything we see. None of this comes from the Father. ¹⁷The world and the desires it causes are disappearing. But if we obey God, we will live forever.

The Enemy of Christ

¹⁸Children, this is the last hour. You heard that the enemy of Christ would appear at this time, and many of Christ's enemies have already appeared. So we know that the last hour is here. ¹⁹These people came from our own group, yet they were not part of us. If they had been part of us, they would have stayed with us. But they left, which proves that they did not belong to our group. ²⁰Christ, the Holy One,ᵈ has blessedᵉ you, and now all of you understand.ᶠ ²¹I did not need to write you about the truth, since you already know it. You also know that liars do not belong to the truth. ²²And a liar is anyone who says that Jesus isn't truly Christ. Anyone who says this is an enemy of Christ and rejects both the Father and the Son. ²³If we reject the Son, we reject the Father. But if we say that we accept the Son, we have the Father. ²⁴Keep thinking about the message you first heard, and you will always be one in your heart with the Son and with the Father. ²⁵The Sonᵍ has promised usʰ eternal life.

²⁶I am writing to warn you about those people who are misleading you. ²⁷But Christ has blessed you with the Holy Spirit.ⁱ Now the Spirit stays in you, and you don't need any teachers. The

---

ᵇ**1.10** *and his message isn't in our hearts*: Or "because we have not accepted his message."
ᶜ**2.10** *and we don't cause problems for them*: Or "and we can see anything that might make us fall." ᵈ**2.20** *Christ, the Holy One*: The Greek text has "the Holy One" which may refer either to Christ or to God the Father. ᵉ**2.20** *blessed*: This translates a word which means "to pour olive oil on (someone's head)." In Old Testament times it was the custom to pour olive oil on a person's head when that person was chosen to be a priest or a king. Here the meaning is not clear. It may refer to the ceremony of pouring olive oil on the followers of the Lord right before they were baptized or it may refer to the gift of the Holy Spirit which they were given at baptism (see verse 27). ᶠ**2.20** *now all of you understand*: Some manuscripts have "you understand all things." ᵍ**2.25** *The Son*: The Greek text has "he" and may refer to God the Father. ʰ**2.25** *us*: Some manuscripts have "you." ⁱ**2.27** *Christ has blessed you with the Holy Spirit*: The Greek text has "You received a pouring on of olive oil from him" (see verse 20). The "pouring on of olive oil" is here taken to refer to the gift of the Holy Spirit, and "he" may refer either to Christ or to the Father.

Spirit is truthful and teaches you everything. So stay one in your heart with Christ, just as the Spirit has taught you to do.

Children of God

²⁸Children, stay one in your hearts with Christ. Then when he returns, we will have confidence and won't have to hide in shame. ²⁹You know that Christ always does right and that everyone who does right is a child of God.

3 Think how much the Father loves us. He loves us so much that he lets us be called his children, as we truly are. But since the people of this world did not know who Christ[j] is, they don't know who we are. ²My dear friends, we are already God's children, though what we will be hasn't yet been seen. But we do know that when Christ returns, we will be like him, because we will see him as he truly is. ³This hope makes us keep ourselves holy, just as Christ[k] is holy.

⁴Everyone who sins breaks God's law, because sin is the same as breaking God's law. ⁵You know that Christ came to take away sins. He isn't sinful, ⁶and people who stay one in their hearts with him won't keep on sinning. If they do keep on sinning, they don't know Christ, and they have never seen him.

⁷Children, don't be fooled. Anyone who does right is good, just like Christ himself. ⁸Anyone who keeps on sinning belongs to the devil. He has sinned from the beginning, but the Son of God came to destroy all that he has done. ⁹God's children cannot keep on being sinful. His life-giving power[l] lives in them and makes them his children, so that they cannot keep on sinning. ¹⁰You can tell God's children from the devil's children, because those who belong to the devil refuse to do right or to love each other.

Love Each Other

¹¹From the beginning you were told that we must love each other. ¹²Don't be like Cain, who belonged to the devil and murdered his own brother. Why did he murder him? He did it because his brother was good, and he was evil. ¹³My friends, don't be surprised if the people of this world hate you. ¹⁴Our love for each other proves that we have gone from death to life. But if you don't love each other, you are still under the power of death.

¹⁵If you hate each other, you are murderers, and we know that murderers do not have eternal life. ¹⁶We know what love is because Jesus gave his life for us. That's why we must give our lives for each other. ¹⁷If we have all we need and see one of our own people in need, we must have pity on that person, or else we cannot say we love God. ¹⁸Children, you show love for others by truly helping them, and not merely by talking about it.

¹⁹When we love others, we know that we belong to the truth, and we feel at ease in the presence of God. ²⁰But even if we don't feel at ease, God is greater than our feelings, and he knows everything. ²¹Dear friends, if we feel at ease in the presence of God, we will have the courage to come near him. ²²He will give us whatever we ask, because we obey him and do what pleases him. ²³God wants us to have faith in his Son Jesus Christ and to love each other. This is also what Jesus taught us to do. ²⁴If we obey God's commandments, we will stay one in our hearts with him, and he will stay one with us. The Spirit that he has given us is proof that we are one with him.

God Is Love

4 Dear friends, don't believe everyone who claims to have the Spirit of God. Test them all to find out if they really do come from God. Many false prophets have already gone out into the world, ²and you can know which ones come from God. His Spirit says that Jesus Christ had a truly human body. ³But when someone doesn't say this about Jesus, you know that person has a spirit that doesn't come from God and is the enemy of Christ. You knew that this enemy was coming into the world and now is already here.

⁴Children, you belong to God, and you have defeated these enemies. God's Spirit[m] is in you and is more powerful than the one that is in the world. ⁵These enemies belong to this world, and the world listens to them, because they speak its language. ⁶We belong to God, and everyone who knows God will listen to us. But the people who don't know God won't listen to us. That is how we can tell the Spirit that speaks the truth from the one that tells lies.

⁷My dear friends, we must love each other. Love comes from God, and when we love each other, it shows that we have been given new life. We are now God's children, and we know him. ⁸God is love, and anyone who doesn't love others has never known him. ⁹God showed his love for us when he sent his only Son into the world to give us life. ¹⁰Real love isn't our love for God, but

---

[j] 3.1 *Christ*: The Greek text has "he" and may refer to God.   [k] 3.3 *Christ*: The Greek text has "that one" and may refer to God.   [l] 3.9 *His life-giving power*: The Greek text has "his seed."
[m] 4.4 *God's Spirit*: The Greek text has "he" and may refer to the Spirit or to God or to Jesus.

his love for us. God sent his Son to be the sacrifice by which our sins are forgiven. [11]Dear friends, since God loved us this much, we must love each other.

[12]No one has ever seen God. But if we love each other, God lives in us, and his love is truly in our hearts.

[13]God has given us his Spirit. That is how we know that we are one with him, just as he is one with us. [14]God sent his Son to be the Savior of the world. We saw his Son and are now telling others about him. [15]God stays one with everyone who openly says that Jesus is the Son of God. That's how we stay one with God [16]and are sure that God loves us.

God is love. If we keep on loving others, we will stay one in our hearts with God, and he will stay one with us. [17]If we truly love others and live as Christ did in this world, we won't be worried about the day of judgment. [18]A real love for others will chase those worries away. The thought of being punished is what makes us afraid. It shows that we have not really learned to love.

[19]We love because God loved us first. [20]But if we say we love God and don't love each other, we are liars. We cannot see God. So how can we love God, if we don't love the people we can see? [21]The commandment that God has given us is: "Love God and love each other!"

Victory over the World

5 If we believe that Jesus is truly Christ, we are God's children. Everyone who loves the Father will also love his children. [2]If we love and obey God, we know that we will love his children. [3]We show our love for God by obeying his commandments, and they are not hard to follow.

[4]Every child of God can defeat the world, and our faith is what gives us this victory. [5]No one can defeat the world without having faith in Jesus as the Son of God.

Who Jesus Is

[6]Water and blood came out from the side of Jesus Christ. It wasn't just water, but water and blood.[n] The Spirit tells about this, because the Spirit is truthful. [7]In fact, there are three who tell about it. [8]They are the Spirit, the water, and the blood, and they all agree.

[9]We believe what people tell us. But we can trust what God says even more, and God is the one who has spoken about his Son. [10]If we have faith in God's Son, we have believed what God has said. But if we don't believe what God has said about his Son, it is the same as calling God a liar. [11]God has also said that he gave us eternal life and that this life comes to us from his Son. [12]And so, if we have God's Son, we have this life. But if we don't have the Son, we don't have this life.

Knowing about Eternal Life

[13]All of you have faith in the Son of God, and I have written to let you know that you have eternal life. [14]We are certain that God will hear our prayers when we ask for what pleases him. [15]And if we know that God listens when we pray, we are sure that our prayers have already been answered.

[16]Suppose you see one of our people commit a sin that isn't a deadly sin. You can pray, and that person will be given eternal life. But the sin must not be one that is deadly. [17]Everything that is wrong is sin, but not all sins are deadly.

[18]We are sure that God's children do not keep on sinning. God's own Son protects them, and the devil cannot harm them.

[19]We are certain that we come from God and that the rest of the world is under the power of the devil.

[20]We know that Jesus Christ the Son of God has come and has shown us the true God. And because of Jesus, we now belong to the true God who gives eternal life.

[21]Children, you must stay away from idols.

---

[n]5.6 *Water and blood came out from the side of Jesus Christ. It wasn't just water, but water and blood:* See John 19.34. It is also possible to translate, "Jesus Christ came by the water of baptism and by the blood of his death! He was not only baptized, but he bled and died." The purpose of the verse is to tell that Jesus was truly human and that he really died.

2 JOHN

ABOUT THIS LETTER

John writes again about the importance of love in a Christian's life. He points out that truth and love must go together. We must also believe that Christ was truly human, and we must love each other.

A QUICK LOOK AT THIS LETTER

Greetings and Prayer (1-3)
Truth and Love (4-11)
Final Greetings (12, 13)

---

¹From the church leader.[a]

To a very special woman and her children.[b] I truly love all of you, and so does everyone else who knows the truth. ²We love you because the truth is now in our hearts, and it will be there forever.

³I pray that God the Father and Jesus Christ his Son will be kind and merciful to us! May they give us peace and truth and love.

Truth and Love

⁴I was very glad to learn that some of your children are obeying the truth, as the Father told us to do. ⁵Dear friend, I am not writing to tell you and your children to do something you have not done before. I am writing to tell you to love each other, which is the first thing you were told to do. ⁶Love means that we do what God tells us. And from the beginning, he told you to love him.

⁷Many liars have gone out into the world. These deceitful liars are saying that Jesus Christ did not have a truly human body. But they are liars and the enemies of Christ. ⁸So be sure not to lose what we[c] have worked for. If you do, you won't be given your full reward. ⁹Don't keep changing what you were taught about Christ, or else God will no longer be with you. But if you hold firmly to what you were taught, both the Father and the Son will be with you. ¹⁰If people won't agree to this teaching, don't welcome them into your home or even greet them. ¹¹Greeting them is the same as taking part in their evil deeds.

Final Greetings

¹²I have much more to tell you, but I don't want to write it with pen and ink. I want to come and talk to you in person, because that will make us[d] really happy.

¹³Greetings from the children of your very special sister.[e]

---

[a]1 *church leader*: Or "elder" or "presbyter" or "priest." [b]1 *very special woman and her children*: A group of the Lord's followers who met together for worship. "The children of your ... sister" (see verse 13) is another group of followers. "Very special" (here and verse 13) probably means "chosen (by the Lord)." [c]8 *we*: Some manuscripts have "you." [d]12 *us*: Some manuscripts have "you." [e]13 *sister*: See the note at verse 1.

3 JOHN

ABOUT THIS LETTER

In this letter the writer reminds Christian readers that they should help support those who go to other parts of the world to tell others about the Lord. The letter is written to an important church member named Gaius, who had been very helpful to Christians who traveled around and preached the good news.

A QUICK LOOK AT THIS LETTER

Greetings to Gaius (1-4)
The Importance of Working Together (5-12)
Final Greetings (13-15)

---

¹From the church leader.[a]
To my dear friend Gaius.
I love you because we follow the truth, ²dear friend, and I pray that all goes well for you. I hope that you are as strong in body, as I know you are in spirit. ³It makes me very happy when the Lord's followers come by and speak openly of how you obey the truth. ⁴Nothing brings me greater happiness than to hear that my children[b] are obeying the truth.

Working Together

⁵Dear friend, you have always been faithful in helping other followers of the Lord, even the ones you didn't know before. ⁶They have told the church about your love. They say you were good enough to welcome them and to send them on their mission in a way that God's servants deserve. ⁷When they left to tell others about the Lord, they decided not to accept help from anyone who wasn't a follower. ⁸We must support people like them, so that we can take part in what they are doing to spread the truth.

⁹I wrote to the church. But Diotrephes likes to be the number-one leader, and he won't pay any attention to us. ¹⁰So if I come, I will remind him of how he has been attacking us with gossip. Not only has he been doing this, but he refuses to welcome any of the Lord's followers who come by. And when other church members want to welcome them, he puts them out of the church.

¹¹Dear friend, don't copy the evil deeds of others! Follow the example of people who do kind deeds. They are God's children, but those who are always doing evil have never seen God.

¹²Everyone speaks well of Demetrius, and so does the true message that he teaches. I also speak well of him, and you know what I say is true.

Final Greetings

¹³I have much more to say to you, but I don't want to write it with pen and ink. ¹⁴I hope to see you soon, and then we can talk in person.

¹⁵I pray that God will bless you with peace!
Your friends send their greetings. Please give a personal greeting to each of our friends.

---

[a]1 *church leader*: Or "elder" or "presbyter" or "priest." [b]4 *children*: Probably persons that the leader had led to be followers of the Lord.

JUDE

ABOUT THIS LETTER

Jude has much to say about false teachers. They are evil! God will punish them, and Christians should not follow their teaching or imitate the way they live.

Jude ends with a beautiful prayer-like blessing:

Offer praise to God our Savior because of our Lord Jesus Christ! Only God can keep you from falling and make you pure and joyful in his glorious presence. Before time began and now and forevermore, God is worthy of glory, honor, power, and authority. Amen. (24, 25)

A QUICK LOOK AT THIS LETTER

Greetings (1, 2)
Defending the Faith against False Teachers (3-23)
Final Prayer (24, 25)

---

¹From Jude, a servant of Jesus Christ and the brother of James.

To all who are chosen and loved by God the Father and are kept safe by Jesus Christ.

²I pray that God will greatly bless you with kindness, peace, and love!

False Teachers

³My dear friends, I really wanted to write you about God's saving power at work in our lives. But instead, I must write and ask you to defend the faith that God has once for all given to his people. ⁴Some godless people have sneaked in among us and are saying, "God treats us much better than we deserve, and so it is all right to be immoral." They even deny that we must obey Jesus Christ as our only Master and Lord. But long ago the Scriptures warned that these godless people were doomed.

⁵Don't forget what happened to those people that the Lord rescued from Egypt. Some of them did not have faith, and he later destroyed them. ⁶You also know about the angels*ᵃ* who didn't do their work and left their proper places. God chained them with everlasting chains and is now keeping them in dark pits until the great day of judgment. ⁷We should also be warned by what happened to the cities of Sodom and Gomorrah*ᵇ* and the nearby towns. Their people became immoral and did all sorts of sexual sins. Then God made an example of them and punished them with eternal fire.

⁸The people I am talking about are behaving just like those dreamers who destroyed their own bodies. They reject all authority and insult angels. ⁹Even Michael, the chief angel, didn't dare to insult the devil, when the two of them were arguing about the body of Moses.*ᶜ* All Michael said was, "The Lord will punish you!"

¹⁰But these people insult powers they don't know anything about. They are like senseless animals that end up

---

*ᵃ*6 *angels*: This may refer to the angels who liked the women on earth so much that they came down and married them (see Genesis 6.2). *ᵇ*7 *Sodom and Gomorrah*: During the time of Abraham the Lord destroyed these cities because the people there were so evil. *ᶜ*9 *Michael . . . the body of Moses*: This refers to what was said in an ancient Jewish book about Moses.

getting destroyed, because they live only by their feelings. [11]Now they are in for real trouble. They have followed Cain's example[d] and have made the same mistake that Balaam[e] did by caring only for money. They have also rebelled against God, just as Korah did.[f] Because of all this, they will be destroyed.

[12]These people are filthy minded, and by their shameful and selfish actions they spoil the meals you eat together. They are like clouds blown along by the wind, but never bringing any rain. They are like leafless trees, uprooted and dead, and unable to produce fruit. [13]Their shameful deeds show up like foam on wild ocean waves. They are like wandering stars forever doomed to the darkest pits of hell.

[14]Enoch was the seventh person after Adam, and he was talking about these people when he said:

Look! The Lord is coming with thousands and thousands of holy angels [15]to judge everyone. He will punish all those ungodly people for all the evil things they have done. The Lord will surely punish those ungodly sinners for every evil thing they have ever said about him.

[16]These people grumble and complain and live by their own selfish desires. They brag about themselves and flatter others to get what they want.

More Warnings

[17]My dear friends, remember the warning you were given by the apostles of our Lord Jesus Christ. [18]They told you that near the end of time, selfish and godless people would start making fun of God. [19]And now these people are already making you turn against each other. They think only about this life, and they don't have God's Spirit.

[20]Dear friends, keep building on the foundation of your most holy faith, as the Holy Spirit helps you to pray. [21]And keep in step with God's love, as you wait for our Lord Jesus Christ to show how kind he is by giving you eternal life. [22]Be helpful to[g] all who may have doubts. [23]Rescue any who need to be saved, as you would rescue someone from a fire. Then with fear in your own hearts, have mercy on everyone who needs it. But hate even the clothes of those who have been made dirty by their filthy deeds.

Final Prayer

[24-25]Offer praise to God our Savior because of our Lord Jesus Christ! Only God can keep you from falling and make you pure and joyful in his glorious presence. Before time began and now and forevermore, God is worthy of glory, honor, power, and authority. Amen.

---

[d]11 *Cain's example*: Cain murdered his brother Abel.   [e]11 *Balaam*: According to the biblical account, Balaam refused to curse the people of Israel for profit (see Numbers 22.18; 24.13), though he led them to be unfaithful to the Lord (see Numbers 25.1-3; 31.16). But by New Testament times, some Jewish teachers taught that Balaam was greedy and did accept money to curse them.   [f]11 *just as Korah did*: Together with Dathan and Abiram, Korah led a rebellion against Moses and Aaron (see Numbers 16.1-35; 26.9, 10).   [g]22 *Be helpful to*: Some manuscripts have "Correct."

REVELATION

ABOUT THIS BOOK

This book tells what John had seen in a vision about God's message and about what Jesus Christ had said and done (1.2). The message has three main parts: (1) There are evil forces at work in the world, and Christians may have to suffer and die; (2) Jesus is Lord, and he will conquer all people and powers who oppose God; and (3) God has wonderful rewards in store for his faithful people, who remain faithful to him, especially for those who lose their lives in his service.

This was a powerful message of hope for those early Christians who had to suffer or die for their faith. In this book they learned that, in spite of the cruel power of the Roman Empire, the Lamb of God would win the final victory. And this gave them the courage to be faithful.

Because this book is so full of visions that use ideas and word pictures from the Old Testament, it was like a book with secret messages for the early Christians. The book could be passed around and be understood by Christians, but an official of the Roman Empire would not be able to understand it. For example, when the fall of Babylon is described (chapter 18), the early Christians knew that this pointed to the fall of the Roman Empire. This knowledge gave them hope.

At the beginning of this book there are seven letters to seven churches. These letters show what different groups of the Lord's followers will do in times of persecution (2.1—3.22).

The author uses many powerful images to describe God's power and judgment. The vision of God's throne (4.1-11) and of the scroll and the Lamb (5.1-14) show that God and Christ are in control of all human and supernatural events. Opening seven seals (6.1—8.5), blowing the seven trumpets (8.6—11.19), and emptying the seven bowls (16.1-21) are among the visions that show God's fierce judgment on the world.

After the suffering has ended, God's faithful people will receive the greatest blessing of all:

> God's home is now with his people. He will live with them, and they will be his own. Yes, God will make his home among his people. He will wipe all tears from their eyes, and there will be no more death, suffering, crying, or pain. These things of the past are gone forever. (21.3b, 4)

A QUICK LOOK AT THIS BOOK

A Prophecy from John (1.1-8)
A Vision of the Living Lord (1.9-20)
Letters to the Seven Churches (2.1—3.22)
A Vision of Worship in Heaven (4.1-11)
A Scroll with Seven Seals (5.1—6.17)
Worship in Front of God's Throne (7.1-17)
Seven Trumpets (8.1—11.19)
A Dragon and Two Beasts (12.1—13.18)
Visions of God's Judgment and Protection (14.1—15.8)
Seven Bowls of God's Anger (16.1-21)
God's Enemies Are Defeated (17.1—20.10)
The Final Judgment (20.11-15)
A New Heaven and a New Earth (21.1-8)
New Jerusalem (21.9—22.5)
Christ Will Soon Return (22.6-21)

Revelation 1.1

1 This is what God showed to Jesus Christ, so that he could tell his servants what must happen soon. Christ then sent his angel with the message to his servant John. ²And John told everything that he had seen about God's message and about what Jesus Christ had said and done.

³God will bless everyone who reads this prophecy to others,[a] and he will bless everyone who hears and obeys it. The time is almost here.

⁴From John to the seven churches in Asia.[b]

I pray that you
    will be blessed
with kindness and peace
from God, who is and was
    and is coming.
May you receive
    kindness and peace
from the seven spirits
    before the throne of God.
⁵ May kindness and peace
    be yours
from Jesus Christ,
    the faithful witness.

Jesus was the first
    to conquer death,
and he is the ruler
    of all earthly kings.
Christ loves us,
    and by his blood
he set us free
    from our sins.
⁶ He lets us rule as kings
and serve God his Father
    as priests.
To him be glory and power
    forever and ever! Amen.
⁷ Look! He is coming
    with the clouds.
Everyone will see him,
even the ones who stuck
    a sword through him.
All people on earth
will weep because of him.
    Yes, it will happen! Amen.

⁸The Lord God says, "I am Alpha and Omega,[c] the one who is and was and is coming. I am God All-Powerful!"

A Vision of the Risen Lord

⁹I am John, a follower together with all of you. We suffer because Jesus is our king, but he gives us the strength to endure. I was sent to Patmos Island,[d] because I had preached God's message and had told about Jesus. ¹⁰On the Lord's day the Spirit took control of me, and behind me I heard a loud voice that sounded like a trumpet. ¹¹The voice said, "Write in a book what you see. Then send it to the seven churches in Ephesus, Smyrna, Pergamum, Thyatira, Sardis, Philadelphia, and Laodicea."[e]

¹²When I turned to see who was speaking to me, I saw seven gold lampstands. ¹³There with the lampstands was someone who seemed to be the Son of Man.[f] He was wearing a robe that reached down to his feet, and a gold cloth was wrapped around his chest. ¹⁴His head and his hair were white as wool or snow, and his eyes looked like flames of fire. ¹⁵His feet were glowing like bronze being heated in a furnace, and his voice sounded like the roar of a waterfall. ¹⁶He held seven stars in his right hand, and a sharp double-edged sword was coming from his mouth. His face was shining as bright as the sun at noon.

¹⁷When I saw him, I fell at his feet like a dead person. But he put his right hand on me and said:

Don't be afraid! I am the first, the last, ¹⁸and the living one. I died, but now I am alive forevermore, and I have the keys to death and the world of the dead.[g] ¹⁹Write what you have seen and what is and what will happen after these things. ²⁰I will explain the mystery of the seven stars that you saw at my right side and the seven gold lampstands. The seven stars are the angels[h] of the seven churches, and the lampstands are the seven churches.

The Letter to Ephesus

2 This is what you must write to the angel of the church in Ephesus:

I am the one who holds the seven stars in my right hand, and I walk among the seven gold lampstands. Listen to what I say.

²I know everything you have done, including your hard work and how you have endured. I know you won't put up with anyone who is evil. When some people pretended to be apostles, you tested them and found out that they were liars. ³You have

---

[a]1.3 *who reads this prophecy to others*: A public reading, in a worship service. [b]1.4 *Asia*: The section 1.4—3.22 is in the form of a letter. Asia was in the eastern part of the Roman Empire and is present day Turkey. [c]1.8 *Alpha and Omega*: The first and last letters of the Greek alphabet, which sometimes mean "first" and "last." [d]1.9 *Patmos Island*: A small island where prisoners were sometimes kept by the Romans. [e]1.11 *Ephesus . . . Laodicea*: Ephesus was in the center with the six other cities forming a half-circle around it. [f]1.13 *Son of Man*: That is, Jesus. [g]1.18 *keys to death and the world of the dead*: That is, power over death and the world of the dead. [h]1.20 *angels*: Perhaps guardian angels that represent the churches, or they may be church leaders or messengers sent to the churches.

endured and gone through hard times because of me, and you have not given up.

⁴But I do have something against you! And it is this: You don't have as much love as you used to. ⁵Think about where you have fallen from, and then turn back and do as you did at first. If you don't turn back, I will come and take away your lampstand. ⁶But there is one thing you are doing right. You hate what the Nicolaitans*ⁱ* are doing, and so do I.

⁷If you have ears, listen to what the Spirit says to the churches. I will let everyone who wins the victory eat from the life-giving tree in God's wonderful garden.

The Letter to Smyrna

⁸This is what you must write to the angel of the church in Smyrna:

I am the first and the last. I died, but now I am alive! Listen to what I say.

⁹I know how much you suffer and how poor you are, but you are rich. I also know the cruel things being said about you by people who claim to be Jews. But they are not really Jews. They are a group that belongs to Satan.

¹⁰Don't worry about what you will suffer. The devil will throw some of you into jail, and you will be tested and made to suffer for ten days. But if you are faithful until you die, I will reward you with a glorious life.*ʲ*

¹¹If you have ears, listen to what the Spirit says to the churches. Whoever wins the victory will not be hurt by the second death.*ᵏ*

The Letter to Pergamum

¹²This is what you must write to the angel of the church in Pergamum:

I am the one who has the sharp double-edged sword! Listen to what I say.

¹³I know that you live where Satan has his throne.*ˡ* But you have kept true to my name. Right there where Satan lives, my faithful witness Antipas*ᵐ* was taken from you and put to death. Even then you did not give up your faith in me.

¹⁴I do have a few things against you. Some of you are following the teaching of Balaam.*ⁿ* Long ago he told Balak to teach the people of Israel to eat food that had been offered to idols and to be immoral. ¹⁵Now some of you are following the teaching of the Nicolaitans.*ᵒ* ¹⁶Turn back! If you don't, I will come quickly and fight against these people. And my words will cut like a sword.

¹⁷If you have ears, listen to what the Spirit says to the churches. To everyone who wins the victory, I will give some of the hidden food.*ᵖ* I will also give each one a white stone*ᑫ* with a new name*ʳ* written on it. No one will know that name except the one who is given the stone.

The Letter to Thyatira

¹⁸This is what you must write to the angel of the church in Thyatira:

I am the Son of God! My eyes are like flames of fire, and my feet are like bronze. Listen to what I say.

¹⁹I know everything about you, including your love, your faith, your service, and how you have endured. I know that you are doing more now than you have ever done before. ²⁰But I still have something against you because of that woman Jezebel.*ˢ* She calls herself a prophet, and you let her teach and mislead my servants to do immoral things and to eat food offered to idols. ²¹I gave her

---

*ⁱ*2.6 *Nicolaitans*: Nothing else is known about these people, though it is possible that they claimed to be followers of Nicolaus from Antioch (see Acts 6.5).   *ʲ*2.10 *a glorious life*: The Greek text has "a crown of life." In ancient times an athlete who had won a contest was rewarded with a crown of flowers as a sign of victory.   *ᵏ*2.11 *second death*: The first death is physical death, and the "second death" is eternal death.   *ˡ*2.13 *where Satan has his throne*: The meaning is uncertain, but it may refer to the city as a center of pagan worship or of Emperor worship.   *ᵐ*2.13 *Antipas*: Nothing else is known about this man, who is mentioned only here in the New Testament.   *ⁿ*2.14 *Balaam*: According to Numbers 22–24, Balaam refused to disobey the Lord. But in other books of the Old Testament, he is spoken of as evil (see Deuteronomy 23.4, 5; Joshua 13.22; 24.9, 10; Nehemiah 13.2).   *ᵒ*2.15 *Nicolaitans*: See the note at 2.6.   *ᵖ*2.17 *hidden food*: When the people of Israel were going through the desert, the Lord provided a special food for them. Some of this was placed in a jar and stored in the sacred chest (see Exodus 16). According to later Jewish teaching, the prophet Jeremiah rescued the sacred chest when the temple was destroyed by the Babylonians. He hid the chest in a cave, where it would stay until God came to save his people.   *ᑫ*2.17 *white stone*: The meaning of this is uncertain, though it may be the same as a ticket that lets a person into God's banquet where the "hidden food" is eaten. Or it may be a symbol of victory.   *ʳ*2.17 *a new name*: Either the name of Christ or God or the name of the follower who is given the stone.   *ˢ*2.20 *Jezebel*: Nothing else is known about her. This may have been her real name or a name that was given to her because she was like Queen Jezebel, who opposed the Lord (see 1 Kings 19.1, 2; 21.1-26).

a chance to turn from her sins, but she did not want to stop doing these immoral things.

²²I am going to strike down Jezebel. Everyone who does these immoral things with her will also be punished, if they don't stop. ²³I will even kill her followers.[t] Then all the churches will see that I know everyone's thoughts and feelings. I will treat each of you as you deserve.

²⁴Some of you in Thyatira don't follow Jezebel's teaching. You don't know anything about what her followers call the "deep secrets of Satan." So I won't burden you down with any other commands. ²⁵But until I come, you must hold firmly to the teaching you have.

²⁶I will give power over the nations to everyone who wins the victory and keeps on obeying me until the end. ²⁷⁻²⁸I will give each of them the same power that my Father has given me. They will rule the nations with an iron rod and smash those nations to pieces like clay pots. I will also give them the morning star.[u]

²⁹If you have ears, listen to what the Spirit says to the churches.

The Letter to Sardis

3 This is what you must write to the angel of the church in Sardis:

I have the seven spirits of God and the seven stars. Listen to what I say.

I know what you are doing. Everyone may think you are alive, but you are dead. ²Wake up! You have only a little strength left, and it is almost gone. So try to become stronger. I have found that you are not completely obeying God. ³Remember the teaching that you were given and that you heard. Hold firmly to it and turn from your sins. If you don't wake up, I will come when you least expect it, just as a thief does.

⁴A few of you in Sardis have not dirtied your clothes with sin. You will walk with me in white clothes, because you are worthy. ⁵Everyone who wins the victory will wear white clothes. Their names will not be erased from the book of life,[v] and I will tell my Father and his angels that they are my followers.

⁶If you have ears, listen to what the Spirit says to the churches.

The Letter to Philadelphia

⁷This is what you must write to the angel of the church in Philadelphia:

I am the one who is holy and true, and I have the keys that belonged to David.[w] When I open a door, no one can close it. And when I close a door, no one can open it. Listen to what I say.

⁸I know everything you have done. And I have placed before you an open door that no one can close. You were not very strong, but you obeyed my message and did not deny that you are my followers.[x] ⁹Now you will see what I will do with those people who belong to Satan's group. They claim to be Jews, but they are liars. I will make them come and kneel down at your feet. Then they will know that I love you.

¹⁰You obeyed my message and endured. So I will protect you from the time of testing that everyone in all the world must go through. ¹¹I am coming soon. So hold firmly to what you have, and no one will take away the crown that you will be given as your reward.

¹²Everyone who wins the victory will be made into a pillar in the temple of my God, and they will stay there forever. I will write on each of them the name of my God and the name of his city. It is the new Jerusalem that my God will send down from heaven. I will also write on them my own new name.

¹³If you have ears, listen to what the Spirit says to the churches.

The Letter to Laodicea

¹⁴This is what you must write to the angel of the church in Laodicea:

I am the one called Amen![y] I am the faithful and true witness and the source[z] of God's creation. Listen to what I say.

¹⁵I know everything you have done, and you are not cold or hot. I wish you were either one or the other. ¹⁶But since you are lukewarm and neither cold nor hot, I will spit you out of my mouth. ¹⁷You claim to be rich and successful and to have everything you need. But you don't know how bad off you are. You are pitiful, poor, blind, and naked.

¹⁸Buy your gold from me. It has

---

[t] *2.23 her followers*: Or "her children."   [u] *2.27,28 the morning star*: Probably thought of as the star that signals the end of night and the beginning of day. In 22.16 Christ is called the "morning star."   [v] *3.5 book of life*: The book in which the names of God's people are written.
[w] *3.7 the keys that belonged to David*: The keys stand for authority over David's kingdom.
[x] *3.8 did not deny that you are my followers*: Or "did not say evil things about me."
[y] *3.14 Amen*: Meaning "Trustworthy."   [z] *3.14 source*: Or "beginning."

been refined in a fire, and it will make you rich. Buy white clothes from me. Wear them and you can cover up your shameful nakedness. Buy medicine for your eyes, so that you will be able to see. ¹⁹I correct and punish everyone I love. So make up your minds to turn away from your sins. ²⁰Listen! I am standing and knocking at your door. If you hear my voice and open the door, I will come in and we will eat together. ²¹Everyone who wins the victory will sit with me on my throne, just as I won the victory and sat with my Father on his throne.

²²If you have ears, listen to what the Spirit says to the churches.

Worship in Heaven

4 After this, I looked and saw a door that opened into heaven. Then the voice that had spoken to me at first and that sounded like a trumpet said, "Come up here! I will show you what must happen next." ²Right then the Spirit took control of me, and there in heaven I saw a throne and someone sitting on it. ³The one who was sitting there sparkled like precious stones of jasper[a] and carnelian.[b] A rainbow that looked like an emerald[c] surrounded the throne.

⁴Twenty-four other thrones were in a circle around that throne. And on each of these thrones there was an elder dressed in white clothes and wearing a gold crown. ⁵Flashes of lightning and roars of thunder came out from the throne in the center of the circle. Seven torches, which are the seven spirits of God, were burning in front of the throne. ⁶Also in front of the throne was something that looked like a glass sea, clear as crystal.

Around the throne in the center were four living creatures covered front and back with eyes. ⁷The first creature was like a lion, the second one was like a bull, the third one had the face of a human, and the fourth was like a flying eagle. ⁸Each of the four living creatures had six wings, and their bodies were covered with eyes. Day and night they never stopped singing,

"Holy, holy, holy is the Lord,
    the all-powerful God,
who was and is
    and is coming!"

⁹The living creatures kept praising, honoring, and thanking the one who sits on the throne and who lives forever and ever. ¹⁰At the same time the twenty-four elders knelt down before the one sitting on the throne. And as they worshiped the one who lives forever, they placed their crowns in front of the throne and said,

¹¹ "Our Lord and God,
    you are worthy
to receive glory,
    honor, and power.
You created all things,
and by your decision they are
    and were created."

The Scroll and the Lamb

5 In the right hand of the one sitting on the throne I saw a scroll[d] that had writing on the inside and on the outside. And it was sealed in seven places. ²I saw a mighty angel ask with a loud voice, "Who is worthy to open the scroll and break its seals?" ³No one in heaven or on earth or under the earth was able to open the scroll or see inside it.

⁴I cried hard because no one was found worthy to open the scroll or see inside it. ⁵Then one of the elders said to me, "Stop crying and look! The one who is called both the 'Lion from the Tribe of Judah'[e] and 'King David's Great Descendant'[f] has won the victory. He will open the book and its seven seals."

⁶Then I looked and saw a Lamb standing in the center of the throne that was surrounded by the four living creatures and the elders. The Lamb looked as if it had once been killed. It had seven horns and seven eyes, which are the seven spirits[g] of God, sent out to all the earth. ⁷The Lamb went over and took the scroll from the right hand of the one who sat on the throne. ⁸After he had taken it, the four living creatures and the twenty-four elders knelt down before him. Each of them had a harp and a gold bowl full of incense,[h] which are the prayers of God's people. ⁹Then they sang a new song,

"You are worthy
    to receive the scroll
and open its seals,
    because you were killed.
And with your own blood
    you bought for God

---

[a] 4.3 *jasper*: Usually green or clear.   [b] 4.3 *carnelian*: Usually deep-red or reddish-white.   [c] 4.3 *emerald*: A precious stone, usually green.   [d] 5.1 *scroll*: A roll of paper or special leather used for writing on. Sometimes a scroll would be sealed on the outside with one or more pieces of wax.   [e] 5.5 *'Lion from the Tribe of Judah'*: In Genesis 49.9 the tribe of Judah is called a young lion, and King David was from Judah.   [f] 5.5 *'King David's Great Descendant'*: The Greek text has "the root of David" which is a title for the Messiah based on Isaiah 11.1, 10.   [g] 5.6 *the seven spirits*: Some manuscripts have "the spirits."   [h] 5.8 *incense*: A material that produces a sweet smell when burned. Sometimes it is a symbol for the prayers of God's people.

people from every tribe,
  language, nation, and race.
[10] You let them become kings
  and serve God as priests,
  and they will rule on earth."

[11] As I looked, I heard the voices of a lot of angels around the throne and the voices of the living creatures and of the elders. There were millions and millions of them, [12] and they were saying in a loud voice,

"The Lamb who was killed
  is worthy to receive power,
riches, wisdom, strength,
  honor, glory, and praise."

[13] Then I heard all beings in heaven and on the earth and under the earth and in the sea offer praise. Together, all of them were saying,

"Praise, honor, glory,
and strength
  forever and ever
to the one who sits
  on the throne
    and to the Lamb!"

[14] The four living creatures said "Amen," while the elders knelt down and worshiped.

Opening the Seven Seals

6 At the same time that I saw the Lamb open the first of the seven seals, I heard one of the four living creatures shout with a voice like thunder. It said, "Come out!" [2] Then I saw a white horse. Its rider carried a bow and was given a crown. He had already won some victories, and he went out to win more.

[3] When the Lamb opened the second seal, I heard the second living creature say, "Come out!" [4] Then another horse came out. It was fiery red. And its rider was given the power to take away all peace from the earth, so that people would slaughter one another. He was also given a big sword.

[5] When the Lamb opened the third seal, I heard the third living creature say, "Come out!" Then I saw a black horse, and its rider had a balance scale in one hand. [6] I heard what sounded like a voice from somewhere among the four living creatures. It said, "A quart of wheat will cost you a whole day's wages! Three quarts of barley will cost you a day's wages too. But don't ruin the olive oil or the wine."

[7] When the Lamb opened the fourth seal, I heard the voice of the fourth living creature say, "Come out!" [8] Then I saw a pale green horse. Its rider was named Death, and Death's Kingdom followed behind. They were given power over one fourth of the earth, and they could kill its people with swords, famines, diseases, and wild animals.

[9] When the Lamb opened the fifth seal, I saw under the altar the souls of everyone who had been killed for speaking God's message and telling about their faith. [10] They shouted, "Master, you are holy and faithful! How long will it be before you judge and punish the people of this earth who killed us?"

[11] Then each of those who had been killed was given a white robe and told to rest for a little while. They had to wait until the complete number of the Lord's other servants and followers would be killed.

[12] When I saw the Lamb open the sixth seal, I looked and saw a great earthquake. The sun turned as dark as sackcloth,[i] and the moon became as red as blood. [13] The stars in the sky fell to earth, just like figs shaken loose by a windstorm. [14] Then the sky was rolled up like a scroll,[j] and all mountains and islands were moved from their places.

[15] The kings of the earth, its famous people, and its military leaders hid in caves or behind rocks on the mountains. They hid there together with the rich and the powerful and with all the slaves and free people. [16] Then they shouted to the mountains and the rocks, "Fall on us! Hide us from the one who sits on the throne and from the anger of the Lamb. [17] That terrible day has come! God and the Lamb will show their anger, and who can face it?"

The 144,000 Are Marked for God

7 [1-2] After this I saw four angels. Each one was standing on one of the earth's four corners. The angels held back the four winds, so that no wind would blow on the earth or on the sea or on any tree. These angels had also been given the power to harm the earth and the sea. Then I saw another angel come up from where the sun rises in the east, and he was ready to put the mark of the living God on people. He shouted to the four angels, [3] "Don't harm the earth or the sea or any tree! Wait until I have marked the foreheads of the servants of our God."

[4] Then I heard how many people had been marked on the forehead. There were one hundred forty-four thousand, and they came from every tribe of Israel:

[5] 12,000 from Judah,
  12,000 from Reuben,

---

[i] **6.12** *sackcloth*: A rough, dark-colored cloth made from goat or camel hair and used to make grain sacks. It was worn in times of trouble or sorrow. [j] **6.14** *scroll*: See the note at 5.1.

12,000 from Gad,
⁶ 12,000 from Asher,
12,000 from Naphtali,
12,000 from Manasseh,
⁷ 12,000 from Simeon,
12,000 from Levi,
12,000 from Issachar,
⁸ 12,000 from Zebulun,
12,000 from Joseph, and
12,000 from Benjamin.

People from Every Nation

⁹After this, I saw a large crowd with more people than could be counted. They were from every race, tribe, nation, and language, and they stood before the throne and before the Lamb. They wore white robes and held palm branches in their hands, ¹⁰as they shouted,

"Our God, who sits
  upon the throne,
has the power
  to save his people,
  and so does the Lamb."

¹¹The angels who stood around the throne knelt in front of it with their faces to the ground. The elders and the four living creatures knelt there with them. Then they all worshiped God ¹²and said,

"Amen! Praise, glory, wisdom,
  thanks, honor, power,
and strength belong to our God
  forever and ever! Amen!"

¹³One of the elders asked me, "Do you know who these people are that are dressed in white robes? Do you know where they come from?"

¹⁴"Sir," I answered, "you must know." Then he told me:

"These are the ones
who have gone through
  the great suffering.
They have washed their robes
  in the blood of the Lamb
  and have made them white.
¹⁵ And so they stand
  before the throne of God
and worship him in his temple
  day and night.
The one who sits on the throne
  will spread his tent
    over them.
¹⁶ They will never hunger
  or thirst again,
and they won't be troubled
  by the sun
  or any scorching heat.

¹⁷ The Lamb in the center
  of the throne
  will be their shepherd.

He will lead them to streams
  of life-giving water,
and God will wipe all tears
  from their eyes."

The Seventh Seal Is Opened

8 When the Lamb opened the seventh seal, there was silence in heaven for about half an hour. ²I noticed that the seven angels who stood before God were each given a trumpet.

³Another angel, who had a gold container for incense,ᵏ came and stood at the altar. This one was given a lot of incense to offer with the prayers of God's people on the gold altar in front of the throne. ⁴Then the smoke of the incense, together with the prayers of God's people, went up to God from the hand of the angel.

⁵After this, the angel filled the incense container with fire from the altar and threw it on the earth. Thunder roared, lightning flashed, and the earth shook.

The Trumpets

⁶The seven angels now got ready to blow their trumpets.

⁷When the first angel blew his trumpet, hail and fire mixed with blood were thrown down on the earth. A third of the earth, a third of the trees, and a third of all green plants were burned.

⁸When the second angel blew his trumpet, something like a great fiery mountain was thrown into the sea. A third of the sea turned to blood, ⁹a third of the living creatures in the sea died, and a third of the ships were destroyed.

¹⁰When the third angel blew his trumpet, a great star fell from heaven. It was burning like a torch, and it fell on a third of the rivers and on a third of the springs of water. ¹¹The name of the star was Bitter, and a third of the water turned bitter. Many people died because the water was so bitter.

¹²When the fourth angel blew his trumpet, a third of the sun, a third of the moon, and a third of the stars were struck. They each lost a third of their light. So during a third of the day there was no light, and a third of the night was also without light.

¹³Then I looked and saw a lone eagle flying across the sky. It was shouting, "Trouble, trouble, trouble to everyone who lives on earth! The other three angels are now going to blow their trumpets."

9 When the fifth angel blew his trumpet, I saw a starˡ fall from the sky to earth. It was given the key to the tunnel that leads down to the deep pit. ²As it opened the tunnel, smoke poured out

---

ᵏ**8.3** *incense*: See the note at 5.8. as living beings, such as angels.

ˡ**9.1** *star*: In the ancient world, stars were often thought of like the smoke of a great furnace. The sun and the air turned dark because of the smoke. ³Locusts*ᵐ* came out of the smoke and covered the earth. They were given the same power that scorpions have.

⁴The locusts were told not to harm the grass on the earth or any plant or any tree. They were to punish only those people who did not have God's mark on their foreheads. ⁵The locusts were allowed to make them suffer for five months, but not to kill them. The suffering they caused was like the sting of a scorpion. ⁶In those days people will want to die, but they will not be able to. They will hope for death, but it will escape from them.

⁷These locusts looked like horses ready for battle. On their heads they wore something like gold crowns, and they had human faces. ⁸Their hair was like a woman's long hair, and their teeth were like those of a lion. ⁹On their chests they wore armor made of iron. Their wings roared like an army of horse-drawn chariots rushing into battle. ¹⁰Their tails were like a scorpion's tail with a stinger that had the power to hurt someone for five months. ¹¹Their king was the angel in charge of the deep pit. In Hebrew his name was Abaddon, and in Greek it was Apollyon.*ⁿ*

¹²The first horrible thing has now happened! But wait. Two more horrible things will happen soon.

¹³Then the sixth angel blew his trumpet. I heard a voice speak from the four corners of the gold altar that stands in the presence of God. ¹⁴The voice spoke to this angel and said, "Release the four angels who are tied up beside the great Euphrates River." ¹⁵The four angels had been prepared for this very hour and day and month and year. Now they were set free to kill a third of all people.

¹⁶By listening, I could tell there were more than two hundred million of these war horses. ¹⁷In my vision their riders wore fiery-red, dark-blue, and yellow armor on their chests. The heads of the horses looked like lions, with fire and smoke and sulfur coming out of their mouths. ¹⁸One-third of all people were killed by the three terrible troubles caused by the fire, the smoke, and the sulfur. ¹⁹The horses had powerful mouths, and their tails were like poisonous snakes that bite and hurt.

²⁰The people who lived through these terrible troubles did not turn away from the idols they had made, and they did not stop worshiping demons. They kept on worshiping idols that were made of gold, silver, bronze, stone, and wood. Not one of these idols could see, hear, or walk. ²¹No one stopped murdering or practicing witchcraft or being immoral or stealing.

The Angel and the Little Scroll

10 I saw another powerful angel come down from heaven. This one was covered with a cloud, and a rainbow was over his head. His face was like the sun, his legs were like columns of fire, ²and with his hand he held a little scroll*ᵒ* that had been unrolled. He stood there with his right foot on the sea and his left foot on the land. ³Then he shouted with a voice that sounded like a growling lion. Thunder roared seven times.

⁴After the thunder stopped, I was about to write what it had said. But a voice from heaven shouted, "Keep it secret! Don't write these things."

⁵The angel I had seen standing on the sea and the land then held his right hand up toward heaven. ⁶He made a promise in the name of God who lives forever and who created heaven, earth, the sea, and every living creature. The angel said, "You won't have to wait any longer. ⁷God told his secret plans to his servants the prophets, and it will all happen by the time the seventh angel sounds his trumpet."

⁸Once again the voice from heaven spoke to me. It said, "Go and take the open scroll from the hand of the angel standing on the sea and the land."

⁹When I went over to ask the angel for the little scroll, the angel said, "Take the scroll and eat it! Your stomach will turn sour, but the taste in your mouth will be as sweet as honey." ¹⁰I took the little scroll from the hand of the angel and ate it. The taste was as sweet as honey, but my stomach turned sour.

¹¹Then some voices said, "Keep on telling what will happen to the people of many nations, races, and languages, and also to kings."

The Two Witnesses

11 An angel gave me a measuring stick and said:

Measure around God's temple. Be sure to include the altar and everyone worshiping there. ²But don't measure the courtyard outside the temple building. Leave it out. It has been given to those people who don't know God, and they will trample all over the holy city for forty-two months. ³My two witnesses will

---

*ᵐ***9.3** *Locusts:* A type of grasshopper that comes in swarms and causes great damage to crops.
*ⁿ***9.11** *Abaddon . . . Apollyon:* The Hebrew word "Abaddon" and the Greek word "Apollyon" each mean "destruction."   *ᵒ***10.2** *scroll:* See the note at 5.1.

wear sackcloth,[p] while I let them preach for one thousand two hundred sixty days.

⁴These two witnesses are the two olive trees and the two lampstands that stand in the presence of the Lord who rules the earth. ⁵Any enemy who tries to harm them will be destroyed by the fire that comes out of their mouths. ⁶They have the power to lock up the sky and to keep rain from falling while they are prophesying. And whenever they want to, they can turn water to blood and cause all kinds of terrible troubles on earth.

⁷After the two witnesses have finished preaching God's message, the beast that lives in the deep pit will come up and fight against them. It will win the battle and kill them. ⁸Their bodies will be left lying in the streets of the same great city where their Lord was nailed to a cross. And that city is spiritually like the city of Sodom or the country of Egypt.

⁹For three and a half days the people of every nation, tribe, language, and race will stare at the bodies of these two witnesses and refuse to let them be buried. ¹⁰Everyone on earth will celebrate and be happy. They will give gifts to each other, because of what happened to the two prophets who caused them so much trouble. ¹¹But three and a half days later, God will breathe life into their bodies. They will stand up, and everyone who sees them will be terrified.

¹²The witnesses then heard a loud voice from heaven, saying, "Come up here." And while their enemies were watching, they were taken up to heaven in a cloud. ¹³At that same moment there was a terrible earthquake that destroyed a tenth of the city. Seven thousand people were killed, and the rest were frightened and praised the God who rules in heaven.

¹⁴The second horrible thing has now happened! But the third one will be here soon.

The Seventh Trumpet

¹⁵At the sound of the seventh trumpet, loud voices were heard in heaven. They said,

"Now the kingdom
of this world
belongs to our Lord
and to his Chosen One!
And he will rule
forever and ever!"

¹⁶Then the twenty-four elders, who were seated on thrones in God's presence, knelt down and worshiped him. ¹⁷They said,

"Lord God All-Powerful,
you are and you were,
and we thank you.
You used your great power
and started ruling.
¹⁸ When the nations got angry,
you became angry too!
Now the time has come
for the dead
to be judged.
It is time for you to reward
your servants the prophets
and all of your people
who honor your name,
no matter who they are.
It is time to destroy everyone
who has destroyed
the earth."

¹⁹The door to God's temple in heaven was then opened, and the sacred chest[q] could be seen inside the temple. I saw lightning and heard roars of thunder. The earth trembled and huge hailstones fell to the ground.

The Woman and the Dragon

12 Something important appeared in the sky. It was a woman whose clothes were the sun. The moon was under her feet, and a crown made of twelve stars was on her head. ²She was about to give birth, and she was crying because of the great pain.

³Something else appeared in the sky. It was a huge red dragon with seven heads and ten horns, and a crown on each of its seven heads. ⁴With its tail, it dragged a third of the stars from the sky and threw them down to the earth. Then the dragon turned toward the woman, because it wanted to eat her child as soon as it was born.

⁵The woman gave birth to a son, who would rule all nations with an iron rod. The boy was snatched away. He was taken to God and placed on his throne. ⁶The woman ran into the desert to a place that God had prepared for her. There she would be taken care of for one thousand two hundred sixty days.

Michael Fights the Dragon

⁷A war broke out in heaven. Michael and his angels were fighting against the dragon and its angels. ⁸But the dragon lost the battle. It and its angels were forced out of their places in heaven ⁹and were thrown down to the earth. Yes, that old snake and his angels were thrown out of heaven! That snake, who fools everyone on earth, is known as the devil

---

[p]11.3 *sackcloth*: See the note at 6.12. [q]11.19 *sacred chest*: In Old Testament times the sacred chest was kept in the tent used for worship. It was the symbol of God's presence with his people and also of his agreement with them.

and Satan. ¹⁰Then I heard a voice from heaven shout,

"Our God has shown
his saving power,
and his kingdom has come!
God's own Chosen One
has shown his authority.
Satan accused our people
in the presence of God
day and night.
Now he has been thrown out!

¹¹ Our people defeated Satan
because of the blood[r]
of the Lamb
and the message of God.
They were willing
to give up their lives.

¹² The heavens should rejoice,
together with everyone
who lives there.
But pity the earth
and the sea,
because the devil
was thrown down
to the earth.
He knows his time is short,
and he is very angry."

¹³When the dragon realized that it had been thrown down to the earth, it tried to make trouble for the woman who had given birth to a son. ¹⁴But the woman was given two wings like those of a huge eagle, so that she could fly into the desert. There she would escape from the snake and be taken care of for a time, two times, and half a time. ¹⁵The snake then spewed out water like a river to sweep the woman away. ¹⁶But the earth helped her and swallowed the water that had come from the dragon's mouth. ¹⁷This made the dragon terribly angry with the woman. So it started a war against the rest of her children. They are the people who obey God and are faithful to what Jesus did and taught. ¹⁸The dragon[s] stood on the beach beside the sea.

The Two Beasts

13 I looked and saw a beast coming up from the sea. This one had ten horns and seven heads, and a crown was on each of its ten horns. On each of its heads were names that were an insult to God. ²The beast that I saw had the body of a leopard, the feet of a bear, and the mouth of a lion. The dragon handed over its own power and throne and great authority to this beast. ³One of its heads seemed to have been fatally wounded, but now it was well. Everyone on earth marveled at this beast, ⁴and they worshiped the dragon who had given its authority to the beast. They also worshiped the beast and said, "No one is like this beast! No one can fight against it."

⁵The beast was allowed to brag and claim to be God, and for forty-two months it was allowed to rule. ⁶The beast cursed God, and it cursed the name of God. It even cursed the place where God lives, as well as everyone who lives in heaven with God. ⁷It was allowed to fight against God's people and defeat them. It was also given authority over the people of every tribe, nation, language, and race. ⁸The beast was worshiped by everyone whose name wasn't written before the time of creation in the book of the Lamb who was killed.[t]

⁹ If you have ears,
then listen!
¹⁰ If you are doomed
to be captured,
you will be captured.
If you are doomed
to be killed by a sword,
you will be killed
by a sword.

This means that God's people must learn to endure and be faithful!

¹¹I now saw another beast. This one came out of the ground. It had two horns like a lamb, but spoke like a dragon. ¹²It worked for the beast whose fatal wound had been healed. And it used all its authority to force the earth and its people to worship that beast. ¹³It worked mighty miracles, and while people watched, it even made fire come down from the sky.

¹⁴This second beast fooled people on earth by working miracles for the first one. Then it talked them into making an idol in the form of the beast that did not die after being wounded by a sword. ¹⁵It was allowed to put breath into the idol, so that it could speak. Everyone who refused to worship the idol of the beast was put to death. ¹⁶All people were forced to put a mark on their right hand or forehead. Whether they were powerful or weak, rich or poor, free people or slaves, ¹⁷they all had to have this mark, or else they could not buy or sell anything. This mark stood for the name of the beast and for the number of its name.

¹⁸You need wisdom to understand the number of the beast! But if you are smart enough, you can figure this out.

---

[r]**12.11** *blood:* Or "death." [s]**12.18** *The dragon:* The text has "he," and some manuscripts have "I." [t]**13.8** *wasn't written ... was killed:* Or "not written in the book of the Lamb who was killed before the time of creation."

Its number is six hundred sixty-six, and it stands for a person.

The Lamb and His 144,000 Followers

14 I looked and saw the Lamb standing on Mount Zion![u] With him were a hundred forty-four thousand, who had his name and his Father's name written on their foreheads. [2]Then I heard a sound from heaven that was like a roaring flood or loud thunder or even like the music of harps. [3]And a new song was being sung in front of God's throne and in front of the four living creatures and the elders. No one could learn that song, except the one hundred forty-four thousand who had been rescued from the earth. [4]All of these are pure virgins, and they follow the Lamb wherever he leads. They have been rescued to be presented to God and the Lamb as the most precious people[v] on earth. [5]They never tell lies, and they are innocent.

The Messages of the Three Angels

[6]I saw another angel. This one was flying across the sky and had the eternal good news to announce to the people of every race, tribe, language, and nation on earth. [7]The angel shouted, "Worship and honor God! The time has come for him to judge everyone. Kneel down before the one who created heaven and earth, the oceans, and every stream."

[8]A second angel followed and said, "The great city of Babylon has fallen! This is the city that made all nations drunk and immoral. Now God is angry, and Babylon has fallen."

[9]Finally, a third angel came and shouted:

Here is what will happen if you worship the beast and the idol and have the mark of the beast on your hand or forehead. [10]You will have to drink the wine that God gives to everyone who makes him angry. You will feel his mighty anger, and you will be tortured with fire and burning sulfur, while the holy angels and the Lamb look on.

[11]If you worship the beast and the idol and accept the mark of its name, you will be tortured day and night. The smoke from your torture will go up forever and ever, and you will never be able to rest.

[12]God's people must learn to endure. They must also obey his commands and have faith in Jesus.

[13]Then I heard a voice from heaven say, "Put this in writing. From now on, the Lord will bless everyone who has faith in him when they die."

The Spirit answered, "Yes, they will rest from their hard work, and they will be rewarded for what they have done."

The Earth Is Harvested

[14]I looked and saw a bright cloud, and someone who seemed to be the Son of Man[w] was sitting on the cloud. He wore a gold crown on his head and held a sharp sickle[x] in his hand. [15]An angel came out of the temple and shouted, "Start cutting with your sickle! Harvest season is here, and all crops on earth are ripe." [16]The one on the cloud swung his sickle and harvested the crops.

[17]Another angel with a sharp sickle then came out of the temple in heaven. [18]After this, an angel with power over fire came from the altar and shouted to the angel who had the sickle. He said, "All grapes on earth are ripe! Harvest them with your sharp sickle." [19]The angel swung his sickle on earth and cut off its grapes. He threw them into a pit[y] where they were trampled on as a sign of God's anger. [20]The pit was outside the city, and when the grapes were mashed, blood flowed out. The blood turned into a river that was about two hundred miles long and almost deep enough to cover a horse.

The Last of the Terrible Troubles

15 After this, I looked at the sky and saw something else that was strange and important. Seven angels were bringing the last seven terrible troubles. When these are ended, God will no longer be angry.

[2]Then I saw something that looked like a glass sea mixed with fire, and people were standing on it. They were the ones who had defeated the beast and the idol and the number that tells the name of the beast. God had given them harps, [3]and they were singing the song that his servant Moses and the Lamb had sung. They were singing,

"Lord God All-Powerful,
you have done great
 and marvelous things.
You are the ruler
 of all nations,

---

[u]**14.1** *Mount Zion*: Another name for Jerusalem.   [v]**14.4** *the most precious people*: The Greek text has "the first people." The Law of Moses taught that the first-born of all animals and the first part of the harvest were special and belonged to the Lord.   [w]**14.14** *Son of Man*: See the note at 1.13.   [x]**14.14** *sickle*: A knife with a long curved blade, used to cut grain and other crops.   [y]**14.19** *pit*: It was the custom to put grapes in a pit (called a wine press) and stomp on them to make juice that would later turn to wine.

and you do what is
  right and fair.
⁴ Lord, who doesn't honor
  and praise your name?
You alone are holy,
and all nations will come
  and worship you,
because you have shown
  that you judge
    with fairness."

⁵After this, I noticed something else in heaven. The sacred tent used for a temple was open. ⁶And the seven angels who were bringing the terrible troubles were coming out of it. They were dressed in robes of pure white linen and wore belts made of pure gold. ⁷One of the four living creatures gave each of the seven angels a bowl made of gold. These bowls were filled with the anger of God who lives forever and ever. ⁸The temple quickly filled with smoke from the glory and power of God. No one could enter it until the seven angels had finished pouring out the seven last troubles.

The Bowls of God's Anger

16 From the temple I heard a voice shout to the seven angels, "Go and empty the seven bowls of God's anger on the earth."

²The first angel emptied his bowl on the earth. At once ugly and painful sores broke out on everyone who had the mark of the beast and worshiped the idol.

³The second angel emptied his bowl on the sea. Right away the sea turned into blood like that of a dead person, and every living thing in the sea died.

⁴The third angel emptied his bowl into the rivers and streams. At once they turned to blood. ⁵Then I heard the angel, who has power over water, say,

"You have always been,
and you always will be
  the holy God.
You had the right
  to judge in this way.
⁶ They poured out the blood^z
  of your people
    and your prophets.
So you gave them blood
  to drink, as they deserve!"
⁷ After this, I heard
  the altar shout,
"Yes, Lord God All-Powerful,
your judgments are honest
  and fair."

⁸The fourth angel emptied his bowl on the sun, and it began to scorch people like fire. ⁹Everyone was scorched by its great heat, and all of them cursed the name of God who had power over these terrible troubles. But no one turned to God and praised him.

¹⁰The fifth angel emptied his bowl on the throne of the beast. At once darkness covered its kingdom, and its people began biting their tongues in pain. ¹¹And because of their painful sores, they cursed the God who rules in heaven. But still they did not stop doing evil things.

¹²The sixth angel emptied his bowl on the great Euphrates River, and it completely dried up to make a road for the kings from the east. ¹³An evil spirit that looked like a frog came out of the mouth of the dragon. One also came out of the mouth of the beast, and another out of the mouth of the false prophet. ¹⁴These evil spirits had the power to work miracles. They went to every king on earth, to bring them together for a war against God All-Powerful. But that will be the day of God's great victory.

¹⁵Remember that Christ says, "When I come, it will surprise you like a thief! But God will bless you, if you are awake and ready. Then you won't have to walk around naked and be ashamed."

¹⁶Those armies came together in a place that in Hebrew is called Armagedon.^a

¹⁷As soon as the seventh angel emptied his bowl in the air, a loud voice from the throne in the temple shouted, "It's done!" ¹⁸There were flashes of lightning, roars of thunder, and the worst earthquake in all history. ¹⁹The great city of Babylon split into three parts, and the cities of other nations fell. So God made Babylon drink from the wine cup that was filled with his anger. ²⁰Every island ran away, and the mountains disappeared. ²¹Hailstones, weighing about a hundred pounds each, fell from the sky on people. Finally, the people cursed God, because the hail was so terrible.

The Prostitute and the Beast

17 One of the seven angels who had emptied the bowls came over and said to me, "Come on! I will show you how God will punish that shameless prostitute who sits on many oceans. ²Every king on earth has slept with her, and her shameless ways are like wine that has made everyone on earth drunk."

³With the help of the Spirit, the angel took me into the desert, where I saw a woman sitting on a red beast. The beast

---

^z16.6 *They poured out the blood*: A way of saying, "They murdered." ^a16.16 *Armagedon*: The Hebrew form of the name would be "Har Megiddo," meaning "Hill of Megiddo," where many battles were fought in ancient times (see Judges 5.19; 2 Kings 23.29, 30).

was covered with names that were an insult to God, and it had seven heads and ten horns. ⁴The woman was dressed in purple and scarlet robes, and she wore jewelry made of gold, precious stones, and pearls. In her hand she held a gold cup filled with the filthy and nasty things she had done. ⁵On her forehead a mysterious name was written:

I AM THE GREAT CITY OF
BABYLON, THE MOTHER
OF EVERY IMMORAL AND FILTHY
THING ON EARTH.

⁶I could tell that the woman was drunk on the blood of God's people who had given their lives for Jesus. This surprising sight amazed me, ⁷and the angel said:

Why are you so amazed? I will explain the mystery about this woman and about the beast she is sitting on, with its seven heads and ten horns. ⁸The beast you saw is one that used to be and no longer is. It will come back from the deep pit, but only to be destroyed. Everyone on earth whose names were not written in the book of life[b] before the time of creation will be amazed. They will see this beast that used to be and no longer is, but will be once more.

⁹Anyone with wisdom can figure this out. The seven heads that the woman is sitting on stand for seven hills. These heads are also seven kings. ¹⁰Five of the kings are dead. One is ruling now, and the other one has not yet come. But when he does, he will rule for only a little while. ¹¹You also saw a beast that used to be and no longer is. That beast is one of the seven kings who will return as the eighth king, but only to be destroyed.

¹²The ten horns that you saw are ten more kings, who have not yet come into power, and they will rule with the beast for only a short time. ¹³They all think alike and will give their power and authority to the beast. ¹⁴These kings will go to war against the Lamb. But he will defeat them, because he is Lord over all lords and King over all kings. His followers are chosen and special and faithful.

¹⁵The oceans that you saw the prostitute sitting on are crowds of people from all races and languages. ¹⁶The ten horns and the beast will start hating the shameless woman. They will strip off her clothes and leave her naked. Then they will eat her flesh and throw the rest of her body into a fire. ¹⁷God is the one who made these kings all think alike and decide to give their power to the beast. And they will do this until what God has said comes true.

¹⁸The woman you saw is the great city that rules over all kings on earth.

The Fall of Babylon

18 I saw another angel come from heaven. This one had great power, and the earth was bright because of his glory. ²The angel shouted,

"Fallen! Powerful Babylon
   has fallen
and is now the home
   of demons.
It is the den
   of every filthy spirit
and of all unclean birds,
   and every dirty
   and hated animal.
³ Babylon's evil and immoral wine
   has made all nations drunk.
Every king on earth
   has slept with her,
and every merchant on earth
is rich because of
   her evil desires."

⁴ Then I heard another voice
   from heaven shout,
"My people, you must escape
   from Babylon.
Don't take part in her sins
   and share her punishment.
⁵ Her sins are piled
   as high as heaven.
God has remembered the evil
   she has done.
⁶ Treat her as she
   has treated others.
Make her pay double
   for what she has done.
Make her drink twice as much
of what she mixed
   for others.
⁷ That woman honored herself
   with a life of luxury.
Reward her now
   with suffering and pain.

"Deep in her heart
Babylon said,
   'I am the queen!
Never will I be a widow
or know what it means
   to be sad.'
⁸ And so, in a single day
she will suffer the pain
   of sorrow, hunger, and death.
Fire will destroy
   her dead body,

---

[b] 17.8 *book of life*: See the note at 3.5.

because her judge
   is the powerful Lord God."

⁹Every king on earth who slept with her and shared in her luxury will mourn. They will weep, when they see the smoke from that fire. ¹⁰Her sufferings will frighten them, and they will stand at a distance and say,

"Pity that great
   and powerful city!
Pity Babylon!
In a single hour
   her judgment has come."

¹¹Every merchant on earth will mourn, because there is no one to buy their goods. ¹²There won't be anyone to buy their gold, silver, jewels, pearls, fine linen, purple cloth, silk, scarlet cloth, sweet-smelling wood, fancy carvings of ivory and wood, as well as things made of bronze, iron, or marble. ¹³No one will buy their cinnamon, spices, incense, myrrh, frankincense,ᶜ wine, olive oil, fine flour, wheat, cattle, sheep, horses, chariots, slaves, and other humans.

¹⁴ Babylon, the things
   your heart desired
have all escaped
   from you.
Every luxury
   and all your glory
   will be lost forever.
You will never
   get them back.

¹⁵The merchants had become rich because of her. But when they saw her sufferings, they were terrified. They stood at a distance, crying and mourning. ¹⁶Then they shouted,

"Pity the great city
   of Babylon!
She dressed in fine linen
   and wore purple
   and scarlet cloth.
She had jewelry
   made of gold
   and precious stones
   and pearls.
¹⁷ Yet in a single hour
   her riches disappeared."

Every ship captain and passenger and sailor stood at a distance, together with everyone who does business by traveling on the sea. ¹⁸When they saw the smoke from her fire, they shouted, "This was the greatest city ever!"

¹⁹They cried loudly, and in their sorrow they threw dust on their heads, as they said,

"Pity the great city
   of Babylon!

Everyone who sailed the seas
   became rich
   from her treasures.
But in a single hour
   the city was destroyed.
²⁰ The heavens should be happy
   with God's people
   and apostles and prophets.
God has punished her
   for them."

²¹A powerful angel then picked up a huge stone and threw it into the sea. The angel said,

"This is how the great city
   of Babylon
will be thrown down,
   never to rise again.
²² The music of harps and singers
   and of flutes and trumpets
   will no longer be heard.
No workers will ever
   set up shop in that city,
and the sound
   of grinding grain
   will be silenced forever.
²³ Lamps will no longer shine
   anywhere in Babylon,
and couples will never again
   say wedding vows there.
Her merchants ruled
   the earth,
and by her witchcraft
   she fooled all nations.
²⁴ On the streets of Babylon
   is found the blood
   of God's people
   and of his prophets,
   and everyone else."

19 After this, I heard what sounded like a lot of voices in heaven, and they were shouting,

"Praise the Lord!
To our God belongs
   the glorious power to save,
² because his judgments
   are honest and fair.
That filthy prostitute
   ruined the earth
   with shameful deeds.
But God has judged her
   and made her pay
the price for murdering
   his servants."

³Then the crowd shouted,

"Praise the Lord!
Smoke will never stop rising
   from her burning body."

⁴After this, the twenty-four elders and the four living creatures all knelt before the throne of God and worshiped him. They said, "Amen! Praise the Lord!"

ᶜ**18.13** *myrrh, frankincense*: Myrrh was a valuable sweet-smelling powder often used in perfume. Frankincense was a valuable powder that was burned to make a sweet smell.

The Marriage Supper of the Lamb

⁵From the throne a voice said,

"If you worship
and fear our God,
give praise to him,
no matter who you are."

⁶Then I heard what seemed to be a large crowd that sounded like a roaring flood and loud thunder all mixed together. They were saying,

"Praise the Lord!
Our Lord God All-Powerful
now rules as king.
⁷ So we will be glad and happy
and give him praise.
The wedding day of the Lamb
is here,
and his bride is ready.
⁸ She will be given
a wedding dress
made of pure
and shining linen.
This linen stands for
the good things
God's people have done."

⁹Then the angel told me, "Put this in writing. God will bless everyone who is invited to the wedding feast of the Lamb." The angel also said, "These things that God has said are true."

¹⁰I knelt at the feet of the angel and began to worship him. But the angel said, "Don't do that! I am a servant, just like you and everyone else who tells about Jesus. Don't worship anyone but God. Everyone who tells about Jesus does it by the power of the Spirit."

The Rider on the White Horse

¹¹I looked and saw that heaven was open, and a white horse was there. Its rider was called Faithful and True, and he is always fair when he judges or goes to war. ¹²He had eyes like flames of fire, and he was wearing a lot of crowns. His name was written on him, but he was the only one who knew what the name meant.

¹³The rider wore a robe that was covered with[d] blood, and he was known as "The Word of God." ¹⁴He was followed by armies from heaven that rode on horses and were dressed in pure white linen. ¹⁵From his mouth a sharp sword went out to attack the nations. He will rule them with an iron rod and will show the fierce anger of God All-Powerful by trampling the grapes in the pit where wine is made. ¹⁶On the part of the robe that covered his thigh was written, "KING OF KINGS AND LORD OF LORDS."

¹⁷I then saw an angel standing on the sun, and he shouted to all the birds flying in the sky, "Come and join in God's great feast! ¹⁸You can eat the flesh of kings, rulers, leaders, horses, riders, free people, slaves, important people, and everyone else."

¹⁹I also saw the beast and all kings of the earth come together. They fought against the rider on the white horse and against his army. ²⁰But the beast was captured and so was the false prophet. This is the same prophet who had worked miracles for the beast, so that he could fool everyone who had the mark of the beast and worshiped the idol. The beast and the false prophet were thrown alive into a lake of burning sulfur. ²¹But the rest of their army was killed by the sword that came from the mouth of the rider on the horse. Then birds stuffed themselves on the dead bodies.

The Thousand Years

20 I saw an angel come down from heaven, carrying the key to the deep pit and a big chain. ²He chained the dragon for a thousand years. It is that old snake, who is also known as the devil and Satan. ³Then the angel threw the dragon into the pit. He locked and sealed it, so that a thousand years would go by before the dragon could fool the nations again. But after that, it would have to be set free for a little while.

⁴I saw thrones, and sitting on those thrones were the ones who had been given the right to judge. I also saw the souls of the people who had their heads cut off because they had told about Jesus and preached God's message. They were the same ones who had not worshiped the beast or the idol, and they had refused to let its mark be put on their hands or foreheads. They will come to life and rule with Christ for a thousand years.

⁵⁻⁶These people are the first to be raised to life, and they are especially blessed and holy. The second death[e] has no power over them. They will be priests for God and Christ and will rule with them for a thousand years.

No other dead people were raised to life until a thousand years later.

Satan Is Defeated

⁷At the end of the thousand years, Satan will be set free. ⁸He will fool the countries of Gog and Magog, which are at the far ends of the earth, and their people will follow him into battle. They will have as many followers as there are

---

[d] 19.13 *covered with:* Some manuscripts have "sprinkled with."   [e] 20.5,6 *second death:* See the note at 2.11.

grains of sand along the beach. ⁹and they will march all the way across the earth. They will surround the camp of God's people and the city that his people love. But fire will come down from heaven and destroy the whole army. ¹⁰Then the devil who fooled them will be thrown into the lake of fire and burning sulfur. He will be there with the beast and the false prophet, and they will be in pain day and night forever and ever.

The Judgment at the Great White Throne

¹¹I saw a great white throne with someone sitting on it. Earth and heaven tried to run away, but there was no place for them to go. ¹²I also saw all the dead people standing in front of that throne. Every one of them was there, no matter who they had once been. Several books were opened, and then the book of life*ᶠ* was opened. The dead were judged by what those books said they had done. ¹³The sea gave up the dead people who were in it, and death and its kingdom also gave up their dead. Then everyone was judged by what they had done. ¹⁴Afterwards, death and its kingdom were thrown into the lake of fire. This is the second death.*ᵍ* ¹⁵Anyone whose name wasn't written in the book of life was thrown into the lake of fire.

The New Heaven and the New Earth

21 I saw a new heaven and a new earth. The first heaven and the first earth had disappeared, and so had the sea. ²Then I saw New Jerusalem, that holy city, coming down from God in heaven. It was like a bride dressed in her wedding gown and ready to meet her husband. ³I heard a loud voice shout from the throne:

God's home is now with his people. He will live with them, and they will be his own. Yes, God will make his home among his people. ⁴He will wipe all tears from their eyes, and there will be no more death, suffering, crying, or pain. These things of the past are gone forever.

⁵Then the one sitting on the throne said:

I am making everything new. Write down what I have said. My words are true and can be trusted. ⁶Everything is finished! I am Alpha and Omega,*ʰ* the beginning and the end. I will freely give water from the life-giving fountain to everyone who is thirsty. ⁷All who win the victory will be given these blessings. I will be their God, and they will be my people.

⁸But I will tell you what will happen to cowards and to everyone who is unfaithful or dirty-minded or who murders or is sexually immoral or uses witchcraft or worships idols or tells lies. They will be thrown into that lake of fire and burning sulfur. This is the second death.*ⁱ*

The New Jerusalem

⁹I saw one of the seven angels who had the bowls filled with the seven last terrible troubles. The angel came to me and said, "Come on! I will show you the one who will be the bride and wife of the Lamb." ¹⁰Then with the help of the Spirit, he took me to the top of a very high mountain. There he showed me the holy city of Jerusalem coming down from God in heaven.

¹¹The glory of God made the city bright. It was dazzling and crystal clear like a precious jasper stone. ¹²The city had a high and thick wall with twelve gates, and each one of them was guarded by an angel. On each of the gates was written the name of one of the twelve tribes of Israel. ¹³Three of these gates were on the east, three were on the north, three more were on the south, and the other three were on the west. ¹⁴The city was built on twelve foundation stones. On each of the stones was written the name of one of the Lamb's twelve apostles.

¹⁵The angel who spoke to me had a gold measuring stick to measure the city and its gates and its walls. ¹⁶The city was shaped like a cube, because it was just as high as it was wide. When the angel measured the city, it was about fifteen hundred miles high and fifteen hundred miles wide. ¹⁷Then the angel measured the wall, and by our measurements it was about two hundred sixteen feet high.

¹⁸The wall was built of jasper, and the city was made of pure gold, clear as crystal. ¹⁹Each of the twelve foundations was a precious stone. The first was jasper,*ʲ* the second was sapphire, the third was agate, the fourth was emerald, ²⁰the fifth was onyx, the sixth was carnelian, the seventh was chrysolite, the

---

*ᶠ***20.12** *book of life*: See the note at 3.5.   *ᵍ***20.14** *second death*: See the note at 2.11.
*ʰ***21.6** *Alpha and Omega*: See the note at 1.8.   *ⁱ***21.8** *second death*: See the note at 2.11.
*ʲ***21.19** *jasper*: The precious and semi-precious stones mentioned in verses 19, 20 are of different colors. *Jasper* is usually green or clear; *sapphire* is blue; *agate* has circles of brown and white; *emerald* is green; *onyx* has different bands of color; *carnelian* is deep-red or reddish-white; *chrysolite* is olive-green; *beryl* is green or bluish-green; *topaz* is yellow; *chrysoprase* is apple-green; *jacinth* is reddish-orange; and *amethyst* is deep purple.

eighth was beryl, the ninth was topaz, the tenth was chrysoprase, the eleventh was jacinth, and the twelfth was amethyst. ²¹Each of the twelve gates was a solid pearl. The streets of the city were made of pure gold, clear as crystal.

²²I did not see a temple there. The Lord God All-Powerful and the Lamb were its temple. ²³And the city did not need the sun or the moon. The glory of God was shining on it, and the Lamb was its light.

²⁴Nations will walk by the light of that city, and kings will bring their riches there. ²⁵Its gates are always open during the day, and night never comes. ²⁶The glorious treasures of nations will be brought into the city. ²⁷But nothing unworthy will be allowed to enter. No one who is dirty-minded or who tells lies will be there. Only those whose names are written in the Lamb's book of life[k] will be in the city.

22 The angel showed me a river that was crystal clear, and its waters gave life. The river came from the throne where God and the Lamb were seated. ²Then it flowed down the middle of the city's main street. On each side of the river are trees[l] that grow a different kind of fruit each month of the year. The fruit gives life, and the leaves are used as medicine to heal the nations.

³God's curse will no longer be on the people of that city. He and the Lamb will be seated there on their thrones, and its people will worship God ⁴and will see him face to face. God's name will be written on the foreheads of the people. ⁵Never again will night appear, and no one who lives there will ever need a lamp or the sun. The Lord God will be their light, and they will rule forever.

The Coming of Christ

⁶Then I was told:

These words are true and can be trusted. The Lord God controls the spirits of his prophets, and he is the one who sent his angel to show his servants what must happen right away. ⁷Remember, I am coming soon! God will bless everyone who pays attention to the message of this book.

⁸My name is John, and I am the one who heard and saw these things. Then after I had heard and seen all this, I knelt down and began to worship at the feet of the angel who had shown it to me.

⁹But the angel said,

Don't do that! I am a servant, just like you. I am the same as a follower or a prophet or anyone else who obeys what is written in this book. God is the one you should worship.

¹⁰Don't keep the prophecies in this book a secret. These things will happen soon.

¹¹Evil people will keep on being evil, and everyone who is dirty-minded will still be dirty-minded. But good people will keep on doing right, and God's people will always be holy.

¹²Then I was told:

I am coming soon! And when I come, I will reward everyone for what they have done. ¹³I am Alpha and Omega,[m] the first and the last, the beginning and the end.

¹⁴God will bless all who have washed their robes. They will each have the right to eat fruit from the tree that gives life, and they can enter the gates of the city. ¹⁵But outside the city will be dogs, witches, immoral people, murderers, idol worshipers, and everyone who loves to tell lies and do wrong.

¹⁶I am Jesus! And I am the one who sent my angel to tell all of you these things for the churches. I am David's Great Descendant,[n] and I am also the bright morning star.[o]

¹⁷The Spirit and the bride say, "Come!"

Everyone who hears this[p] should say, "Come!"

If you are thirsty, come! If you want life-giving water, come and take it. It's free!

¹⁸Here is my warning for everyone who hears the prophecies in this book:

If you add anything to them, God will make you suffer all the terrible troubles written in this book. ¹⁹If you take anything away from these prophecies, God will not let you have part in the life-giving tree and in the holy city described in this book.

²⁰The one who has spoken these things says, "I am coming soon!"

So, Lord Jesus, please come soon!

²¹I pray that the Lord Jesus will be kind to all of you.

---

[k]**21.27** *book of life*: See the note at 3.5.   [l]**22.2** *trees*: The Greek has "tree," which is used in a collective sense of trees on both sides of the heavenly river.   [m]**22.13** *Alpha and Omega*: See the note at 1.8.   [n]**22.16** *David's Great Descendant*: See the note at 5.5.   [o]**22.16** *the bright morning star*: Probably thought of as the brightest star (see 2.27, 28).   [p]**22.17** *who hears this*: The reading of the book of Revelation in a service of worship.

Word List

Aaron The brother of Moses. Only he and his descendants were to serve as priests and offer sacrifices for the people of Israel.

Abel The second son of Adam and Eve and the younger brother of Cain, who killed him, after God accepted Abel's offering and refused Cain's.

Abijah A descendant of Aaron. King David divided the priests into twenty-four groups, and Abijah was head of the eighth group.

Abimelech The Philistine king of Gath when David escaped from there by pretending to be crazy. See the title of Psalm 34. He is called Achish in 1 Samuel 21.10—22.1.

Abraham The first great ancestor of the people of Israel. He was the husband of Sarah and the father of Isaac. Abraham put his faith in God, and God promised to bless everyone on earth because of Abraham.

Adam The first man and the husband of Eve.

Agrippa (1) Herod Agrippa was king of Judea A.D. 41–44 and mistreated Christians (Acts 12.1–5). (2) Agrippa II was the son of Herod Agrippa and ruled Judea A.D. 44–53. He and his sister Bernice listened to Paul defend himself (Acts 25.13–26, 32).

Agur, Son of Jakeh A wise man, otherwise unknown. Agur wrote some of the proverbs. See Proberbs 30.1.

Ahimelech A priest at Nob who gave food and a sword to David when he fled from Saul. See the title of Psalm 52.

aloes A sweet-smelling spice that was mixed with myrrh and used as a perfume.

altar A raised structure where sacrifices and offerings were presented to God or gods. Altars could be made of rocks, packed earth, metal or pottery.

amen A Hebrew word used after a prayer or a blessing and meaning, "Let it be that way."

ancestor Someone born one or more generations earlier in a family line, such as a grandparent or great-grandparent.

angel A supernatural being who tells God's messages or protects God's people.

Antipas The father of Herod the Great and ruler of Judea 55–43 B.C. He was also known as Antipater.

apostle A person chosen by Christ to take his message to others.

Aram-naharaim A territory in northern Mesopotamia. The name means Arameans from the land of the Two Rivers. See the title of Psalm 60.

Aram-zobah An Aramean kingdom north of Damascus. See the title of Psalm 60 and 2 Samuel 8.3–13.

Aramaic A language closely related to Hebrew. It was spoken by many Jews including Jesus during New Testament times.

Asaph One of David's musicians. He wrote many psalms and also sang at the dedication of Solomon's temple. See the titles of Psalms 50 and 73–83.

Asia A Roman province in what is today modern Turkey.

Augustus This is the title meaning "honored" that the Romans gave to Octavian when he began ruling the Roman world in 27 B.C. He was Emperor when Jesus was born (Luke 2.1).

Babylon A large city in south-central Mesopotamia, the capital of the kingdom of Babylonia. The Babylonians defeated the southern kingdom of Judah in the sixth century B.C. and forced many of its people to live in Babylonia.

barley A grain something like wheat and used to make bread.

Bashan Flatlands and wooded hills in southern Syria, northeast of Lake Galilee. It was known for its fat cattle and fine grain. See Psalm 68.15, 16.

Benjamin One of the tribes of Israel. It occupied land between Bethel and Jerusalem. The people of this tribe descended from Benjamin, the younger of Jacob and

Word List

Rachel's two sons. When the ten northern tribes of Israel broke away following the death of Solomon, only the tribes of Benjamin and Judah were left to form the southern kingdom.

Cain The first son of Adam and Eve and the brother of Abel.

Christ A Greek word meaning "the Chosen One" and used to translate the Hebrew word "Messiah." It is used in the New Testament both as a title and a name for Jesus.

circumcise To cut off the foreskin from the male organ. This is done for Jewish boys as part of a religious ceremony eight days after they are born to show that they belong to God's people. God's command to Abraham (Genesis 17.9–14) was to circumcise all males on the eighth day. Jesus' circumcision on the eighth day is reported in Luke 2.21.

citizen A person who is given special rights and privileges by a nation or state. In return, a citizen was expected to be loyal to that nation or state.

commandments God's rules for his people to live by.

council A leading group of Jewish men who were allowed by the Roman government to meet and make certain decisions for their people.

cumin A plant with small seeds used for seasoning food.

David The most famous ancestor of the Jewish people and the most powerful king Israel ever had. They hoped that one of his descendants would always be their king.

Day of Atonement The one day each year (the tenth day after the Jewish new year's day in the fall) when the high priest went into the most holy part of the temple and sprinkled some of the blood of a sacrificed bull on the sacred chest. This was done so that the people's sins would be forgiven. This holy day is called Yom Kippur in Hebrew.

demons and *evil spirits* Supernatural beings that do harmful things to people and sometimes cause them to do bad things. In the New Testament they are sometimes called "unclean spirits," because people under their power were thought to be unclean and unfit to worship God.

descendant Someone born one or more generations later in a family line, such as a grandchild or great-grandchild.

devil The chief of the demons and evil spirits, also known as "Satan."

disciple Someone who was a follower of Jesus and learned from him.

Doeg of Edom An Edomite who worked for King Saul as the head of his shepherds. He was known to be ruthless and conniving. See the title of Psalm 52 and 1 Samuel 21–22.

Edom A kingdom south of the Dead Sea as far as the Gulf of Aqaba. The Edomites descended from Esau, the twin brother of Jacob.

Elijah A prophet who spoke for God in the ninth century B.C. Many Jews in later centuries thought Elijah would return to get things ready for the coming of the Lord.

elders Men whose age and wisdom made them respected leaders.

Emperor The ruler who lived in the city of Rome and governed all the land around the Mediterranean Sea.

Ephraim One of the most important tribes of northern Israel. It occupied the land north of Benjamin and south of Manasseh. The people of this tribe descended from Ephraim, Joseph's second son.

Epicureans People who followed the teachings of a man named Epicurus, who taught that happiness should be a person's main goal in life.

eternal life Life that is the gift of God and never ends.

Ethan the Ezrahite One of David's musicians. See the title of Psalm 89.

Ethiopia The extensive territory south of Egypt called Cush in Hebrew, traditionally translated as Ethiopia. In Bible times it included within its borders most of modern Sudan and present day Ethiopia.

evil spirits See "demons."

exile The time in Jewish history (597–539 B.C.) when the Babylonians took away most of the people of Jerusalem and Judah as prisoners of war and made them live in Babylonia.

Feast of Thin Bread The days after Passover when Jews eat a kind of thin, flat bread made without yeast to remember how God freed the people of Israel from

Word List

slavery in Egypt and give them a fresh start.

Felix The Roman governor of Judea A.D. 52–60, who listened to Paul speak and kept him in jail.

Festival of Shelters This festival celebrates the period of forty years when the people of Israel walked through the desert and lived in small shelters. This happy celebration takes place each year in connection with the fall harvest season. Its name in Hebrew is Sukkoth.

Festus The Roman governor after Felix, who sent Paul to stand trial in Rome.

Gath One of the five major Philistine towns on the coastal plain of southern Palestine.

Generation One way of describing a group of people who live during the same period of time. The time of one generation is often understood to be about forty years. See Psalm 95.10.

Gentile Someone who is not a Jew.

Glory The magnificence of God's presence that inspires awe and worship.

God's kingdom God's rule over people, both in this life and in the next.

God's Law God's rules for his people to live by. They are found in the Old Testament, especially in the first five books.

God's Tent The tent where the people of Israel worshiped God before the temple was built.

Greek The language in which the New Testament was written.

Hagar A personal servant of Sarah, the wife of Abraham. When Sarah could not have any children, she followed the ancient custom of letting her husband have a child by Hagar, her servant woman. The boy's name was Ishmael.

Hebrew The language used by the people of Israel and for the writing of most of the Old Testament.

Heman the Ezrahite One of David's musicians. See the title of Psalm 88.

Hermes The Greek god of skillful speaking and the messenger of the other Greek gods.

Herod (1) Herod the Great was the king of all Palestine 37–4 B.C. He ruled Judea at the time Jesus was born. (2) Herod Antipas was the son of Herod the Great and the ruler of Galilee 4 B.C.–A.D. 39, during the time of John the Baptist and Jesus. (3) Herod Agrippa I, the grandson of Herod the Great, ruled Palestine A.D. 41–44.

Hezekiah King of Judah during the Assyrian attack on Jerusalem in 701 B.C., known for his loyalty to the LORD.

high priest See "priest."

Holy One A name for the Savior that God had promised to send. See "Savior."

hyssop A bush with bunches of small, white flowers. A bunch of hyssop was used for sprinkling blood and water in religious ceremonies. These ceremonies made people rightly prepared to worship God after having a bad skin disease. In a similar way, Psalm 51.7 mentions using hyssop in making a person rightly prepared to worship God by taking away sin.

incense A material that makes a sweet smell when burned and is used in the worship of God.

Isaac The second of the three great ancestors of the people of Israel. He was the son of Abraham and father of Jacob.

Isaiah A prophet from Jerusalem, who lived during the eighth century B.C. He served as a prophet during the rule of four different kings of Judah, between the years 740–700 B.C.

Israel See Jacob/Israel.

Jacob/Israel The third great ancestor of the people of Israel. He was the son of Isaac. His name was changed to Israel when he struggled with God at the Jabbok River.

Jeduthun One of David's musicians. See the titles of Psalms 39, 62, 77.

Joab The commander of David's army during most of his reign. See the title of Psalm 60.

Joseph The older son of Jacob and Rachel. He was the father of Ephraim and Manasseh, whose descendants formed two of the most important northern tribes.

Judah One of the tribes of Israel. It occupied the hill country between the Dead Sea and the coastal flatlands. The people of this tribe descended from Judah, the fourth son of Jacob and Leah. When the ten northern tribes of Israel broke away following the death of Solomon, only the tribes of Judah and Benjamin were left to form the southern kingdom.

Word List

judges Leaders chosen by the Lord for the people of Israel after the time of Joshua and before the time of the kings.

Kadesh A town in the desert of Paran southwest of the Dead Sea, also known as Kadesh-Barnea. It was near the southern border of Israel and the western border of Edom.

King Lemuel of Massa King of Massa, a country possibly located in northern Arabia. King Lemuel wrote a few of the proverbs. See Proverbs 31.1.

Korah A Levite family of the clan of Kohath whose people formed one of the major groups of temple singers. The Korahites were also known as temple gatekeepers (1 Chronicles 9.19) and temple bakers (1 Chronicles 9.31).

Law and the Prophets The sacred writings of the Jews in Jesus' day (the first two of the three sections of the Old Testament).

Law of Moses and *Law of the Lord* Usually refers to the first five books of the Old Testament, but sometimes to the entire Old Testament.

Leviathan A legendary sea monster representing revolt and evil, also known from Canaanite writings. Psalm 74.14 celebrates its defeat by God.

Levite A member of the tribe of Levi, from which priests were chosen. Men from this tribe who were not priests helped with the work in the temple.

Lord The word "Lord" in capital letters stands for the Hebrew consonants YHWH, the personal names of God. The word "Lord" represents the Hebrew term *Adonai*, the general word for "Lord." By late Old Testament times Jews considered God's personal name too holy to be pronounced. So they said *Adonai*, "Lord," whenever they read the Hebrew consonants YHWH. When the Jewish scribes first translated the Hebrew Scriptures into ancient Greek, they translated the personal name of God as *Kurios*, "Lord." Since then most translations, including the *Contemporary English Version*, have followed the Jewish example and avoided using the personal name of God.

Manasseh One of the most important tribes of northern Israel. It occupied two areas of land. One was east of the Jordan River, from the Jabbok River north to include all of Bashan. The other was on the west side of the Jordan River and went all the way to the Mediterranean Sea. Its northern boundary began a few miles south of Lake Galilee and went as far south as the border with Ephraim. The people of this tribe descended from Manasseh, Joseph's first son.

Messiah A Hebrew word meaning "the Chosen One." See "Christ."

mint A garden plant used for seasoning and medicine.

Moab A country east of the Dead Sea. Its people descended from Moab, the son of Lot, who was Abraham's nephew.

Moses The leader of the people of Israel when God rescued them from Egypt.

Mt. Hermon One of the highest mountains in the Near East, with an elevation of 9,230 feet. Located about 45 miles north of Lake Galilee, its three peaks tower over the upper Jordan River valley. In Hebrew the name means "sacred" or "forbidden."

Mt. Lebanon A mountain range that stretches about 100 miles north and south along the coast of Phoenicia. In Hebrew the name means "white," and it was known for its white peaks and cedar forests.

Mt. Mizar Probably a name for one of the lesser peaks of Mt. Hermon. Possibly a way of referring to the small size of Mt. Zion. In Hebrew the name means "small." See Psalm 42.6.

myrrh A valuable sweet-smelling powder used in perfume.

Naphtali One of the tribes of Israel. Its people descended from Naphtali, the second son of Jacob and Bilhah. The tribe occupied land north and west of Lake Galilee.

Nazarenes A name that was sometimes used for the followers of Jesus, who came from the small town of Nazareth.

Noah When God destroyed the world by a flood, Noah and his family were kept safe in a big boat that God had told him to build.

paradise The place where God's people go when they die, often understood as another name for heaven.

Passover A day each year in the spring when Jews celebrate the time God rescued them from slavery in Egypt.

Pentecost A Jewish festival fifty days

after Passover to celebrate the wheat harvest.

Pharisees A large group of Jews who thought they could best serve God by strictly obeying the laws of the Old Testament as well as their own teachings.

Philistia The fertile strip of land along the Mediterranean coast controlled by the Philistine people. This land began at the Brook of Egypt, below Gaza in the south, and ended at the town of Joppa in the north. Philistia was often at war with Israel.

Phoenicia The territory along the Mediterranean Sea controlled by the cities of Tyre, Sidon, Arvad and Byblos. The coast of modern Lebanon covers about the same area.

pit or **deep pit** The place of punishment for demons and evil spirits.

priest A man who led the worship in the temple and offered sacrifices. Some of the more important priests were called "chief priests," and the most important priest was called the "high priest."

Promised One A title for the Savior that God promised to send. See "Savior."

prophesy See "prophet."

Prophet A person who delivers a message from God to another person or to a group. Often a prophet's message tells what will happen in the future. To speak as a prophet is thus to "prophesy."

Proverb A wise saying that is short and easy to remember.

Psalm A Hebrew poem that could be used as a song or a prayer. Psalms could be prayed by individuals or sung by groups in worship of God. Some of the psalms thank and praise God. Others ask God to take away sins or to give protection, comfort, vengeance or mercy.

rue A garden plant used for seasoning and medicine.

Sabbath The seventh day of the week when Jews worship and do not work, in obedience to the commandment.

Sacrifice/Offering Gifts to God of certain animals, grains, fruits, and sweet-smelling spices. Israelites offered sacrifices to give thanks to God, to beg for forgiveness, to make a payment for a wrong, or to ask for God's blessing. Some sacrifices were completely burned on the altar. In other sacrifices, a portion was offered to the LORD and the remaining portions were eaten by the priests or ordinary people.

Sadducees A small and powerful group of Jews who were closely connected with the high priests and who accepted only the first five books of the Old Testament as their Bible. They also did not believe in life after death.

Samaria A district between Judea and Galilee. The people of Samaria, called Samaritans, worshiped God differently from the Jews and did not get along with them.

Sarah The wife of Abraham and the mother of Isaac. When she was very old, God promised her that she would have a son.

Satan See "devil."

save To rescue people from the power of evil, to give them new life, and to place them under God's care. See "Savior."

Savior The one who rescues people from the power of evil, gives them new life, and places them under God's care. See "save."

Scriptures The sacred writings known as the Old Testament. These were first written in Hebrew and Aramaic, then translated into Greek about two centuries before the birth of Jesus. This Greek translation, known as the Septuagint, was used both by Jews and Christians in the first century.

Sin Turning away from God and disobeying the teachings of God.

Solomon One of King David's sons. After David's death, Solomon took his place as king and became widely known for his wisdom. He wrote many of the proverbs and two of the psalms. See Proverbs 10.1 and 25.1; Psalms 72 and 127.

Son of Man A name often used by Jesus to refer to himself. It is also found in the book of Daniel and refers to the one to whom God has given the power to rule.

Stoics Followers of a man named Zeno, who believed that nature was controlled by the gods and who taught that people should learn self-control.

taxes and **tax collectors** Special fees collected by rulers, usually part of the value of a citizen's crop, property, or income. There were also market taxes to be paid, and customs taxes were collected at ports and border crossings. The wealthy Zacchaeus (Luke 19.1–10) was a tax collector who collected taxes at a border crossing near Jericho. Jews hired by the Roman government to collect taxes from other Jews were hated by their own people.

temple A building used as a place of worship. The Jewish temple was in Jerusalem.

Temple Festival In 165 B.C. the Jewish people recaptured the Jerusalem temple from their enemies and made it fit for worship again. They celebrate this event in December of each year by a festival which they call "dedication" (Hanukkah). In the New Testament it is mentioned only in John 10.22.

Theophilus The name means "someone God loves" and is found only in Luke 1.3 and Acts 1.1. Nothing else is known about him.

Way In the book of Acts the Christian religion is sometimes called "the Way" or "the Way of the Lord" or "God's Way."

Wisdom The cleverness, common sense, and practical skill needed to solve the everyday problems of life. Wisdom is sometimes pictured as a wise woman who invites people to use good judgment. In Proverbs 8, Wisdom is pictured as helping God plan and build the universe.

Zebulun One of the tribes of Israel. It occupied land that was north of Manasseh and that stretched from the eastern end of Mt. Carmel to Mt. Tabor. The people of this tribe descended from Zebulun, the sixth son of Jacob and Leah.

Zeus The chief god of the Greeks.

Zion Another name for Jerusalem. It can also refer to the hill in Jerusalem where the temple was built.

Ziph A town in the hill country of southern Judah where David hid while running away from King Saul. See the title of Psalm 54 and 1 Samuel 23.19; 26.1.

SPECIAL READER'S HELPS

Rejoice!

You have in your hands a message of hope and Good News. It is called the New Testament. It is made up of 27 different books. Each one tells of God's great love and how he has made it possible, through the death and resurrection of Jesus Christ, to unite every person to himself, so that anyone who desires it may discover spiritual guidance and joy.

You are invited to begin reading this Good News today. The section of special helps provided here will help you begin this rewarding journey of discovery.

- *What's in the New Testament* gives you a brief summary of every book in the New Testament along with a handy chart.
- *How to Read the New Testament* provides simple suggestions on how to read the New Testament devotionally and to keep notes on the many lessons you'll learn.
- *Read through the New Testament* is a reading plan that suggests a simple way to read everything the New Testament has to say about Jesus' life, death and resurrection and the spread of the new religion which became known as Christianity.
- *Famous Passages of the New Testament* helps you to quickly locate passages you've heard time and again, but may never have read for yourself.
- *Finding Help in the New Testament* leads you to those passages that can help you when you're facing a difficult problem or special challenge.
- *What the New Testament Says about God's Forgiveness* will lead you to places in the New Testament where you can learn how much God loves each one of us and what he has done to put us right with himself.

So begin your journey of discovery today! Use any one of these special reader's helps to get you started on a daily habit of Scripture reading. And when you finish the New Testament, read the Old Testament, which you will find in any edition of the Bible. Discover for yourself the joy and hope God's Holy Scriptures have to offer.

The Bible

The word "Bible" comes from the Greek word *biblia*, which means "books." So the Bible is really a collection or library of many books. These books are divided into two main parts, the Old Testament and the New Testament.

Old Testament

The Old Testament tells the history of the people of Israel. This history is based on their faith in the God of Israel and on their religious life as the people of God. The authors of these books wrote about what God had done for them as a people and how they were to worship and obey God in return. The following chart shows the different groups of books that make up the Old Testament.

The Law
Genesis, Exodus, Leviticus, Numbers, Deuteronomy

History
Joshua, Judges, Ruth, 1 Samuel, 2 Samuel, 1 Kings, 2 Kings, 1 Chronicles, 2 Chronicles, Ezra, Nehemiah, Esther

Poetry and Wisdom
Job, Psalms, Proverbs, Ecclesiastes, Song of Songs

Major Prophets
Isaiah, Jeremiah, Lamentations, Ezekiel, Daniel

Minor Prophets
Hosea, Joel, Amos, Obadiah, Jonah, Micah, Nahum, Habakkuk, Zephaniah, Haggai, Zechariah, Malachi

Deuterocanonicals/Apocrypha

The books that comprise the Deuterocanonicals/Apocrypha formed part of the ancient Greek translation of the Old Testament known as the Septuagint. They were located at various places among the other books of the Old Testament. They cover the period in between the Old Testament and New Testament and provide significant knowledge of developments during this period.

History
1 Esdras, Esther (Greek), 1 Maccabees, 2 Maccabees

Letters
Baruch, Letter of Jeremiah

Wisdom
Wisdom of Solomon, Sirach

Devotional
Song of the Three Young Men, Prayer of Manasseh

Teaching Stories
Tobit, Judith, Susanna, Bel and the Dragon

Prophecy
2 Esdras

New Testament

The books of the New Testament were written by the followers of Jesus Christ. These followers wanted others to know the Good News about Jesus Christ and the possibility of a "new" life available to them through his death and resurrection. The following chart shows the different groups of books that make up the New Testament. Although scholarly opinion has varied, Paul has traditionally been identified as the author of the letters indicated below.

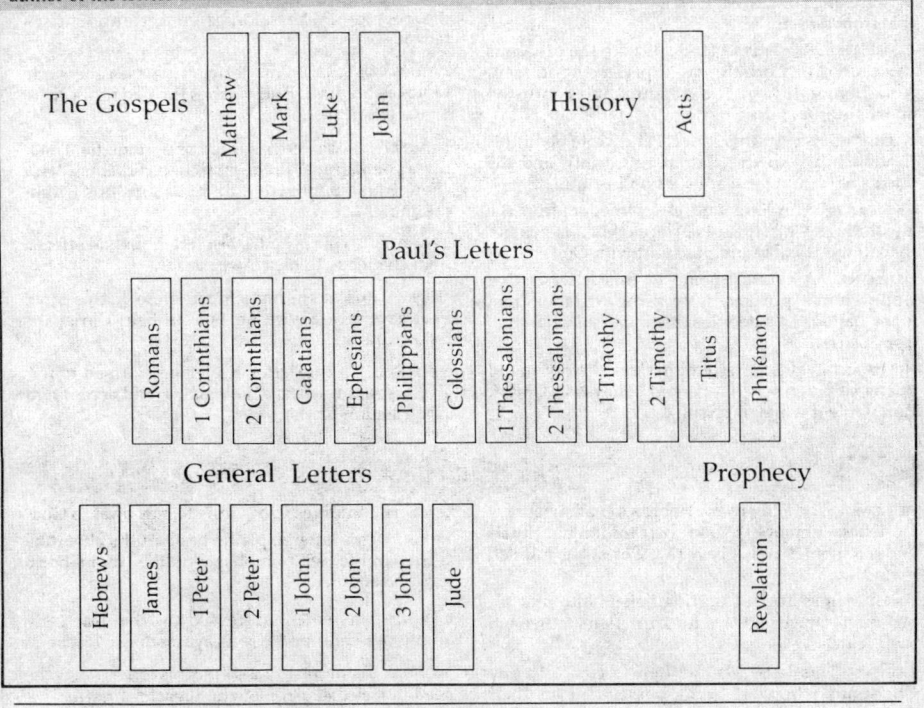

The Gospels: Matthew, Mark, Luke, John

History: Acts

Paul's Letters: Romans, 1 Corinthians, 2 Corinthians, Galatians, Ephesians, Philippians, Colossians, 1 Thessalonians, 2 Thessalonians, 1 Timothy, 2 Timothy, Titus, Philemon

General Letters: Hebrews, James, 1 Peter, 2 Peter, 1 John, 2 John, 3 John, Jude

Prophecy: Revelation

What's in the New Testament

The following are summaries of each book of the New Testament. It will be obvious from how brief the descriptions are that they are not complete. They should, however, serve as a quick and handy guide to the content of the New Testament. The grouping of the books by sections follows the divisions of the books as they are organized in the English Bible.

The Gospels

MATTHEW: This Gospel includes many Old Testament quotations, thus appealing to a Jewish audience and presenting Jesus as the Messiah promised in the Hebrew Scriptures. Matthew told the story of Jesus from birth to resurrection and placed emphasis on his teaching.

MARK: Mark wrote a short, action-packed Gospel. He emphasized Jesus' miracles and his life of suffering. His aim was to deepen the faith and commitment of the believers in the community to which he wrote.

LUKE: In this Gospel, the availability of salvation for all people is emphasized. Luke proclaimed this message by showing Jesus' involvement with people who are poor, needy, and on the fringes of society.

JOHN: The Gospel of John stands apart from the others. John organized his message around seven signs that point to Jesus as the Son of God. His writing style is reflective and filled with striking images.

History

ACTS: When Jesus left his disciples, the Holy Spirit came to abide with them. Written by Luke as the sequel to his Gospel, Acts records key events in the history of the work of the early Christian Church to spread the Gospel throughout the Mediterranean world.

Paul's Letters

ROMANS: In this important letter, Paul wrote to the Romans about life in the Spirit, which is given to believers in Christ through faith. The apostle tells them about God's great kindness and declares that because of Jesus Christ, God accepts us and sets us free from our sins.

1 CORINTHIANS: This letter deals with the problems the church in Corinth was experiencing: dissension, immorality, public worship, and confusion about spiritual gifts.

1 CORINTHIANS: In this letter, Paul wrote about his relationship with the church of Corinth and the effects of certain false apostles on his ministry.

GALATIANS: This letter addresses freedom from the law through Christ. Paul declares that it is by faith that all who believe are put right with God.

EPHESIANS: A central theme to this letter is that God's eternal purpose is to bring together from many nations and peoples the universal Church of Jesus Christ.

PHILIPPIANS: This letter emphasizes the joy found in any situation when a person believes in Christ. Paul wrote it while in prison.

COLOSSIANS: In this letter Paul tells the people of Colossae to make Christ the center of their faith and to put aside their superstitions.

1 THESSALONIANS: In this letter Paul gives advice to the people of Thessalonica concerning Christ's return.

2 THESSALONIANS: This letter discusses the same topics as the first. Paul teaches the people a way to be ready for the Lord.

1 TIMOTHY: This letter served as a guide for Timothy, a young leader in the church. It contains advice about worship, ministry, and relationships within the church.

2 TIMOTHY: This is Paul's last letter. In it he offers a final challenge to his co-worker.

TITUS: Titus was ministering in Crete. In this letter, Paul gave him advice on how to help Christians follow Christ.

PHILEMON: In this letter, Philemon is urged to forgive his runaway slave, Onesimus, and accept him as a friend in Christ.

General Letters

HEBREWS: The letter to the Hebrews challenges new Christians to move beyond their traditional rituals and ceremonies and believe that Christ has fulfilled them all.

JAMES: James advises putting beliefs into practice and offers practical ways for Christians to live out their faith.

1 PETER: This letter was written to comfort early Christians who were being persecuted for their faith.

2 PETER: In this letter Peter warns against false teachers and urges Christians to stay loyal to God.

1 JOHN: This letter explains basic truths about the Christian life, with emphasis on the command to love one another.

2 JOHN: This letter, addressed to "the dear Lady and to her children," warns against false teachers.

3 JOHN: In contrast to 2 John, this letter states the need to welcome people who preach Christ.

JUDE: Jude warns against the influence of evil ones outside the fellowship of believers.

Prophecy

REVELATION: This book was written to encourage persecuted believers and affirm their faith that God will care for them. Using visions and symbols, the writer illustrates the triumph of good over evil and the creation of a new heaven and new earth.

How to look up a New Testament reference.

Every verse in this New Testament is marked by its own *verse number*. To find any one of the passages listed in these reader's helps, you need to find the book, the chapter in the book, and the verse or verses within that chapter. The chapter number immediately follows the name of the book. This is followed by a period (.) which is followed by the number or range of numbers for the verses you seek. For example: 1 Corinthians 12.1-11 is the First Letter of Paul to the Corinthians, chapter twelve, verses one through eleven.

How to Read the New Testament

Set aside time each day to read from your New Testament. Try to make it the same time each day. Be realistic. Commit yourself only to as much time as you honestly feel that you can stick to on an ongoing basis. Before you begin reading ask for God's guidance and blessing. Some people have found that keeping a daily notebook is helpful. Use the following steps to get the most out of your daily Scripture reading:

1. Select a passage of Scripture (perhaps one from the *Read through the New Testament* section that follows). It is probably best not to try to read more than one to three chapters at one sitting.
2. Examine its context:
   a. What kind of book is it drawn from? A biographical book such as one of the Gospel accounts of Jesus' life; a long historical book, such as *The Acts of the Apostles*; a brief letter to a person (*The Letters of Paul to Timothy*) or to a specific church (*The Letters of Paul to the Corinthians*).
   b. What is the overall purpose/intent of this book? (Do not do lengthy research, but feel free to read the opening and closing paragraphs as well as section headings.)
   c. What occurs or is discussed in the passages immediately preceding and following the passage you chose?
3. Read the passage quickly for sense.
4. Identify key words or phrases. Are there words or thoughts that are repeated throughout the passage? Are any cause and effect relationships established? (These are often signaled by words like *if* and *then*, *therefore*, *because*, *since*, and *so*.) Are any comparisons made or similarities pointed out? Are any two people, things or concepts contrasted?
5. Read the passage again and ask yourself what is the intent or purpose of the passage. Try to find out what the author is saying. Be honest; don't just look for what you want to hear. The New Testament has many strong messages that can change lives!
6. What do you learn about God from this passage? What do you learn about human nature? Ask yourself how this message applies to you. Is there anything you need to change in your life in order to be a more faithful child of God or more loving toward your neighbor? Ask for God's help in making this change.
7. Re-read the passage one more time. Is there one verse you would like to commit to memory? Why not write it on an index card and carry it with you throughout the day as a study aid?
8. Thank God for what he has shown you, and ask for his help as you seek to apply this lesson in your life.
9. Share what you have learned with someone else.

Read through the New Testament

The books of the New Testament were written by the followers of Jesus Christ. The reading plan given here will help you to learn more about Jesus' life and ministry and about what his death and resurrection means to his followers. This Good News was so important to Jesus' first followers that they traveled great distances and took great risks to share it with others. They also wrote many letters to encourage one another to hold fast to their faith in Jesus.

The Life of Jesus

The New Testament gives four accounts of Jesus' life. They are called Gospels, which means "good news." They tell of his birth, baptism, ministry of teaching and healing, death and resurrection. Although similar in many ways, these books offer four different looks at the life of Jesus. Choose one of the following reading plans to learn more about Jesus and then go on to read the rest of the New Testament.

Plan A
Read:
- Mark 1-16
- John 1-21
- Luke 1-24
- Matthew 1-28

Plan B
Read:
- The birth of Jesus
  - Matthew 1, 2; Luke 1, 2
- The public ministry of Jesus
  - Matthew 3-20; Mark 1-10; Luke 3.1-19.27; John 1-12
- The last days of Jesus' life
  - Matthew 21-27; Mark 11-15; Luke 19.28-23.56; John 13-19
- The resurrection of Jesus
  - Matthew 28; Mark 16; Luke 24; John 20-21

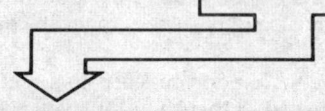

The Early Church

Jesus speaks to his followers and is taken up to heaven
  Acts 1.1-11
The beginning of the Christian movement in Jerusalem
  Acts 1.12-8.3
The spread of the Christian movement into Judea and Samaria
  Acts 8.4-12.25

The Ministry of Paul

Paul's first missionary journey
  Acts 13, 14
An important conference in Jerusalem
  Acts 15.1-35
  Also read what Paul had to say about the issues discussed at this conference: Galatians.

Paul's second missionary journey
Acts 15.36-18.22
- After Acts 16.5 read 1 Timothy and 2 Timothy to learn more about the young man Timothy who was to become an important assistant to Paul.
- After Acts 18.17 read 1 Thessalonians and 2 Thessalonians.

Paul's third missionary journey
Acts 18.23-21.16
- After Acts 19.41 read 1 Corinthians, Philippians and Philemon.
- After Acts 20.6 read 2 Corinthians and Titus.
- After Acts 20.38 read Romans.

Paul's imprisonments in Jerusalem, Caesarea and Rome
Acts 21.17-28.31
- After Acts 28.31 read Ephesians and Colossians.

The Spread of Christianity under Roman Persecution

Read:
Hebrews
James
1 Peter
2 Peter
Jude
1 John
2 John
3 John
Revelation

How to look up a New Testament reference.

Every verse in this New Testament is marked by its own *verse number*. To find any one of the passages listed in these reader's helps, you need to find the book, the chapter in the book, and the verse or verses within that chapter. The chapter number immediately follows the name of the book. This is followed by a period (.) which is followed by the number or range of numbers for the verses you seek. For example: 1 Corinthians 12.1-11 is the First Letter of Paul to the Corinthians, chapter twelve, verses one through eleven.

Famous Passages from the New Testament

THE LIFE OF JESUS

The Birth of Jesus
Matthew 1.18-2.15; Luke 2.1-20
Jesus Is Named and Presented
in the Temple
Luke 2.21-40
The Young Jesus
Luke 2.41-52
The Baptism of Jesus
Matthew 3; Mark 1.1-11; Luke 3.21, 22
The Temptation of Jesus
Matthew 4.1-11; Mark 1.12, 13;
Luke 4.1-13
Jesus Calls His First Disciples
Matthew 4.18-22; Mark 1.16-20;
Luke 5.1-11
Jesus Chooses Twelve Apostles
Matthew 10.1-4; Mark 3.13-19;
Luke 6.12-16
The Transfiguration of Jesus
Matthew 17.1-13; Mark 9.2-13

JESUS' DEATH AND RESURRECTION

Jesus' Entry into Jerusalem
Matthew 21.1-11; Mark 11.1-11;
Luke 19.29-44; John 12.12-19
The Last Supper of Jesus
Matthew 26.17-35; Mark 14.12-26;
Luke 22.1-38
Jesus Prays in Gethsemane
Matthew 26.36-46; Mark 14.32-42;
Luke 22.39-46
Jesus' Trial and Crucifixion
Matthew 26.47-27.66; Mark 14.43-15.47;
Luke 22.47-23.56; John 18; 19
The Resurrection of Jesus
Matthew 28.1-10; Mark 16;
Luke 24.1-12; John 20
The Great Commission
Matthew 28.16-20
The Ascension of Jesus
Luke 24.50-53; Acts 1.1-12

MIRACLES AND HEALINGS OF JESUS

Jesus Turns Water into Wine
John 2.1-11
Jesus Feeds Many People
Matthew 14.13-21; Mark 6.30-44;
Luke 9.10-17; John 6.1-15;
Matthew 15.32-39; Mark 8.1-10
Jesus Calms a Storm
Matthew 8.23-27; Mark 4.35-41;
Luke 8.22-25
The Great Catch of Fish
Luke 5.1-11
Jesus Walks on Water
Matthew 14.22-33; Mark 6.45-52;
John 6.16-21
Jesus Heals People with
Skin Diseases
Matthew 8.1-4; Mark 1.40-45;
Luke 5.12-16; Luke 17.11-19
Jesus Casts Out Demons
Matthew 8.28-34; Mark 5.1-20;
Luke 8.26-39; Matthew 12.22-37;
Mark 3.20-30; Luke 11.14-23;
Matthew 17.14-21; Mark 9.14-29;
Luke 9.37-43; Mark 1.21-28;
Luke 4.31-37
Jesus Heals the Blind
Matthew 9.27-31; Matthew 20.29-34;
Mark 10.46-52; Luke 18.35-43
Jesus Heals a Deaf Man
Mark 7.31-37
Jesus Heals the Paralyzed and Crippled
Matthew 12.9-14; Mark 3.1-6;
Luke 6.6-11; John 5.1-8;
Luke 14.1-6; Matthew 9.1-8;
Mark 2.1-12; Luke 5.17-26
Jesus Heals Many Women
Matthew 9.18-26; Mark 5.21-43;
Luke 8.1-3; Luke 8.40-56;
Luke 13.10-17; Matthew 15.21-28;
Mark 7.24-30
Jesus Heals the Centurion's Servant
Matthew 8.5-13; Luke 7.1-10
Jesus Heals Peter's Mother-in-law
Matthew 8.14, 15; Mark 1.29-31;
Luke 4.38, 39
Jesus Heals an Official's Son
John 4.46-54
Jesus Revives an Official's Daughter
Matthew 9.18,19,23-26;
Mark 5.21-24,35-42; Luke 8.40-42,49-56
Jesus Raises the Dead
Luke 7.11-17; John 11.1-44

THE TEACHINGS AND PARABLES OF JESUS

The Sermon on the Mount
Matthew 5-7; Luke 6.20-49
The Beatitudes
Matthew 5.3-11; Luke 6.20-26
The Great Commandment
Matthew 22.37-39; Mark 12.29-31; Luke 10.27
The Golden Rule
Matthew 7.12; Luke 6.31
The Grain of Mustard Seed
Matthew 13.31, 32; Mark 4.30-32; Luke 13.18, 19
The Parable of the Sower
Matthew 13.1-23; Mark 4.1-20; Luke 8.4-15
The Parable of the Growing Seed
Mark 4.26-29
Some Parables About the Kingdom of Heaven
Matthew 13.24-52
The Parable of the Unforgiving Servant
Matthew 18.23-35
The Parable of the Workers in the Vineyard
Matthew 20.1-16
The Parable of the Tenants in the Vineyard
Matthew 21.33-46; Mark 12.1-11; Luke 20.9-18
The Parable of the Wedding Feast
Matthew 22.1-14; Luke 14.15-24
The Parable of the Ten Young Women (Virgins)
Matthew 25.1-13
The Parable of the Three Servants and Their Coins
Matthew 25.14-30; Luke 19.11-27
The Parable of the Sheep and the Goats
Matthew 25.31-46

The Parable of the Good Samaritan
Luke 10.25-37
The Parable of the Shepherd
John 10.1-21
The Parable of the Rich Fool
Luke 12.16-21
The Parable of the Watchful Servants
Luke 12.35-48
The Parable of the Barren Fig Tree
Luke 13.6-9
The Parable of the Lost Sheep
Matthew 18.12-14; Luke 15.3-7
The Parable of the Lost Coin
Luke 15.8-10
The Parable of the Lost Son
Luke 15.11-32
The Parable of the Shrewd Manager
Luke 16.1-13
The Rich Man and Lazarus
Luke 16.19-31
The Parable of the Widow and the Judge
Luke 18.1-8
The Parable of the Pharisee and the Tax Collector
Luke 18.9-14

OTHER NEW TESTAMENT STORIES

The Birth of John the Baptist
Luke 1.57-66
John the Baptist Is Executed
Matthew 14.1-12; Mark 6.14-29
Peter Receives the Keys of the Kingdom
Matthew 16.13-20
The Holy Spirit Comes on Pentecost
Acts 2
Stephen, the First Martyr
Acts 6.5-15; 7.54-60
Philip Baptizes the Ethiopian Official
Acts 8.26-39
The Conversion of Paul
Acts 9.1-31
Peter and Cornelius
Acts 10
Peter in Prison
Acts 12.1-19
The Baptism of Lydia
Acts 16.11-15
Paul in Prison
Acts 16.16-40
The Riot at Ephesus
Acts 19.23-41
Paul's Voyage to Rome
Acts 27; 28

What is a parable?

Parables are stories that use typical, everyday situations in order to teach important truths. Jesus used many parables to teach his followers about the Kingdom of God.

NEW TESTAMENT PRAYERS

The Lord's Prayer
   Matthew 6.9-13
Jesus' Prayer in Gethsemane
   Matthew 26.36-44
Jesus' Prayer for His Disciples
   John 17
The Disciples' Prayer
   Acts 4.24-31
Paul's Prayer for Believers
   Ephesians 3.14-21

SPECIAL BLESSINGS FROM THE NEW TESTAMENT

Invocations and Openings
   1 Corinthians 1.3; 1 Timothy 1.2;
   2 John 3; Revelation 1.4-6
Dismissals and Closings
   Romans 15.5,6,13; Romans 16.25-27;
   2 Corinthians 13.13; Ephesians 6.23,24;
   Philippians 4.7; Hebrews 13.20,21;
   Jude 24,25

How to look up a New Testament reference.

Every verse in this New Testament is marked by its own *verse number*. To find any one of the passages listed in these reader's helps, you need to find the book, the chapter in the book, and the verse or verses within that chapter. The chapter number immediately follows the name of the book. This is followed by a period (.) which is followed by the number or range of numbers for the verses you seek. For example: 1 Corinthians 12.1-11 is the First Letter of Paul to the Corinthians, chapter twelve, verses one through eleven.

Finding Help in the New Testament

Help in Special Circumstances

Being a friend
Luke 10.25-37; John 15.11-17; Romans 16.1-2

Being a leader
1 Timothy 3.1-7; 2 Timothy 2.14-26; Titus 1.5-9

Caring for the aged and widowed
1 Timothy 5.3-8

Celebrating the birth/adoption of a child
Luke 18.15-17; John 16.16-22

Celebrating a graduation
Galatians 5.16-26; Philippians 4.4-9

Celebrating a marriage
Ephesians 5.21-33; Colossians 2.6-7

Celebrating a wedding anniversary
1 Corinthians 13

Controlling your temper
Galatians 5.16-26

Controlling your tongue
2 Thessalonians 2.16-17; James 3.1-12

Discovering God's will
Matthew 5.14-16; Luke 9.21-27; Romans 13.8-14; 2 Peter 1.3-9; 1 John 4.7-21

Encountering a cult
Matthew 7.15-20; 2 Peter 2; 1 John 4.1-6; Jude

Encountering peer pressure
Romans 12.1-2; Galatians 6.1-5; Ephesians 5.1-20

Entering college
Romans 8.1-17; 1 Corinthians 1.18-31

Entering military service
Ephesians 6.10-20; 2 Timothy 2.1-13

Experiencing the death of a loved one
John 11.25-27; John 14.1-7; Romans 8.31-39; Romans 14.7-9; 1 Thessalonians 4.13-18

Experiencing illness
Mark 1.29-34; Mark 6.53-56; James 5.14-16

Experiencing suffering and persecution
Matthew 5.3-12; John 15.18-16.4; Romans 8.18-30; 2 Corinthians 4.1-15; Hebrews 12.1-11; 1 Peter 4.12-19

Facing a difficult decision
Colossians 3.12-17

Facing a divorce
Matthew 19.1-9; Philippians 3.1-11

Facing homelessness
Luke 9.57-62; Revelation 21.1-4

Facing imprisonment
Matthew 25.31-46; Luke 4.16-21

Facing life alone
1 Corinthians 7.25-38; 1 Corinthians 12.1-31

Facing a natural disaster
Romans 8.31-39; 1 Peter 1.3-12

Facing a trial or lawsuit
Matthew 5.25-26; Luke 18.1-8

Losing your job
Luke 16.1-13; Philippians 4.10-13

Losing your property and possessions
Romans 8.18-39

Managing your time
Mark 13.32-37; Luke 21.34-36; 1 Timothy 4.11-16; Titus 3.8-14

Moving into a new home
John 14.1-7; Ephesians 3.14-21; Revelation 3.20, 21

Overcoming addiction
2 Corinthians 5.16-21; Ephesians 4.22-24

Overcoming a grudge
Matthew 5.23-26; Luke 6.27-36; Ephesians 4.25-32

Overcoming prejudice
Matthew 7.1-5; Acts 10.34-36; Galatians 3.26-29; Ephesians 2.11-22; Colossians 3.5-11; James 2.1-13

Overcoming pride
Mark 9.33-37; Luke 14.7-11; Luke 18.9-14; Luke 22.24-27; Romans 12.14-16; 1 Corinthians 1.18-31; 2 Corinthians 12.1-10

Overcoming procrastination
Matthew 22.1-14; Matthew 25.1-13; 2 Corinthians 6.1-2

Raising children
Ephesians 6.4; Colossians 3.21

Respecting civil authorities
Mark 12.13-17; Romans 13.1-7; Titus 3.1-2; 1 Peter 2.13-17

Respecting parents
Ephesians 6.1-3; Colossians 3.20

Retiring from your job
Matthew 25.31-46; Romans 12.1-2; Philippians 3.12-21; 2 Peter 1.2

Seeking forgiveness
Matthew 6.14-15; Luke 15; Philemon; Hebrews 4.14-16; 1 John 1.5-10

Seeking God's help
Matthew 7.7-12

Seeking salvation
John 3.1-21; Romans 1.16-17; Romans 3.21-31; Romans 5.1-11; Romans 10.5-13; Ephesians 1.3-14; Ephesians 2.1-10

Seeking strength
Ephesians 6.10-20; 2 Thessalonians 2.16-17

Seeking truth
John 8.31-47; John 14.6-14; John 16.4b-15;
1 Timothy 2.1-7

Sharing your gifts
Luke 21.1-4; Acts 2.43-47; Acts 4.32-37;
Romans 12.9-13; 1 Corinthians 16.1-4;
2 Corinthians 8.1-15; 2 Corinthians 9.6-15

Starting a new job
Romans 12.3-11; 1 Thessalonians 5.12-18;
2 Thessalonians 3.6-13; 1 Peter 4.7-11

Understanding your relationship with God
John 15.1-17; Romans 5.1-11; Romans 8.1-17

Understanding your relationship with others
Matthew 18.15-17; Matthew 18.21-35;
Romans 14.13-23; Romans 15.1-16;
Galatians 6.1-10; Colossians 3.12-17;
1 John 4.7-12

Worrying about the future
1 Peter 1.3-5; Revelation 21.1-8

Worrying about money
Matthew 6.24-34; Luke 12.13-21;
1 Timothy 6.6-10

Experiencing Troublesome Feelings

Afraid?
Mark 4.35-41; Hebrews 13.5-6; 1 John 4.13-18

Afraid of death?
John 6.35-40; Romans 8.18-39;
1 Corinthians 15.35-57; 2 Corinthians 5.1-10;
2 Timothy 1.8-10

Angry?
Matthew 5.21-24; Romans 12.17-21;
Ephesians 4.26-32; James 1.19-21

Anxious? Worried?
Matthew 6.24-34; Matthew 10.26-31;
1 Peter 1.3-5; 1 Peter 5.7

Depressed?
John 3.14-17; Ephesians 3.14-21

Discouraged?
Romans 15.13; 2 Corinthians 4.16-18;
Philippians 4.10-13; Colossians 1.9-14;
Hebrews 6.9-12

Doubting your faith in God?
Matthew 7.7-12; Luke 17.5-6; John 20.24-31;
Romans 4.13-25; Hebrews 11; 1 John 5.13-15

Frustrated?
Matthew 7.13-14

Impatient?
Hebrews 6.13-20; James 5.7-11

Insecure? Lacking confidence?
Philippians 4.10-20; 1 John 3.19-24

Jealous?
James 3.13-18

Lonely?
John 14.15-31a

Overwhelmed? Experiencing stress?
Matthew 11.25-30; John 4.1-30;
2 Corinthians 6.3-10; Revelation 22.17

Rejected?
Matthew 9.9-13; Luke 4.16-30; John 15.18-16.4;
Ephesians 1.3-14; 1 Peter 2.1-10

Tempted?
Luke 4.1-13; Hebrews 2.11-18;
Hebrews 4.14-16; James 1.12-18

Tempted by sex?
1 Corinthians 6.12-20; Galatians 5.16-26

Tired? Weary?
Matthew 11.25-30; 2 Thessalonians 3.16;
Hebrews 4.1-11

Feeling useless? Inferior?
Galatians 1.11-24; Ephesians 4.1-16;
1 Peter 2.4-10

Vengeful?
Matthew 5.38-42; Romans 12.17-21

How to look up a New Testament reference.

Every verse in this New Testament is marked by its own *verse number*. To find any one of the passages listed in these reader's helps, you need to find the book, the chapter in the book, and the verse or verses within that chapter. The chapter number immediately follows the name of the book. This is followed by a period (.) which is followed by the number or range of numbers for the verses you seek. For example: 1 Corinthians 12.1-11 is the First Letter of Paul to the Corinthians, chapter twelve, verses one through eleven.

What the New Testament Says about God's Forgiveness

Every person is separated from God because of sin.
    Romans 3.9-20
    Romans 5.12-21
    Romans 7.14-25

God has always sought to form a close relationship with people.
    Ephesians 1.3-14
    1 Peter 1.1-10
    1 John 3.1-10

God has reached out to people in a personal way by sending Jesus Christ.
    Colossians 1.15-23
    Romans 5.1-11
    1 Peter 2.10-25
    John 3.1-21
    2 Timothy 1.3-10
    Ephesians 2.1-10

God's forgiveness through Jesus Christ is available to every person.
    1 John 1.5-10
    Romans 10.5-13
    Romans 8.31-39
    Romans 3.21-26

New life in Christ calls a person to live in a Christ-like way.
    Romans 6.1-14
    Matthew 20.20-28
    Ephesians 4.17-32
    Galatians 5.16-26
    1 John 4.7-21
    Romans 12.1-21

MAPS

THE WORLD OF THE NEW TESTAMENT

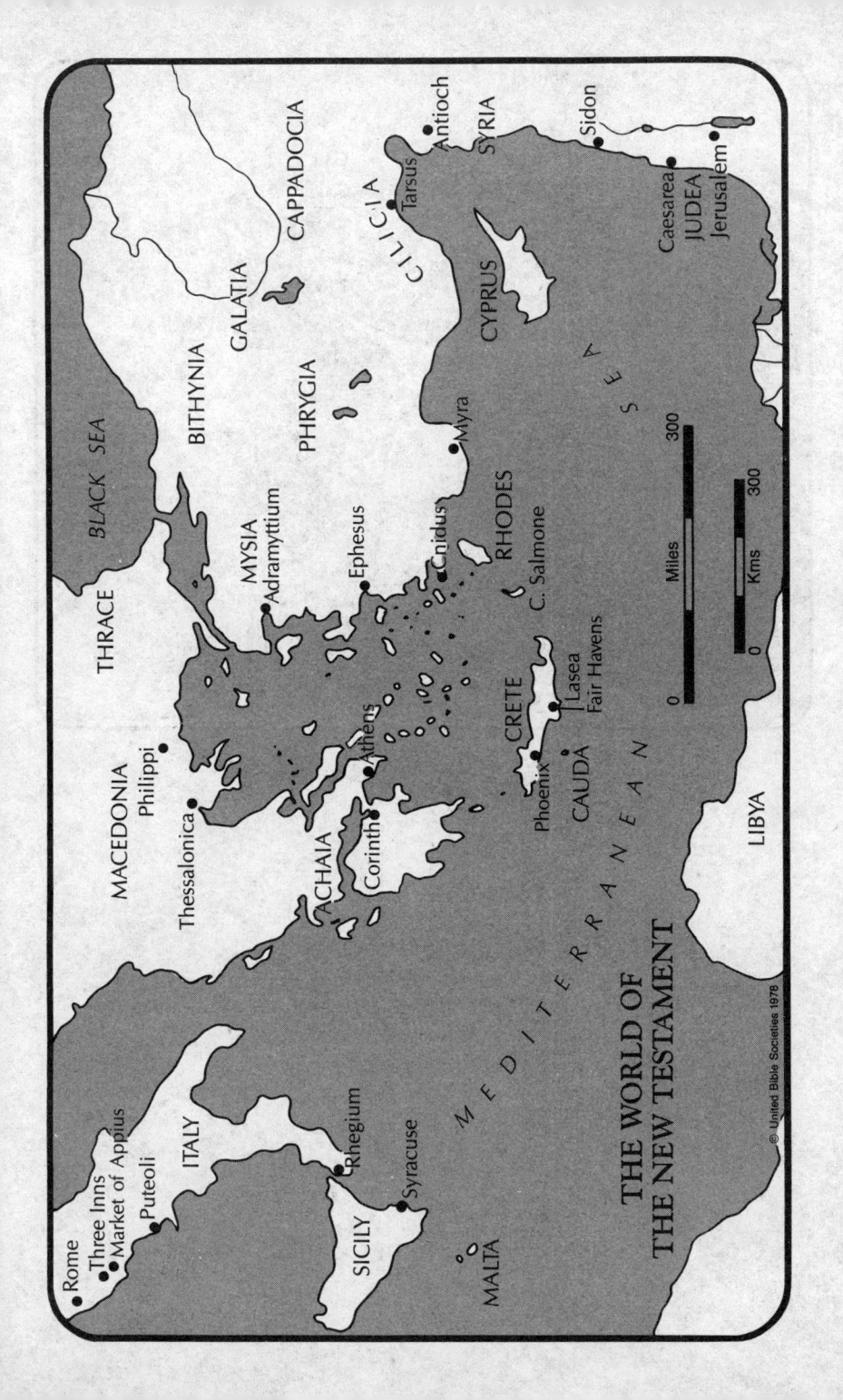

PALESTINE AND SYRIA

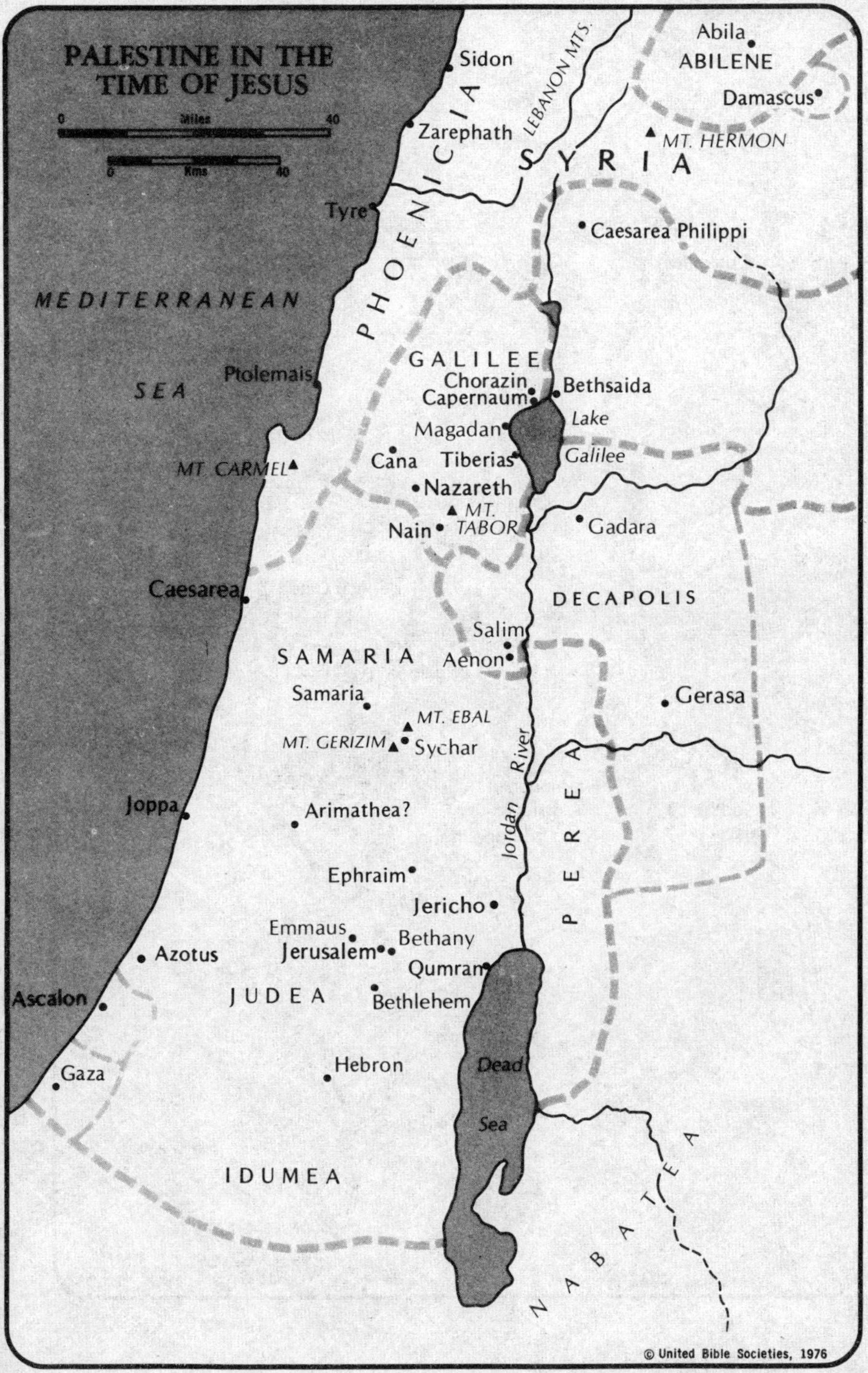
PALESTINE IN THE TIME OF JESUS
0
Miles
40
0
Kms
40
MEDITERRANEAN
SEA
PHOENICIA
LEBANON MTS.
SYRIA
ABILENE
Abila
Damascus
MT. HERMON
Sidon
Zarephath
Tyre
Caesarea Philippi
GALILEE
Ptolemais
Chorazin
Capernaum
Bethsaida
Lake
Galilee
Magadan
Cana
Tiberias
MT. CARMEL
Nazareth
MT. TABOR
Nain
Gadara
Caesarea
DECAPOLIS
Salim
Aenon
SAMARIA
Samaria
MT. EBAL
MT. GERIZIM
Sychar
Gerasa
Jordan River
PEREA
Joppa
Arimathea?
Ephraim
Jericho
Emmaus
Bethany
Jerusalem
Azotus
Qumran
Ascalon
JUDEA
Bethlehem
Hebron
Gaza
Dead Sea
IDUMEA
NABATEA

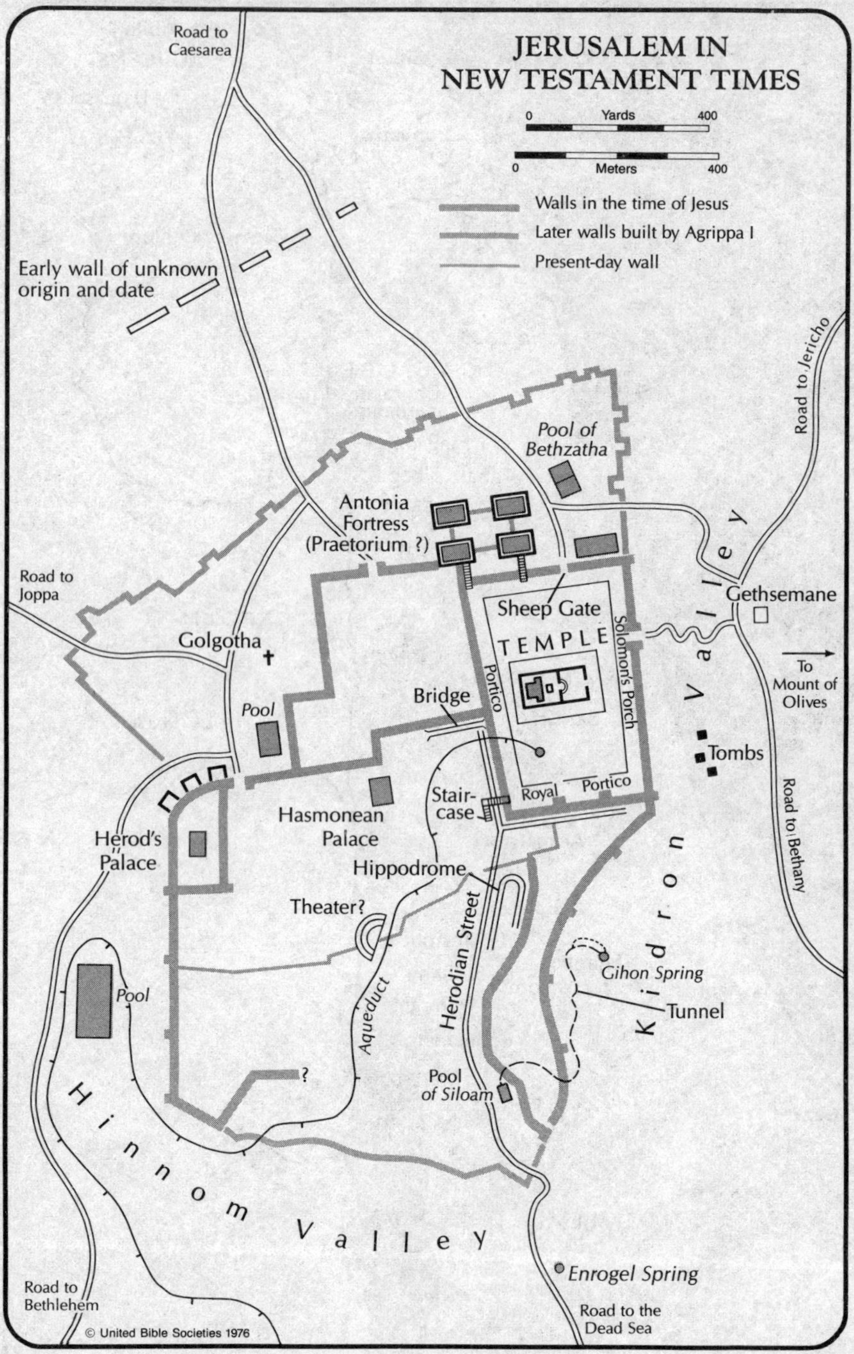
JERUSALEM IN NEW TESTAMENT TIMES
0 Yards 400
0 Meters 400
Walls in the time of Jesus
Later walls built by Agrippa I
Present-day wall
Road to Caesarea
Early wall of unknown origin and date
Road to Jericho
Pool of Bethzatha
Antonia Fortress (Praetorium ?)
Road to Joppa
Sheep Gate
Gethsemane
TEMPLE
Solomon's Porch
Portico
Golgotha
To Mount of Olives
Bridge
Pool
Tombs
Stair-case
Royal Portico
Hasmonean Palace
Herod's Palace
Hippodrome
Road to Bethany
Kidron Valley
Theater?
Herodian Street
Gihon Spring
Pool
Aqueduct
Tunnel
?
Pool of Siloam
Hinnom Valley
Enrogel Spring
Road to Bethlehem
Road to the Dead Sea
© United Bible Societies 1976

NOTES

NOTES

NOTES

NOTES

PROGRAM SYLLABUS AND RESOURCES

STAND IN THE GAP

On the Mall
October 4, 1997

*Let my words and my thoughts
be pleasing to you, LORD,
    because you are my mighty rock and my protector.*

Psalm 19.14

PREPARATION THOUGHTS FOR STAND IN THE GAP

Four principles for personal revival that Evan Roberts used to prepare for the Welsh revival:

1. Confess every known sin.
   (I know I am seeking revival when I stop confessing the sins of others and confess my own instead.)
2. Put aside every doubtful habit.
3. Obey the Holy Spirit promptly.
4. Confess Jesus Christ publicly.

The seven indicators for spiritual awakening from Charles Finney:

1. When the sovereignty of God indicates that revival is near.
2. When wickedness grieves and humbles Christians.
3. When there is a spirit of prayer for revival.
4. When the attention of ministers is directed toward revival and spiritual awakening.
5. When Christians confess their sins to one another.
6. When Christians are willing to make sacrifices necessary to carry out the new movements of God's Spirit.
7. When the ministers and laity are willing for God to promote spiritual awakening by whatever instrument he pleases.

If my people, which are called by my name, shall humble themselves, and pray, and seek my face, and turn from their wicked ways; then will I hear from heaven, and will forgive their sin, and will heal their land.

2 Chronicles 7.14 KJV

And I sought for a man among them, that should make up the hedge, and stand in the gap before me for the land, that I should not destroy it; but I found none.

Ezekiel 22.30 KJV

PROGRAM OVERVIEW

This gathering is about God. The program of the Sacred Assembly is designed to bring us, his men, before almighty God.

We will be led in worship and prayer, and we will be challenged from the Word of God by various people and groups, some in person, and others by video. Our desire is that God will direct the activities of this day as he chooses.

Our hope and prayer is that none of us will leave unchanged. The goal is that we would each become agents of revival, renewed to bless and serve the church, and empowered to bring hope to our land.

SECTION I   AN EXTRAORDINARY GOD

Americans in the United States are caught up with God—often several gods. In our view of an extraordinary God, we will re-focus on the God of creation, the God of the Bible, and the God of history.

Thoughts you may want to note:

_____

_____

_____

_____

_____

_____

_____

_____

_____

_____

SECTION II   AN EXTRAORDINARY RESPONSE

When the prophet Isaiah saw God accurately, his response was expressed, "I'm doomed! Everything I say is sinful, and so are the words of everyone around me. Yet I have seen the King, the Lord All-Powerful." (Isaiah 6.5)

As Isaiah, we must see ourselves in comparison to the Lord; when we do so our sin becomes evident. We have a need to deal with our own sin personally. Together, we have a need to deal with sin against others, against each other, and against God.

Notes of issues I need to process with God:

_____

_____

_____

_____

_____

SECTION III   AN EXTRAORDINARY HOPE

When men are cleansed they can be usable to God. All of us desire significance. Our hope is in God. Our future is his. The hopes and aspirations of us personally and together in our nations find fulfillment and hope in the extraordinary God. He alone is the hope for the church. His spirit in each of us shares the hope with the non-believing world.

What is God impressing on my mind?

_____

_____

_____

_____

_____

Declare a holy fast;
   call a sacred assembly.
Summon the elders
   and all who live in the land
to the house of the LORD your God,
   and cry out to the LORD.

Joel 1.14 NIV

"Rend your heart
   and not your garments.
Return to the LORD your God,
   for he is gracious and compassionate,
slow to anger and abounding in love,
   and he relents from sending calamity.
Who knows? He may turn and have pity
   and leave behind a blessing—
grain offerings and drink offerings
   for the LORD your God.
Blow the trumpet in Zion,
   declare a holy fast,
   call a sacred assembly.
Gather the people,
   consecrate the assembly;
bring together the elders,
   gather the children,
   those nursing at the breast.
Let the bridegroom leave his room
   and the bride her chamber.
Let the priests, who minister before the LORD,
   weep between the temple porch and the altar.
Let them say, "Spare your people, O LORD.
   Do not make your inheritance an object of scorn,
   a byword among the nations.
Why should they say among the peoples,
   'Where is their God?'"

Joel 2.13-17 NIV

PRAYER OF CONFESSION

PUBLIC PRAYER OF CONFESSION:
PRAY TOGETHER.

God our father, we kneel before you guilty of sin. / As a group, we have failed to reflect your glory / to those in our families and to others around us. / We have been preoccupied with our own concerns. / We have ignored or even resented the needs of others, / those outside of our own people or church groups. / As for your world with all its opportunity to be reached and blessed, we have "bailed out" on your commands. / Lord, it is dismal inside our hearts except for your promise / to forgive us if we will confess and repent of our sin. / We are not very good at owning up to sin. / For so long we have practiced shifting the blame or denying reality. / Today we stop! / One by one, we acknowledge our sins before you. / Each one of us has his own list of offenses before a holy God. / We do not compare ourselves by our neighbor's standard, / but by your standard. You said, "be holy as I am holy." We invite your conviction in each area of our life, / not only will we address our sin, / but we pledge to seek forgiveness and reconciliation with those we have sinned against. Amen.

PERSONAL ISSUES OF LIFE:
PRAY PRIVATELY.

Express your own prayer of confession and repentance of sins. Wait before the Lord in silence. Make sure you are totally honest and open; God already knows your sins. Include each topic, plus any others you need.

- My personal integrity, my speech, my behavior, my promise keeping.
- My morality, sexual behavior, lust, pornography, victimization.
- My loyalty to God, to worship, to my local church, to my pastor.
- My outreach to others, in evangelism, in sharing resources to minister, to break down walls of offense and sin, to restore and be restored to others.

ASSURANCE OF FORGIVENESS:
PRAY TOGETHER.

Lord, thank you for hearing our prayers./ Thank you for forgiving all of our sin. Help us to accept your forgiveness/ and allow us to be free of guilt and shame./ Lord, let our lives each day be lives of confession, openness, and repentance so that you may direct and control us. In the name of Jesus, Amen.

God's Love Never Fails

Praise the LORD! He is good.
  God's love never fails.
Praise the God of all gods.
  God's love never fails.
Praise the Lord of lords.
  God's love never fails.

Only God works great miracles.
  God's love never fails.
With wisdom he made the sky.
  God's love never fails.
*The Lord stretched the earth
over the ocean.*
  God's love never fails.
*He made the bright lights
in the sky.*
  God's love never fails.
He lets the sun rule each day.
  God's love never fails.
*He lets the moon and the stars
rule each night.*
  God's love never fails.

*God struck down the first-born
in every Egyptian family.*
  God's love never fails.
He rescued Israel from Egypt.
  God's love never fails.
*God used his great strength
and his powerful arm.*
  God's love never fails.
He split the Red Sea apart.
  God's love never fails.

The Lord brought Israel safely
through the sea.
> God's love never fails.

He destroyed the Egyptian king
and his army there.
> God's love never fails.

The Lord led his people
through the desert.
> God's love never fails.

Our God defeated mighty kings.
> God's love never fails.

And he killed famous kings.
> God's love never fails.

One of them was Sihon,
king of the Amorites.
> God's love never fails.

Another was King Og of Bashan.
> God's love never fails.

God took away their land.
> God's love never fails.

He gave their land to Israel,
the people who serve him.
> God's love never fails.

God saw the trouble we were in.
> God's love never fails.

He rescued us from our enemies.
> God's love never fails.

He gives food to all who live.
> God's love never fails.

Praise God in heaven!
> God's love never fails.

Psalm 136

PRAY FOR THE MEN

... KEEP ON PRAYING AND NEVER GIVE UP. LUKE 18.1

The goal of Promise Keepers prayer department is two-fold:

1) To increase prayer for all aspects of the Christian men's movement and
2) To encourage men to pray more effectively, personally with other men, with their wives and families, and in their churches.

These goals hold a common basis. We men and those who pray for us need to better understand our needs and temptations so that our praying is strong and on target. We need to sense God's heart for what he wants to accomplish in and through the Christian men in our country.

The following are specific requests which we want to encourage you to pray for the men in your church. The more specific requests are, the more powerful and focused the praying will be. Please be sure that your prayer is without judgment. God is the change agent!

PRAYER ISSUES TO PRAY FOR MEN SPECIFICALLY

- Submission to the Spirit
- Conviction of Personal Sin
- Hunger for the Word
- Clarity in understanding the Bible
- Obedience to the Word
- Joy in the Lord
- Men committed to children
- Nurture of children by fathers
- Oneness among believers
- Purity of thought life
- Purity of speech and action
- Freedom from unwholesome habits
- Building relationships with other men
- A spirit of reconciliation
- Honor to spiritual leaders
- Blessing and cooperation to pastors
- Salvation of non-Christian men
- Understand and fulfill his role
- Men's love for their wives
- Freedom to express affirmation
- Christlike emotional expressions
- Moral courage and integrity
- A humble spirit
- More focus in prayer
- Openness to God

PRAYER ISSUES FOR ALL CHRISTIANS TO PRAY FOR THE HEALTH OF THE CHURCH

1. For unreserved worship and adoration of the Lord.
2. For a loving servant spirit of humility among Christians in obedience to the Lord
3. For an openness to conviction of sin by the Spirit of God.
4. For genuine repentance and godly sorrow for sin.
5. For fresh power and blessing on all leadership.
6. For God to move in revival and spiritual awakening.
7. For reconciliation, affirmation and cooperation among Christians of various denominations and ethnic groups.

STAND IN THE GAP: WHAT HAPPENS AFTER THIS HISTORIC EVENT?

Events such as Stand in the Gap act as a catalyst in our lives to move us to greater commitments, more clearly defined vision and a greater understanding of our need for each other. Promise Keepers believes that you will best live out these new commitments in the context of your local church. If you connect with or help create a vibrant men's ministry in your church, you are better equipped to keep promises that last a lifetime.

When Promise Keepers was formed in 1991, the leadership sensed that men across the country had abdicated their responsibilities to their families and in the church. It is PK's desire to serve the local church by helping them to disciple men through vibrant men's ministries to become godly influences in their world.

PK wants to come alongside the churches that desire support in establishing or maintaining their men's ministry in the following ways:

- To implement a critical follow-up plan after catalytic events;
- To pursue relationships with Christian denominational leaders to help build men's ministries in their member churches;
- To pursue relationships with cultural ministry leaders. PK desires to come alongside many churches which are connected by their common cultures and/or language and recruit trainers to build men's ministries within these churches;
- To pursue relationships with members of city-wide networks. From coast to coast, clergy from different denominations are organizing networks to pray for the salvation of those in their city. Promise Keepers wants to become involved in these networks to assist pastors in impacting the men in their churches.

In addition, PK will provide men's ministry resources, seminars and ongoing rallies for clergy and men's ministry leaders. In particular, we want to build a relationship with the local church through the Key Man and Ambassador network. A Key Man is a clergy-appointed layman, trained in men's ministry, who works with his pastor to implement a men's ministry strategy for his church. An Ambassador is a trained volunteer who works with 5-10 churches in an area to provide support for the pastors and Key Men of those churches as they seek to establish and strengthen their men's ministries.

There is no doubt that God is doing a new work in men today. As he continues to draw men to him, let us do all that we can to prepare his bride, the church, for Christ's return.

For more information on Promise Keepers field ministry, call 1-800-888-7595.

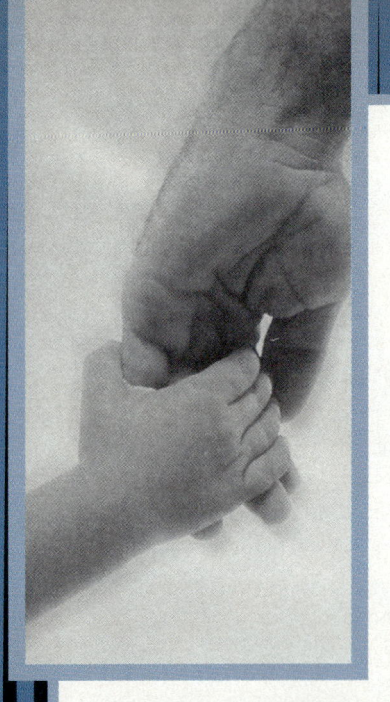

MAN TO MAN ABOUT BEING A SON OF GOD

A man's relationship with his father is basic. The benefit of a strong, affirming bond with "Dad" is powerful.

On the other hand, the pain of a lost or nonexistent relationship with a father can last a lifetime. Insecurity and crippled relationships with others are often traced back to what wasn't gained from a loving, accepting father.

GOD LOVES HIS SONS

God's love is strong, fatherly and complete. Men from all over the country are coming to understand this relationship for the very first time.

Many of us, some for years, have been trying to gain God's approval by performance—doing good things. But it is impossible to live like God's sons before we're in a relationship with him. A wall of separation has come between God and man. Instead of a relationship, we find a barrier. But there is good news!

RECONCILIATION IS THROUGH CHRIST

Do you need to be reconciled? The wall that separated us from our Father God has been broken down. Reconciliation is now possible. If you are not in a family relationship with God as a son to his Father, this is your primary need.

Here are some questions you may have:

If God made me, why would I need to be reconciled?

What happened to the original relationship?

If I choose to stay the way I am, what are the consequences?

The following pages will answer these and other questions. This invitation is for you, whether your background is religious or nonreligious. If you are distanced from God and his acceptance, keep reading to learn more about the relationship that's available.

WHAT WE LOST! A RELATIONSHIP

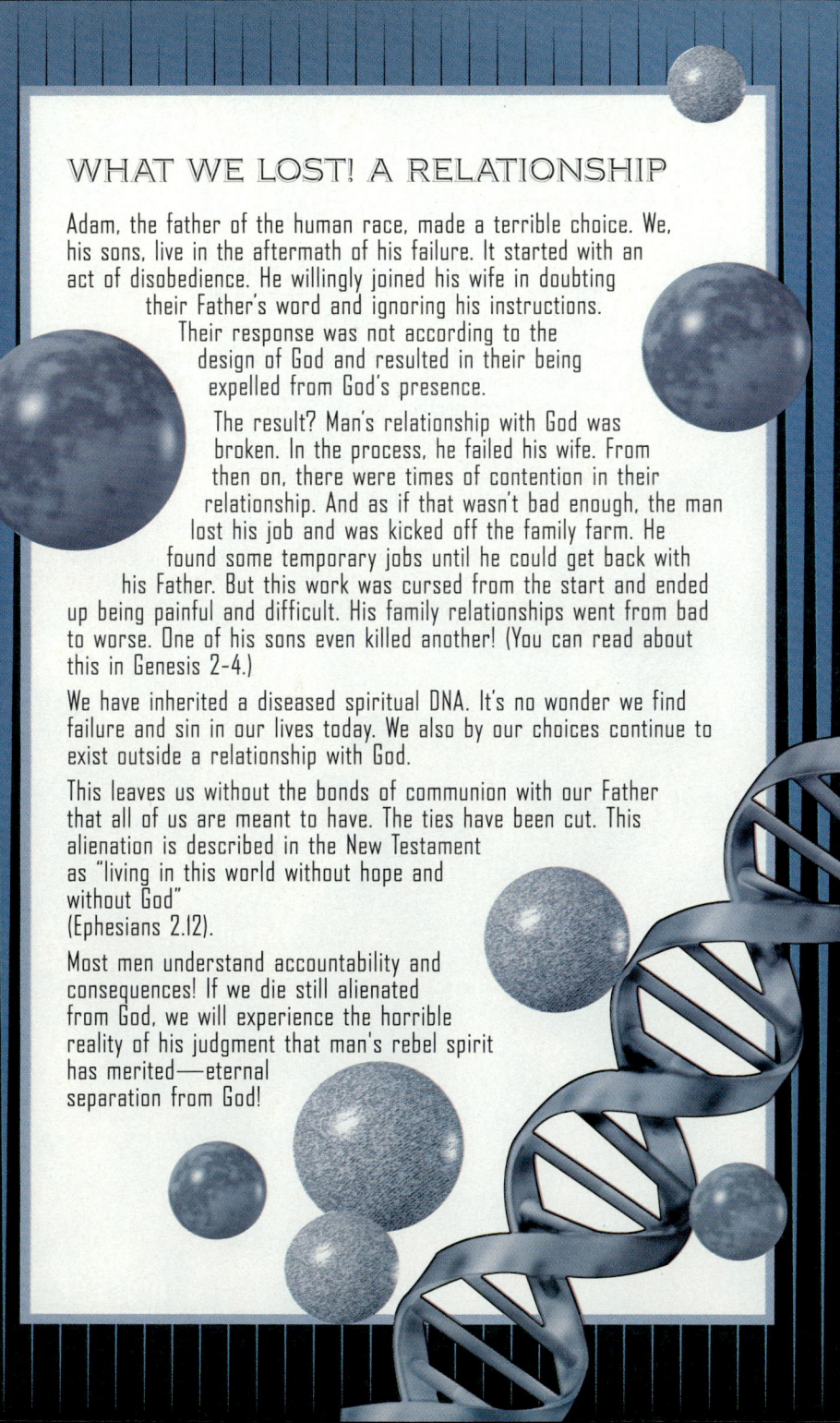

Adam, the father of the human race, made a terrible choice. We, his sons, live in the aftermath of his failure. It started with an act of disobedience. He willingly joined his wife in doubting their Father's word and ignoring his instructions. Their response was not according to the design of God and resulted in their being expelled from God's presence.

The result? Man's relationship with God was broken. In the process, he failed his wife. From then on, there were times of contention in their relationship. And as if that wasn't bad enough, the man lost his job and was kicked off the family farm. He found some temporary jobs until he could get back with his Father. But this work was cursed from the start and ended up being painful and difficult. His family relationships went from bad to worse. One of his sons even killed another! (You can read about this in Genesis 2-4.)

We have inherited a diseased spiritual DNA. It's no wonder we find failure and sin in our lives today. We also by our choices continue to exist outside a relationship with God.

This leaves us without the bonds of communion with our Father that all of us are meant to have. The ties have been cut. This alienation is described in the New Testament as "living in this world without hope and without God" (Ephesians 2.12).

Most men understand accountability and consequences! If we die still alienated from God, we will experience the horrible reality of his judgment that man's rebel spirit has merited—eternal separation from God!

WHAT WE NEED!
A RESTORED RELATIONSHIP

Jesus Christ is the only one able to restore the relationship we lost by giving us life. Note: we are dead and God is alive—so we must be made alive to be able to have a relationship with him.

There's another obstacle to our becoming God's sons. Men tend to be "fix it myself" people. We can admit we're weak in establishing relationships. We admit we're far from perfect. We are, in fact, sinners! But the problem is that our theme song is "I did it my way."

When we do it our way, we remain isolated by our own sins. We separate ourselves not only from God, but also from right relationships with our families and others. In our relationship with God, we can't be do-it-your selfers. We can't fix what's wrong by our own efforts.

greed

lust

malice

adultery

porn   envy

ego

murder

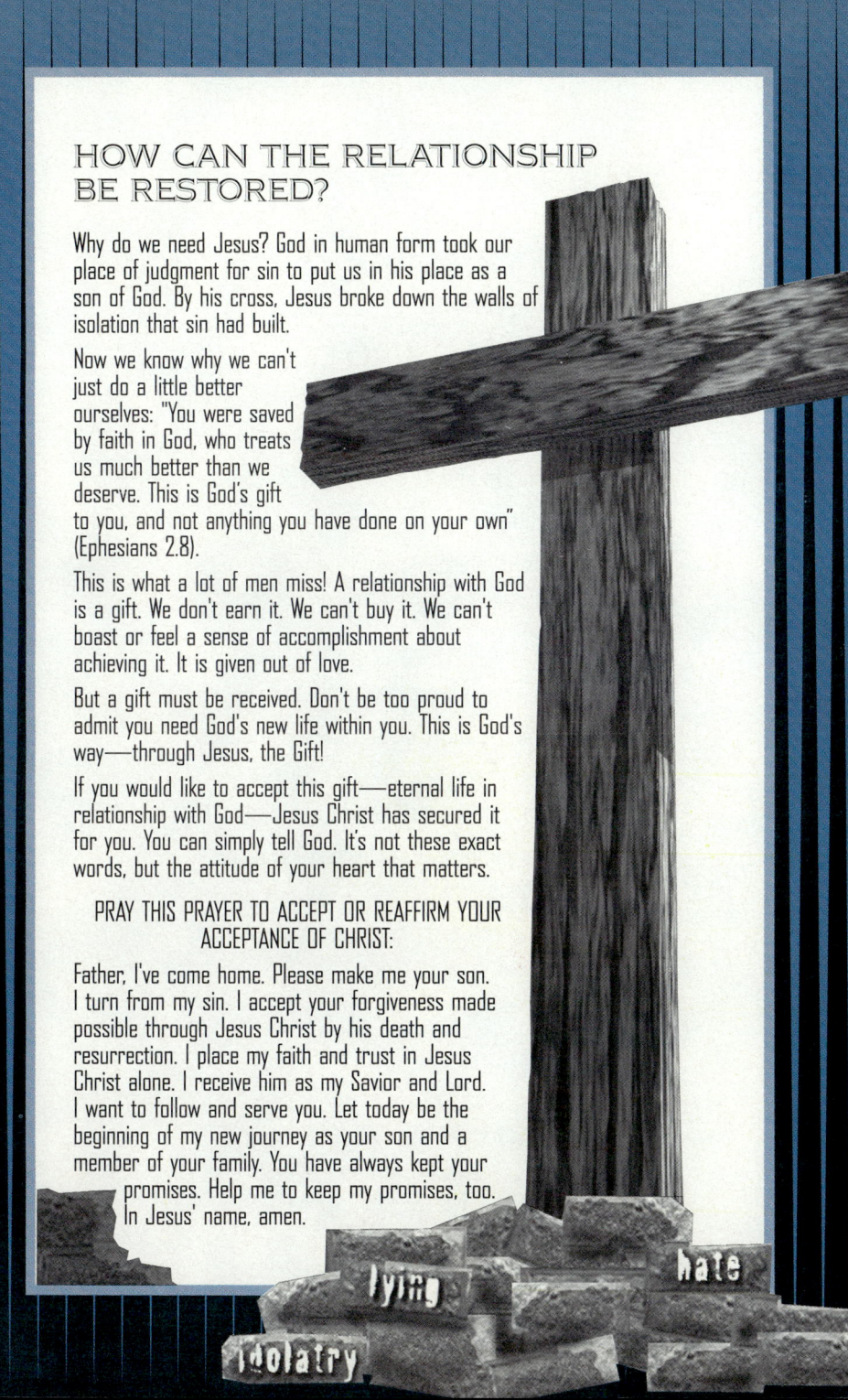

HOW CAN THE RELATIONSHIP BE RESTORED?

Why do we need Jesus? God in human form took our place of judgment for sin to put us in his place as a son of God. By his cross, Jesus broke down the walls of isolation that sin had built.

Now we know why we can't just do a little better ourselves: "You were saved by faith in God, who treats us much better than we deserve. This is God's gift to you, and not anything you have done on your own" (Ephesians 2.8).

This is what a lot of men miss! A relationship with God is a gift. We don't earn it. We can't buy it. We can't boast or feel a sense of accomplishment about achieving it. It is given out of love.

But a gift must be received. Don't be too proud to admit you need God's new life within you. This is God's way—through Jesus, the Gift!

If you would like to accept this gift—eternal life in relationship with God—Jesus Christ has secured it for you. You can simply tell God. It's not these exact words, but the attitude of your heart that matters.

PRAY THIS PRAYER TO ACCEPT OR REAFFIRM YOUR ACCEPTANCE OF CHRIST:

Father, I've come home. Please make me your son. I turn from my sin. I accept your forgiveness made possible through Jesus Christ by his death and resurrection. I place my faith and trust in Jesus Christ alone. I receive him as my Savior and Lord. I want to follow and serve you. Let today be the beginning of my new journey as your son and a member of your family. You have always kept your promises. Help me to keep my promises, too. In Jesus' name, amen.

WHAT SHOULD I EXPECT OF REVIVAL AND SPIRITUAL AWAKENING?

- Passion for God
- Abounding joy in the Lord
- Increased intercessory prayer
- Regular commitment to fasting
- Hunger for the Bible
- Increased family spiritual life
- Generous support of God's work in money and time
- Concern for reconciliation (biblical unity)
- Regular pattern of confessing sin and repentance
- The Body of Christ becomes my team, not my competition

STAND IN THE GAP